Lecture Notes in Computer Science 9945

Commenced Publication in 1973
Founding and Former Series Editors:
Gerhard Goos, Juris Hartmanis, and Jan van Leeuwen

More information about this series at http://www.springer.com/series/7407

Michela Taufer · Bernd Mohr
Julian M. Kunkel (Eds.)

High Performance Computing

ISC High Performance 2016 International Workshops
ExaComm, E-MuCoCoS, HPC-IODC, IXPUG, IWOPH, P^3MA, VHPC, WOPSSS
Frankfurt, Germany, June 19–23, 2016
Revised Selected Papers

 Springer

Editors
Michela Taufer
University of Delaware
Newark, DE
USA

Bernd Mohr
Forschungszentrum Jülich
Jülich
Germany

Julian M. Kunkel
DKRZ
Hamburg
Germany

ISSN 0302-9743 ISSN 1611-3349 (electronic)
Lecture Notes in Computer Science
ISBN 978-3-319-46078-9 ISBN 978-3-319-46079-6 (eBook)
DOI 10.1007/978-3-319-46079-6

Library of Congress Control Number: 2016942512

LNCS Sublibrary: SL1 – Theoretical Computer Science and General Issues

Printed on acid-free paper

This Springer imprint is published by Springer Nature
The registered company is Springer International Publishing AG
The registered company address is: Gewerbestrasse 11, 6330 Cham, Switzerland

Preface

A separate workshop day attached to the ISC High Performance, formerly known as the International Supercomputing Conference, was first added to the technical program in 2015 under the leadership of Bernd Mohr (Forschungszentrum Jülich GmbH). Supported by the success of the last year, ISC High Performance renewed and further extended the workshop program in 2016. This year Michela Taufer (University of Delaware, USA) joined Bernd Mohr to co-lead the workshop organization. Julian Kunkel (German Climate Computing Center) joined the team as the proceedings chair and managed the organization of proceedings for the workshops.

As in 2015, the 21 workshops at ISC High Performance provided a focused, indepth platform with presentations, discussions, and interaction on topics related to all aspects of research, development, and application of large-scale, high-performance experimental and commercial systems. Workshop topics included: HPC computer architecture and hardware; programming models, system software, and applications; solutions for heterogeneity, reliability, power efficiency of systems; virtualization and containerized environments; big data and cloud computing; as well as international collaborations. Workshops were selected via a peer-review process by an international committee of 10 experts in the field from Europe, the USA, and Asia.

For the first time, ISC High Performance provided a platform for workshops with their own call for papers and individual peer-review process through an early deadline in December 2015. In all, 13 workshop proposals were submitted before this deadline from organizers all over the world; the committee accepted 10 workshops (seven full-day and two half-day workshops) after a rigorous review process in which each proposal received three reviews. Additionally, each reviewer was given the possibility to discuss all the submissions.

Workshops without a call for papers were invited to submit their proposals in February 2016. For this second deadline, 13 workshop proposals were submitted and 11 workshops (two full-day and nine half-day workshops) were accepted by the committee with the same rigorous peer-review process as for workshops with proceedings.

The 21 workshops were held on Thursday, June 26, 2016, at the Frankfurt Marriott Hotel with over 600 registered attendees, about 170 presentations, and over a dozen panel discussions. Workshop organizers were asked to collect the slides of all presentations at their workshops. PDF versions of the presentation slides were included in the ISC 2016 online proceedings, which were made available online to conference attendees a few days after the conference.

The workshop proceedings volume collects all the accepted papers of the workshops with a call for papers. Each chapter of the book contains the accepted and revised papers for one of the workshops. For some workshops, an additional preface describes the review process for the workshop and provides a summary of the outcome.

June 2016

Michela Taufer
Bernd Mohr
Julian M. Kunkel

Organization

ISC High Performance Workshops Co-chairs

Bernd Mohr — Forschungszentrum Jülich GmbH, Germany
Michela Taufer — University of Delaware, USA

ISC High Performance Workshops Committee

Rosa M. Badia — Barcelona Supercomputing Center, Spain
Franois Bodin — University of Rennes, France
Bronis R. de Supinski — Lawrence Livermore National Laboratory, USA
Jay Lofstead — Sandia National Laboratories, USA
Craig Lucas — NAG, UK
Naoya Maruyama — RIKEN, Japan
Satoshi Matsuoka — Tokyo Institute of Technology, Japan
Marie-Christine Sawley — Intel, France
Seetharami Seelam — IBM T.J. Watson Research Center, USA
John Shalf — Lawrence Berkeley National Laboratory, USA
Antonino Tumeo — Pacific Northwest National Laboratory, USA

ISC High Performance Workshops Proceedings Chair

Julian Kunkel — DKRZ, Germany

International Workshop on OpenPOWER for HPC (IWOPH)

Organizing Committee

Dirk Pleiter — Jülich Supercomputing Centre, Germany
Jack Wells — Oak Ridge National Laboratory, USA

Program Committee

Zaid Al-Ars — TU Delft, The Netherlands
Mike Ashworth — STFC, UK
Costas Bekas — IBM, Switzerland
Sunita Chandrasekaran — University of Delaware, USA
Norbert Eicker — Jülich Supercomputing Centre, Germany
Oscar Hernandez — Oak Ridge National Laborator, USA (Co-chair)
Guido Juckeland — TU Dresden, Germany

Graham Lopez	Oak Ridge National Laboratory, USA (Co-chair)
Barney Maccabe	Oak Ridge National Laboratory, USA
Marek Michaelewicz	A-Star, Singapore
Rob Neely	Lawrence Livermore National Laboratory, USA
Kevin O'Brien	IBM, USA
Duncan Poole	NVIDIA, USA
Swaroop Pophale	Oak Ridge National Laboratory, USA
Maciej Remiszewski	ICM, Poland
Vivek Sarkar	Rice University, USA
Jim Sexton	IBM, USA
Gilad Shainer	Mellanox, Israel
Pavel Shamis	Oak Ridge National Laboratory, USA
Sameer Shende	University of Oregon, USA
Tjerk Straatsma	Oak Ridge National Laboratory, USA
Bronis de Supinski	Lawrence Livermore National Laboratory, USA
Michael Wolfe	PGI, USA

Workshop on Performance & Scalability of Storage Systems (WOPSSS)

Organizing Committee

Jean-Thomas Acquaviva	DDN, USA

Program Committee

Francisco J. Alfaro	University of Castilla-La Mancha, Spain
André Brinkmann	Mainz University, Germany
Jason Chun Xue	City University of Hong Kong, Hong Kong, SAR China
Toni Cortes	Barcelona Supercomputing Centre, Spain
Stefano Cozzini	NR, Italy
Liu Duo	Chongqing University, China
Juan Piernas	University of Murcia, Spain
Rekha Singhal	Tata CS Innovation Labs, India

International Workshop on Performance Portable Programming Models for Accelerators (P^3MA)

Organizing Committee

Sunita Chandrasekaran	University of Delaware, USA
Graham Lopez	Oak Ridge National Laboratory, USA

Program Committee

Samuel Thibault	Inria, University of Bordeaux, France
James Beyer	NVIDIA, USA
Wei Ding	AMD, USA
Saber Feki	King Abdullah University, Saudi Arabia
Robert Henschel	Indiana University, USA
Michael Klemm	Intel, USA
Eric Stotzer	Texas Instruments, USA
Amit Amritkar	University of Houston, USA
Guido Juckeland	HZDR, Germany
Will Sawyer	ETH, Zurich
Sameer Shende	University of Oregon, USA
Costas Bekas	IBM Zurich, Switzerland
Toni Collis	University of Edinburgh, UK
Adrian Jackson	University of Edinburgh, UK
Henri Jin	NASA, USA
Andreas Knuepfer	TU Dresden, Germany
Steven Olivier	Sandia National Laboratory, USA
Suraj Prabhakaran	TU Darmstadt, Germany
Bora Ucar	ENS Lyon, France
Sandra Wienke	Aachen University, Germany

Application Performance on Intel Xeon Phi – Being Prepared for KNL & Beyond (IXPUG)

Organizing Committee

Richard Gerber	NERSC and Lawrence Berkeley National Laboratory, USA
Kent Milfeld	TACC, USA
Chris Newburn	Intel, USA
Thomas Steinke	ZIB, Germany

Program Committee

Damian Alvarez-Mallon	Forschungszentrum Jülich GmbH, Germany
Ryan Coleman	Sandia National Laboratories, USA
Douglas Doerfler	NERSC and Lawrence Berkeley National Laboratory, USA
Antonio Gomez	TACC, USA
Simon Hammond	Sandia National Laboratories, USA
Rahul Hardikar	Indian Institute of Science, India
Helen He	NERSC and Lawrence Berkeley National Laboratory, USA

Dave M. Hiatt
Michael Klemm   Intel, Germany
Lars Koesterke   TACC, USA
Rakesh Krishnaiyer   Intel, USA
Olli-Pekka Lehto   CSC - IT Center for Science Ltd., Finland
John Linford   ParaTools, Inc., USA
Simon McIntosh-Smith   Bristol University, UK
John Michalakes   NREL, USA
Dmitry Prohorov   Intel, USA
Karthik Raman   Intel, USA
Carlos Rosales   TACC, USA
Hideki Saito   Intel, USA
Abhinav Sarje   Lawrence Berkeley National Laboratory, USA
Estella Suarez   Forschungszentrum Jülich GmbH, Germany
Srinath Vadlamani   Paratools, Inc., USA
Jerome Vienne   TACC, USA

HPC I/O in the Data Center (HPC-IODC)

Organizing Committee

Julian Kunkel   DKRZ, Germany
Jay Lofstead   Sandia National Laboratories, USA
Colin McMurtrie   CSCS, Switzerland

Program Committee

Wolfgang Frings   Jülich Supercomputing Centre, Germany
Javier Garcia Blas   University Carlos III of Madrid, Spain
Rob Ross   Argonne National Laboratory, USA
Carlos Maltzahn   University of California, Santa Cruz, USA
Kathryn Mohror   Lawrence Livermore National Laboratory, USA
Xiaosong Ma   North Carolina State University and Oak Ridge
                               National Laboratory, USA

Second International Workshop on Communication Architectures at Extreme Scale (ExaComm)

Organizing Committee

Khaled Hamidouche   Ohio State University, USA
Dhabaleswar K. Panda   Ohio State University, USA
Hari Subramoni   Ohio State University, USA

Program Committee

Taisuke Boku	University of Tsukuba, Japan
Ron Brightwell	Sandia National Laboratories, USA
Hans Eberle	NVIDIA, Germany
Ada Gavrilovska	Georgia Tech, USA
Brice Goglin	Inria, France
Dror Goldenberg	Mellanox Technologies, Israel
R. Govindarajan	Indian Institute of Science, Bangalore, India
Hai Jin	Huazhong University of Science and Technology, Wuhan, China
Yutong Lu	National University of Defense Technology, China
Takeshi Nanri	University of Kyushu, Japan
Sebastien Rumley	Columbia University, USA
Martin Schulz	Lawrence Livermore National Laboratory, USA
John M. Shalf	National Energy Research Scientific Computing Center and Lawrence Berkeley National Laboratory, USA
Tor Skeie	Simula Research Laboratory, Norway
Sayantan Sur	Intel, USA
Xin Yuan	Florida State University, USA

Workshop on Exascale Multi/Many Core Computing Systems (E-MuCoCoS)

Organizing Committee

Sabri Pllana	Linnaeus University, Sweden
Achim Streit	KIT, Germany

Program Committee

Erika Abraham	RWTH Aachen University, Germany
Siegfried Benkner	University of Vienna, Austria
Alécio Binotto	IBM Research, Brazil
Eduardo Cesar	UAB, Spain
Jiri Dokulil	University of Vienna, Austria
Samir Genaim	Universidad Complutense de Madrid, Spain
Einar Broch	University of Oslo, Norway
Ivan Kondov	Karlsruhe Institute of Technology, Germany
Renato Miceli	SENAI CIMATEC, Brazil
Hiroyuki Takizawa	Tohoku University, Japan
Samuel Thibault	LaBRI, University of Bordeaux 1, France

Workshop on Virtualization in High-Performance Cloud Computing (VHPC'16)

Organizing Committee

Michael Alexander (Chair)	TU Wien, Austria
Anastassios Nanos (Co-chair)	NTUA, Greece
Balazs Gerofi (Co-chair)	RIKEN, Japan

Program Committee

Stergios Anastasiadis	University of Ioannina, Greece
Costas Bekas	IBM Zurich Research Laboratory, Switzerland
Jakob Blomer	CERN
Ron Brightwell	Sandia National Laboratories, USA
Roberto Canonico	University of Napoli Federico II, Italy
Julian Chesterfield	OnApp, UK
Stephen Crago	USC ISI, USA
Christoffer Dall	Columbia University, USA
Patrick Dreher	MIT, USA
Robert Futrick	Cycle Computing, USA
Robert Gardner	University of Chicago, USA
William Gardner	University of Guelph, Canada
Wolfgang Gentzsch	UberCloud, USA
Kyle Hale	Northwestern University, USA
Marcus Hardt	Karlsruhe Institute of Technology, Germany
Krishna Kant	Temple University, USA
Romeo Kinzler	IBM, Switzerland
Brian Kocoloski	University of Pittsburgh, USA
Kornilios Kourtis	IBM Research, Switzerland
Nectarios Koziris	National Technical University of Athens, Greece
John Lange	University of Pittsburgh, USA
Nikos Parlavantzas	IRISA, France
Kevin Pendretti	Sandia National Laboratories, USA
Che-Rung Roger Lee	National Tsing Hua University, Taiwan
Giuseppe Lettieri	University of Pisa, Italy
Qing Liu	Oak Ridge National Laboratory, USA
Paul Mundt	Adaptant, Germany
Amer Qouneh	University of Florida, USA
Carlos Reaño	Technical University of Valencia, Spain
Seetharami Seelam	IBM Research, USA
Dieter Suess	TU Wien, Austria
Josh Simons	VMWare, USA
Borja Sotomayor	University of Chicago, USA

Contents

IXPUG

P^3MA

WOPSSS

VHPC

E-MuCoCoS

2016 Workshop on Exascale Multi/Many Core Computing Systems (E-MuCoCoS)

Sabri Pllana[1] and Achim Streit[2]

[1] Department of Computer Science, Linnaeus University, Vaxjo, Sweden
[2] Steinbuch Centre for Computing, Karlsruhe Institute of Technology, Karlsruhe, Germany

Overview

Exascale computing will revolutionize computational science and engineering by providing 1000x the capabilities of currently available computing systems, while having a similar power footprint. The HPC community is working towards the development of the first Exaflop computer after reaching the Petaflop milestone in 2008. There are concerns that computer designs based on existing multi-core and many-core solutions will not scale to Exascale considering technical challenges (such as, productivity, energy consumption or reliability) and reasonable economic constraints. Therefore, novel multi-core and many-core solutions are required to reach Exascale.

The E-MuCoCoS workshop series focuses on multi/many core languages, system software and architectural solutions for extreme-scale systems towards Exascale. The topics of the workshop include but are not limited to:

- Methods and tools for preparing applications for Exascale
- Extreme-scale data analysis and visualization
- Extreme-scale performance visualization, analysis, modeling, and tuning
- Adaptive run-time systems for extreme-scale
- Architectures for extreme-scale computing

E-MuCoCoS 2016 is organized in conjunction with the International Supercomputing Conference (ISC), Frankfurt, Germany, June 23, 2016.

Earlier editions of E-MuCoCoS workshop have not emphasized extreme-scale computing and the workshop was known as MuCoCoS. Previous MuCoCoS workshops include MuCoCoS 2014 (Porto, PT), MuCoCoS 2013 (Edinburgh, UK), MuCoCoS 2012 (Salt Lake City, US), MuCoCoS 2011 (Seoul, KR), Mu-CoCoS 2010 (Krakow, PL), MuCoCoS 2009 (Fukuoka, JP), and MuCoCoS 2008 (Barcelona, ES).

Program Chairs

Sabri Pllana   Linnaeus University, SE
Achim Streit   Karlsruhe Institute of Technology, DE

Program Committee

Erika Abraham	RWTH Aachen University, DE
Siegfried Benkner	University of Vienna, AT
Alecio Binotto	IBM Research, BR
Eduardo Cesar	UAB, ES
Jiri Dokulil	University of Vienna, AT
Samir Genaim	Universidad Complutense de Madrid, ES
Einar Broch Johnsen	University of Oslo, NO
Ivan Kondov	Karlsruhe Institute of Technology, DE
Renato Miceli	SENAI CIMATEC, BR
Sabri Pllana	Linnaeus University, SE
Achim Streit	Karlsruhe Institute of Technology, DE
Hiroyuki Takizawa	Tohoku University, JP
Samuel Thibault	LaBRI, Universite Bordeaux 1, FR

Program

E-MuCoCoS 2016 workshop program included two keynotes, four selected speakers, and two invited talks of the European Exascale projects. The academic keynote speech was given by Ivona Brandić, who is Professor at the Vienna University of Technology and member of the Young Academy of Austrian Academy of Sciences. Hans-Christian Hoppe, who is Principal Engineer with Intel and director of the ExaCluster Lab at Jülich Supercomputing Centre, gave the industrial keynote speech.

In what follows in this section we list the workshop program.

- **Session 1: Towards Exascale Computing**
  Chair: Sabri Pllana (LNU, SE)

- *Welcome to E-MuCoCoS 2016*
  Sabri Pllana (LNU, SE) and Achim Streit (SCC, KIT, DE)
- Academic Keynote: *Exascale System Management - What can we learn from efficient management of Ultra-scale Distributed Systems?*
  Ivona Brandić (Vienna University of Technology, AT)
- *Extreme-Scale In-Situ Visualization of Turbulent Flows on IBM Blue Gene/Q JUQUEEN*
  Jens Henrik Göbbert (Jülich Supercomputing Centre, DE)
- *Behavioral Emulation for Scalable Design-Space Exploration of Algorithms and Architectures*
  Nalini Kumar (University of Florida, US)
- *Energy Efficient Runtime Framework for Exascale Systems*
  Yousri Mhedheb (Karlsruhe Institute of Technology, DE)
- *Work Distribution of Data-parallel Applications on Heterogeneous Systems*
  Suejb Memeti (Linnaeus University, SE)

- **Session 2: Invited Talks of European Exascale Projects**
  Chair: Achim Streit (SCC, KIT, DE)

- Industrial Keynote: *Intel HPC Co-Design Activities in Europe*
  Hans-Christian Hoppe (Intel Deutschland GmbH, DE)
- *EPiGRAM: Preparing Message-Passing and PGAS Programming Models for Exascale*
- Stefano Markidis (KTH, SE)
- *AllScale: Closing the Performance Gap with Modern C++*
  Thomas Heller (Friedrich-Alexander-Universität Erlangen-Nürnberg, DE)

Behavioral Emulation for Scalable Design-Space Exploration of Algorithms and Architectures

Nalini Kumar$^{(\boxtimes)}$, Carlo Pascoe, Christopher Hajas, Herman Lam, Greg Stitt, and Alan George

Department of ECE, PSAAP II Center for Compressible Multiphase Turbulence, NSF Center for High-Performance Reconfigurable Computing, University of Florida, Gainesville, FL 32608, USA
{nkumar,pascoe,hajas,hlam,stitt,george}@chrec.org

Abstract. This paper presents a simulation methodology called Behavioral Emulation (BE) for scalable design-space exploration of algorithms and architectures. By design, BE is independent of simulation vehicle (e.g., simulation in software or emulation in hardware) and addresses system-simulation complexity with a coarse-grained, multi-scale approach. We describe the BE methodology, component models, and simulation workflow from calibration to validation of applications simulated on existing architectures and present a device-level case study with roughly 10 % relative error. Finally, we discuss the extension of validated models to predict application performance on notional architectures.

Keywords: Behavioral Emulation · Performance modeling · Coarse-grained simulation · Design space exploration

1 Introduction

Large-scale simulations are vital scientific tools, especially when direct experimentation is expensive or infeasible [1–3]. Over several decades, these simulations have required constant growth in high-performance computing (HPC) to simulate more complex phenomena, with emerging applications [4] now requiring Exascale performance. In a rapidly evolving landscape of HPC systems [5], it is increasingly difficult for application developers to optimize code across system generations, a fact worsened by the trend towards many-core architectures and hardware accelerators (e.g., Intel Xeon Phi and Nvidia GPUs) [6]. Efficient optimization will require *co-design*, where application developers work with computer scientists and engineers to explore the design space to better design and optimize algorithms on different architectures and systems [7,8].

For design-space exploration (DSE) to be effective, it is important that turnaround between application performance analysis and code development be timely [9]. Architectural simulation/emulation plays a key role in design trade-off evaluation, but traditional approaches face several challenges, key among them optimizing the delicate balance between simulation speed, model accuracy, and design scalability. Unfortunately, traditional cycle-accurate simulators [10–12]

© Springer International Publishing AG 2016
M. Taufer et al. (Eds.): ISC High Performance Workshops 2016, LNCS 9945, pp. 5–17, 2016.
DOI: 10.1007/978-3-319-46079-6_1

and even functional simulators [13,14], while highly accurate, lack scalability for DSE at extreme scales [15]. At the other extreme, purely analytical models [16–18] can provide quick performance estimates, but limit one's ability to gain detailed insight into the behavior of individual system components. As existing simulation methods do not provide an appropriate combination of fast turn-around time, scalability, and accuracy for large-scale system simulation, there is a need for a simulation framework that can fulfill these requirements.

In this paper, we present a novel multi-scale and coarse-grained methodology for large-scale system simulation called Behavioral Emulation (BE). The term *emulation* often refers to pre-fabrication simulation of architecture designs in hardware, but we use it to mean mimicking (i.e., emulating) behavior of the system under study. BE handles the complexity of extreme-scale system modeling and simulation by reducing it to a problem of modeling system components and their interactions at different levels of system organization—micro, meso, and macro—and by abstracting away low-level operational details at each of these levels. After a brief discussion of related research (Sect. 2), we expand our discussion of BE with more details on the approach (Sect. 3), modeling workflow and underlying BE component models (BE Objects or BEOs) (Sect. 4). Although our ultimate goal is prediction on large-scale systems, in this paper we limit our focus to establishing the BE methodology by presenting proof-of-concept design, calibration, and validation results for device-level experiments. In Sect. 5, we discuss our application (Spectral Element Solver kernel from CMT-nek) and architecture (mesh-based Tile-Gx36 many-core processor) case studies used in Sect. 6.1 to showcase validated BE simulation results with roughly 10 % relative error for an existing system. Additionally, to demonstrate the applicability of BE for architecture DSE, in Sect. 6.2 we expand our "library" of BEOs by modeling additional devices, then mix, match, and modify components to model more notional architectures. Finally, in Sect. 7, we present conclusions and our future work towards realizing Exascale application and architecture DSE with BE.

2   Related Research

Various modeling and simulation approaches, varying greatly in their accuracy and scalability, have been developed and used for design space exploration. Cycle-accurate simulation approaches (e.g., Gem5 [10], SimpleScalar [12], Simics [11] etc.) offer high accuracy but are prohibitively slow for simulating complex systems. Cycle-accurate emulation in hardware (e.g., Palladium [19], Veloce [20]) is a faster alternative, but it requires more resources, effort, and expertise that can be impractical for study of entire extreme-scale systems. While these approaches are impractical for use in isolation, they are complementary to Behavioral Emulation. Results of high-fidelity simulations of some system components can be used to calibrate models that be used in BE.

In addition to the cycle-accurate and analytical simulators already mentioned, functional simulation attempts to balance the tradeoff between simulation time and accuracy by modeling systems at a higher level of granularity. Manifold [14,21], an execution-based simulator, follows a component-based approach, allowing users to piece together in-built (cycle-level models) or user-generated components and tools to perform system performance, power, thermal, and reliability analysis. BigSim [13], a trace-driven simulator, analyzes the performance of sequential code-segments with variable-resolution architecture models that can be swapped to tune simulation speed/accuracy. FASE [22], another trace-driven simulator, characterizes the behavior of performance-critical components and allows users to build virtual system prototypes for analysis. BE uses a component-based approach similar to these simulators, but further decomposes the simulation into device-, node-, and system-level while using coarser-grained models for system components and a minimal application representation (as opposed to traces or application source). The fine-grained simulation approaches mentioned above can complement BE by providing data for calibrating BE component models.

SST (Structural Simulation Toolkit) [23,24] is a popular component-based simulation framework, with a parallel discrete-event simulation back-end and a standardized front-end used to interface various models (component simulators) to build a larger system. While high-fidelity models for system components are frequently used (e.g., gem5 [10]) within the SST framework, it is not a requirement. Because of the "plug-and-play" infrastructure and the freedom to model components at different granularities, we have adopted SST as the platform (backend) for our BE simulations.

3   Behavioral Emulation: Overview and Approach

Behavioral Emulation (BE) is a coarse-grained modeling and simulation approach that aims to provide timely, flexible, and scalable estimates of application performance on existing and future system architectures. In BE, the complexity of large-scale system simulation is handled by simultaneously dividing the simulation into different levels of system abstraction (e.g., device, node, rack, system) and abstracting the behavior of the components at each of these levels. The coarse-grained component models mimic or emulate the observed execution behavior of the component instead of its cycle-accurate operation. Key features present within the BE approach (Fig. 1) are summarized below:

Coarse-grained. Coarse-grained application and architecture models allow BE to tradeoff acceptable accuracy for speed to enable fast DSE. High-level application models enable rapid prototyping of candidate algorithms and negate the need for working code. In addition, because BE coarse-grained performance models are pre-trained from samples of actual execution, they provide sufficiently accurate analysis in a short amount of time.

Multi-scale. Rather than simulate the entire HPC system, simulation is divided into separate levels of system organization such that the lower levels appear as a black box to the higher levels. We define device-, node-, and system-level simulations as micro-, meso-, and macro-scale simulations. Decomposing the problem in this manner allows us to prune the design space independently at

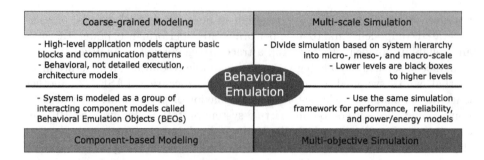

Fig. 1. Key features of Behavioral Emulation

lower scales (i.e., micro- and meso-) and evaluate only promising configurations at the macro-scale.

Component-based. In BE simulations, a system is modeled as a collection of interacting component models called Behavioral Emulation Objects (BEOs) (detailed in Sect. 4). For example, a micro-scale device simulation can be modeled as a combination of several parallel processing cores each able to communicate with their local L1 cache, the shared L2 and L3 caches, and memory all modeled as separate BEOs. At macro-scale, a simulation may consist of interacting devices or nodes, network switches, routers, and storage BEO models.

Multi-objective. The BE approach chiefly deals with various ways of reducing system simulation complexity and can be applied to study any aspect of system behavior such as performance, power, and reliability concerns.

In this paper, we focus on demonstrating the component-based and coarse-grained modeling aspects of BE by limiting ourselves to performance (execution time) modeling and simulation at micro-scale (device-level), while our ultimate goal remains to scale beyond device-level and study performance, power, and reliability tradeoffs.

4   BE Modeling and Workflow

Figure 2 illustrates three key steps of the BE workflow: (1) design and calibration of application and architecture component models (i.e., BEOs), (2) validation of simulation (architecture and application model interactions) results against testbed measurements, and (3) using the verified models for performance prediction and HW/SW co-design. Each BEO from step (1) models the observed high-level behavior of the component it represents, interacts with other BEOs in the simulation via event tokens, and gathers metrics of interest for post-simulation analysis. We classify these BEOs in two groups—Application BEOs (AppBEO) and Architecture BEOs (ArchBEOs).

AppBEOs are high-level, architecture-agnostic representations for the computation and communication blocks in a target application provided by the user

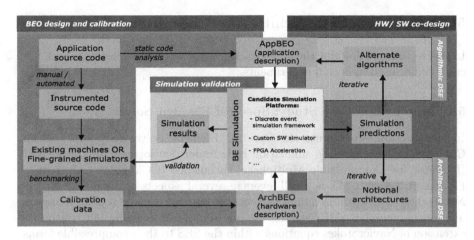

Fig. 2. BE workflow outlining major steps: (1) BEO design and calibration, (2) Validation of BE simulations, and (3) BE predictions for HW/SW co-design

(Fig. 3(c)). They are described in a simple, extensible, platform-independent, high-level API and compiled into events for ArchBEOs to interpret and process. By doing so, algorithms of interest can be easily prototyped at the expense of exact execution details which, in some cases, may be of interest to the user.

ArchBEOs are coarse-grained models crafted to mimic the behavior of various systems components such as processors (ProcBEO), network switches and routers (CommBEO), memory (MemBEOs), processing nodes (NodeBEO), storage (DiskBEO) etc. ArchBEOs have two functions—emulation and management. Emulation tasks include processing event queues, handling and creating events, updating simulation timestamps, and interacting with other BEOs in the simulation. Management tasks include tracking results and statistics for run-time or post-simulation analysis.

In a BE simulation, operations defined in the AppBEO (e.g., matrix multiply, fast fourier transform) are compiled into events (e.g., update timestamp, wait, generate event token) to be handled by ArchBEOs. The events are processed and simulation clocks are updated based on multi-dimensional performance models (surrogates [25]) when an event is processed. Data collected from micro-benchmarked testbeds (or external fine-grained architecture simulation tools) is used to calibrate surrogates for existing systems. By tweaking ArchBEO simulation parameters (e.g., network bandwidths, latencies, or topology) or replacing BEO models with other validated BEO models, it becomes possible to simulate notional architectures. These BEOs use a parallel discrete-event simulation back-end for event handling and synchronization. We use Lamport clocks [26] to maintain event ordering.

5   Application and Architecture Case Study

In this section, we describe the application (Sect. 5.1) and architecture (Sect. 5.2) case-studies used in Sect. 6 experiments.

5.1   Application Case Study: Spectral Element Solver

In this Section, we discuss the Spectral Element Solver (SES) [27] within CMT-nek [4], a large-scale simulation code under development by the PSAAP II Center for Compressible Multiphase Turbulence (CCMT) at University of Florida. Although CMT-nek will leverage several aspects of the petascale code Nek5000 [1] (e.g., optimized linear algebra operations, element topology, approximation polynomials, MPI strategies), one significant contribution will be the extension of NavierStokes equations within the SES to their compressible forms. With many possible implementations, early algorithm DSE for target systems (current and future) will help to maximize application performance and minimize wasted effort.

The majority of CMT-nek execution time is spent computing the *flux divergence* terms within the SES (Fig. 3(a)). Flux divergence is essentially a dot product of the gradient operator and the flux vector implemented as the multiplication of the derivative operator matrix *(N, N)* and the element matrix *(N, N, N, E)*

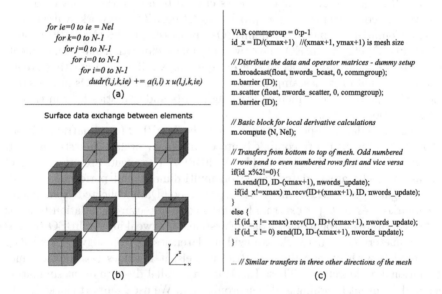

Fig. 3. (a) Pseudo-code for the partial derivative calculation for estimating the flux-divergence term, (b) Pairwise exchange communication between the neighboring elements located on processes in X, Y and Z directions, and (c) Partial AppBEO for the spectral element solver

to calculate the partial derivatives along the three Cartesian coordinate dimensions (r, s, t). Here $N \in [5, 25]$ is the number of grid points along a direction in a cubic reference element and E is the total number of elements in the computational domain. For our case study, we use a straightforward implementation of this operation where explicit optimizations, such as loop fusion or loop unroll, are not applied. *Numerical flux* is evaluated to ensure continuity on the element boundaries and requires exchanging surface data between neighboring elements. Currently, CMT-nek uses a *pairwise exchange* communication strategy, a simple implementation of which is used for crafting our AppBEOs (Fig. 3(b) and (c)).

5.2   Architecture Case Study: Mesh-Based Many-Core Device

As previously mentioned, in this paper we limit our focus to the design, calibration, and validation of device-level models. For our experiments we use TILE-Gx36, a 36-core many-core processor [28] from Mellanox (Tilera corporation before acquisition). The 36 cores, or *tiles*, are arranged as a 6×6 2D mesh. Each tile contains a 64-bit SIMD processor core, L1 and L2 cache, and a non-blocking switch for connection to the *iMesh* network. The iMesh interconnect has five independent low-latency mesh networks for memory, I/O, and user communication. Of these, explicit transfer of data between tiles occurs via packets on the User Dynamic Network (UDN). The packets are routed in dimension-order and cut-through switching with each hop taking a single clock cycle.

The BE description of TILE-Gx36 consists of 36 ProcBEOs (model for a single tile) and 36 CommBEOs (model for a single iMesh switch) connected as a 2D mesh. The ProcBEO is responsible for sequentially processing

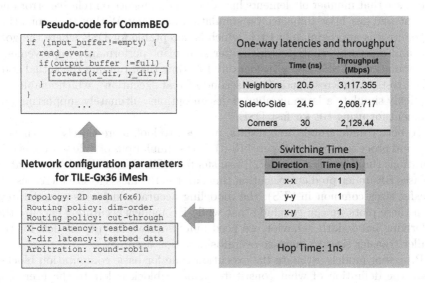

Fig. 4. Pseudo-code for CommBEO and data obtained from the TILE-Gx36 testbed to calibrate iMesh model for BE simulation

AppBEO instructions (events), estimating the performance of computation events, sending/receiving communication events to/from CommBEOs, updating local simulation clocks, and logging of event outcomes for future analysis or visualization. Each ProcBEO has models calibrated for setup times, overheads, and the time taken for several computation operations (e.g., addition, multiplication, dotproduct). CommBEOs interface with each other to model communication over the mesh network. Each CommBEO is calibrated with tile-to-tile one-way transfer latencies, hop times, and routing procedures as shown in Fig. 4.

6   Experiments: BE Validation and Prediction

In this Section, we evaluate the BE approach by validating simulations of SES (Sect. 5.1) executed on TILE-Gx36 by comparing the simulation results with device benchmarking measurements. We then extend our architecture models to predict the performance of the same kernel on notional device architectures.

6.1   Simulation Validation

We compare BE simulations of SES on TILE-GX36 against benchmarking data collected by running the same SES configurations on the TILE-Gx36 platform. For processor loads of $E = 10$ and $E = 100$ elements, BE predicted the execution times for varied element sizes (i.e., gridpoints) from $N = 5$ to 20. This setup is representative of experiments used to identify the optimal N value for SES on a particular architecture (i.e., algorithm and architecture DSE). Figure 5(a) shows the relative error between predicted and actual execution times. From the plot we can see that number of elements has almost no influence on relative error and element size has little influence on simulation accuracy. Within the simulation range, error is approximately 10 %, which is acceptable for DSE where the goal is to find design alternatives which offer significant performance improvement. BE simulations of SES take considerably less time than running the actual code on the testbed (microseconds for a second of real execution), which enables us to quickly simulate a large number of design options, ultimately supporting our argument for using BE for fast DSE.

To better understand these results, we need to look more closely at our network and processor models. Figure 5(b-d) shows simulations of different collective operations (implemented using P2P transfers) on Tile iMesh. We observe that in all cases BE under-predicts execution time, and as the message size increases (to transfer sizes common in SES), the modeling accuracy improves considerably. From these plots we can conclude that while BE models accurately capture the underlying bandwidth behavior, we need more accurate latency models for the smaller transfer sizes to increase overall simulation accuracy.

Processor models estimate the execution time for basic computation blocks, where the definition of what constitutes a basic block is left to the user. For example, a parallel matrix multiplication can be thought of as each processor computing several smaller matrix multiplies (coarse-grain decomposition) or as computing several dot products (fine-grained decomposition). While BE gives

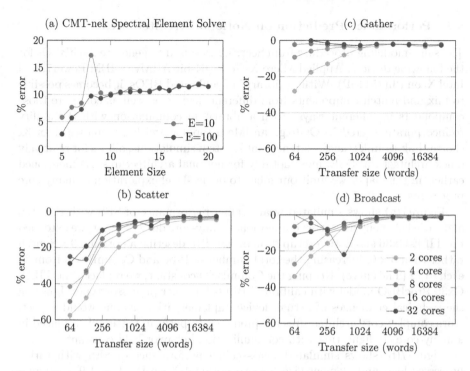

Fig. 5. Percent relative error in simulations of (a) Spectral Element Solver on TILE-Gx36, (b) Scatter over iMesh, (c) Gather over iMesh, and (d) Broadcast over iMesh

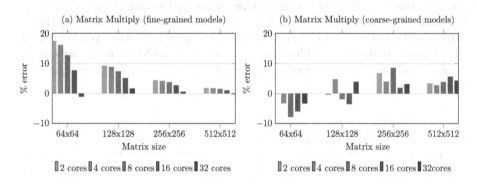

Fig. 6. Percent relative error in simulations of matrix multiplication configured as (a) fine-grained vector dot-products, and (b) smaller coarse-grained matrix multiplications

the flexibility of using either decomposition, we observed using coarse-grained models can improve simulation accuracy as shown in Fig. 6 and improve simulation speed by reducing the total number of processed events. The SES App-BEO used for simulation in Fig. 5(a) followed the coarse-grained decomposition approach.

6.2   Performance Prediction on Notional Architectures

The same modeling procedure from Sect. 5.2 was used to generate ArchBEOs for the following devices: Applied Micro X-Gene (64-bit ARMv8), IBM Power7, and Intel Xeon Phi (5110P). With a "library" of calibrated BEOs, it becomes possible to mix and match components from different devices as well as configure those components in different ways. Such a library, in combination with the ability to incorporate altered BEOs (e.g., an iMesh topology with 2x bandwidth or 3x shorter link-to-link transfer latency) into system simulations, allows for relatively quick architectural DSE, most notably for notional architectures. As mentioned earlier, in this paper we limit our focus to device-level exploration of many-core processors.

Figure 7(a) shows simulated weak-scaling performance of SES with E = 100 and varied element size for several notional many-core devices. First, we extended the TILE-Gx36 simulation setup from Sect. 6.1 to describe a notional 9 × 8 mesh rather than 6 × 6, increasing the total number of Proc and CommBEOs from 36 each to 72 (Tile curve). Keeping the CommBEO constant, we replaced the TILE-Gx36 ProcBEO model with calibrated BEOs for other processor types. Ignoring the technical challenges of actual device implementation, as one would expect, more complex core architectures are predicted to perform better when placed in a many-core configuration with communication behavior held constant.

Figure 7(b) shows simulated weak-scaling performance of SES with varied processor load and element size for two notional Xeon-Phi-based 9 × 8 many-core devices. One device is configured with the same link-to-link transfer latency from Fig. 7(a) experiments and the other with half of that latency. We observed that, for these application configurations, reducing the link-to-link latency by half increased the overall application performance between 28 and 78 percent depending upon the exact computation to communication ratios. While we used 50 % latency reduction for illustrative purposes, it would be advantageous to insert actual numbers from existing product data sheets or upcoming product press releases.

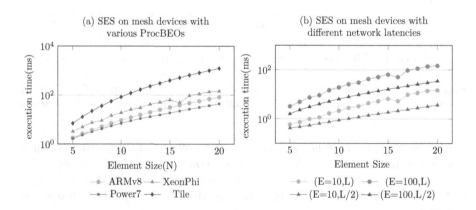

Fig. 7. Architecture DSE of SES on notional device architectures

7 Conclusions and Future Work

In this paper, we introduced Behavioral Emulation, a coarse-grained, component-based, multi-scale simulation methodology for fast and scalable DSE of algorithms and architectures. We demonstrated the value of such an approach for kernel optimization by modeling the SES used within CMT-nek and predicting its performance for an existing many-core device (TILE-Gx36). We then extended the models for performance prediction to notional mesh-based many-core devices and demonstrated the ease and utility of BE methodology for DSE.

Although this paper was limited to device-level experiments, we discussed the extensibility of our methods to node- and system-levels. Working towards this goal, we are modeling a larger portion of the current CMT-nek implementation (than described in this paper) and its execution on contemporary HPC systems (e.g., Vulcan [29], CAB [30]). Furthermore, we are beginning to model several candidate implementations of certain CMT-nek kernels and exploring their performance on HPC systems utilizing accelerators such as GPUs. In the future, we plan to model additional metrics (e.g., reliability, power) to enable multi-objective DSE.

Determining the optimal degree of behavioral abstraction becomes more difficult at the system-level prompting us to employ more robust uncertainty quantification and analysis techniques when evaluating new design decisions (e.g., sophistication of performance interpolation techniques, detail of network congestion models). We have incorporated mechanisms for Monte-Carlo-based (MC) uncertainty propagation [31] into the BE framework, greatly improving model development and simulation accuracy. The increased computation required for MC-based simulations may limit the practical scale of BE simulations in software; we are currently investigating the use of FPGA acceleration techniques to alleviate this issue. Our early functioning prototype running on Novo-G [32,33] is capable of performing simulations in Sect. 6 about 100x faster than our software simulator and we are currently integrating functionality for random distribution sampling to enable MC simulations in hardware.

Acknowledgment. This work is supported by the U.S. Department of Energy, National Nuclear Security Administration, Advanced Simulation and Computing Program, as a Cooperative Agreement under the Predictive Science Academic Alliance Program, under Contract No. DE-NA0002378. This work was supported in part by the I/UCRC Program of the National Science Foundation under Grant Nos. EEC-0642422 and IIP-1161022.

References

1. Fischer, P.F., Lottes, J.W., Kerkemeier, S.G.: Nek5000 (2008). http://nek5000.mcs.anl.gov
2. Berna, G., Beyer, G., Davis, K., Lanning, D.: FRAPCON-3: a computer code for the calculation of steady-state, thermal-mechanical behavior of oxide fuel rods for high burnup, December 1997

3. Hamidouche, T., Bousbia-Salah, A., Adorni, M., D'Auria, F.: Dynamic calculations of the iaea safety mtr research reactor benchmark problem using relap5/3.2 code. Ann. Nucl. Energy **31**(12), 1385–1402 (2004)
4. CCMT: Psaap-ii center for compressible multiphase turbulence. https://www.eng.ufl.edu/ccmt/
5. Kogge, P., Bergman, K., Borkar, S., Campbell, D., Carson, W., Dally, W., Denneau, M., Franzon, P., Harrod, W., Hill, K., et al.: Exascale computing study: technology challenges in achieving exascale systems (2008)
6. Top500: The top500 list, November 2015. http://www.top500.org/lists/2015/11/
7. Barrett, R.F., Borkar, S., Dosanjh, S.S., Hammond, S.D., Heroux, M.A., Hu, X.S., Luitjens, J., Parker, S.G., Shalf, J., Tang, L.: On the role of co-design in high performance computing, vol. 24, pp. 141–155 (2013)
8. Dosanjh, S., Barrett, R., Doerfler, D., Hammond, S., Hemmert, K., Heroux, M., Lin, P., Pedretti, K., Rodrigues, A., Trucano, T., et al.: Exascale design space exploration and co-design. Future Gener. Comput. Syst. **30**, 46–58 (2014)
9. Ang, J.A., Hoang, T.T., Kelly, S.M., McPherson, A., Neely, R.: Advanced simulation and computing co-design strategy. Technical report, Sandia National Laboratories (SNL-NM), Albuquerque, NM (United States) (2015)
10. Binkert, N., Beckmann, B., Black, G., Reinhardt, S.K., Saidi, A., Basu, A., Hestness, J., Hower, D.R., Krishna, T., Sardashti, S., Sen, R., Sewell, K., Shoaib, M., Vaish, N., Hill, M.D., Wood, D.A.: The gem5 simulator. SIGARCH Comput. Archit. News **39**(2), 1–7 (2011)
11. Magnusson, P.S., Christensson, M., Eskilson, J., Forsgren, D., Hallberg, G., Hogberg, J., Larsson, F., Moestedt, A., Werner, B.: Simics: a full system simulation platform. Computer **35**(2), 50–58 (2002)
12. Austin, T., Larson, E., Ernst, D.: Simplescalar: an infrastructure for computer system modeling. Computer **35**(2), 59–67 (2002)
13. Zheng, G., Kakulapati, G., Kalé, L.V.: Bigsim: a parallel simulator for performance prediction of extremely large parallel machines. In: Proceedings of the 18th International Symposium on Parallel and Distributed Processing, vol. 78. IEEE (2004)
14. Wang, J., Beu, J., Yalamanchili, S., Conte, T.: Designing configurable, modifiable and reusable components for simulation of multicore systems. In: 2012 SC Companion: High Performance Computing, Networking, Storage and Analysis (SCC), pp. 472–476. IEEE (2012)
15. Tan, Z., Waterman, A., Avizienis, R., Lee, Y., Cook, H., Patterson, D., Asanović, K.: Ramp gold: an fpga-based architecture simulator for multiprocessors. In: Proceedings of the 47th Design Automation Conference, pp. 463–468. ACM (2010)
16. Culler, D., Karp, R., Patterson, D., Sahay, A., Schauser, K.E., Santos, E., Subramonian, R., von Eicken, T.: Logp: towards a realistic model of parallel computation. In: Proceedings of the Fourth ACM SIGPLAN Symposium on Principles and Practice of Parallel Programming, PPOPP 1993, New York, NY, USA, pp. 1–12. ACM (1993)
17. Alexandrov, A., Ionescu, M.F., Schauser, K.E., Scheiman, C.: Loggp: incorporating long messages into the logp modelone step closer towards a realistic model for parallel computation. In: Proceedings of the Seventh Annual ACM Symposium on Parallel Algorithms and Architectures, pp. 95–105. ACM (1995)
18. Ino, F., Fujimoto, N., Hagihara, K.: Loggps: a parallel computational model for synchronization analysis. In: ACM SIGPLAN Notices, vol. 36, pp. 133–142. ACM (2001)

19. Cadence palladium ii
20. Mentor graphics corporation. veloce emulation platform
21. Dong, Z., Wang, J., Riley, G., Yalamanchili, S.: An efficient front-end for timing-directed parallel simulation of multi-core system. In: Proceedings of the 7th International ICST Conference on Simulation Tools and Techniques, ICST (Institute for Computer Sciences, Social-Informatics and Telecommunications Engineering), pp. 201–206 (2014)
22. Grobelny, E., Bueno, D., Troxel, I., George, A.D., Vetter, J.S.: Fase: a framework for scalable performance prediction of hpc systems and applications. Simulation **83**(10), 721–745 (2007)
23. Rodrigues, A.F., Hemmert, K.S., Barrett, B.W., Kersey, C., Oldfield, R., Weston, M., Risen, R., Cook, J., Rosenfeld, P., CooperBalls, E., et al.: The structural simulation toolkit. ACM SIGMETRICS Perform. Eval. Rev. **38**(4), 37–42 (2011)
24. Janssen, C.L., Adalsteinsson, H., Cranford, S., Kenny, J.P., Pinar, A., Evensky, D.A., Mayo, J.: A simulator for large-scale parallel computer architectures. Technol. Integr. Advancements Distrib. Syst. Comput. **179**, 179–195 (2012)
25. Rudolph, D., Stitt, G.: An interpolation-based approach to multi-parameter performance modeling for heterogeneous systems. In: 2015 IEEE 26th International Conference on Application-specific Systems, Architectures and Processors (ASAP), pp. 174–180. IEEE (2015)
26. Lamport, L.: Time, clocks, and the ordering of events in a distributed system. Commun. ACM **21**(7), 558–565 (1978)
27. Kumar, N., Sringarpure, M., Banerjee, T., Hackl, J., Balachandar, S., Lam, H., George, A., Ranka, S.: CMT-bone: a mini-app for compressible multiphase turbulence simulation software. In: Proceedings of the 2015 IEEE International Conference on Cluster Computing (CLUSTER 2015), pp. 785–792. IEEE Computer Society, Washington, DC (2015)
28. Tilera: Tile-gx8036 processor specification brief (2012). http://www.tilera.com/sites/default/files/productbriefs/TILE-Gx8036PB033-02.pdf
29. Barney, B.: Using the sequoia and vulcan bg/q systems, Tutorial Lawrence Livermore National Laboratory, Lawrence Livermore National Laboratory, **8** (2014). https://computing.llnl.gov/tutorials/bgq/#ParallelIO
30. LLNL: Open computing facility-ocf, resource overview: Cab, October 2014
31. Helton, J.: Uncertainty and sensitivity analysis in the presence of stochastic and subjective uncertainty. J. Stat. Comput. Simul. **57**(1–4), 3–76 (1997)
32. George, A., Lam, H., Stitt, G.: Novo-g: at the forefront of scalable reconfigurable supercomputing. Comput. Sci. Eng. **13**(1), 82–86 (2011)
33. Lawande, A.G., George, A.D., Lam, H.: Novo-g#: a multidimensional torus-based reconfigurable cluster for molecular dynamics. Concurrency Comput. Pract. Experience **28**, 2374–2393 (2015)

Closing the Performance Gap with Modern C++

Thomas Heller[1,5(✉)], Hartmut Kaiser[2,5], Patrick Diehl[3,5], Dietmar Fey[1], and Marc Alexander Schweitzer[3,4]

[1] Computer Science 3, Computer Architectures,
Friedrich-Alexander-University, Erlangen, Germany
thom.heller@gmail.com
[2] Center for Computation and Technology,
Louisiana State University, Baton Rouge, USA
[3] Institute for Numerical Simulation, University of Bonn, Bonn, Germany
[4] Meshfree Multiscale Methods, Fraunhofer SCAI,
Schloss Birlinghoven, Sankt Augustin, Germany
[5] The STELLAR Group, Baton Rouge, USA
hpx-users@stellar.cct.lsu.edu
http://stellar-group.org

Abstract. On the way to Exascale, programmers face the increasing challenge of having to support multiple hardware architectures from the same code base. At the same time, portability of code and performance are increasingly difficult to achieve as hardware architectures are becoming more and more diverse. Today's heterogeneous systems often include two or more completely distinct and incompatible hardware execution models, such as GPGPU's, SIMD vector units, and general purpose cores which conventionally have to be programmed using separate tool chains representing non-overlapping programming models. The recent revival of interest in the industry and the wider community for the C++ language has spurred a remarkable amount of standardization proposals and technical specifications in the arena of concurrency and parallelism. This recently includes an increasing amount of discussion around the need for a uniform, higher-level abstraction and programming model for parallelism in the C++ standard targeting heterogeneous and distributed computing. Such an abstraction should perfectly blend with existing, already standardized language and library features, but should also be generic enough to support future hardware developments. In this paper, we present the results from developing such a higher-level programming abstraction for parallelism in C++ which aims at enabling code and performance portability over a wide range of architectures and for various types of parallelism. We present and compare performance data obtained from running the well-known STREAM benchmark ported to our higher level C++ abstraction with the corresponding results from running it natively. We show that our abstractions enable performance at least as good as the comparable base-line benchmarks while providing a uniform programming API on all compared target architectures.

© Springer International Publishing AG 2016
M. Taufer et al. (Eds.): ISC High Performance Workshops 2016, LNCS 9945, pp. 18–31, 2016.
DOI: 10.1007/978-3-319-46079-6_2

1   Introduction

The massive local parallelism available on today's and tomorrow's systems poses one of the biggest challenges to programmers, especially on heterogeneous architectures, where conventional techniques require to develop and tune independent code bases for each of the separate parts of the machine. This paper focuses on how to address portability in terms of code and performance when developing applications targeting heterogeneous systems. More and more systems come online which consist of more than one hardware architecture, all of it made available to the developers through often independent and orthogonal tool-chains.

With the recently growing interest in the community in C++ and the increased activity towards making all of the available parallelism of the machine available through native C++ language features and library facilities, we see an increasing necessity in developing higher level C++ APIs which ensure a high level of portability of code while providing the best possible performance. At the same time, such APIs have to provide a sufficient amount of generality and flexibility to provide a solid foundation for a wide variety of application use cases. GPGPU vendors have started to make their C++ tool chains more conforming with the newest C++11/C++14 Standards [17], as demonstrated for instance by recent versions of NVidia's CUDA [6] or the newer HCC compiler [3] as provided by AMD. Unfortunately, there are no usable standards-conforming library solution available yet which would help in writing C++ code which is portable across heterogeneous architectures.

One of the key problems to solve while developing such higher level library abstractions is to provide facilities to control and coordinate the placement of data in conjunction with the location of the execution of the work on this data. We describe the result of our research in this direction, provide a proof of concept optimization, and present performance results gathered from comparing native implementations of the STREAM benchmark for OpenMP [16] and CUDA [9] with an equivalent application written based on our design. We show that there is essentially no performance difference between the original benchmarks and our results.

Our presented implementation of C++ algorithms is fully conforming to the specification to be published as part of the C++17 Standard [18]. It is based on HPX [13], a parallel runtime system for applications of any scale. For our comparisons with the native OpenMP and CUDA benchmarks we use the same sources demonstrating a high degree of portability of code and performance. The used parallel algorithms are conforming to the latest C++17 Standard and are designed to be generic, extensible and composable.

In the remaining part of this paper we describe related work (Sect. 2), talk about locality of data and work (Sect. 3), describe our implementations (Sect. 4), show the results (Sect. 5), and summarize our findings (Sect. 6).

2   Related Work

The existing solutions for programming accelerators mostly have in common that they are based either on OpenCL [5] or on CUDA [6] as their backends.

Table 1 shows an overview of the different approaches existing today. The most prominent in that regard are pragma based language extensions such as OpenMP and OpenACC [4]. The pragma solutions naturally don't offer good support for C++ abstractions. In order to get better C++ language integration, software has to directly rely on newer toolchains directly supporting C++, such as recent versions of CUDA, the newer HCC compiler [3], or SYCL [2].

Generic higher level abstractions are also provided by various library based solutions such as Kokkos [10], raja [12], Thrust [11], and Bolt [1]. Those attempt to offer higher level interfaces similar but not conforming to the parallel algorithms specified in the upcoming C++17-Standard [19]. One of the contributions of this paper is to provide standards-conforming implementations of those parallel algorithms combined with truly heterogeneous solutions enabling transparent locality control, a feature not available from the listed existing libraries.

In addition, we aim to provide a solution for all existing accelerator architectures, that is not limited to either OpenCL or CUDA based products providing a modern C++ programming interface.

Table 1. overview of different approaches: pragma based solutions, low level compiler and libraries to leverage different architectures.

Name	Type	Hardware support	
OpenMP	pragmas	cpu, accelerators	[5]
OpenACC	pragmas	accelerators	[4]
HCC	compiler	OpenCL, HSA	[3]
CUDA	compiler	CUDA	[6]
SYCL	compiler	OpenCL	[2]
Kokkos	library	OpenMP, CUDA	[10]
Raja	library	OpenMP, CUDA	[12]
Thrust	library	CUDA, TBB, OpenMP	[11]
Bolt	library	C++Amp, OpenCL, CPU	[1]

3   Locality of Work and Data

Modern computing architectures are composed of various different levels of processing units and memory locations. Figure 1 shows an example for such architectures that are a common in today's nodes for GPU accelerated supercomputers. Tomorrow's systems will be composed of even more complex memory architectures. In addition, when for instance looking at autonomous driving applications requiring a huge amount of processing power, the diversity of different processing units as well as different memory locations will increase.

In order to program these architectures efficiently it is important to place the data as close as possible to the site where the execution has to take place. As such, we need APIs that are able to effectively and transparently express the data placement on and data movement to concrete memory locations

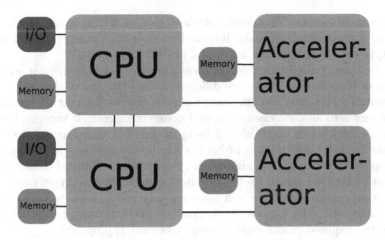

Fig. 1. This Figure shows an example of a typical heterogeneous architecture that is composed of multiple CPUs containing different physical blocks of memory as well as Accelerators and Network Interfaces with their own discrete memory locations, which are connected through a common bus.

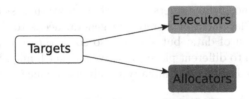

Fig. 2. This figure shows the relation between targets, memory allocation and work execution; A target is the link between co-locating memory allocation and execution of tasks close to the memory location. It is used to transparently express the notion of a 'place' in the system to both, allocation and execution.

(or places) in a system. We also need APIs allowing to coordinate the desired data placement with fine control over defining the execution site from where the code will access the data.

This paper proposes concepts and APIs that are rooted within the C++ language and Standard Library to create an expressive, performant, and extensible way to control locality of work and data by refining the *allocator* concept already defined in the C++ standard as well as using the proposed *executor* concept. These are tied together by defining *targets*, which represent places in a system, to properly co-locate placement of data and execution of work (see Fig. 2).

3.1   Defining Places in a System

In order to define a place in a system, or a *target*, we first need to evaluate the landscape of all available different targets. Examples for targets are: Sets of CPU cores, which can be used to solve NUMA related problems; Different memory areas, such as scratch pads, used to access high bandwidth or other special purpose memory; Accelerator devices, such as GPUs, which can be used to offload compute intensive tasks; Remote Processes in a distributed application; Other types of special purpose hardware, like FPGAs; etc.

Since all the examples for different targets given above have distinct use cases in terms of their ability to execute different tasks (data parallelism, code with many control structures) and different properties such as different address spaces or mechanisms to allocate memory as well as executing code, it becomes obvious that the definition of a target should be in the form of an concept that doesn't define the behavior directly, but rather is a handle to an opaque implementation defined place in the system. This does not require any additional constraints or specification for the concept itself, since an implementation is directly operating on target properties specific to a in place memory and to execute work. By not having those artificially imposed limitations, we allow for maximal flexibility by defining the required customization points wherever appropriate.

For supporting the richer functionality to dispatch memory placement and work execution, the implementation is based on the interfaces described in Sects. 3.2 and 3.3.

3.2 Controlling Memory Placement

After creating a concept for targets (see Sect. 3.1), we discuss the actual placement of memory. Placement of memory in general needs to first and foremost handle the allocation of data, but should also cover the transparent migration (movement) of data to different places of a given target family. For memory allocation purposes, we leverage the already widely used concept of the Allocator.

```
template <typename Allocator >
struct allocator_traits
  : std::allocator_traits<Allocator>
{
  typedef unspecified reference;
  typedef unspecified const_reference;

  typedef unspecified access_target;
  typedef typename access_target::target_type target_type;

  static target_type target(Allocator const& alloc);

  template <typename ...Ts>
  static void bulk_construct(Allocator& alloc, pointer p,
    size_type count, Ts &&... vs);

  static void bulk_destroy(Allocator& alloc, pointer p,
    size_type count) noexcept;
};
```

Listing 1.1. Extensions to std::allocator_traits to support efficient memory allocation and construction operations for targets as described in Sect. 3.1.

Allocators are already widely used within the C++ standard library (for example with containers or smart pointers) with the main purpose of encapsulating memory allocation. This allows for great reuse of the defined concepts in already existing code and serves our purpose of hiding memory allocation on opaque targets perfectly. For the sake of making memory allocations efficient on various targets, such as for discrete GPU memory or remote processes, we introduced backwards compatibly extensions. Listing 1.1 outlines the traits class which supports our extensions, the remaining interface follows `std::allocator_traits`. The extensions are optional, and fall back to the requirements for C++ standard allocators. The extensions introduced, serve the purpose to perform bulk construction and destruction of C++ objects. This is necessary to either avoid overheads of offloading the constructor or destructor code or to support first-touch policies (as used for ccNUMA architectures) efficiently.

The topic of transparent data migration is not covered within this paper and does not fall within the realm of memory allocation. Another mechanism would need to be created with appropriate customization points to support different target use cases. One example within the HPX runtime system is the migration of objects between different localities (where a locality is a HPX specific target).

3.3   Controlling Execution Locality

The previous sections described the mechanisms to define targets (Sect. 3.1) and memory allocation (Sect. 3.2). The missing piece, execution of work close to targets, is based on the `Executor` concept. Executors are an abstraction which define where, how, and when work should be executed, in a possibly architecture specific way (see also [7]).

```
template <typename Executor>
struct executor_traits
{
  typedef Executor executor_type;

  template <typename T>
  struct future { typedef unspecified type; };

  template <typename Executor_, typename F, typename ... Ts>
  static void apply_execute(Executor_ && exec, F && f,
    Ts &&... ts);

  template <typename Executor_, typename F, typename ... Ts>
  static auto async_execute(Executor_ && exec, F && f,
    Ts &&... ts);

  template <typename Executor_, typename F, typename ... Ts>
  static auto execute(Executor_ && exec, F && f,
    Ts &&...ts);
```

```
template <typename Executor_, typename F, typename Shape,
    typename ... Ts>
static auto
bulk_async_execute(Executor_ && exec, F && f,
  Shape const& shape, Ts &&... ts);

template <typename Executor_, typename F, typename Shape,
    typename ... Ts>
static auto
bulk_execute(Executor_ && exec, F && f,
  Shape const& shape, Ts &&... ts);
};
```

Listing 1.2. std::executor_traits to support efficient execution on targets as described in Sect. 3.1

Executors follow the same principle as Allocators in such that they are accessible through the trait executor_traits (see Listing 1.2), in a similar fashion to allocator_traits. It is important to note that an implementation for a given executor is not required to implement all functions as outlined but the traits are able to infer missing implementations. The only mandatory function an executor needs to be implement is async_execute. The remaining facilities are, if not provided otherwise, automatically deduced from that. However, it is important to note that architectures like GPGPUs benefit tremendously by implementing the bulk execution features.

Specific executor types are then specialized, architecture dependent implementations of the executor concept which use this architecture dependent knowledge to provide the target specific mechanisms necessary to launch asynchronous tasks. We introduce a selection of special purpose executors in Sect. 4.

3.4 Parallel Algorithms and Distributed Data Structures

Now that we have all the necessary ingredients to co-locate work and data, we are going to make it usable by providing a specialized implementation of a vector. This vector is exposing the same high level interface as std::vector<T>. This data structure encapsulates an array of elements of the same type and enables accessing the stored data element-wise, through iterators, and using other supporting facilities like resizing data, giving the user an abstraction over contiguous data using the API as described in Sect. 3.2.

The exposed iterators can be used directly with the parallel algorithms [14] already existing in HPX. Additionally, HPX's parallel algorithms allow us to pass executors (see Sect. 3.3) which will in turn execute the algorithm on the designated resources. By using compatible targets for both, the executor and the allocator, the co-location of tasks and data is guaranteed.

Listing 1.3 is providing an example that transforms the string "hello world" to all uppercase. Note that this example is omitting actual targets and specific allocators/executors which will be introduced in Sect. 4.

```
auto target = ...;

target_allocator<char> alloc(target);
vector<char, target_allocator<char>> s(
   {'h', 'e', 'l', 'l', 'o', 'w', 'o', 'r', 'l', 'd'},
   alloc);

target_executor exec(target);
transform(par.on(exec), s.begin(), s.end(),
   [](char c){ return to_upper(c); });
```

Listing 1.3. Hello world example using the introduced concepts `Target`, `Allocator` and `Executor`

4 Implementation

This Section describes specific implementations for the concepts we defined in Sect. 3 to demonstrate the feasibility of our claims. As a proof of concept we implemented special allocators and executors to support NUMA architectures as well as an allocator and various executors for CUDA devices.

4.1 Support for NUMA Aware Programming

Contemporary compute nodes nowadays usually consist of two or more sockets. Within this architecture, co-locating work and data is an important ingredient to leverage the full memory bandwidth within the whole system to avoid NUMA related bottlenecks and to reduce cross-NUMA-domain (cross-socket) memory accesses.

For this purpose of identifying cores, the target (see Sect. 3.1) is a numeric identifier for a specific CPU (see Fig. 3). To identify the various cores in the system we use hwloc [8]. This allows us to use bit-masks to define multiple CPUs as one single target, making up a convenient way to build targets for whole NUMA domains. For convenience, two functions are provided: `get_targets()` which returns a vector containing all processing units found in the system and `get_numa_domains()` which is returning a vector with targets, where each element in that vector represents the cpuset (bit-mask) identifying the respective NUMA domain. The targets returned from those functions can then easily be transformed as necssary, for instance to construct finer grained sets.

After having the targets defined to support our CPU based architecture we need a target specific allocator to support a vector of separate targets. As a proof of concept we chose to implement a block allocation scheme by dividing the number of bytes to be allocated evenly across the passed elements in the target vector.

The same scheme as described above is used to implement the executor. This ensures that work that is to be executed on data using the block allocator is

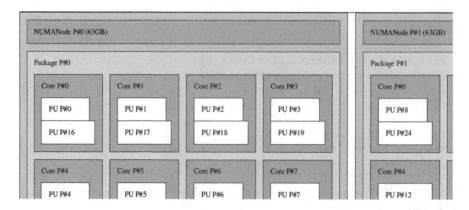

Fig. 3. Graphical output from `hwloc-ls` showing a two-socket Ivy Bridge system. The Figure shows the different identifiers for the different processing units and groups them in their respective NUMA domain.

co-located with the data. The cpusets in the associated targets are used as an affinity mask to pin the executed tasks to the cores accordingly.

4.2 Leveraging CUDA Based GPGPUs

Since more and more supercomputers are equipped with NVIDIA based GPG-PUs as accelerators, this section will cover a prototypical solution based on CUDA.

Within the CUDA based implementation, the choice for how to define a target is determined by the underlying programming model. The devices are represented by numerical identifiers and in order to support asynchronous operations such as kernel invocations and memory copies, CUDA streams are used. That means a CUDA target is implemented as a wrapper for an integer representing the device and a CUDA stream attached to that device.

For memory placement, an `Allocator` (see Listing 1.1) are specialized to allocate memory on the given device and the (bulk) construct/destruct functions offload directly to the GPU. In terms of transparent memory access via references to a given object we introduce a special proxy object that allows to hide the implementation specific details on how to read and write memory and as such seamlessly supports the interfaces described in Sect. 3.4. For copying data between host and device, we extended the parallel copy algorithm to provide a internal specialization that is able to directly call the respective CUDA memcpy functions for maximum efficiency.

The executor support (see Sect. 3.3) is exploiting the dual compilation mode of CUDA's nvcc compiler and is therefore able to execute any callable that is marked with the CUDA specific `__device__` attribute. This gives great flexibility since code that is supposed to be offloaded needs to be, in theory, only marked with the __device__ (in addition to __host__) attribute and can be used immediately with the new executor.

The executor itself implements all functions as outlined in Listing 1.2. For one, the implemented bulk execution facility ensures best-possible performance for executing kernels on an array of data-elements. Secondly, we implemented both, the synchronous and asynchronous versions of the executor interfaces as the synchronous versions can be implemented more efficiently than they could be generated by the traits class. The asynchronous versions additionally need to attach a callback to the stream in order to notify the returned future about the completion of the operation on the GPU.

In practice however, this way of programming leads to unforeseen problems during compilation since not all features of C++ are supported on devices and the need to mark up every function does not scale well especially for third party code. Newer compiler technologies such as hcc are more promising in this regard and a truly single source solution without additional mark up can be implemented there in the near future.

5   Results

For the sake of giving a first evaluation of our abstractions defined in the previous sections, we are using the STREAM Benchmark [16]. As a proof of concept, the presented APIs have been implemented with the HPX parallel runtime system, and have been ported to the parallel algorithms as defined in the newest C++ Standard [19] (see Listing 1.4).

```
template <typename Executor, typename Vector>
void stream(Executor& e, Vector const& as, Vector const& bs,
    Vector const& cs)
{
  double scalar = 3.0
  // Copy
  copy(e, as.begin(), as.end(), cs.begin());
  // Scale
  transform(e, cs.begin(), cs.end(), bs.begin(),
      [scalar](double c){ return c * scalar;});
  // Add
  transform(e, as.begin(), as.end(), bs.begin(), cs.begin(),
      [](double a, double b){ return a + b;});
  // Triad
  transform(e, bs.begin(), bs.end(), cs.begin(), as.begin(),
      [scalar](double b, double c){ return b + c*scalar;});
}
```

Listing 1.4. Generic implementation of the STREAM benchmark using HPX and C++ standards conforming parallel algorithms.

It is important to note that the benchmark is parameterized on the allocaor used for the arrays (vectors) and the given executor, which allows to design an portable implementation of the benchmark ensuring best possible performance across heterogeneous architecturs in plain C++. For any of the tested architectures, the used Executor and Vector is are using the same target. In our case, we use the NUMA target as defined in Sect. 4.1 and a CUDA target as described in Sect. 4.2. The test platform we use is a dual socket Intel Xeon CPU E5-2650v2 with 2.60 GHz together with a NVIDIA Tesla K40m GPU. As a reference implementation for the NUMA based benchmark, we used the original STREAM benchmark [15], The GPU version was compared with the CUDA based GPU-STREAM [9]. For the CPU based experiments, we used two sockets and 6 cores per socket, that is a total of 12 CPU Cores, which has been determined to deliver the maximal performance for the benchmark

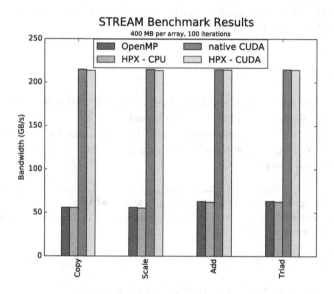

Fig. 4. Results for STREAM Benchmark on the host and GPU. The figure shows the resulting bandwidth achieved with the native implementations and the HPX port showed in Listing 1.4. The achieved performance for all tests is approximately the same for the respective architectures. The benchmark on the CPU used 2 NUMA domains with 6 cores each, the GPU version ran on a single Tesla K40m.

The results we obtained from running our benchmark show that the utilized memory bandwidth is essentially equivalent to that achieved by the native benchmarks. Figure 4 is showing results comparing to the respective reference implementations. What can be seen is that our CPU based implementation is about 1.1% slower than the reference and our CUDA implementation are about 0.4% slower. Figure 5 is giving an impression on the overheads involved with the parallel algorithms abstractions. For small array sizes, the overhead is

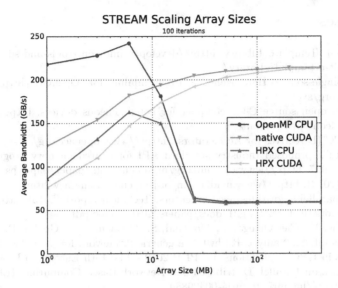

Fig. 5. Results for STREAM Benchmark on the host and GPU. This graph shows the average performance of the entire benchmark suite with varying input sizes, from 10 to 400 MB. While the native implementations provide lower overhead for small input sizes, all implementations converge to the same maximum. The benchmark on the CPU used 2 NUMA domains with 6 cores each, the GPU version ran on a single Tesla K40m.

noticeable within the HPX implementation, however, for reasonable large extents of the array, the implementations are almost similar again.

6   Conclusion

This paper presented a coherent design and implementation based on the foundation of the upcoming C++17 Standard and provided extensions to ensure locality of work and data. We showed that the performance of the introduced higher-level parallelism framework is does not significantly reduced compared to the performance of today's prevalent programming environments. The benefit of our presented solution is to provide a single source, generic, and extensible abstraction for expressing parallelism, together with no loss in performance.

For future work, we are going to extend the number of targets to include more support for different memory hierarchies (e.g. Intel Knights Landing High Bandwitdth Memory) as well as improving the support for GPGPU based solutions by implementing other back ends such as HCC and SYCL.

Acknowledgement. This work is supported by the NSF awards 1240655 (STAR), 1447831 (PXFS), and 1339782 (STORM), and the DoE award DE-SC0008714 (XPRESS) and by the European Union's Horizon 2020 research and innovation program under grant agreement No 671603.

References

1. Bolt C++ Template Library. http://developer.amd.com/tools-and-sdks/opencl-zone/bolt-c-template-library/
2. C++ Single-source Heterogeneous Programming for OpenCL. https://www.khronos.org/sycl
3. HCC: an open source C++ compiler for heterogeneous devices. https://github.com/RadeonOpenCompute/hcc
4. OpenACC (Directives for Accelerators). http://www.openacc.org/
5. OpenMP: a proposed Industry standard API for shared memory programming, October 1997. http://www.openmp.org/mp-documents/paper/paper.ps
6. CUDA (2013). http://www.nvidia.com/object/cuda_home_new.html
7. N4406: parallel algorithms need executors. Technical report (2015). http://www.open-std.org/jtc1/sc22/wg21/docs/papers/2015/n4406.pdf
8. Broquedis, F., Clet-Ortega, J., Moreaud, S., Furmento, N., Goglin, B., Mercier, G., Thibault, S., Namyst, R.: hwloc: a generic framework for managing hardware affinities in HPC applications. In: PDP 2010 - The 18th Euromicro International Conference on Parallel, Distributed and Network-Based Computing. IEEE, Pisa, Italy. https://hal.inria.fr/inria-00429889
9. Deakin, T., McIntosh-Smith, S.: GPU-STREAM: benchmarking the achievable memory bandwidth of graphics processing units. In: IEEE/ACM SuperComputing (2015)
10. Edwards, H.C., Trott, C.R., Sunderland, D.: Kokkos: enabling manycore performance portability through polymorphic memory access patterns. J. Parallel Distrib. Comput. **74**(12), 3202–3216 (2014). Domain-Specific Languages and High-Level Frameworks for High-Performance Computing
11. Hoberock, J., Bell, N.: Thrust: a parallel template library, vol. 42, p. 43 (2010). http://thrust.googlecode.com
12. Hornung, R., Keasler, J., et al.: The Raja portability layer: overview andstatus. Lawrence Livermore National Laboratory, Livermore, USA (2014)
13. Kaiser, H., Adelstein-Lelbach, B., Heller, T., Berg, A., Biddiscombe, J., Bikineev, A., Mercer, G., Schfer, A., Habraken, J., Serio, A., Anderson, M., Stumpf, M., Bourgeois, D., Grubel, P., Brandt, S.R., Copik, M., Amatya, V., Huck, K., Viklund, L., Khatami, Z., Bacharwar, D., Yang, S., Schnetter, E., Bcorde5, Brodowicz, M., Bibek, atrantan, Troska, L., Byerly, Z., Upadhyay, S.: hpx: HPX V0.9.99: a general purpose C++ runtime system for parallel and distributed applications of any scale, July 2016. http://dx.doi.org/10.5281/zenodo.58027
14. Kaiser, H., Heller, T., Bourgeois, D., Fey, D.: Higher-level parallelization for local and distributed asynchronous task-based programming. In: Proceedings of the First International Workshop on Extreme Scale Programming Models and Middleware, pp. 29–37. ACM (2015)
15. McCalpin, J.D.: Stream: sustainable memory bandwidth in high performance computers. Technical report, University of Virginia, Charlottesville, Virginia (1991–2007), a continually updated Technical report. http://www.cs.virginia.edu/stream/
16. McCalpin, J.D.: Memory bandwidth and machine balance in current high performance computers. IEEE Comput. Soc. Tech. Committee Comput. Archit. (TCCA) Newsl. **59**, 19–25 (1995)

17. The C++ Standards Committee: ISO International Standard ISO/IEC 14882: 2014, Programming Language C++. Technical report, Geneva, Switzerland: International Organization for Standardization (ISO) (2014). http://www.open-std. org/jtc1/sc22/wg21
18. The C++ Standards Committee: N4578: Working Draft, Technical Specification for C++ Extensions for Parallelism Version 2. Technical report (2016). http:// open-std.org/JTC1/SC22/WG21/docs/papers/2016/n4578.pdf
19. The C++ Standards Committee: N4594: Working Draft, Standard for Programming Language C ++. Technical report (2016). http://open-std.org/JTC1/SC22/ WG21/docs/papers/2016/n4594.pdf

Energy Efficient Runtime Framework for Exascale Systems

Yousri Mhedheb$^{(\boxtimes)}$ and Achim Streit

Steinbuch Centre for Computing, Karlsruhe Institute of Technology,
Karlsruhe, Germany
{yousri.mhedheb,achim.streit}@kit.edu

Abstract. Building an Exascale computer that solves scientific problems by three orders of magnitude faster as the current Petascale systems is harder than just making it huge. Towards the first Exascale computer, energy consumption has been emerged to a crucial factor. Every component will have to change to create an Exascale syestem, which capable of a million trillion of computing per second. To run efficiently on these huge systems and to take advantages of every computational power, software and underlying algorithms should be rewritten. While many computing intensive applications are designed to use Message Passing Interface (MPI) with two-sided communication semantics, a Partitioned Global Address Space (PGAS) is being designed, through providing an abstraction of the global address space, to treat a distributed system as if the memory were shared. The data locality and communication could be optimized through the one sided communication offered by PGAS. In this paper we present an energy aware runtime framework, which is PGAS based and offers MPI as a substrate communication layer.

Keywords: Exascale · Energy efficiency · Data locality · PGAS · Runtime system · MPI

1 Introduction

Most performance studies of large-scale HPC systems and their workloads have focused primarily on flops, bandwidth, and latency. However, moving forward Exascale computing, energy consumption is expected to be the most crucial factor. In order to achieve the Exascale challenges, as presented in Table 1, power consumption should be increased by only an integer factor. The U.S Department of Energy targets 20 MW as the ceiling for power consumption for an exaflop system. So energy efficiency is being the most crucial factor for Exascale computing. As today's applications are being more data driven as compute driven, and to achieve the Exascale goals [9] for the energy efficiency, only changing the hardware architecture is not sufficient. Also a radical programming rethinking is needed here. To support the future Exascale systems a wide range of scientific data intensive applications are being designed. Most of them are written with the de facto Message Passing Interface (MPI) [2]. Because Exascale systems will

© Springer International Publishing AG 2016
M. Taufer et al. (Eds.): ISC High Performance Workshops 2016, LNCS 9945, pp. 32–44, 2016.
DOI: 10.1007/978-3-319-46079-6_3

Table 1. Exascale challenges

HPC systems	Petascale	Exascale
Peak flops	100–200 Peta	1 Exa
Memory	5 PB	10 PB
Node performance	400 GF	1–10 TF
Node memomry BW	100 GB/s	200–400 GB/s
Interconnect BW	25 GB/s	50 GB/s
Node concurrency	O(100)	O(1000)
System size (nodes)	500000	O(Million)
Total concurrency	50 Million	O(Billion)
Storage	150 PB	300 PB
I/O	10 TB/s	20 TB/s
Power	10 MW	20 MW

be more hierarchical [6] and data locality is being an important deal, Partitioned Global Address Space (PGAS) [16] will be more fitting for these domains. In the context of the DASH [10] project, we have developed a runtime system interface for supporting shared memory style programming on distributed memory systems called DART [23] (the DASH runtime). In an earlier paper [23], we have described DART-MPI, a portable implementation of the DASH runtime, that uses MPI-3 as low-level communication substrate. In this work, we extend DART and we propose an optimized version toward energy efficiency as a new feature of the DART runtime framework. We also explore the different mechanisms for energy efficiency and integrate them in the DART runtime. We will also show how PGAS approaches are well suitable for the Exascale systems.

The remainder of the paper is organized as follows: In Sect. 2, we present the background and the relevant related works, followed by the proposing of our thermal and power aware runtime system DART in Sect. 3. Section 4 describes the implementation using MPI-3. In Sect. 5 benchmark results are shown and discussed. Finally, the paper concludes with a short summary and future work in Sect. 6.

2   Related Work

Energy consumption on Exascale systems has been a hot topic in various research domains. As a result, a lot of research works have been performed for investigating the mechanisms of the energy efficiency with traditional features like Dynamic Voltage and Frequency Scaling (DVFS) [14], load-balancing. Other runtime systems, which are supporting PGAS and energy efficiency, have been proposed in the literature. The work described in [5] presents a runtime framework for HPC systems without any knowledge of applications. In this paper, the authors propose and implement an online methodology for phase detection and identification in HPC systems. Moreover they introduce a partial phase recognition technique that guides the usage of green capabilities. The green capability is here defined as any action that can save energy in an HPC system, such as: CPU frequency scaling, spinning down disks, scaling the speed of network interconnections, and task migration. An important feature of this work is that it does not require prior knowledge of the applications running on the system. The work described in [20] presents a design for Power Aware One-Sided Communication Library. The proposed design detects communication slack, leverage of DVFS and interrupt driven execution to exploit the detected slack for energy efficiency. Besides PGAS languages there are also approaches that implement PGAS in the form of an API and a library. An example is SHMEM, a library API that allows its participating processes to view a partitioned global address space. It was started by Cray Inc. in 1993 and adopted by other vendors later. Currently, the OpenSHMEM community project is building a new and open specification to consolidate the various existing SHMEM [17] versions into a widely accepted standard. Global Arrays (GA) [7] has originally been developed over 20 years ago and provides one-sided global data access for regularly structured one- or multi-dimensional arrays. Many of PGAS languages, which are an extension of C like UPC [8] or Fortran like CAF [21], are designed and proposed in the last years.

2.1   One Sided Communication

In this section, we introduce the various features of MPI and different power conservation approaches which influence our design decisions. The most common use of MPI calls is for two-sided communication [2]. In this communication models, both sender and receiver have to participate in data exchange operations explicitly, which requires synchronization between the processes. For example,

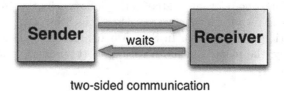

two-sided communication

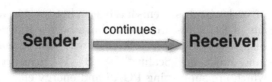

one-sided communication

Fig. 1. MPI one- and two-sided communication send/receive

on the sender's side, it is common to use MPI_Send() or MPI_Isend() calls. On the receiver's side, it is common to use MPI_Recv() or MPI_Irecv() calls. An MPI_Sendrecv() call specifies both a send and a receive. Even collective calls, such as MPI broadcasting, require that every process that contributes or receives data must explicitly do so with the correct MPI call. To overcome this drawback, the MPI-2 standard introduces one-sided communication. In these communication model MPI_Put and MPI_Get allow a direct access to a process without any explicit system synchronization. So that one-sided communication has more advantages like reducing synchronization to improve performance, reducing the data movement and the simplicity of programming. The Fig. 1 demonstrate the difference between one and two sided communication mechanisms.

3   Energy Efficiency in DART

3.1   DASH: Data Structures and Algorithms with Support for Hierarchical Locality

The DASH project funded by the German research foundation (DFG) in the context of the priority program Software for Exascale SPPEXA [18]. It consists of four German partner institutions (LMU Munich, KIT Karlsruhe, HLRS Stuttgart, and TU Dresden) and an associated partner at CEODE in Beijing, China. DASH is a data-structure oriented C++ template library based on PGAS languages. Figure 2 shows the big picture of the structure of the DASH library.

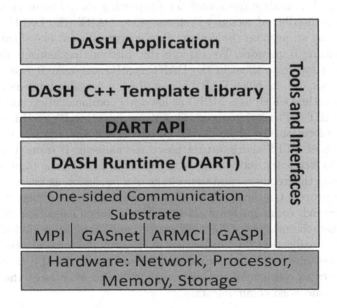

Fig. 2. DASH architecture

The DASH applications are enabled to use the provided data structures that is given in the from of a C++ library. One of the most important features of DASH is making irregular data, stored in memories at several nodes, accessible as if it were a regular data structure. In the context of the DASH project, we have developed a runtime system interface for supporting shared memory style programming on distributed memory systems called DART (the DASH runtime). DASH is a C++ template library to efficiently work with distributed data structures. DASH implements PGAS semantics [10] through operator overloading, supports the allocation over large data sets and provides means of achieving multilevel hierarchical data locality. DART provides the C++ library DASH with services and abstracts from a variety of underlying communication substrates. For our scalable DART runtime implementation we chose MPI, more specifically MPI-3, as the underlying communication mechanism and we call this implementation DART-MPI, while DART-SHMEM and DART-CUDA [22] are other implementations currently under development at the authors' organizations. We chose MPI because it is a standard, well-developed communication substrate, with support for different network technologies. In general, MPI implementations, in particular those provided by system vendors, are highly optimized for their particular network fabric. MPI introduced the concept of one-sided communication, called RMA (Remote Memory Access), in the second version of its specification. The RMA features were improved in the third version (MPI-3). Our PGAS runtime benefits from the optimized implementations of MPI-3 on different architectures as well as its support for one-sided non-blocking inter-node communications. In the context of the DASH project, we have developed a runtime framework for supporting shared memory style programming on distributed memory systems called DART (the DASH runtime). In this section, we propose the design of an energy efficient one-sided communication runtime framework. We explore the different mechanisms for energy efficiency and integrate them in the DART runtime to make it energy aware. As in the paper [23], in which DART is described, a portable implementation of the DASH runtime which uses MPI-3 as low-level communication substrate. To make the DART-MPI runtime more efficient, we integrate DVFS [13] and interrupt based execution. To make DART an energy efficient runtime system, we combine both of DVFS and interrupt based mechanisms. If transitioning overhead between frequency and voltage is negligible in front of the communication slack, reducing the frequency and the voltage of a processor, an energy efficiency would be improved. On the other side, as an alternative to polling specially by exploiting enough communication slack, interrupt based execution [20] mechanism has been the most used for high performance computing and allows the minimal CPU utilization. In this section we present the implementation of an energy efficient one-sided communication runtime system. In this case we classify data-types as contiguous and non-contiguous and we present the different scenarios for one-sided communication.

3.2 Data Locality in DART

As today's applications are being more data driven as compute driven, and as the future Exascale systems will be multi-hierarchical as the today's Petascale systems, the data locality is expected to be the most important factor to achieve the design of an energy efficient system. Due to the increasing complexity of HPC server architectures and networks topology- and affinity-awareness has become a critical component of HPC application optimization. The most important abstraction provided by DART is that of a virtual global memory space and a mechanism to refer to data items residing in this space (a global pointer). A global pointer in DART is a structure of 128 bits, it has a 32 bit field for identifying the unit owning the memory, a 64 bit offset or address field and 32 bits for flags and segment identifiers. Crucially, the global pointer on the DART level has no phase information associated with it, its only purpose on the DART level is to name and refer to memory in the global address space abstraction provided by DART. DASH provides its own global memory class which does contain appropriate phase information needed to decide when to switch between units.

4 Thermal- and Power-Aware Management

DART group, as shown in Fig. 3, should be maintained in an ascending order based on the absolute unit ID. The DART global memory is composed of the memory segments contributed by the units of an application. Visibility and accessibility to memory is based on the team concept in DART. The team-collective operation dart team memalloc aligned allocates n bytes in each unit's memory.

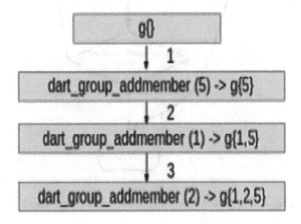

Fig. 3. DART group creation

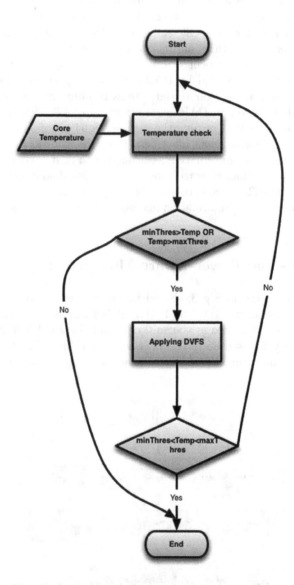

Fig. 4. Thermal aware scheme for temperature check

This memory is accessible only by the members of team t and this particular function allocates team-aligned and symmetric memory. Symmetric refers to the property that all units allocate the same amount of memory, while team-aligned denotes to the property that any unit can compute the global pointer to any location in the global memory chunk by simple arithmetic. The second memory allocation function supported at the moment is dart memalloc, a local (global) memory allocation that allocates n bytes accessibly memory by any unit (the memory has implicit associativity with DART TEAM ALL, but the call is local). Our energy-aware scheduling concept is based on several existing strategies, which are applied for the requirement of different scheduling scenarios. These strategies are individually integrated in our framework at the run-time based on the current load and temperature state.

In this section, we propose a novel approach that reduces the power consumption of a large scale system. It is based on reducing the core temperature [15] using DVFS, task migration and data locality awareness. We choose here DASH and DART as our framework for the parallel programming as it allows a data locality awareness with low overhead. The design of our thermal aware scheme is based on the following strategies, which are individually integrated in our framework at the runtime based on the current load and temperature state. The main tasks of this scheme can be summarized as shown in Fig. 4. The first purpose is to schedule tasks with respect to the temperature of the processors. Such scheduling strategy needs temperature values of the node that describes the changes of this parameter as applications are running. We use here the HOTSPOT tool described at [1] to get temperature values. By an incoming of a task request our temperature check scheme starts first with an initial task of allocating the task's data to one of the nodes that meets the requirement described in the request. In the following, it performs the runtime tuning with respect to load and temperature. The first step for runtime tuning is to detect the critical hosts with either higher temperature or workloads. The pseudo-code in Algorithm 1 illustrates how the scheduler performs this task. In the second step, described by line 11–23, the list of critical nodes, which has been created by the scheduler in the first step, is processed again for finding the tasks running on them. These tasks are the concrete candidates for migration. The candidate tasks are then sorted by their CPU usage and those with minimal CPU usage are marked with a higher priority of migration for the reason of not to bring high workload on the target node, thus to avoid possible further migrations. For the same reason the scheduler must also ensure that the temperature on the target node does not exceed the threshold with a maximal possible frequency. At the end of processing, this scheduling step creates a task list that contains all tasks, which are the actual migration objects.

The third and last step, described by lines 24–40 is to find an appropriate target node for allocation of the migration objects in the list created in the second step. Here, the workload requirements (e.g., needed resources) have to be taken into account. The proposal scheme first observes the temperature on the destination. If this temperature is between the maximal and minimal threshold values (temperature threshold) and the requirement of the task is fulfilled, the observed node is selected as the target node. In case that several target nodes are found, the one with the minimal energy consumption will be chosen.

Since the power consumption depends on the CPU usage, this metric has to be measured periodically, before each task scheduling step in the whole execution process in order to calculate the current consumed energy by the CPU. And since the temperature of each core depends of his dynamic power, we apply here the DVFS technique for maintaining all cores working at their maximum frequency [12] as long as their temperature is between the minimal and the maximal allowed temperature values (temperature thresholds). To verify the concept and to validate the functionality of the proposed scheduling strategies, we extend the implementation of DART with a scheduling Interface.

5   Energy and Performance Evaluation of DART

In this section, we evaluate the performance of DART-MPI using a set of benchmarks which includes low-level communication and application benchmarks. We describe also the evaluation methodology and experimental setup that we use to evaluate the effectiveness of our runtime scheduling algorithm.

5.1   Experimental Test Bed

We performed all experiments on BwUniCluster [4], a 512-node Intel Xeon E5-2670 cluster at Steinbuch Centre for Computing (KIT) with an InfiniBand 4X FDR interconnect. Each cab node is composed of 2 Octa-Core processors and 64 GB of DRAM. To study the impact of the approaches proposed in Sect. 4, we use a designed MPI communication benchmarks available at [3]. This benchmark was selected because it exhibits performance and scaling behaviour typical for a wide range of HPC applications. There are two different evaluation metrics used for the evaluation of DART to compare the performance of various approaches presented above, and we compare them with the polling approach, which is the default methodology for most one-sided communication runtime systems. The fundamental metric is the latency observed by each of the approaches. Another metric of interest is the power consumption of the approaches. We specifically focus on the thresholds beyond which the power and energy/mbyte may be improved without an increase in latency. To estimate the potential power benefits, we use the power consumption data gathered from the benchmark results.

Algorithm 1. Algorithm for detecting critical nodes

Input: nodes, tasks
Output: CriticalNodes
1: **for** each node in nodes **do**
2:     **if** isNodeOverThresholdTemperature (node) **then**
3:         $overThresholdTempNodes \leftarrow addnode$
4:     **else**
5:         **if** isNodeUnderThresholdTemperature (node) **then**
6:             $underThresholdTempNodes \leftarrow addnode$
7:         **end if**
8:     **end if**
9:     $overunderNodes \leftarrow overThresholdTempNodes + underThresholdTempNodes$
10:    $CriticalNodes \leftarrow overunderNodes$
11:    **for** each node in CriticalNodes **do**
12:        **while** true **do**
13:            $vm \leftarrow getTasks(node)$
14:            **if** **then**$task = Null$
15:                break
16:            **end if**
17:            $TaskstoMigrateList \leftarrow addtask$
18:            $node \leftarrow deallocatetask$
19:            **if** **then**$isNodeOverThresTemp(node)\ AndisNodeUnderThresTemp(node)$
20:                break
21:            **end if**
22:        **end while**
23:    **end for**
24:    **for** each task in TasksToMigrateList **do**
25:        $allocatednode \leftarrow null$
26:        $minPower \leftarrow Max$
27:        **for** each node not in CriticalNodes **do**
28:            **if** node has enough resources for task **then**
29:                $power \leftarrow estimatePower(node, task)$
30:            **end if**
31:            **if** **then**$power < minPower$
32:                $allocatedNode \leftarrow node$
33:                $minPower \leftarrow power$
34:            **end if**
35:            **if** **then**$allocatedNode! = NULL$
36:                allocate task to allocatedNode
37:            **end if**
38:        **end for**
39:        $MigrationMap \leftarrow add(task, allocatedNode)$
40:    **end for**
41: **end for**

5.2   Experimental Results

In this section, we present the evaluation of DART for each of the communication primitives using the metrics presented above, while comparing the performance of the approaches using native DART and thermal-aware, which is combined with DVFS. Figures 5 and 6 show latency and power consumption for the shift

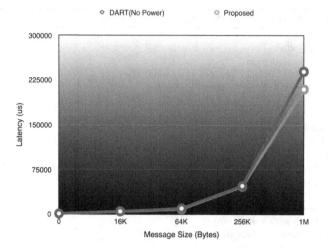

Fig. 5. Alltoall performance (64 processors)

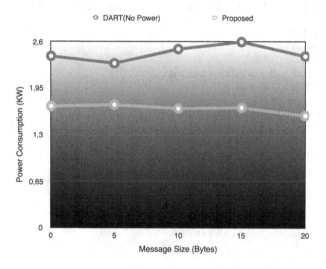

Fig. 6. Power consumption (64 processors)

communication benchmark using the Alltoall on 64 processes, respectively. All benchmarks are averaged over multiple executions and the measurement errors are estimated from the statistical standard deviation. In Fig. 5, we compare the performance of our proposed thermal-aware algorithm with DART_Alltoall algorithm for data locality. We observe that there is a little bit latency difference between the default algorithm, DVFS and our proposed algorithm. In the Fig. 6 we compare the power consumption characteristics of the proposed algorithm with the primitive DART. In the native DART algorithm, each node consumes circa 2.4 KW. However, our thermal-aware algorithm allows a minimizing of a power consumption to circa 1.6 KW for big size of messages.

6   Conclusion

In this paper we have designed a Power and Thermal Aware One-sided Communication Runtime Framework, based on PGAS, that utilises DVFS and the temperature threshold to maintain the system working with his peak frequency. The main challenge of our approach is to minimize the power amount being consumed without any remarkable performance degradation. We have demonstrated through an application benchmark that our proposed algorithm outperforms the native DART runtime algorithm and can deliver better power saving results. We plan to continue development of energy-efficient runtime and we also plan to evaluate it with a real DASH application on a bigger system like JUQUEEN [11] and SuperMUC [19].

Acknowledgement. We gratefully acknowledge funding by the German Research Foundation (DFG) through the German Priority Programme 1648 Software for Exascale Computing (SPPEXA).

References

1. HOTSPOT. http://lava.cs.virginia.edu/HotSpot/
2. MPI. http://www.mpi-forum.org/
3. OSU MPI Benchmarks: OSU MVPICH. http://mvapich.cse.ohio-state.edu/benchmarks/
4. BwUniCluster: BwUniCluster. http://www.bwhpc-c5.de/wiki/index.php
5. Chetsa, G.L.T., Lefevre, L., Pierson, J.M., Stolf, P., Da Costa, G.: A runtime framework for energy efficient HPC systems without a priori knowledge of applications. In: Proceedings of the International Conference on Parallel and Distributed Systems - ICPADS, pp. 660–667 (2012)
6. Daily, J., Vishnu, A., Palmer, B., Van Dam, H., Kerbyson, D.: On the suitability of MPI as a PGAS runtime. In: 2014 21st International Conference on High Performance Computing, HiPC 2014 (2015)
7. Dinan, J., Balaji, P., Hammond, J.R., Krishnamoorthy, S., Tipparaju, V.: Supporting the global arrays PGAS model using MPI one-sided communication. In: Proceedings of the 2012 IEEE 26th International Parallel and Distributed Processing Symposium, IPDPS 2012, pp. 739–750 (2012)
8. El-Ghazawi, T., Carlson, W., Sterling, T., Yelick, K.: UPC: Distributed Shared Memory Programming. Wiley, New York (2005)
9. EXACHA: Exascale challenges. http://science.energy.gov/ascr/research/scidac/exascale-challenges/
10. Fürlinger, K., Glass, C., Gracia, J., Knüpfer, A., Tao, J., Hünich, D., Idrees, K., Maiterth, M., Mhedheb, Y., Zhou, H.: DASH: data structures and algorithms with support for hierarchical locality. In: Lopes, L., et al. (eds.) Euro-Par 2014. LNCS, vol. 8805, pp. 542–552. Springer, Heidelberg (2014). doi:10.1007/978-3-319-14313-2_46

11. Juqueen
12. Kandalla, K., Mancini, E.P., Sur, S., Panda, D.K.: Designing power-aware collective communication algorithms for infiniband clusters. In: Proceedings of the International Conference on Parallel Processing, pp. 218–227 (2010)
13. Krawezik, G., Cappello, F.: Performance comparison of MPI and OpenMP on shared memory multiprocessors. Concurr. Comput. Pract. Exp. **18**(1), 29–61 (2006)
14. Mametjanov, A., Min, M., Norris, B., Hovland, P.D.: Accelerating performance of NekCEM with MPI and CUDA. In: Super Computing (SC13) (2013)
15. Mhedheb, Y., Streit, A.: Energy-efficient Task Scheduling in Data Centers (2014)
16. PGAS. http://www.pgas.org/
17. Shmem: OpenSHMEM. http://openshmem.org/site/
18. SPPEXA: Software for Exascale SPPEXA. http://www.sppexa.de
19. SuperMuc: SuperMUC. https://www.lrz.de/services/compute/supermuc/
20. Vishnu, A., Song, S., Marquez, A., Barker, K., Kerbyson, D., Cameron, K., Balaji, P.: Designing energy efficient communication runtime systems: a view from PGAS models. J. Supercomput. **63**(3), 691–709 (2013)
21. Yang, C., Bland, W., Mellor-Crummey, J., Balaji, P.: Portable, MPI-interoperable coarray fortran. In: Proceedings of the 19th ACM SIGPLAN Symposium on Principles and Practice of Parallel Programming - PPopp 2014, pp. 81–92 (2014)
22. Zhou, H., Idrees, K., Gracia, J.: Leveraging MPI-3 shared-memory extensions for efficient PGAS runtime systems. In: Träff, J.L., Hunold, S., Versaci, F. (eds.) Euro-Par 2015. LNCS, vol. 9233, pp. 373–384. Springer, Heidelberg (2015). doi:10.1007/978-3-662-48096-0_29
23. Zhou, H., Mhedheb, Y., Idrees, K., Glass, C.W.: DART-MPI: an MPI-based implementation of a PGAS runtime system. In: PGAS 2014 (2014)

Extreme-Scale In Situ Visualization of Turbulent Flows on IBM Blue Gene/Q JUQUEEN

Jens Henrik Göbbert[1]([✉]), Mathis Bode[2], and Brian J.N. Wylie[1]

[1] Jülich Supercomputing Centre, Forschungszentrum Jülich GmbH,
Jülich, Germany
{j.goebbert,b.wylie}@fz-juelich.de
[2] Institute for Combustion Technology, RWTH Aachen University,
Aachen, Germany
m.bode@itv.rwth-aachen.de
http://www.fz-juelich.de, http://www.itv.rwth-aachen.de

Abstract. Extracting and analyzing detailed information from large simulations is of crucial importance for science. However, with the increasing problem size of current simulations, the process of visualizing and understanding big simulation raw data becomes more difficult and needs additional effort. More precisely, the gap between compute and I/O performance is widening with current supercomputers. Thus, the classical approach of visualizing simulation results in a post-processing step is limited or even impossible for extreme-scale scenarios. One promising technique to overcome this issue is in situ visualization, which visualizes and analyzes simulation data during simulation runtime. Within this work, in situ visualization using VisIt/Libsim has been added to the CIAO code framework for interactive- and batch-mode visualization on JUQUEEN, an IBM Blue Gene/Q system with 458 752 cores. Full-system runs are demonstrated and early results of performance measurements of an extreme-scale multiphase case are discussed.

Keywords: In-Situ visualization · VisIt/Libsim · Blue Gene/Q · Scalasca

1 Introduction

Storing simulation results on disk and post-processing them after the simulation has finished is still the dominant processing paradigm for analysis and visualization on supercomputers. However, with each generation of supercomputers, available memory and FLOPs increase resulting in simulations of higher fidelity and larger data, while I/O bandwidth and storage do not keep up. Hence, from an energy point of view, FLOPs are cheap, but moving data is expensive. This trend hampers the traditional offline post-processing paradigm as the time to compute relevant simulation results decrease much faster than the time required to dump the data to disk. Consequently, extreme-scale simulations often have to reduce the amount of stored data and subsequent processing algorithms have to

© Springer International Publishing AG 2016
M. Taufer et al. (Eds.): ISC High Performance Workshops 2016, LNCS 9945, pp. 45–55, 2016.
DOI: 10.1007/978-3-319-46079-6_4

reduce the amount of read data from storage devices as file I/O performance is a critical scalability constraint.

The "slow I/O" issue has been addressed through a variety of techniques encountered in highly optimized I/O frameworks [1,2] or just by reducing the data size through coarse-grained temporal resolution, data subsetting, or simply fewer dumps of simulation results to disk. However, as the exascale-computing era approaches, transferring of raw simulation data is increasingly cumbersome. Scientists are most often forced to limit the time for I/O and abstain from meaningful intermediate results of their simulations, when they are preparing their simulations for extreme-scale.

One way to reduce the need for I/O is sparing some supercomputing time to process, structure, reduce, or visualize the data in real-time (in situ/in transit processing) during the simulation [3]. In particular, when data reduction becomes inevitable, only during the simulation all relevant data about the simulated fields and any embedded geometry is readily available at the highest resolution and fidelity for critical decision making. The key aspect of real-time processing on the same machine (in situ processing) is that data is used while it is still in memory. By transforming the data in situ, analysis can extract and preserve all salient features in the raw data that would be lost as a result of aggressive data reduction or much fewer file dumps. It can characterize the full extent of data to enable runtime monitoring, steering, analyzing, and visualizing of the simulation on-the-fly as it does not require to transfer large quantities of raw data to the storage devices.

Especially visualization benefits from in situ methods as I/O performance limits are a major bottleneck in extreme-scale scenarios and makes post-processing of high fidelity simulations impractical. Different tools are available to add in situ visualization to simulation codes. For example, two widespread open-source tools for in situ visualization are ParaView/Catalyst [4,5] and VisIt/Libsim [6–8].

Motivated by the I/O bottleneck of current extreme-scale cases, the CIAO code framework developed at the Institute for Combustion Technology, RWTH Aachen University, for multiscale, multiphysics simulations has been coupled with VisIt/Libsim within this work. An extreme-scale multiphase case was chosen for demonstrating successful in situ visualization in batch and interactive mode on all racks of the IBM Blue Gene/Q JUQUEEN. Early results of performance measurements using Scalasca will be shown and discussed for the remaining part of this paper.

2   Motivation

The efficiency of direct injection combustion engines is strongly affected by the corresponding fuel injection processes. Thus, a more detailed understanding of the fuel injection, especially the droplet formation, would help to improve the design and performance of current engines in order to reduce their emission and pollutant formation. However, studying these processes is very difficult due

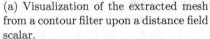

(a) Visualization of the extracted mesh from a contour filter upon a distance field scalar.

(b) Final image raytraced from the extracted mesh in a post-processing step using Blender [9].

Fig. 1. Zoomed view on a droplet forming from a ligament in a primary breakup simulation of a multiphase jet using CIAO [14].

to the overall complexity and the involved small length and time scales. Especially the primary breakup, which happens immediately after the liquid exits the nozzle, is experimentally hardly accessible, but a clear understanding of it is particularly important, because it is the first process to be modeled and impacts all other physical processes [10]. Therefore high-fidelity Direct Numerical Simulation (DNS) of two phase flows providing detailed information about temporal and spatial evolution of multiphase mixing is of crucial importance.

Studying the breakup of ligaments over time (Fig. 1) is one example for high-fidelity multiphase simulations [11–13]. Due to the required resolution, classical post-processing is impossible since the size of a data set representing only a single breaking ligament would already reach ∼850.0 TiB assuming a spatial jet case with 2560^3 grid and a breaking time of 100 time steps. Because many data sets would be required for computing converged statistics, the overall amount of data would be not manageable with conventional post-processing techniques. In order to overcome this issue, in situ visualization is an essential method [14,15] for reducing the amount of data tremendously by focusing only on relevant spatial locations while locally preserving the full temporal resolution.

3 System Setup

JUQUEEN [17] is an IBM Blue Gene/Q system consisting of 28 racks each with two midplanes comprising 512 compute nodes with 1.6 GHz PowerPC A2 processors and 16 GB RAM, connected via a custom five-dimensional torus network. Compute node processors provide 16 cores to applications, each capable of running four hardware threads. Consequently, JUQUEEN offers a total of 458 752 cores and can concurrently run 1 835 008 processes or threads. Additional 248 I/O nodes are connected via Cisco network switches to the JUST GPFS filesystem. A lightweight Linux-based Compute-Node Kernel (CNK) runs on each compute node along with an optimized MPI library.

4   Application Setup

CIAO (**C**ompressible/**I**ncompressible **A**dvanced reactive turbulent simulations with **O**verset) is a multiphysics, multiscale Navier-Stokes solver for turbulent reacting flows in complex geometries. It is a member of the High-Q Club [18], a collection of the highest scaling codes on JUQUEEN. CIAO performs Direct Numerical Simulations (DNS) as well as Large-Eddy Simulations (LES) based on the Navier-Stokes equations along with multiphysics effects (multiphase, combustion, soot, spark, ...). It is a structured, finite difference code, which enables the coupling of multiple domains and their simultaneous computation. Moving meshes are supported and overset meshes can be used for local mesh refinement.

A fully compressible (called *arts_cf*) as well as an incompressible/low-Mach solver (called *arts*) are available within the code framework. Spatial and temporal staggering of flow variables are used in order to increase the accuracy of stencils. The sub-filter model for the momentum equations is an eddy viscosity concept in form of the dynamic Smagorinsky model with Lagrangian averaging along fluid particle trajectories. The fully compressible solver uses equation of states or tabulated fluid properties, a transport equation for internal/total energy, and a low-storage five-stage, explicit Runge-Kutta method for time integration. The incompressible/low-Mach solver uses Crank-Nicolson time advancement and an iterative predictor corrector scheme. The resulting Poisson equation for pressure is solved by HYPRE's [19] highly-scalable multi-grid solver (AMG) or a BiCGStab method. The momentum equations are spatially discretized with central schemes of arbitrary order and various different schemes are available for the scalar equations (WENO, HOUC, QUICK, BQUICK).

The code is written in Fortran90 and parallelized with MPI. The code has been used for production on multiple supercomputers (eg. JUQUEEN, SuperMUC, MareNostrum III). It shows good scaling (Fig. 2 left) up to the full JUQUEEN with all 28 racks and 458 752 cores as long as the limit of about 25 000 cells per core is not undershot, which is a quite common behavior for

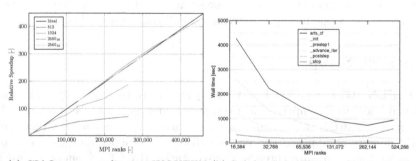

(a) CIAO strong scaling on JUQUEEN for different problem sizes excluding I/O.

(b) Subdivided wall time of a setup with 1024^3 cells and one file dump in _stop every 100 iterations.

Fig. 2. Scaling and timing of the compressible solver 'arts_cf' of CIAO on JUQUEEN

compressible flow solvers. Direct MPI I/O and HDF5 is implemented in CIAO. For performance reasons direct MPI I/O is used for writing the simulation state to the file system. But for large-scale simulations with high-frequency file dumps the I/O performance becomes a major bottleneck.

In Fig. 2(right) the wall time of the major components of the solver are shown exemplary for a setup with 1024^3 grid cells. Here, writing a the raw simulation data file every 100 iterations (as required) dramatically increases the compute time. The simulation becomes even slower for the job size of 262 144 MPI processes. This is related to the small problem size, but at the same time the I/O wall time is rising the wall time for the parts of the compute kernel of the code is still dropping. Hence, the code scales very well on JUQUEEN as long as the I/O is not considered. To get a deeper understanding of the I/O bottleneck performance measurement of CIAO/arts_cf execution performance on JUQUEEN was done with Scalasca using the community-developed Score-P instrumentation and measurement infrastructure [22].

Scalasca, the open-source toolset for scalable performance analysis of large-scale parallel applications [21] is widely deployed on HPC systems including some of the largest in the world. Its runtime summarization and event trace analyses of MPI and OpenMP primarily focus on locating and quantifying communication and synchronization inefficiencies in C/C++/Fortran applications. While most analyses are adequate at modest scales (e.g., a single BGQ rack with 64 k processes/threads), occassionally it is necessary to investigate performance issues that only manifest at larger scales.

All sources were instrumented with the IBM XLF compiler directed to instrument application routines and interposing on the MPI library. Initial profiles collected from executions of the instrumented executable were scored to identify an appropriate routine filter for subsequent measurements, both reducing measurement overheads and generating a more compact profile. Post-processing derived a rich hierarchy of metrics, and also allowed extraction of sub-profiles. One such Scalasca profile of CIAO/arts_cf execution on the 28 racks of JUQUEEN with 458 752 MPI ranks is shown in Fig. 3.

The strong scaling graph in Fig. 2(b) shows the overall execution time of CIAO/arts_cf and its major components for a fixed problem size (1024^3 grid, 10 scalars, 100 iterations) with different numbers of MPI ranks (16 ranks per compute node). Overall execution time decreases with up to 262 144 MPI ranks before becoming slower again with the largest configuration of 458 752 MPI ranks. While `advance_iter` with the WENO5 solver continues to scale well, it is a breakdown in performance of the `_stop` routine dumping the final simulation state that is responsible.

But only 19 % of total CPU time is local computation and 70 % of which is for advancing 100 iterations. The remaining CPU time is used for MPI, of which 77 % is stopping the simulation and dumping the final output with collective file writes. Focusing the profile examination on the `_stop` routine (Fig. 3) reveals that 99 % of its total CPU time is spent in `MPI_File_write_all` calls, with two of these in the `write_sd_data_v003` routine constituting over 94 %. While MPI

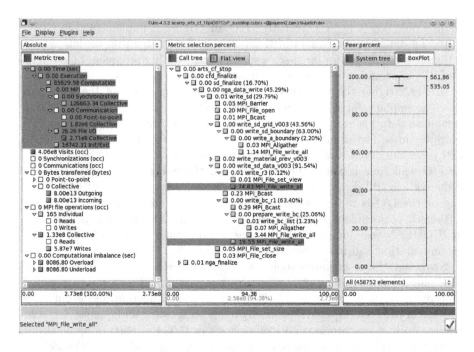

Fig. 3. Scalasca profile of CIAO arts_cf execution on the 28 racks of JUQUEEN Blue Gene/Q with 458 752 MPI ranks. 19 % of total CPU time is local computation, 70 % of which is for advancing 100 iterations. The remaining CPU time is used for MPI, of which 77 % is stopping the simulation and dumping the final output with collective file writes. Within the `arts_cf_stop` routine, 99 % of total CPU time is spent in `MPI_File_write_all` calls, with two of them in `write_sd_data_v003` constituting over 94 %. (Display hiding callpaths with less than 0.5 % of time.)

collective file I/O routines are much more efficient than associated individual file writes, they remain constrained by the bandwidth achievable when all ranks are writing to a single shared file. Libraries such as SIONlib [1] which are optimised for scalable native file I/O achieve significantly higher performance by writing separate files from each BG/Q IONode which serves 2048 cores.

But even with optimized I/O the required high frequency of file dumps would significantly slow down the simulation for extreme-scale scenarios. Therefore, VisIt/Libsim was coupled to CIAO in the step.

Coupling VisIt/Libsim

It takes considerable effort to couple a parallel simulation code like CIAO with a real-time processing code. In general there are two primary coupling strategies: loose coupling using a general purpose approach or close coupling of simulation and processing code via dedicated custom code. For close coupling simulation and visualization codes are sharing the same compute and memory resources and run as a single process for each MPI rank.

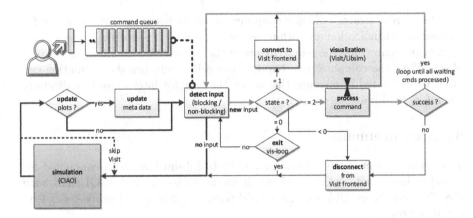

Fig. 4. Coupling mechanism between simulation CIAO and visualization VisIt/Libsim for interactive mode after connection to the VisIt client has been established. The blue line represents the code path for a simulation iteration. The orange line represents the code path to process a visualization command. (Color figure online)

In this case a coupling layer (Fig. 4) for close coupling has been developed to add the parallel in situ VisIt/Libsim to the simulation code CIAO. This layer is independent of CIAO and already in use by two other simulations codes of the High-Q club (ZFS and psOpen) for in situ visualization. It has been developed as a separate module and is linked to the application as VisIt/Libsim only supports static linkage on Blue Gene/Q. Coupling methods for in situ visualization in interactive- and batch-mode have been integrated to CIAO.

If the desired visualization is known before the simulation starts the visualization commands can be batched and an interactive session is not required. This batch mode is often preferable as it is in general not known in advance when a job will start on the supercomputer. Batch mode has been added to CIAO+VisIt/Libsim and used partly for the measurements.

In contrast the interactive mode allows to control the visualization while the simulation is running. In Fig. 4 the coupling mechanism is sketched for interactive mode after connection to the VisIt client running on a local workstation has been established. Here the blue line (simulation loop) represents the code path for a simulation iteration and the orange line (visualization loop) the code path to process a visualization command. After each CIAO iteration it can be checked if new visualization commands have been send from a connected VisIt client. If new input is detected the visualization loop cycles until all commands are processed.

Although in situ processing reduces the amount of time required for I/O, there is a slight overhead which has to be discussed. The VisIt client communicates to MPI rank 0 which broadcasts the information to all other ranks. To limit this overhead in each iteration, the frequency for executing checks (and the MPI broadcast) can be reduced at runtime. Hence, the overhead is negligible.

The current strategy of close coupling can easily result in load imbalance for the parallel visualization algorithms as the numerical grid is distributed over all MPI ranks concerning the requirements of the simulation algorithms in the first place. While the compute time required per cell to advance the simulation can often be estimated in advance this is not the case for interactive visualization. Therefore load imbalances are expected.

5 Measurements

Two measurement campaigns of CIAO+VisIt/Libsim have been conducted for visualization in interactive- and batch mode up to the full JUQUEEN with 458 752 cores. Since CIAO is not hybrid-parallelized one MPI process was executed per core.

VisIt/Libsim version 2.10.0 has been used for the first measurement campaign and 2.10.1 for the second. Required patches, e.g. for the JUQUEEN specific network configuration, have been added to enable the communication between a VisIt client running on an external workstation and VisIt/Libsim on rank 0. All required source code modifications to compile and run VisIt on JUQUEEN have been added to the official branch of VisIt and are contained in version 2.10.2 [16] released March 2016.

With one MPI process per core the available main memory is limited to 1 GiB on JUQUEEN less the memory required by the system. For the setup the binary size increases from 84 MiB without VisIt/Libsim to 167 MiB with statically linked VisIt/Libsim. As the binary is loaded only once per node to the main memory (16 GiB) the additional 83 MiB huge but acceptable. Even though the simulation data could be zero-copied between simulation and visualization engine, it was copied as this ensures that no modification is done accidentally by VisIt. This is a requirement by the developers and users of CIAO and increases the memory footprint additionally.

A turbulent channel setup with droplets and Reynolds number 13760 with two periodic directions as the target case has been used and iteratively simulated using the compressible CIAO solver. In more detail, Large-Eddy Simulation (LES) with Lagrangian averaging, 4th order velocity scheme, WENO5 scalar scheme, and 5 time step subiterations was performed. A Cartesian grid was used, which was uniformly distributed over all MPI ranks and shared between simulation and in situ visualization. Three different test cases from small to production size (Table 1) using CIAO's compressible flow solver have been tested. As well as the flow field, one additional active scalar has been transported. In each case plots with ten isocontours and pseudo-color plots on the pressure field are computed and visualized in addition to volume rendering for the interactive mode.

Interactive Visualization

In the first measurement campaign the interactive in situ visualization on the full system has been tested. The required runs have been conducted during the JUQUEEN Extreme Scaling Workshop 2016 [20].

Table 1. The different CIAO test cases running with VisIt or Scalasca on the full JUQUEEN.

Case	Grid		In situ visualization		Score-P
	Grid size	Cells per rank	Interactive	Batch	
1	640^3	571	x	x	
2	1024^3	2340		x	x
3	2560^3	36571		x	

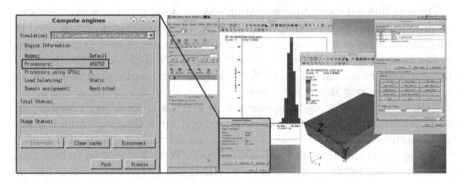

Fig. 5. Interactive in situ visualization of a CIAO+VisIt/Libsim simulation with 458 752 MPI processes. The figure shows the VisIt client on a workstation connected to the simulation running on the full JUQUEEN.

Figure 5 shows a screenshot of the full JUQUEEN run. It visualizes the simulation state after running for 9 units of simulation time. Beside the VisIt overview window (on the left), Window 1 showing a histogram of the pressure, Window 2 visualizing the turbulent kinetic energy within the channel, the compute engines window giving information about the simulation on JUQUEEN and the simulation window allowing to give instructions to the simulation are visible.

The additional memory of $\sim$440 MiB required on rank 0 for interactive in situ visualization limited the problem size to 640^3 grid cells.

Batch Visualization

In the second measurement campaign the visualization was processed in batch mode. Again all tests have been conducted on 28 racks. The additional memory allocated on rank 0 was at any time less than 100 MiB. Hence, the contour filter could be executed on larger problem sizes up to 2560^3 grid. The rendering performance required to generate an image from the resulting contour mesh was not scaling in contrast to the interactive mode. The contour mesh had to be saved to the storage device and rendered in a post-processing step.

6   Conclusions and Future Work

Many extreme-scale applications are facing an I/O bottleneck, which limits their overall performance or the accuracy of the resulting data. One way to deal with this issue is to use in situ visualization benefiting from full memory access during simulation runtime. By coupling VisIt/Libsim and the CIAO code framework it was possible to realize in situ visualization of a turbulent channel flow simulation on 28 racks of JUQUEEN in fully-interactive and batch modes. This setup avoids the need for I/O completely.

The coupling interface implementation was analyzed with the help of Scalasca and promising results presented. Furthermore, the implementation was used to study the breakup of a liquid spatial round jet in a gaseous environment during the Big Blue Gene Week 2016 on the full JUQUEEN. This simulation featured 6144 grid cells in streamwise and 4096 cells in each crosswise direction in order to resolve even finest liquid structures.

Even though the successful application of extreme-scale in situ visualization was demonstrated, issues with respect to memory and scaling were found, which will be addressed in future work. Currently, memory shortage on MPI rank 0 is limiting the grid size for the interactive mode. Work has started to overcome this issue adding hybrid parallelization to CIAO using OpenMP. In batch mode the scaling of the visualization engine has to be analyzed in more detail in order to further improve the communication patterns.

The introduced coupling interface has been generalized in order to simply couple arbitrary code frameworks and visualization libraries like VisIt/Libsim. It is part of the JUSITU library for in situ visualization and available from the authors.

Acknowledgments. The authors gratefully acknowledge the computing time granted for the project JHPC18 by the JARA-HPC Vergabegremium and provided on the JARA-HPC Partition part of the supercomputer JUQUEEN [17] at Forschungszentrum Jülich.

References

1. Frings, W., Wolf, F., Petkov, V.: Scalable massively parallel I/O to task-local files. In: Proceedings of the Conference on High Performance Computing Networking, Storage and Analysis. IEEE (2009)
2. The HDF Group Hierarchical data format (hdf), version 5 (1997–2015). http://www.hdfgroup.org/HDF5
3. Ma, K.-L.: In-situ visualization at extreme scale: challenges and opportunities. IEEE Comput. Graphics Appl. **29**(6), 14–19 (2009)
4. Kitware: ParaView (2002–2016). http://www.paraview.org
5. Ayachit, U., et al.: Paraview catalyst: enabling in-situ data analysis and visualization. In: Proceedings of the First Workshop on In Situ Infrastructures for Enabling Extreme-Scale Analysis and Visualization, pp. 25–29. ACM (2015)
6. LLNL: VisIT Visualization Tool (2002–2016). https://wci.llnl.gov/codes/visit

7. Childs, H., et al.: VisIt: an end-user tool for visualizing and analyzing very large data. In: High Performance Visualization - Enabling Extreme-Scale Scientific Insight, pp. 357–372 (2012)
8. Whitlock, B., Favre, J.M., Meredith, J.S.: Parallel in-situ coupling of a simulation with a fully featured visualization system. In: Eurographics Symposium on Parallel Graphics and Visualization, pp. 101–109 (2011)
9. Blender Online Community: Blender - a 3D modelling and rendering package (2016). http://www.blender.org/
10. Marmottant, P., Villermaux, E.: On spray formation. J. Fluid Mech. **498**, 73–111 (2004)
11. Bode, M., Falkenstein, T., Chenadec, V.L., Pitsch, H., Arima, T., Taniguchi, H.: A new Euler/Lagrange approach for multiphase simulations of a multi-hole GDI injector, SAE Paper 2015–01-0949 (2015)
12. Bode, M., Falkenstein, T., Pitsch, H., Kimijima, T., Taniguchi, H., Arima, T.: Numerical study of the impact of cavitation on the spray processes during gasoline direct injection. In: ICLASS 2015, 13th Triennial International Conference on Liquid Atomization and Spray Systems, Tainan, Taiwan (2015)
13. Bode, M., Deshmukh, A., Kirsch, V., Reddemann, M.A., Kneer, R., Pitsch, H.: Direct numerical simulations of novel biofuels for predicting spray characteristics. In: ICLASS 2015, 13th Triennial International Conference on Liquid Atomization and Spray Systems, Tainan, Taiwan (2015)
14. Bode, M., Göbbert, J.H., Pitsch, H.: Novel multiphase simulations investigating cavitation by use of in-situ visualization and Euler/Lagrange coupling. In: PRACE-days15, Dublin (2015)
15. Bode, M., Göbbert, J.H., Pitsch, H.: High-fidelity multiphase simulations and in-situ visualization using CIAO. In: NIC Symposium, Jülich (2016)
16. LLNL: VisIT Visualization Tool: Release Notes for VisIt 2.10.2 (2016). https://wci.llnl.gov/simulation/computer-codes/visit/releases/release-notes-2.10.2
17. Jülich Supercomputing Centre. JUQUEEN: IBM Blue Gene/Q Supercomputer System at the Jülich Supercomputing Centre. Journal of large-scale research facilities, 1, A1 (2016). http://dx.doi.org/10.17815/jlsrf-1-18
18. High-Q Club. http://www.fz-juelich.de/ias/jsc/high-q-club. Accessed 01 April 2016
19. Falgout, R.D., Jones, J.E., Yang, U.M.: Pursuing scalability for hypre's conceptual interfaces. ACM Trans. Math. Softw. (TOMS) **31**(3), 326–350 (2005)
20. Brömmel, D., Frings, W., Wylie, B.J.N.: JUQUEEN Extreme Scaling Workshop 2016, Technical Report FZJ-JSC-IB-2016-01, Jülich Supercomputing Center (2016)
21. Geimer, G., et al.: The Scalasca performance toolset architecture. Concurrency Comput. Pract. Experience **22**(6), 702–719 (2010). http://www.scalasca.org/
22. Knüpfer, K., et al.: Score-P: a joint performance measurement run-time infrastructure for Periscope, Scalasca, TAU, and Vampir. In: Brunst, H., Müller, M.S., Nagel, W.E., Resch, M.M. (eds.) Tools for High Performance Computing 2011, pp. 79–91. Springer, Heidelberg (2012). http://www.score-p.org/

The EPiGRAM Project: Preparing Parallel Programming Models for Exascale

Stefano Markidis[1]([✉]), Ivy Bo Peng[1], Jesper Larsson Träff[2], Antoine Rougier[2],
Valeria Bartsch[3], Rui Machado[3], Mirko Rahn[3], Alistair Hart[4], Daniel Holmes[5],
Mark Bull[5], and Erwin Laure[1]

[1] KTH Royal Institute of Technology, Stockholm, Sweden
s.markidis@gmail.com
[2] Vienna University of Technology (TU Wien), Vienna, Austria
[3] Fraunhofer ITWM, Kaiserslautern, Germany
[4] Cray UK, Edinburgh, UK
[5] Edinburgh Parallel Computing Center, Edinburgh, UK
http://www.epigram-project.eu/

Abstract. EPiGRAM is a European Commission funded project to improve existing parallel programming models to run efficiently large scale applications on exascale supercomputers. The EPiGRAM project focuses on the two current dominant petascale programming models, message-passing and PGAS, and on the improvement of two of their associated programming systems, MPI and GASPI. In EPiGRAM, we work on two major aspects of programming systems. First, we improve the performance of communication operations by decreasing the memory consumption, improving collective operations and introducing emerging computing models. Second, we enhance the interoperability of message-passing and PGAS by integrating them in one PGAS-based MPI implementation, called *EMPI4Re*, implementing MPI endpoints and improving GASPI interoperability with MPI. The new EPiGRAM concepts are tested in two large-scale applications, iPIC3D, a Particle-in-Cell code for space physics simulations, and Nek5000, a Computational Fluid Dynamics code.

1 Introduction

Exascale supercomputers will deliver 10^{18} floating-point operations per second (FLOPS) in double precision using the High Performance Linpack (HPL) benchmark. Today, the two fastest supercomputers are the Chinese *Sunway TaihuLight* and *Tianhe-2* supercomputers delivering respectively 93 and 33.8 petaFLOPS. The next American supercomputers from the *Corral* initiative will deliver between 100 and 200 petaFLOPS. Current projections of future supercomputers estimate the delivery of exascale machine in 2024.

While the race to exascale resulted in faster and larger supercomputers that today are only a factor of ten far from exascale, the software stack to support parallel applications on supercomputers has remained almost unchanged with

M. Taufer et al. (Eds.): ISC High Performance Workshops 2016, LNCS 9945, pp. 56–68, 2016.
DOI: 10.1007/978-3-319-46079-6_5

respect to the software present on petascale machines. In fact, almost all applications use MPI as main library to support parallel communication. Some of the applications use Partitioned Global Address Space (PGAS) languages, such as Coarray Fortran and UPC, with MPI [19,22]. Several applications employ OpenMP in combination with MPI for programming intra-node communication [13]. Despite the proposal of new disruptive programming models and systems [1,3,5], it is unlikely that such programming systems will reach a level of maturity and reliability to be readily deployed on the full exascale machine. The programming system dominating the exascale era will be MPI, possibly in combination with PGAS and OpenMP. For this reason, it is important both to improve the performance of these existing programming systems and to enhance their interoperability.

The size of next exascale supercomputers and their hardware pose difficult challenges to development of programming models. One of the main challenges is to handle the amount of parallelism that an exascale supercomputer will provide. The current fastest supercomputer *Sunway TaihuLight* provides 10,649,600 cores for parallel computation. Extrapolating this value to future more powerful supercomputers, it is reasonable to expect that an exascale machine will provide an 100 million-way parallelism. While communication cost decreases as part of communication operations is offloaded to the NIC and network technologies improve, still a large amount of memory is needed for storing process and communicator information on 100 million processes and memory footprint becomes a serious bottleneck [2]. In addition, collective operations and synchronization of such a large amount of processes [24] require the development and implementation of more sophisticated collective algorithms. A second main challenge is to guarantee that all the programming systems, such MPI, OpenMP and PGAS approaches efficiently interoperate sharing fairly all the hardware resources. It is therefore important to improve the performance of communication operations on a very large number of process potentially in presence of a combination of different programming systems.

Exascale ProGRAmming Models (EPiGRAM) is a European Commission funded project with the goal of addressing these exascale challenges in programming models. The EPiGRAM consortium consists of KTH Royal Institute of Technology, Vienna University of Technology (TU Wien), Fraunhofer ITWM, Cray UK, University of Edinburgh and University of Illinois (associate partner).

EPiGRAM focuses on the improvement of MPI and GASPI performance on exascale systems. MPI is currently the most used approach for programming parallel applications on supercomputers [11]. Global Address Space Programming Interface (GASPI) is the standard [12] for a PGAS API. GASPI uses one-sided Remote Direct Memory Access (RDMA) driven communication in combination with remote completion in a PGAS environment. Global address space Programming Interface (GPI) is a GASPI implementation, developed by Fraunhofer ITWM. Since GPI-2, Fraunhofer ITWM provides an open-source GPI implementation under GPL v3.

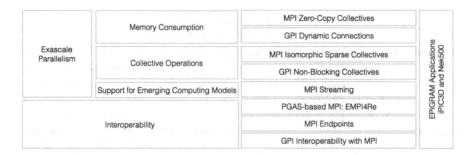

Fig. 1. Overview of the EPiGRAM project.

Figure 1 provides an overview of the different topics that have been investigated during the EPiGRAM project and the remaining part of the paper will describe these topics more in detail.

The paper is organized as follows. The second section presents the EPiGRAM work to address the challenge of exascale parallelism. In particular, we present how MPI and GASPI are further developed to reduce the memory footprint, to improve collective algorithms and implementations and to support emerging computing models. The third section describes the EPiGRAM research on MPI and GASPI interoperability, presenting MPI endpoints, GPI interoperability with MPI and the PGAS-based MPI implementation, called *EMPI4Re*, that integrates message-passing and PGAS in one framework. The fourth section presents the EPiGRAM applications. Finally, the fifth section concludes the paper summarizing the work done in EPiGRAM.

2   The *Exascale Parallelism* Challenge

Some important issues and obstacles that might prevent an effective use of MPI and GASPI programming systems on exascale machines are:

1. Memory-footprint and efficient memory usage. The available memory per core or even per (heterogeneous) shared-memory node will not, as was the case to a large extent in the past, scale linearly with the number of cores or nodes. Thus, implementations and specifications of MPI and GASPI functionalities must use sub-linear space per core or per node.
2. Algorithms and implementations for collective communication. Commonly used implementations often assume a fully connected network, and have relatively dense communication patterns. Better implementations, and in particular, new, space efficient algorithms for sparse collective communication and for collective communication on sparse networks are needed. In addition, current MPI interfaces for sparse collective communication are still limited.
3. Support for emerging computing models on massively parallel supercomputers. Computing models, such streaming models, lack of a convenient interface in MPI to run efficiently on large scale supercomputers. This might prevent the use of emerging computing models on exascale supercomputers.

2.1   Memory-Footprint and Efficient Memory Usage

The first issue EPiGRAM addresses is the memory consumption of MPI and GPI at exascale. This is done by designing and implementing *zero-copy* MPI collectives and GPI dynamic connections.

MPI Zero-Copy Collectives. The MPI datatype mechanism allows application programmers to describe the structure of the data to be communicated in a concise way [11]. In particular, non-consecutive layouts of data can be described as vectors, indexed or structured types, allowing a compact representation of complex layouts. The application programmer describes the layout of the data to be communicated, and the MPI library implementation performs the actual access of the data.

An efficient MPI implementation of data types can save memory copy operations. In fact, an explicit pack operation, implemented by the application programmer, copies data into some intermediate communication buffer, and then the MPI library may entail another copy of this buffer. This extra copy can be sometimes eliminated completely with datatypes, or in part for large data where pipelining may be applied by the library. In particular, the MPI datatype mechanism permits so-called *zero-copy* implementations, in which no explicit data movements are present in the application and all data access and manipulation are carried out implicitly by the MPI library implementation.

In EPiGRAM, we studied the design and implementation of different *zero-copy* collective operations, focusing on obstacles that might prevent the design and implementation of such operations in an efficient way. We have investigated the use of the derived datatype mechanism of MPI in the implementation of the classic all-to-all communication algorithm of Bruck et al. [4]. Through a series of improvements to the canonical implementation of the algorithm we gradually eliminated initial and final processor-local data reorganizations, culminating in a *zero-copy* version that contains no explicit, process-local data movement or copy operations [35, 37]. In this case, all necessary data movements are carried out as part of the communication operations. We also showed how the improved algorithm can be used to solve irregular all-to-all communication problems. In particular, in EPiGRAM we used and implemented three new derived datatypes (`bounded_vector`, `circular_vector`, and `bucket`) that are not in MPI. On two supercomputers at the Vienna University of Technology, we experimentally compared the algorithmic improvements to the Bruck et al. algorithm when implemented on top of MPI, showing the zero-copy version to perform significantly better than the initial, straight-forward implementation. One of our variants has also been implemented inside `mvapich`, and we showed it to perform better than the `mvapich` implementation of the Bruck et al. algorithm for the range of processes and problem sizes where it is enabled. Details about this work are provided in [35, 37].

However, we showed in EPiGRAM that current collective interfaces cannot support *zero-copy* implementations in all cases [36]. The problem is that the regular collective interfaces use a receive datatype to specify a per-process layout, whereas sometimes a different layout is needed for each process. Such cases cannot be accounted for; only for applications using all-to-all communication, the required flexibility is provided in the form of the tedious, non-scalable MPI_Alltoallw operation. In [36] we show a simple, and in many cases backwards compatible and mostly non-intrusive solution to the problems in the form of slightly changed collective interfaces (all other communication interfaces would have to be reinterpreted in a similar way). The key to the solution is to separate the number of elements to be communicated from the overall structure of the data. The latter is described by a datatype; the former by an element count. The current MPI specification mixes these two concerns, leading to the problems discussed.

GPI Dynamic Connections. We have identified GPI memory consumption as one of the main aspects to be improved for large scale execution of GPI applications. The memory consumption is strongly related to the management of the communication infrastructure in GPI. The GASPI specification, that GPI implements, defines that the communication infrastructure should be either built during initialization or performed explicitly by the application. This can be set through a configuration parameter where the default value is TRUE. In this case, the communication infrastructure is built at start-up by default. In fact, details of the initialization of the GPI communication infrastructure are left to the implementation.

Before EPiGRAM, communication infrastructure was built-up statically in GPI. In this case, each computing node (a GPI rank) establishes a connection to all the other computing nodes during initialization. This results in an all-to-all communication topology. Despite this is acceptable on small scale and typical executions, the problem becomes evident when running large-scale GPI applications. For this reason, we have extended GPI to allow three modes of topology building: GASPI_TOPOLOGY_NONE where the application explicitly handles the infrastructure setup, GASPI_TOPOLOGY_STATIC where, as before, an all-to-all connection is established and GASPI_TOPOLOGY_DYNAMIC where connections are dynamically established as the first communication request between two nodes is performed. We were able to verify and measure the effects of such GPI extension during the Extreme Scale Workshop using the full SuperMUC iDataPlex supercomputer, consisting of 3,072 nodes, at the Leibniz Supercomputing Centre. The establishment of dynamic connections provides a much more efficient and scalable resource consumption in terms of memory footprint. Panel a of Fig. 2 presents the memory consumption (per rank) after initialization using static and dynamic connections. The non-scalable behavior of the GPI all-to-all connection is evident. We can now alleviate that using GPI dynamic connections.

2.2   Algorithms and Implementations for Collective Communication

The second issue EPiGRAM addresses is the performance of collective communication operations at exascale by investigating improved sparse collectives and studying non-blocking collectives in GPI.

MPI Isomorphic Sparse Collectives. The MPI specification has functionality for sparse collective communication where processes communicate with a subset of other processes in a local neighborhood. Sparse neighborhoods can be explicitly specified using the general graph topology functionalities or Cartesian topology [10]. However, both approaches have problems. In the first case, this mechanism is cumbersome to use, and the necessary collective communication and computation to create the local neighborhoods as well as the creation of a new, possibly reordered communicator can be very expensive. Alternatively, neighborhoods can be given implicitly with a Cartesian communicator. On Cartesian MPI communicators, neighborhood collective communication is possible with these implicit neighborhoods. Although neighborhood collective communication should be oblivious to how neighborhoods are set up, there are some differences between explicit and implicit neighborhoods in the MPI standard. For instance, non-existing neighbors are possible for Cartesian neighborhoods and buffer space needs to be calculated for such non-existing neighbors; this is neither possible nor allowed for graph topologies. On the other hand, graph topologies can associate weights with the graph edges (that may reflect communication costs in different ways and thus can permit better process mappings), but this is not possible for Cartesian topologies.

EPiGRAM provides a middle ground between these two approaches: a mechanism for structured, sparse collective communication with a much smaller overhead than the general graph topology mechanism but with more flexibility and expressivity than the Cartesian neighborhoods. In EPiGRAM, we introduced the concept of *isomorphic* sparse collective [33,34]: isomorphic sparse collective communication is a form of collective communication in which all involved processes communicate in small, identically structured neighborhoods of other processes. Isomorphic sparse collective communication is useful for implementing stencil and other regular, sparse distributed computations, where the assumption that all processes behave symmetrically is justified. The concept of isomorphic neighborhood extends and generalizes what is possible with the limited MPI Cartesian topologies.

In EPiGRAM, a library for isomorphic sparse collective communication has been implemented. The library supports the navigation and query functionality, creation of isomorphic neighborhoods (by attaching the neighborhood information to a Cartesian communicator), functions for using relative neighbor lists to set up MPI graph communicators, and sparse isomorphic collective operations of the `allgather`, `alltoall` and reduction types. The performance improvements that can be achieved by using *isomorphic* sparse collectives are presented in [33,34].

GPI Non-blocking Collectives. Non-blocking collectives have been recently introduced in MPI-3 as a mean to overlap communication and computation during collective operations [10,14]. In EPiGRAM, we have investigated the development of non-blocking collectives in GPI. Currently there are only two collective operations in GASPI: `gaspi_barrier` and `gaspi_allreduce`. Both collective operations in GASPI have a timeout argument that specifies after

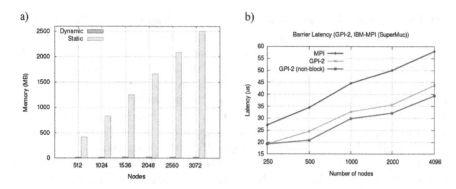

Fig. 2. Panel *a* shows the memory consumption using GPI static all-to-all connection (green bars) and dynamic connections (red bars) when using different number of computing nodes. Panel *b* shows the execution time for MPI blocking (red line), GPI blocking (green line) and non-blocking (blue line) barriers increasing the number of nodes. The tests have been performed on SuperMUC iDataPlex supercomputer at the Leibniz Supercomputing Centre. (Color figure online)

which period of time the collective operation can be interrupted. This timeout argument can be used as a form of non-blocking call. For instance, the time out argument can be set to `GASPI_TEST`. Each GPI process can call a collective function and when the function is interrupted as a consequence of the timeout other work can be performed, effectively implementing a non-blocking collective. In EPiGRAM, we added the support for this kind of non-blocking collectives and we performed performance tests of blocking and non-blocking GPI barriers and a comparison with MPI blocking barrier on the SuperMUC iDataPlex supercomputer up to 4,096 nodes (corresponding to a total of 65,536 cores) at the Leibniz Supercomputing Centre. Panel *b* of Fig. 2 presents the execution time for the different implementations of barriers, showing a reduced execution time for GPI non-blocking barrier (blue line) with respect to the execution of blocking GPI (green line) and MPI (red line) implementations.

2.3   MPI Support for Streaming Computing

EPiGRAM also investigated the support for emerging computing models that will be likely used on massively parallel supercomputers in the future. An example of such computing models is the data streaming computing model that is an effective way to tackle challenges from data-intensive applications. However, streaming computing is not naturally supported in MPI.

In EPiGRAM, we have designed and implemented a library called *MPIStream* [25] that allows HPC applications to globally allocate data producers and consumers on MPI processes, to stream data continuously or irregularly, to receive and process data and to terminate the streaming operations. Use cases of enabling HPC applications to carry out threshold collective operations, to monitor and control applications and to perform parallel I/O of irregular events are illustrated in [25].

Our MPI streaming library targets the streaming model for distributed systems, where MPI is the dominant programming system. The *MPIStream* library is written in C and built on the top of MPI. A stream is a continuous flow of stream elements, which is the basic unit of transmission between data producer and streamer. MPI data types are used to describe the memory layout of the elements on data producers to achieve *zero-copy* streaming and consequently saving memory consumption on large systems. MPI persistent communication is used to reduce the overhead of repeatedly calling receive routines.

The performance of the *MPIStream* library has been evaluated using a parallel STREAM benchmark [25] on two supercomputers: Beskow Cray CX40 at KTH and Mira BlueGene/Q at the Argonne National Laboratory. The performance results show that the library can achieve acceptable performance (52 %–65 % of the maximum available bandwidth) and demonstrate its potential by reaching as high as 200 GB/s and 80 GB/s processing rate using 2,048 data producers over 2,048 data consumers on the Blue Gene/Q and Cray XC40 supercomputers respectively. Additional performance results of the *MPIStream* library are reported and discussed in [21,25].

3   The *Interoperability* Challenge

Interoperability of programming systems, such as MPI, OpenMP and PGAS, is a key aspect in exascale computing as it is likely that exascale applications will use a combination of programming systems to use efficiently different kind of communications, i.e. inter-node and intra-node communications. In EPiGRAM, we implemented a PGAS-based MPI to fully integrate message-passing and PGAS programming models, we introduced MPI endpoints in this MPI implementation and improved the GPI interoperability with MPI.

EMPI4Re: A PGAS-based MPI Implementation. EPiGRAM integrates and combines message-passing and PGAS programming models in one MPI implementation. The EPiGRAM MPI library for Research (EMPI4Re) is an MPI-1 library created by EPCC at the University of Edinburgh as a vehicle for research into new MPI functionality. The library adopts the conceptual model of PGAS and assumes hardware support for RDMA operations. This conceptual model enables efficient implementation of remotely accessible double buffered first-in first-out (FIFO) queues, used for point-to-point operations, and distributed state control structures, used for collective operations.

The code-base for the EMPI4Re library currently consists of 55,495 lines of C code (OpenMPI version 1.8.6 consists of 933,889 lines for comparison). The current implementation of EMPI4Re is based on DMAPP (a Cray one-sided communication API) [31] and there is an ongoing effort in EPiGRAM to replace DMAPP with GPI. Overall, we found in EPiGRAM that the EMPI4Re library is a useful research vehicle for rapidly prototyping and assessing code changes to MPI functionality without the complexity of managing a large code-base or production MPI implementation.

MPI Endpoints. MPI is typically targeted at communication between distributed memory spaces. For a pure MPI programming approach, multi-core nodes require an OS process per core in order to take advantage of the available compute capability. This requires multiple instances of the MPI library per shared-memory node including communication buffers, topology informations and connection resources. Hybrid programming, commonly referred to as *MPI+X*, where *X* is programming model that supports threads, only requires a single instance of the MPI library per shared-memory node and so it should scale with increasing per-node core-count better than pure MPI. However, there are restrictions on how MPI can be used in multi-threaded OS processes that make it difficult to efficiently achieve high performance with hybrid programming. In particular, threads cannot be individually identified as the source or target of MPI messages [15].

MPI endpoints have been designed to remove or alleviate threading restrictions in MPI and facilitate high performance communication between multi-threaded OS processes. MPI endpoints allow the programmer to create additional ranks at each MPI process. Each endpoint rank can be then distributed to threads in system-level programming models enabling these threads to act as MPI processes and interoperate with MPI directly [6]. For an initial implementation study, see also [17,30].

The EPiGRAM project is implementing the MPI endpoints in EMPI4Re. The initial approach taken in the EMPI4Re library is to create each communicator handle as normal: generating a new structure for each one, including a full mapping of all ranks to their associated location. This is exactly what would happen if each of the members of the new communicator were individual MPI processes each in their own OS processes. EMPI4Re is already designed to be able to cope with each member of a communicator using a different context identifier for a particular communicator so this approach does not cause a conflict. The next step is to de-duplicate the internal data-structures so that multiple MPI endpoints in the same OS process share a single copy of the mapping information and share a reduced number of matching data-structures and communication buffers. In EMPI4Re, various design choices, such as having a different context identifier at each MPI process for a communicator thereby avoiding the use of a distributed agreement algorithm, simplify the addition of new features.

GPI Interoperability with MPI. Large parallel applications that have been developed over several years often reach several thousands or even millions of lines of code. Moreover, there is a large set of available libraries and tools which run with MPI. For this reason, it is important to enable GPI full cooperation with MPI so that both can be used simultaneously in an efficient way. This interoperability allows an incremental porting of large applications to GPI and an effective usage of existing MPI libraries and infrastructure. This tighter support for MPI interoperability was integrated in GPI during the EPiGRAM project (GPI release v1.1.0 in June 2014) by introducing the so-called *mixed-mode*.

In this mode, GPI sets its environment reusing MPI instead of relying on its own startup mechanism (`gaspi run`). The only constraint is that MPI must be initialized (`MPI_Init`) before GPI (`gaspi_proc_init`). In this mode, as MPI and GPI both follow a Single Program Multiple Data (SPMD) model, there is a direct match between the MPI the GPI ranks. This simplifies the reasoning about the hybrid GPI-MPI application.

In addition, an interface allowing memory management interoperability has been recently established in the GASPI standard [12]. GASPI handles memory spaces in so-called *segments*, which are accessible from every thread of every GASPI process. The GASPI standard has been extended to allow users to provide an already existing memory buffer as the memory space of a GASPI segment. This new function will allow future applications to communicate data from memory that is not allocated by the GASPI runtime system but provided to it, i.e. by MPI. If an MPI program calls GPI libraries, the GPI libraries need to be isolated, so that the communication in a library does not interfere with the communication in the main application, or any other library. This is required to guarantee correct results. The GASPI interface has been extended to offer a clear separation: a library is now able to create its own communication queues and thus have an isolated communication channel. For all other resources, i.e. segments, GPI already provides some mechanism to query their usage and to select an unused resource.

4 EPiGRAM Applications

The effectiveness of concepts that have been developed in EPiGRAM have been tested against two real-world open-source codes, iPIC3D [20,29] and Nek5000 [7]. iPIC3D is a massively parallel Particle-in-Cell code that is written in C++ and using MPI. Nek5000 is a semi-spectral Computational Fluid Dynamics (CFD) code for solving fluid dynamics problems, such as the study of turbulence arising on the surface of airplane wings. Nek5000 is written in large part in Fortran and in a small part in C and it uses MPI for parallel communication.

The EPiGRAM codes have been used for providing feedback to development of the programming systems in EPiGRAM: they have been employed to test new features in MPI and GASPI programming systems, to provide feedback to the developers of EMPI4Re library, and to compare the performance of the EPiGRAM programming system implementations in real-world applications [16].

The new EPiGRAM communication kernel of iPIC3D is now included in the release version of the code [29] and enabled large scale simulations of magnetospheric physics [23,26,27,32]. Together with the improvement of the communication kernels of the applications, also OpenACC/OpenMP porting of the applications to GPU systems [8,9,13,18,28] and new algorithmic strategies [38,39] have been implemented in EPiGRAM.

5 Conclusions

In summary, EPiGRAM is a European Commission project with the goal of improving the performance and the integration of existing parallel programming models. The EPiGRAM project focuses on the two current dominant petascale programming models, message-passing and PGAS, and on the improvement of two of their associated programming systems, MPI and GASPI. In EPiGRAM, we addressed two major exascale challenges: large-scale parallelism and interoperability of programming systems. First, we improve the performance of communication operations on a very large number of processes by decreasing their memory consumption, improving collective operations and introducing emerging computing models. Second, we enhance the interoperability of MPI and GPI by integrating message-passing and PGAS in one implementation, called *EMPI4Re*, implementing MPI endpoints and improving GPI interoperability with MPI. The new EPiGRAM concepts have been validated with experiments in two large-scale applications, iPIC3D, a Particle-in-Cell code for space physics simulations, and Nek5000, a CFD code.

Acknowledgments. This work was funded by the European Commission through the EPiGRAM (grant agreement no. 610598, www.epigram-project.eu) project.

References

1. Balaji, P.: Programming Models for Parallel Computing. MIT Press, Cambridge (2015)
2. Balaji, P., Buntinas, D., Goodell, D., Gropp, W., Kumar, S., Lusk, E., Thakur, R., Träff, J.L.: MPI on a million processors. In: Ropo, M., Westerholm, J., Dongarra, J. (eds.) EuroPVM/MPI 2009. LNCS, vol. 5759, pp. 20–30. Springer, Heidelberg (2009). doi:10.1007/978-3-642-03770-2_9
3. Bauer, M., Treichler, S., Slaughter, E., Aiken, A.: Legion: expressing locality and independence with logical regions. In: Proceedings of the International Conference on High Performance Computing, Networking, Storage and Analysis, p. 66. IEEE Computer Society Press (2012)
4. Bruck, J., Ho, C.T., Kipnis, S., Upfal, E., Weathersby, D.: Efficient algorithms for all-to-all communications in multiport message-passing systems. IEEE Trans. Parallel Distrib. Syst. 8(11), 1143–1156 (1997)
5. Chamberlain, B.L., Callahan, D., Zima, H.P.: Parallel programmability and the Chapel language. Int. J. High Perform. Comput. Appl. 21(3), 291–312 (2007)
6. Dinan, J., Balaji, P., Goodell, D., Miller, D., Snir, M., Thakur, R.: Enabling MPI interoperability through flexible communication endpoints. In: Proceedings of the 20th European MPI Users' Group Meeting, pp. 13–18. ACM (2013)
7. Fischer, P.F., Lottes, J.W., Kerkemeier, S.G.: Nek5000 web page. mcs.anl.gov(2008). http://nek5000.mcs.anl.gov
8. Gong, J., Markidis, S., Laure, E., Otten, M., Fischer, P., Min, M.: Nekbone performance on GPUs with OpenACC and CUDA Fortran implementations. J. Supercomput. 1–21 (2016). doi:10.1007/s11227-016-1744-5D

9. Gong, J., Markidis, S., Schliephake, M., Laure, E., Henningson, D., Schlatter, P., Peplinski, A., Hart, A., Doleschal, J., Henty, D., Fischer, P.: Nek5000 with OpenACC. In: Markidis, S., Laure, E. (eds.) EASC 2014. LNCS, vol. 8759, pp. 57–68. Springer, Heidelberg (2015). doi:10.1007/978-3-319-15976-8_4

10. Gropp, W., Hoefler, T., Thakur, R., Lusk, E.: Using Advanced MPI: Modern Features of the Message-Passing Interface. MIT Press, Cambridge (2014)

11. Gropp, W., Lusk, E., Skjellum, A.: Using MPI: Portable Parallel Programming with the Message-Passing Interface, vol. 1. MIT Press, Cambridge (1999)

12. Grünewald, D., Simmendinger, C.: The GASPI API specification and its implementation GPI 2.0. In: 7th International Conference on PGAS Programming Models, vol. 243 (2013)

13. Hart, A.: First experiences porting a parallel application to a hybrid supercomputer with OpenMP4.0 device constructs. In: Terboven, C., Supinski, B.R., Reble, P., Chapman, B.M., Müller, M.S. (eds.) IWOMP 2015. LNCS, vol. 9342, pp. 73–85. Springer, Heidelberg (2015). doi:10.1007/978-3-319-24595-9_6

14. Hoefler, T., Lumsdaine, A., Rehm, W.: Implementation and performance analysis of non-blocking collective operations for MPI. In: Proceedings of the 2007 ACM/IEEE Conference on Supercomputing, 2007, SC 2007, pp. 1–10. IEEE (2007)

15. Ibrahim, K.Z., Yelick, K.: On the conditions for efficient interoperability with threads: an experience with PGAS languages using cray communication domains. In: Proceedings of the 28th ACM International Conference on Supercomputing, pp. 23–32. ACM (2014)

16. Ivanov, I., Gong, J., Akhmetova, D., Peng, I.B., Markidis, S., Laure, E., Machado, R., Rahn, M., Bartsch, V., Hart, A., et al.: Evaluation of parallel communication models in Nekbone, a Nek5000 mini-application. In: 2015 IEEE International Conference on Cluster Computing,. pp. 760–767. IEEE (2015)

17. Luo, M., Lu, X., Hamidouche, K., Kandalla, K., Panda, D.K.: Initial study of multi-endpoint runtime for MPI+ OpenMP hybrid programming model on multi-core systems. In: ACM SIGPLAN Notices, vol. 49, pp. 395–396. ACM (2014)

18. Markidis, S., Gong, J., Schliephake, M., Laure, E., Hart, A., Henty, D., Heisey, K., Fischer, P.: OpenACC acceleration of the Nek5000 spectral element code. Int. J. High Perform. Comput. Appl. 29(3), 311–319 (2015)

19. Markidis, S., Lapenta, G.: Development and performance analysis of a UPC particle-in-cell code. In: Proceedings of the Fourth Conference on Partitioned Global Address Space Programming Model, p. 10. ACM (2010)

20. Markidis, S., Lapenta, G.: Rizwan-uddin: multi-scale simulations of plasma with iPIC3D. Math. Comput. Simul. 80(7), 1509–1519 (2010)

21. Markidis, S., Peng, I.B., Iakymchuk, R., Laure, E., Kestor, G., Gioiosa, R.: A performance characterization of streaming computing on supercomputers. Procedia Comput. Sci. 80, 98–107 (2016)

22. Mozdzynski, G., Hamrud, M., Wedi, N., Doleschal, J., Richardson, H.: A PGAS implementation by co-design of the ECMWF integrated forecasting system (IFS). In: High Performance Computing, Networking, Storage and Analysis (SCC), 2012 SC Companion, pp. 652–661. IEEE (2012)

23. Olshevsky, V., Deca, J., Divin, A., Peng, I.B., Markidis, S., Innocenti, M.E., Cazzola, E., Lapenta, G.: Magnetic null points in kinetic simulations of space plasmas. Astrophys. J. 819(1), 52 (2016)

24. Peng, I.B., Markidis, S., Laure, E.: The cost of synchronizing imbalanced processes in message passing systems. In: 2015 IEEE International Conference on Cluster Computing, pp. 408–417. IEEE (2015)

25. Peng, I.B., Markidis, S., Laure, E., Holmes, D., Bull, M.: A data streaming model in MPI. In: Proceedings of the 3rd Workshop on Exascale MPI, p. 2. ACM (2015)
26. Peng, I.B., Markidis, S., Laure, E., Johlander, A., Vaivads, A., Khotyaintsev, Y., Henri, P., Lapenta, G.: Kinetic structures of quasi-perpendicular shocks in global particle-in-cell simulations. Phys. Plasmas (1994-Present) **22**(9), 092109 (2015)
27. Peng, I.B., Markidis, S., Vaivads, A., Vencels, J., Amaya, J., Divin, A., Laure, E., Lapenta, G.: The formation of a magnetosphere with implicit particle-in-cell simulations. Procedia Comput. Sci. **51**, 1178–1187 (2015)
28. Peng, I.B., Markidis, S., Vaivads, A., Vencels, J., Deca, J., Lapenta, G., Hart, A., Laure, E.: Acceleration of a particle-in-cell code for space plasma simulations with OpenACC. In: EGU General Assembly Conference Abstracts, vol. 17, p. 1276 (2015)
29. Peng, I.B., Vencels, J., Lapenta, G., Divin, A., Vaivads, A., Laure, E., Markidis, S.: Energetic particles in magnetotail reconnection. J. Plasma Phys. **81**(02), 325810202 (2015)
30. Sridharan, S., Dinan, J., Kalamkar, D.D.: Enabling efficient multithreaded MPI communication through a library-based implementation of MPI endpoints. In: Proceedings of the International Conference for High Performance Computing, Networking, Storage and Analysis, pp. 487–498. IEEE Press (2014)
31. Ten Bruggencate, M., Roweth, D.: DMAPP - an API for one-sided program models on Baker systems. In: Cray User Group Conference (2010)
32. Tóth, G., Jia, X., Markidis, S., Peng, I.B., Chen, Y., Daldorff, L.K., Tenishev, V.M., Borovikov, D., Haiducek, J.D., Gombosi, T.I., et al.: Extended magnetohydrodynamics with embedded particle-in-cell simulation of Ganymede's magnetosphere. J. Geophys. Res. Space Phys. **121**, 1273–1293 (2016)
33. Träff, J.L., Carpen-Amarie, A., Hunold, S., Rougier, A.: Message-combining algorithms for isomorphic, sparse collective communication. arXiv preprint arXiv:1606.07676 (2016)
34. Träff, J.L., Lübbe, F.D., Rougier, A., Hunold, S.: Isomorphic, sparse MPI-like collective communication operations for parallel stencil computations. In: Proceedings of the 22nd European MPI Users' Group Meeting, p. 10. ACM (2015)
35. Träff, J.L., Rougier, A.: MPI collectives and datatypes for hierarchical all-to-all communication. In: Proceedings of the 21st European MPI Users' Group Meeting, p. 27. ACM (2014)
36. Träff, J.L., Rougier, A.: Zero-copy, hierarchical gather is not possible with MPI datatypes and collectives. In: Proceedings of the 21st European MPI Users' Group Meeting, p. 39. ACM (2014)
37. Träff, J.L., Rougier, A., Hunold, S.: Implementing a classic: zero-copy all-to-all communication with MPI datatypes. In: Proceedings of the 28th ACM International Conference on Supercomputing, pp. 135–144. ACM (2014)
38. Vencels, J., Delzanno, G.L., Johnson, A., Peng, I.B., Laure, E., Markidis, S.: Spectral solver for multi-scale plasma physics simulations with dynamically adaptive number of moments. Procedia Comput. Sci. **51**, 1148–1157 (2015)
39. Vencels, J., Delzanno, G.L., Manzini, G., Markidis, S., Peng, I.B., Roytershteyn, V.: SpectralPlasmaSolver: a spectral code for multiscale simulations of collisionless, magnetized plasmas. J. Phys. Conf. Ser. **719**, 012022 (2016). IOP Publishing

Work Distribution of Data-Parallel Applications on Heterogeneous Systems

Suejb Memeti[✉] and Sabri Pllana

Department of Computer Science, Linnaeus University, 351 95 Vaxjo, Sweden
{suejb.memeti,sabri.pllana}@lnu.se

Abstract. Heterogeneous computing systems offer high peak performance and energy efficiency, and utilizing this potential is essential to achieve extreme-scale performance. However, optimal sharing of the work among processing elements in heterogeneous systems is not straightforward. In this paper, we propose an approach that uses combinatorial optimization to search for optimal system configuration in a given parameter space. The optimization goal is to determine the number of threads, thread affinities, and workload partitioning, such that the overall execution time is minimized. For combinatorial optimization we use the Simulated Annealing. We evaluate our approach with a DNA sequence analysis application on a heterogeneous platform that comprises two Intel Xeon E5 processors and an Intel Xeon Phi 7120P co-processor. The obtained results demonstrate that using the near-optimal system configuration, determined by our algorithm based on the simulated annealing, application performance is improved.

1 Introduction

Heterogeneous computing systems consist of general-purpose CPUs and accelerators – such as, graphical processing units (GPUs) or Intel Xeon Phi – which offer high performance and energy efficiency. Some of the most powerful supercomputers in the TOP500 [1] list are heterogeneous at their node level. For example, Tianhe-2 nodes consist of two Intel IvyBridge CPUs and three Intel Xeon Phi co-processors, whereas a node of Titan contains one AMD Opteron CPU and one Nvidia Tesla GPU. Mapping computations to processing elements of the heterogeneous node in an optimal way is an important step to efficiently utilize the large-scale computing systems [2,24].

Due to the different performance characteristics of heterogeneous processing elements, distributing the workload across such elements to utilize the aggregate power of heterogeneous systems depends on many parameters and is a non-trivial task. Using enumeration of all possible parameters to determine the optimal system configuration is prohibitively time-consuming. Equation 1 shows the product function of the parameter value ranges that determines the number

---

This research has received funding from the Swedish Knowledge Foundation under Grant No. 20150088.

M. Taufer et al. (Eds.): ISC High Performance Workshops 2016, LNCS 9945, pp. 69–81, 2016.
DOI: 10.1007/978-3-319-46079-6_6

of all possible configurations, where $C = \{c_1, c_2, \ldots, c_m\}$ is a set of parameters and each parameter c_i has a value range R_{c_i}.

$$\prod_{i=1}^{m} R_{c_i} = R_{c_1} \times R_{c_2} \times \ldots \times R_{c_m} \tag{1}$$

Various techniques have been proposed for utilization of heterogeneous computing systems. CoreTSAR [27] is an adaptive work-sharing library for scheduling computations across multiple devices. Qilin [17] is an off-line based profiling technique for automatic mapping of computations to processing elements. Grewe and O'Boyle [11] use a static partitioning approach based on machine learning methods to distribute OpenCL programs on heterogeneous computing systems. A task splitting and distribution dynamic scheduling technique was proposed by Ravi and Agrawal [26]. Albayrak et al. [3] use the Greedy Algorithm to determine the near-optimal mapping for applications designed as sequence of kernels.

So far not much research has addressed combinatorial optimization approaches for workload distribution across resources of heterogeneous systems. Furthermore, related research focuses on heterogeneous systems that are accelerated with GPUs. Platforms accelerated with the Intel Xeon Phi deserve our attention because of their capability to deliver high performance, energy efficiency, and the ease of programmability and portability [6,8,12].

In this paper we propose an optimization approach that uses combinatorial optimization to determine near-optimal system configuration parameters (including the number of threads, thread affinity, and the workload distribution ratio) of a heterogeneous systems. To search for the optimal system configuration in the given large discrete search space we use Simulated Annealing [25]. The optimization goal is to minimize the application's execution time. For empirical evaluation we use a parallel application for DNA sequence analysis of real world DNA sequences of various animals. We perform our experiments on a heterogeneous platform that comprises two Intel Xeon E5 CPUs and an Intel Xeon Phi7120P co-processor.

Results demonstrate that by running only about 5 % of all the possible experiments we can determine a near-optimal system configuration, which yields with 1.74× speedup and 2.2× compared to the case when only the cores of host or device are used.

The major contributions of this paper include:

1. a heuristic based optimization approach to determine the near-optimal system configuration (such as, workload distribution ratio between host and device, number of threads and thread allocations),
2. a parallel algorithm for matching patterns in DNA sequences that efficiently utilizes the resources of the host and device in heterogeneous systems,
3. an experimental evaluation of our approach for DNA sequence analysis using real-world DNA sequences.

The rest of the paper is organized as follows. Section 2 provides background information with respect to meta-heuristics and heterogeneous computing systems. In Sect. 3.2 we describe the methodology, including the heuristic-guided approach for optimization of workload distribution in heterogeneous systems, and our algorithm for DNA sequence analysis. Section 4 presents the experimentation environment and discusses the experimental evaluation results. The related work will be discussed in Sect. 5. Section 6 provides a conclusion and discusses the future work.

2   Background

In this section we provide background information on the meta-heuristics and a heterogeneous computing platform that is accelerated with the Intel Xeon Phi co-processor.

2.1   Meta Heuristics

Meta-heuristics are designed for finding, generating or selecting the global optimum on some class of problems with less computation effort, which in general is a very difficult problem. A well known problem that can be solved using meta-heuristics is the Traveling Salesman Problem (TSP) where the search-space grows exponentially as the problem size increases. Brute-force (or enumeration) approaches are infeasible to deal with such complex problems.

As there are many different heuristic-based optimization methods, such as Genetic Algorithms, Ant Colony Optimization, Simulated Annealing, Local Search, and Tabu Search, which differ substantially in their underlying concepts, choosing the most convenient requires to consider different characteristics [7]. Such characteristics include: generation of new solutions, treatment of the new solutions, number of search agents, limitations of the search space, prior knowledge, flexibility for specific constraints, ease of implementation, computational complexity, convergence speed, reliability, type of optimization problem and search space, the available computational time, or the demanded solution quality [25].

2.2   Heterogeneous Systems – Intel Xeon Phi

A typical heterogeneous node that uses the Intel Xeon Phi as accelerator may consist of one or two CPUs on the host, and one to eight accelerators. Our *Emil* system that is used for experimentation in this paper comprises two Intel Xeon E5 2695 v2 and one Intel Xeon Phi 7120P co-processor. The E5 CPUs comprise 12 Ivy Bridge cores. These cores are connected using a ring topology, which features low latency and high throughput. The L3 cache size is 30 MB. The CPUs are connected to the memory using the Quad channel memory controller. The two host CPUs are linked through the QuickPath Interconnect, which offers up to 8.0 GT/s.

The Intel Xeon Phi is a many-core share memory processor. The lightweights Linux Operating System running on the card enables communicating with it over ssh. In the current version (Knights Landing, used in this paper) there are

61 cores, each of them has four hardware threads. The base core's frequency is 1.2 GHz, and 1.3 GHz max turbo frequency [8]. A 30.5 MB unified L2 cache is formed through a bidirectional ring bus interconnect that connects these cores. The 16 memory channels offer a theoretical maximum memory bandwidth of 352 GB/s.

The Intel Xeon Phi supports 512-bit wide Single Instruction Multiple Data (SIMD) registers that can perform 16 single precision floating point operations, or eight double precision floating point operations per cycle. The theoretical single and double performance capability of the Intel Xeon Phi is one and two teraFLOP/s, respectively. The practical performance capabilities of the Intel Xeon Phi, and its accessibility from the programmability point of view have been investigated in different articles [9,16,28].

3 Methodology

This section describes our heuristic-guided approach for optimization of workload distribution on heterogeneous computing systems. Furthermore, it describes our parallel algorithm for DNA sequence analysis that is able to utilize the aggregate power of host CPUs and accelerators in heterogeneous computing systems.

3.1 Using Simulated Annealing for Optimization of Heterogeneous Systems

Simulated Annealing (SA) is an optimization technique used to approximate global optimization in large discrete search space. A fundamental property of SA is its ability to accept worse solutions that allows a more extensive search of the optimal space.

The method and its name is inspired by the process of material cooling and annealing, where the slow cooling is interpreted as a slow decrease in the probability of accepting worse solutions.

While the temperature T is higher, it is more likely to accept new solutions. Therefore, there is a corresponding chance to get out of a local minimum, in favor of searching for a global optimum. The lower the temperature, less likely it accepts new solutions [25].

In the context of optimizing the workload distribution on heterogeneous systems, the configuration space is as follows:

- workload fraction is a discrete value from 0–100
- number of threads used for the host (1–48) and device (1–244);
- thread allocation strategy for the host (none, compact, scatter) and device (balanced, compact, scatter).

The objective function E (analog of *energy*) that we are trying to minimize is the total *execution time* of the application running on the host and the device, which basically is determined by the maximum of the t_{host} and t_{device}:

$$E = max(t_{host}, t_{device}) \qquad (2)$$

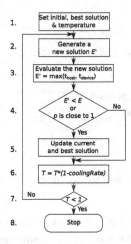

Fig. 1. The major steps of the simulated annealing based algorithm.

Figure 1 shows the major steps of the simulated annealing algorithm. First, we set the initial value of T (temperature) and generate a random initial solution (step 1). Thereafter, we generate a new solution (step 2), and evaluate it (step 3). If the newly generated solution is better than the current one, or the probability distribution is close to 1 (step 4) we update the current and best solution (step 5), otherwise we decrease the temperature (step 6). Unless the temperature has cooled down, the steps 2–6 will be repeated.

The annealing schedule *coolingRate* is defined as follows:

$$T = T * (1 - coolingRate); \tag{3}$$

Equation 4 shows the Boltzmann probability distribution [25] (acceptance function) used to decide whether or not to accept a worse solution. If the energy of the newly generated solution E' is lower than the energy of the current solution E, then we accept it unconditionally, otherwise we consider temperature and the time difference between the two solutions being compared. The higher the temperature, it is more likely that the system accepts worse solutions.

$$p = exp((E - E')/T) \tag{4}$$

3.2   DNA Sequence Analysis on Heterogeneous Computing Nodes

The current version of Intel Xeon Phi co-processor (Knights Corner) offers two programming models:

- *offload* - where parts of the code are offloaded to the co-processor
- *native* - where the code is compiled specifically for running natively on the co-processor. The code and dependent libraries are transferred to the device.

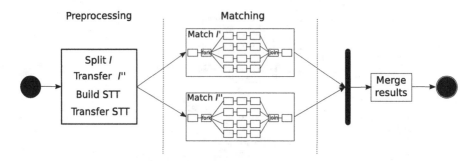

Fig. 2. Using resources of the host and device for DNA sequence analysis.

Our approach for parallel DNA Sequence analysis is based on the *offload* programming model, which allows using the resources of the host and the device at the same time. Figure 2 depicts workload distribution (that is partitioning) strategy of the DNA Sequences to be analyzed in heterogeneous systems. In the preprocessing phase the input DNA sequence I is split based on the fraction ratio F (selected by SA) into the part $I' = (F/100) * I$ that will be processed on host CPUs, and $I'' = I - I'$ processed on device. During this phase the construction of the State Transition Table (STT) takes place. When ready, both I'' and the STT are transferred to the device.

Our application takes advantage of the double advantage of transforming-and-tunning [8] of the Intel Xeon Phi, which means that with not much invest-ment we can use the same algorithm for matching patterns in both host and device. When the process of matching I'' on the device is completed, we trans-fers the result (the total number and the location of matched patterns) to the host memory, and a merge of the results is performed.

4   Evaluation

In this section we empirically evaluate our heuristic-guided approach for opti-mization of DNA sequence analysis on heterogeneous platforms. We describe the following,

- the experimentation environment,
- performance comparison of our heuristic-guided approach with the enumera-tion approach (also known as brute force),
- the performance improvement when using the selected solution by our app-roach (that uses both resources of host and device) compared to host-only (48-threads) and device-only (244-threads) executions.

4.1   Experimentation Environment

In this section we provide information related to the experimentation environ-ment including: (1) system configuration, (2) benchmark application, (3) data sets used for evaluation of our approach, and (4) parameter values that define the system configuration space.

System Configuration. The heterogeneous system used for the performed experiments consists of two Intel Xeon E5 processors and one Intel Xeon Phi 7120P co-processor.

Benchmark Application. We used a DNA sequence analysis application with real-world DNA sequences. The major features of our *Emil* system at the Linnaeus University and implementation details of our algorithm for DNA sequence analysis are described in [19,20].

Data Sets. Real world DNA sequences of human (3.17 GB), mouse (2.77 GB), cat (2.43 GB), and dog (2.38 GB) extracted from the GenBank sequence database of the National Center for Biological Information [22]. We use patterns from the *regex-dna* benchmark for matching and extracting specific k-mers from a DNA sequence. The PaREM [18] tool is used to generate the STT for the used patterns.

System Configuration Space. The parameters and their value ranges that define the system configuration for our combinatorial optimization approach are shown in Table 1.

Table 1. The parameters that define the system configuration

Parameter Name	Type	Value range	
		Host	Device
Number of threads	Discrete	{2, 6, 12, 24, 36, 48}	{2, 4, 8, 16, 30, 60, 120, 180, 240}
Thread affinity	Discrete	{none, compact, scatter}	{balanced, compact, scatter}
DNA sequence fraction	Discrete	{0,...,100}	100 - (Host sequence fraction)

4.2 Performance Comparison of Our Heuristic-Guided Optimization Approach with Enumeration

The enumeration approach certainly determines the optimal system parameter values, which results with the best performance by trying all the possible parameter values. However, for large search space of real-world problems, this approach is prohibitively time consuming. For example, despite the fact that we tested only what we considered reasonable parameter values (see Table 1), a total of 19926 experiments were required by enumeration to determine the optimal system configuration. We have achieved comparatively good performance results by using our heuristic-guided approach based on Simulated Annealing by trying only a relatively small subset of the total experiments involved in enumeration.

For performance comparison, we use the absolute difference $|t_{EM} - t_{SA}|$ and the percent difference $100 \cdot absolute\_difference/t_{EM}$, where t_{EM} indicates the best execution time determined using enumeration, and t_{SA} indicates the execution time of our algorithm with a system configuration suggested by the simulated annealing approach.

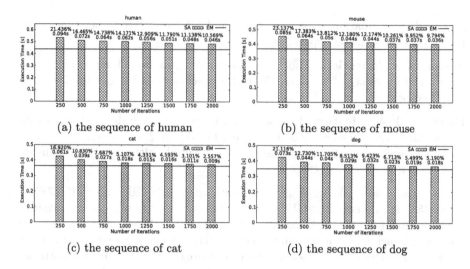

Fig. 3. Performance comparison between the best system configuration determined by the enumeration [EM] approach and the near to optimal one determined by the Simulated Annealing [SA]. The labels at the top of each bar depicts the percent difference [%] and absolute difference [s].

The results in Fig. 3 show the execution time of our algorithm when using the system configuration suggested by SA for various iterations (experiments performed by SA) compared to the best performance achieved using the system configuration determined by enumeration. The labels on top of each bar indicate the percent difference and absolute difference. The horizontal line indicates the execution time of the system configuration determined with enumeration.

By running about 1000 experiments (that is $100 \times 1000/19926 = 5\%$ of the total experiments required by enumeration) SA suggests system configuration that yields with a performance that is close to the optimal one determined by enumeration. Please note that SA is a global optimization approach and to avoid ending at a local optima during the space exploration, sometimes it accepts worse system configuration that results with a higher execution time compared to previous iterations.

The percent difference is shown in the labels on top of the bars (row 1) of Fig. 3. While the average percent difference of SA with 250 iterations is high (20.6%) compared to enumeration, it decreases significantly by increasing the number of iterations. For example by increasing the number of iterations to 500, 750 and 1000 the percent difference decreases to 14.3%, 11.9% and 9.9% respectively.

The second row of the labels on top of the bars of Fig. 3 shows the absolute difference of SA compared to enumeration. The average absolute difference for 250 iterations is 0.078 s, whereas for 500, 750 and 1000 iterations it is only 0.055, 0.045, and 0.038 s, respectively.

4.3   Performance Improvement

This section presents the performance improvement achieved in case all available resources of the host and device are used for the DNA sequence analysis compared to host- and device-only.

The results in Fig. 4 expose the accomplished performance improvement (speedup) when the system configuration determined by the simulated annealing algorithm or the enumeration approach is used for DNA sequence analysis compared only to the host. We may observe that as we increase the number of iterations the speedup of simulated annealing approaches the maximal speedup determined by enumeration. The average speedup achieved for 250, 500, and 1000

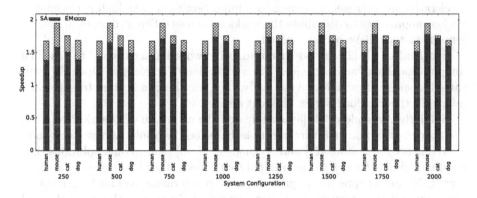

Fig. 4. Speedup achieved when host and device are used for the DNA sequence analysis compared with the host only. We consider 19926 system configurations determined by enumeration (EM) and by Simulated Annealing after 250, 500, 750, 1000, 1250, 1500, 1750, 2000 iterations.

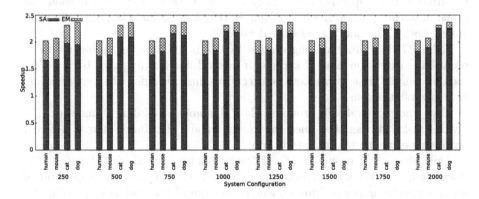

Fig. 5. Speedup achieved when host and device are used for the DNA sequence analysis compared with the device only. We consider system configurations determined by enumeration (EM) and by Simulated Annealing after 250, 500, 750, 1000, 1250, 1500, 1750, 2000 iterations.eps

iterations is $1.46\times$, 1.54, and $1.63\times$ whereas the maximal achieved speedup with enumeration is $1.77\times$.

Figure 5 depicts the achieved speedup when the system configuration determined by the simulated annealing algorithm or the enumeration approach is used for the DNA sequence analysis compared only to the device. The average speedup achieved for 250, 500, and 1000 iterations is $1.82\times$, 1.92, and $2.0\times$ whereas the maximal achieved speedup with enumeration is $2.2\times$.

5 Related Work

Utilizing the combined computation power of multi-core CPUs and many-core accelerators in heterogeneous systems is important to achieve high performance. Various approaches to distribute the workload across different devices in heterogeneous systems have been proposed.

Scogland et al. [27] proposed an adaptive worksharing library to schedule computational load across devices. Their extension of accelerated OpenMP evaluates the speed of each device statically, then use these indicators to automatically split the workload across different devices.

Similarly Ayguadé et al. [5] investigated the extension of OpenMP to allow workload distribution on future iterations based on the results of first static ones.

While Scogland et al. [27] and Ayguadé et al. [5] tend to offer solutions that require minimal changes to the original source code, task block models, such as StarPU [4] and OmpSs [10] require the user to determine workload distribution manually and may require significant structural changes to the original serial code.

Odajima et al. [23] proposed an approach that combines the pragma-based XcalableMP (XMP) [21] programming language with the runtime system by StarPU to utilize both GPU and CPU resources on each node for work distribution of the loop executions. They use the XMP for data distribution and synchronization purposes, whereas the StarPU is used for scheduling the tasks among host CPUs and accelerating devices.

Qilin [17] is a programming system that is based on a regression model to predict the execution time of kernels. It uses off-line learning that is thereafter used in compile time to predict the execution time for different input sizes and system configurations.

Ravi and Agrawal [26] proposed their dynamic scheduling framework that divides tasks into smaller ones that later on are distributed across different processing elements in a task-farm way.

Dokulili et al. [9] proposed a C++ framework for dynamic distribution of the work among the host CPUs and co-processor devices. The workload is distributed using a priority queue technique, where one core of the host is responsible for the queue management.

Grewe and O'Boyle [11] proposed a static partitioning approach to distribute OpenCL programs on heterogeneous systems. Their approach is based on static analysis to extract code features from OpenCL programs. These features are then used to determine the best partitioning across the different devices. Their approach relies on the architectural characteristics of a system.

In comparison to the aforementioned approaches, we use combinatorial optimization to determine the near-optimal system configuration.

Albayrak et al. [3] propose a profiling-based approach for mapping kernel computations to heterogeneous platforms. Their approach extracts profiling information by running each application on each device (including host CPUs and accelerators), to collect information such as execution time and data transfer time. This information is then passed to solvers such as Greedy Algorithm to select the optimal mapping for a specific kernel.

In contrast to Albayrak et al. [3] we use Simulated Annealing to minimize the overall execution cost. Furthermore, they work focuses on applications that are designed as sequence of kernels, whereas we target data-parallel applications.

In the context of Grid computing environments, Kołodziej et al. [15] have studied the use of meta-heuristics for efficient data scheduling. Khan et al. [14] address *parameter sensitivity* [13] of workflows and propose to use the Ant-Colony Optimization to identify parameters of workflow activities that affect more the overall result of the workflow.

6   Conclusion and Future Work

In this paper we have presented a combinatorial optimization approach to determine the system configuration (the number of threads, thread affinity, and the DNA sequence fraction for the host and device) such that the overall execution time is minimized. Furthermore, we presented an approach for DNA sequence analysis that is designed to efficiently utilize the available resources of heterogeneous systems accelerated with Intel Xeon Phi.

Determining the best system configuration using enumeration is prohibitively time consuming because it requires many experiments. Using our approach we were able to determine a near optimal system configuration by executing only about 5 % of experiments, which results with comparable performance to the one determined with enumeration. When using the near-optimal system configuration selected by our approach we achieved a maximal speedup of 1.74× compared to host-only execution, and up to 2.2× speedup compared to device-only execution.

Future work will study multi-objective optimization (energy consumption and performance efficiency) of DNA sequence analysis using platforms accelerated with the second generation of the Intel Xeon Phi (Knights Landing).

References

1. TOP500 Supercomputer Sites. http://www.top500.org/. Accessed Jan 2016
2. Abraham, E., Bekas, C., Brandic, I., Genaim, S., Johnsen, E.B.,Kondov, I., Pllana, S., Streit, A.: Preparing HPC applications for exascale: challenges and recommendations. In: 2015 18th International Conference on Network-Based Information Systems (NBiS), pp. 401–406, September 2015

3. Albayrak, O.E., Akturk, I., Ozturk, O.: Improving application behavior on heterogeneous manycore systems through kernel mapping. Parallel Comput. **39**(12), 867–878 (2013). http://dx.doi.org/10.1016/j.parco.2013.08.011

4. Augonnet, C., Thibault, S., Namyst, R., Wacrenier, P.A.: StarPU: a unified platform for task scheduling on heterogeneous multicore architectures. Concurr. Comput. Pract. Exp. **23**(2), 187–198 (2011)

5. Ayguadé, E., Blainey, B., Duran, A., Labarta, J., Martínez, F., Martorell, X., Silvera, R.: Is the *Schedule* clause really necessary in OpenMP? In: Voss, M.J. (ed.) WOMPAT 2003. LNCS, vol. 2716, pp. 147–159. Springer, Heidelberg (2003). doi:10.1007/3-540-45009-2_12

6. Benkner, S., Pllana, S., Traff, J., Tsigas, P., Dolinsky, U., Augonnet, C., Bachmayer, B., Kessler, C., Moloney, D., Osipov, V.: PEPPHER: efficient and productive usage of hybrid computing systems. IEEE Micro **31**(5), 28–41 (2011)

7. Braun, T.D., Siegel, H.J., Beck, N., Bölöni, L.L., Maheswaran, M., Reuther, A.I., Robertson, J.P., Theys, M.D., Yao, B., Hensgen, D., et al.: A comparison of eleven static heuristics for mapping a class of independent tasks onto heterogeneous distributed computing systems. J. Parallel Distrib. Comput. **61**(6), 810–837 (2001)

8. Chrysos, G.: Intel® Xeon Phi Coprocessor-the Architecture. Intel Whitepaper (2014)

9. Dokulil, J., Bajrovic, E., Benkner, S., Pllana, S., Sandrieser, M.,Bachmayer, B.: High-level support for hybrid parallel execution of C++ applications targeting Intel Xeon Phi coprocessors. In: ICCS. Procedia Computer Science, vol. 18, pp. 2508–2511. Elsevier (2013)

10. Duran, A., Ayguadé, E., Badia, R.M., Labarta, J., Martinell, L., Martorell, X., Planas, J.: OmpSs: a proposal for programming heterogeneous multi-core architectures. Parallel Process. Lett. **21**(02), 173–193 (2011)

11. Grewe, D., O'Boyle, M.F.P.: A static task partitioning approach for heterogeneous systems using OpenCL. In: Knoop, J. (ed.) CC 2011. LNCS, vol. 6601, pp. 286–305. Springer, Heidelberg (2011). doi:10.1007/978-3-642-19861-8_16

12. Kessler, C.W., Dastgeer, U., Thibault, S., Namyst, R., Richards, A., Dolinsky, U., Benkner, S., Traff, J.L., Pllana, S.: Programmability and performance portability aspects of heterogeneous multi-/manycore systems, pp. 1403–1408. IEEE (2012)

13. Khan, F., Han, Y., Pllana, S., Brezany, P.: Estimation of parameters sensitivity for scientific workflows. In: 2009 International Conference on Parallel Processing Workshops, pp. 457–462, September 2009

14. Khan, F., Han, Y., Pllana, S., Brezany, P.: An ant-colony-optimization based approach for determination of parameter significance of scientific workflows. In: 2010 24th IEEEInternational Conference on Advanced Information Networking and Applications (AINA), pp. 1241–1248, April 2010

15. Kołodziej, J., Khan, S.U.: Data scheduling in data grids and data centers: a short taxonomy of problems and intelligent resolution techniques. In: Nguyen, N.-T., Kołodziej, J., Burczyński, T., Biba, M. (eds.) Transactions on Computational Collective Intelligence X. LNCS, vol. 7776, pp. 103–119. Springer, Heidelberg (2013). doi:10.1007/978-3-642-38496-7_7

16. Liu, Y., Pan, T., Aluru, S.: Parallel pairwise correlationcomputation on intel xeon phi clusters. arXiv preprint arXiv:1605.01584 (2016)

17. Luk, C.K., Hong, S., Kim, H.: Qilin: exploiting parallelism on heterogeneous multiprocessors with adaptive mapping. In: 42nd Annual IEEE/ACM International Symposium on Microarchitecture, 2009, MICRO-42, pp. 45–55. IEEE (2009)

18. Memeti, S., Pllana, S.: PaREM: a novel approach for parallel regular expression matching. In: 17th International Conference on Computational Science and Engineering (CSE 2014), pp. 690–697, December 2014
19. Memeti, S., Pllana, S.: Accelerating DNA sequence analysis using Intel Xeon Phi. In: PBio at the 2015 IEEE International Symposiumon Parallel and Distributed Processing with Applications (ISPA). IEEE (2015)
20. Memeti, S., Pllana, S.: Analyzing large-scale DNA sequences on multi-core architectures. In: 18th IEEE International Conference on Computational Science and Engineering (CSE 2015). IEEE (2015)
21. Nakao, M., Lee, J., Boku, T., Sato, M.: XcalableMP implementationand performance of NAS parallel benchmarks. In: Proceedings of the Fourth Conference on Partitioned Global Address Space Programming Model, p. 11. ACM (2010)
22. NCBI: National Center for Biotechnology Information U.S. NationalLibrary of Medicine (2015). http://www.ncbi.nlm.nih.gov/genbank. Accessed Dec 2015
23. Odajima, T., Boku, T., Hanawa, T., Lee, J., Sato, M.: GPU/CPU work sharing with parallel language XcalableMP-dev for parallelized accelerated computing. In: 2012 41st International Conference on Parallel Processing Workshops (ICPPW), pp. 97–106. IEEE (2012)
24. Pllana, S., Benkner, S., Xhafa, F., Barolli, L.: Hybrid performance modeling and prediction of large-scale computing systems. In: International Conference on Complex, Intelligent and Software Intensive Systems, 2008, CISIS 2008, pp. 132–138, March 2008
25. Press, W.H., Teukolsky, S.A., Vetterling, W.T., Flannery, B.P.: Numerical Recipes in C: The Art of Scientific Computing, 3rd edn. Cambridge University Press, Cambridge (2007)
26. Ravi, V.T., Agrawal, G.: A dynamic scheduling framework for emerging heterogeneous systems. In: 2011 18th International Conference on High Performance Computing (HiPC), pp. 1–10. IEEE (2011)
27. Scogland, T.R.W., Feng, W., Rountree, B., Supinski, B.R.: CoreTSAR: adaptive worksharing for heterogeneous systems. In: Kunkel, J.M., Ludwig, T., Meuer, H.W. (eds.) ISC 2014. LNCS, vol. 8488, pp. 172–186. Springer, Heidelberg (2014). doi:10.1007/978-3-319-07518-1_11
28. Viebke, A., Pllana, S.: The potential of the Intel (R) Xeon Phi forsupervised deep learning. In: 2015 IEEE 17th International Conference on High Performance Computing and Communications (HPCC), pp. 758–765. IEEE (2015)

ExaComm

Reducing Manipulation Overhead of Remote Data-Structure by Controlling Remote Memory Access Order

Yuichiro Ajima[✉], Takafumi Nose, Kazushige Saga, Naoyuki Shida, and Shinji Sumimoto

Fujitsu Limited/JST-CREST, Kawasaki, Japan
{aji,nose.takafumi,saga.kazushige,shidax,
sumimoto.shinji}@jp.fujitsu.com

Abstract. The Advanced Communication Primitives (ACP) is a communication library which provides the PGAS programming model to existing programming languages. The communication primitives of ACP include remote-to-remote data transfer and atomic operations. The reference implementation of communication primitives of ACP uses connectionless sockets over UDP and agent threads. The remote-to-remote data transfer is implemented as a protocol. The ACP data library (ACPdl) is a utility library using the communication primitives that include interfaces to create and manipulate several types of remote and distributed data structures. In the current implementation of ACP, there is a performance issue in the erase and insert functions of vector-type data structures due to the in-place data movement algorithm. This paper proposes a new technique called 'remote ordering' for the remote-to-remote data transfer protocol. The remote ordering technique overlaps the progresses of the protocol for the data movement simultaneously. The evaluation results show that the average execution times of the functions were reduced to about one seventh.

Keywords: Communication library · Partitioned global address space · Data structure

1 Introduction

The Partitioned Global Address Space (PGAS) programming model provides the shared global address space of which each portion has an affinity for a particular process. The global address space provides an appropriate mean to describe irregular data transfer to manipulate unstructured data, and the affinity for a particular process provides the capability to exploit the locality of inter-process data placement. In the PGAS model, inter-node data transfer is described as a memory access to the global address space, and both the source and destination addresses are determined before the data transfer. This approach not only eliminates the destination-side communication buffer to store data until determination of the destination address, which is required in the message passing and active message models, but also allows communication primitives to be implemented in hardware. In actual fact, the remote direct memory

© Springer International Publishing AG 2016
M. Taufer et al. (Eds.): ISC High Performance Workshops 2016, LNCS 9945, pp. 85–97, 2016.
DOI: 10.1007/978-3-319-46079-6_7

access (RDMA) protocol implemented in hardware is the basis of almost all existing PGAS languages and communication libraries.

The Advanced Communication Primitives (ACP) is a PGAS communication library which is being developed to provide the PGAS programming model to existing programming languages. [1] The communication primitives of ACP allow remote-to-remote data transfer, which is nearly the same abstraction level as the PGAS languages, and a higher level than local-to-remote and remote-to-local data transfer of the existing RDMA protocols. However, there is a drawback for the higher abstraction level that even inefficient algorithms would be written easily. To make matters worse, no compiler optimizations would be available, because the ACP is a library. Therefore, optimizations for each communication primitive are vitally important to the ACP.

The ACP provides not only the communication primitives, but also utility libraries using the communication primitives. [2, 3] For example, the ACP data library (ACPdl) is a utility library that includes interfaces to create and manipulate several types of remote and distributed data structures. The implementations of utility libraries are device independent and portable, although those of the communication primitives are device dependent. In the development phase, the utility libraries are also important as the common test sets to optimize each implementation of communication primitives.

In this paper, a new technique for the implementation of remote-to-remote data transfer protocol is proposed. The specifications of the ACP library corresponding to the new method are summarized in Sect. 2, and the issue to address is described in Sect. 3. The new technique is proposed in Sect. 3, and the evaluation results are shown in Sect. 4. Future work, related work, and a summary are presented in Sects. 5, 6, and 7, respectively.

2 Advanced Communication Primitives

The ACP is a communication library which provides the PGAS programming model to existing programming languages. The global address space is partitioned into memory regions. Each memory region is exposed by a particular process, and accessed from other processes. Each process dynamically and independently registers and unregisters memory regions to the global address space. A pre-allocated and zero-cleared global memory region is provided for each process that is intended to be used to place static shared variables.

The communication primitives of ACP include data transfer and atomic operations. The remote-to-remote data transfer function is '**acp_copy**' and the atomic operation functions include '**acp_cas8**' and '**acp_add4**.' Each function name of ACP starts with prefix '**acp_**', and the atomic operation functions end with a postfix digit '4' or '8' which represents the data size of the value. The communication primitive functions have arguments to specify source and destination global addresses; therefore, any process can transfer data from a remote process to another remote process without involving both source- and destination-side processes.

The ACPdl provides a global memory allocator and data structure interfaces. The global memory allocation function is '**acp_malloc**' and the data structure functions include '**acp_create_vector**' and '**acp_destroy_list**.' The data structure functions end with a postfix that represents the type of data structure, which includes vector, deque, list, set, and map; vector is a dynamic array, deque is a bidirectional queue, list is a bidirectional linked-list, set is a dictionary, and map is an associative array.

The following subsections describe the remote-to-remote data transfer and the vector-type data structure.

2.1 Data Transfer and Ordering

The acp_copy function transfers data from source global address to destination global address. For the **acp_copy** function, remote-to-remote, remote-to-local, local-to-remote, and even local-to-local data transfers do not differ in terms of syntax. The left image of Fig. 1 shows a conceptual model of remote-to-remote transfer. Process 1 initiates a data transfer from the memory of process 2 to that of process n, while neither process 2 nor n calls an ACP function. Because existing protocol stack or interconnect hardware does not support remote-to-remote data transfer, the typical implementation of the remote-to-remote data transfer is that each process has an agent thread to process the protocol of the remote-to-remote data transfer.

If an ordinary RDMA protocol is supported by the underlying interconnect hardware, the remote-to-remote data transfer protocol can be simplified by executing the local-to-remote data transfer on the source process. Even an implementation without agent threads is possible. The right image of Fig. 1 shows an example of the implementation without agent threads. The initiator process executes the remote-to-local RDMA transfer from the source process to a local buffer, and then executes the local-to-remote RDMA transfer from the local buffer to the destination process.

The implementation without agent threads requires less computing resources. However, transferring data twice consumes more bandwidth and electrical power. The difference between implementation with and without agent threads gets larger when both the source and destination addresses are in the same process. Figure 2 shows images of the case. No inter-process data transfer is required for the typical implementation with agent threads, because the agent thread on the source or destination process can copy the data locally.

The **acp_copy** is a non-blocking function that returns immediately, before the data transfer starts or completes. The '**acp_complete**' function waits for the completion of a data transfer. The **acp_complete** function requires an argument of handle type '**acp_handle_t**' to instruct the data transfer to wait, and **acp_copy** function returns a

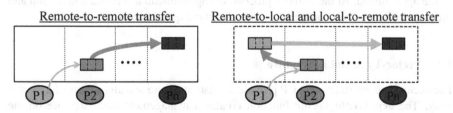

Remote-to-remote transfer   Remote-to-local and local-to-remote transfer

P1   P2   Pn   P1   P2   Pn

Fig. 1. Images of a conceptual model and an example implementation of the remote-to-remote data transfer.

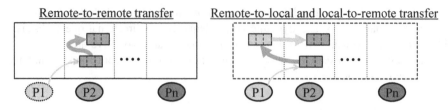

Fig. 2. Images of implementations of the remote-to-remote data transfer when both the source and the destination addresses are in the same process.

value of the **acp_handle_t** type handle. For an implementation without agent threads, it is another disadvantage that the **acp_copy** function is blocked until the completion of the former remote-to-local data transfer.

Moreover, the **acp_copy** function also has an argument of **acp_handle_t** type handle itself, although that is used for a different functionality than that of the **acp_-complete** function. The start of the data transfer is delayed until after the completion of the indicated data transfer. If a data transfer is executed out of order, the **acp_copy** call should indicate the pre-defined handle **ACP_HANDLE_NULL**. If multiple data transfers are required to be executed in sequential order, each **acp_copy** call should indicate the pre-defined handle **ACP_HANDLE_ALL**, or the handle returned by the previous call. This non-blocking ordering feature is also difficult to be implemented without agent threads, and an implementation without agent threads might fall down to execute all data transfers in sequential order, regardless of the indicated handles.

The reference implementation of the device dependent layer of ACP uses connectionless sockets over UDP/IP [4] and agent threads. The other implementations, including InfiniBand, [5] Tofu interconnect, [6, 7] and Tofu interconnect 2 [8, 9] versions, also use agent threads implemented similarly to the UDP version. At the initiator process of the remote-to-remote data transfer, the main thread enqueues a command which includes arguments of a data transfer to the command queue of the process. The agent thread of the initiator process transfers the command from the command queue to the source process or the destination process. The agent thread that received a command enqueues the command to the delegation queue of the process. The agent thread dequeues a command from the delegation queue and starts the communication protocol between the source and the destination processes. When the protocol is done, the agent thread transfers a notification of the completion of the data transfer to the initiator process. The order of the remote-to-remote transfer is controlled by the agent thread. At the initiator process, the agent thread receives a notification and checks whether the top command on the command queue can be started or not.

2.2   Vector-Type Data Structure

The vector type interfaces of ACP provide the data structure and algorithms of dynamic array. The **acp_create_vector** function creates a management data structure on the specified process, and returns **acp_vector_t** type reference of vector. The vector manipulation functions such as **acp_push_back_vector** store data to it. The vector is

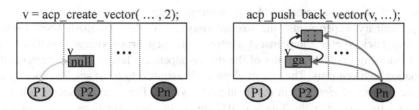

Fig. 3. Images of creation and data storage of a vector

created as empty and it has no data storage. The memory for data storage is dynamically allocated on the same process as the management data structure. Figure 3 shows images of creation and data storage of a vector. Process 1 creates an empty vector on process 2 in the left image. In the right image, process *n* stores data to the vector. If the memory for data storage is not allocated, it is allocated before storing data. The management data structure is also updated.

The vector iterator **acp_vector_it_t** consists of the reference of the corresponding vector and an offset value which indicates a relative address from the start of the stored data in the vector. The **acp_begin_vector** function returns a vector iterator including an offset value zero. The offset value can be changed by the **acp_advance_vector_it** function. The **acp_dereference_vector_it** function returns the global address of the data specified by the indicated vector iterator.

The **acp_push_back_vector** function inserts data at the end, and the **acp_pop_back_vector** function erases data at the end. Inserting or erasing data at the end of the data of a vector is a low overhead manipulation, because the size of the storage is maintained to keep a reserved area. The size of the storage is rounded up to a particular value according to the required size, and it is not truncated when a part of the data is removed.

The **acp_erase_vector** function erases data at an arbitrary offset indicated by a vector iterator. The latter part of the remained data is moved forward to the erasure point to keep the data continual. Because the original and the new placement of the remained data may be overlapped, the remained data are moved by an in-place algorithm. The data are divided into chunks of the same size as the size of erasing data, and the chunks are moved sequentially in order ascending from the erasure point to the end. The **acp_insert_vector** function inserts data at an arbitrary offset indicated by a vector iterator. The existing data after the insertion point is moved backward by the size of insertion data to concatenate the insertion data with the existing data. The data to move is also divided into chunks of the same size as the insertion size, and the chunks are moved sequentially in order descending from the end to the insertion point.

3   Issue

The in-place data movement algorithm described in the previous section is memory efficient. However, the algorithm causes a performance issue when the size of a data element is small and the number of elements in a vector increases. The execution time of the function may be dominated by the sequential movement of small chunks of data. As preliminary experiments, the execution times of the **acp_push_back_vector**, **acp_pop_back_vector**, **acp_insert_vector**, and **acp_erase_vector** functions are measured using the UDP version of the device-dependent layer. Table 1 presents the evaluation environments. The size of elements is assumed to be as small as four bytes, and the number of elements in the input vector varies. The average execution time is measured by executing the function 100 times. In the evaluations of the **acp_insert_vector** and **acp_erase_vector** functions, the input iterator marks the start of the data.

Figure 4 shows the results. When the number of elements is the minimum, the average execution times of the **acp_pop_back_vector** and **acp_erase_vector** functions are nearly the same, and those of the **acp_push_back_vector** and **acp_insert_vector** functions are also nearly the same. As the number of elements increases, the average execution times of the **acp_erase_vector** and **acp_insert_vector** functions increase proportionally to the number of elements in the input vector at a rate of about 0.1 ms per element.

A data movement algorithm that copies the data twice via a temporal buffer, may address the performance issue. Figure 5 shows the results of preliminary experiments that measured the execution time of erasing the first element from a vector by three different algorithms. The first used the acp_erase_vector function. The second copies the data to a temporary vector on the remote process which is a process in which the target vector is placed, then copies back the remained portion of the data to the target vector. The third copies the data to a temporary vector on the local process which is a process that executes the erasure, then copies back the remained portion of the data to the target vector.

The results of the two-copy algorithms are almost constant regardless of the number of elements in the input vector. When the number of elements in the input vector is four or below, the two-copy algorithms are slower than the in-place algorithm due to the overhead of the two copies. However, if the number of elements in the input vector is seven or above, the two-copy algorithms are faster than the in-place algorithm. The difference between the two-copy algorithms using a remote temporal buffer and a local temporal buffer mainly derives from the difference of the overhead of the protocol. If the total size of the input vector exceeds the maximum size of a UDP datagram, the average execution times of the two-copy algorithm using a local temporal buffer may get longer compared with that of the two-copy algorithm using a remote temporal buffer to copy the data locally by the agent thread on the remote process.

Figure 6 shows the results of preliminary experiments that measured the execution time of inserting an element at the start of a vector by the in-place two-copy algorithms using a remote buffer and a local buffer. When the number of elements in the input

Table 1. Evaluation environment

Node	Fujitsu PRIMERGY RX200 S5
CPU	Intel Xeon E5520 (4 cores, 2.27 GHz), 2 sockets
Memory	DDR3 SDRAM 48 GB, 51.2 GB/s
Network	Gigabit Ethernet (125 Mbyte/sec)

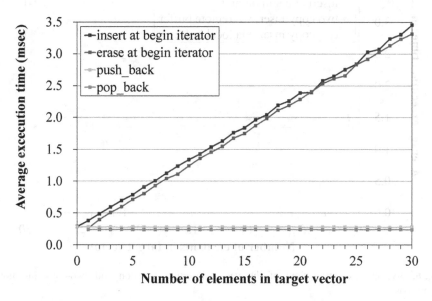

Fig. 4. Average execution times of the vector insertion, erasure, push_back and pop_back functions

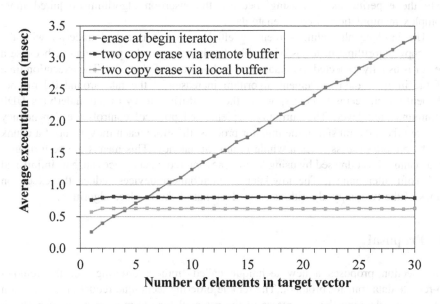

Fig. 5. Average execution times of the vector erasure function and two-copy erasure algorithms

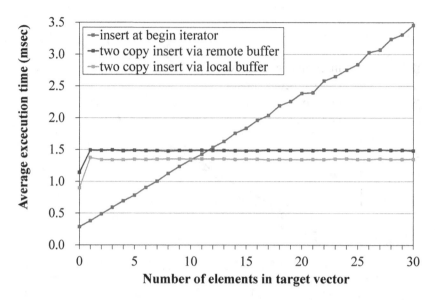

Fig. 6. Average execution time of the vector insertion function and two-copy insertion algorithms

vector is twelve or above, the two-copy algorithms are faster than the in-place algorithm. The average execution times of the two-copy algorithms got longer compared with the experiments of erasing, because the insertion algorithms required more complex manipulation to concatenate data.

The in-place algorithm is memory efficient, but it is a bad trade-off with the two-copy algorithms in terms of the big disadvantage of the performance, because a vector is usually expected to contain tens or hundreds of elements. The execution time of the in-place data movement algorithm increased at the rate around 0.1 ms per element which seems to correspond to the round-trip latency of the underlying UDP communication layer. The currently implemented protocol controls the dependency between the data transfer at the initiator process; therefore, each movement of a chunk on the remote process takes a whole round-trip latency. This means the performance issue cannot be addressed by using low-latency interconnect devices such as InfiniBand and Tofu interconnect. The low-latency interconnect devices reduce the execution times of the two-copy algorithms as well as that of the in-place algorithm.

4   Proposal

This section proposes a new technique called 'remote ordering' for the remote-to-remote data transfer protocol. The remote ordering technique reduces the execution time by overlapping the progresses of the protocol for the movement of each chunk simultaneously. The command transferred from the initiator process to the source or the destination process contains the dependency information, and the agent thread that received the command controls the order of execution of commands. The detail algorithm to implement the remote ordering differs for each device dependent layer of ACP. In this paper, a remote ordering algorithm is introduced to the remote-to-remote data transfer protocol of the UDP version of ACP.

The agent thread at the initiator process memorizes the source and the destination processes of the last transferred command. When the next command indicates the sequential execution order, and the source and the destination processes identical to the previous command, the agent thread at the initiator process sets 'remote fence flag' to the command and transfers it right after the previous command is successfully transferred, instead of waiting for the notification of the completion of the data transfer of the previous command. The agent thread at the source or the destination process delays the execution of a command with the remote fence flag until all preceding commands in the delegation queue are completed.

5   Evaluation

In this section, the average execution times of the **acp_erase_vector** and **acp_insert_vector** functions improved by the remote ordering feature are evaluated. The evaluation environment and the experimental method are as described in Sect. 3. Figure 7 shows the results. The average execution times still increase proportionally to the number of elements in the input vector, but the rate of increase is reduced from about 0.1 ms per element to about 0.015-ms per element.

Figure 8 shows the average execution times of erasing data at the start of data using two-copy algorithms. The results are almost identical to those of the preliminary

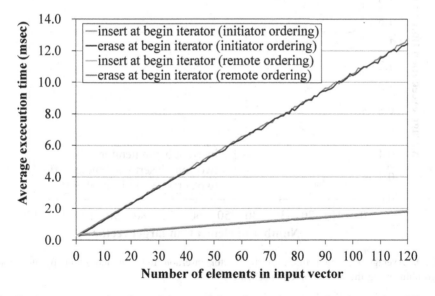

Fig. 7. Average execution time of the vector insertion and erasure functions using different ordering scheme

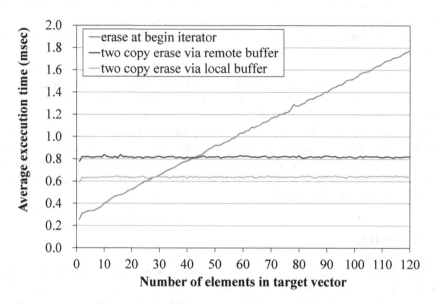

Fig. 8. Average execution times of the vector erasure function and two-copy erasure algorithms using the remote ordering scheme

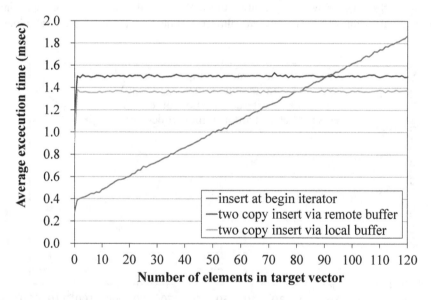

Fig. 9. Average execution times of the vector insertion function and two-copy insertion algorithms using the remote ordering scheme

experiments, because the two-copy algorithms do not include the sequence of data transfer that can be overlapped by the remote ordering feature. The in-place algorithm is faster than the two-copy algorithm using a remote buffer when the number of elements in the input vector is 42 or below, and is faster than the two-copy algorithm using a local buffer when the number of elements in the input vector is 27 or below.

Figure 9 shows the average execution times of inserting data at the start of data using two-copy algorithms. The results are also almost identical to those of the preliminary experiments. The in-place algorithm is faster than the two-copy algorithm using a remote buffer when the number of elements in the input vector is 90 or below, and is faster than the two-copy algorithm using a local buffer when the number of elements in the input vector is 79 or below.

The remote ordering feature introduced to the remote-to-remote data transfer protocol of the UDP version of ACP device dependent layer reduces the average execution time of the **acp_erase_vector** and the **acp_insert_vector** functions which use the in-place data movement algorithm to about one seventh. The improved execution times are faster or comparable to those using two-copy algorithms when the input vector contains elements of tens or below.

6 Future Work

The **acp_erase_vector** and the **acp_insert_vector** functions still cause the performance issue if the input vector contains hundreds or above elements. Therefore, more sophisticated and adaptive algorithms should be investigated, such as a semi-in-place partial two-copy algorithm.

Protocols for the remote-to-remote data transfer also need further investigation to exploit the locality and to hide the latency.

7 Related Work

A number of communication libraries to underlie PGAS programming language runtimes have been developed. The Aggregate Remote Memory Copy Interface (ARMCI) [10] is a low-level communication library designed to be used by the Global Arrays Toolkit. The Global-Address Space Networking (GASNet) [11] is a low-level communication interface intended for use in implementing the runtime system for global address space languages such as UPC [12]. OpenFabrics Interface (OFI) [13] is a collection of communication functions to underlie applications and middleware such as MPI, SHMEM, PGAS and Database Management System. Unified Communication X (UCX) [14] is a collection of communication interfaces for multiple middleware domains, including MPI, PGAS, Task-based and I/O. These communication libraries do not support remote-to-remote data transfer such as the **acp_copy** function and employ a one-sided communication model that reflects the RDMA protocol directly.

8 Summary

The ACP is a communication library which provides the PGAS programming model to existing programming languages. The communication primitives of ACP include remote-to-remote data transfer and atomic operations. The reference implementation of communication primitives of ACP uses connectionless sockets over UDP and agent threads. The remote-to-remote data transfer is implemented as a protocol. The ACPdl is a utility library using the communication primitives that include interfaces to create and manipulate several types of remote and distributed data structures. In the current implementation of ACP, there is a performance issue in the erase and insert functions of vector-type data structures due to the in-place data movement algorithm. This paper proposes a new technique called 'remote ordering' for the remote-to-remote data transfer protocol. The remote ordering technique overlaps the progresses of the protocol for the data movement simultaneously. The evaluation results show that the average execution times still increase proportionally to the number of elements in the input vector, but the rate of increase is reduced from about 0.1 ms per element to about 0.015-ms per element.

Acknowledgement. The development of the ACP library is a part of the Advanced Communication for Exa (ACE) project, [15] which is a research theme in the CREST research area 'Development of System Software Technologies for post-Peta Scale High Performance Computing,' sponsored by JST (Japan Science and Technology Agency).

References

1. Sumimoto, S., Ajima, Y., Saga, K., Nose, T., Shida, N., Nanri, T.: The design of advanced communication to reduce memory usage for exa-scale systems. In: 12th International Meeting on High Performance Computing for Computational Science (VECPAR) (2016, in press)
2. Ajima, Y., Nose, T., Saga, K., Shida, N., Sumimoto, S.: ACPdl: data-structure and global memory allocator library over a thin PGAS-layer. In: The First International Workshop on Extreme Scale Programming Models and Middleware (ESPM 2015), pp. 11–18 (2015)
3. Nanri, T., Soga, T., et al.: Channel interface: a primitive model for memory efficient communication. In: 23rd Euromicro PDP, pp. 177–181 (2015)
4. Postel, J.B. (ed.): User Datagram Protocol, RFC 768 (1980)
5. InfiniBand Trade Association. http://www.infinibandta.org
6. Ajima, Y., Sumimoto, S., Shimizu, T.: Tofu: a 6D mesh/torus interconnect for exascale computers. IEEE Comput. **42**(11), 30–40 (2010)
7. Ajima, Y., Inoue, T., et al.: The tofu interconnect. IEEE Micro **32**(1), 21–31 (2012)
8. Ajima, Y., et al.: Tofu interconnect 2: system-on-chip integration of high-performance interconnect. In: Kunkel, J.M., Ludwig, T., Meuer, H.W. (eds.) ISC 2014. LNCS, vol. 8488, pp. 498–507. Springer, Heidelberg (2014)
9. Ajima, Y., Inoue, T., et al.: The tofu interconnect 2. In: IEEE 22nd High-Performance Interconnects, pp. 57–62 (2014)
10. ARMCI – Aggregate Remote Memory Copy Interface. http://hpc.pnl.gov/armci/
11. GASNet Communication System. http://gasnet.lbl.gov/

12. Berkeley UPC – Unified Parallel C. http://upc.lbl.gov/
13. Libfabric. http://ofiwg.github.io/libfabric/
14. UCX – Unified Communication X. http://www.openucx.org/
15. ACE Project. http://ace-project.kyushu-u.ac.jp/index.html

SONAR: Automated Communication Characterization for HPC Applications

Steffen Lammel$^{(\boxtimes)}$, Felix Zahn, and Holger Fröning

Computer Engineering Group, Ruprecht-Karls University of Heidelberg,
Heidelberg, Germany
s.lammel@stud.uni-heidelberg.de,
{felix.zahn,holger.froening}@ziti.uni-heidelberg.de
http://www.ziti.uni-heidelberg.de/compeng

Abstract. Future computing systems will need to operate within hard power and energy constraints, this is particularly true for Exascale-class systems. These constraints are hard for technical, economical and ecological reasons, thus, such systems have to operate within given power and energy budgets. Therefore, we anticipate the need for modeling tools that help to predict power and energy consumption. In particular, such modeling tools would allow for detailed explorations of various alternatives when designing systems. While processing and memory already receives a large amount of interest from the research community, power modeling of scalable interconnection networks is rather neglected. However, analyses show that the network contributes about 20 % to the overall power consumption of HPC systems. Considering the increasing energy efficiency of other components, this fraction is likely to increase. While models for processing and memory typically rely on performance counters to model power and energy, we observe that the distributed nature of networks leads to significantly more complex metrics. Selecting the right set of abstract metrics, which will be used as input for such a prediction, is crucial for prediction performance.

In this work we introduce our tool called Simple Offline Network Analyzer (SONAR) to derive complex metrics from communication traces of HPC applications. We explain the motivation behind choosing this concept, the implementation, and the ability of the tool to easily support the integration of new metrics. We also show exemplary explorations using an initial set of metrics for a representative range of HPC applications, including contemporary as well as emerging Exascale workloads. In particular, we use SONAR to characterize the communication of applications in terms of verbosity and network utilization, as we believe both to be important metrics for power prediction.

Keywords: Exascale · HPC · MPI · Communication · Characterization · Automated tooling

© Springer International Publishing AG 2016
M. Taufer et al. (Eds.): ISC High Performance Workshops 2016, LNCS 9945, pp. 98–114, 2016.
DOI: 10.1007/978-3-319-46079-6_8

1   Introduction

Following the end of Dennard scaling, power and energy consumption turned into hard constraints that limit a computing system's computational power. Key to a continuing performance scaling is improving energy efficiency, which means more computations per Joule can be performed.

This is particularly true for Exascale systems, which will be severely limited by power consumption. Presently, it is estimated that a power dissipation between 20 MW and 100 MW is anticipated for those systems. Since processors make up a large fraction of the overall power consumption, the majority of current work focuses on understanding and optimizing their power efficiency. Additionally, we believe the network component has historically received too little attention. Analyses show that the network consumes up to 30 % of the overall power [1]. This fraction increases if processors become more energy-proportional, i.e. the actually consumed power is linked linearly to the component's load. Therefore, there is an urgent need to understand power consumption in scalable interconnection networks in order to design optimizations.

In order to achieve an understanding of power consumption, we believe the most suitable option is using power-aware network simulations and power models. The first method excels in an accurate prediction, the latter allows for much faster predictions. Therefore, it enables explorations of topology, link configuration and other abstract aspects. While our initial version of a power-aware network simulator already exists [2], we are currently working on a network power model. For such models it is crucial to select the right set of metrics that describe the traffic in a way that is suitable for an abstracted power prediction.

Understanding the communication behavior of large scale HPC applications is essential for our research regarding power consumption and possible optimizations. Therefore, it is mandatory to provide realistic input for simulators and models. Traces of real HPC applications meet this demand and allow simulations of different hardware configurations under realistic conditions. Additionally, traces are examined post-run, which enables analysis for different metrics without running the application again.

There are a variety of tools that generate traces for post-run examination. Some popular examples are VampirTrace[1], TAU[2] and Score-P[3]. Once the traces have been created, tools like Vampir or Jumpshot-4 take a look at the inner workings of the applications. These tools are designed to discover and fix programming weaknesses of applications such as waiting phases, bottlenecks, contention, etc. to maximize the performance.

In this work we introduce our communication characterization tool called SONAR (Simple Offline Network Analyzer), which allows us to easily derive

---

[1] https://tu-dresden.de/die_tu_dresden/zentrale_einrichtungen/zih/forschung/ projekte/vampirtrace/.

[2] https://www.cs.uoregon.edu/research/tau/home.php.

[3] https://www.vi-hps.org/Tools/Score-P.html.

complex metrics from communication traces. Furthermore, it is simple to introduce new metrics based on these traces. In particular, we make the following contributions:

- Introduce SONAR as an open-source tool to automatically generate complex metrics of HPC communication traces
- Provide reasoning behind the methodology for our approach
- Exemplary characterization of a representative set of HPC workloads, including metrics like verbosity and network load

The remainder of this work is structured as follows: We continue with providing background information including a brief review of related work. Then, we detail our methodology, our analyzed metrics, and how we generate and examine our traces. This is followed by short overview of SONAR's tool-design. Finally, the results of our first analysis of six different HPC application are shown, followed by a conclusion in which we summerize our results and outline possible future directions.

2   Background

Today, power consumption is one of the most important aspects when designing and operating HPC systems. Analyses have shown that a large fraction of the power consumption originates from data movements, and that associated costs significantly increase with distance [3]. Predictions indicate that the gap between energy costs for computation and data movement will actually widen in the future [4].

Power saving strategies in the area of networks are based on reducing link frequency or link width, both of which result in a decreased bandwidth. Since transition times of several microseconds are common, it is important to know when a link can operate with lower bandwidth without reducing performance. Therefore it is essential to analyze and understand applications regarding their communication behavior.

In order to examine the impact of different network configurations on power consumption and performance simulations and models are essential. Synthetic traffic is a commonly used for such simulators. This approach is a good first-order approximation, but some peculiarities of real application are neglected. Therefore, real application traces are mandatory for a deep understanding of certain communication patterns. Furthermore, traces can be used for post execution analyses. This allows to examine new metrics without running applications again.

2.1   Communication Pattern

Applications in high performance computing exhibit various different communication patterns. Figure 1 depicts the injection pattern of one particular node over the normalized run time. It is apparent that these different communication pattern have differing suitability for various power saving strategies. While the

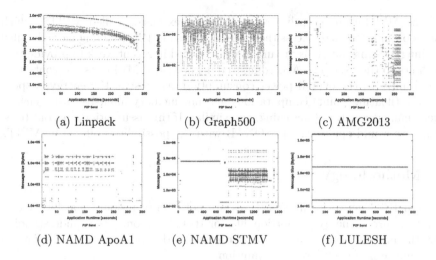

(a) Linpack   (b) Graph500   (c) AMG2013

(d) NAMD ApoA1   (e) NAMD STMV   (f) LULESH

Fig. 1. P2P injection plots of exemplary workloads

Graph500 workload (b) has a very irregular and dense pattern, the network is idling periodically for the AMG2013 (c) and NAMD (d, e) workload.

Analyzing communication patterns and other metrics is mandatory for future interconnection network power models. These models are much faster than accurate simulations of a complete cluster. This enables the possibility to test a variety of different parameters in a reasonable time. Since these models are not cycle accurate, they are not taking full event-based traces as input data but simpler metrics. Therefore, tools such as SONAR are used to derive different metrics that affect power consumption directly from the traces.

2.2 Related Work

There is a large set of existing tools that gear to profile MPI applications. The most important ones include TAU [5], HPCToolKit[4], Intel VTune[5], IPM[6], mpiP[7], INAM [6] and INAM2 [7]. However, they rather focus on reporting and visualizing MPI communication behavior for profiling purposes instead of generating aggregated metrics like SONAR. In fact, they can be seen as being one level below SONAR, i.e. SONAR builds on top of such tools.

Tools that monitor and analyze MPI jobs also have a large history, such as Lightweight Distributed Metric Service (LDMS) [8] by Sandia National Labs, the HOlistic Performance System Analysis (HOPSA) [9], and TACC STATS [10]. Compared to SONAR, they tend to be more abstract and are geared towards monitoring the behavior of complete MPI jobs.

---

[4] http://hpctoolkit.org/.
[5] https://software.intel.com/en-us/intel-vtune-amplifier-xe.
[6] http://ipm-hpc.sourceforge.net/.
[7] http://www.llnl.gov/CASC/mpip/.

The MPI forum recently proposed a new extension called MPIT[8], which allows profiling tools to access the internal states of MPI, enabling more detailed profiling information. This feature is already used in recent work to provide tuning hints to the user [11]. According to our knowledge MPI does not contribute significantly to the overall power consumption, as most of the energy is spent for core (floating point) computations and not memory-intensive tasks such as queue management, tag matching, and similar. If this assumption turn out to be wrong we would opt to extend SONAR with the possibilities offered by MPIT.

3   Methodology

Modern HPC network infrastructures are not energy proportional [2]. A first step to improve energy-proportionality for HPC interconnects is understanding how the interconnect behaves during runtime and what is a suitable approach to minimize network power consumption.

To determine how an application utilizes the provided network resources, we have postulated a set of metrics which give us a qualitative and quantitative insight to the communication behavior of an HPC application. The following metrics have been found to be important:

Network Activity Map: This metric visualizes all point-to-point and collective messages by size and relation to the application runtime in a graph. Each data-point in the plot indicates a particular event. Figure 2 (a) depicts the network activity map of of an exemplary workload (AMG2013).

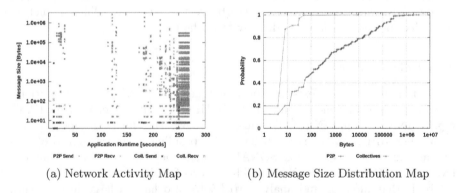

(a) Network Activity Map   (b) Message Size Distribution Map

Fig. 2. Examples of the visual metrics SONAR derives from an application trace

MPI idle time: We determine the minimum, maximum and average times during which a node does not have to handle any messages to or from the interconnect. This values represent the white spots in the message activity map

---

[8] http://cscads.rice.edu/workshops/summer-2010/slides/performance-tools/
2010-08-cscads-mpit.pdf.

in Fig. 2 (a). A good example in the plot can be seen in Fig. 2 (a) from second 50 to 100. In this region, the network is completely idle on this node.

Message Distribution: We use a cumulative distribution function graph (CDF) to visualize the message sizes, which occur in a trace. This metric shows the probability of a message having a size X or smaller. Figure 2 (b) shows the CDF-graph of an exemplary workload (AMG2013).

Verbosity: This represents the ratio of work and the total amount of data which has been consumed by the application. The work is quantified by the number of floating point operations (Flops) issued, as many HPC applications are depending on floating point arithmetic. The Flops are determined via the hardware performance counters of the CPUs. For integer based workloads (such as graph algorithms), the verbosity is defined by their number of integer operations instead of Flops.

Message Rate: The message rate indicates how many messages are sent by one node in a given time period. This metric can be interpreted as a single-value approximation of the network activity map.

All the described metrics are MPI process based. This means we get $N \times P$ results for each metric, where N is the number of nodes and P is the number of MPI processes launched per node. Derived from these metrics, we are able to estimate how the application utilizes the cluster. Largely differing numbers indicate an over- or under utilization of specific nodes in the cluster. Metrics which can be quantified by a single number, such as the verbosity, will also be reported as a global average value.

3.1   The Open Trace Format (OTF)

The open trace format (OTF) stores application activities as events. Each event is associated with a time stamp and additional event-specific information. For example, the *MessageSent*-event contains information such as source, destination and length of the message, whereas the *FunctionEnter*-event requires the function's signature and the ID of the concerning node. All non-numeric values, e.g. the function signatures, are encoded as integer values to minimize the trace's size. To refer these encodings to their respective values, the OTF trace contains a section with definitions. These definition provide the mapping of the encodings to their actual meaning, e.g. the function with the ID 42 belongs to the function with the signature `void foo(int bar)`.

3.2   Trace Generation

The development of SONAR is motivated by the need to efficiently gather information from application traces. Depending on the number of nodes, the complexity of the underlying problem, the communication characteristics, and other factors, these traces can become very large. The traces we have generated for this paper require between 5 and 50 GBs of disk space each. In order to be able to store such traces efficiently, an appropriate format is necessary.

We have tested the Tuning and Analysis Utilities (TAU) and the Vampir-Trace frameworks. In both cases, an application can be compiled with code instrumentation to examine specific parts. They provide also the possibility to run existing binaries without any modifications. With this black-box approach, the traces contain only a reduced amount of information. Application-specific functions are opaque in this case. The only data that can be gathered with this method is the entry and exit point of the application's `main()`-function as well as the entry and exit points of the MPI library functions used by the application.

As mentioned before, instead of looking at specific parts of an application, we want to examine the behavior of the whole application with special attention to the communication aspects. Since all information regarding MPI and communication are retained when running an existing application with the run-wrappers, this method is sufficient for our experiments.

For our purposes, the VampirTrace framework proved to be the better fit. It stores traces directly in the compressed Open-Trace-Format (OTF), whereas TAU requires an intermediate format. The collective records are stored in a more convenient way with VampirTrace. TAU uses OTF counters to encode the collective's payload. The involved nodes have to be recovered with the functions's entry and exit points. VampirTrace utilizes the OTF collective handlers, so that all information regarding collective events are available and accessible from a single location.

Figure 3 shows the abstract steps needed to acquire metrics from an application trace with SONAR.

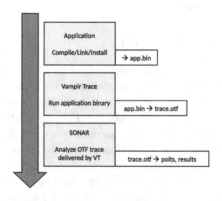

Fig. 3. Schematic view of the workflow of acquiring metrics with SONAR

3.3   Trace Post-processing and Exploration

Once the trace has been obtained with VampirTrace, it contains, among others, the following events:

1. Definitions: Nodes, Functions, Communicators
2. Function Enter/Leave Events

3. Point-to-point Messages: Send/Receive Events
4. Collective Messages: Begin/End Events

All these events are associated with a time stamp and additional information regarding this event, such as, the message length or type. VampirTrace stores the time stamp as ticks and provides a trace-specific ticks-per-second value to convert the time stamps into a reasonable unit. This should be considered when handling the raw OTF data.

When viewing the trace with the *otfprint* tool of the OTF library, the information looks like this:

```
$ otfprint mytrace.otf

// Functions:
(#38271) 5719742052 Enter: function 82, process 10, source 0
(#38272) 5719742504 Leave: function 0, process 9, source 0

// Point-to-point communication:
(#23768) 5708630907 SendMessage: sender 4, receiver 14, group
    1000000004, type 1375, length 80, source 0, KeyValue:
    1:5709047177
(#23812) 5708664706 ReceiveMessage: receiver 14, sender 4, group
    1000000004, type 1375, length 80, source 0

// Collective communication:
(#2536) 5689898534 BeginCollective: process 13, collective 6, group
    1000000004, matchingId 5, root 0, sent 0, received 0, source 0
(#2567) 5691141019 EndCollective: process 4, matchingId 5
```

Listing 1.1. OTF Events

This textual representation of the trace can be used to get an overview of the trace. Specific informations can be found and processed with the GNU tools *grep*, *sed*, *awk* and alike. To characterize traces automatically with a set of multiple metrics, this approach is not feasible, as the GNU tools tend to be very slow on large amounts of data and cumbersome to use when implementing new metrics. To be more efficient, we need to be able to process the trace's data as-it-is instead of the detour with the textual representation. SONAR uses the OTF library functions to access the numerical values shown in Listing 1.1 directly as their respective data type, e.g. integers.

4   Tool-Design

For SONAR, we used the C based OTF library[9]. It provides fast and convenient interfaces to access OTF traces from C/C++ and Python applications. SONAR itself has been implemented in C++.

---

[9] https://tu-dresden.de/die_tu_dresden/zentrale_einrichtungen/zih/forschung/ projekte/otf/.

4.1 Implementation and Prerequisites

In order to access traces, the high-level OTF library functions expect one handler function for each event. SONAR uses these handler functions as an interface to acquire data from the traces. Since a trace usually contains more events than needed, a selection of chosen events can be set up in the reader of the OTF library.

We provide a script that downloads the OTF library, configures, builds, and installs it to the current working directory. The OTF library has some dependencies itself, such as the *zlib* for the trace's compression. If this build process fails, these dependencies have to be resolved manually. The same holds true for the Boost C++ Libraries, which are used to handle the program options.

Gnuplot is used to generate the graphs. If gnuplot is not present on the system, this part will be skipped and SONAR generates only data files. These files are encoded as comma-separated values (CSV) to be (re-)used by any other data processing tool.

4.2 Custom Metrics

SONAR can easily be extended with new metrics. To do so, we need to identify the data which is required for the metric. For example, we want to count all messages which are exactly 42 bytes in size. The data for this new metric is located in the handler function which is called on every outgoing messages.

The class *OTF_Handler* in the file "otf_handler.h" contains stub implementations of all available OTF handlers. In his function the location of the data of interest is handled. For a new metric, a new class must be derived from this base class and re-implement the relevant functions.

```
static int
handleSendMsg(void* userData, uint64_t time, uint32_t sender,
    uint32_t receiver, uint32_t group, uint32_t type,
    uint32_t length, uint32_t source, OTF_KeyValueList *list)
{
    if (length == 42)
        *((int*)userData)++;
    return OTF_RETURN_OK;
}
```

Listing 1.2. Example implementation to derive a new metric from the OTF-trace

The code Listing 1.2 show the implementation of the new metric. The *userData*-pointer is defined as an integer to be incremented at ever message which is exactly 42 bytes in size. Metrics, which are more complex than this simple example, are likely to depend on several values. In this case, it is advisable to use a structure or class to organize the data.

5 Results

In this section, we present results that are generated by SONAR after an analysis of MPI traces of the following applications: HPL, Graph500, NAMD, LULESH, and AMG2013.

5.1 Test System

We use an HPC system that consists of 8 nodes. Each node hosts two six-core *Intel Xeon E5-2630 v2* CPUs and 64 GBs of RAM and runs a standard Linux distribution. The nodes are connected to each other with Gigabit Ethernet. All the traces and measurements were acquired with this system.

5.2 Benchmarks and Workloads

We used a set of benchmarks to evaluate the output of SONAR. The workloads represent the typical demands of an HPC environment. We chose the configuration of these applications in a way to keep the total runtime low and the resulting traces small.

HPL (High-Performance Linpack) is the benchmark used to determine the Top500-List[10]. It solves a dense $N \times N$ system of linear equations. The performance is reported in GFlops/s. In our test we used a dimension of $N = 50000$.

The **Graph500 Benchmark** is used to determine the Graph500-List. The workload is a breadth-first search (BFS) graph traversal. Unlike HPL, the Graph500 Benchmark relies more on the communication abilities of the cluster. For our tests, we used the reference implementation[11] with emulated one-sided communication and a scale factor of 12.

NAMD (Nanoscale Molecular Dynamics program) is a molecular dynamics simulation program[12]. Two widely known workloads are the *Apolipoprotein A1 (ApoA1)* and the *Satellite Tobacco Mosaic Virus (STMV)*. These workloads are publicly available and are commonly used to compare different systems against each other. The number of computational steps was limited to 100 for each workload to keep the traces small.

LULESH (Livermore Unstructured Lagrange Explicit Shock Hydrodynamics) represents the field of hydrodynamic simulations[13]. LULESH uses a stencil code to calculate the physical forces. The problem size parameter was set to 100, which results in one million elements per node. The number of iterations was limited to 500.

AMG2013 (Algebraic Multigrid Solver) solves linear systems of unstructured grids with the algebraic multigrid method[14]. For our tests we used the

---

[10] http://www.netlib.org/benchmark/hpl/.
[11] http://www.graph500.org/referencecode.
[12] http://www.ks.uiuc.edu/Research/namd/.
[13] https://codesign.llnl.gov/lulesh.php.
[14] https://codesign.llnl.gov/amg2013.php.

default problem and adjusted the problem scaling parameter to prolong the runtime of the application.

LULESH and AMG2013 are part of a collection of proxy applications[15] which
represent current and future HPC workloads.

5.3   SONAR Measurements

In this section, we present the insights we have gathered with SONAR. We ran
the workloads described in Subsect. 5.2 on our cluster. The traces were acquired
using the *vtrun* wrapper of VampirTrace. The following metrics were selected
for first analyses.

Network activity: The graphics in Fig. 4 depict the network activity footprints of the High-Performance Linpack, Graph500, LULESH and AMG2013
benchmarks.

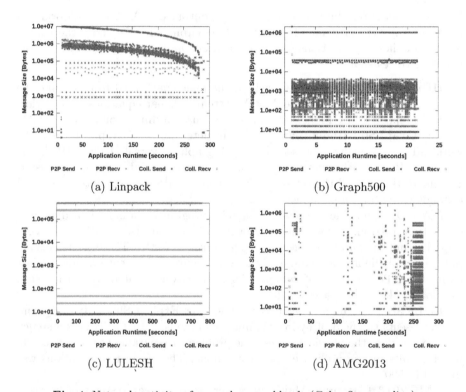

Fig. 4. Network activity of exemplary workloads (Color figure online)

Each data point in the graphs represents a distinct event in the network. The
position on the X and Y axis indicates the time of occurrence and respectively
the size of the message. The colors visualize point-to-point (red, green) and

---

[15] https://codesign.llnl.gov/proxy-apps.php.

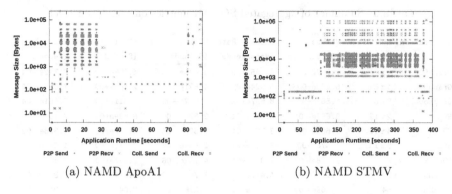

(a) NAMD ApoA1   (b) NAMD STMV

Fig. 5. Network activity of the same application, but with different workloads

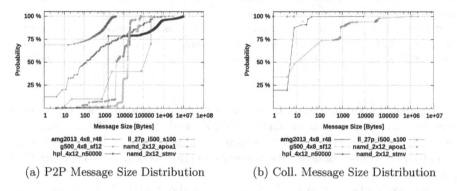

(a) P2P Message Size Distribution   (b) Coll. Message Size Distribution

Fig. 6. Message distribution of different workloads for point-to-point (a) and collective (b) messages

collectives messages (purple, blue). SONAR produces such one graph for each node, recorded in the trace. Here, we selected only one graph per node, which we think is representative.

It is apparent that the communication characteristics vary widely between the different applications. This is not surprising for workloads, which are inherently different from each other such as the ones shown in Fig. 4. Figure 5 depicts the NAMD application with two different sets of input data. Although both show periodic communication behavior, their network activity maps differ a lot.

The ApoA1 workload causes dense communication patterns in the first third of the application's runtime. There are also some white spots which indicate no network activity at all. STMV communicates heavily from the middle to the end of the application and has fewer idle gaps.

Message Distribution: Figure 6 shows the message distribution of our selected workloads as a cumulative distribution function (CDF). SONAR reports one CDF graph for each trace. For a better comparability, we merged them into one graph.

Table 1. Summary of aggregated SONAR metrics on the cluster level

Application	MPI Processes	Verbosity [Bytes/Flop]	Message Rate [Messages/s]	MPI Idle min. [Seconds]	MPI Idle max. [Seconds]	MPI Idle avg. [Seconds]
Graph500	2 x 8	2.087e+01	4.795e+02	4.096e−06	1.256e+00	8.742e−04
Graph500	4 x 8	6.180e+00	5.924e+02	4.821e-06	2.849e+00	7.096e−04
Graph500	8 x 8	1.560e+00	8.697e+02	4.902e−06	3.411e+00	5.161e−04
HPL	2 x 12	9.597e−01	6.885e+01	2.528e−06	6.629e+00	7.160e−03
HPL	4 x 12	1.602e+00	3.729e+01	2.609e−06	6.250e+00	1.328e−02
HPL	8 x 12	1.478e+00	3.032e+01	2.654e−06	7.589e+00	1.638e−02
LULESH	8	9.398e−04	1.027e+01	4.132e−06	1.327e+00	4.695e−02
LULESH	27	1.236e−03	1.417e+01	3.764e−06	1.914e+00	3.825e−02
LULESH	64	1.409e−03	1.712e+01	3.536e−06	2.648e+00	3.210e−02
AMG2013	2 x 8	3.690e−03	1.598e+01	0.000e+00	8.757e+00	3.004e−02
AMG2013	4 x 8	1.009e−02	1.508e+01	0.000e+00	6.917e+01	3.290e−02
NAMD ApoA1	2 x 12	6.020e−03	8.501e+01	4.117e−06	4.317e+00	6.023e−03
NAMD ApoA1	4 x 12	8.651e−03	2.181e+01	4.453e−06	5.920e+00	2.356e−02
NAMD STMV	2 x 12	4.543e−03	6.861e+01	4.142e−06	1.375e+01	7.197e−03
NAMD STMV	4 x 12	6.274e−03	1.262e+01	4.389e−06	1.419e+01	3.951e−02

The most important insight is that point-to-point communication is preferred over collective communication. Only AMG2013 and the Graph500 are using collective messages to transfer data, which are larger than 10 Bytes. This suggests that the other workloads use collective operations only for synchronization purposes.

The second observation in Fig. 6 (a) is that about 80 % of all point-to-point messages we gathered with our workloads are smaller than 20 kbyte. One exception is Graph500, in which most messages are smaller than one kbyte. The other one is LULESH with most messages being smaller than 200 kbyte.

Aggregated Metrics: The results, which can be represented as numerical values, have been summarized in Table 1. The presented data are averaged values of all nodes. This table provides an overview how an application utilizes the cluster's components such as processors and interconnection network.

The information about sending and receiving of messages is measured at MPI level. Therefore, the MPI idle time represents the time period between two successive MPI events. As we take the send, as well as the associated receive event into account, these numbers give a reasonably accurate idea of the behavior of the underlying network interface.

Node divergence: To show how evenly an application utilizes the different nodes, SONAR produces also graphics that represent the data from Table 1 at node level. The box plots in Figs. 7 and 8 show the variance of these metrics spread over all nodes. Workloads with a low box and short whiskers indicate an even utilization of each cluster node. This means the bigger the boxes the bigger the larger variance between all nodes.

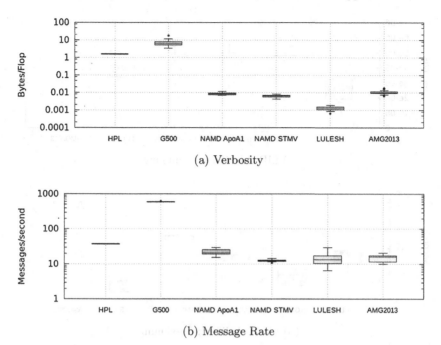

Fig. 7. Verbosity and message rate variance of tested workloads for all nodes

Figure 7 depicts the variance of the metrics verbosity and message rate. The high verbosity of the Linpack benchmark surprises, respectively reveals the huge amounts of data this workload needs to transfer. Graph500 has the highest verbosity, as this work does not rely on floating point operations. Otherwise, the message rate is the largest of all tested workloads. This is because the Graph500 relies heavily on communication. NAMD, LULESH and AMG2013 show similar behavior regarding the verbosity and the message rate. They seem to be more efficient than Linpack, as they show a lower verbosity. This is in line with the message rate, which for these workloads is lower than on HPL.

Figure 8 shows the distribution of idle times on the MPI layer. The minimum idle time depends on the actual interconnect hardware. In our measurements, we see gaps of a few microseconds for successive messages. This is within the expected capabilities of the Gigabit Ethernet network we have used.

The average idle time between successive networks is between $20\,ms$ and $80\,ms$. The Graph500 is the outlier with an average gap of about $80\,\mu s$. Once again, this shows the communication demands of this workload.

A hypothetical energy-proportional network must be able to switch its power state much faster than the average message gap to save energy and retain the application's performance. The maximum idle time reveals, that many of the

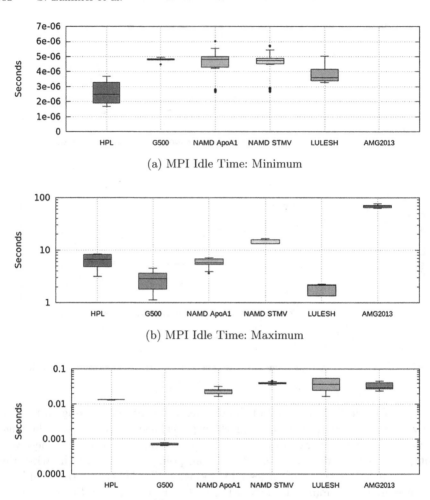

(a) MPI Idle Time: Minimum

(b) MPI Idle Time: Maximum

(c) MPI Idle Time: Average

Fig. 8. Idle time variance of tested workloads for all nodes

tested applications have at least one phase, where the network is not used at all for more than five seconds (HPL, NAMD, AMG2013). The apparently missing box of AMG2013's minimum idle time is in fact zero seconds on each node. This is likely caused by overlapping messages. AMG2013 shows a maximum idle time of even more than one minute for each node. We assume this is the result of an unfavorable configuration of the application. For a energy-proportional network, this means, during this idle time the network can be set to the lowest energy state or even be switched off completely.

6   Conclusion

With SONAR, we introduced a tool to derive advanced communication characteristics from traces of common HPC applications. These traces were obtained with VampirTrace, a well-known MPI trace generator.

Using these trace, we demonstrated the capabilities of SONAR by extracting various metrics, which we believe are crucial to develop a power-aware network model. For example, the generated network activity maps show a wide range of different communication patterns. Energy-proportional networks show significant power saving potential on workloads, such as NAMD or AMG2013. Various opportunities exist to save power without any loss in performance by dynamically reducing the link width or even by switching them off completely. Similar potentials are seen with LULESH and its highly regular communication pattern and fixed message sizes. Although links cannot be switched off completely, fine tuning the network is sufficient to save power for this workload.

Our observations of the network activity maps are also proven by other metrics, such as MPI idle times of the single nodes. SONAR revealed that the gaps between MPI events provide a possibility to put less active links into a reduced power state for the duration of these inactivity periods.

Supporting all these scenarios, however, requires an energy-proportional network infrastructure. Therefore, further research in this area is mandatory and we believe SONAR to be a first and important step in this direction.

Acknowledgements. We thank the anonymous reviewers for their constructive and detailed reviews. We would also like to express our thanks to Alexander Matz for his support. Furthermore, we want to thank Pedro J. Garcia and Jesus Escudero-Sahuquillo for our insightful technical discussions.

References

1. Saravanan, K.P., Carpenter, P.M., Ramirez, A.: Power/performance evaluation of energy efficient ethernet (eee) for high performance computing. In: 2013 IEEE International Symposium on Performance Analysis of Systems and Software (ISPASS), pp. 205–214, April 2013

2. Zahn, F., Yebenes, P., Lammel, S., Garcia, P.J., Froning, H.: Analyzing the energy (dis-) proportionality of scalable interconnection networks. In: HiPINEB, 2016, 2016 2nd IEEE International Workshop on High-Performance Interconnection Networks in the Exascale and Big-Data Era (HiPINEB), pp. 25–32 (2016)

3. Borkar, S.: Exascale computing - a fact or a fiction? (invited talk). In: IPDPS, vol. 3. IEEE Computer Society (2013)

4. Shalf, J., Dosanjh, S., Morrison, J.: Exascale computing technology challenges. In: Palma, J.M.L.M., Daydé, M., Marques, O., Lopes, J.C. (eds.) VECPAR 2010. LNCS, vol. 6449, pp. 1–25. Springer, Heidelberg (2011). doi:10.1007/978-3-642-19328-6_1

5. Malony, A.D., Shende, S.: Performance technology for complex parallel and distributed systems. In: Kacsuk, P., Kotsis, G. (eds.) Distributed and Parallel Systems: From Instruction Parallelism to Cluster Computing, pp. 37–46. Springer, Boston (2000)

6. Dandapanthula, N., Subramoni, H., Vienne, J., Kandalla, K., Sur, S., Panda, D.K., Brightwell, R.: INAM - a scalable infiniband network analysis and monitoring tool. In: Alexander, M., et al. (eds.) Euro-Par 2011. LNCS, vol. 7156, pp. 166–177. Springer, Heidelberg (2012). doi:10.1007/978-3-642-29740-3_20
7. Subramoni, H., Augustine, A.M., Arnold, M., Perkins, J., Lu, X., Hamidouche, K., Panda, D.K.: Inam2̂: infiniband network analysis & monitoring with mpi (2016)
8. Agelastos, A., Allan, B., Brandt, J., Cassella, P., Enos, J., Fullop, J., Gentile, A., Monk, S., Naksinehaboon, N., Ogden, J., Rajan, M., Showerman, M., Stevenson, J., Taerat, N., Tucker, T.: The lightweight distributed metric service: a scalable infrastructure for continuous monitoring of large scale computing systems and applications. In: Proceedings of the International Conference for High Performance Computing, Networking, Storage and Analysis, SC 2014, Piscataway, NJ, USA, pp. 154–165. IEEE Press (2014)
9. Mohr, B., Voevodin, V., Giménez, J., Hagersten, E., Knüpfer, A., Nikitenko, D.A., Nilsson, M., Servat, H., Shah, A., Winkler, F., Wolf, F., Zhukov, I.: The HOPSA workflow and tools. In: Cheptsov, A., Brinkmann, S., Gracia, J., Resch, M.M., Nagel, W.E. (eds.) Tools for High Performance Computing 2012, pp. 127–146. Springer, Berlin (2013)
10. Evans, T., Barth, W.L., Browne, J.C., DeLeon, R.L., Furlani, T.R., Gallo, S.M., Jones, M.D., Patra, A.K.: Comprehensive resource use monitoring for hpc systems with tacc stats. In: Proceedings of the First International Workshop on HPC User Support Tools, HUST 2014, Piscataway, NJ, USA, pp. 13–21. IEEE Press (2014)
11. Gallardo, E., Vienne, J., Fialho, L., Teller, P., Browne, J.: Mpi advisor: a minimal overhead tool for mpi library performance tuning. In: Proceedings of the 22Nd European MPI Users' Group Meeting, EuroMPI 2015, pp. 6:1–6:10. ACM, New York (2015)

HPC-IODC

HPC I/O in the Data Center Workshop (HPC-IODC)

Julian M. Kunkel[1], Jay Lofstead[2], and Colin McMurtrie[3]

[1] Deutsches Klimarechenzentrum, Bundesstraße 45a, 20146 Hamburg, Germany
kunkel@dkrz.de
[2] Center for Computing Research,
Sandia National Laboratories, Albuquerque, USA
[3] Swiss National Computing Center (CSCS), Lugano, Switzerland

1 Introduction

Many public and privately funded data centers host supercomputers for running large scale simulations and analyzing experimental and observational data. These super-computers run usually tightly coupled parallel applications that require hardware components that deliver the best performance. In contrast, commercial data centers, such as Facebook and Google, execute loosely coupled workloads with a broad assumption of regular failures. The dimension of the data centers is enormous. A 2013 article summarizes commercial data centers' dimensions [1]. It estimates, for example, that Facebook hosts around 100PB of storage and Google and Microsoft manage around 1 million servers each – although the hardware is split among several physical data centers – a modus operandi not suitable for HPC centers. With the hunger for information, the globally installed storage capacity increases exponentially and is expected to hit 7,235 exabytes by 2017 [2]. This trend is visible in the sales reports of companies such as the disk drive manufacturer Seagate. Within 5 years, they shipped 1 billion HDDs, which means 700.000 units every day [3]. With state-of-the-art 8TB disks, this would already account for 5.5 exabyte of capacity by day.

Management of the huge amount of data is vital for effective use of the contained information. However, with limited budgets, it is a daunting task for data center operators, especially as design and storage system required hardware depends heavily on the executed workloads. A co-factor of the increasing difficulty is the increase in complexity of the storage hierarchy with the adoption of SSD and memory class storage technology. The US Department of Energy recognizes the importance of data management, listing it among the top 10 research challenges for Exascale [4].

There are several initiatives, consortia and special tracks in conferences that target RD&E audiences. Examples are the Storage Networking Industry Association (SNIA) for enterprises, the Big Data and Extreme-Scale Computing (BDEC) initiative[1], the Exascale10 workgroup [5], the Parallel Data Storage Workshop (PDSW) and the HEC FSIO workshop [6].

---

[1] http://www.exascale.org/bdec/.

There are many I/O workloads studies and performance analysis reports for parallel I/O available. Additionally, many surveys of enterprise technology usage include predictions of analysis for future storage technology and the storage market such as [7]. However, analysis conducted for HPC typically focuses on applications and not on the data center perspective. Information about data center operational aspects is usually described in file system specific user groups and meetings or described partially in research papers as part of the evaluation environment.

In this workshop, we bring together I/O experts from data centers and application workflows to share current practices for scientific workflows, issues and obstacles for both hardware and the software stack, and R&D to overcome these issues.

2 Organization of the Workshop

The workshop content was built on three tracks:

- **Research paper presentations** – authors needed to submit a paper regarding relevant research for I/O in the datacenter.
- **Talks from I/O experts** – authors needed to submit a rough outline for the talk related to the operational aspects of the data center.
- **Invited track** for a keynote and two moderated discussion slots.

The CFP has been issued beginning of January. Important deadlines were:

- Submission deadline: 28-02-2016 AoE
- Author notification: 23-03-2016
- Workshop: 23-05-2016
- Camera-ready papers: 23-06-2016

From all submissions, the programm committee selected four talks from I/O experts and four research papers for presentation during the workshop.

2.1 Programm Committee

Wolfgang Frings	Jülich Supercomputing Center, Germany
Javier Garcia Blas	University Carlos III of Madrid, Spain
Rob Ross	Argonne National Laboratory, USA
Carlos Maltzahn	University of California, Santa Cruz, USA
Kathryn Mohror	Lawrence Livermore National Laboratory, USA
Xiaosong Ma	North Carolina State University, Oak Ridge National Laboratory, USA
Julian Kunkel	DKRZ, Germany
Jay Lofstead	Sandia National Laboratory, USA
Colin McMurtrie	CSCS, Switzerland

3   Workshop Summary

Throughout the day, on average 33 participants attended the workshop. We had a good mix of talks from I/O experts, data center relevant research and also discussions. A short summary of the presentations is given in the following. The slides of the presentations are available on the workshop's webpage: http://wr.informatik.uni-hamburg.de/events/2016/iodc.

The keynote from Rob Ross advocated the use of tools to study I/O actities from the data center perspective. He presented results from I/O monitoring using Darshan, that point out the benefit of centralized monitoring and the continuing challenge to accurately monitor all I/O activity. Application authors use a much more extensive set of I/O interfances than expected making the job of understanding how to address I/O challenges even harder. Also, he presented some studies with the I/O simulation tool Codes for understanding object storage and the dragon fly network topology. Finally, the recently started Tokio project is introduced that will lift I/O monitoring to a next level.

3.1   Research Papers

In the research paper "Delta: Data Reduction for Integrated Application Workflows and Data Storage", the ADIOS middleware is extended with a compression method. It compresses a time series of data with delta encoding by comparing data to the initial values. A result of the study is that already this approach reduces the data volume for in-situ analysis significantly for applications.

In the second research paper "The Effect of Python and NetCDF on the Read Performance when using HPC Parallel Filesystems", evaluates various aspects of NetCDF performance on several storage systems. It is shown that there are some issues in the Python libraries which reduce performance significantly.

Next, in the paper "Analyzing Data Properties using Statistical Sampling Techniques", a method is presented to evaluate data characteristics such as scientific file formats and compression ratio on a subset of data to estimate the value for the full system. It turns out, that a small subset of data is sufficient to predict the true value of characteristics that are computed by file numbers or storage capacity accurately.

The last paper, "An Overview of the Sirocco Parallel Storage System", introduces the Sirocco distributed object storage. In contrast to parallel file systems, the consistency model is relaxed and there is a-priori no explicit central index for the data. This allows writers to proceed independetly and even adjust their storage targets based on system utilization.

3.2   Talks from Experts

The four talks from experts included information about the site and typical application profiles but also contained information regarding I/O tools and strategies. In the first talk, we heard about LRZ's storage system and strategy. Utilizing file system monitoring and the Persyst tool an overview of the bottleneck for an application is gained. Additionally, Darshan, Scalasca and VampirTrace is used for I/O characterisation and analysis. An emphasis was made to present and demonstrate a methodology to identify I/O bottlenecks that is applied in the data center with success.

Then, we heard an update of HLRS data management plans. It was demonstrated, that the storage system's peak performance is barely utilized from typical applications. Additionally, potential strategies and architectures for a future system has been sketched relying on NVRAM.

The third talk described work on the SIRIUS US DOE funded storage stack and I/O research project. This project is relatively new and is seeking community feedback about the research plans. The current strategy is to spread a single data set across all available storage resources, organized by data utility. This will optimize the desired information density within the scare resources, such as NVM, while still offering full datasets. The audience seemed accepting of the approach and did not have any significant input to offer.

The next talk described I/O monitoring at Jülich Supercomputing Center. The LLview tool provides a good overview of ongoing jobs but also a history. This includes system statistics and I/O activity and can be used to analyze the overall system behavior and utilization. Next, SIONlib has been introduced, which manages shared files for task-local data. Finally, the activities in the DEEP-ER project where described, in which SIONlib manages buddy checkpoints.

Our final talk covered CSCS storage system and ... TODO: Colin....

3.3 Discussion rounds

The major distinguishing feature for this workshop compared to other venues is the discussion rounds. The opportunity for themed, open discussions about issues both pressing and relevant to the data center community facilitates sharing experiences, solutions, and problems. The forum has lively discussion with few reservations about maintaining secrecy.

The first discussion starter is based on the community effort of the Virtual Institute for I/O (VI4IO)[2]. VI4IO aims to provide a community hub containing research groups, relevant tools to monitor and benchmark HPC storage behavior, events. Finally it hosts and manages the High-Performance Storage List (HPSL), which currently contains 30 high-performance storage systems including their characteristics. In contrast to existing lists, operators of a data center can create and manage the list themselves and can provide additional prosa text describing site, system and storage. Since it is very difficult to find detailed information about existing storage systems, there are still a lot of characteristics missing, still the first analysis of storage capacity have been made and presented during the talk. The discussion with the attendees revealed optimization potential in the presentation of the characteristics that are already resolved in the current list.

The second discussion was on the impact of Non-Volatile Memory (NVM) on storage activities. The current set of machines being deployed at supercomputing centers in the USA all have such a layer in the form of flash-based devices. The discussion centered around sereral topics: (1) the opportunity to pre-empt a running job on a node via swapping memory contents to a node local SSD to support urgent computation requirements is seen as a priority. There are serveral issues, such as

---

[2] http://vi4io.org.

security, that still need to be considered for this to be a viable idea. (2) The audience agreed that NVM resources are most useful when they can be treated as either slow memory or fast storage, depending on application needs. Ideally, this will be supported on an application-by-application basis rather than requiring any system configuration changes. (3) The audience agreed that because of the performance characteristics, it is important to have explicit use options. Some participants suggested that they would rather support invisible use, such as for a TLB swap space or have the software stack be able to predict which pages are no longer imminently needed and swap them for those that are. How to do this effectively was unknown. (4) The concept of the burst buffer offering the fast cache for the file system was universally acknowledged to not be able to address the I/O performance issues. The key issue is that, as last year's workshop revealed, the major concern is the use of I/O libraries like NetCDF and HDF5 and the very low I/O performance they obtain in their default configuration. Multiple other pieces of research have shown that the overheads involved in the data rearrangement phase of two-phase collective I/O with data sieving can completely dominate, on the order of 99 % of the I/O time. Until this issue is solved, accelerating the bandwidth to the storage array will not address the performance issues. (5) Having NVM in multiple locations, such as compute area as well as on every node, is seen as critical for performance. Interference effects that plague our current storage arrays will still exist for NVM sources making only having centralized resources problematic. And (6) Because the hardware is evolving so rapidly and how and where the NVM is deployed in machines, the software interface is largely undefineable. Until the locations and hardware interfaces settle down, the best we can hope to do is to have solutions to address a single platform generation with the expectation it may have to be completely rethought for the next generation.

References

1. StorageServers Blog: Facts and stats of world's largest data centers (2013). https://storageservers.wordpress.com/2013/07/17/facts-and-stats-of-worlds-largest-data-centers/. Accessed July 2013
2. International Data Corporation. http://www.businesswire.com/news/home/20131021005243/en/IDCs-Outlook-Data-Byte-Density-Globe-Big
3. Seagate: Storage Solutions Guide. http://www.seagate.com/files/www-content/product-content/_cross-product/en-us/docs/seagate-storage-and-application-guide-apac.pdf
4. Lucas, R., Committee Members: Top ten exascale research challenges (2014). http://science.energy.gov/~/media/ascr/ascac/pdf/meetings/20140210/Top10reportFEB14.pdf. Accessed February 2014
5. Brinkmann, A., Cortes, T., Falter, H., Kunkel, J., Narasimhamurthy, S.: E10 – Exascale IO (2014)
6. Bancroft, M., Bent, J., Felix, E., Grider, G., Nunez, J., Poole, S., Ross, R., Salmon, E., Ward, L.: Hec fsio 2008 workshop report. In: High End Computing Interagency Working Group (HECIWG), Sponsored File Systems and I/OWorkshop HEC FSIO (2009)
7. IDC: Enterprise storage services survey. http://www.idc.com/getdoc.jsp?containerId=254468

An Overview of the Sirocco Parallel Storage System

Matthew L. Curry[1]([✉]), H. Lee Ward[1], Geoff Danielson[2], and Jay Lofstead[1]

[1] Sandia National Laboratories, Albuquerque, NM 87186, USA
{mlcurry,lee,gflofst}@sandia.gov
[2] Hewlett Packard Enterprise, Palo Alto, CA 94304, USA
geoffrey.danielson@hpe.com

Abstract. Sirocco is a massively parallel, high performance storage system that breaks from the classical Zebra-style file system design paradigm. Its architecture is inspired by peer-to-peer and victim-cache architectures, and emphasizes client-to-client coordination, low server-side coupling, and free data movement and placement. By leveraging these ideas, Sirocco natively supports automatic migration between several media types, including RAM, flash, disk, and archival storage.

Sirocco provides advanced storage interfaces, enabling clients to efficiently use key-value storage or block-based storage through a single interface. It also provides several levels of transactional data updates, up to and including ACID-compliant updates across several objects. Further support is provided for concurrency control, enabling greater performance during safe concurrent modification.

By pioneering these and other techniques, Sirocco is well-poised to fulfill a need for a massively scalable, write-optimized storage system. This paper provides an overview of Sirocco's current system design.

Keywords: Parallel file systems · High performance computing · I/O

1 Introduction

Existing parallel file systems, such as Lustre, GPFS, Panasas, and PVFS, all offer storage for very large files with high performance by striping data across devices. Each of these systems have been optimized in different ways, but are at their cores inspired by the Zebra file system [1], which also statically stripes data across servers. For upcoming large scale systems, the explosion of devices (in number and type) presents a challenge to the inherently flat nature of striped organizations.

The aim of the Sirocco project is to completely rethink storage system design, moving away from the current status quo. Instead of offering a rigid striping

Sandia National Laboratories is a multi-program laboratory managed and operated by Sandia Corporation, a wholly owned subsidiary of Lockheed Martin Corporation, for the U.S. Department of Energy's National Nuclear Security Administration under contract DE-AC04-94AL85000.

© Springer International Publishing AG 2016
M. Taufer et al. (Eds.): ISC High Performance Workshops 2016, LNCS 9945, pp. 121–129, 2016.
DOI: 10.1007/978-3-319-46079-6_9

model with a separate metadata service, Sirocco provides a storage fabric with the assumption that resources are transient and data is fluid. This fundamental rethinking is being done with a nod to backwards compatibility by offering a POSIX client that can work with Sirocco, allowing legacy and next-generation APIs to coexist. The native interface, a low-level I/O API that is designed to be used by both POSIX and non-POSIX clients, is object-based: Containers hold objects, objects hold data forks, and each fork has a key-value store accessed through a 64-bit address space. These four abstract levels offer flexibility to address HPC, cloud, and large scale data analytics needs.

This paper describes the mechanisms and facilities provided by the Sirocco storage system. We begin with a discussion of Sirocco's origin and design principles. We then compare and contrast Sirocco with its inspiration, unstructured peer-to-peer (P2P) file sharing systems. We then discuss reading under free placement. Finally, we describe concurrency control mechanisms in Sirocco.

2   Sirocco's Design Principles

Sirocco's design is focused on fast checkpoints, so the overall philosophy is based on enabling clients to write data into Sirocco quickly. One way to accomplish that is to eschew system-global views of storage. Instead, clients view Sirocco as a federated group of storage servers offering a symmetric API, but different performance and resilience characteristics. Each client is likely to see a different set of servers than other clients, but can discover other servers in the system to improve quality of service. Figure 1 demonstrates how and why data can move from clients through the Sirocco storage system. Based on visibility, durability, and performance, clients can choose the best target for its writes.

The roots of Sirocco originate from the Lightweight File Systems (LWFS) project [2]. LWFS sought to strip down a file system to the bare, required components and allow users to add additional capabilities as needed. This philosophy allows some compute jobs to opt-in to services that are considered a burden to others. The LWFS core consists of an object store with authentication and authorization services only. Other features, such as naming and consistency control, are left to separate services. Sirocco follows this philosophy as well.

To maximize scalability and generality, there are a small number of guiding principles for Sirocco's design.

1. There is no central index that determines where a piece of data must be (or is currently) stored. Clients of the storage system are allowed to place data within any server they can reach. As a consequence, the location of a required piece of data may not be known at the time it is needed.
2. Data will be continually moving within the system to ensure longevity, integrity, and system health. Replicas will be created and destroyed, and servers will eject data into more durable or less burdened stores. Clients will not be notified of these events. Consequently, growing and shrinking a Sirocco store is trivial.

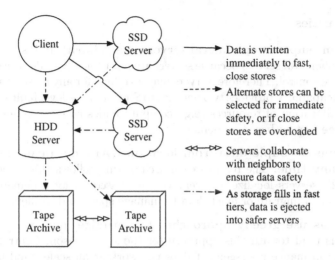

Fig. 1. Data moves from clients through Sirocco based on load, capacity, and desired safety. Note that these behaviors are based on local decisions; there are no explicit tiers, but tiered behavior follows from safety-motivated victim caching.

3. Sirocco's design emphasizes scalability over legacy concerns. Support for legacy storage system semantics, like POSIX, are required; however, scalability should not be harmed by POSIX considerations. A client implementing more scalable semantics than POSIX should see better scalability on Sirocco.
4. Heterogeneous media (including temporary RAM-based stores, flash-based burst buffers, disk, tape, and others as they become available) should be supported transparently, with symmetric APIs for data access.
5. All data are not created equal, and some need more resilience. Clients should be able to define the level at which Sirocco protects specific data.
6. Server-side operations should be as scalable as possible, particularly when running on faulty hardware. Servers should not couple during any operation.

3   Comparison with Unstructured P2P Systems

The simplest way to illustrate how Sirocco works is by contrasting it with an architecture it was inspired by, unstructured P2P systems. Unstructured P2P systems are well-regarded for their ability to handle web-scale file sharing [3]. While Sirocco is P2P-inspired, it must function in a completely different environment with different requirements. This creates some significant similarities and differences between the two types of system.

Note that this comparison is specifically with unstructured P2P systems. Structured P2P systems, such as those based on distributed hash tables [4], have a different set of constraints that do not conform to all points in the following discussion. Note that this discussion uses the term "servers" instead of "seeds" in the P2P context, to draw a more direct comparison.

3.1   Similarities

Both systems support ephemeral servers (i.e., churn). P2P systems have to support ephemeral servers because servers are not typically under the system's administrative control. Therefore, servers may go offline for any reason (including whim). This capability provides two benefits to Sirocco: Low-level fault tolerance, and elastic allocation of resources (e.g., compute nodes as RAM-based caches) by the storage system based on demand.

Both systems decouple data from location - Any data can exist anywhere, at any time. The reasons each architecture follows this principle are different: P2P servers localize and remove data based on local demand, while Sirocco hosts can migrate or evict data to manage space and resilience.

Both systems use greedy approaches to optimize quality of service. Both systems tend toward this approach for the same reason: Central coordination for performance management does not work at all scales, and may cost more than they gain. For very large scale systems, it can be better to make local, sub-optimal decisions than to coordinate and make a globally optimal decision.

Both systems use popularity to drive copy creation, enhancing performance. Here, the motivation is the same, but the mechanism is different. In P2P systems, popularity automatically drives copy creation, as servers create local copies upon user request. In contrast, Sirocco servers reactively create copies on other nodes in response to high demand from clients.

3.2   Differences

P2P systems publish constant data. Sirocco allows data to be modified. This embodies the distinction between a content addressable store, as most P2P systems implement, and a general-purpose storage system like Sirocco. This implies that different revisions of the same data may exist in multiple locations, requiring some effort to determine which portions of data are current.

P2P systems disseminate data with pulling. Sirocco relies on pushing. A client will store data within a P2P system by simply publishing its presence, allowing other clients download it as they wish. Sirocco enables clients to push data into the system, while also specifying a resilience level for the data. This causes servers within the system to further push data to other stores to attain and maintain resilience.

P2P systems use centralized directories or structured subnetworks to find servers and files [5]. Sirocco relies on searching. BitTorrent employs trackers to enable a system to quickly find seeds holding a particular file. Sirocco does not include these types of facilities, as they can harm ultimate write scalability of the system.

P2P systems do not function well with excessive numbers of leeches. Sirocco must support large numbers of leeches (i.e., clients). Significant research in the P2P community focuses on thwarting leeches, also known as free-riders [6]. Leeches do not contribute resources to the system, but instead act in selfish ways, imposing load. In contrast, a parallel file system client does not typically have storage to offer, so nearly any interaction it has with the system is considered to be leeching. As parallel file system clients tend to outnumber servers at a ratio of at least 10-to-1, Sirocco must effectively cope.

P2P systems are not concerned with the lifetime of a file. Sirocco must actively preserve data. P2P systems are not considered archival, and are not designed to preserve unpopular data. Sirocco is intended for data that is to be kept indefinitely, so space management is crucial.

4   Logical Structure of Storage

Sirocco's logical storage organization is based on the Advanced Storage Group (ASG) interface [7], which was partially developed for and motivated by Sirocco. The address space is made up of four 64-bit values. These values denote a container ID, object ID, fork ID, and record ID, which can be expressed as $\langle container, object, fork, record \rangle$ (Fig. 2). Loosely, container IDs usually map to file systems within the storage system, object IDs map to files, and fork IDs map to data forks within a file. The hierarchy and relationships are static; forks cannot move between objects, for example. A record is a variable length atomic unit of up to 2^{64} bytes, and represents an "atom" of storage. This may be a single byte of a flat file, a floating point number, a text string, etc.

Sirocco reserves forks within the name space for security information. Each container x such that $x \neq 0$ has security information recorded in the KV store located in $\langle 0, 0, 0 \rangle$, record x. Each object y in container x has security information stored in the KV store $\langle x, 0, 0 \rangle$, record y. Each fork z in object y in container

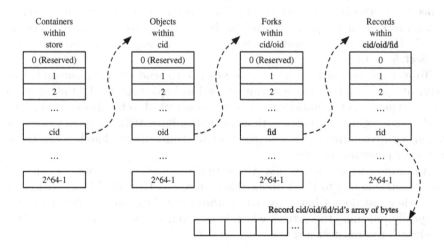

Fig. 2. An illustration of address space organization

x has security information stored in record z of $\langle x, y, 0 \rangle$. Access to the records within a fork is protected by the security attributes of the fork. If not present, attributes are inherited from the object or container.

Each record has an update ID, a 64-bit user-modifiable attribute. It is a logical clock that is expected to increase by at least one after each write, and is used to determine the most recently written instance of a particular record. Specifically, Sirocco will use the update ID to reconcile two instances of a record during migration from one server to another, or when multiple copies of data are located for reading. If the update IDs are different, the largest update ID determines which record is used. The client is expected to know (or determine) an appropriate update ID to use for a record for each write.

4.1   Data Interfaces

Sirocco provides the following types of operations:

Write: Given a data buffer, container ID, extent (i.e., range of records), record length, and update ID, the range will be overwritten on the server transactionally (i.e., all data is written to the record range, or none of it is). Optionally, one can provide an update condition (see Sect. 6) and an update ID to use with it. A user can omit the update ID, and instead use an automatically incremented update ID on that store.

Read: Sirocco supports sparse data within forks, creating a need for obtaining a map that describes the data present. Such a map describes the extents returned. The read operation allows for the user to obtain the map, the data within the requested range, or both. The map will, for all extents present, indicate the size and update ID of each record. Optionally, one can provide an update condition and an update ID to use with it. One can provide special IDs for the fork, object, and/or container ID to obtain a map of an object, a container, or containers, respectively. Another optional flag, the location flag, can specify that the server should invoke location protocols to find the most recently written copies of the record. This can be an expensive operation, but its expense can be mitigated. See Sect. 5 for more information.

To increase network efficiency, it is possible to send several commands to a server at once in a batch. These can be used to implement list I/O [8] or other non-contiguous I/O operations, even across different objects. Sirocco also allows batches to be specified as transactional, enabling fully ACID updates to records. Paired with concurrency control (see Sect. 6), transactional batches can be an extremely powerful construct.

An interesting feature of this API is that there are no "create" or "delete" operations. One way to think about this is to reason that all objects exist at all times, they just do not have any data within them. Likewise, a deletion of data is logically punching the extent, which is procedurally accomplished by writing zero-length records over a range.

5   Where Is the Data?

One side effect of the free placement enabled by the Sirocco model is that data can be initially written to a location that is not ultimately considered safe enough to hold the data. This is a typical behavior in a write-back caching model. For instance, in a local POSIX file system, bulk I/O contents can be temporarily held in memory. The user is only guaranteed that I/O requests will reach full durability if she calls "sync." Sirocco enables a similar technique. However, the location of data written in this way is not predictable, and makes reads challenging. We do not consider read-heavy workloads a solved problem. However, Sirocco provides two facilities to make reads possible.

The first facility enables reading data that the client did not predict it would need, i.e. a random, one-off read. Such a read requires an extensive search over the population of storage servers, which Sirocco servers will perform on behalf of the client. We are conducting research on how best to reduce the expense of such searches [9], improving the efficiency over exhaustive broadcast searches.

The second facility, proxying, enables efficient reading in the case of data that we can predict will be read, especially by multiple clients. Data like file system structures and metadata can be quite efficiently supported through this mechanism. Another potential application is to use proxying to pre-locate data that will be required for a job to launch (e.g., input decks).

Each server, when initially started, considers itself non-authoritative for all records in the store. "Non-authoritative" simply means that the server can make no assumptions about the freshness or location of any data. Therefore, if the client is requesting data, the full location process must be executed to provide a guarantee of up-to-date data. However, in cooperation with other clients, a server may be deemed authoritative for ranges of records. Once authoritative, clients must direct all write requests for that range to that server. This enables the server to cache data and/or other metadata, including location.

6   Concurrency Control

Concurrency control is the ability to ensure a correct outcome to concurrent updates to shared data by multiple clients. There are two well-known methods for accomplishing concurrency control. Pessimistic concurrency control (i.e., locking) is the most common form found in storage systems. Other systems, including database management systems, employ optimistic concurrency control, where operations can be attempted, then rolled back in the event of an invalid concurrent modification [10]. Optimistic concurrency control is beneficial in cases where the likelihood of conflicting operations is low, and locking would incur a significant overhead on the operation. An example is a read-modify-write operation on a remote store. Taking and releasing a lock would double the number of network round trips to complete the operation.

Sirocco implements optimistic concurrency control for a more general workload. Instead of inspecting data, the server executing the operations compare the incoming update IDs with those already present. If the transaction contains a *conditional operation*, the server will ensure that the stored update ID conforms to the expectations specified by the conditional operation. Conditional operations work within transactional batches, extending their applicability to more complex workloads. If a conditional write fails, the enclosing transaction is also failed, rolling back any changes. More information on uses and performance of conditional updates are available [11].

Sirocco also provides a mechanism that a client can leverage to implement pessimistic concurrency control via traditional leased locks, the trigger. Triggers are similar to conditional operations, but with three important differences. First, a trigger is only able to be registered on a single record. Second, a trigger does not modify data, but is instead associated with a batch that is executed when the trigger is activated. Third, a trigger does not fail when its condition is not true. Instead, the operation is placed on a per-record queue. Operations are removed from the head of the queue and executed when that operation's trigger becomes true. This happens when another non-triggered write operation modifies the update ID of the record.

A few additional considerations are allowed for triggers to enable failure recovery if a client fails to release a lock. During a triggered operation, the client is notified of progress: First when the operation is deferred for later execution, and then when the queued operation is next in line to be executed. This allows the client with an operation at the head of a trigger queue to detect when progress is not made in a timely manner, which can be interpreted as a lease expiration in a locking protocol.

Triggered operations allow clients implement locking protocols against storage servers without requiring discrete lock services. Further, a variety of locking schemes can be implemented in clients and libraries without increasing the complexity of the lock service itself. In the current prototype, migration and reconciliation can potentially cause unwelcome changes to the update ID that can obviate its utility for locking. We are investigating a variety of ways to overcome this limitation.

7   Conclusions

Sirocco is a fundamental departure from traditional storage system designs for high end computing environments. By rejecting the current Zebra model for a P2P-style model, resilience features can be incorporated more easily. While some of the limitations of this approach may complicate the file system interaction built on top of Sirocco, the flexibility and features make considerations worth the trouble.

Future materials will be made available at http://www.cs.sandia.gov/Scal able_IO/sirocco.

References

1. Hartman, J.H., Ousterhout, J.K.: The Zebra striped network file system. ACM Trans. Comput. Syst. **13**(3), 274–310 (1995). http://doi.acm.org/10.1145/210126. 210131
2. Oldfield, R., Ward, L., Riesen, R., Maccabe, A., Widener, P., Kordenbrock, T.: Lightweight I/O for scientific applications. In: 2006 IEEE International Conference on in Cluster Computing, pp. 1–11, September 2006
3. BitTorrent.org
4. Stoica, I., Morris, R., Karger, D., Kaashoek, M.F., Balakrishnan, H.: Chord: a scalable peer-to-peer lookup service for internet applications. In: SIGCOMM 2001, pp. 149–160 (2001)
5. Timpanaro, J., Cholez, T., Chrisment, I., Festor, O.: Bittorrent's mainline DHT security assessment. In: 2011 4th IFIP International Conference on New Technologies, Mobility and Security (NTMS), pp. 1–5, February 2011
6. Feldman, M., Papadimitriou, C., Chuang, J., Stoica, I.: Free-riding and whitewashing in peer-to-peer systems. IEEE J. Sel. Areas Commun. **24**(5), 1010–1019 (2006)
7. Karakoyunlu, C., Kimpe, D., Carns, P., Harms, K., Ross, R., Ward, L.: Toward a unified object storage foundation for scalable storage systems. In: Proceedings of the 5th Workshop on Interfaces and Architectures for Scientific Data Storage (IASDS 2013) (2013)
8. Ching, A., Choudhary, A., Liao, W.-K., Ross, R., Gropp, W.: Noncontiguous I/O through PVFS. In: Proceedings of 2002 IEEE International Conference on Cluster Computing, 2002, pp. 405–414 (2002)
9. Sun, Z., Skjellum, A., Ward, L., Curry, M.L.: A lightweight data location service for nondeterministic exascale storage systems. Trans. Storage **10**(3), 1–22 (2014). http://doi.acm.org/10.1145/2629451
10. Kung, H.T., Robinson, J.T.: On optimistic methods for concurrency control. ACM Trans. Database Syst. **6**(2), 213–226 (1981). http://doi.acm.org/10.1145/319566.319567
11. Carns, P., Harms, K., Kimpe, D., Wozniak, J., Ross, R., Ward, L., Curry, M., Klundt, R., Danielson, G., Karakoyunlu, C., Chandy, J., Settlemyer, B., Gropp, W.: A case for optimistic coordination in HPC storage systems,. In: 2012 SC Companion in High Performance Computing, Networking, Storage and Analysis (SCC), pp. 48–53, November 2012

Analyzing Data Properties Using Statistical Sampling Techniques – Illustrated on Scientific File Formats and Compression Features

Julian M. Kunkel[✉]

Deutsches Klimarechenzentrum, Bundesstraße 45a, 20146 Hamburg, Germany
kunkel@dkrz.de

Abstract. Understanding the characteristics of data stored in data centers helps computer scientists in identifying the most suitable storage infrastructure to deal with these workloads. For example, knowing the relevance of file formats allows optimizing the relevant formats but also helps in a procurement to define benchmarks that cover these formats. Existing studies that investigate performance improvements and techniques for data reduction such as deduplication and compression operate on a small set of data. Some of those studies claim the selected data is representative and scale their result to the scale of the data center. One hurdle of running novel schemes on the complete data is the vast amount of data stored and, thus, the resources required to analyze the complete data set. Even if this would be feasible, the costs for running many of those experiments must be justified.

This paper investigates stochastic sampling methods to compute and analyze quantities of interest on file numbers but also on the occupied storage space. It will be demonstrated that on our production system, scanning 1 % of files and data volume is sufficient to deduct conclusions. This speeds up the analysis process and reduces costs of such studies significantly. The **contributions** of this paper are: (1) the systematic investigation of the inherent analysis error when operating only on a subset of data, (2) the demonstration of methods that help future studies to mitigate this error, (3) the illustration of the approach on a study for scientific file types and compression for a data center.

Keywords: Scientific data · Compression · Analyzing data properties

1 Introduction

Understanding the characteristics of data stored in the data center helps computer scientists optimizing the storage. The quantities of interest could cover proportions, i.e. the percentage of files with a certain property, or means of certain metrics such as achievable read/write performance, compression speed and ratio. For example, knowing the relevance of file formats may shift the effort towards the most represented formats. When 80 % of the capacity is utilized by

© Springer International Publishing AG 2016
M. Taufer et al. (Eds.): ISC High Performance Workshops 2016, LNCS 9945, pp. 130–141, 2016.
DOI: 10.1007/978-3-319-46079-6_10

NetCDF4 files, performance analysis and optimization should target this file format first. Understanding the achievable compression ratio of available compression schemes helps in choosing not only the best one for user-specific compression but also for file system compression as provided by ZFS.

Assessing the benefit of any modification in production systems requires to either deploy those system-wide, or to evaluate its potential in advance on a small data set. For data centers with storage capacity of tens of Petabytes and file numbers in the order of hundreds of millions, it is not feasible to change the production system frequently. Thus, prototyping and evaluation on small scale is necessary. However, as a scientist involved in such prototyping, how can we estimate the benefit from small scale to large scale? Usually, this is done by picking a representative or relevant set of data for the evaluation and assuming those values can be scaled up to the full system.

In the literature, studies can be found that investigate compression ratio, deduplication factor or improve performance of scientific middleware. Due to the long running time to apply any improvement on large amounts of data, many studies assume the benefit measured on a small data sample can be transferred to the scale on the data center. However, usually these studies do not pay attention if the data set is actually representative, with other words, they do not take into account the fraction of the workload that can actually benefit from the advancement. In statistics, the big field of sampling theory addresses this issue. Due to the law of large numbers, there are methods to draw instances appropriately and deduce properties from the sample set to the population with high confidence. However, this process is non-trivial and a research discipline in statistics by itself [1,2].

This paper investigates statistical sampling to estimate file properties on the scale of data centers using small data sets and statistical simulation. The computation time used for this project was 517 core days. With 24 cores per node, a complete system scan of DKRZ's system would have needed about 475 node days which would have cost at least about 4000 €[1] – while not revealing additional insight. Instead with 1 % of scanned files or capacity, similar results are achievable.

The paper is structured as follows: an excerpt to related studies analyzing scientific data is given in Sect. 2. The method to create test data for this research is described in Sect. 3. To show the variability of data and importance of proper sampling, the data is explored in Sect. 4. It also describes some interesting properties of DKRZ's scientific data. The strategies to pick appropriate samples for studies analyzing data by file count and by occupied space is given in Sect. 5. Finally, the paper is concluded.

---

[1] The value is an estimate based on the TCO of the system for 5 years. It is conservative and does not include secondary costs such as jitter introduced to other models by the caused I/O.

2   State of the Art

Existing research that analyzes properties of scientific data can be classified into performance analysis, compression ratio and data deduplication. Effort that investigates and optimizes performance usually picks a certain workload to demonstrate that the new approach is superior than existing strategies. A few studies analytically analyze typical patterns and optimize for a large range of access patterns. An example is the study in [3], which analyzes the access pattern for several workloads and discusses general implications. Research for optimization techniques, as far as known to the author, do not check how many people actually benefit from these optimizations and the implications on system level.

In the field of compression, many studies have been conducted on pre-selected workloads, for example, see [4–7]. Some of those studies are used to estimate the benefit of the compression on the data center level, for example, Hübbe et al. investigate the cost-benefit for long-term archival. Similarly in [6], the compression ratio is investigated. However, in this case the selected data is a particular volume from a small system.

Modern file systems such as BTRFS and ZFS offer compression on system-side [8]. It is also considered to embed compression into storage devices such as SSDs [9] and evaluate it for OLTP workloads. In [10], Jin et al. investigate the benefit for compressing and de-duplicating data for virtual machines. They created a diverse pool of 52 virtual images and analyze the impact.

The de-duplication study for data centers in [11], analyzes a larger fraction of scientific data on different sites, but due to the long run-time did not manage to analyze the full data set. When looking at all these studies, one may ask the question how would those techniques behave on a full system?

3   Sampling of Test Data

To assess and demonstrate the impact of statistical sampling, firstly, a subset of data of DKRZ's supercomputer Mistral is scanned and relevant data properties about data compression and scientific file types are extracted. The goal of the following strategy was not to gain a completely representative sample, since this is to be developed within this paper. Since the global Lustre file system hosts about 320 million files and 12 Petabytes of space is occupied, only a subset is scanned: 380 k (0.12 %) accounting for an (aggregated size) of 53.1 TiB of data (0.44 %). Note that the mean file size scanned is about 145 MiB but on our single file system it is 38.8 MiB. The discrepancy is due to the fact that project directories contain usually larger files compared to home directories that were not scanned. To prevent data loss and ensure data privacy, the scanning process is performed using a regular user account and, thus, it cannot access all files. There are still 58 million files and 160 out of 270 project directories accessible.

The scanning process used as baseline in the paper works as follows:

1. Run a parallel scan for accessible files of each project directory independently using `find`; store them in individual file lists.

2. Select 10.000 files from each project directory randomly (or all, if less files exist in a project directory) and merge them into a single file list.
3. Create a random permutation of the file list and partition the result into one process list for each thread that shall be used.
4. Distribute the threads across different nodes, each thread processes its fixed file list sequentially and writes an individual output file.
5. After 300 k files have been scanned, the threads are prematurely terminated and the resulting data from all threads is ingested into a SQLlite database.

The strategy increases the likelihood, that a representative sample of files is chosen from accessible projects[2]. It is to be expected that projects differ in their file characteristics as they may use different scientific simulations and analysis workflows. From perspective of statisticians, this process creates a simple random sample [1] but incorporates a systematic stratified sampling approach to balance between projects. The limitations of this sampling strategy to investigate properties based on occupied file size, will be shown later.

Processing of the threads: a few threads are started concurrently on the system, to prevent overwhelming the file system and exploit compute time on interactive nodes that is not utilized by users. Since the file list is created only once, but the threads are executed over the course of several weeks, the processing ignores non-existing files. A thread iterates through the file list, for each file it first copies it to a temporary location – this prevents concurrent file modifications, then it runs: (1) the CDO [12] command to identify the scientific file type, (2) the `file` command to identify file types checking the file header, and (3) each compressor under investigation (LZMA, GZIP, BZIP2, ZIP) in compression and de-compression mode. The `time` command is used to capture runtime information of each step. To assess compression speed, user time is extracted – this covers the actual computing time and ignores system and I/O times as well as competing jobs.

4   Exploring Analyzed Data

In this section, we investigate several quantities of interest on the complete data set, they are computed either on file count, i.e. each file is weighted identically, or by weighting each file with its occupied size. This section will show that both types of analyses lead to different results.

In Fig. 1, the distribution of file sizes is shown. Figure 1(a) shows a histogram with logarithmic file sizes. In Fig. 1(b) the relation between file size and file count is illustrated; to construct the figure, files have been sorted by size in ascending order and then the cumulative sum is computed. While the histogram suggests similarities between size distribution and a normal distribution, this is due to

---

[2] Obviously, if those 160 projects are not representative, deducing properties for the full data is not valid. Still the introduced analysis and approaches are correct. The number of 10 k files was choosen as it would ensure to scan at most 0.5 % of the files.

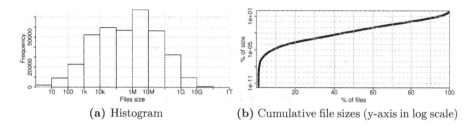

(a) Histogram   (b) Cumulative file sizes (y-axis in log scale)

Fig. 1. Distribution of file sizes

the logarithmic x-axis. In the cumulative view, it can be seen that aggregated 20 % of files consume one millionth of storage space and 90 % still consume less than 10 % space (these files are below 100 MiB in size). If a study takes small files as representatives, those fail to represent the storage capacity. Similar large files fail to represent the typical (small) file that must be handled by the storage.

4.1   Scientific File Formats

The usage of file formats is shown in Fig. 2. The figure shows the relative relevance in terms of occupied space and number of files of each file format. About 60 % of the number of files and 47 % of aggregated file size is non-scientific and cannot be resolved with the CDO tool. The dominant scientific formats are NetCDF3, GRIB1 and NetCDF2. The `file` command cannot identify and distinguish scientific formats as reliable as CDO but can shed light over the distribution of the 60 %. Looking at its output, the 60 % of capacity seems to be dominated by TAR (7 %) and GZIP compressed files (5 %)[3] – it classifies 43 % of capacity as "data" and 40 % as NetCDF (no version information provided). Looking at the proportions in terms of file count, roughly 30 % are classified as data, 30 % as text (e.g., code), 24 % as NetCDF files, 4 % as HDF5 and 3.5 % as images. Other file types are negligible.

4.2   Compression Ratio

To evaluate compression ratio, files with a size below 4 KiB (about 15 % of all files) are not taken into consideration, as compressing them is not expected to be beneficial because of the additional header and file system block size. As metric we will use the inverse of the compression ratio that is the fraction the compressed file occupies in comparison to the original, e.g., after compressing a file might be down to 10 % of its original size. For simplicity, we label this metric as **compressed %**; it is computed as $c_\%(f) = \dfrac{\text{compressed size}(f)}{\text{file size}(f)}$. The mean compression can be determined as the arithmetic mean ratio all files c_{files}

---

[3] From the GZIP files, the extension tar.gz is observed on 9 % of files, representing 53 % of GZIP data overall size. Thus most GZIP files are also TAR files.

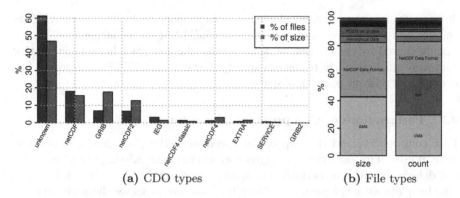

(a) CDO types   **(b)** File types

Fig. 2. Relative usage of file formats determined using CDO and `file`.

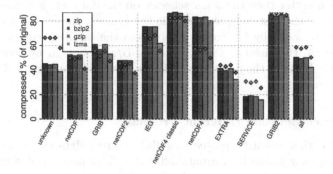

Fig. 3. Arithmetic mean compression of the full data set for each scientific file format computed on file number. The column "all" shows the mean values for the whole data set. Yellow diamonds show compress % computed by file size. (Color figure online)

(Eq. 1), i.e. averaging it by file number; or, by file size, i.e. considering the total space saved c_{size} (Eq. 2).

$$c_{files} = \frac{\sum_{f=1}^{files} \frac{\text{comp. size}(f)}{\text{file size}(f)}}{\text{file count}} \tag{1}$$

$$c_{size} = \frac{\sum_f \text{compr. size}(f)}{\sum_f \text{file size}(f)} \tag{2}$$

In Fig. 3, both, the mean relative compression by count and by size is shown for each compression scheme and file format. The column "all" shows the reduction when compressing the full data set. In average, the compressors except LZMA achieve similar results – but a compression scheme can be slightly better than another on individual file sets. LZMA, performs much better on all data except GRIB2. While overall the computation by file and by size is similar, there are differences in details. For example, in average LZMA packs each file down to

40 % of its size, but in terms of overall storage space only 50 % is saved. Thus, smaller files typically compress better with LZMA than the larger files. This is mainly caused by the fraction of non-scientific file formats (the unknowns) that compress much worse in terms of capacity. For example, GZIP compressed files occupy a significant portion of space.

4.3   Performance of Compression Algorithms

Fast compression and decompression speed and, thus, required computation time, is crucial for embedding compression schemes into existing workflows without delaying them. The performance spectrum across the files is shown in Fig. 4. The boxplots show the median as black line; the box indicates the limits of quartile 1 and quartile 3, whiskers can go up to 1.5 interquartile range. Many outliers with faster performance are not visualized. While on average, BZIP2 does not perform much better than the other schemes on the data set, it is much slower. LZMA achieved the best compression ratio but is much slower than gzip. Again, the compression ratio by file count differs from the mean speed computed by size. For LZMA, the mean is 38.4 and 21.7 MiB/s, computed by count and by size, respectively. Thus the difference in decompression is roughly 50 % as bigger files need more time to compress and decompress.

4.4   Variance Between Different Projects

It is expected that scientific projects exhibit different data characteristics, for example, they may utilize file formats differently. This makes it difficult to pick a random sample from just a few projects. To investigate this issue, all projects for which more than 1,000 files have been scanned were analyzed individually. A few characteristics across the projects are shown in the boxplot in Fig. 5: The file count indicates how many files have been scanned for each project, how much storage is occupied by the files, the compression % of LZMA, proportion of NetCDF and GRIB files in terms of the projects overall file count and occupied size. It can be seen that while between 2,000 and 3,000 files have been scanned due to random file selection, other metrics vary significantly. For example, some projects have nearly 100 % of NetCDF files while others use other formats. Thus, it is very important to sample properly across projects.

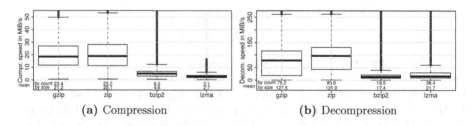

(a) Compression   (b) Decompression

Fig. 4. Boxplots showing compression/decompression speed per file, the arithmetic means are shown as text under the plot.

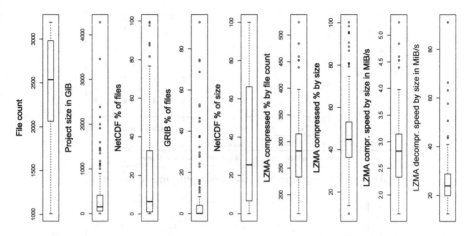

Fig. 5. Several quantities of interest, this barchart covers 125 individual projects. Each point represents the arithmetic mean value computed on one project.

5 Stochastic Sampling of Data

The way the quantities of interest are computed are either by file count, i.e. we predict properties of the population based on individual files, or by weighting the individual files with their size. From the perspective of statistics, we analyze variables for quantities that are continuous values or proportions, i.e. the fraction of samples for which a certain property holds. To select the number of observations that allows inference about the population, statistics knows methods for determining sample size. These methods require that we can make certain assumptions about the distribution of values such as normally distributed data. To determine the number of samples needed, the tolerable error between prediction and real value must be chosen, it depends on the used analysis method and distribution of values. Usually the error is defined by the size of an interval with the predicted value as center in which is extremely likely (e.g., 95 %), that the true value resides. The interval is called confidence interval and the probability is the confidence level.

For estimating proportions there are easy approaches – that work regardless of probability distribution: With Cochran's sample size formula, to achieve an error bound of ±5 % and ±1 %, roughly 400 and 10000 samples are needed, respectively [1]. Note that the sample number does not increase even for large population sizes.

Estimating a continuous variable, e.g., the arithmetic mean compression ratio or performance, is more complex as sampling ratio is based on the expected distribution of values. But we do not know it a-priori, and not necessarily the property we are looking for is normally distributed. All these methods have in common that they determine the mean value, i.e., the proportion in all files and not weight them by occupied storage size. As the size is a-priori is unbounded, it is not unlikely that file size distribution follows heavy-tailed distributions,

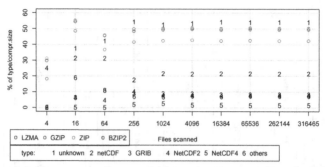

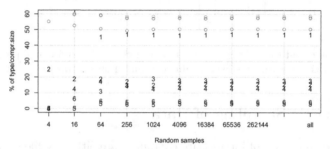

(a) Correct sampling method to compute mean by count

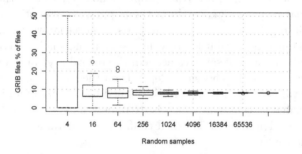

(b) Correct sampling method to compute mean by size

Fig. 6. Evaluating various metrics (proportions and compressed %) for an increasing number of samples. Only one simulation is done for each count.

Fig. 7. Simulation of sampling by file count to compute compr. % by file count.

increasing the analysis of sample size determinination [13,14]. The detailed analysis is out of scope of this paper, but we will show that the means are converging for typical use cases. The methods to obtain a representative sample are as follows.

Sampling method to compute by file count. When computing the proportion or the mean of a variable for files, a strategy is to enumerate all files on the storage system and then create a simple random sample, i.e., choose a number of files

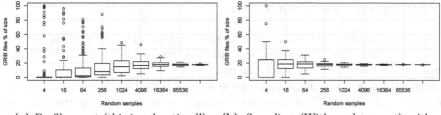

(a) By file count (this is suboptimal!)   (b) Sampling (With replacement) with a probability proportional to size

Fig. 8. Simulation of sampling to compute proportions of types by size.

for which the property is computed. For proportion variables, Cochran's sample size formula is applicable and the number of files can be easily deducted.

Sampling method to compute by file size. Estimating values and weighting them based on file size requires to enumerate all files and determine their size, then pick a random sample from the file list based on the probability defined by filesize/totalsize. Draws from the list must be done with replacement, i.e., we never remove any picked file. Once all chosen files are determined, the quantities of interest are computed once for each unique file. Then, each time we have chosen a file, we add our quantity of interest without weighting the file size, e.g., the arithmetic mean can be computed just across all samples. Thus large files are more likely to be picked but each time their property is accounted identically as for small files.

Evaluation for mean compressed file size and proportions of file types. To demonstrate this approach, a simulation has been done by drawing a variable number of samples from the data. The result is shown in Fig. 6. It can be seen that this quickly converges to the correct mean value of the full data. With 4096 samples, that are slightly more than 1 % of files, the value is close to the correct mean.

Robustness. To illustrate the stability of the approach, the simulation is repeated 100 times and a boxplot is rendered with the deviations. Naturally, the repeats of a robust method should have little variance and converge towards the correct mean value. The result for the proportion of GRIB files are given as an example but the results for all variables behave similar. In Fig. 7, it can be clearly seen that the error becomes smaller but Cochran's approximation is yield.

The sampling strategy to compute quantities on file size is shown in Fig. 8(b). Similarly, to the correct method for sampling by file count it converges quickly. However, if we would simply use a file scanner to compute the metrics on size but it would choose files randomly without considering file sizes, we would achieve highly unstable results (Fig. 8a). Indeed the error margin with even one fifth of all files (64 k) is comparable to the correct sampling strategy with only 1024 samples. Thus, it is vital to apply the right sampling method, and, therefore, the initial approach used to gather the test data as described in Sect. 3 is suboptimal.

6   Summary and Conclusions

In this paper, sampling techniques from statistics are applied to estimate data properties. These techniques are demonstrated to be useful approximate the proportions of scientific file types, the compressed % and speed. The paper also highlighted some interesting data properties of DKRZ's data. It has been demonstrated that a random file scanner is not efficient to estimate quantities that are computed on file size. Instead, sampling with replacement and a probability equal to the proportion of file size leads to stable results. Tools using such techniques can estimate properties of data robust without the need to analyze the huge data volumes of data centers. We will be working on such tools to evaluate the benefit of optimization strategies.

Acknowledgements. I thank Charlotte Jentzsch for the fruitful discussions.

References

1. Kotrlik, J., Higgins, C.: Organizational research: determining appropriate sample size in survey research appropriate sample size in survey research. Inf. Technol. Learn. Perform. J. **19**(1), 43 (2001)
2. Newcombe, R.G.: Two-sided confidence intervals for the single proportion: comparison of seven methods. Stat. Med. **17**(8), 857–872 (1998)
3. Lofstead, J., Polte, M., Gibson, G., Klasky, S., Schwan, K., Oldfield, R., Wolf, M., Liu, Q.: Six degrees of scientific data: reading patterns for extreme scale science IO. In: Proceedings of the 20th International Symposium on High Performance Distributed Computing, pp. 49–60. ACM (2011)
4. Lakshminarasimhan, S., Shah, N., Ethier, S., Ku, S.H., Chang, C.S., Klasky, S., Latham, R., Ross, R., Samatova, N.F.: ISABELA for effective in situ compression of scientific data. Concurrency Comput. Pract. Experience **25**(4), 524–540 (2013)
5. Kunkel, J., Kuhn, M., Ludwig, T.: Exascale storage systems - an analytical study of expenses. Supercomputing Front. Innovations **1**(1), 116–134 (2014)
6. Kuhn, M., Chasapis, K., Dolz, M., Ludwig, T.: Compression By Default - Reducing Total Cost of Ownership of Storage Systems, June 2014
7. Hübbe, N., Kunkel, J.: Reducing the HPC-datastorage footprint with MAFISC - multidimensional adaptive filtering improved scientific data compression. Comput. Sci. Res. Dev. **28**, 231–239 (2013)
8. Legesse, S.D.: Performance Evaluation of File Systems Compression Features. Master's thesis, University of Oslo (2014)
9. Zuck, A., Toledo, S., Sotnikov, D., Harnik, D.: Compression and SSDs: where and how? In: 2nd Workshop on Interactions of NVM/Flash with Operating Systems and Workloads (INFLOW 2014), Broomfield, CO. USENIX Association, October 2014
10. Jin, K., Miller, E.L.: The effectiveness of deduplication on virtual machine disk images. In: Proceedings of SYSTOR 2009: The Israeli Experimental Systems Conference, **7**. ACM (2009)
11. Meister, D., Kaiser, J., Brinkmann, A., Kuhn, M., Kunkel, J., Cortes, T.: A study on data deduplication in HPC storage systems. In: Proceedings of the ACM/IEEE Conference on High Performance Computing (SC). IEEE Computer Society, November 2012

12. Schulzweida, U., Kornblueh, L., Quast, R.: CDO Users guide: Climate Data Operators Version 1.6. 1 (2006)
13. Resnick, S.I.: Heavy-Tail Phenomena: Probabilistic and Statistical Modeling. Springer Science & Business Media, New York (2007)
14. Tursunalieva, A., Silvapulle, P.: Estimation of Confidence Intervals for the Mean of Heavy Tailed Loss Distributions: A Comparative Study Using a Simulation Method (2009)

Delta: Data Reduction for Integrated Application Workflows and Data Storage

Jay Lofstead[1]([✉]), Gregory Jean-Baptiste[2], and Ron Oldfield[1]

[1] Sandia National Laboratories, Albuquerque, NM, USA
{gflofst,raoldfi}@sandia.gov
[2] Florida International University, Miami, FL, USA
gjean011@fiu.edu

Abstract. Data sizes are growing far faster than storage bandwidth. To address this growing gap, Integrated Application Workflows (IAWs) are being investigated as a potential to replace using a centralized storage array for storing intermediate data. IAWs run multiple simulation workflow components concurrently on an HPC resource connecting these components using compute area resources. These IAWs require high frequency and high volume data transfers between compute nodes and staging area nodes during the lifetime of a large parallel computation. The available network bandwidth between the two areas may not be enough to efficiently support the data movement. As the processing power available to compute resources increases, the requirements for this data transfer will become more difficult to satisfy and perhaps will not be satisfiable at all since network capabilities are not expanding at a comparable rate. It is necessary to reduce the volume of data without reducing the quality of data when it is being processed and analyzed. Delta resolves the issue by addressing the lifetime data transfer operations. Delta removes subsequent identical copies of already transmitted data prior to transfer and restores those pieces once the data has reached the destination using previously transmitted data. Delta is able to identify duplicated information and determine the most space efficient way to represent it. Initial tests show about 50 % reduction in data movement while maintaining the same data quality and transmission frequency. Given the simplicity of the approach and the log-based format employed by ADIOS, the approach can also be used to write less data to the storage array outside of IAW considerations.

1 Introduction

Addressing limited storage bandwidths requires considering required data quality, alternative storage locations for intermediate data, and distributed processing to avoid bottlenecks. One approach is moving offline workflows online as Integrated Application Workflows (IAWs). Ideally, any data management technique would also be usable for data storage to a central storage array rather than just from node to node. Delta offers such a system. First, consider IAWs.

© Springer International Publishing AG 2016
M. Taufer et al. (Eds.): ISC High Performance Workshops 2016, LNCS 9945, pp. 142–152, 2016.
DOI: 10.1007/978-3-319-46079-6_11

The concept of an IAW is striaghtforward. Traditional scientific simulation workflows all use the centralized scratch storage to stage intermediate data between workflow components. An IAW potentially uses the same components, but uses in compute area storage of some sort, such as another node's RAM or in compute area NVM on compute nodes, in a different configuration, such as per rack, or both. By using this in compute area storage, bandwidth limitations rise to near or at network bandwidths enabling moving vastly larger data in the same time period. With this concept, consider how scientific simulation workflows could work.

Scientific simulation workflows are becoming increasingly complex as the data size and the computation speed accelerate. With disk-based storage array performance falling behind these trends and faster alternatives, such as SSDs, still too expensive as a general solution, a move to using IAWs instead is starting. An illustration of such an IAW is in Fig. 1. The general idea for the staging area, or burst buffer as they are sometimes called, is to offer a place to temporarily store intermediate data between IAW components. Data analytics or visualization components can retrieve this data both when it becomes available and when they have capacity. Current trends in extreme scale OS design suggest that this is better thought of as a logical rather than physical model as node partitioning is expected to offer a loosely coupled, nearly in-place data movement environment. This offers a degree of asynchrony while keeping data movement at interconnect speeds, or faster, rather than being limited by the storage array bandwidth. While shifting data movement online reduces the IO bottleneck, it is not a panacea.

The amount of relevant data produced during the run of such an application is large and is getting larger as the simulation ensembles use finer resolutions and more complex physics. Given the presence of unchanged data from previous transmission(s), it is possible to remove this data and restore it at the destination using prior transmission data. Transferring such a high data volume repeatedly during runtime can have a severely negative impact on the network, where the improvement in bandwidth cannot match the growing data size, or on data storage due to a performance mismatch between data generators and consumers. The resulting backlog could affect performance on both the compute area and the staging area. Compounding the issue is the amount of energy consumed over the course of such an application including the cost of transferring data. Currently, computation is the single largest contributor to energy usage [7] but if the data volume grows at the same rate, the cost of moving data can easily become the limiting factor. Not only is writing to a storage array problematic, but also is moving data to other places within the compute resource. This energy cap prompts new work into managing various energy use sources throughout the scientific simulation workflow process.

Since data transmission from node to node is little different from writing to a storage array on an energy use perspective, an ideal technique would offer the ability to reduce data sizes with low computational overhead while offering the flexibility use an IAW or to the storage array for offline processing. This paper examines one such project focusing on managing data movement.

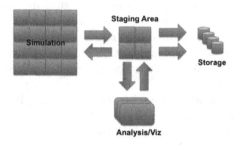

Fig. 1. Overall IAW architecture

For at least two different scientific simulation application classes, there are opportunities to reduce data movement with little to no negative IAW impact. For molecular dynamics and finite element codes, the data proportion that changes with each calculation iteration is significantly smaller than the entire working set size. Our measurements showed that only 40 % to 75 % of the data changed from iteration to iteration. Usually, the same type of data is produced every timestep (e.g., temperature, velocity, position), but the value may or may not change from timestep to timestep offering opportunities to avoid data movement and the associated energy costs.

Using this observation, an application developer could adjust the application such that if a particular element does not change between timesteps, it is not sent to any downstream consumer. When the analysis software receives a "no change" or even no value at all instead of the element, it can assume that it has not changed from the previous value and use the old value instead. An even better and easier approach for application developers would be for an underlying system that did this for any application running on top of it. We developed such a system to effectively eliminate any data unchanged between output steps and yielded approximately a 50 % reduction in aggregate data movement over the simulation lifetime.

The ADIOS IO API [8] offers an ideal vehicle for such a system. The replaceable transport methods offers a flexibile way to incorporate new ways to move data without requiring any application changes. For reading, it does not matter other than a small data sourcing difference, where the data comes from. Given the simpler in memory operation option of using an IAW rather than writing to the storage array, we investigate this aspect of the Delta approach. There is nothing that prevents using the Delta encoded ADIOS BP format from being written to the storage array and later read and decoded just as it is done for the IAW approach.

The rest of the paper is organized as follows. First is a short discussion of related work in Sect. 2. Next is a design overview in Sect. 3. An evaluation follows in Sect. 4. Section 5 has a short discussion of the evaluation implications and future work.

2   Related Work

General workflow systems such as Pegasus [12], Kepler [9], and DAGMan [10] manage the inter-component scheduling for an effective workflow. In general, they assume that each component is a separate application and typically disk is used to store intermediate data. These facts makes these systems less useful for constructing an online workflow system. Hand-coded systems using a language like Python generally suffer the same limitations.

Data transmission or storage related solutions are infesible for this environment. Many other older approaches towards using deduplication-like techniques have been investigated in conjuction with networking protocols [15] or more specifically web browsing. WebExpress [4] is similar in that it offers differencing between the same transmission between two end-points, however, it is optimized for web traffic and requires extra software and storage space installed. Delta is part of a client linked library on both the client and server and requires at most $O(n)$ overhead on the server since it is focused on a single dataset. The other consideraiton is the data sizes we are addressing. If a multi-TB output is pushed into a staging area, there must be sufficient storage across a sufficient number of nodes to handle the data load. The inherent data replication is also undesirable. Further, each record is treated as a separate or full replacement entity. While Delta's concepts could be incorporated into such a system, it would require more semantic changes because an update can come from any source eliminating the ability to effectively determine on the client side what data has changed since the last update.

More directly related work includes the ConCORD [16] project. This work observed that data in memory could be better thought of based on the accesses made against it affording opportunities to reduce data duplication. While this works well in the target virtual machine environment, it does not address data moving off a node.

AI-Ckpt [13] evaluated memory changes for scientific simulations to only move data pages that change between output steps. While this is an admirable first step in this direction, our observations showed that far greater data movement reductions could be achieved by making decisions on an element-by-element basis because portions of every simulation variable generally changed every iteration while certain portions did not. With these static and dynamic elements intermixed, data pages are generally all moved even though only a portion of the data has changed.

On a post-processing basis, a climate science team evaluated lossy data compression techniques to determine how much a data set could be compressed while still maintaining sufficient validity to keep application scientists confident [1]. This project yielded good results, but is intended for long-term archival rather than the immediacy required by IAWs. The additional steps for data compression may be appropriate as an alternative to this approach, but would require considerably more computation, but at a lesser local storage cost. Further investigation would be required to determine which solution is preferable for which situations and if this globally optimized compression could be done on a node-by-node basis.

Isabella [6] provides lossy compression after data sorting. This time overhead is at least $O(nlogn)$ and introduces errors. Delta seeks to offer an $O(n)$ time overhead and be lossless. Sif [11] offered deduplication for general Unix files rather than the uncompressible and frequently randomly changed scientific data sets. Burns and Long [3] proposed using version chains for efficient version storage at a cost of data reconstruction time. With Delta, we need rapid reconstruction since all compressed objects are needed uncompressed at the destination. While wavelet compression [5] can match the $O(n)$ overhead, it introduces errors we seek to avoid.

3   Design

One of the simplest way to examine the potential impact for this approach is to adapt an existing IO library to automatically handle both the data compression and expansion. The easiest library in which to add these sorts of data processing techniques is ADIOS [8]. The ability to install a new transport method that receives raw data with full name and type information makes it easy to replace any IO operation with data processing and then IO. ADIOS' BP file format is flexible enough to support writing to the storage array of the Delta modified format. With the index blocks at the end of the BP file, direct access can still be offered to variables by linking to each instance in the BP file. If a variable has not changed since the last output, there is no index entry. While this requires a smarter index processing engine, it is a small increment over the existing reading system. Alternatively, the HDF5 Virtual Object Layer (VOL) offers similar functionality, but with potentially more rigid programming semantics.

Delta is a prototype ADIOS transport method that caches the last whole data set transferred for each output group and creates and expands compressed data sets only transferring the reduced data between the source and destination. As far as the end user is concerned, the IAW writes and reads data normally, but using the Delta transport method instead. The architecture is illustrated in Fig. 2. The ADIOS transport is currently undergoing internal copyright review and will be released as open source on github once these reviews are completed.

In order to reduce data transferred over the network, Delta must determine how much data is changed between every computation output. Each node in the system keeps track of the local full output from the previous full output from which it generates the difference. When the current round completes, the new output is compared to the cached full output. During the first round, there is no comparison because there is no old output with which to compare. Every subsequent round compares each variable element against its matching predecessor including both scalars and vectors. Delta calculates the difference between the rounds. Anything that has not changed is not included in the new payload

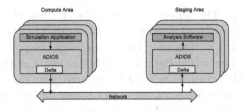

Fig. 2. A diagram of the IAW architecture, including ADIOS and Delta

and is instead replaced by metadata to describe what is left out. Once the payload arrives at its destination, the full, current data set can be recreated. The unchanged elements can be found in a previous payload. If the number of changed elements is too large, then the cost of the metadata summed with the changed data will be greater than the cost of just sending the data plainly. Therefore, if the amount of change is above a certain threshold, all the data is sent as is.

Packing the data for transport requires several steps. At top of each payload, certain pieces of information are required. Some of these data items are artifacts of how ADIOS encodes data. For example, because ADIOS uses a log-based format by default that annotates every log entry with information about the source process rank, this additional data is required. Using HDF5 VOL instead would eliminate some of these values, but would require more communication to coordinate among the participating processes to determine what has changed with each output step.

To keep the complexity low, the payload construction is largely driven by the ADIOS BP format and uses some of this information to encode the differences. Delta attempts to address the entire output, including the header overheads, rather than just the variables.

In the BP format overhead, some of the values can be sent once while others must be sent with each output. An ADIOS Group ID is assigned as the XML file is processed and is used to determine which cached full dataset should be used for the difference operation. This allows multiple variables of the same name to be used in different output operations without worrying about name collisions causing poor data differencing. Fields like Epoch change with every output and are sent each during each output setup. Other fields like Group Name Length, and Group Name are almost exclusively static and only need to be sent once. Since some variables may be static between output steps, the Variable Count cannot be sent a single time.

After the header section, the individual variables for the designated group are added. Each variable has two required components:

First is a variable status. The status has a value of NONE, SOME or NEW. If the status is SOME, there was a change in the variable between the rounds. If the status is NONE, there was no change and no data should be sent besides the required metadata. If the status is NEW, that means that the variable in question is being written for the first time and all the necessary metadata will be sent along with it. The second is a variable id. This id number is used to identify the variable once it is delivered by the receiver.

If the status is NONE, then only these two fields are sent as metadata for a particular variable. The actual data is exactly the same as the previous round. If the status is SOME, then more data is required, but since this variable was previously written, some pieces of information can be left out. Otherwise, the variable is new and will be padded accordingly.

On the first, full output, a few fields for each variable are sent. These include Name Length, Name, Dim Count, Dim Sizes, Global (distributed vs. local only variable), Type, and Type Size. Should a variable change over time by expanding the dimensions or shrinking or growing from a single node to multi-nodes (or vice-versa), corresponding values would be sent again.

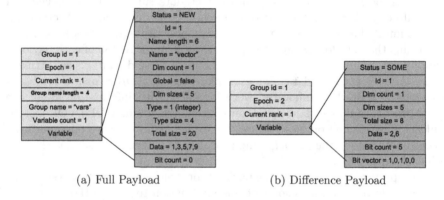

(a) Full Payload   (b) Difference Payload

Fig. 3. Payload descriptions

Next, it must be determined whether all of the data should be sent or if a portion should be left out with some metadata that describes it. If there are no copies of the variable, then all of the information is sent. If the variable is a scalar, this is not an issue. If a scalar changed, it must be sent. If it did not change, it is not sent. Vectors present a challenge. Delta represents a vector variable using a bit vector. The bit vector is set to the size of the full output from the round. For example, if the variable is question was an array with 100 elements, the bit vector would consist of 100 bits. Each element in the output is compared to an element in the same position in the previous round. If it is the same as before, the value of the matching bit is set to 0 and the element is excluded from the payload. Otherwise, the bit is set to 1 and the data remains in the payload. If the new output vector is larger than the last, then the overflow is all represented by '1's. All of the extra new data is included in the payload. The output from the last round is then replaced by the current output. Next, the size of the current rounds output is compared to the size of the reduced payload plus the bit vector. If the reduction summed with the bit vector is larger than the original output size, then the bit vector is discarded and all of the data is sent. Otherwise, the reduction and the bit vector are prepared for transport.

There are a few remaining fields in the BP format, including some new pieces custom to the Delta transport method. Total Size and Data correspond to the payload of the full and/or compressed variable encoded. The new fields are a Bit Count and Bit Vector for cases where a difference is being output.

This is the format for every variable in every output group. When complete, the buffer is written to whatever the destination is. Figure 3(a) illustrates a full data set with all of the associated metadata included. Figure 3(b) shows the same data set in the following epoch. Some of its data values have changed, so a bit vector has been added to describe the change. Much of the metadata is no longer necessary at that point since it is unchanging and has already been written previously.

In order to unpack the payload, there are a set of data structures to manage the parts of the payload. At the top is the Delta_Data_Struct, which keeps track of two different types of information: The information that can change from epoch to epoch and the information that stays the same.

For the changing information, The Delta_Data_Struct (or DDS) keeps a linked list of Group_Struct structures. Each Group_Struct represents a different group and contains a linked list of Epoch structures. An Epoch structure represents a single timestep in the associated group's lifespan. It also keeps track of the process (rank) that submitted the group data during that timestep. Finally, each Epoch has a vector of Var_Struct structures that hold the state of each variable during that particular epoch such as its value and size (if it is a vector, for example).

For the unchanging information, the DDS has a linked list of Group_Record structures that hold the group name and the number of variables for that group since those don't change. Also, each contains a vector of Variable_Record structures that hold information such as the variable name, data type, and whether or not it is global.

The data could be stored as the difference or reconstituted into the full data set. For this first test case, we simply regenerated the whole data set each time removing complexity from read operations.

4   Evaluation

The evaluation is performed on the Chama capacity cluster at Sandia National Laboratories. It consists of 1232 nodes each with 2 2.6 GHz Intel Sandy-Bridge CPUs with 8 cores/socket. Each node has 64 GB of DDR3 RAM and connects with a 4X QDR InfiniBand network configured in a fat tree. The file system is the site shared Lustre offering 1 PB of storage. There are also 8 login nodes each with the same hardware as the compute nodes. All nodes run RHEL 6.

To evaluate this approach's potential, two separate scientific applications were modified to measure the change of output between timesteps. The first is

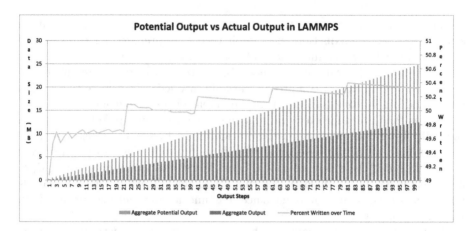

Fig. 4. A graph showing the pattern of reduced writes in LAMMPS for the "Crack" example. Aggregate Potential Output is uncompressed size; Aggregate Output is Delta compressed size

the molecular dynamics code LAMMPS [14]. It can simulate a number of inter-actions and events at a fine level by applying physics to atom positions based on the simulation setup. The user can define the interaction in an application specific manner and let it run over a number of timesteps. Here, the modified code was run with and example called "crack", which simulates a crack propagating through some solid. Roughly 40 % of the data changed between output timesteps, getting as high as 60 % at times. Figure 4 displays the changes aggregated over time. Another example, which simulated a melting solid had 60 % of its variables changing between output timesteps, getting as high as 75 %. Similar results were found when running an example built using the DEAL.II [2] finite element library. It is easy to see that this strategy will work better with some simulations that others. Simulations that have some form of propagation (such as a crack or melting) would have many of its parts remain static for some period of time. Other simulations even have parts that don't change at all (such as the ground over which a liquid is flowing). These kinds of simulations would benefit the most from applying Delta or an application specific version. Since ADIOS can be used to support such applications, Delta aims to be an application independent version.

5 Conclusion

As supercomputers continue gaining ground on the road to exascale, many of the currently acceptable practices when it comes to managing data will become obsolete because of the resulting bottlenecks and the associated energy consumption. One of these practices involves taking up bandwidth to transfer information that was already previously transmitted and already exists at the destination. Delta makes an attempt to prevent that by keeping track of changes between timesteps in a computation in order to detect stagnant data. By blocking the transfer of such data, the extra bandwidth that would have been consumed is now available to the rest of the application or not used at all. In that process, no data is lost to the staging area for IAWs. The reader in Delta can rebuild the reduced data using previously obtained information, giving a complete picture of the output produced during computation. With the demonstrated advantages for IAWs, offering a full ADIOS transport method that writes to the storage array in the Delta format should be addressed. Since it would only change where the data comes from and have a slightly more complicated index processing step to find the full data, this is a relatively small effort.

There are many avenues to continue this work. First, ADIOS has an inherent assumption that the variables represented in an output can change. The current design does not take this into account. There are also considerations related to static metadata. For example, global or local array dimensions for structure meshes may not change over the simulation lifetime. Retransmitting these values each time could be eliminated further reducing data sizes.

Different data encoding techniques, such as using a sparse map when few elements change could also be incorporated along with a flag identifying which encoding technique is employed.

Maintaining a fixed "full" data copy is sufficient for a prototype, but not an optimal solution. Ideally, this "full" data copy would update with each output step reducing the frequency of full data set transfers.

Other higher computational cost techniques such as lossless or lossy data compression could be used instead. The performance, space, and energy tradeoffs must be investigated to see when these more complex approaches would be superior to this simple approach. There are some indications that lossy approaches may be sufficient for at least some scientific simulations, such as was demonstrated for the climate simulation. Other low overhead techniques should be investigated.

Acknowledgments. Sandia National Laboratories is a multi-program laboratory managed and operated by Sandia Corporation, a wholly owned subsidiary of Lockheed Martin Corporation, for the U.S. Department of Energy's National Nuclear Security Administration under contract DE-AC04-94AL85000. SAND2014-17090 C.

References

1. Baker, A.H., Xu, H., Dennis, J.M., Levy, M.N., Nychka, D., Mickelson, S.A., Edwards, J., Vertenstein, M., Wegener, A.: A methodology for evaluating the impact of data compression on climate simulation data. In: The 23rd International Symposium on High-Performance Parallel, pp. 203–214 (2014)
2. Bangerth, W., Hartmann, R., Kanschat, G.: deal.II - a general purpose object oriented finite element library. ACM Trans. Math. Softw. **33**(4), 24/1–24/27 (2007)
3. Burns, R.C., Long, D.D.E.: Efficient distributed backup with delta compression. In: Proceedings of the Fifth Workshop on I/O in Parallel and Distributed Systems, IOPADS 1997, New York, NY, USA, pp. 27–36. ACM (1997)

4. Housel, B.C., Lindquist, D.B.: Webexpress: a system for optimizing web browsing in a wireless environment. In: Proceedings of the 2nd Annual International Conference on Mobile Computing and Networking, MobiCom 1996, New York, NY, USA, pp. 108–116. ACM (1996)
5. Klappenecker, A., May, F.U.: Evolving better wavelet compression schemes. In: Proceedings of Wavelet Applications in Signal and Image Processing III, vol. 1214, pp. 614–622 (1995)
6. Lakshminarasimhan, S., Shah, N., Ethier, S., Klasky, S., Latham, R., Ross, R., Samatova, N.F.: Compressing the incompressible with ISABELA: in-situ reduction of spatio-temporal data. In: Jeannot, E., Namyst, R., Roman, J. (eds.) Euro-Par 2011. LNCS, vol. 6852, pp. 366–379. Springer, Heidelberg (2011). doi:10.1007/978-3-642-23400-2_34
7. Laros III, J.H., Pedretti, K.T., Kelly, S.M., Shu, W., Vaughan, C.T.: Energy based performance tuning for large scale high performance computing systems. In: Proceedings of the 2012 Symposium on High Performance Computing. Society for Computer Simulation International, p. 6 (2012)
8. Lofstead, J., Zheng, F., Klasky, S., Schwan, K.: Adaptable, metadata rich IO methods for portable high performance IO. In: IPDPS, Rome, Italy (2009)
9. Ludäscher, B., Altintas, I., Berkley, C., Higgins, D., Jaeger, E., Jones, M., Lee, E.A., Tao, J., Zhao, Y.: Scientific workflow management and the Kepler system: research articles. Concurr. Comput. Pract. Exper. **18**(10), 1039–1065 (2006)
10. Malewicz, G., Foster, I., Rosenberg, A., Wilde, M.: A tool for prioritizing DAGMan jobs and its evaluation. In: 2006 15th IEEE International Symposium on High Performance Distributed Computing, pp. 156–168 (2006)
11. Manber, U., Manber, U.: Finding similar files in a large file system. In: Proceedings of the USENIX Winter 1994 Technical Conference, pp. 1–10 (1994)
12. Mullender, S.J., Leslie, I.M., McAuley, D.: Operating-system support for distributed multimedia. In: Proceedings of the USENIX Summer 1994 Technical Conference on USENIX Summer 1994 Technical Conference, vol. 1, pp. 209–219 (1994)
13. Nicolae, B., Cappello, F.: Ai-ckpt: leveraging memory access patterns for adaptive asynchronous incremental checkpointing. In: Proceedings of the 22nd International Symposium on High-Performance Parallel and Distributed Computing, pp. 155–166. ACM (2013)
14. Plimpton, S.: Fast parallel algorithms for short-range molecular dynamics. J. Comput. Phys. **117**(1), 1–19 (1995)
15. Spring, N.T., Wetherall, D.: A protocol-independent technique for eliminating redundant network traffic. ACM SIGCOMM Comput. Commun. Rev. **30**(4), 87–95 (2000)
16. Xia, L., Hale, K.C., Dinda, P.A.: Concord: easily exploiting memory content redundancy through the content-aware service command. In: The 23rd International Symposium on High-Performance Parallel, pp. 25–36 (2014)

Investigating Read Performance of Python and NetCDF When Using HPC Parallel Filesystems

Matthew Jones[1]([✉]), Jon Blower[1], Bryan Lawrence[1,2,3], and Annette Osprey[1,3]

[1] Department of Meteorology, University of Reading, Reading, UK
m.jones3@pgr.reading.ac.uk
[2] STFC Rutherford Appleton Laboratory,
Centre for Environmental Data Analysis, Didcot, UK
[3] National Centre for Atmospheric Science, Manchester, UK

Abstract. New methods need to be developed to handle the increasing size of data sets in atmospheric science - traditional analysis scripts often inefficiently read and process the data. NetCDF4 is a common file format used in atmospheric and ocean sciences, and Python is widely used in atmospheric and ocean science data analysis. The aim of this work is to provide insight into which read patterns and sizes are most effective when using the netCDF4-python library. Quantitative information on these would be useful information for scientists, library developers, and data managers.

Three different read patterns were compared to simulate different types of reads: sequential, strided, and random, with each tested across three file systems - Panasas, Lustre, and GPFS. Read rate and standard deviation were measured using Python and C, reading from plain binary files and NetCDF4 files. Read performance for netCDF4-python was compared with the performance of native Python, the C NetCDF library, and the C Posix library.

As expected, comparison between the different read modes shows that access pattern and read size significantly affect achieved performance. The results also show read performance profiles that are similar for the C, C NetCDF, and Python tests, however netCDF4-python performs less efficiently.

1 Introduction

The efficiency of atmospheric data analysis scripts can be affected by many different factors in the software-hardware stack. Understanding these factors is paramount when designing efficient analysis scripts. This paper quantifies the effect of some of these elements. The remainder of this section describes these elements and provides motivation for this work.

As the resolution of atmospheric numerical models increase, so does the amount of data to be processed. This will become particularly prevalent with the sixth community model inter-comparison project (CMIP6 [4]) expected to produce 10–20 PB of data [14]. This volume of data means that high performance

© Springer International Publishing AG 2016
M. Taufer et al. (Eds.): ISC High Performance Workshops 2016, LNCS 9945, pp. 153–168, 2016.
DOI: 10.1007/978-3-319-46079-6_12

I/O is a critical requirement for efficient analysis code, and therefore productive scientific workflows [15].

The size of data sets means that traditional, serial data processing is a suboptimal solution; parallel processing data analysis methods are a solution to this. In order for parallel analysis scripts to be efficient, a scientist needs to be able to assess how best to decompose the reading of the data in terms of looping, and access patterns, without necessarily having the computer science background to know how the these would theoretically effect the read rate.

To understand how to efficiently implement a parallel analysis script one needs an appreciation of the bottlenecks that will affect each individual parallel process - from our experience of data analysis scripts in atmospheric science, most can be implemented in a pleasingly parallel way (easily paralellisable into non communicating jobs), so each concurrent job is independent. Therefore it is paramount to understand the I/O performance of each task. The initial step for this is to consider only the serial read performance with netCDF4-python on a parallel file system.

For data intensive algorithms, the slowest part of the algorithm is typically the I/O, so the read rate of the data from disk into memory becomes very important. File type, IO bandwidth, and the type of file system can all affect the read performance. Typically however, scientists do not have control over the hardware they run on, therefore performance benefits come from optimisation of the analysis code and carefully determining the layout of the data on the storage devices.

For many large data sets in atmospheric science, a file is generally written once and read from many times, so the work in this paper focusses on data reading. Since the structure of files can greatly affect the efficiency of analysis, it may be useful for data managers to know whether it is worth the extra initial overhead to organise the file in a way that will enable faster analysis; by chunking, compression, array order, file size and how the data is split into files.

The software contributions to the performance that need to be understood are depicted in Fig. 1. In order to understand the performance of the user application, the contribution of each layer needs to be accounted for.

One of the most widely used data formats in atmospheric science is the Network Common Data Format (NetCDF) [11] (for example two thirds of the data at the Centre for Environmental Data Analysis, CEDA [2] is in NetCDF format), and Python is often used to implement data analysis using scientific libraries in atmospheric science. NetCDF4 is used because it is a self describing, platform independent binary file format. NetCDF4 uses HDF5 (Hierarchical Data Format version 5). NetCDF3 is an older format of NetCDF but is not built on HDF5, so we have not tested NetCDF3.

HDF5 is a versatile, portable data format which can be used to store large data sets [6]. It allows NetCDF files to be chunked and compressed [20]. Chunking allows files to be reorganised on disk for different access patterns [24]. These chunks can be compressed to reduce the size of data on disk. Chunking and compression can have a large effect on the read rate [10].

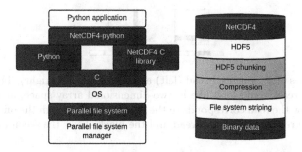

Fig. 1. The left image shows the software stack for applications built on NetCDF4-python. The netCDF4-python library relies on Python (some of which is written in C) and the C NetCDF library. C interfaces with the operating system (OS) which interfaces with the parallel file system to access the NetCDF4 data files. The right image depicts the NetCDF4 data format. NetCDF is built on HDF5, which is a type of binary file. Areas shaded in black are being tested in this paper, and areas shaded in grey will be covered in future work.

Data can be split across multiple disk in a parallel file system by striping. This can increase the access rate by exploiting all the disks the file is split across [21].

Scientists working with large data sets often have to decide what subsections of data to analyse and how their code will read, and possibly stream (here meaning reading a section at a time in 'buffers'), the data from disk using libraries. The libraries then determine how the file is read from the raw bytes, often employing a buffer to read the data into memory. The data managers have also decided the structure and organisation of the data on disk. All of these factors can effect the read rate, so it would be useful to know where in this workflow inefficiencies in performance lie.

Since analysis is often over part of the data set, it is useful to know what read sizes offer best performance. Bartz et al. [10] show that the read size has a significant effect on the read rate. Quantitative information about what read buffer sizes work well would also be useful in the future when exploiting tiered memory.

Accessing slices in two dimensional or higher data may require non-sequential access which can significantly affect the read rate, although this can be reduced by using a sensible read pattern strategy [11]. Figure 2 shows two potential read patterns. The read pattern which is sequential on disk is expected to have have a much higher read rate than the one which strides through the file.

To provide a broader more widely relevant testing base, more than a single platform is used in this study. The focus of this paper is on the extent that different layers in the software-hardware stack affect the read rate, rather than a rigorous comparison between the platforms. The aim of this work is to understand the read performance of netCDF4-python in different realistic situations, on multiple analysis platforms, so that environmental big data can be analysed more efficiently.

Fig. 2. Examples of a sequential read (left) and a strided read (right). The top images show what the read would look like in two-dimensional array space, and the bottom images show how the read corresponds to the read pattern through the one-dimensional file space. The grey shows the first read and the black shows the second read.

Tests were run on three analysis platforms which are available to the UK atmospheric science research community: JASMIN which uses the Panasas file system [19], the UK Research Data Facility (RDF) which uses the GPFS file system, and ARCHER which uses the Lustre file system [1]. JASMIN and RDF are specialised data analysis systems and ARCHER is a general purpose high performance computer. The methodology of the tests and architectures of the analysis platforms is discussed in Sect. 2. The initial stage of the investigation to determine the baseline performance of each of the platforms is detailed in Sect. 3, Python and NetCDF on JASMIN are evaluated in Sect. 4. Related work is covered in Sect. 5 and finally, overall conclusions are drawn in Sect. 6.

2   Methodology

Performance can be lost at different layers of the software stack, so the contributions of software layers thought to be key to the performance were evaluated. Firstly the baseline read performance of each system was measured by reading a plain binary file using a C program. This was compared to a plain binary file read from Python, and reads of a NetCDF file from C and Python. The netCDF4-python library is built on the NetCDF4 C library (as shown in Fig. 1) so understanding what contribution the C library has is paramount in completing the picture.

Three read methods were evaluated: sequential reads, strided reads (also known as striding reads), and random reads. Examples of the sequential and strided reads are shown in Fig. 2. The sequential reads access the whole file sequentially, reading sections of a given read buffer size until the whole file is read. The buffer sizes used started at 512 b and doubled up to the largest block size of 1 GiB - a complete file read for each buffer size composed a single experiment. Strided reads read one buffer size then a new read offset is calculated to skip the amount of data equal to three times the buffer size, this process is repeated for the entire file, i.e. reading one buffer then skipping three. For the random reads, a set of uniformly distributed numbers were generated for the read offsets, the read is then for the required buffer size. 100 reads are completed for the random reads to keep the chance of re-reading a section of the file from cache low (reading from cache would artificially decrease the read time from disk). The random reads differ from the other reads in that the direction of the read is not always forward and the size of the strides through the file vary. A summary of the tests performed is included in Table 1. Below is a pseudo code example of each read.

```
# Sequential read
f = open(filename)
for number of buffers:
    data = f.read(buffersize)

# Strided read
f = open(filename)
readoffset = 0
for number of buffers:
    f.seek(readoffset)
    data = f.read(buffersize)
    readoffset = readoffset + 4*buffersize

# Random read
f = open(filename)
readoffsets = genrandoffsets(length=100)
for offset in readoffsets:
    f.seek(offset)
    data = f.read(buffersize)
```

The reads from 'plain' binary files include the seek shown. For the NetCDF4 files the buffer size is converted into a number of floats, as is the read offset, so that each read is described by start and stop indices.

Table 1. Variables which compose each test in this paper. The tests using C and Python read from plain binary files, and the tests using NetCDF C and netCDF4-python read from NetCDF4 files. Not all the combinations possible here were done on all platforms - Python plain binary tests and NetCDF tests were only done on JASMIN due to resource constraints.

Filesystem	Language and library	Read mode	Read block size
Panasas	C	sequential	512 b
Lustre	NetCDF C	strided	doubling
GPFS	Python	random	to 1 GiB
	netCDF4-python		

The sequential reads were designed to simulate a best case scenario where the read from the file is contiguous - a read where the bytes in the file are stored next to each other. The strided reads are designed to simulate a read which is not contiguous in the file with a regular stride pattern through the file. This is representative of a slice through a dimension which is not stored contiguously in the file (where there are two or more dimensions). The random reads simulate a worst case scenario, where the direction of the reads through the file are not consistent, and neither is the size of the hop.

For the binary tests using C and Python, a plain binary file was created on each system using the Linux dd command. To avoid disk buffering as much as possible, the file size was set to be over twice the size of the RAM of the system. The file size on all platforms was 256 GiB (275 GB). The plain binary file was read using fseek() and fread() in C and f.seek() and f.read() in Python.

The netCDF4-python library was used to create the NetCDF4 files for testing. The file, as with the binary files, was created to be over twice the size of the RAM on the compute nodes. The file size on each platform was 257 GiB, and the file contained a single 1D contiguous (not chunked) variable consisting of 8 byte floating point numbers. Each read size was converted into a number of elements to stream from the file on each read.

2.1   Testing Platforms

A parallel (or distributed) file system differs from a non-parallel file system in that the data can be distributed across multiple storage devices which can be accessed simultaneously to increase the bandwidth to the file system [21].

JASMIN (Panasas Platform). The JASMIN system at the Science and Technology Facilities Council (STFC) uses a Panasas storage system [19]. The Panasas sub-system is composed of bladesets, composed of shelves, that in turn contain blades, that are each made up of two disks. The blades are connected to the shelf via 1 Gb/s ports, and the shelves are connected to the local area network via one 10 Gb/s port (newer options have two 10 Gb/s connections). The compute cluster is composed of nodes, with each connected to the storage system and to each other via a non blocking 10 Gb/s network. The Panasas file system handles how to physically store the objects on disk and the most efficient way to access them, i.e. giving the shortest possible access time [24]. This gives a theoretical maximum bandwidth to a single processing node of 1.25 GB/s. The compute nodes used here have 128 GB RAM. In Panasas, files can be striped using the RAID6 method, in which a large file is split across multiple blades (small files are copied) with included redundancy [21]. This means that the file can be read from multiple different blades increasing the read performance, theoretically, by a factor of the number of blades and bladesets. The manager nodes have the metadata describing where and how the files are stored [24].

RDF (GPFS Platform). The UK Research Data Facility (UK-RDF) HPC platform uses GPFS (General Parallel File System), with Infiniband connections between the storage and compute nodes. The compute nodes used have 128 GB RAM. Filesystem metadata is stored on solid state drives (SSDs), with the data stored on hard disk drives (HDDs) on four storage arrays [1]. GPFS is a parallel file system that can increase bandwidth by exploiting multiple network shared disks [17]. The storage for GPFS is connected to network shared disk servers, which are connected to the local area network which is in turn connected to the processing nodes [17].

ARCHER (Lustre Platform). The ARCHER platform (a Cray XC30) uses a high performance Lustre file system. The compute nodes used have 64 GB RAM, and are connected by Cray Aries interconnect [1]. Lustre is an open source parallel file system which uses many object storage servers with metadata servers to store data [9]. The object storage targets are connected to object storage servers which are all connected to the local area network, and there is a manager node which is connected to all the object storage severs. Metadata servers are connected directly to the local area network, and to the object storage serves via the manager node [9].

3 Baseline Performance

3.1 JASMIN (Panasas)

Figure 3 shows the plain binary read performance using C and Python on JAS-MIN. The Python rate is lower at higher read block size than the C results possibly because Python has to convert the raw bytes into a native Python type, a string in this case, indicated by more time spent in CPU than IO compared to the C case.

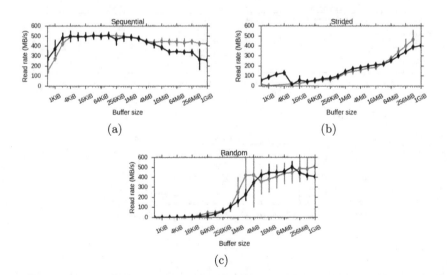

(a)

(b)

(c)

Fig. 3. Average read rate (diamonds) and one standard deviation (error bars) for the tests reading from a binary file on JASMIN. Grey lines show the results using C and black lines show the results using Python. (a) shows the sequential reads, (b) shows strided reads, and (c) shows random reads.

Strace [7] was used to look at reads in more detail. For the C sequential reads, there is one slow read of about 100 MB/s followed by read of around 460 MB/s and then 6 fast reads of about 3 GB/s, repeating throughout the file. This behaviour was not seen on the strided or random reads, each read following a seek and being slow.

The profiles of the strided read with C and Python are very similar throughout the whole range of read block sizes starting with very low read rates, increasing to around 400 MB/s at 512 MiB. The variability for the remaining read block sizes for each remains low.

The random read profile increases in a similar way to the strided reads, although with much higher variability when using C. It is not clear what has caused this variability.

The Python tests were not run on the other platforms because of the similarity between the C read rate and the Python read rate on JASMIN.

3.2   RDF (GPFS)

The results for the C plain binary reads on RDF are shown in Fig. 4. The profile for the sequential reads is similar to the JASMIN results, albeit at higher bandwidth because of the Infiniband used on RDF compared to 10 Gb/s Ethernet in JASMIN. The variability for the strided reads is high which makes the profile more difficult to interpret. It is interesting however that the average strided reads are consistently higher than the random reads.

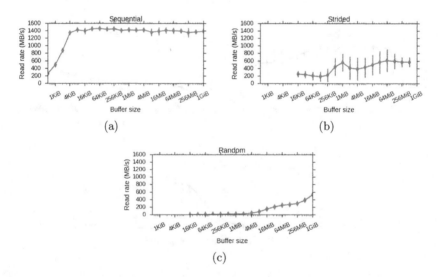

Fig. 4. Average read rate (diamonds) and one standard deviation (error bars) for the tests reading from a binary file on RDF using the C script. (a) shows the sequential reads, (b) shows the strided reads, and (c) shows the random reads.

3.3   ARCHER (Lustre)

The results for the binary read on ARCHER are shown in Fig. 5. The results are similar to the JASMIN results.

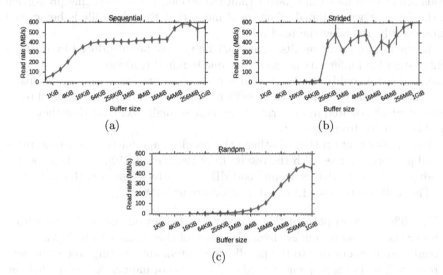

(a)   (b)

(c)

Fig. 5. Average read rate (diamonds) and one standard deviation (error bars) for the tests reading from a binary file on ARCHER using the C script. (a) shows the sequential reads, (b) shows the strided reads, and (c) shows the random reads.

3.4   Discussion

The JASMIN and ARCHER results have similar characteristics. All the results show the same increase at the start of the sequential results at low buffer size. This is likely to be due to the reads being smaller than disk sector size, although we have not verified this. For all platforms the sequential reads are the fastest. The random reads and strided reads have similar profiles and have a lower read rate partly because of having to seek through the file. The effect of this is reduced at large buffer size due to larger read sizes.

The strace results also explain some of the difference between the read rate. The 3 GB/s read could not have come from disk (1.25 GB/s bandwidth to processing nodes) so the 3 GB/s read is due to a read from memory on the processing node; the filesystem is anticipating what data is needed ahead of time. This behaviour is not seen for the strided or random reads, so could explain the reduced read rate, because the file system not being able to anticipate the location of the next required sections of data.

The RDF results, however, show a different relationship between the sequential, strided and random reads, with the sequential reads being a similar profile to the other results but with a much larger magnitude, due to the Inifiniband LAN. The strided read rate is much lower than the sequential read rate and the random reads are of even lower magnitude. It is unclear why the relationship between the read rates is not more similar to the other platforms. The sequential reads are around four times faster than the strided reads, the same proportion of the file that was skipped. This could mean that the whole file is being read unnecessarily, reducing the read rate.

In the random read results, some variability may be introduced by inadvertent system file buffer hits because only one hundred reads were involve in each case, and some could have been from very close to previous reads in file space. This interpretation is supported by evidence from additional constant seed tests, some of which resulted in data rates that were so high (3 GiB/s) that they must have been reads from memory.

Our results confirm that of others: the profile shape for the sequential reads for all platforms agrees with the results from Bartz et al. [10], and the expected bandwidth on ARCHER is around 500 MB/s [16] which agrees with our results.

The main conclusions from this section are as follows:

- The different read patterns have a very large effect on the read rate, with a lesser effect at larger buffer sizes. The cause of this is likely to be because of a read from memory due to the parallel file system anticipating where the next reads will be in the sequential reads. This does not happen in the strided and random reads, which are also slower due to having to seek through the file much more frequently.
- Read rate drops significantly at very small buffer size which agrees with results from Bartz et al. [10].
- There is very little difference between C and Python when reading plain binary files.
- Read rate profiles between the different platforms were similar, but different in magnitude.

4   NetCDF Performance

To investigate the effect of NetCDF, the experiment from Sect. 3.1 was repeated using the C NetCDF library and the netCDF4-python library (on JASMIN only due to resource constraints). Figure 6 shows the results. The C results look similar to the results when reading from a plain binary file, but the Python performance is reduced. A reduction in performance is seen in the Python profile for read block sizes less than 64 KiB.

The drop in read rate above 1 MiB buffer size could be caused by Numpy arrays - netCDF4-python uses them. To eliminate Numpy as a factor in the performance drop a test was run using Numpy to read the plain binary files. This gave similar results to the Python profile in Fig. 3, indicating that the significantly lower read rate seen in the netCDF4-python results was not caused by Numpy.

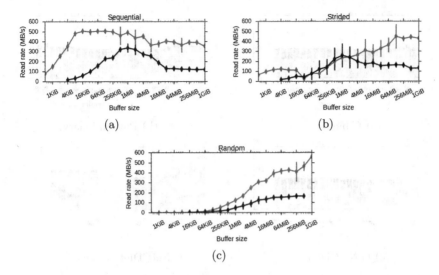

Fig. 6. Average read rate (diamonds) and one standard deviation (error bars) for the tests reading from a NetCDF4 file on JASMIN. Grey lines show the results using C and black lines show the results using Python. (a) shows the sequential reads, (b) shows strided reads, and (c) shows random reads.

To further investigate the reasons for the drop in performance of netCDF4-python, the CPU time was measured using the POSIX `clock` [3] function in C and the equivalent function from the Python time library [8]. Figure 7 shows the comparison between wall time and CPU time for the sequential read tests on JASMIN. The results for the C tests reading from plain binary files and NetCDF4 files show a very similar pattern, with the CPU time decreasing as the buffer size increases, the CPU time not being a limiting factor after 4 KiB. For the Python test reading from a plain binary file the pattern is similar, but the CPU increases after 16 MiB (also seen in the Numpy tests previously mentioned), but not to be a limiting factor. The netCDF4-python results, however, show that the CPU is the limiting factor for the reads, causing the performance reduction.

The strided reads with netCDF4-python follow a similar profile to the sequential reads, albeit with much higher variability and are similar to the C strided read until 16 MiB where the CPU overhead has a more significant effect. The similarity between the netCDF4-python strided reads and the sequential reads is due to the CPU limited behaviour of both read types. The random C profile looks similar to the Python, and the other JASMIN results, with the netCDF4-python results performing worse, especially at large buffer size.

The CPU limited behaviour explains the significantly reduction in the read rate for netCDF4-python compared to the other tests (being I/O limited).

Brief testing with another Python library reading from NetCDF4 files using the HDF5 library h5netcdf [5], shown in Fig. 8, indicate that this extra CPU use is not needed; when using h5py the read rate is I/O limited, not CPU limited.

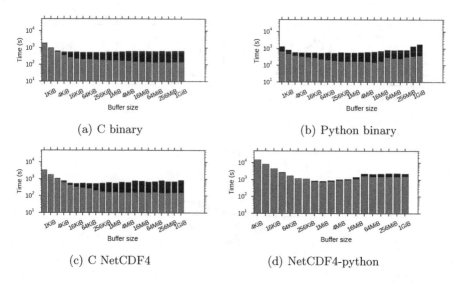

Fig. 7. Comparison between average wall time and CPU time for the different sequential read tests on JASMIN. Black bars show wall time, and grey bars show CPU time. (Note: bars overlap, and CPU time in these tests will not be greater than wall time)

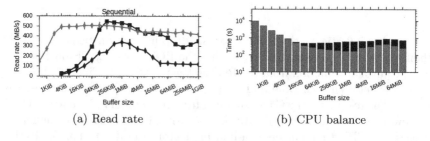

Fig. 8. Comparison between sequential rates for C binary read (grey), netCDF4-python read (black diamonds), and read using h5py Python library (black squares); and CPU wall time balance for reads using h5netcdf; black bars show wall time, and grey bars show CPU time.

The balance between CPU use and wall time show that this is I/O bound rather than CPU bound.

The Linux utility strace was also used to retrieve some more information about the I/O calls when using the netCDF4-python library. The pattern for the read types is similar to the plain binary test; the difference between read types is caused by read ahead for the sequential reads. The read sizes below 64 KiB have a reduction in performance because a read below this is always at least 64 KiB, i.e. even a for a 4 KiB read, the netCDF4-python library sends a read I/O call for 64 KiB, therefore reducing the effective read rate for low read sizes.

The main conclusions from this section are as follows:

- The C NetCDF4 read performance is very similar to read performance when reading plain binary files using C and Python.
- Using netCDF4-python the performance is lower generally, but is significantly reduced at buffer sizes of 8 MiB and higher.
- The results from the HDF5 Python library and CPU balance indicate that the performance of netCDF4-python could be improved by making more efficient use of CPU.
- Peak read rate using netCDF4-python is at around 1 MiB buffer size.
- The performance below 64 KiB for Python reading from NetCDF4 files is due to the library always reading at least 64 KiB.

5 Related Work

A solution for high speed, efficient I/O is to use a parallel data model, such as parallel-netcdf [15], or MPI-IO. The focus here is on what effect the non-parallel libraries have on the performance on a parallel HPC file system, so as to advise scientists on better read sizes and patterns to improve design of parallel data analysis code, therefore the parallel libraries were not used. Also here we have concentrated on a single processing node, with intent to extend this to multiple nodes in future work. The parallel I/O library approach would mean that scientists would have to rewrite much of their analysis script, which may not mean an efficient development workflow.

Compression can reduce the amount of data stored and reduce the size of data being transferred from disk, therefore increasing read performance. Compression can also reduce the cost of storing data [18].

In theory an object store (such as CEPH, [23]) might be able to provide high performance I/O, since if the file were chunked those chunks could be stored in an object store and retrieved in parallel in an arbitrary order - meaning that no particular order would be preferential. However, we are not aware of any practical instances of NetCDF files being stored in this manner - although we are involved in building a test bed to investigate this possibility.

A Hadoop framework could also be used to increase the I/O performance - the compute nodes have the data locally on the node rather than stored separately. Data being on the processing node is an efficient solution if the analysis always requires the same data layout. In atmospheric science, however, different analysis may have very different dimensional dependencies so the possible need for repeated transfer of data for Hadoop-type processing on different data layouts might lead to significant inefficiency.

Hadoop and MapReduce grew out of the need to analyse large volumes of data whereas in HPC the focus was on processing speed. However now that scientific datasets are getting so large a link between these two paradigms would be useful [13]. There are groups working on using Hadoop and MapReduce for scientific problems (for example [12,22]), but the focus in our work is on advising end users about effective analysis of large data sets on HPC-type architectures with parallel file systems. Also, there are large conceptual differences between HPC-type analysis and Hadoop-type analysis, namely that in Hadoop the data is on the processing nodes, and in HPC the data is not.

6   Conclusions

We identified the performance loss in the NetCDF4 performance stack by running tests using C and Python when reading from plain binary files and NetCDF4 files. The drop in read rate performance was found to be in the netCDF4-python library, and not due to either Python or the NetCDF4 file format. The main conclusions from this work are:

- The netCDF4-python library performs less efficiently than the other tests, giving a lower read rate, which was especially prevalent at small (less than 64 KiB) and large (greater than 8 MiB) buffer size, with peak performance at a buffer size of about 1 MiB. This drop in read rate could have a significant performance impact on analysis scripts which use netCDF4-python. This decrease in performance is caused by the netCDF4-python library reads being CPU bound so not utilising the bandwidth of the node.
- There is little difference between the performance of C reading from plain binary files, Python reading from plain binary files, and C reading from NetCDF4 files.
- The read pattern has a large effect on the performance of a read, meaning that any seeking done in an analysis script is very expensive. Therefore, keeping as many reads as possible contiguous on disk is very important.

These results could have implications in the design of analysis scripts, and choices made when deciding what sized chunks to use in NetCDF4. The buffer size of around 1 MiB may be the most efficient size for reads and chunk sizes, but the compromise between more efficient reads and higher quantity of reads needs discerning. Also, avoiding any reads of less than 64 KiB would benefit performance.

The results showing that sequential reads are significantly more efficient means that for analysis script to be most efficient as much of the reading done from a file should be contiguous. This could be taken advantage of in strided reads by splitting the read into parallel threads.

Another important implication is that NetCDF4 is read at the same rate as plain binary files. This means that there is no disadvantage to reading from NetCDF4 files.

The effects of chunking, compression, and multithreading will be investigated in future work. This would then mean that a quantitative cost model could be built to estimate how much time would be spent doing I/O tasks, which could potentially be overlapped with CPU tasks. Knowledge of all of these things would then inform the end user designing parallel data analysis code enabling more efficient code to be written with less trial and error, hence optimising the development workflow.

Other interesting results which could come from this are from the perspective of data managers. They would need to decide if having chunked and compressed files benefit scientists enough to justify the overhead of implementation when formatting large multi-user datasets.

References

1. ARCHER User Guide. http://www.archer.ac.uk/documentation/user-guide/
2. Centre for Environmental Data Analysis. http://www.ceda.ac.uk/
3. clock. http://pubs.opengroup.org/onlinepubs/009695399/functions/clock.html
4. CMIP6. http://www.wcrp-climate.org/wgcm-cmip/wgcm-cmip6
5. h5netcdf 0.2.2. https://pypi.python.org/pypi/h5netcdf/
6. HDF Group. https://www.hdfgroup.org/HDF5/
7. strace(1) - Linux man page. http://linux.die.net/man/1/strace
8. time - Time access and conversions. https://docs.python.org/2/library/time.html
9. Barton, E., Dilger, A.: High Performance Parallel I/O. CRC Press, Boca Raton (2015). Chap. 8, pp. 91–106
10. Bartz, C., Chasapis, K., Kuhn, M., Nerge, P., Ludwig, T.: A best practice analysis of HDF5 and NetCDF-4 using Lustre. In: Kunkel, J.M., Ludwig, T. (eds.) ISC High Performance 2015. LNCS, vol. 9137, pp. 274–281. Springer, Heidelberg (2015). doi:10.1007/978-3-319-20119-1_20
11. Blower, J., Gemmell, A., Griffiths, G., Haines, K., Santokhee, A., Yang, X.: A Web Map Service implementation for the visualization of multidimensional gridded environmental data, September 2013. http://centaur.reading.ac.uk/31396/12/ncWMS_paper_EMS_2013.pdf
12. Buck, J.B., Watkins, N., Lefevre, J., Maltzahn, C., Brandt, S.: SciHadoop : array-based query processing in Hadoop categories and subject descriptors. In: Proceedings of 2011 International Conference for High Performance Computing, Networking, Storage and Analysis, p. 66 (2011)
13. Castain, R.H., Kulkarni, O., Zhenyu, X.: MapReduce and running Hadoop in a high performance computing environment Lustre : Agenda. In: Lustre User Group 2013, China and Japan (2013)
14. Cinquini, L., Crichton, D.J., Braverman, A.J., Kyo, L., Fuchs, T., Turmon, M.: Dawn: A Simulation Model for Evaluating Costs and Tradeoffs of Big Data Science Architectures. AGU Fall Meeting Abstracts, p. 3, December 2014
15. Gao, K., Jin, C., Choudhary, A., Liao, W.K.: Supporting computational data model representation with high-performance I/O in parallel netCDF. In: 18th International Conference on High Performance Computing, HiPC 2011 (2011)
16. Henty, D., Jackson, A., Moulinec, C., Szeremi, V.: Performance of Parallel IO on ARCHER (2015). http://www.archer.ac.uk/documentation/white-papers/parallelIO/ARCHER_wp_parallelIO.pdf
17. Hildebrand, D., Schmuck, F.: High Performance Parallel I/O. CRC Press, Boca Raton (2015). Chap. 9, pp. 91–106
18. Hübbe, N., Kunkel, J.: Reducing the HPC-datastorage footprint with MAFISC multidimensional adaptive filtering improved scientific data compression. Comput. Sci. Res. Dev. 28(2–3), 231–239 (2012)
19. Lawrence, B.N., Bennett, V.L., Churchill, J., Juckes, M., Kershaw, P., Pascoe, S., Pritchard, M., Stephens, A., Pepler, S.: Storing and manipulating environmental big data with JASMIN. In: IEEE Big Data 2013 (2013)

20. Lee, C., Yang, M., Aydt, R.: NetCDF-4 Performance Report. Technical report, HDF Group (2008)
21. Silberschatz, A., Baer Galvin, P., Gagne, G.: Operating System Concepts, 9th edn. Wiley, Hoboken (2013)
22. Srirama, S.N., Jakovits, P., Vainikko, E.: Adapting scientific computing problems to clouds using MapReduce. Future Gener. Comput. Syst. **28**(1), 184–192 (2012)
23. Weil, S.A., Brandt, S.A., Miller, E.L., Long, D.D.E., Maltzahn, C.: Ceph: a scalable, high-performance distributed file system. In: Proceedings of the 7th Symposium on Operating Systems Design and Implementation, pp. 307–320. USENIX Association, November 2006
24. Welch, B., Unangst, M., Abbasi, Z., Gibson, G., Mueller, B., Small, J., Zelenka, J., Zhou, B.: White paper scalable performance of the Panasas parallel file system. In: 6th USENIX Conference on File and Storage Technologies (FAST 2008), pp. 1–22, May 2010

IWOPH

International Workshop on OpenPOWER for HPC (IWOPH)

Oscar R. Hernandez[1], M. Graham Lopez[1], Dirk Pleiter[2],
and Jack Wells[1]

[1] Oak Ridge National Laboratory, Oak Ridge, TN 37831, USA
{oscar,lopezmg,wellsjc}@ornl.gvo
[2] Forschungszentrum Jülich, 52425 Jülich, Germany
d.pleiter@fz-juelich.de

Abstract. The InternationalWorkshop on OpenPOWER for HPC Proceedings provided a venue for broader community to explore OpenPOWER technologies for their research and development activities. It allowed both application experts and experts on different technologies to exchange experiences with using technologies from this new ecosystem.

Keywords: OpenPOWER · POWER8 · GPU acceleration · Applications · Programming models · Data analytics · Energy efficiency

The OpenPOWER Foundation was established as a non-profit consortium to give its members the ability to innovate on software and hardware solutions based on the POWER architecture. About half of the members are from academia. One of the Foundation's goals is for OpenPOWER technologies to drive innovation within HPC. As scientific workloads and demands increase, advances are being enabled by Open-POWER member collaborations throughout the HPC software stack from the low-level hardware architecture up through application and next generation programming model designs. The goal of this workshop was to provide a venue for the broader HPC community to further understand OpenPOWER technologies and discuss how they can be harnessed for HPC applications needs.

Most of the contributions reported on experiences made during porting to and optimization for POWER8-based architectures with or without GPU acceleration. Furthermore, insight was provided on the obtained performance. In several papers the results are compared to other architectures, namely Intel E5-2600 v3 processors. Application portfolios, which have been analysed, range from a set of skeleton, financial and CFD benchmarks [5], CFD applications based on the Lattice Boltzmann method and FFT benchmarks [1] to 3-dimensional combustion simulation codes [2]. A significant amount of efforts have already been invested into bringing molecular dynamics applications to the new architecture, e.g. CPMD [8] as well as NAMD and VMD [7].

Another topic addressed during this workshop was the use of programming models for enabling portability, as well as programming frameworks for data analytics applications. The heterogeneous OpenPOWER platform is used to demonstrate the effectiveness of the porting interface 'cupla' for the particle-in-cell code PIConGPU [9]. To address graph-based applications using OpenPOWER hardware, Spark/GraphX has been evaluated as a processing framework for several important graph kernels [4].

For any new HPC architecture, the ability to measure power and determine energy efficiency characteristics are of keen interest. The AMESTER framework, which has recently been open-sourced, is capable of performing such measurements [6]. This technology was also the basis for the energy efficiency analysis and modeling results that have been presented for different applications for designing optical elements as well as explore materials [3].

Within an overall view, the contributions give a good overview on the status of exploitation of OpenPOWER architectures and technologies for both, scientific computing as well as industrial applications. Sharing a common background given by the technology ecosystem facilitated fruitful interactions, which extended far beyond what could be documented in these proceedings.

References

1. Ashworth, M., Meng, J., Novakovic, V., Siso-Enric, S.: Early application performance at the Hartree Centre with the OpenPOWER architecture. In: Taufer, M., et al. (Eds.) ISC High Performance Workshops 2016. LNCS, Vol. 9945, pp. 173–187. Springer, Switzerland (2016)
2. Berreth, A., Risio, B., Bühler, M., Anlauf, B., Vezolle, P.: Performance of the 3D combustion simulation code RECOM-AIOLOS on IBM POWER8 architecture. In: Taufer, M., et al. (Eds.) ISC High Performance Workshops 2016. LNCS, Vol. 9945, pp. 286–294. Springer, Switzerland (2016)
3. Hater, T., Anlauf, B., Baumeister, P., Bühler, M., Kraus, J., Pleiter, D.: Exploring energy efficiency for GPU-accelerated POWER servers. In: Taufer, M., et al. (Eds.) ISC High Performance Workshops 2016. LNCS, Vol. 9945, pp. 207–227. Springer, Switzerland (2016)
4. Que, X., Schneidenbach, L., Checconi, F., Costa, C.H., Buono, D.: Performance analysis of Spark/GraphX on POWER8 cluster In: Taufer, M., et al. (Eds.) ISC High Performance Workshops 2016. LNCS, Vol. 9945, pp. 268–285. Springer, Switzerland (2016)
5. Reguly, I.Z., Keita, A.K., Zurob, R., Giles, M.: High performance computing on the IBM Power8 platform. In: Taufer, M., et al. (Eds.) ISC High Performance Workshops 2016. LNCS, Vol. 9945, pp. 235–254. Springer, Switzerland (2016)
6. Rosedahl, T., Lefurgy, C., Broyles, M.: Measuring and managing energy in OpenPOWER. In: Taufer, M., et al. (Eds.) ISC High Performance Workshops 2016. LNCS, Vol. 9945, pp. 255–265. Springer, Switzerland (2016)
7. Stone, J.E., Hynninen, A.P., Phillips, J.C., Schulten, K.: Early experiences porting the NAMD and VMD molecular simulation and analysis software to GPU-accelerated Open-POWER platforms. In: Taufer, M., et al. (Eds.) ISC High Performance Workshops 2016. LNCS, Vol. 9945, pp. 188–206. Springer, Switzerland (2016)

8. Weber, V., Cristiano, A., Malossi, I., Tavernelli, I., Laino, T., Bekas, C., Modani, M., Wilner, N., Heller, T., Curioni, A.: First experiences with ab initio molecular dynamics on OpenPOWER: the case of CPMD. In: Taufer, M., et al. (Eds.) ISC High Performance Workshops 2016. LNCS, Vol. 9945, pp. 228–234. Springer, Switzerland (2016)
9. Zenker, E., Widera, R., Hübl, A., Juckeland, G., Andreas, K., Nagel, W.E., Bussmann, M.: Performance-portable many-core plasma simulations: porting PICon-GPU to OpenPower and beyond. In: Taufer, M., et al. (Eds.) ISC High Performance Workshops 2016. LNCS, Vol. 9945, pp. 293–301. Springer, Switzerland (2016)

Early Application Performance at the Hartree Centre with the OpenPOWER Architecture

Mike Ashworth$^{(\boxtimes)}$, Jianping Meng, Vedran Novakovic,
and Sersi Siso

Scientific Computing Department, STFC Daresbury Laboratory,
Sci-Tech Daresbury, Warrington WA4 4AD, UK
{mike.ashworth,jianping.meng,vedran.novakovic,
sergi.siso}@stfc.ac.uk

Abstract. The Hartree Centre has been established as a UK focus for indus-trial engagement. STFC has acquired a new IBM system based on the Open-POWER architecture, comprising 32 nodes with POWER8 CPUs and NVIDIA Kepler K80 GPUs. We report early evaluation of the system using some real applications based on the Lattice Boltzmann Method, Direct Numerical Sim-ulation of Turbulence and using FFTs. No optimisation has been carried out yet, but results are encouraging with performance comparable or better on a per core basis to Intel IvyBridge CPUs. Use of the GPUs for suitable algorithms such as Lattice Boltzmann kernels and for FFTs provides further performance enhancements.

1 The Hartree Centre

STFC's Hartree Centre was established in 2012 located at STFC Daresbury Laboratory, near Warrington, United Kingdom. Initial funding for the centre came from the UK Government department for Business Innovation and Skills (BIS) as a result of rec-ommendations for increased funding for e-infrastructure made in the Tildesley report [13]. The Hartree Centre was established with a focus on industrial engagement, using modelling and simulation capabilities accelerated by high-performance computing to deliver economic impact.

In 2013 there was a further injection of funding focusing on energy efficiency and data analytics. A major announcement followed in 2015 with significant further UK Government investment in extended industrial and scientific reach through the exploitation of data centric and cognitive computing technologies. This latest devel-opment of the Hartree Centre is underpinned by a five-year agreement with IBM establishing a significant presence of IBM Research staff on the Daresbury site.

The Hartree Centre is enabling companies of all sizes to tackle diverse challenges using the latest developments in high-performance and data-intensive computing, with many returning customers bringing new projects. The value and insight provided to

© Springer International Publishing AG 2016
M. Taufer et al. (Eds.): ISC High Performance Workshops 2016, LNCS 9945, pp. 173–187, 2016.
DOI: 10.1007/978-3-319-46079-6_13

businesses is demonstrated by a set of case studies which are available at the Hartree Centre website[1].

The Hartree Centre has a mission to bring the benefits of high-performance computing and data science to industry and commerce, using hardware and software capabilities exploited by skilled and experienced staff. The centre works in tandem with STFC's Scientific Computing Department, which has about 180 staff roughly equally divided between STFC's Daresbury Laboratory and the Rutherford Appleton Laboratory. Key areas of specialisation include applications expertise in a wide range of science areas such as computational chemistry, CFD and engineering, materials science, life sciences and environmental modelling, underpinned by technical expertise in data management, energy efficient computing, numerical analysis, performance optimisation, software engineering, and visualisation.

We provide services to clients from across industry, government and academia based upon a service model comprising:

- access to HPC platforms
- consultancy & professional services
- software development
- collaborative R&D
- training & education

This instruction file for Word users (there is a separate instruction file for LaTeX users) may be used as a template. Kindly send the final and checked Word and PDF files of your paper to the Contact Volume Editor. This is usually one of the organizers of the conference. You should make sure that the Word and the PDF files are identical and correct and that only one version of your paper is sent. It is not possible to update files at a later stage. Please note that we do not need the printed paper.

2   POWER Application Design Centre

STFC is a member of the OpenPOWER Foundation[2]. On 22 October 2015 the Hartree Centre was announced as the UK's first POWER Acceleration and Design Centre (PADC). The aim of the PADC is to improve modelling, simulation and big data analytical capabilities on IBM's OpenPOWER systems.

The STFC PADC is working on the design and optimisation of applications across a range of HPC and data intensive workloads for modelling and simulation and data analytics. Simulations cover almost the full range of length and time scales from sub-atomic processes to environmental modelling at global scales, with a strong focus on bridging length and time scales through coupled multi-scale and multi-physics capabilities.

---

[1] Hartree Centre Case Studies http://www.stfc.ac.uk/about-us/our-impacts-achievements/case-studies/hartree-centre-case-studies/.

[2] OpenPOWER Foundation http://openpowerfoundation.org/.

3   The POWER8 System 'Panther'

STFC has recently taken delivery of an IBM compute platform 'Panther' using the OpenPOWER architecture, comprising POWER8 CPUs and NVIDIA K80 GPUs supported by InfiniBand interconnect and disk and flash storage (Fig. 1). The specification of the system is as follows:

- 32 compute nodes
- 2 sockets × 8 cores @ 3.32 GHz
- 28 nodes with 512 GB RAM
- 4 nodes with 1 TB RAM
- 2 × NVIDIA K80 GPU
- 2 × 1 TB HDD
- InfiniBand (FDR)
- 2 × IBM ESS GS4 storage arrays,
- 96 × 800 GB SSD
- IBM FlashStorage 900 57 TB (InfiniBand QDR attached)
- IBM FlashStorage 900 57 TB (CAPI attached)

Fig. 1. The Panther system shortly after delivery to STFC Daresbury Laboratory; ribbons and bows courtesy of OCF plc.

Some results presented were obtained using an earlier pre-production system 'Palmerston'. In this system there are four 8-core sockets giving 24 POWER8 physical cores per node running at 3.32 GHz and two NVIDIA Tesla K40 GPU accelerators. For the POWER8 system, we use the IBM XL C/C++ V13.1.2 compiler for the POWER8 CPU and the NVIDIA CUDA 7.0 SDK for the K40 GPU on Palmerston and CUDA 7.5 for the K80 on Panther. OpenMPI 1.10.1 is used for message passing of both multiple-CPU and multiple-GPU calculations.

Comparisons are made with performance of the Hartree Centre IBM iDataPlex cluster which is equipped with Intel Ivy Bridge E5-2697v2 2.7 GHz CPUs, each node comprising two 12-core processors. Software included the Intel C/C++ version 15.2.164 compiler, Intel Fortran 16.0.0 and Intel MPI 5.03.

4   The DL_MESO Lattice Boltzmann Code

DL_MESO is a C++ general purpose mesoscopic simulation package which comes with two different simulation methods: Dissipative Particle Dynamics (DPD) and Lattice Boltzmann equations (LBE) [1, 11]. The current work is concerned with a simplified version of the LBE method exclusively.

The LBE is a computational fluid dynamics method which has emerged from the lattice-gas automata and is used to simulate a multitude of flow problems. In LBE a fluid can be represented by using the probability of finding one of its particles at a given position in space and time with a given momentum, described by a density distribution function, $f(x,p,t)$, depending on the position, x, the momentum, p, and time, t. Over a single time-step Δt the distribution function at each lattice point x evolves initially by collisions and then by propagation between neighbouring lattice sites.

The advantage of DL_MESO over other packages implementing the Lattice Boltzmann equation is that it allows computing multiple components and/or fluid phases and coupling them with other physics like the heat transfer function or solute diffusion equations. This flexibility to plug in different physics makes DL_MESO LBE ideal to simulate applications such as the cavity flow problem [4], or subjecting an initially stationary fluid to a temperature difference between two solid boundaries [2].

The Lattice Boltzmann method is generally suitable for parallel computing and it is easy to code, however, the aforementioned flexibility in the physics comes with some performance constraints. The necessity for computing the pseudo-potentials in each time step and therefore having non-local collision computations complicates the algorithm compared to other LBE implementations. The simplified version of LBE code [12] has the main advantage that the algorithm can be expressed in just two loops, one for the pre-computation of the pseudo-potentials and another for the collision and streaming steps. Consequently, the data-structure is only traversed twice leading to high data re-use and a high ratio of computation to data movement.

4.1   Porting to POWER8

To port DL_MESO to the POWER8 platform we used the IBM XL compiler set. DL_MESO uses OpenMP capabilities to distribute the work between different threads using static scheduling and among the vector lanes using the SIMD directive available since OpenMP 4.0 [6]. However, the XL Compiler only has partial support for OpenMP 4.0 and the pragmas regarding the SIMD vectorisation of the code were not recognized. Other strategies like setting the –qsimd = auto flag and the IBM #pragma simd_level() statements were introduced, but this produced incorrect output results for DL_MESO. Similarly, setting the optimisation flags to high levels also produced incorrect results. The best times with correct outputs were obtained using the –O2 optimisation flag.

4.2   Performance Results

Figure 2 shows a comparison of the performance of DL_MESO on several platforms. On the Intel platforms DL_MESO was compiler using Intel Compiler Suite with the – fopenmp, –Ofast and –xHost and -mmic flags. On the POWER8 the executable was produced with the IBM xlc++ compiler version 13.1, in this case with the –O2 - qsmp = omp -qsimd = noauto -qarch = auto flags.

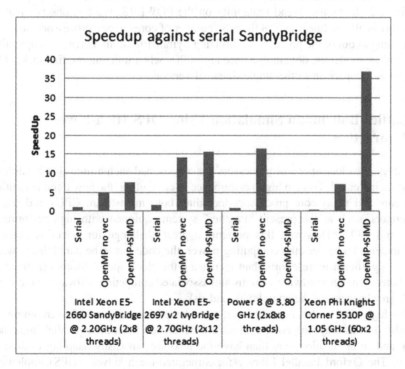

Fig. 2. Speedup of the DL_MESO LBM code on POWER8, SandyBridge, IvyBridge and Xeon Phi systems compared to the serial SandyBridge execution time.

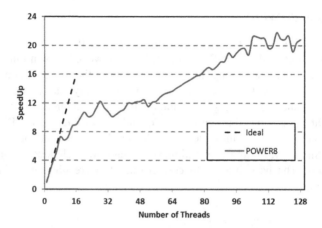

Fig. 3. Speedup of the DL_MESO LBM code on a single POWER8 node with 16 physical cores. Beyond 16 cores Symmetric Multithreading is used.

Performance is compared against the serial time of the Intel SandyBridge. The chart shows how, the POWER8 execution without vectorisation is slightly better than the Intel IvyBridge Platform with SIMD (x16.5 vs x15.7), however, it still stands far below an accelerated architecture such as the Xeon Phi (x16.5 vs x26.8).

Figure 3 shows the thread scalability on the POWER8. We can observe that the scalability is almost linear until 8 threads (number of cores in one processor), however, when going to out of the processor or utilizing Symmetric Multi-Threading capabilities the gains are moderate, obtaining a speedup of 20x when utilizing the full socket (128 threads) in comparison to the single-threaded version.

5 Lattice Boltzmann Simulation Using OPS High-Level Abstraction

Nowadays, the clock speed of processors has approached such a limit that is harder to be further increased. To gain high performance in computing, the new trend is to utilise multi-core and many-core processors including both mainstream CPUs and add-on accelerators, such as the present "Panther" system equipped with high-performance CPUs and GPUs. However, this presents a great challenge for scientific software development. To harness the computing power, the code has to be parallelised, which requires significant more efforts than increasing the clock speed. Moreover, there are often heterogeneous hardware systems and associated competing software frameworks, which greatly increase the complexity and risk.

The high-level abstraction approach provides a potential way of overcoming this difficulty. In this way, the computations are decoupled from their parallel implementation, and an application may then have the flexibility of easily adapting to different system. The Oxford Parallel Library for Structured-mesh solvers (OPS) implements this idea for developing block-structured applications [6]. Through careful design, the library provides concise but sufficient abstraction to hide the complexity of both parallelisation and managing multi-block meshes, which is very attractive for an application point of view.

Here we test the two-dimensional OPS based lattice Boltzmann code using a single node of the "Panther" for both multiple-CPU and multiple-GPU calculations. For the CPU calculations with a 4096 × 4096 mesh, the code is compiled using the IBM XL C/C++ V13.1.3 compiler and OpenMPI 1.10.2 is used for message passing. As shown in Fig. 4, we observe nearly linear scalability and nice speedup when using up to 16 physical cores. For larger thread counts Symmetric Multi-Threading (SMT) is used, delivering a significant performance boost to attain a speedup of 24x on 16 physical cores with eight-way multi-threading (SMT = 8). This appears to be consistent with the fact that a LBM code tends to be memory bound [5].

For the multiple-GPU calculations, we carried out a weak-scaling test. Although there are only two K80 boards on a single-node, we use a 2048 × 4096 mesh for "a half" of K80 (one of the two GPUs in a K80 board), a 4096 × 4096 mesh for 1 K80 and a 8192 × 4096 mesh for 2 K80 s. The code is compiled with the above mentioned IBM compiler and the NVIDIA CUDA 7.5 SDK. For reference, we also present the computation time measured for a K40 calculation on the "Palmerston" system using a 4096 × 4096 mesh, for which the code is compiled with the tool sets are the IBM XL C/C++ V13.1.2, the NVIDIA CUDA 7.0 SDK, and OpenMPI 1.10.1. From Fig. 5, we see nearly optimal weak scaling behaviour across the K80 s. One K80 board can achieve twice the performance of one K40 GPU, which is consistent with the specifications of two cards.

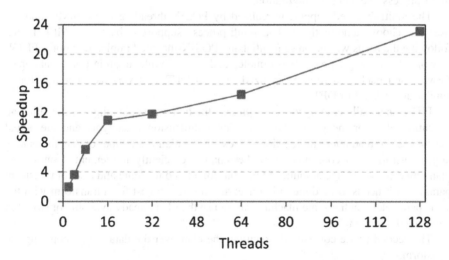

Fig. 4. Speedup of the OPS-based LBM code on a single node of the POWER8 Panther system. There are 16 physical cores. Larger numbers of threads use Symmetric Multi-Threading (SMT), with 2, 4 and 8 threads per core.

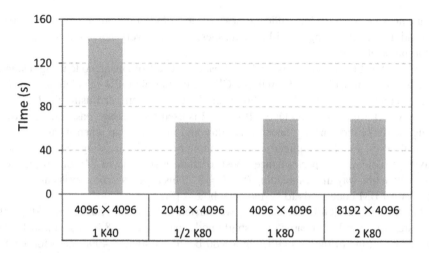

Fig. 5. Execution time of the OPS-based LBM code with different grid sizes on IBM POWER8 systems with NVIDIA K40 and K80 GPUs.

6 Fast Fourier Transforms

FFTW[3] is a widely used, free software library for computing the discrete Fourier transform (DFT) in one or more dimensions of real or complex data [2], with C and Fortran interfaces, and supporting single-threaded (sequential), multi-threaded, and multi-process execution configurations.

The multi-threaded support is realized by POSIX threading or OpenMP, and the user can choose among them. The multi-process support is based on MPI. In the following the focus will be on sequential and POSIX-threaded implementations. FFTW supports float (single-precision), double, and long double floating-point datatypes; forward and backward (non-normalized inverse) DFT, and various other transforms similar and related to DFT.

FFTW is usually employed in two phases; the first one is planning, i.e., creating an execution plan for the given transform, input dimensions, datatype, and the actual machine and thread count in question. An execution plan is a recipe for decomposing a large transform into combination of the smaller, efficiently implemented ones. The planning can take a huge amount of time, but for a fixed machine and a set of transform parameters it needs to be done only once; any further request for a transform with the same parameters on the same machine can re-use the plan already available or stored in a so-called "wisdom" file.

The second phase consists of executing the plan over the data, i.e., computing the transform.

---

[3] FFTW Home Page http://www.fftw.org .

The source code distribution comes with a benchmarking tool, which enables measuring of time required for particular phases of a computation, calculates the FLOP rate (see [2] for details), and can check for accuracy of the results.

6.1 Porting to POWER8

The porting and testing platform consists of a single node with 16 physical POWER8 cores running on 3857 MHz, with 8-way SMT per core. The software environment is Red Hat Enterprise Linux 7.2 with IBM XL C compiler version 13.1.3.

FFTW can be compiled from source without any code modifications, but the binaries obtained by specifying various levels of optimisation, at least in the single-precision case, cannot sustain the post-build accuracy self-checking by the benchmarking tool, invoked by the *make check* command. The similar is true for GNU C compiler version 4.8.5 with the library's default settings for the compiler flags. Therefore, our choice of was to omit any optimisation flags for IBM XL compiler, save for "-qtune = pwr8:smt8", bearing in mind that suboptimal code might be produced.

6.2 Performance Results

We have measured running time and FLOP rate for the 2D single-precision DFT, forward and backward, real and complex, in-place (overwriting the input) and out-of-place transforms, with 1, 2, 4, 8, and 16 POSIX threads, over 10 runs for each transform. In order to distribute the workload evenly across the cores, the *taskset* command was used to limit the number of available virtual processors to one per a physical core.

Out-of-place transforms are generally faster than the in-place ones, and forward transforms perform better than their backward counterparts. Therefore, only the results for out-of-place forward transforms are presented herein.

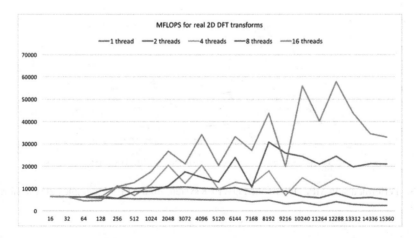

Fig. 6. Performance in MFLOPS on the POWER8 system of the FFTW real 2D transform.

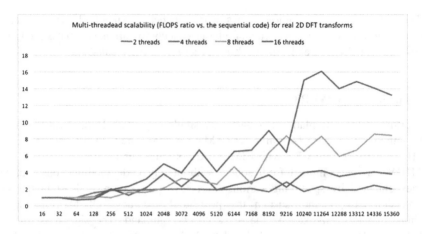

Fig. 7. Scalability on the POWER8 system of the FFTW multi-threaded real 2D transform.

Figure 6 shows the raw performance of FFTW real 2D transforms in terms of the best achieved MFLOPS rate per a given number of threads, while Fig. 7 demonstrates reasonable scalability achieved for 8 and 16 threads. Figures 8 and 9 depict similar measurements for the complex 2D transforms.

The planning time, using the recommended "patient" method, can be huge, and increases with the number of threads. For example, planning for 9216 × 9216 complex DFT for 1 thread takes 2693.25 s, for 4 threads 11519.70 s, and for 16 threads 12866.52 s. The transform itself runs in 2.39 s sequentially, or in 289.19 ms with 16 threads available.

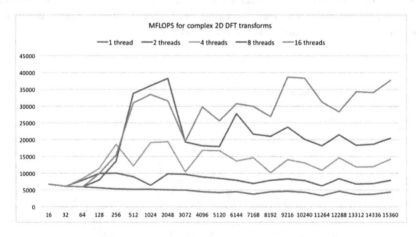

Fig. 8. Performance in MFLOPS on the POWER8 system for the FFTW complex 2D transform.

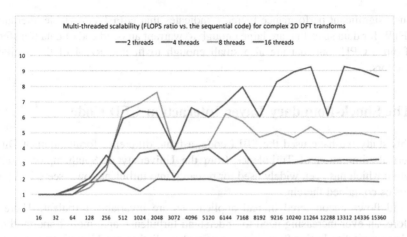

Fig. 9. Performance in MFLOPS on the POWER8 system for the FFTW complex 2D transform.

6.3 GPU FFT

The POWER architecture supports NVIDIA CUDA technology for general-purpose computation on the graphics processors (GPUs). As a part of CUDA software distribution, cuFFT – a library for computing FFT on the GPUs – is provided. With an interface similar to FFTW, cuFFT offers a massively parallel counterpart of the CPU-based DFT libraries, which is especially well tuned for the transforms of data sizes that factorize as a product of powers of small primes.

We have compared cuFFT and FFTW with 16 threads on 2D complex datasets, and obtained 5 to 15-fold speedup, as shown in Fig. 10, using NVIDIA Tesla K80 GPU and CUDA 7.5.

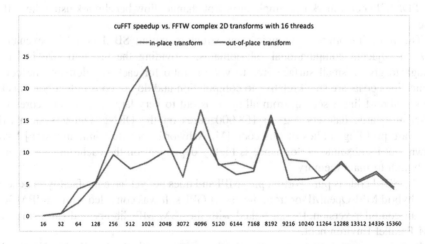

Fig. 10. Speedup of cuFFT on the Kepler K80 GPU compared with FFTW running on the POWER8 CPUs.

Such significant performance increase indicates that cuFFT is a viable alternative for FFTW for data sizes that are large enough to warrant an overhead of data transfer to and from a GPU, but that are also small enough to fit into RAM of the available accelerators.

7 The Shock-Boundary Layer Interaction CFD Code

For this study we have used the SBLI code, a finite difference formulation of Direct Numerical Simulation of Turbulence from the University of Southampton, United Kingdom which has been widely used for research into turbulent flows, see e.g. [9] and references contained therein.

Fluid flows encountered in real applications are invariably turbulent. There is, therefore, an ever-increasing need to understand turbulence and, more importantly, to be able to model turbulent flows with improved predictive capabilities. As computing technology continues to improve, it is becoming more feasible to solve the governing equations of motion, the Navier-Stokes equations, from first principles. The direct solution of the equations of motion for a fluid, however, remains a formidable task and simulations are only possible for flows with small to modest Reynolds numbers.

Within the United Kingdom, the UK Turbulence Consortium (UKTC) has been at the forefront of simulating turbulent flows by direct numerical simulation (DNS). UKTC has developed a parallel version of a code to solve problems associated with shock/boundary-layer interaction.

The SBLI code was originally developed for the Cray T3E and is a sophisticated DNS code that incorporates a number of advanced features: namely high-order central differencing; a shock-preserving advection scheme from the total variation diminishing (TVD) family; entropy splitting of the Euler terms and the stable boundary scheme. The code has been written using standard Fortran 90 code together with MPI in order to be efficient, scalable and portable across a wide range of high-performance platforms. The PDNS3D benchmark is a simple turbulent channel flow benchmark using the SBLI code.

The most important communications structure within SBLI is a halo-exchange between adjacent computational sub-domains. Providing the problem size is large enough to give a small surface area to volume ratio for each sub-domain, the communications costs are small relative to computation and do not constitute a bottleneck. We see almost linear scaling from all systems out to very large numbers of cores for sufficiently large datasets, e.g. to 168,000 cores on the ORNL Jaguar system [8]. Hardware profiling studies of this code [M. Ashworth, private communication] have shown that its absolute performance is highly dependent on the cache utilisation and bandwidth to main memory.

The SBLI code is pure Fortran plus MPI and does not yet have the facility to benefit from hybrid MPI-OpenMP or from the use of GPUs. It was compiled with the IBM XL Fortran compiler version 15.1.3, linked with the IBM MPI library and run using the IBM Parallel Environment.

We compare performance on the Panther system with the Ivy Bridge NextScale system using a turbulent channel flow benchmark case which has a mesh of 120 cubed points run for 100 timesteps. This is a relatively small problem size and so tends to stress the communications network.

Execution times were measured using the standard Fortran 90 system clock procedure system_clock. A performance metric is shown which is computed by dividing the execution time in seconds into a constant of 1000. As an inverse time metric this means that ideal performance increases linearly with the number of cores and deviations from ideal performance are easily visible.

Figure 11 shows performance on a single node from 1 to 16 cores. For small core counts, the POWER8's faster clock and memory delivers superior performance, but by the time the node is fully populated, performance is equivalent. Using Symmetric Multi-Threading (SMT) of 2, 4 and 8 threads per core gives an advantage due to the ability to mask memory latency. SMT with eight threads on 16 cores delivers a 1.5x speed-up.

In Fig. 12 we see the performance across multiple-nodes out to 256 cores. Performance is limited by communications and there is little dependence on processor type. Again SMT was tried: 2-way multi-threading gave some speed-up, four-way was better but eight-way was much worse; therefore only performance for SMT = 4 is shown, delivering a 25 % speed-up on 256 cores. One disadvantage of using SMT for a pure MPI code is that it results in a large increase in the number of MPI tasks, e.g. on 256 cores with SMT = 8 there are 2048 MPI tasks with resulting increase in communications albeit much of it within a node. We believe that a hybrid OpenMP-MPI approach would improve the speedup obtained from SMT.

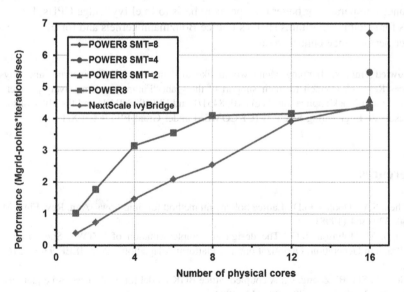

Fig. 11. Performance of the SBLI CFD code on POWER8 and NextScale systems for a turbulent channel benchmark: single node 1 to 16 cores.

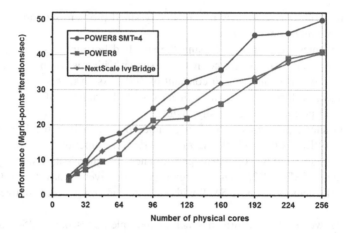

Fig. 12. Performance of the SBLI CFD code on POWER8 and NextScale systems for a turbulent channel benchmark across multiple nodes.

8   Conclusions

We have shown early performance results for some applications and for some FFT kernels on the OpenPOWER architecture with POWER8 CPUs and NVIDIA Kepler K80 GPUs.

No optimisation has been carried out yet, but results are encouraging with performance comparable or better on a per core basis to Intel IvyBridge CPUs. Use of the GPUs for suitable algorithms such as Lattice Boltzmann kernels and for FFTs provides further performance enhancements.

Acknowledgements. Jianping Meng would like to thank the UK Engineering and Physical Sciences Research Council for their support of the grant "Future-proof massively-parallel execution of multi-block applications" (EP/K038451/1 and EP/K038494/1) and the UK Consortium on Mesoscale Engineering Sciences (UKCOMES) under Grant EP/L00030X/1.

References

1. Chen, S.Y., Doolen, G.D.: Lattice boltzmann method for fluid flows. Ann. Rev. Fluid Mech. **30**, 329–364 (1998)
2. Frigo, M., Johnson, S.G.: The design and implementation of FFTW3, Special issue on "Program Generation, Optimization, and Platform Adaptation". Proc. IEEE **93**(2), 216–231 (2005)
3. Guo, Z., Shi, B., Zheng, C.: A coupled lattice BGK model for the Boussinesq equations. Int. J. Num. Meth. Fluids **39**, 325–342 (2002)
4. Hou, S., Zou, Q., Chen, S., Doolen, G., Cogley, A.C.: Simulation of cavity flow by the lattice Boltzmann method. J. Comp. Phys. **118**, 329–347 (1995)

5. Lee, V.W., Kim, C, Chhugani, J, Deisher, M., Kim, D., Nguyen, A.D., Satish, N., Smelyanskiy, M., Chennupaty, S., Hammarlund, P., Singhal, R., Dubey, P.: Debunking the 100x GPU vs. CPU myth: an evaluation of throughput computing on CPU and GPU. In: Proceedings of the 37th Annual International Symposium on Computer Architecture, ser, ISCA 2010, pp. 451–460. ACM, New York (2010)

6. Mudalige, G.R., Reguly, I.Z., Giles, M.B., Mallinson, A.C., Gaudin, W.P., Herdman, J.A.: Performance analysis of a high-level abstractions-based hydrocode on future computing systems. In: Proceedings of the 5th International Workshop on Performance Modeling, Benchmarking and Simulation of High Performance Computing Systems (PMBS 2014) (2014)

7. OpenMP Application Program Interface Version 4.0, July 2013. http://www.openmp.org/mp-documents/OpenMP4.0.0.pdf. Accessed 14 Apr 2016

8. Redford, J.A., Sandham, N.D., Roberts, G.T.: Direct numerical simulation of transitional flow at high Mach number coupled with a thermal wall model. Comput. Fluids **45**, 37–46 (2011)

9. Sandham, N.D., Schuelein, E., Wagner, A., et al.: Transitional shock-wave/boundary-layer interactions in hypersonic flow. J. Fluid Mech. **752**, 1–33 (2014). doi:10.1017/jfm.2014.333

10. Seaton, M.A., Anderson, R.L., Metz, S., Smith, W.: DL_MESO: highly scalable mesoscale simulations. Mol. Sim. **39**(10), 796–821 (2013)

11. Seaton, M.A., Smith, W.: DL_MESO User Manual. http://www.scd.stfc.ac.uk/SCD/resources/PDF/USRMAN.pdf. Accessed 14 Apr 2016

12. Siso, S., Seaton, M.A., Mason, L.: Code modernization of DL_MESO LBE to achieve good performance on the Intel Xeon Phi. In: Emit Conference Proceedings (2016)

13. Tildesley, D.: A strategic vision for UK e-infrastructure: a roadmap for the development and use of advanced computing, data and networks. Report for the Department of Business Innovation and Skills, UK, pp. 1–33, 4 January 2012. https://www.gov.uk/government/publications/e-infrastructure-strategy-roadmap-for-development-of-advanced-computing-data-and-networks. Accessed 14 Apr 2016

Early Experiences Porting the NAMD and VMD Molecular Simulation and Analysis Software to GPU-Accelerated OpenPOWER Platforms

John E. Stone[1]([✉]), Antti-Pekka Hynninen[2], James C. Phillips[1], and Klaus Schulten[1,3]

[1] Beckman Institute for Advanced Science and Technology, University of Illinois at Urbana-Champaign, Urbana, IL, USA
jestone@illinois.edu, johns@ks.uiuc.edu
[2] Oak Ridge Leadership Computing Facility, Oak Ridge National Laboratory, Oak Ridge, TN, USA
[3] Department of Physics, University of Illinois at Urbana-Champaign, Urbana, IL, USA

Abstract. All-atom molecular dynamics simulations of biomolecules provide a powerful tool for exploring the structure and dynamics of large protein complexes within realistic cellular environments. Unfortunately, such simulations are extremely demanding in terms of their computational requirements, and they present many challenges in terms of preparation, simulation methodology, and analysis and visualization of results. We describe our early experiences porting the popular molecular dynamics simulation program NAMD and the simulation preparation, analysis, and visualization tool VMD to GPU-accelerated OpenPOWER hardware platforms. We report our experiences with compiler-provided autovectorization and compare with hand-coded vector intrinsics for the POWER8 CPU. We explore the performance benefits obtained from unique POWER8 architectural features such as 8-way SMT and its value for particular molecular modeling tasks. Finally, we evaluate the performance of several GPU-accelerated molecular modeling kernels and relate them to other hardware platforms.

1 Introduction

Atomic-detail molecular dynamics (MD) simulation provides researchers with a powerful computational microscope that permits the study of biomedically-relevant processes that are too fast to observe first-hand, and that occur in the crowded molecular environment of living cells, that cannot be seen with even the most advanced experimental microscopes. Many societal challenges are addressed by biomolecular modelers employing state-of-the-art parallel computing platforms, for example, treatment of viral infections [1,2] and addressing the antibiotic resistance crisis [3]. The cellular processes of interest to biomedical researchers take place in molecular assemblies made of millions to hundreds of

M. Taufer et al. (Eds.): ISC High Performance Workshops 2016, LNCS 9945, pp. 188–206, 2016.
DOI: 10.1007/978-3-319-46079-6_14

millions of atoms. Such simulations are extremely demanding in terms of preparation, computation, storage, analysis, and visualization, and they continue to push the limits of parallel computing.

State-of-the-art petascale supercomputing platforms such as Blue Waters [4] and Titan [5] contend with significant challenges posed by constraints on space, power, and cooling. To achieve higher application performance, future systems must directly address these challenges with performant and energy efficient computing technologies that take maximal advantage of many-core CPUs, GPU accelerators, non-volatile storage systems, and new intra- and inter-node interconnects. One of the upcoming leadership-class computing systems for open science will be Summit, a pre-exascale supercomputer to be composed of roughly 3,400 GPU-accelerated compute nodes, fielded by the U.S. Department of Energy, and housed at the Oak Ridge Leadership Computing Facility. While a development environment directly comparable to the final Summit system is not yet available, existing OpenPOWER platforms support GPU accelerators and associated compilers and libraries, allowing application porting to begin today.

Below we describe the adaptation of representative and performance-critical algorithms in the widely used molecular dynamics program NAMD [6,7], and the molecular analysis and visualization tool VMD [8–10], on an IBM S822L OpenPOWER hardware platform with NVIDIA Tesla K40m GPUs.

2   Overview of ORNL Crest Test System

Except where noted, the application porting and performance evaluation activities reported here were performed using the "Crest" development systems made available through the Center for Accelerated Application Readiness (CAAR) at the Oak Ridge National Laboratory (ORNL), in preparation for the next-generation Summit supercomputer. The ORNL Crest system is currently composed of four compute nodes and an associated login node for software development and testing. The Crest compute nodes are IBM S822L servers configured with two 3.7 GHz 10-core POWER8 dual-chip CPU modules (DCMs), 256 GB of RAM among four NUMA nodes, four NVIDIA Tesla K40m GPUs, and two Mellanox Connect-IB FDR InfiniBand (56 Gbit/s) NICs. Figure 1 shows a simplified block diagram of the S822L hardware used in the Crest compute nodes.

The current software environment on Crest supports several compilers including GCC 4.9.3 and IBM XLC 13.1.2, both supporting compile-time auto-vectorization of performance critical loops using POWER8 VSX SIMD instructions. Although NAMD and VMD are both endianism-independent, the little-endian byte ordering used by the Linux operating system for OpenPOWER is beneficial for applications originally developed on popular little-endian platforms such as Intel x86, and it is necessary for efficient use of GPU accelerators. The NVIDIA Tesla K40m GPUs are supported by natively-hosted CUDA 7.5 compilers, and an assortment of GPU-accelerated subroutine libraries. At the time of writing, the CUDA 7.5 implementation for OpenPOWER does not yet support peer-to-peer GPU transfers. Below we discuss the use of specific compiler optimization features in the context of NAMD and VMD algorithms.

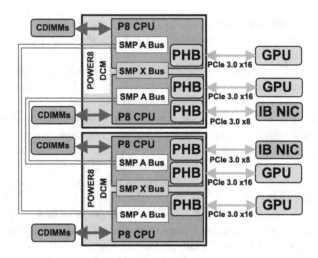

Fig. 1. Simplified block diagram of the IBM S822L compute nodes used in the ORNL Crest development system. Two POWER8 dual-chip CPU modules (DCMs) are shown with associated NUMA CPU and PCIe bus topology interconnecting the CPUs, PCIe host bridge (PHB) I/O channels, NVIDIA Tesla K40m GPUs, and Mellanox Connect-IB InfiniBand network adapters (IB NIC). The two DCMs contain two 5-core POWER8 processors, each with 8-way hardware simultaneous multithreading (SMT), for a total of 20 CPU cores and 160 SMT threads. Each CPU contains its own memory controller with a 96 GB/s bandwidth channel to a set of four CDIMMs (DIMMs paired with a so-called "Centaur" DIMM controller), giving each DCM 192 GB/s DRAM bandwidth, yielding a full system peak DRAM memory bandwidth of 384 GB/s. The two CPUs on a DCM are linked by a 32 GB/s SMP "X" bus, and the two DCMs communicate using four 12.8 GB/s SMP "A" bus links. Each of the four NVIDIA Tesla K40m GPUs are directly connected to the on-chip PCIe 3.0x16 PCIe host bridge (PHB) channel on a corresponding CPU. System components and peripherals less relevant to molecular dynamics simulation and analysis workloads are not shown.

3   NAMD: Parallel Molecular Dynamics Simulation

For the current Titan system and the future Summit system the majority of arithmetic performance is provided by GPU accelerators. NAMD currently exploits GPU acceleration for the two most compute intensive parts of molecular dynamics simulation: non-bonded force computation and Particle Mesh Ewald (PME) reciprocal computation. The remaining computations, e.g., bonded forces, are performed on the CPU. Continuing this existing GPU acceleration model, here we focus on further optimization of the two GPU parts. The starting point for our work is the NAMD CVS repository version 2015-04-23, which is essentially NAMD 2.10 with CUDA kernels modified to stream results incrementally to the CPU. In the following discussion, all changes and comparisons are made with respect to this version of NAMD. The algorithm changes described below are all new and are planned for inclusion in the NAMD 2.12 release.

3.1   Non-bonded Force Computation

Three major changes were made to the way non-bonded force computation is performed in NAMD. First, we broke up the compute objects that used to be on a single thread block, into "tile lists" that can be computed by any thread block. Second, Newton's third law was applied to eliminate duplicate calculation of pairwise forces. Third, we removed synchronization from the thread blocks to allow individual warps to perform the computation independently. We discuss each of these changes in further detail below.

Non-bonded forces in NAMD are calculated in compute objects that define all pairwise interactions between two sets of atoms. In the GPU-accelerated version of NAMD, computes are further split into 32×32 tiles as illustrated in Fig. 2(a). In Fig. 2(a), gray tiles do not have any atom pairs that interact and will be skipped. In the previous version of NAMD, a single thread block was assigned per compute. In the new version of the kernel, computes are broken into tile lists as shown in Fig. 2(b). Tile lists from different computes can be mixed and executed on any thread block. This gives rise to more flexible execution and a better opportunity for load balancing within warps in the thread block.

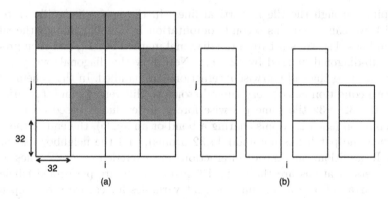

Fig. 2. (a) A so-called compute object consists of 32×32 tiles. Gray tiles have no interactions and are skipped. The previous version of the non-bonded force kernel executed an entire compute on a single thread block. (b) The new non-bonded kernel splits the compute into tile lists that can be executed on any thread block.

The total non-bonded force acting on atom i is given as a sum of all pairwise forces $\boldsymbol{f}_i = \sum_j \boldsymbol{f}_{ij}$. Due to Newton's third law, once $\boldsymbol{f}_{ij}$ are known, the force acting on atom j can be obtained from $\boldsymbol{f}_j = \sum_i -\boldsymbol{f}_{ij}$. In the previous version of the non-bonded force kernel, forces $\boldsymbol{f}_{ij}$ were computed on each thread of a warp and then accumulated to form $\boldsymbol{f}_i$. This is illustrated in Fig. 3(a) for warp size 4, where a warp of threads loops through the tile in horizontal lines starting at line $j = 1$ and ending at $j = 4$. Trying to accumulate to $\boldsymbol{f}_j$ during this loop would give rise to a race condition since all threads in the warp are storing to the same variable. Therefore, a second computation was necessary to compute forces $\boldsymbol{f}_j$

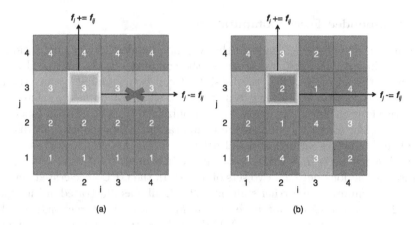

Fig. 3. Pairwise force computation in a 4 × 4 tile (a) previously and (b) in the new scheme. In (a) tile is looped in horizontal lines, while in (b) tile is looped in diagonal lines. The looping index is indicated on the tile elements and elements with the same index belong to the same warp.

by looping through the tile in vertical lines. In the new scheme illustrated in Fig. 3(b), we can avoid this second computation by looping though the tile in diagonal lines [11]. We start from the diagonal marked by "1", and then proceed to the sub-diagonal marked by "2", etc. Note how the diagonals wrap around the tile ensuring that all pairwise interactions are handled. In this scheme there is no race condition since every thread stores to different f_i and f_j variables. Within the 32 × 32 tile some pairwise forces are excluded based on the force field definition (such as atoms sharing a bond or an angle), the end of the atom list (when the patch has non-modulo 32 atoms), and the neighbor list cut-off radius. In addition, one half of interactions are excluded on "self" tiles where the two sets of atoms are the same. Exclusions tests are performed efficiently using an array of 32 × 32-bit unsigned int variables for each tile to keep track of the exclusions, where a 0-bit means "exclude" and 1-bit means "compute". The exclusion bit masks are created during the neighbor list build using a compressed lookup table [7]. For each of the 32 iterations through the tile, we must shift the input (atom coordinates, charges, etc.) and output (force) variables between threads within the warp. We use the _shfl() instructions first introduced in the Kepler GPU architecture to do this shifting with warp-synchronous programming entirely in GPU registers, thereby eliminating the need for shared memory and the additional synchronization operations it requires.

After the 32 × 32 tile is computed, forces f_j are stored in a global memory buffer using the atomicAdd() instruction and the kernel proceeds to the next tile with different j atoms but the same i atoms. Keeping i atoms constant reduces the number of memory accesses since for each tile only the j atoms must be loaded from global memory. After the warp finishes all tiles it was assigned, forces f_i are stored in global memory using the atomicAdd() instruction.

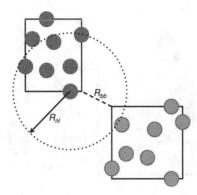

Fig. 4. Bounding boxes for two sets of eight atoms. Bounding box distance R_{bb} is well within the neighbor list cut-off distance R_{nl}, however none of the atoms are within the neighbor list cut-off.

In the previous version of NAMD, the neighbor list was built by the non-bonded force kernel by checking all atom pair distances in every 32×32 tile. We implemented a more efficient neighbor list builder that first builds an approximate neighbor list based on the bounding boxes of sets of 32 atoms, and then using that approximate list as input, builds the atom-based neighbor list in the non-bonded force kernel. The bounding-box approximation always overestimates the true neighbor list, as is illustrated in Fig. 4 where, although the bounding box distance R_{bb} is well within the neighbor list cut-off distance R_{nl}, none of the atoms are actually within the neighbor list cut-off. In the situation illustrated in Fig. 4, the bounding-box neighbor list would contain the two sets of atoms, but this entry would be pruned away in the atom-based distance check in the non-bonded force kernel.

We have also implemented the neighbor list for the Generalized Born implicit solvent (GBIS) kernels. Since the GBIS method does not use force-field exclusions and includes self-energies (explicit solvent calculations do not), a separate GBIS version of the neighbor list must be created. The bounding-box neighbor lists for both the GBIS and explicit solvent calculations are the same. During the atom-based neighbor list build in the non-bonded force kernel, we keep track of both the regular and the GBIS tile lists by assigning their indicators to the lower and upper 16-bits of a 32-bit integer, respectively. The two lists are finally separated in the neighbor list sorting step where the GBIS list is produced by choosing the upper bits, and the regular list by choosing the lower bits.

Benchmarks of the non-bonded force kernel were performed on a single Tesla K40m GPU of the Crest system for explicit solvent and GBIS systems. The explicit solvent systems included DHFR with 23,588 atoms, ApoA1 with 92,224 atoms, and STMV with 1,066,628 atoms, while the implicit solvent systems included GP (rabbit muscle glycogen phosphorylase, PDB ID 2GJ4) with 13,340 atoms and an empty HIV capsid with 5,662,344 atoms. For the explicit solvent cases, the benchmarks were performed using the non-streaming versions

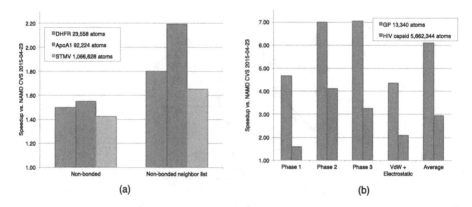

Fig. 5. Speedup of non-bonded force kernels vs. NAMD CVS version 2015-04-23 for (a) explicit solvent regular and neighbor list versions and (b) Generalized Born implicit solvent kernels.

of the kernels and we disabled the GPU PME reciprocal computation (NAMD script command `PMEOffload no`) to ensure that it did not interfere with the non-bonded force kernel timings. The kernel timings were obtained from the average kernel run time reported by the CUDA `nvprof` profiler.

Figure 5 shows the speedup observed for both explicit and implicit solvent cases. In the explicit solvent case shown in Fig. 5(a) we observe 1.4× to 1.6× speedup for the regular non-bonded force kernel and 1.7× to 2.2× speedup for the non-bonded neighbor list builder kernel. The neighbor list version gets a larger speedup due to the use of the bounding box neighbor list approximation, which reduces the number of tiles that must be checked at atom level.

In the case of explicit solvent, shown in Fig. 5(b), we observe much larger speedups: 6× speedup for the smaller GP system and 3× speedup for the HIV capsid system. Figure 5(b) also shows the breakdown of speedups for the three phases of the GBIS computation as well as the Van der Waals (VdW) and electrostatic parts.

3.2   PME Reciprocal Force Computation

NAMD uses the smooth particle mesh Ewald version [12] of the famous particle mesh Ewald (PME) method [13]. The PME method consists of five main parts: (1) spread charges on to grid, (2) 3-D Fast Fourier Transform (FFT) from direct to reciprocal space, (3) solve Poisson equation on the grid in the reciprocal space, (4) 3-D FFT back from reciprocal to direct space, and (5) gather atom forces from the direct space grid. In the previous version of NAMD, only charge spreading (1) and force gathering (5) were performed on the GPU while the 3-D FFT and Poisson solve were performed on the host CPUs. In the new version, we moved all of the PME computation to the GPU and changed the way the charge spreading and force gathering is done, as detailed below. We implemented a multi-GPU 3-D FFT solver that uses a pencil, slab, or box decomposition depending on the

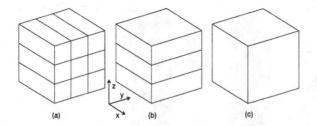

Fig. 6. PME (a) pencil, (b) slab, and (c) box decompositions for the direct to reciprocal space FFT. A single GPU is assigned to each pencil, slab, or box, respectively.

number of GPUs in use. These decompositions are illustrated in Fig. 6 for the direct to reciprocal space FFT step. We assign a single GPU for each pencil, slab or box. This means that we would use nine GPUs for the pencil decomposition in Fig. 6(a), three GPUs for the slab decomposition in Fig. 6(b), and a single GPU for the box decomposition in Fig. 6(c).

For the pencil decomposition in Fig. 6(a), we perform 1-D FFTs in x, y, and z directions in order to compute the full 3-D FFT. After each 1-D FFT, we need to 3-D transpose the grid such that the current FFT direction is contiguous in memory. For example, after 1-D FFT in the x direction, we transpose the grid to (y, z, x) order and then proceed with the 1-D FFT in the y direction. For the slab decomposition in Fig. 6(b), we perform 2-D FFT in a xy slab, and then 1-D FFT in the z direction. For the box decomposition in Fig. 6(c), we simply perform a single 3-D FFT on the entire grid. The 1-D, 2-D, and 3-D FFTs are computed using NVIDIA's cuFFT library. For the reciprocal to direct space FFT, we perform the same steps in reverse. For example in the case of PME pencil decomposition, we would first perform 1-D FFT in the z direction, then in the y direction, and finally in the x direction. The 3-D transposes are now performed in the reverse order as well.

The 3-D transpose involves communication between GPUs and can therefore become the most time consuming part of the PME reciprocal computation. For communication within a Crest node, we use the CUDA `cudaMemcpyPeerAsync()` function. We were not able to use direct GPU-to-GPU (known as peer-to-peer) communication since this is not currently enabled on the IBM POWER8 platform. We expect future NVLink GPU interconnect technology to enable direct GPU-to-GPU transfers and to make communication between GPUs on the same node much faster. For communication between nodes, we copy the GPU memory to a CPU buffer and then use the Charm++ communication layer to send the buffer to the receiving node. On the receiving node, we then copy the CPU buffer to the GPU. Future versions of Charm++ will hopefully enable direct GPU-to-GPU communication between nodes on capable hardware.

As mentioned earlier, we also changed the way the charges are spread on the grid. In the previous version of NAMD, charges on an atom patch were spread into a sub-grid and then the sub-grids were communicated among the PEs to form the PME pencils (with similar operation for PME slabs and boxes).

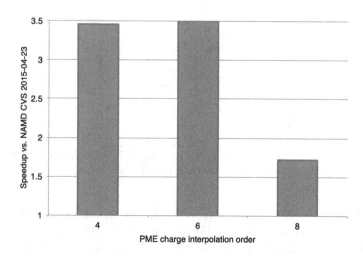

Fig. 7. Speedup for PME force computation vs. NAMD CVS version 2015-04-23 for DHFR system with 23,588 atoms and PME grid of size $64 \times 64 \times 64$. Benchmarks were run on a single node of the Titan supercomputer.

We changed the charge spreading such that instead of communicating grid points, we communicate the charges to the GPU that needs them. The GPU will then spread the charges and start working on the 3-D FFT. Note that since atoms near neighboring PME pencils boundaries spread to multiple pencils, we need to communicate a halo of atoms of the width of the PME interpolation order to obtain correct results.

Similarly to charge spreading, force gathering was changed to communicate forces instead of grid points. In detail, force gathering is now done on the GPU for all atoms that are within its PME pencil. Since atoms share neighboring PME pencils, some of the gathered forces will be partial at this stage. Therefore, after force gathering, the GPU communicates the partial forces to the CPU, and then the CPU combines the forces from multiple neighboring pencils to form the total PME reciprocal force acting on each atom.

In particular for small systems, where there is only a single GPU performing the PME reciprocal computation (i.e. box decomposition), the GPU can perform the entire PME reciprocal force computation on its own. This greatly improves PME reciprocal computation for single GPU runs, as is shown in Fig. 7.

3.3   NAMD Performance on Crest Versus Titan

In Fig. 8 we compare NAMD performance on a single node of Crest versus four nodes of Titan. Based on the difference in the underlying GPU hardware performance, K40m on Crest and K20X on Titan, one would expect about 7 % better kernel performance on Crest (for K40m without GPU Boost since users are not allowed to change the GPU settings on the Crest cluster). We see from Fig. 8 that the non-bonded force kernel performance on Crest is always somewhat less

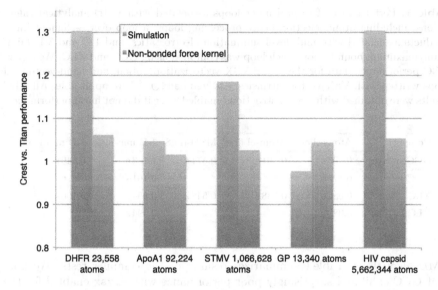

Fig. 8. Relative performance of a single Crest node vs. four nodes of Titan.

than the theoretical maximum, which is to be expected. We also see that Crest runs some of the simulations up to 30 % faster than Titan, while others (GP) actually have lower performance on Crest. Further work is necessary to see why the performance on Crest sometimes dips below the performance on Titan.

4   VMD: Simulation Preparation and Analysis

VMD [8] is a popular tool for MD simulation preparation, analysis, and visualization. In concert with a sophisticated atom selection language and a wide variety of data structures and algorithms for visualization, analysis, and structure manipulation, VMD incorporates built-in Tcl and Python scripting that can be used to perform large scale molecular modeling and analysis tasks in parallel on clouds [14], clusters, and petascale computers [9,10,15–17]. VMD provides a wide variety of tools for assembling large macromolecular complexes from constituent proteins, and combining these with solvent and ions to replicate biological conditions in vivo, and it can emit the completed system for simulation with popular GPU-accelerated MD simulation tools such as NAMD [6,7,18] and GROMACS [19,20]. The performance of VMD for a user's molecular modeling and visualization work is not well-characterized by any single kernel or time-critical loop, so we report performance for a variety of algorithms that capture key characteristics of VMD workloads.

4.1   Compiler Performance Comparisons

To evaluate the merits of GCC and XLC for POWER8 CPUs, we compared the performance of exemplary performance-critical loops from internal

Table 1. Performance of several inner loops associated with VMD analytical calculations, including atom selection array processing loops, a loop over 8-element inner products associated with multilevel summation electrostatics, and 1-D and 3-D minimum/maximum bounds loop. Each loop was compiled using GCC and XLC. We report GCC performance data for the -mvsx VSX vectorization option, and hand-vectorized loops written with VSX vector intrinsics, e.g. vec_madd(), where applicable. All XLC results were obtained with VSX instructions enabled since it did not harm performance.

Compiler	Atomsel cnt	Atomsel first	MSM-dot8	1-D min-max	3-D min-max
GCC -mvsx	0.123 s	0.061 s	0.571 s	1.163 s	0.649 s
GCC intrinsics	0.123 s			0.101 s	
XLC	0.082 s	0.038 s	0.548 s	0.094 s	0.106 s
XLC intrinsics	0.082 s			0.094 s	

VMD algorithms. Table 1 summarizes results for the compiler tests. We note that GCC exhibited surprisingly poor performance with -mvsx enabled for the 1-D min-max test case, but that when provided with hand-written vectorized loops using VSX intrinsics, the generated code approached the performance of XLC. We found that the code generated by XLC ran at the same speed as the hand-coded VSX loops. Our general experience during porting of VMD was that XLC provided higher overall performance on average, but particularly for cases with significant opportunity to exploit VSX instructions. As such, all subsequent VMD performance measurements were performed using XLC.

4.2 Tachyon Ray Tracing Engine

VMD incorporates the Tachyon ray tracing (RT) engine for high quality rendering on all supported platforms, including clouds, clusters, and supercomputers [9,21]. The rise of ray tracing for high-fidelity scientific visualization has led to the development of hardware-optimized RT libraries and frameworks [22,23], in combination with SPMD languages and compilers such as CUDA [24] and ISPC [25] that generate highly-optimized code for wide SIMD vector units. VMD contains a GPU-accelerated RT engine [10,15,26], however OptiX [22] is not yet available for OpenPOWER platforms, so Tachyon is currently the highest performance VMD RT engine on OpenPOWER. Figure 9 shows a visualization of the HIV-1 capsid with host cell factor cyclophilin A (CypA) [2], docked with a cryo-electron density map of the nuclear pore complex, which was used as a representative test case for Tachyon on multi-core CPUs.

Tachyon is an interesting performance test case since it is widely used for high quality VMD figure and movie renderings as a result of its speed and availability on all platforms supported by VMD. Even on platforms that support the GPU-accelerated TachyonL-OptiX [10,15,26] RT engine, it is still occasionally necessary to use the CPU-based Tachyon RT engine for scenes that greatly exceed GPU physical memory capacity. Tachyon uses a variety of linked lists

Fig. 9. Visualization of the HIV-1 capsid with pentamers highlighted in yellow, host cell factor cyclophilin A (CypA) shown in blue [2], docked with a cryo-electron density map of the nuclear pore complex shown in white. The scene, incorporating direct lighting, ambient occlusion lighting, and depth of field with large sample counts, was used to measure Tachyon ray tracing performance on the POWER8 CPU, as shown in Fig. 11. (Color figure online)

and hierarchical data structures that share some performance characteristics with molecular structure traversal algorithms in other areas of VMD. Tachyon currently does not make explicit use of POWER8 VSX vector instructions, and present-day compilers and languages are not capable of effectively autovectorizing RT algorithms, so effective use of SMT is of particular interest at present.

Tachyon CPU RT performance was measured for two very different test scenes and execution conditions, with varying counts of SMT threads per core. In the first case, shown in Fig. 10, a standalone Tachyon build was run on a simple scene containing a short DNA segment, but with very high stochastic sample counts, thereby creating a workload that emphasized floating point arithmetic and CPU cache performance. The DNA scene is small enough to expect that all performance-critical Tachyon data structures would be cached entirely on each CPU, and that NUMA-related performance effects would be minimized. Figure 10 shows that for the small DNA scene, the use of SMT is beneficial for performance all the way up to 8 threads per CPU core, or 160 threads in total, yielding a peak speedup 2.2× the performance achieved using a single thread per core.

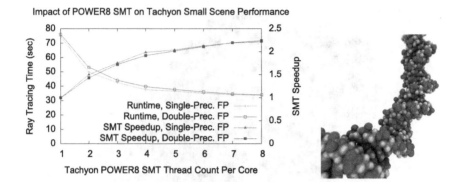

Impact of POWER8 SMT on Tachyon Small Scene Performance

Fig. 10. Evaluation of the impact of varying per core SMT thread counts on Tachyon small scene ray tracing performance on POWER8.

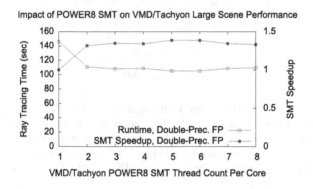

Impact of POWER8 SMT on VMD/Tachyon Large Scene Performance

Fig. 11. Evaluation of the impact of varying per core SMT thread counts on VMD/Tachyon ray tracing performance on POWER8, for the HIV-1 scene in Fig. 9.

In the second test case, shown in Figs. 9 and 11, the Tachyon engine built into VMD was used to render a large scale geometrically complex scene of the HIV-1 capsid and host cell factor cyclophilin A docked with a cryo-electron density map of the nuclear pore complex [2]. The HIV-1 scene is representative of routine visualizations created from ongoing petascale molecular dynamics simulations. Due to the large size of the HIV-1 scene and the fact that Tachyon is linked into VMD, the impact of NUMA locality and inter-processor SMP bus bandwidth are much greater. Since Tachyon inherits the existing distribution of VMD memory allocations among NUMA nodes and the HIV-1 scene size is very large, Tachyon's runtime memory allocations are less uniformly distributed than when Tachyon is run standalone, and this also leads to increased run-to-run performance variation. As a result of these effects, the maximum SMT performance observed for the HIV-1 test case was roughly 1.3× that of using a single thread per CPU core. Table 2 summarizes performance results obtained for varying degrees of SMT threading for the large HIV-1 test case with double-precision floating point arithmetic on POWER8 and Intel Xeon E5-2660v3. The POWER8

Table 2. VMD/Tachyon HIV-1 double precision CPU ray tracing performance for varying numbers of SMT threads per core. The table shown here provides numeric values for the plot in Fig. 11, and adds performance results for the Xeon E5-2660v3.

SMT Count	POWER8			Xeon E5-2660v3		
	Threads	DNA	HIV-1	Threads	DNA	HIV-1
1	20	76.0 s	143.1 s	20	63.7 s	104.9 s
2	40	53.1 s	110.9 s	40	48.4 s	87.1 s
4	80	39.6 s	108.9 s			
8	160	33.9 s	109.8 s			

system outperformed the Xeon by 1.43× for the (cache-friendly, arithmetic bound) DNA scene rendered standalone, the Xeon outperforms POWER8 by 1.26× for the large HIV-1 scene rendered by Tachyon within VMD.

4.3 Molecular Dynamics Flexible Fitting Cross Correlation

Molecular dynamics flexible fitting combines molecular structure data from cryo-electron microscopy and X-ray crystallography with molecular dynamics simulations, to determine all-atom structures of large biomolecular complexes such as the HIV-1 capsid [1,2]. The calculation of quality-of-fit for structures obtained from hybrid fitting approaches is computationally demanding, and particularly when run on tens of thousands of MDFF trajectory frames and when multiple structural conformations need to be evaluated. To address this challenge, VMD implements fast algorithms for computing quality-of-fit between all-atom structures and experimental cryo-electron density maps using hand-coded CPU SIMD vector instructions and data-parallel CUDA kernels on NVIDIA GPUs [16].

Table 3 reports cross correlation performance for a single trajectory frame from a large rabbit hemorrhagic disease virus (RHDV) capsid test case [16,27]. The reported cross correlation performance results were obtained using density map simulation algorithms implemented using hand-coded POWER8 VSX and Intel Xeon E5-2660v3 SSE vector intrinsics. The POWER8+Tesla K40m result demonstrates performance closely approaching the Xeon E5-2687W+Quadro K6000 result previously reported [16]. The closely comparable GPU performance results are expected since the two GPUs share the same architecture but the Quadro K6000 has a core clock rate that is roughly 20 % higher.

4.4 Molecular Orbital Calculation

Calculation and display of molecular orbitals (MOs), electron densities, and molecular electrostatic potentials are helpful steps in the analysis of quantum chemistry calculations. The key challenge involved in the calculation and display of MOs and related quantities is the rapid evaluation of complex wavefunctions on a three-dimensional lattice; the resulting data can then be used for plotting

Table 3. VMD molecular dynamics flexible fitting (MDFF) quality-of-fit cross correlation analysis performance for the rabbit hemorrhagic disease virus (RHDV) capsid solved with a 6.5 Å resolution density map [16,27]. On POWER8 platforms, hand-coded VSX vector instructions are used, providing a 20 % overall performance gain relative to xlC autovectorization. The use of SMT has negligible performance benefit on POWER8. On the Intel platforms hand-coded SSE vector instructions are used, yielding a 12 % performance gain compared to the best autovectorization achieved by the Intel XE 2015 compiler. The difference between the GPU-accelerated performance results is likely attributable solely to the higher Quadro K6000 GPU clock rate.

SMT Count	POWER8 hand-coded VSX		Xeon E5-2660v3 hand-coded SSE		POWER8 + Tesla K40m		Xeon E5-2687W + Quadro K6000	
	Threads	CC time	Threads	CC time	GPUs	CC time	GPUs	CC time
1	20	1.354 s	20	0.922 s	1	0.488 s	1	0.458 s
2	40	1.345 s	40	0.905 s				
4	80	1.334 s						
8	160	1.364 s						

isocontours or isosurfaces as shown in Fig. 12, and for other analyses. VMD contains data-parallel CPU and GPU kernels for computing MOs on Intel x86 CPUs optionally paired with NVIDIA GPUs [28,29], and on a variety of ARM SoCs and CPUs paired with integrated (on-chip) or discrete (add-in board) GPUs [30].

VMD evaluates MOs on a 3-D lattice by decomposing the lattice points into 2-D planes which are computed independently by different CPU threads or different GPUs. The workload is dynamically scheduled across the pool of workers to balance load on hardware of varying capability and in the presence of external load or operating system interference. Table 4 lists performance results for the VMD CPU and GPU-accelerated molecular orbital kernels run on a C_{60} test case. While the use of POWER8 SMT was beneficial for the plain

Fig. 12. VMD rendering of the atomic structure and molecular orbitals for a vibrating C_{60} simulation produced by Terachem.

Table 4. VMD C_{60} molecular orbital kernel performance for varying grid sizes, CPU thread counts and SMT utilization, vectorization approach, and GPU counts. Execution times are reported in seconds. Speedups within each platform are shown normalized to the base test case for each platform: vs. plain C++ on POWER8 CPU, vs. plain C++ on Xeon CPU, and vs. a single Tesla K40m GPU. The 4-GPU run achieved performance about 9× faster than the best POWER8 hand-coded VSX CPU results for both tests, and 5× and 8× faster than the Xeon E5-2660v3 hand-coded SSE results for medium and high resolution grid sizes, respectively. POWER8 SMT threading increases performance by up to 1.85× for the non-vectorized plain C++ implementation, but it had no measurable impact on the hand-coded VSX implementation.

C_{60} Grid Size	POWER8 160 Threads		Xeon E5-2660v3 40 Threads		POWER8 + Tesla K40m GPUs		
	C++	VSX	C++	SSE	1	2	4
$172 \times 173 \times 169$	1.09 s	0.52 s	2.42 s	0.301 s	0.190 s	0.099 s	0.058 s
	1.0×	2.10×	1.0×	8.01×	1.0×	1.91×	3.27×
$516 \times 519 \times 507$	17.57 s	8.03 s	59.18 s	7.14 s	3.49 s	1.76 s	0.91 s
	1.0×	2.18×	1.0×	8.28×	1.0×	1.98×	3.83×

C++ algorithm, the lack of impact on the hand-vectorized implementation likely indicates that it already effectively utilizes all of the POWER8 arithmetic units even with only 1 thread per core. The 4-way Tesla K40m performance result for high resolution test case closely matches performance results obtained on the same GPU hardware on Intel x86 systems. The 4-GPU result outperforms the POWER8 CPU results using hand-coded VSX instructions by a factor of 9× and it runs 5× to 8× faster than the Xeon E5-2660v3 CPU results using hand-coded SSE instructions. The hand-coded VSX and SSE MO kernels for POWER8 and Intel x86 hardware outperform the best autovectorized C++ loops in each case by 2× and 8× respectively. We note that it may be possible to further increase the performance of the hand-vectorized POWER8 VSX loop with additional tuning work.

5   Conclusions and Future Work

We have presented the adaptation of NAMD and VMD to GPU-accelerated POWER8 platforms and we have reported performance results for a variety of algorithms and test cases, and we have provided results for relevent comparison platforms. The CPU-focused test results presented here demonstrate the potential for POWER8 SMT to allow non-vectorized code to better utilize CPU functional units. Conversely, we observe that fully-vectorized code does not appear to benefit from SMT. Further developments that make use of explicit NUMA-aware memory allocations from private memory arenas should improve VMD-integrated Tachyon RT performance for large scenes such as HIV-1 by mitigating the impact of pre-existing memory fragmentation and NUMA locality. We noted that the lack of horizontal-add and other vector instructions found on competing CPUs made development of some VSX kernels more challenging than initially expected, but that substantial performance gains were still possible relative to the best compiler-generated code.

The ORNL Crest development system models key attributes of the future Summit supercomputer. The future Summit system will provide larger memory capacity, faster POWER9 CPUs and Volta GPUs, and higher performance intra-node communication paths between the CPUs and GPUs by virtue of the future NVLink interconnect. While the Crest system provides a programming environment representative of the future Summit system, not all of the desired capabilities of Summit are available yet on Crest. At the time of writing, it was not yet possible to evaluate the performance benefits associated with peer-to-peer GPU transfers as they are not yet implemented by CUDA 7.5 for Open-POWER. Several GPU-accelerated graphics-related features of VMD were similarly unavailable for testing due to lack of OpenPOWER versions of the OpenGL or Vulkan APIs for rasterization, and the associated GLX or EGL context management APIs [14], the OptiX GPU ray tracing framework [22], or the NVENC GPU-accelerated video encoding library.

Acknowledgments. The authors acknowledge support from NIH grants 9P41GM10 4601 and 5R01GM098243-02, the CUDA Center of Excellence at the University of Illinois, the Blue Waters sustained-petascale computing project supported by NSF awards OCI-0725070 and ACI-1238993, the state of Illinois, "The Computational Microscope" NSF PRAC awards OCI-0832673 and ACI-1440026, and the Oak Ridge Leadership Computing Facility at Oak Ridge National Laboratory supported by the Department of Energy under Contract DE-AC05-00OR22725.

References

1. Zhao, G., Perilla, J.R., Yufenyuy, E.L., Meng, X., Chen, B., Ning, J., Ahn, J., Gronenborn, A.M., Schulten, K., Aiken, C., Zhang, P.: Mature HIV-1 capsid structure by cryo-electron microscopy and all-atom molecular dynamics. Nature **497**, 643–646 (2013)

2. Liu, C., Perilla, J.R., Ning, J., Lu, M., Hou, G., Ramalho, R., Bedwell, G., Byeon, I.J., Ahn, J., Shi, J., Gronenborn, A., Prevelige, P., Rousso, I., Aiken, C., Polenova, T., Schulten, K., Zhang, P.: Cyclophilin A stabilizes HIV-1 capsid through a novel non-canonical binding site. Nat. Commun. **7**, Article no. 10714, 10 pages (2016)

3. Sothiselvam, S., Liu, B., Han, W., Klepacki, D., Atkinson, G.C., Brauer, A., Remm, M., Tenson, T., Schulten, K., Vázquez-Laslop, N., Mankin, A.S.: Macrolide antibiotics allosterically predispose the ribosome for translation arrest. Proc. Natl. Acad. Sci. USA **111**, 9804–9809 (2014)

4. Mendes, C.L., Bode, B., Bauer, G.H., Enos, J., Beldica, C., Kramer, W.T.: Deploying a large petascale system: the Blue Waters experience. Procedia Comput. Sci. **29**, 198–209 (2014)

5. Joubert, W., Archibald, R., Berrill, M., Brown, W.M., Eisenbach, M., Grout, R., Larkin, J., Levesque, J., Messer, B., Norman, M., Philip, B., Sankaran, R., Tharrington, A., Turner, J.: Accelerated application development: the ORNL Titan experience. Comput. Electr. Eng. **46**, 123–138 (2015)

6. Phillips, J.C., Braun, R., Wang, W., Gumbart, J., Tajkhorshid, E., Villa, E., Chipot, C., Skeel, R.D., Kale, L., Schulten, K.: Scalable molecular dynamics with NAMD. J. Comp. Chem. **26**, 1781–1802 (2005)
7. Phillips, J.C., Stone, J.E., Schulten, K.: Adapting a message-driven parallel application to GPU-accelerated clusters. In: Proceedings of the 2008 ACM/IEEE Conference on Supercomputing, SC 2008, 9 pages. IEEE Press, Piscataway, NJ, USA (2008)
8. Humphrey, W., Dalke, A., Schulten, K.: VMD - visual molecular dynamics. J. Mol. Graph. **14**, 33–38 (1996)
9. Stone, J.E., Isralewitz, B., Schulten, K.: Early experiences scaling VMD molecular visualization and analysis jobs on Blue Waters. In: Extreme Scaling Workshop (XSW 2013), pp. 43–50 (2013)
10. Stone, J.E., Sener, M., Vandivort, K.L., Barragan, A., Singharoy, A., Teo, I., Ribeiro, J.V., Isralewitz, B., Liu, B., Goh, B.C., Phillips, J.C., MacGregor-Chatwin, C., Johnson, M.P., Kourkoutis, L.F., Hunter, C.N., Schulten, K.: Atomic detail visualization of photosynthetic membranes with GPU-accelerated ray tracing. Parallel Comput. **55**, 17–27 (2016)
11. Götz, A.W., Williamson, M.J., Xu, D., Poole, D., Grand, S.L., Walker, R.C.: Routine microsecond molecular dynamics simulations with AMBER on GPUs. 1. Generalized Born. J. Chem. Theory Comput. **8**, 1542–1555 (2012)
12. Essmann, U., Perera, L., Berkowitz, M.L., Darden, T., Lee, H., Pedersen, L.G.: A smooth particle mesh Ewald method. J. Chem. Phys. **103**, 8577–8593 (1995)
13. Darden, T., York, D., Pedersen, L.: Particle mesh Ewald: an N·log(N) method for Ewald sums in large systems. J. Chem. Phys. **98**, 10089–10092 (1993)
14. Stone, J.E., Messmer, P., Sisneros, R., Schulten, K.: High performance molecular visualization: In-situ and parallel rendering with EGL. In: 2016 IEEE International Parallel and Distributed Processing Symposium Workshop (IPDPSW) (2016, in Press)
15. Stone, J.E., Vandivort, K.L., Schulten, K.: GPU-accelerated molecular visualization on petascale supercomputing platforms. In: Proceedings of the 8th International Workshop on Ultrascale Visualization. UltraVis 2013, pp. 6:1–6:8. ACM, New York (2013)
16. Stone, J.E., McGreevy, R., Isralewitz, B., Schulten, K.: GPU-accelerated analysis and visualization of large structures solved by molecular dynamics flexible fitting. Faraday Discuss. **169**, 265–283 (2014)
17. Phillips, J.C., Stone, J.E., Vandivort, K.L., Armstrong, T.G., Wozniak, J.M., Wilde, M., Schulten, K.: Petascale Tcl with NAMD, VMD, and Swift/T. In: Workshop on High Performance Technical Computing in Dynamic Languages, SC 2014, pp. 6–17. IEEE Press (2014)
18. Ribeiro, J.V., Bernardi, R.C., Rudack, T., Stone, J.E., Phillips, J.C., Freddolino, P.L., Schulten, K.: QwikMD-integrative molecular dynamics toolkit for novices and experts. Sci. Rep. **6**, 26536 (2016)
19. Pronk, S., Páll, S., Schulz, R., Larsson, P., Bjelkmar, P., Apostolov, R., Shirts, M.R., Smith, J.C., Kasson, P.M., van der Spoel, D., Hess, B., Lindahl, E.: Gromacs 4.5: a high-throughput and highly parallel open source molecular simulation toolkit. Bioinformatics **29**, 845–854 (2013)
20. Vermaas, J.V., Hardy, D.J., Stone, J.E., Tajkhorshid, E., Kohlmeyer, A.: TopoGromacs: automated topology conversion from CHARMM to GROMACS within VMD. J. Chem. Inf. Model. (2016, in Press)
21. Stone, J.E.: An efficient library for parallel ray tracing and animation. Master's thesis, Computer Science Department, University of Missouri-Rolla (1998)

22. Parker, S.G., Bigler, J., Dietrich, A., Friedrich, H., Hoberock, J., Luebke, D., McAllister, D., McGuire, M., Morley, K., Robison, A., Stich, M.: OptiX: a general purpose ray tracing engine. In: ACM SIGGRAPH 2010 papers, SIGGRAPH 2010, pp. 66:1–66:13. ACM, New York (2010)

23. Wald, I., Woop, S., Benthin, C., Johnson, G.S., Ernst, M.: Embree: a kernel framework for efficient CPU ray tracing. ACM Trans. Graph. **33**, 143:1–143:8 (2014)

24. Nickolls, J., Buck, I., Garland, M., Skadron, K.: Scalable parallel programming with CUDA. ACM Queue **6**, 40–53 (2008)

25. Pharr, M., Mark, W.: ispc: A SPMD compiler for high-performance CPU programming. In: Innovative Parallel Computing (InPar 2012), pp. 1–13 (2012)

26. Stone, J.E., Sherman, W.R., Schulten, K.: Immersive molecular visualization with omnidirectional stereoscopic ray tracing and remote rendering. In: 2016 IEEE International Parallel and Distributed Processing Symposium Workshop (IPDPSW) (2016, in Press)

27. Wang, X., Xu, F., Liu, J., Gao, B., Liu, Y., Zhai, Y., Ma, J., Zhang, K., Baker, T.S., Schulten, K., Zheng, D., Pang, H., Sun, F.: Atomic model of rabbit hemorrhagic disease virus by cryo-electron microscopy and crystallography. PLoS Pathog. **9**, e1003132 (2013). (14 pages)

28. Stone, J.E., Saam, J., Hardy, D.J., Vandivort, K.L., Hwu, W.W., Schulten, K.: High performance computation and interactive display of molecular orbitals on GPUs and multi-core CPUs. In: Proceedings of the 2nd Workshop on General-Purpose Processing on Graphics Processing Units, ACM International Conference Proceeding Series, vol. 383, pp. 9–18. ACM, New York (2009)

29. Stone, J.E., Hardy, D.J., Saam, J., Vandivort, K.L., Schulten, K.: GPU-accelerated computation and interactive display of molecular orbitals. In: Hwu, W. (ed.) GPU Computing Gems, pp. 5–18. Morgan Kaufmann Publishers, San Francisco (2011)

30. Stone, J.E., Hallock, M.J., Phillips, J.C., Peterson, J.R., Luthey-Schulten, Z., Schulten, K.: Evaluation of emerging energy-efficient heterogeneous computing platforms for biomolecular and cellular simulation workloads. In: 2016 IEEE International Parallel and Distributed Processing Symposium Workshop (IPDPSW) (2016, in Press)

Exploring Energy Efficiency
for GPU-Accelerated POWER Servers

Thorsten Hater[1], Benedikt Anlauf[2], Paul Baumeister[1], Markus Bühler[2],
Jiri Kraus[3], and Dirk Pleiter[1(✉)]

[1] Forschungszentrum Jülich, JSC, 52425 Jülich, Germany
{t.hater,p.baumeister,d.pleiter}@fz-juelich.de
[2] IBM Deutschland Research and Development GmbH, 71032 Böblingen, Germany
{anlaufb,buehler}@de.ibm.com
[3] NVIDIA GmbH, Würselen, Germany
jkraus@nvidia.com

Abstract. Modern servers provide different features for managing the
amount of energy that is needed to execute a given work-load. In this
article we focus on a new generation of GPU-accelerated servers with
POWER8 processors. For different scientific applications, which have in
common that they have been written for massively-parallel computers,
we measure energy-to-solution for different system configurations. By
combining earlier developed performance models and a simple power
model, we derive an energy model that can help to optimise for energy
efficiency.

Keywords: POWER8 · GPU acceleration · Power measurements ·
Power modelling · Energy efficiency

1 Introduction

The power consumption of supercomputers has become a major limiting factor
for further increases in performance. For particularly compute intensive workloads like the high-performance Linpack benchmark, currently a power efficiency
of 7 GFlop/s/W can be reached on (smaller) supercomputers [13].

With the goal of keeping the power consumption of an exascale system below
20 MW, an improvement in power efficiency of at least a factor seven is required.
Achieving this goal will require combining multiple strategies.

Leveraging existing system features that impact performance and power consumption (and thus energy-to-solution) is one of them. We review some of these
features available on GPU-accelerated servers based on POWER8 processors.
This includes, e.g., the core clock frequencies of processor and accelerator. Higher
frequencies typically lead to a reduction in time-to-solution and (due to the
behaviour of CMOS technology) unavoidably to an increase in power consumption. In line with previous observations, we observe a reduction of energy-to-
solution for increasing the clock speed, i.e. a "run to idle" clock tuning strategy to be beneficial. For the considered system this effect is particularly large

© Springer International Publishing AG 2016
M. Taufer et al. (Eds.): ISC High Performance Workshops 2016, LNCS 9945, pp. 207–227, 2016.
DOI: 10.1007/978-3-319-46079-6_15

because of the high idle power consumption. The memory sub-system attached to the POWER processor comprising a larger number of memory buffer chips contributes significantly to that.

To identify the setting for which energy-to-solution becomes minimal performance and power models can be helpful. Performance models enable prediction of time-to-solution for different parts of a work-load, while the power model is needed to predict the power that is consumed on average while executing a particular part of the work-load. Combining both multiplicatively allows to predict energy-to-solution.

For this paper we consider three different applications that come from different research areas. They have in common that they are used to target research questions, for which significant HPC resources are required. Their performance characteristics, however, differ significantly. B-CALM is an application for simulating electro-magnetic fields in dispersive media, which is relevant for developing photonic products. From the area of materials research we selected the application KKRnano, which implements the Density Functional Theory (DFT) method in a particularly scalable way. Finally, we also consider the molecular dynamics package GROMACS.

With this article we make the following contributions:

1. An overview on opportunities for optimising energy-to-solution on GPU-accelerated POWER8 servers is given.
2. Results for energy-to-solution measurements for kernels of several relevant scientific applications and different system configurations are given.
3. A simple power model is derived and combined with available performance models to model energy-to-solution.

After providing background on the relevant technologies in Sect. 2 we discuss the considered applications in Sect. 3 and the options to tune for energy-efficiency in Sect. 4. In Sect. 5 we present results from power measurements for different configurations. Based on these results we derive power and energy models with empirically determined parameters in Sect. 6. Before presenting our conclusions in Sect. 8, we give an overview on related work in Sect. 7.

2   Technology Background

All results presented in this paper have been obtained on a single POWER8 8247-42L Server [8]. This server, which comprises 2 POWER8 Dual-Chip Modules (DCM), was the first to support acceleration by NVIDIA GPUs. The server considered here is equipped with 2 Tesla K40m cards.

Each of the POWER8 modules comprises 5 cores, i.e. there are 20 cores per node. Each core offers two sets of the following instruction pipelines: fixed point (FXU), floating-point (VSU), pure load (LU) and a load-store unit (LSU). Instructions are processed out-of-order to increase instruction level parallelism. The cores feature 8-way Simultaneous Multi-threading. The two VSU support

VSX (Vector-Scalar eXtensions) instructions, including two-way SIMD, double-precision fused multiply-add instructions. This results in a theoretical peak performance per node

$$B_{\mathrm{fp}}^{(\mathrm{CPU})} = N_{\mathrm{core}} \cdot f_{\mathrm{CPU}} \cdot 8\,\mathrm{Flop} \leq 590\,\mathrm{GFlop/s}, \tag{1}$$

where N_{core} denotes the number of cores (here $N_{\mathrm{core}} = 20$) and f_{CPU} is the core clock frequency.

Each POWER8 processor is connected to eight external memory buffer chips (Centaur chips). Each of these 16 chips is connected with one link to one of the POWER8 processors, which has a bandwidth of 16 GByte/s and 8 GByte/s for reading and writing, respectively.

Each Tesla K40m hosts a GK110B GPU of the Kepler generation that comprises $N_{\mathrm{SM}} = 15$ streaming multi-processors. Each streaming multi-processors has 64 double precision floating point pipelines capable of executing one fused multiply-add instruction every clock. This results in a theoretical peak performance per GPU

$$B_{\mathrm{fp}}^{(\mathrm{GPU})} = N_{\mathrm{SM}} \cdot f_{\mathrm{GPU}} \cdot 128\,\mathrm{Flop} \leq 1622\,\mathrm{GFlop/s}, \tag{2}$$

where f_{GPU} is the GPU's clock frequency. The device memory is based on GDDR5 memory technology and is directly attached to GK110B GPU with a theoretical maximum bandwidth of 288 GByte/s.

The POWER8 processor provides an on-chip controller (OCC) to measure a set of sensors in the hardware. The data is available out-of-band via a service processor and can be read out by a tool called Amester [15,28], which recently has been made available open-source.[1] The power sensors considered in this publication are sampled with an interval of 0.25 ms. The read-out granularity depends on the number of sensors, each requires an additional latency of typically 200 ms. The data is, therefore, gathered in irregular intervals and is re-sampled at evenly spaced intervals of $\Delta\tau = 0.1$ s. To calculate the overall energy consumption we have to aggregate the power consumption measurements P_i and multiply this with the measurement interval $\Delta\tau$. The sensor does not allow for exactly attributing consumed power to individual server components. For instance, the sensor for the 12 V domain includes different I/O devices, also covering part of the power consumed by the GPUs. We combine the values of these sensors when presenting power traces, thus overestimating the actual power consumed by the GPU.[2]

As can be seen from Fig. 4, the read-out time interval can be large compared to the time scale on which power consumption changes. We verified, however, that energy-to-solution values determined from repeated measurements for the same application kernel are consistent with a reasonable bound[3], which we take as an indication that the power sensor sampling rates are sufficiently fine.

---

[1] https://github.com/open-power/amester.

[2] Comparison with `nvidia-smi` indicates an overhead of roughly 40 W measured with idle system.

[3] Less than 15 % of the mean value in pathological cases.

3 Applications

KKRnano is an application from materials research and features a very high level of scalability [39]. It is based on the Density Functional Theory (DFT) method that enables an accurate description of the electronic properties of a material. Instead of solving for the many-electron wave-function, an effective potential is utilised, treating the problem as a single electron system via the Kohn-Sham equation $\hat{H}\Psi = E\Psi$. Here $\hat{H}$ denotes the Hamilton operator, E the energy and Ψ the electron wave functions. KKRnano finds solutions to this equation in the form of the Green function $\hat{G}(E) = (E - \hat{H})^{-1}$, as proposed by Korringa, Kohn and Rostoker (KKR) [4, 24, 25].

In large systems, where the number of atoms $N_{\mathrm{atom}} \gg 1000$, the Green function formulation can be approximated by systematically truncating long-ranged interactions between well-separated atoms. This reduces the overall complexity of the method from cubic to linear and, hence, large systems with $100{,}000$ atoms and more become feasible. The high level of exposed parallelism can be exploited using MPI plus OpenMP or MPI plus compute accelerators, like GPUs.

Most of the computational efforts are spent on solving a linear system $\Lambda\gamma = \omega$ for each atom. The matrix Λ is block-sparse with a typical block size $b = 16$. The inversion is done locally on a single node using the Quasi Minimal Residual (QMR) method, an iterative solver [16], modified to work over matrices and vectors with block structure. For the following discussion, we focus on the application of the operator to a block-structured dense vector as the central part of the QMR solver. KKRnano utilises double-precision complex numbers, requiring 16 Byte per element and 8 Flop to perform a complex multiply-accumulate operation.

Our performance modelling approach is based on the information exchange function concept [5, 30], which captures as a function of the problem size the amount of information that has to be exchanged within a computer architecture. On a single node the most important factors are the number of floating-point operations I_{fp} as well as the amount of data loaded and stored, namely I_{ld} and I_{st}. We further need to consider the data exchanged between the accelerator and its host, I_{acc}. For the KKRnano kernel we previously derived these information exchange functions:

$$I_{\mathrm{fp}} = 2N_{\mathrm{iter}} \cdot \frac{N_{\mathrm{atom}}}{N_{\mathrm{node}}} \cdot N_{\mathrm{tr}} \cdot N_{\mathrm{cl}} \cdot b^3 \cdot 8\,\mathrm{Flop}\,, \tag{3}$$

$$I_{\mathrm{ld}} = 2N_{\mathrm{iter}} \cdot \frac{N_{\mathrm{atom}}}{N_{\mathrm{node}}} \cdot N_{\mathrm{tr}} \cdot N_{\mathrm{cl}} \cdot b^2 \cdot 16\,\mathrm{Byte}\,, \tag{4}$$

$$I_{\mathrm{st}} = 2N_{\mathrm{iter}} \cdot \frac{N_{\mathrm{atom}}}{N_{\mathrm{node}}} \cdot N_{\mathrm{cl}} \cdot b^2 \cdot 16\,\mathrm{Byte}\,, \tag{5}$$

$$I_{\mathrm{acc}} = \frac{N_{\mathrm{atom}}}{N_{\mathrm{node}}} \cdot (2 + N_{\mathrm{cl}}) \cdot N_{\mathrm{tr}} \cdot b^2 \cdot 16\,\mathrm{Byte}\,. \tag{6}$$

To construct a performance model, we follow a procedure described in [3], where we made the assumption that latency depends linearly on the amount

Table 1. Parameters used for all KKRnano benchmark runs.

Implementation	$N_{\text{atom}}/N_{\text{node}}$	N_{iter}	N_{tr}	N_{cl}	b
CPU	20	1000	1000	13	16
GPU	20	10000	1000	13	16

of exchanged information. When executing the application on the POWER8 processors, we expect it to be bound by floating-point operation throughput, because of the relatively high memory bandwidth. On the GPU, however, we expect the memory bandwidth to be the limiting factor. Additionally, we have to take the time needed to exchange data between host and device into account. We, therefore, make the following semi-empirical modelling ansatz:

$$\Delta t_{\text{solver}}^{\text{CPU}} = a_0^{\text{CPU}} + a_{1,\text{fp}}^{\text{CPU}} I_{\text{fp}} \tag{7}$$

$$\Delta t_{\text{solver}}^{\text{GPU}} = a_0^{\text{GPU}} + a_{1,\text{mem}}^{\text{GPU}}(I_{\text{ld}} + I_{\text{st}}) + a_{1,\text{acc}}^{\text{GPU}} I_{\text{acc}}, \tag{8}$$

where the coefficients have to be determined by fitting this ansatz to performance measurements. As the constants offsets are sufficiently small, we set $a_0^{\text{CPU}} = 0$ and $a_0^{\text{GPU}} = 0$.

B-CALM (Belgium-California Light Machine) is a research application for studying photonics or in general electromagnetic waves in media [41]. It implements the Finite-Difference Time-Domain (FDTD) numerical method for simulating classical electrodynamic interaction, that is to solve Maxwell's equations in a medium [37]. The evolution of the discretised electromagnetic fields is described by a first-order spatial and temporal difference equation, alternating between magnetic and electrostatic components.

B-CALM exploits the inherently high level of parallelism in the FDTD algorithm by making use of GPUs. Significant gains in performance compared to CPU-only-implementations have been reported for FDTD in general [27,33,41]. Realistic problems require the use of multiple distributed GPUs due to the memory footprint.

We apply a similar semi-empirical performance modelling approach as for KKRnano [3]. We consider a single node where the simulation domain is parallelised over $p = 2$ GPUs in z-direction. The total time taken for an update step Δt can be decomposed into three contributions: boundary update Δt_{bnd}, update of the interior domain Δt_{bulk} and exchange of the boundary Δt_{com} between the direct neighbours of the p processes, where the last two operations are overlapped. Our semi-empirical performance model ansatz is:

$$\Delta t = \Delta t_{\text{bnd}} + \max\left(\Delta t_{\text{bulk}}, \Delta t_{\text{com}}\right), \tag{9}$$

$$\Delta t_{\text{bulk}} = a_{\text{bulk}} + V \cdot b_{\text{bulk}}\, 168\,\text{Byte}, \tag{10}$$

$$\Delta t_{\text{com}} = a_{\text{com}} + S \cdot b_{\text{com}}\, 48\,\text{Byte}, \tag{11}$$

$$\Delta t_{\text{bnd}} = a_{\text{bnd}} + S \cdot b_{\text{bnd}}\, 336\,\text{Byte}, \tag{12}$$

Table 2. Parameters used for all B-CALM benchmark runs.

$p = N_{\mathrm{proc}}/N_{\mathrm{node}}$	L_x	L_y	L_z
2	512	512	96

where $V = (L_x/p - 2) \cdot L_y \cdot L_z$ is the local sub-domain's volume excluding halo layers and $S = L_y \cdot L_z$ corresponding halo volume. For our benchmarks, we utilise a one-dimensional domain decomposition with the parameters summarised in Table 2.

GROMACS simulates Newtonian equations of motion to perform molecular dynamics. It is primarily designed for biochemical molecules like proteins, lipids and nucleic acids. A very important design goal of GROMACS is high performance which is achieved through algorithmic optimisations and by exploiting all available hardware resources. To achieve the latter it uses intrinsic functions for SIMD vectorisation and supports MPI and OpenMP for parallelisation on CPUs. CUDA C is used to accelerate the calculation of the non-bonded force components on NVIDIA accelerators. GPU accelerated runs of GROMACS utilise task parallelism between different force components to maximise resource utilisation, i.e. overlap CPU and GPU work. GROMACS applies a dynamic CPU/GPU load balancing, however, for optimal efficiency both parts – CPU and GPU – in the system need to be balanced [1].

For all runs of GROMACS in this article a water box with 1 million water molecules, i.e. 3 million particles, was simulated for 12000 time steps corresponding to 24 pico seconds of simulation time. We selected the Particle Mesh Ewald method for the long-range electrostatics and applied a domain decomposition with 40 domains. Each domain is processed by one MPI rank with 4 OpenMP threads and respectively 20 domains share a GPU.

4   Tuning for Energy Efficiency

The energy E required to execute a computational task is given by

$$E = \int_{t_0}^{t_0 + \Delta t} d\tau \, P(\tau) , \qquad (13)$$

where t_0 is the time when the computational task is started, Δt the time needed to execute the task, and $P(\tau)$ the power consumed by the system at time τ. If we assume the power consumption during execution of the kernel to be constant, i.e. $P(\tau) = \overline{P}$ then the relation simplifies to $E = \overline{P} \cdot \Delta t$.

For the given node architecture, we identify the following options for changing the implementation or the execution environment such that Δt and P change:

1. Dynamic voltage and frequency scaling (DVFS) capabilities of the POWER8 processor.
2. Exploitation per POWER8 core DVFS settings and low-power states.

3. Modification of the GPU's clock frequency f_{GPU}.
4. Change of GPU driver settings.
5. Use of algorithms optimised for energy-to-solution.

The frequency f a processing element is running at is exerting a significant influence on its power drain as voltage has to be increased when f is raised. The power consumption effectively scales as $P \propto f^{\gamma}$, with $\gamma \simeq 3$. On POWER8 the clock frequency can be managed by restricting the range of frequencies used by the Linux[4] kernel governor. The strategy employed by the governor follows the on-demand setting and results in the highest available frequency being chosen during our kernel's runtime and a power saving state in between runs. The available frequencies are distributed almost uniformly between 2.061 GHz and 3.690 GHz in 50 steps, out of which we chose $f_{CPU} \in \{2.061, 2.294, 2.493, 2.693, 2.892, 3.092, 3.291, 3.491, 3.690\}$ GHz.

The POWER8 processor comprises a PowerPC[5]-based On-Chip Controller (OCC), which provides for real-time control of per-core clock frequency and power states [17]. Additionally, cores can be switched off under control of the operating system enabling software to reduce the number of active cores. Instead of user selection of active cores, one may use thread pinning to move all workload to a subset of cores and rely on the OS to detect unused cores and adjust frequency and power settings accordingly.

Recently, also GPUs became able to operate at different clock frequencies. For the K40 GPU we considered 4 different clock states, namely $f_{GPU} \in \{666, 745, 810, 845\}$ MHz. Changing the GPU frequency of the K40 GPU is possible via application clock settings which are accessible from the NVIDIA Management Library (NVML) or the `nvidia-smi` command line tool [26].

The architecture considered here is best used from an energy-efficiency point-of-view if significant parts of the application can be off-loaded to the GPUs. The reason is that the GPU typically requires less energy per floating-point operation. In many cases, there is no concurrent execution of tasks both, on CPU and GPU, i.e. the CPU should be largely inactive while a kernel is executed on the GPU. However, by default the GPU driver is polling on an active lock while waiting for a kernel to complete. Alternatively, the driver can yield its thread to the Linux kernel scheduler and thus avoid polling, which is achieved by changing the device flags from `cudaDeviceScheduleSpin` to `cudaDeviceScheduleYield`. This might come with a small cost penalty for the driver as notification through the kernel may be delayed.

Recently, optimisation of algorithms for energy-efficiency attracted increasing attention. In particular, in case of solving linear systems often a choice between different algorithms exists (see, e.g., [22] for a recent investigation). We have not pursued this option within the scope of this paper.

---

[4] Linux is a registered trademark of Linus Torvalds in the United States, other countries, or both.

[5] Trademark of IBM in USA and/or other countries.

5   Measurements Results

Exploitation per POWER8 core DVFS settings and low-power states. In Fig. 1 we show power measurements for the KKRnano solver running either on 20 or 10 cores. We observe that the additional power consumed by the processor after starting the execution of the kernel is reduced by almost a factor 2. At the same time, the execution time Δt almost doubles. Given the high base power load for the processors, memory and GPUs, the overall reduction in power consumption is less than 15 % and thus energy-to-solution increases by more than 70 %.

Change of GPU driver settings. For the same application kernel, we analysed the power consumption when off-loading this to the GPUs. While a kernel is running on the GPU, there are no application tasks running on the CPU. Nevertheless, a significant increase of the power consumption beyond what is consumed without the user application running, as can be seen in Fig. 2. Between kernel launches the CPU performs tasks for steering the solvers progress. We investigated the effect of advising the CUDA driver to yield its thread to the operating system scheduler when possible. No effect was observed, consistently for both KKRnano and BCALM.

Modification of clock frequencies. Next we consider the power consumed by applications running on the POWER8 processor at different clock frequencies f_{CPU}. In Fig. 3 we show the power consumed by the processors, the memory subsystem as well as the GPU (including the other I/O devices attached to the 12 V power rail) during execution of the KKRnano solver on the CPU. As expected, the power consumption increases with f_{CPU}, while the execution time reduces.

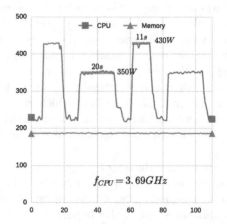

Fig. 1. Power consumption for four invocations of the KKRnano solver running on the CPU, only. 40 threads are distributed either over 20 (1st and 3rd invocation) or 10 cores (2nd and 4th).

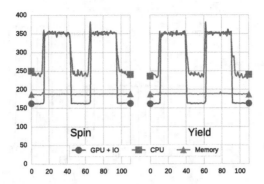

Fig. 2. Power consumption for two invocations of the KKRnano solver running on the GPU with the GPU driver polling for completion of the kernel (Spin) or yielding its thread to the operating system (Yield).

Table 3. Energy-to-solution for the KKRnano solver running on the CPU in units of kJ.

f_{CPU} (GHz)	CPU	Disk	Fan	GPU	IO	Memory	Total
2.06	20.6	2.6	5.8	1.9	4.2	15.5	50.5
2.29	20.3	2.4	5.4	1.7	3.8	14.2	47.8
2.49	20.2	2.2	5.0	1.6	3.5	13.3	45.8
2.69	20.2	2.1	4.7	1.5	3.3	12.5	44.4
2.89	20.3	1.9	4.4	1.4	3.1	11.8	42.9
3.09	20.4	1.8	4.1	1.3	2.9	11.1	41.7
3.29	20.5	1.7	4.0	1.2	2.8	10.5	40.7
3.49	21.5	1.7	3.8	1.2	2.7	10.2	41.1
3.69	23.0	1.6	3.5	1.2	2.6	9.8	41.6

Results for energy-to-solution as a function of f_{CPU} are documented in Table 3. For small clock frequencies the increase in time-to-solution overcompensates the reduction in power consumption, which causes energy-to-solution to increase. It is thus beneficial to use a higher clock frequency.

As shown in Fig. 4, a similar effect is observed for B-CALM, where the kernels are running on the GPU. Since the kernels are completely running on the GPU, we consider here only the case where the processor clock is kept fixed at minimal value and f_{GPU} is varied. In Tables 4 and 5 we show our results for energy-to-solution for B-CALM as well as the GPU-accelerated version of the KKRnano solver when using different GPU clock settings. In both cases we observe that larger f_{GPU} result in smaller energy-to-solution.

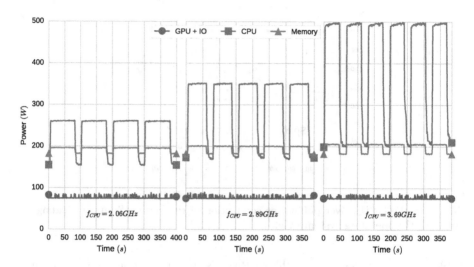

Fig. 3. Power consumption for multiple invocations of the KKRnano solver running on the CPU for different settings of f_{CPU}.

Table 4. Energy-to-solution for B-CALM in units of kJ.

f_{CPU} (GHz)	f_{GPU} (MHz)	CPU	Disk	Fan	GPU	IO	Memory	Total
2.06	666	4.1	0.8	1.8	3.8	2.9	4.5	17.8
2.06	745	4.0	0.8	1.8	3.8	2.8	4.5	17.7
2.06	810	3.5	0.7	1.7	3.7	2.5	3.9	15.9
2.06	875	3.2	0.6	1.5	4.0	2.5	3.5	15.2

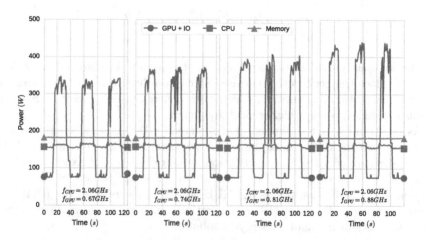

Fig. 4. Example of a GPU power trace over multiple invocations of B-CALM. GPU clocks are set to each of the available values.

Table 5. Energy-to-solution for the KKRnano solver running on the GPU in units of kJ.

f_{CPU} (GHz)	f_{GPU} (MHz)	CPU	Disk	Fan	GPU	IO	Memory	Total
2.06	666	7.1	1.1	2.5	6.3	4.0	5.9	26.8
2.06	745	6.0	1.0	2.2	6.4	3.8	5.4	24.8
2.06	810	5.9	0.9	2.0	6.6	3.6	5.0	24.0
2.06	875	5.6	0.8	1.9	7.1	3.5	4.7	23.7

As opposed to the other two codes, GROMACS has a task parallelisation scheme that allows to execute tasks on CPU and GPU concurrently. Data is exchanged at defined points in the algorithm [29]. As both, the CPU and the GPU consume a significant amount of power even when not being in use, an imperfect overlap of tasks running on any of the 4 processing devices will result in a loss in energy efficiency. Table 6 shows the energy consumption and time to solution for a single run as a function of f_{GPU} for different processor frequencies f_{CPU}. We observe that changing the processor frequency f_{CPU} has a much larger effect on energy-to-solution than changing the frequency of the GPU f_{GPU}. The energy to solution is reduced by 8 % to 17 % when using the higher CPU frequency, while variations of f_{GPU} change the energy to solution by at maximum 7 %. While the energy consumed by the GPU increases for larger clock frequencies (up to 40 % with low f_{CPU}, up to 22 % for high f_{CPU}), the energy consumed by the remaining parts of the compute node is reduced (by up to 11 %) due to the shorter time to solution (see Fig. 5). On the other hand, increasing f_{CPU} has a even more significant effect on time-to-solution (up to 32 %), which overcompensates the increase in CPU power consumption (up to 20 %). The net effect is a reduction of energy-to-solution at higher clock speed, ranging between 8 % and 20 %.

Finally, we give power measurements for the behaviour of the STREAM benchmark at different clock settings in Table 7 and the corresponding power trace in Fig. 6. Notably, the achieved performance does not depend on the core

Table 6. GROMACS energy to solution in kJ.

f_{CPU} (GHz)	f_{GPU} (MHz)	CPU	Disk	Fan	GPU	IO	Memory	Total	Time (s)
2.06	666	365.6	44.6	101.3	203.0	181.4	303.2	1199.2	1395
2.06	745	363.6	45.1	103.2	247.2	191.1	304.4	1254.6	1410
2.06	810	352.1	43.4	98.7	259.7	187.1	293.4	1234.4	1359
2.06	875	349.8	43.0	97.6	284.0	188.7	290.9	1253.8	1344
3.69	666	457.2	33.1	75.4	168.5	139.7	234.0	1108.0	1041
3.69	745	426.3	30.2	69.0	170.1	130.1	215.1	1040.8	949
3.69	810	426.7	30.2	68.3	175.0	129.9	215.1	1045.2	949
3.69	875	403.3	28.9	65.3	205.6	130.7	203.5	1037.2	907

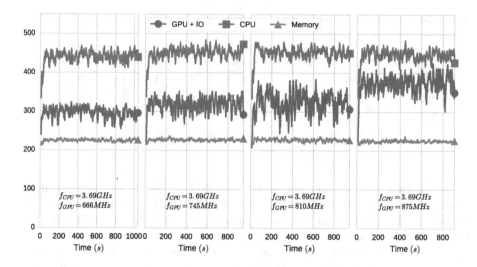

Fig. 5. GROMACS power trace for different GPU clock settings.

Table 7. Performance of STREAM as a function of the CPU frequency.

f_{CPU} (GHz)	Add (GB/s)	Copy (GB/s)	Scale (GB/s)	Triad (GB/s)
2.061	195.1	222.1	338.5	289.7
2.294	197.0	221.8	338.4	293.5
2.493	195.0	221.4	334.5	291.8
2.693	197.4	221.7	337.9	293.9
2.891	196.3	218.6	327.0	293.4
3.291	197.6	222.1	334.3	296.5
3.690	196.0	219.2	330.0	293.1

clock. This is explained by the fact that the serial link between CPU and off-chip memory controller runs at a fixed speed. In line with previous observations [12,31], one can conclude that for purely memory bandwidth bound operations the clock speed can be reduced without impacting performance.

6 Power and Energy Modelling

Our strategy to derive an energy model is as follows. We only consider the case where all options for tuning for energy efficiency except for changing clock speeds of CPU and GPU are applied. Furthermore, we make the assumption that power consumption during application kernel execution is constant. The challenge thus reduces to the design of a performance model and a power model to determine time-to-solution Δt and power consumption $\overline{P}$, which we assume to be constant

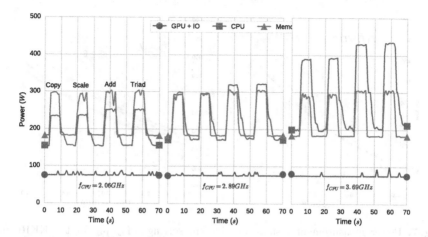

Fig. 6. Example of a CPU power trace over the four tasks in the STREAM micro-benchmark. Three of used values for the CPU clock are shown.

during the time interval Δt, as a function of the CPU and GPU clock frequencies f_{CPU} and f_{GPU}, respectively.

For deriving a power model we choose for a phenomenological approach, which has the advantage of being sufficient simple to be of practical use. The concerned compute devices are based on CMOS circuits, where power is typically split in two components: A static power consumption due to leakage currents and a dynamic contribution due to charging and de-charging the capacitive elements of the circuit. The latter is assumed to depend linearly on the clock frequency and quadratically on the supply voltage. Since the latter needs to be increased for higher clock frequencies, we can in first approximation assume a cubic dependency on the frequency. We therefore make the following generic ansatz in terms of the frequency f:

$$\overline{P}(f) = p_0 + p_3 f^\gamma, \tag{14}$$

with $\gamma = 3$ fixed.[6] The parameters p_0 and p_3 will be determined through least-square fits to experimental data.

In Fig. 7 we show results for power consumption of the KKRnano solver as well as 4 different STREAM benchmarks, which are all executed on the POWER8 processor, as a function of f_{CPU}. Multiple measurements have been obtained by executing the application kernels and benchmarks multiple times in sequence. Active phases were selected based on thresholding the power for the GPU halfway between minimum and maximum values. We observe that Eq. (14) using $f = f_{CPU}$ parametrises the measurements very well.

The instruction mix for the KKRnano kernel is similar to the triad micro-benchmark. However, the KKRnano kernel achieves a significantly higher instruction throughput when compared to triad (instruction-per-cycle IPC = 1.44 versus 0.24 when using 40 threads). The higher throughput is mainly

---

[6] We also performed fits with γ as a free parameter, where we found $\gamma \simeq 3$.

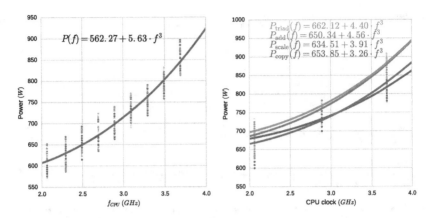

Fig. 7. Power measurement results for different settings of f_{CPU} for the KKRnano kernel running on the CPU (left) and the STREAM benchmarks (right). The solid lines show results from fits to Eq. (14).

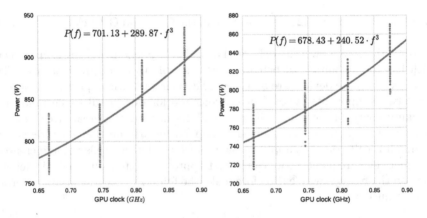

Fig. 8. Fitting the model against KKRnano GPU (left) and B-CALM (right) experimental results

due to the data reuse in the matrix-matrix multiplication and the resulting cache efficiency. This is consistent with the observation that p_3 is larger for KKRnano than for the STREAM benchmarks.

We extended the analysis to the GPU-accelerated application kernels, where we varied f_{GPU}. Results for KKRnano and B-CALM are summarised in Fig. 8. Again we observe that Eq. (14) provides a good parametrisation of the measured power.

Next, we extend the performance model for KKRnano introduced in Eq. (7) by considering the parameter $a_{1,fp}^{CPU}$ to be a function of the clock frequency f_{CPU}. We observe from Fig. 10 that the results for different f_{CPU} can be parametrised as follows:

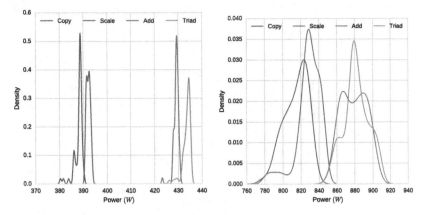

Fig. 9. Estimated distributions of power drain for $f_{CPU} = 3.69\,\text{GHz}$ for the four STREAM micro-benchmarks on the CPU level (left) and on the node level (right).

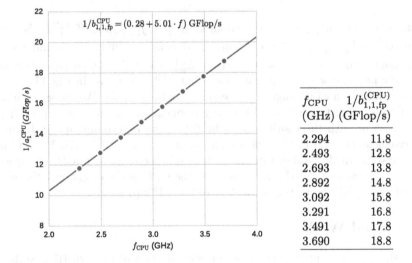

f_{CPU} (GHz)	$1/b_{1,1,fp}^{(CPU)}$ (GFlop/s)
2.294	11.8
2.493	12.8
2.693	13.8
2.892	14.8
3.092	15.8
3.291	16.8
3.491	17.8
3.690	18.8

Fig. 10. KKRnano performance model results versus processor clock f_{CPU}.

$$\frac{1}{a_{1,fp}^{CPU}(f_{CPU})} = b_{1,0,fp}^{CPU} + b_{1,1,fp}^{CPU} \cdot f_{CPU} \qquad (15)$$

with the empirical factors $b_{1,0,fp}^{CPU} = 0.28\,\text{GFlop/s}$ and $b_{1,1,fp}^{CPU} = 5.01\,\text{GFlop}$.

Plugging this result into Eq. (7) gives us Δt_{solver}^{CPU} as a function of the processor clock speed f_{CPU}. We combine this with the power model of Eq. (14) to derive the following energy model:

$$E_{solv}^{CPU} = \overline{P}(f_{CPU}) \cdot \Delta t(f_{CPU}) = I_{fp}\frac{p_0 + p_3 \cdot f_{CPU}^3}{b_{1,0,fp}^{CPU} + b_{1,1,fp}^{CPU} \cdot f_{CPU}} \cdot \qquad (16)$$

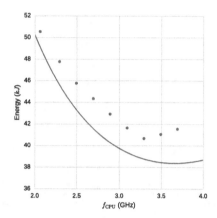

Fig. 11. Modelled energy-to-solution metric for the KKRnano CPU solver as a function of the processor core clock f_{CPU}. In comparison the measured data from Table 5 is shown.

In particular, if p_0 is large compared to $p_3 \cdot f_{\text{CPU}}^3$ and if $b_{1,0,\text{fp}}^{CPU}$ is small compared to $b_{1,1,\text{fp}}^{CPU} \cdot f_{\text{CPU}}$ the frequency dependence may be dominated by the denominator. In this case we expect $E_{\text{solv}}^{\text{CPU}} \propto f_{\text{CPU}}^{-1}$. Once f_{CPU} becomes large, the numerator will dominate such that $E_{\text{solv}}^{\text{CPU}} \propto f_{\text{CPU}}^2$. In Fig. 11 we plot model results for a wide range of processor clock frequencies. We observe initially energy-to-solution to drop, until for large frequencies the numerator prevails.

Consistent with the results shown in Table 3 we determine an – in terms of energy-efficiency – optimal clock setting, namely $f_{\text{CPU}} = 3.5\,\text{GHz}$. We find our model systematically underestimating the required energy by maximally around 7 % over the range 2–4 GHz. KKRnano on the CPU achieves energy efficiencies of around 45 J/GFlop or the equivalent of 22.2 MFlop/J.

7   Related Work

Given the growing importance of power consumption of modern HPC systems, there is a growing number of papers reporting on work related to power measurements as well as power modelling.

An early framework for accurate and scalable power profiling is PowerPack [18], which relies however on power data acquisition devices to be added to all cluster nodes. Another framework is PowerScope, which was developed for mobile compute platforms [14]. Some node architectures feature fine-grained power measurements capabilities, which are often based on reconfigurable hardware components for high-frequency read-out of power sensors (see, e.g., [20]). Demmel and Gearhart proposed to use on-chip counters, more specifically Intel's Running Average Power Limit (RAPL) interface, for measuring energy consumption at subroutine level [10]. Investigations about the use of the RAPL interface for measuring memory power can be found in the literature [9]. Such kind of measurements using counters that can be read-out from the processor have become easier with the integration into performance measurements frameworks like PAPI [42]. An integration of the the node-level power measurement framework Amester into Vampir has been reported by Knobloch and others [23]. Another approach is taken, where power measurement capabilities are integrated into a Linux kernel module [32]. Both, the PowerPack as well as the PAPI framework have been used to explore the energy footprint of linear algebra algorithms [11].

Other work aims on modelling power consumption at processor level. For instance, a power measurement and runtime power modeling framework for the Intel Netburst architecture is presented [21]. Processor level power models have also been proposed and used in the context of processor selection to identify, e.g., processors that yield a certain frequency in a given power budget [45]. At a time, when direct power measurement capabilities were largely non-existing, Van Bui and others advocated using power models that used performance counters as input, for estimating power consumed by applications [6]. Such approaches can be exploited for dynamic profitability estimation of dynamic voltage and frequency scaling (DVFS) [12,31].

With GPUs becoming more widely used as computational devices, research was started on power models for GPUs. Statistical methods to model power and energy consumption of common high performance kernels have been employed successfully [19]. In a new approach hardware performance counter data is combined with machine learning to model power and performance for modern GPU-based systems [34]. Also Wu and others applied machine learning in their work [44].

Other approaches to power modelling target numerical kernels. Statistical methods like multi-variable regression are used to model the power and performance of the High-Performance Linpack benchmark [36]. Model parameters are application parameters like matrix size or block size. The same numerical kernel is also considered [7]. Power models for another important numerical kernel, namely Cholesky factorisation, are considered using a semi-analytical approach [2]. Machine learning techniques are also employed to create application specific power models [40]. Input parameters include application specific plus system parameters, like clock frequency. For an extensive survey of power and energy efficient techniques for high performance numerical linear algebra operations we refer to the work of Tan and others [38].

Performance models for more complex applications are, e.g., considered in [43]. Here Wittmann and others use models to explore energy efficiency of a computational fluid-dynamics (CFD) application based on the Lattice Boltzmann method on Intel Sandy Bridge multi-core processors. They combined an analytic performance model with a simple phenomenological power model. A semi-analytical performance and power model for another CFD application, namely a mini-application version of the spectral element method based code Nek5000, is presented in [35].

8 Summary and Conclusions

In this paper we investigated for several scientific applications, how energy efficiency of currently available, GPU-accelerated POWER8 servers can be optimised. We discussed several options for how to change application and/or system configuration such that energy-to-solution for a given workload could be reduced. We found that, in particular, adjusting processor or GPU clock have major impact on energy-to-solution. Except for the STREAM benchmarks we found that applications typically benefit from higher clock speeds. This behaviour can be explained by the relatively high base power consumption. Within a certain range of clock frequencies it is thus more beneficial to reduce time-to-solution by using higher clock frequencies. For applications running on the processor only, this applies, however, only to applications that are limited by instruction throughput.

Furthermore, we found that the measured power consumption can be described by a simple phenomenological power model, which describes power consumption as a function of the CPU or GPU clock frequency. For one of the application kernels, the KKRnano solver, we extended a performance model to include variations of the processor clock frequency. By combining the performance and power model we derived a simple energy model. The curve shown in Fig. 11 is based on four parameters, only, which are relatively easy to determine. This can be used to tune the clock frequency. For KKRnano the model results and measurements lead to a reasonably consistent results for the CPU clock frequency f_{CPU} that minimises energy-to-solution.

A significant fraction of the base power consumption, i.e. the power that is consumed without an application running, is due to the memory subsystem. The base power consumption on servers based on POWER8 processors with a smaller number of memory buffer chips is lower and therefore the clock frequency, for which power consumption is minimised, is likely to be smaller. The picture is expect to change again for the recently announced POWER9-SO processors with directly attached memory.

Acknowledgements. This work has been carried out in the context of the *POWER Acceleration and Design Center*, a joined project between IBM, Forschungszentrum Jülich and NVIDIA. We acknowledge generous support from IBM by providing early access to GPU-accelerated POWER8 systems.

References

1. Abraham, M.J., Murtola, T., Schulz, R., Páll, S., Smith, J.C., Hess, B., Lindahl, E.: GROMACS: high performance molecular simulations through multi-level parallelism from laptops to supercomputers. SoftwareX **1**, 19–25 (2015)
2. Alonso, P., Dolz, M.F., Mayo, R., Quintana-Ortí, E.S.: Modeling power and energy of the task-parallel Cholesky factorization on multicore processors. Comput. Sci. Res. Dev. **29**(2), 105–112 (2012). doi:10.1007/s00450-012-0227-z

3. Baumeister, P.F., Hater, T., Kraus, J., Pleiter, D., Wahl, P.: A performance model for GPU-accelerated FDTD applications. In: 2015 IEEE 22nd International Conference on High Performance Computing (HiPC), pp. 185–193, December 2015
4. Beeby, J.: The density of electrons in a perfect or imperfect lattice. Proc. R. Soc. Lond. A Math. Phys. Eng. Sci. **302**(1468), 113–136 (1967). The Royal Society
5. Bilardi, G., Pietracaprina, A., Pucci, G., Schifano, F., Tripiccione, R.: The potential of on-chip multiprocessing for QCD machines. In: Bader, D.A., Parashar, M., Sridhar, V., Prasanna, V.K. (eds.) HiPC 2005. LNCS, vol. 3769, pp. 386–397. Springer, Heidelberg (2005). doi:10.1007/11602569_41
6. Bui, V., Norris, B., Huck, K., McInnes, L.C., Li, L., Hernandez, O., Chapman, B.: A component infrastructure for performance and power modeling of parallel scientific applications. In: Proceedings of the 2008 compFrame/HPC-GECO Workshop on Component Based High Performance, CBHPC 2008, pp. 6:1–6:11. (2008). http://doi.acm.org/10.1145/1456190.1456199
7. Cabrera, A., Almeida, F., Blanco, V., Giménez, D.: Analytical modeling of the energy consumption for the High Performance Linpack. In: 2013 21st Euromicro International Conference on Parallel, Distributed and Network-Based Processing (PDP), pp. 343–350, February 2013
8. Caldeira, A.B., et al.: IBM Power System S824L technical overview and introduction (2014). http://www.redbooks.ibm.com/Redbooks.nsf/RedbookAbstracts/redp5139.html
9. David, H., Gorbatov, E., Hanebutte, U.R., Khanna, R., Le, C.: RAPL: memory power estimation and capping. In: 2010 ACM/IEEE International Symposium on Low-Power Electronics and Design (ISLPED), pp. 189–194, August 2010
10. Demmel, J., Gearhart, A.: Instrumenting linear algebra energy consumption via on-chip energy counters. Technical report, UCB/EECS-2012-168, EECS Department, University of California, Berkeley, June 2012. http://www.eecs.berkeley.edu/Pubs/TechRpts/2012/EECS-2012-168.html
11. Dongarra, J., Ltaief, H., Luszczek, P., Weaver, V.M.: Energy footprint of advanced dense numerical linear algebra using tile algorithms on multicore architecture. In: The 2nd International Conference on Cloud and Green Computing, November 2012
12. Eyerman, S., Eeckhout, L.: A counter architecture for online DVFS profitability estimation. IEEE Trans. Comput. **59**(11), 1576–1583 (2010)
13. Feng, W.C., et al.: Green500 list, November 2015. http://green500.org
14. Flinn, J., Satyanarayanan, M.: PowerScope: a tool for profiling the energy usage of mobile applications. In: Proceedings of the Second IEEE Workshop on Mobile Computer Systems and Applications, WMCSA 1999, p. 2 (1999). http://dl.acm.org/citation.cfm?id=520551.837522
15. Floyd, M., et al.: Introducing the adaptive energy management features of the POWER7 chip. IEEE Micro **31**(2), 60–75 (2011)
16. Freund, R.W., Nachtigal, N.: QMR: a quasi-minimal residual method for non-Hermitian linear systems. Numer. Math. **60**(1), 315–339 (1991)
17. Friedrich, J., Le, H., Starke, W., Stuechli, J., Sinharoy, B., Fluhr, E., Dreps, D., Zyuban, V., Still, G., Gonzalez, C., Hogenmiller, D., Malgioglio, F., Nett, R., Puri, R., Restle, P., Shan, D., Deniz, Z., Wendel, D., Ziegler, M., Victor, D.: The POWER8^{TM} processor: designed for big data, analytics, and cloud environments. In: 2014 IEEE International Conference on IC Design Technology (ICICDT), pp. 1–4, May 2014
18. Ge, R., Feng, X., Song, S., Chang, H.C., Li, D., Cameron, K.W.: PowerPack: energy profiling and analysis of high-performance systems and applications. IEEE Trans. Parallel Distrib. Syst. **21**(5), 658–671 (2010)

19. Ghosh, S., Chandrasekaran, S., Chapman, B.: Statistical modeling of power/energy of scientific kernels on a multi-GPU system. In: 2013 International Green Computing Conference (IGCC), pp. 1–6, June 2013

20. Hackenberg, D., Ilsche, T., Schuchart, J., Schöne, R., Nagel, W.E., Simon, M., Georgiou, Y.: HDEEM: high definition energy efficiency monitoring. In: Energy Efficient Supercomputing Workshop, E2SC 2014, pp. 1–10, November 2014

21. Isci, C., Martonosi, M.: Runtime power monitoring in high-end processors: methodology and empirical data. In: 2003 Proceedings of the 36th Annual IEEE/ACM International Symposium on Microarchitecture, MICRO-36, pp. 93–104, December 2003

22. Klavík, P., Malossi, A.C.I., Bekas, C., Curioni, A.: Changing computing paradigms towards power efficiency. Philos. Trans. R. Soc. Lond. A: Math. Phys. Eng. Sci. 372(2018), 20130278 (2014)

23. Knobloch, M., Foszczynski, M., Homberg, W., Pleiter, D., Böttiger, H.: Mapping fine-grained power measurements to HPC application runtime characteristics on IBM POWER7. Comput. Sci. Res. Dev. 29(3), 211–219 (2013). doi:10.1007/s00450-013-0245-5

24. Kohn, W., Rostoker, N.: Solution of the Schrödinger equation in periodic lattices with an application to metallic Lithium. Phys. Rev. 94, 1111–1120 (1954)

25. Korringa, J.: On the calculation of the energy of a Bloch wave in a metal. Physica 13(6), 392–400 (1947)

26. Kraus, J.: Increase performance with GPU boost and K80 autoboost (2014). https://devblogs.nvidia.com/parallelforall/increase-performance-gpu-boost-k80-autoboost/

27. Lee, K.H., Ahmed, I., Goh, R.S., Khoo, E.H., Li, E.P., Hung, T.G.: Implementation of the FDTD method based on Lorentz-Drude dispersive model on GPU for plasmonics applications. Prog. Electromagnet. Res. 116, 441–456 (2011)

28. Lefurgy, C., Wang, X., Ware, M.: Server-level power control. In: 2007 Fourth International Conference on Autonomic Computing, ICAC 2007, p. 4, June 2007

29. Lindahl, E.: Molecular simulation with GROMACS on CUDA GPUs (2013). http://on-demand.gputechconf.com/gtc/2013/webinar/gromacs-kepler-gpus-gtc-express-webinar.pdf

30. Pleiter, D.: Parallel computer architectures. In: 45th IFF Spring School 2014 "Computing Solids Models, ab-initio methods and supercomputing". Schriften des Forschungszentrums Jülich, Reihe Schlüsseltechnologien, vol. 74 (2014)

31. Rountree, B., Lowenthal, D.K., Schulz, M., de Supinski, B.R.: Practical performance prediction under dynamic voltage frequency scaling. In: 2011 International Green Computing Conference and Workshops (IGCC), pp. 1–8, July 2011

32. Ryffel, S.: LEA^{2}P: the Linux energy attribution and accounting platform. Master's thesis, Swiss Federal Institute of Technology (ETH) (2009). http://ftp.tik.ee.ethz.ch/pub/students/2009-FS/MA-2009-04.pdf

33. Shahmansouri, A., Rashidian, B.: GPU implementation of split-field finite-difference time-domain method for Drude-Lorentz dispersive media. Prog. Electromagnet. Res. 125, 55–77 (2012)

34. Song, S., Su, C., Rountree, B., Cameron, K.W.: A simplified and accurate model of power-performance efficiency on emergent GPU architectures. In: 2013 IEEE 27th International Symposium on Parallel Distributed Processing (IPDPS), pp. 673–686, May 2013

35. Song, S.L., Barker, K., Kerbyson, D.: Unified performance and power modeling of scientific workloads. In: Proceedings of the 1st International Workshop on Energy Efficient Supercomputing, E2SC 2013, pp. 4:1–4:8. (2013). http://doi.acm.org/10.1145/2536430.2536435

36. Subramaniam, B., Feng, W.C.: Statistical power and performance modeling for optimizing the energy efficiency of scientific computing. In: Green Computing and Communications (GreenCom), pp. 139–146, December 2010

37. Taflove, A., Hagness, S.C.: Others: Computational Electrodynamics: The Finite-Difference Time-Domain Method. Artech House, Norwood (1995)

38. Tan, L., Kothapalli, S., Chen, L., Hussaini, O., Bissiri, R., Chen, Z.: A survey of power and energy efficient techniques for high performance numerical linear algebra operations. Parallel Comput. **40**(10), 559–573 (2014)

39. Thiess, A., et al.: Massively parallel density functional calculations for thousands of atoms: KKRnano. Phys. Rev. B **85**, 235103 (2012)

40. Tiwari, A., Laurenzano, M.A., Carrington, L., Snavely, A.: Modeling power and energy usage of HPC kernels. In: 2012 IEEE 26th International Parallel and Distributed Processing Symposium Workshops PhD Forum (IPDPSW), pp. 990–998, May 2012

41. Wahl, P., Ly-Gagnon, D., Debaes, C., Miller, D., Thienpont, H.: B-CALM: an open-source GPU-based 3D-FDTD with multi-pole dispersion for plasmonics. In: 2011 11th International Conference on Numerical Simulation of Optoelectronic Devices (NUSOD), pp. 11–12, September 2011

42. Weaver, V.M., Johnson, M., Kasichayanula, K., Ralph, J., Luszczek, P., Terpstra, D., Moore, S.: Measuring energy and power with PAPI. In: 2012 41st International Conference on Parallel Processing Workshops (ICPPW), pp. 262–268, September 2012

43. Wittmann, M., Hager, G., Zeiser, T., Treibig, J., Wellein, G.: Chip-level and multi-node analysis of energy-optimized lattice Boltzmann CFD simulations. Concur. Comput. Pract. Exper. **28**, 2295–2315 (2016). doi:10.1002/cpe.3489

44. Wu, G., Greathouse, J.L., Lyashevsky, A., Jayasena, N., Chiou, D.: GPGPU performance and power estimation using machine learning. In: 2015 IEEE 21st International Symposium on High Performance Computer Architecture (HPCA), pp. 564–576, February 2015

45. Zyuban, V., Taylor, S.A., Christensen, B., Hall, A.R., Gonzalez, C.J., Friedrich, J., Clougherty, F., Tetzloff, J., Rao, R.: IBM POWER7+ design for higher frequency at fixed power. IBM J. Res. Dev. **57**(6), 1:1–1:18 (2013)

First Experiences with *ab initio* Molecular Dynamics on OpenPOWER: The Case of CPMD

Valéry Weber[1], A. Cristiano I. Malossi[1(✉)], Ivano Tavernelli[1],
Teodoro Laino[1], Costas Bekas[1], Manish Modani[2], Nina Wilner[3],
Tom Heller[3], and Alessandro Curioni[1]

[1] IBM Research–Zurich, Zurich, Switzerland
{vwe,acm,ita,teo,bek,cur}@zurich.ibm.com
[2] IBM India, Bengaluru, India
mamodani@in.ibm.com
[3] IBM, Armonk, USA
{new_nina,tjheller}@us.ibm.com

Abstract. In this article, we present the algorithmic adaptation and code re-engineering required for porting highly successful and popular planewave codes to next-generation heterogeneous OpenPOWER architectures that foster acceleration and high bandwidth links to GPUs. Here we focus on CPMD as the most representative software for *ab initio* molecular dynamics simulations. We have ported the construction of the electronic density, the application of the potential to the wavefunctions and the orthogonalization procedure to the GPU. The different GPU kernels consist mainly of fast Fourier transforms (FFT) and basic linear algebra operations (BLAS). The performance of the new implementation obtained on Firestone (POWER8/Tesla) is discussed. We show that the communication between the host and the GPU contributes a large fraction of the total run time. We expect a strong attenuation of the communication bottleneck when the NVLink high-speed interconnect will be available.

Keywords: CPMD · POWER8 · CUDA · NVlink · FFT · Gram–Schmidt

1   Introduction

Ab initio molecular dynamics (AIMD) is still one of the most commonly used approaches for calculating the time evolution of molecular and solid state systems under ambient conditions of temperature and pressure. Specifically, AIMD is particularly suited for the simulation of complex molecular systems that undergo

M. Taufer et al. (Eds.): ISC High Performance Workshops 2016, LNCS 9945, pp. 228–234, 2016.
DOI: 10.1007/978-3-319-46079-6_16

important reorganizations of their electronic structure (bond breaking and bond forming), and for which the design of a classical force field is very cumbersome. Essential to all AIMD techniques is the calculation of the molecular potential and the corresponding forces obtained from the derivatives of the potential with respect to the nuclear coordinates. These forces are then used to solve the Newton equation of motion for calculating of the nuclear trajectories.

Within density functional theory (DFT), the molecular Hamiltonian is mapped (in principle exactly) into a system of noninteracting particles subject to a compensating local external potential (the exchange-correlation (xc) potential), for which we need approximations.

CPMD [1] uses a pseudopotential-based Kohn–Sham DFT description of the electronic structure in which the Kohn–Sham orbital and the electronic density are expanded in a plane-wave basis set. In addition, working with plane waves has the important advantage of simplifying the calculation of energies and forces; thus some parts of the total energy (such as the kinetic term) are efficiently computed in the Fourier (reciprocal) space, whereas other parts, like the Hartree energy and the interaction with external fields, are accurately evaluated in the real (direct) space. The limiting steps in the plane-wave implementation of AIMD codes consist in (a) the forward and backward Fourier transforms (FFT) [3] (wavefunctions, potentials, and energy terms) and (b) the orthogonalization of the wavefunctions.

The combined use of plane waves and pseudopotential together with highly optimized algorithms for the computation of energies and forces made CPMD one of the most efficient DFT-based AIMD codes, with a documented scaling performance that extends to one million computing cores [5].

The advent of data-centric OpenPOWER systems based on the IBM, NVIDIA and MELLANOX collaboration offers a new potential for scalability and performance that leads to Exascale systems. Here, we present our strategy plans in migrating CPMD to the data-centric systems and summarize our progress so far.

2   Methodology

The basic task in Kohn–Sham based DFT is the minimization of the energy density functional with respect to the Kohn–Sham orbitals $\{\phi_i(\mathbf{r})\}$

$$E_{\text{tot}} = \min_{\{\phi_i\}} E^{KS}\left[\{\phi_i(\mathbf{r})\}\right], \tag{1}$$

where

$$E[\{\phi_i(\mathbf{r})\}] = T_s[\{\phi_i(\mathbf{r})\}] + \int d\mathbf{r}\, V_{ext}[\{\phi_i(\mathbf{r})\}]\rho(\mathbf{r})$$
$$+ \int d\mathbf{r}\, V_H[\{\phi_i(\mathbf{r})\}]\rho(\mathbf{r}) + E_{\text{XC}}[\{\phi_i(\mathbf{r})\}],$$

and $T_s[\{\phi_i(\mathbf{r})\}]$ is the kinetic energy, $V_{ext}[\{\phi_i(\mathbf{r})\}]$ is the external potential generated by the nuclei, $V_H[\{\phi_i(\mathbf{r})\}]$ is the Hartree (Coulomb) term, $E_{\text{XC}}[\{\phi_i(\mathbf{r})\}]$ is the exchange correlation energy, and $\rho(\mathbf{r}) = \sum_{i=1}^{N} |\phi_i(\mathbf{r})|^2$ is the electronic density. Index i runs through the N states of the system. The minimization of (1) leads to a self-consistent set of Kohn–Sham equations

$$\left[-\frac{1}{2}\nabla_i^2 + V_{\text{eff}}[\rho] \right] \phi_i^{KS}(\mathbf{r}) = \epsilon_i \phi_i(\mathbf{r})^{KS},$$
$$V_{\text{eff}}[\rho] = V_{ext} + V_H[\rho] + V_{xc}[\rho], \qquad (2)$$
$$V_{xc}[\rho] = \frac{\delta E_{xc}[\rho(\mathbf{r})]}{\delta\rho(\mathbf{r})}.$$

Numerically, the solution of the Kohn–Sham equations (2) requires a direct minimization algorithm that preserves the orthogonality among the Kohn–Sham orbitals. To optimize this process, Bekas and Curioni [2] recently proposed a block variant of Gram–Schmidt that ensures high processor performance and excellent scaling. The new method exploits data locality to allow the best mapping on the cache-memory hierarchies of modern processors and also enable optimal utilization of the memory subsystem of hardware accelerators such as GPUs. Unlike the current state of the art, the simplicity of the new schemes, inherited from the original Gram–Schmidt method, renders them ideal for enabling much needed fault-tolerance properties when they are deployed on massively parallel computing systems.

High efficiency and numerical scalability in CPMD are achieved thanks to the use of the plane-wave basis set for the expansion of the Kohn–Sham orbitals

$$\phi_i(\mathbf{r}) = \frac{1}{\sqrt{\Omega}} \sum_{\mathbf{G}} \tilde{\phi}_i(\mathbf{G}) e^{i\mathbf{G}\cdot\mathbf{r}},$$

where Ω is the volume of the simulation box, and $\mathbf{G}$ is the index that runs through the reciprocal space vectors. The Fourier coefficients $\tilde{\phi}_i(\mathbf{G})$ are then related to the Kohn–Sham orbital through the inverse FFT

$$\tilde{\phi}_i(\mathbf{G}) = \frac{1}{\sqrt{\Omega}} \sum_{\mathbf{r}} \phi_i(\mathbf{r}) e^{-i\mathbf{G}\cdot\mathbf{r}}.$$

The number of operations required for the conversion of a general function f

$$f(\mathbf{r}) \underset{\text{invFFT}}{\overset{\text{FFT}}{\Longleftrightarrow}} \tilde{f}(\mathbf{G}),$$

using 3d FFT is approximately on the order of $5N\log N$, where N is the number of grid points in the direct space.

3   GPU Implementation

Achieving overlap between data transfer and computation requires the use of CUDA streams. A stream is a sequence of operations that are executed on the

GPU in the same order as they are launched from the host. Operations between streams can be interleaved and potentially run concurrently. Below we summarize the three main computational kernels that we have ported to CUDA so far. In the following, on-GPU FFT transforms and BLAS operations kernels are implemented in the cuFFT and cuBLAS libraries, respectively.

Construction of the Electronic Density. The reverse Fourier transform of the N states $\phi_i(\mathbf{r})$ is distributed over the N_S streams that work concurrently. Each stream is assigned to a CPU thread and performs the sequence of operations needed to transform a state $\tilde{\phi}_i(\mathbf{G})$ to the corresponding state density $\rho_i(\mathbf{r}) = |\phi_i(\mathbf{r})|^2 = |\text{invFFT}(\tilde{\phi}_i(\mathbf{G}))^2|$. The summation over i of the N state densities finally gives the desired electronic density $\rho(\mathbf{r})$.

The computation of a state density starts with an asynchronous communication of a state $\phi_i(\mathbf{G})$ from the host to the device; the GPU performs an 1-D FFT and then back copies the data to the host. The host proceeds to the interprocess communication (MPI all-to-all) while taking care of packing/unpacking operations. We note that a specific MPI communicator is assigned to each CPU thread. In the last phase, the data is transferred to the GPU, which performs a 2d FFT before pushing the direct-space state to the host. The host finally adds up the N contributions to the electronic density.

Applying the Potential to the Wavefunctions. The reverse and forward Fourier transforms as well as the application of the potential $V_{\text{eff}}[\rho]$ to the N states are distributed over N_S streams that work concurrently. Each stream is again assigned to a CPU thread and performs the sequence of operations needed to apply the potential to a state $V\phi_i(\mathbf{G}) = \text{FFT}(V\text{invFFT}(\tilde{\phi}_i(\mathbf{G})))$. Thus the reverse FFT of a state from reciprocal to direct space is identical to the construction of the electronic density. The direct-space state is then copied to the host, and the potential is applied. The forward transform takes place by performing the 2d FFT (on the GPU), followed by the interprocess communication (on the host) and the last 1d FFT (on the GPU).

Orthogonalization. We modified the block Gram–Schmidt scheme introduced in [2] to make use of the GPU. Let us assume that only one MPI task is used (generalization to multiple MPI tasks is trivial). The coefficient matrix (which corresponds to the coefficients of the expansion of ϕ_i on the plane-wave basis) is block-partitioned column-wise into n blocks of size b as $C = [C_1, C_2, \ldots, C_n]$. We seek the orthogonalized coefficient matrix $\tilde{C} = \text{ortho}(C)$. The rows of the coefficient matrix C are block distributed over CPU threads. Each CPU thread is assigned three streams. The first stream, which we refer to as S_{cmp}, is used for computation, while the other two streams are in charge of host-to-device (S_{h2d}) and device-to-host (S_{d2h}) asynchronous communications of the C and $\tilde{C}$ matrices, respectively. The key idea of the block Gram–Schmidt scheme is to loop over the n blocks C_i and to orthogonalize them one after the other.

The orthogonalization is done by first projecting out the previously orthogonalized blocks $[\tilde{C}_1, \tilde{C}_2, \ldots, \tilde{C}_{i-1}]$ and then using a Cholesky (of size $b \times b$) based orthogonalization to produce the $\tilde{C}_i$. In each iteration, intermediate reductions among the threads (the row distribution of the matrix) are needed. The stream S_{cmp} is in charge of performing the BLAS operations as well as the intermediate communication for reductions. The role of the stream S_{h2d} is to asynchronously copy the block C_{i+1} to the GPU for the next orthogonalization iteration. The stream S_{d2h} is used to copy $\tilde{C}_{i-1}$ back to the host.

4   Results

To illustrate the progress on porting CPMD to OpenPOWER systems, we show the strong scaling of the construction of the density, the application of the potential to the wavefunctions and the orthogonalization process for a box of 128 water molecules at normal liquid density and under periodic boundary conditions. We use the GTH pseudopotential [4] and plane-wave and density cutoffs of 100 Ry and 400 Ry, respectively.

The code is compiled using the IBM XL Fortran compiler for Linux 15.1.4 with optimization flags: `-O3 -qhot -qstrict -qprefetch=aggressive:dscr=7 -qsimd=auto -qaltivec -qmaxmem=-1 -qsmp=omp`. The C-code was compiled with the GNU compiler collections 4.9.3. The runs are performed on two IBM POWER8 systems: Tuleta and Firestone. Both servers are equipped with two POWER8 processors. Each POWER8 core supports 8 hardware threads, has 64 kBytes L1 cache, 512 kBytes L2 cache, and 8 MBytes of shared L3 cache. Tuleta runs 12 cores in total at 4.2 GHz, whereas Firestone equips 20 cores at 3.42 GHz. Tuleta has one Nvidia Tesla K40, with 2880 CUDA cores; Firestone has two Nvidia Tesla K80 GPUs, each composed of two devices with 2496 CUDA cores. All computations are performed with CUDA compute capability 3.5 (on Tuleta) and 3.7 (on Firestone), both with driver version 7.5. On Firestone, our calculations use only one device of one K80, i.e., 2496 CUDA cores.

The performance comparison for the three computational blocks described in Sect. 3 is shown in Fig. 1. First, we observe that the Firestone CPU performance is better than that of the earlier Tuleta processor for the two FFT computational blocks. Concerning the GPU results, we observe a dependence on the number of streams used. The PCI-E bandwidth in the two systems is equivalent; therefore once it is saturated, the K40 tends to run slightly faster than half-K80, because of the slightly greater number of CUDA cores. The optimal number of streams varies between 4 and 6, depending on the type of computational block. Using more streams does not help, as memory bandwidth becomes the limiting factor. By analyzing the output of NVprof, we summarize, in Table 1, the time percentage spent in computation and memory copies for the construction of the electronic density and applying the potential to the wavefunctions. Although all operations are performed asynchronously, the time spent in memory copies exceeds the computation time by far (about 1/3 of the total time), so that for at least 2/3 of the total time the GPU cores are idle, waiting for data.

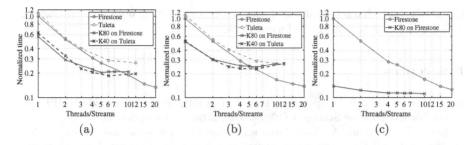

Fig. 1. Log-scale performance comparison of three CPMD computational blocks run on IBM Firestone (20-cores vs. 1-device K80) and IBM Tuleta (12-cores vs. K40). Time is normalized w.r.t. one core CPU time on Firestone. All CPU runs are performed with one thread per core. All GPU runs are performed with one stream per thread per core. (a) Construction of the electronic density. (b) Applying the potential to wavefunctions. (c) Orthogonalization (results on Tuleta are not available)

Table 1. Time percentage spent in computation and memory copy from device to host (D2H) and host to device (H2D) for constructing the electronic density and applying the potential to the wavefunctions. Computation and memory copies are performed asynchronously.

Kernel	Computation [%]	D2H [%]	H2D [%]
Electronic density	27	95	76
Applying potential	30	92	89

At the current state of development, maximum performance is achieved by the 2-socket CPU of Firestone for the FFT computational kernels. We expect that future improvements in the CUDA implementation, including the generalization to multi-GPUs, will change this picture in favor of the accelerators.

5   Future Works

Our initial porting phase of CPMD to OpenPOWER architectures highlights the negative impact of a limited PCI-E bandwidth between the CPU and the GPU. To alleviate this problem, we will tackle the issue from multiple directions: at the implementation level, we will move the calculation of the electronic density and the application of the potential to the wavefunctions to the GPUs and, more generally, we will minimize data transfer whenever possible. At the architecture level, we expect a significant improvement from the NVLink high-speed interconnect equipped by next-generation Garrison POWER8' systems. NVLink will enable ultra-fast communication between the CPU and GPU, allowing data transfer at rates more than 2.5 times faster than traditional PCI-E interconnects. This should be tremendously beneficial for scenarios such as the one summarized in Table 1, where multiple streams have overlapped operations, but communication time is left exposed. Garrison's systems will be available in Q3–Q4 2016:

the study and characterization of the performance gain obtained on such an architecture will be subject of future work.

References

1. CPMD ver. 4.1: Copyright IBM Corp.1990–2016, Copyright MPI für Festkörperforschung Stuttgart (1997–2001). http://www.cpmd.org
2. Bekas, C., Curioni, A.: Very large scale wavefunction orthogonalization in density functional theory electronic structure calculations. Comput. Phys. Commun. **181**(6), 1057–1068 (2010)
3. Goedecker, S.: Fast radix 2, 3, 4, and 5 kernels for fast Fourier transformations on computers with overlapping multiply-add instructions. SIAM J. Sci. Comput. **18**(6), 1605–1611 (1997)
4. Goedecker, S., Teter, M., Hutter, J.: Separable dual-space Gaussian pseudopotentials. Phys. Rev. B **54**, 1703–1710 (1996)
5. Weber, V., Bekas, C., Laino, T., Curioni, A., Bertsch, A., Futral, S.: Shedding light on lithium/air batteries using millions of threads on the BG/Q supercomputer. In: 2014 IEEE 28th International Parallel and Distributed Processing Symposium, pp. 735–744 (2014)

High Performance Computing on the IBM Power8 Platform

István Z. Reguly[1]([✉]), Abdoul-Kader Keita[2], Rafik Zurob[2],
and Michael B. Giles[3]

[1] Faculty of Information Technology and Bionics,
Pázmány Péter Catholic University, Budapest, Hungary
reguly.istvan@itk.ppke.hu
[2] IBM Toronto Lab, Toronto, Canada
{akkeita,rzurob}@ca.ibm.com
[3] Mathematics Institute, University of Oxford, Oxford, UK
mike.giles@maths.ox.ac.uk

Abstract. This paper discusses the performance of IBM's Power8
CPUs, on a number of skeleton, financial and CFD benchmarks and
applications. Implicitly, the performance of the software toolchain is also
tested - the bare-bones Little-Endian Ubuntu, the GNU 5.3 and the XL
14.1.3 compilers and OpenMP runtimes. First, we aim to establish some
roofline numbers on bandwidth and compute throughput, then move
on to benchmark explicit and implicit one-/three-factor Black-Scholes
computations, and CFD applications based on the OP2 and OPS frameworks, such as the Airfoil and BookLeaf unstructured-mesh codes, and
the CloverLeaf 2D/3D structured mesh simulations. These applications
all exhibit different characteristics in terms of computations, communications, memory access patterns, etc. Finally we briefly discuss performance of an industrial CFD code, Rolls-Royce Hydra, and we show
initial results from IBM's CUDA Fortran compiler. Both absolute and
relative performance metrics are computed and compared to NVIDIA
GPUs and Intel Xeon CPUs.

1 Introduction

So far, only a few reports have discussed the performance of the Power8 on
scientific workloads [2,6], and there is very little know-how available about how
to configure, compile and execute such applications in order to maximise the
achieved performance. Indeed, the software stack is still fairly new, generally
compilers are still very much in development for little-endian configurations -
the primary configuration type for future systems (e.g. CORAL).

In this paper, we investigate the performance of the hardware, the software
stack and various programming approaches in order to determine the strong
and weak points for a variety of computational patterns and to offer suggestions
about best practices to application developers.

The skeleton benchmarks tested serve to establish a roofline performance
model, both in terms of computational throughput and memory bandwidth,

© Springer International Publishing AG 2016
M. Taufer et al. (Eds.): ISC High Performance Workshops 2016, LNCS 9945, pp. 235–254, 2016.
DOI: 10.1007/978-3-319-46079-6_17

that is practically achievable. Using the STREAM benchmark, we determine the maximum achievable bandwidth on the platform, at different SMT settings and data chunks - this will give an upper limit for performance on later benchmarks that are bandwidth-limited. Similarly, we test realistically achievable computational throughput with the single and double precision general matrix-matrix multiply operations in the IBM ESSL library.

The one-factor Black-Scholes benchmark evaluates computational throughput and bandwidth to L1/L2 cache, the three-factor Black-Scholes benchmark stresses both the computational and the memory sub-systems; it uses a 13-point stencil, therefore it has good data reuse. The unstructured mesh applications, based on the OP2 framework – Airfoil and BookLeaf – are finite-volume/element codes that are primarily bandwidth-bound, and have irregular memory access patterns. The structured mesh applications are based on the OPS framework (CloverLeaf 2D/3D), these perform stencil computations and have highly regular memory access patterns and relatively few computations per grid point, thus they are also primarily bandwidth-limited, but also affected by the efficiency of domain-decomposition and MPI messaging. Several benchmarks have implementations available both in C and Fortran, which helps in comparing performance of different compilers.

All tests were evaluated five times and the results were averaged. Aside from the STREAM benchmark at relatively low NTIMES values, the results had low variance (less than 5 % different from the mean), therefore for most figures we do not show the variance.

2   The Power8 Architecture

The Power8 is the latest RISC CPU from IBM, it uses a 22 nm manufacturing process and supports up to 12 cores per chip. Each core has support for up to 8 hardware threads, and has 64 KB L1, 512 KB L2 and 8 MB L3 cache. Each core has 16 execution pipelines, two fixed-point, two load/store, two load, four floating-point, two vector pipelines, one cryptographic, one branch execution, one condition register logical and one decimal floating-point pipeline. Each of the four floating-point pipelines are capable of executing a multiply-add operation per clock cycle, which corresponds to 8 double precision or 16 single precision floating point operations per cycle.

A processor core can perform two load operations and two load or store operations in the load and the load/store pipelines. The bandwidth to L2 cache is up to 256 GB/s read and 64 GB/s write, and 128/128 GB/s to the L3 cache, at 4 GHz. Each chip has 8 high-speed channels to off-chip memory, and the bandwidth per socket is 128 GB/s read and 64 GB/s write.

The core supports dynamic Simultaneous Multithreading (SMT) for up to 8 hardware threads - a software thread can execute in any hardware thread position, even in Single Thread (ST) mode, the SMT mode can therefore dynamically be switched. There are two Unified Issue Queues (UniQueues) per core, each with a dedicated set of general-purpose and vector-scalar registers. Execution pipelines (fixed-point, floating-point, etc.) are also associated to one of

Table 1. Characteristics of the POWER8 and the Intel system. Base characteristics are described per socket

	POWER8	Intel E52650 v3
Cores	10	10
Clock	3.69 GHz	2.3(3.0) GHz
L1/L2	64/512 KB	64/256 KB
L3	80 MB	25 MB
Bandwidth to DRAM	128 + 64 GB/s	68 GB/s
SP/DP flop/core/cycle	16/8	32/16
Threads/core	8	2
Sockets	2	2
Release date	Q2'14	Q3'14
Compilers	XL 14.1.3, GNU 5.0	Intel 2016 SP1
Compiler options	xl: -O5 -qarch=pwr8 -qtune=pwr8 gnu: -Ofast -march=power8 -mtune=power8	icc: -O3 -xCORE_AVX2 -fno-alias

the UniQueues. In ST, both halves can dispatch instructions to any execution pipeline, but in SMT modes, threads will be associated with either half, and the UniQueues can only dispatch instructions to the execution pipelines associated with them.

The machine being tested has 20 cores at 3.69 GHz and 256 GB of memory, in 16 16GB modules. The machine is running bare-bones little-endian Ubuntu 14.10.

Throughout the paper, we test performance against an Intel E5-2650 v3 (Haswell) CPU, using the 2016 Intel compilers. A summary of the two architectures is described in Table 1.

2.1 Compilers

On the POWER8, we use the IBM XL C/C++ 14.1.3 and Fortran 16.1.3 compilers (as well as the 16.1.4 beta for CUDA Fortran), and the GNU 5.0 compilers with the options listed in Table 1. The flags used enable platform-specific optimisations, the use of fused multiply-adds and re-ordering of code considered unsafe from the IEEE floating-point perspective, this however had insignificant impact on the end results. Additional flags used with the XL compilers include -qaltivec when vector intrinsics are used, and -qsmp=omp -qthreaded when OpenMP is enabled. The flag -qlist can be used to get optimisation reports from the compiler.

On the Intel platform, we use the Intel 2016 SP1 compilers, enabling the AVX2 instruction set.

3   STREAM

The STREAM benchmark [5] measures bandwidth between the CPU and memory; depending on the data set size to on-chip cache or off-chip DRAM. There are four kinds of tests: (1) *copy* moves all data from one array to an other, (2) *scale* moves all data from one array to an other while multiplying all elements by a given value, (3) *add* adds the contents of two arrays and puts the results in a third array, and (4) *triad* adds the values of one array to the scaled values of an other and puts the results in a third array.

The key difference between the first two and the last two benchmarks is that the first two read and write the same amount of data, while the last two read twice as much as they write. This is key in understanding performance of the Power8; each core has two symmetric load pipelines and two symmetric load/store pipelines, and the interface to off-chip memory supports twice the number of load requests than store requests; therefore the achievable bandwidth on the last two benchmarks is 50 % higher. Each Power8 chip has 8 memory channels, with up to 128 GB/s read and 64 GB/s write aggregated bandwidth, thus a full two-socket machine is theoretically capable of delivering 384 GB/s bandwidth to off-chip memory.

Figure 1 shows the bandwidth measured by the triad benchmark; as long as data is read from off-chip DRAM memory, the best performance is achieved at a low number of threads: 1 thread per code (SMT1 or ST), there seem to be bottlenecks at higher levels when using more threads. The other important observation is the amount of data required to saturate the available bandwidth; the highest achieved is just below 300 GB/s, when each of the three arrays are 1.5 GB is size, and as the array size goes down, there is a clear reduction in achieved bandwidth, and an increasing level of noise in the measurements (up to 30 %).

When the dataset can be fully contained in the cache however, the trend reverses; more threads are required to saturate bandwidth. This suggests that the previously discussed bottleneck is in managing requests to off-chip memory. A total bandwidth of up to 1080GB/s is achieved to the L3 cache at SMT4,

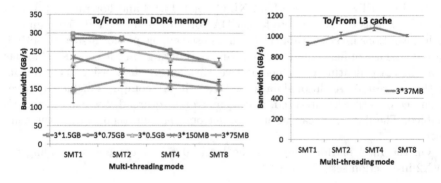

Fig. 1. STREAM Triad bandwidth on different size arrays and different number of threads

regardless of which of the four benchmarks is used; the two-to-one ratio of load and store requests only applies to requests to DRAM.

Execution with `OMP_NUM_THREADS=XX OMP_PROC_BIND=TRUE ./stream`, with XX set to 20/40/80/160, depending on the desired SMT setting. Thread/process binding is key to achieving performance on this system, there is an up to five-fold decrease in performance if threads are allowed to migrate between cores and sockets. Between cores on the same socket the penalty is less, only up to 70 %.

In comparison, an Intel Xeon E5-2650 v3 (Haswell) CPU has a theoretical maximum bandwidth of 136 GB/s and achieves 95 GB/s, using 256-bit AVX2.

4   Balance of Computations and Data Movement

One of the key machine parameters when determining the theoretical maximum performance is the balance of computations and data movement. As we have seen in the previous section, the Power8 can deliver up to 300 GB/s bandwidth. The 20-core machine, running at 3.69 GHz can do 16 single or 8 double precision floating point operations per core per clock cycle, when the vector units are utilised and multiply-add operations are used. This reduces to 2 operations when multiply is used on scalars (either single or double precision). This translates to 1180 GFLOPS/s vectorised single, 590 GFLOPS/s vectorised double precision throughput with multiply-adds, and 147 GFLOPS/s non-vectorised single operations. For computations and data movement to be in balance, 3.93, 1.96 or 0.49 FLOPS/Byte have to be carried out respectively. However, these are only theoretical peak values; Fig. 2a shows actually achieved computational throughput on a general dense matrix-matrix multiplication kernel (using the IBM ESSL library); these kernels are commonly used to evaluate the practically achievable peak computational performance. In single precision, SGEMM achieves 931 GFLOPS, or 78 % of the theoretical peak, and in double precision DGEMM achieves 501 GFLOPS, or 85 % of theoretical peak, on 4096^2 matrices. It is important to note however, that this is only achieved at SMT1 (ST)

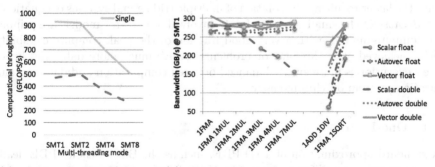

(a) Achieved GFLOPS on DGEMM and SGEMM

(b) Bandwidth with increasing number of operations per 3 values

Fig. 2. Computational performance

or SMT2 settings, at a higher number of threads per core, performance drops rapidly, by up to 50 % at SMT8.

Following this logic, for the single precision scalar case, the balance should be around 6 FLOPS per 3 values moved, up to which point full bandwidth should be utilised, and beyond which computations would dominate, reducing achieved bandwidth. This value for scalar double precision values is near 12 FLOPS per 3 values moved. Figure 2b shows bandwidth numbers when the number and type of operations is varied: using just 1 FMA, adding further MUL instructions and finally testing more expensive division and square root operations. These are also evaluated when compiler auto-vectorization is disabled or enabled, and there is a variant which uses Altivec vector types. In order to achieve auto-vectorization, the loops were outlined and all pointer arguments were decorated with `restrict` and `const` where applicable. Previous compiler versions failed to vectorize these loops when OpenMP was enabled, but the latest one does vectorize the loops. Performance when increasing the number of multiply operations holds steady as expected for most variants except for the non-vectorized single precision case - it is currently not clear why. The figure also shows some inconsistency in the behaviour of the square root and division operations between single and double precision; hand-vectorized and auto-vectorized double precision performance is almost the same, but it's very different for single precision.

The figure highlights the importance of vectorization especially when computationally expensive operations are used; it is easy to become compute-bound on this architecture.

In comparison the Intel E5-2650 v3 (using 256-bit AVX2) achieves 1280/523 GFLOPS in single/double precision on the general matrix-matrix multiply benchmark using 4096^2 matrices.

5   Black-Scholes

This section discusses the performance of one-factor and three-factor PDE models, after [3]. Both explicit and implicit time-marching methods are considered, with the latter requiring the solution of multiple tridiagonal systems of equations.

Because of the small amount of data involved, one-factor models are primarily compute-limited, with a very good fraction of the peak compute capability being achieved. The three-factor problems involve much more data, and hence their execution is more evenly balanced between computation and data communication to/from off-chip memory.

5.1   One-Factor

A standard approximation of a 1D PDE, such as the Black-Scholes PDE, leads to an *explicit* finite difference equation of the form

$$u_j^{n+1} = u_j^n + a_j\, u_{j-1}^n + b_j\, u_j^n + c_j\, u_{j+1}^n, \quad j = 0, 1, \ldots J - 1$$

with $u_{-1} = u_J = 0$. Here n is the timestep index which increases as the computation progresses, so u_j^{n+1} is a simple combination of the values at the nearest neighbours at the previous timestep, a common stencil computation pattern. All of the numerical results are for a grid of size $J = 256$ which corresponds to a fairly high resolution grid in financial applications. Additional parallelism is achieved by solving multiple one-factor problems at the same time, with each one having different model constants, or a different financial option payoff.

A standard *implicit* time-marching approximation leads to a tridiagonal set of equations of the form

$$a_j\, u_{j-1}^{n+1} + b_j\, u_j^{n+1} + c_j\, u_{j+1}^{n+1} = u_j^n, \quad j = 0, 1, \ldots J - 1$$

with $u_{-1} = u_J = 0$. This is then solved using the Thomas algorithm, a sequential algorithm for each option at each timestep.

The baseline implementations for both explicit and implicit algorithms have an outermost loop over all options, and then after initialising the a,b, and c coefficient arrays, iterate for a number of timesteps (50000 explicit 2500 implicit, due to the latter converging faster) updating the values of all 256 grid points - this is the *explicit1/implicit1* implementation. Various compilers may or may not vectorise over either the outer loop, in which case different lanes of the vector represent different options, or in the explicit case, over the finite-difference update of grid points, with each lane representing a different gridpoint. Hand-written vectorisations are created for all of these, using vector intrinsics on Intel and the Altivec types on the Power8. Scalar and vectorised versions (over different options) are named *explicit1, implicit1*, explicit vectorisation over the iterations of the inner loop for a single option is named *explicit2*.

Evaluating single-threaded performance using both XL and GNU compilers yields results shown in Fig. 3; for scalar versions, both compilers report having

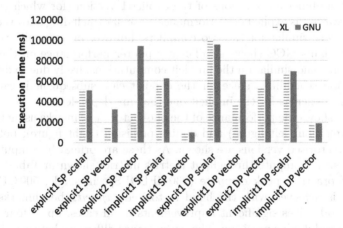

Fig. 3. One-factor Black-Scholes performance on a single core of the Power8. The timings are for 50000 (explicit) or 2500 (implicit) timesteps, for 6144 options each on a grid of size 256.

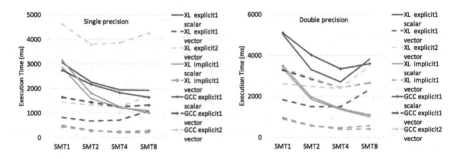

Fig. 4. One-factor hand-vectorised Black-Scholes performance on the Power8. The timings are for 50000 (explicit) or 2500 (implicit) timesteps, for 6144 options each on a grid of size 256.

Table 2. One-factor hand-vectorised Black-Scholes performance on the Power8 and Intel. The timings are for 50000 (explicit) or 2500 (implicit) timesteps, for 6144 options each on a grid of size 256.

	POWER8				Intel E5-2650 v3			
	Single prec.		Double prec.		Single prec.		Double prec.	
	ms	GFlop/s	ms	GFlop/s	ms	GFlop/s	ms	GFlop/s
explicit1 scalar	1923	244	2704	173	942	499	1593	293
explicit1 vector	666	706	1468	319	1512	311	2805	167
explicit2 vector	1229	381	2373	198	756	620	1359	346
implicit1 scalar	1098	71	993	67	1191	65	1524	44
implicit1 vector	243	320	465	145	288	270	756	89

vectorised the inner stencil loops of the explicit1 version (for which the hand-vectorised variant is explicit2). Performance on scalar (including auto-vectorised) versions is very similar for the two compilers, however on manually vectorised (Alitvec) variants GCC shows significantly poorer performance on the explicit computations, and similar on the implicit computations; likely due to differences in instruction scheduling, since for the explicit case subsequent iterations are independent, whereas for the implicit one they are dependent.

Figure 4 shows the performance of the one-factor benchmarks using OpenMP in single precision (left figure) and double precision (right figure), both scalar and hand-vectorised versions are shown. As these are primarily compute-bound benchmarks, we compute throughput metrics metrics shown in Table 2; around 60–65% of practical peak compute (930 GFLOPS/s in single, 500 GFLOPS/s in double) is achieved with the hand-vectorised *explicit1* benchmarks. Hand-vectorised code gives significant improvements in all cases; up to four times in both single and double precision. The performance difference between single and double precisions for both implicit and explicit hand-vectorised versions is close to 2×. In the implicit case, during the Thomas algorithm a reciprocal value has to be computed at each grid point, here the fast approximate reciprocal is used (vec_re), which gives a 15 % improvement in overall performance. Overall, GCC gives very similar performance in most cases, except for the manually vectorised explicit versions as seen in the case of the single-threaded test.

In comparison, on Intel Xeon E5-2950 v3 (Haswell) the Intel compiler does auto-vectorize the *explicit1*, although it is less performant than the hand-vectorised variant. Overall, it achieves about 50 % of the benchmarked peak, slightly outperforming the POWER8 on the explicit benchmark, but it is 20–60% slower on the implicit benchmark.

5.2 Three-Factor

The three-factor test application uses the Black-Scholes PDE for 3 underlying assets, each corresponding to Geometric Brownian Motion and with positive correlation between the 3 driving Brownian motions. This leads to a parabolic PDE which spatial cross-derivative terms with positive coefficients. The spatial approximation of this leads to a 13-point stencil involving offsets $\pm(1, 0, 0)$, $\pm(0, 1, 0)$, $\pm(0, 0, 1)$, $\pm(1, 1, 0)$, $\pm(0, 1, 1)$ and $\pm(1, 0, 1)$, relative to a point with 3D indices (i, j, k). The test case uses a grid of size 256^3, with all data stored in the main memory in 1D arrays.

The implementation of the explicit solution is very similar to the one-factor implementation; a nested loop over the different dimensions (explicit1: z-y-x, explicit2: y-x-z, explicit3: z-x-y), applying the 13-point stencil. The hand-vectorised implementation vectorises over adjacent grid points in the x dimension. The implicit version has to use the Alternating Direction Implicit (ADI) method to solve the system of linear equation, which means solving along the x, y, or z dimensions using the Thomas algorithm.

In the three-factor benchmarks, the one of the primary concerns is data locality, especially with respect to NUMA regions; during initialisation, different threads initialise different z-slices of the 256^3 domain, which means that according to the first-touch allocation policy, these are allocated on pages and DRAM closest to where the thread is running. This does not pose major problems in the explicit case, because during computations threads compute on the same grid points that they initialised, the only time they may have to access memory allocated to a different NUMA regions is when accessing adjacent grid points for the 13-point stencil. However, in the implicit case threads iterate over different dimensions, therefore during the y and z solves a large chunk of data is allocated on different NUMA regions (on the Power 8, which has 4 regions, 3/4).

Figure 5 shows the performance of the full Power8 machine, with both scalar and hand-vectorised code in either single or double precision. The first thing to note is that the scalar code performs very similarly in both precisions, and the code does not auto-vectorize - with the sole exception of the single precision explicit1 version with the GCC compiler. This suggests that performance is limited by computations (for which the throughput is the almost the same in single and double precision). With the hand-vectorised code the performance difference between the two precisions is close to 2× as expected, because the

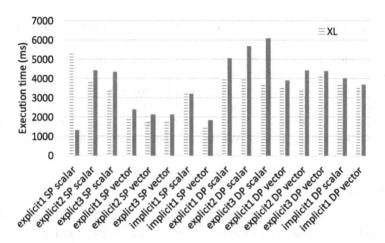

Fig. 5. Three-factor hand-vectorised Black-Scholes performance on the Power8. The timings are for 500 (explicit) or 100 (implicit) timesteps, for one three-factor option on a grid of size 256^3.

vectors hold twice as many values in single precision, and half as much memory has to be transferred. Nevertheless, vector code is still very inefficient in utilizing the system's resources, and only achieves a fraction of the peak bandiwdth.

There were several steps taken to achieve this performance using altivec instructions however, which were not needed in previous tests. Firstly, we needed to use the `vec_xlw4` instruction for loading, instead of the `vec_ld` instruction, which improved performance by up to 2× with the XL compiler (this intrinsic is not available in the GCC compiler). Furthermore, we had to move some iteration-independent code out of the innermost for loop, because it was not done by the compiler automatically. Lastly, in some cases it was advantageous to manually

Table 3. Three-factor performance on the Power8 and Intel. The timings are for 500 (explicit) or 100 (implicit) timesteps, for one three-factor option on a grid of size 256^3. Comp - GFlops/s, BW - GB/s

	POWER8						Intel E5-2650 v3					
	Single prec.			Double prec.			Single prec.			Double prec.		
	ms	Comp	BW	ms	Comp	BW	ms	Comp	BW	ms	Comp	BW
explicit1 scalar	1342	322	45	3643	121	35	1746	248	35	3482	127	37
explicit1 altivec	1684	263	38	3476	127	37	-	-	-	-	-	-
implicit1 scalar	3204	65	19	3632	57	31	1397	149	43	2722	76	41
implicit1 altivec	1582	132	38	3566	58	32	-	-	-	-	-	-

inline the main body of computations into `main()`, which were otherwise placed in separate functions of their own. The latter two optimizations, when applied to scalar code, had no effect on performance.

Overall, it is not clear what the limiting factors for performance are; as shown in Table 3 the achieved computational throughput in the explicit testcase is a fourth of the theoretical and a half of the results achieved by the one-factor model, and the achieved bandwidth in all testcases is between 10–20% of the maximum, measured by the STREAM benchmark.

In comparison, on Intel Xeon E5-2650 v3 (Haswell) CPU, the Intel compiler does auto-vectorize the explicit benchmark. Due to the issues described above, it does slightly outperform the POWER8 platform, despite the latter's much higher bandwidth.

6 Structured Meshes - OPS

OPS [9] is a framework and active library developed at the University of Oxford that is targeting structured mesh stencil-based computations. It uses a high-level approach to enable application developers to describe their computational problems at a high level and then, using a combination of code generation and backend logic, it enables efficient parallel execution on a range of modern hardware, such as multicore CPUs or GPUs, using the MPI, OpenMP, CUDA, OpenACC and OpenCL parallelisation techniques. The two key benchmarks are CloverLeaf 2D and CloverLeaf 3D, structured hydrodynamics codes, also available separately, with vanilla Fortran and C implementations. CloverLeaf is open source software and forms part of Sandia National Laboratory's Mantevo project [4]. Both codes move a lot of data and perform relatively few computations per grid point, therefore we expect performance to be bound by bandwidth to off-chip memory, as well as the efficiency of the software stack: the compiler translating different parallelisation approaches to machine code, and then the runtime managing it.

6.1 CloverLeaf 2D

Here, we benchmark the pure MPI and MPI+ OpenMP versions of the 2D and the 3D applications, using the reference implementation (denoted as ref) with computational kernels implemented in C or Fortran (denoted as Fortran or C) with both the XL and the GNU compilers (denoted as XL or GNU). We also evaluate performance using the OPS framework (denoted as OPS), with both compilers. Corresponding to different SMT settings we have two times four results with each: 20/40/80/160 MPI processes for pure MPI and 20 MPI processes and 1/2/4/8 OpenMP threads each for hybrid MPI+OpenMP.

The reference implementations use straightforward nested `for` loops in C and `DO` loops in Fortran, they have not been optimised specifically for the Power8 platform. The OPS implementation generates C code specifically optimised to enable auto-vectorisation by the XL compiler. Due to the large number of loops, a manually-vectorised (with altivec) version was not developed.

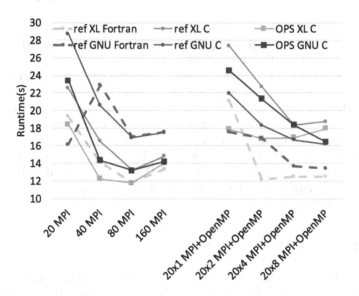

Fig. 6. Performance of the Power8 on CloverLeaf 2D: 3840^2 grid, 87 iterations.

The code is available at:
https://github.com/gihanmudalige/OPS/tree/feature/power8 in the `apps/c/CloverLeaf` directory.

Figure 6 shows the performance of the 2D version on a 3840^2 mesh (with a total footprint of 2914 MB); when running on the full machine, pure MPI execution performs the best, and the amount of time spent in MPI communications is less than 10 %. In case of pure MPI execution, the performance of Fortran and C code are very similar (at most 10 % difference), and on the reference implementation, the GNU version is up to 25 % slower than XL, but only 12 % slower on the OPS implementation, showing that optimisations introduced by the OPS library are beneficial for both compilers. The best performance in all cases is achieved at an SMT4 setting.

Moving to hybrid MPI+OpenMP changes the relative performance of different implementations significantly; there is now an up to 50 % difference between Fortran and C versions, particularly in case of the XL compilers - clearly some optimisations are disabled in C when OpenMP is enabled; all C OpenMP versions slow down compared to their pure MPI counterparts, whereas Fortran versions speed up in most cases. The overheads likely come from the process of outlining code within the OpenMP region to a function, and the reduced number of loops SIMD vectorised, as reported by the compiler. The optimal SMT setting in some cases is also shifted to SMT8 - using 8 OpenMP threads per MPI process.

The total bandwidth averaged through the whole of the execution, but excluding time spent in MPI communications, is 160 GB/s, for some computational phases it reaches 250–270 GB/s (revert, fluxes, reset), but on some it is only 70–110 GB/s (update halo, timestep, ideal gas, viscosity), most of which are more computationally intensive, except for update halo, which updates the boundaries, therefore has poor memory access patterns. These results confirm that the application is primarily bound by bandwidth to main memory, however there is an overhead in C+OpenMP and in MPI communications. Furthermore, computationally heavier kernels are also significantly slower; the compiler does not auto-vectorise over different grid points.

In comparison, an Intel Xeon E5-2650 v3 (Haswell) CPU, completes execution in 32 s, about 3× slower, however, the difference between MPI and MPI+OpenMP execution is less than 1 %. An NVIDIA K20 GPU completes execution in 15 s, 40 % slower than the best performance on the Power8.

6.2   CloverLeaf 3D

The 3D application is essentially the straightforward extension of the 2D application, with a very similar code structure. The total memory footprint on the 192^3 mesh is 1624 MB. MPI runs show a significant amount of time spent in MPI communications - around 20–25% of total for the best performing cases. This is however not unreasonable, considering that the relative number of grid points on the interfaces of the domain decomposition to the total number of grid points is almost 10 times more than in 2D. Average bandwidth over the total execution, excluding the time spent in MPI, is 267 GB/s, with different computational phases behaving similar to the 2D version.

For the 3D version, there was no reference implementation in C, but as Fig. 7 shows, in case of pure MPI, performance is very close for both compilers and both reference (Fortran) and OPS (C) implementations, with the best performance achieved at SMT4. Moving to a hybrid MPI+OpenMP version changes relative performance once again, with Fortran versions slightly improving over pure MPI, but C versions slowing down significantly.

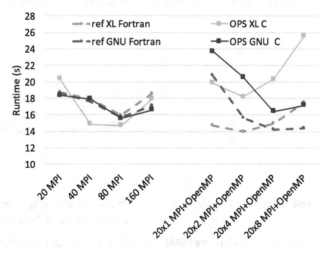

Fig. 7. Performance of the Power8 on CloverLeaf 3D: 192^3 grid.

In comparison, an Intel Xeon E5-2650 v3 CPU, completes execution of the 192^3 problem in 34.5 s, 2.3× slower. An NVIDIA K20 GPU completes execution in 17.2 s, slightly lower overall performance as the Power8.

7   Unstructured Mesh Computations - OP2

OP2 is a framework and active library developed at the University of Oxford that targets the domain of unstructured meshes. In a similar way to OPS, it defines a high-level abstraction and then uses code generation and backend logic to enable execution on a variety of platforms. OP2 was initially aimed at replacing OPlus - the parallel library running under Rolls-Royce Hydra. There are currently several codes utilising OP2: the Airfoil benchmark, the Volna tsunami simulation code and Rolls-Royce Hydra. These applications tend to be data-movement heavy, however in many phases of computations indirect memory accesses are used to either read or update data. Thus this class of applications will test caching behaviour and the performance of random memory access patterns.

Here, we benchmark the MPI, OpenMP and hybrid MPI+OpenMP performance, and compare it to the performance achieved on Intel CPUs.

7.1   Airfoil

Airfoil is the best understood testcase under OP2: it consists of five kernels, two direct ones (save_soln, update), one over the boundary (bres), one that is computationally intensive (2 reciprocals, 5 sqrt ops) and reads data indirectly (adt), and one that both reads and writes data indirectly (res).

Figure 8 shows the overall performance of the Power8 running the Airfoil benchmark on a 2.8 million cell problem. The memory footprint of this problem is fairly small (373 MB in double precision), but tests on a 24 million cell problem

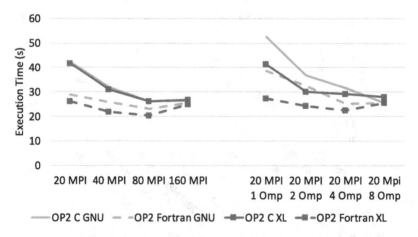

Fig. 8. Performance of the Power8 on Airfoil: 2.8m cell problem for 1000 iteration, on the full machine.

Table 4. Useful bandwidth (BW - GB/s) and computational (Comp - GFops/s) throughput of baseline implementations on Airfoil

Kernel	POWER8						Intel E5-2650 v3					
	Double precision			Single precision			Double precision			Single precision		
	Time	BW	Comp	Time	BW	Comp	Time	BW	Comp	Time	BW	Comp
save_soln	0.61	301	18.6	0.14	641	80	2.86	64	4.1	1.44	64	8.0
adt_calc	8.39	38	38.4	7.49	22	49	5.89	55	62.6	6.44	25	57.2
res_calc	8.94	77	93.9	8.29	42	101	11.92	58	60.5	10.95	32	76.7
bres_calc	0.02	133	41.3	0.01	57	56	0.05	53	16.3	0.03	27	27.2
update	4.55	172	21.5	3.39	115	29	9.52	82	10.3	4.49	87	21.8

give the same performance. The best performance in double precision is achieved at SMT8, 20.28 s with the pure MPI backend and Fortran, with 1.83 s spent in MPI (9 %). The best performance achieved in both precisions is almost exactly the same, which suggests that performance is not limited by bandwidth, rather latency. Performance with the two compilers is again similar, with XL narrowly outperforming GCC, and Fortran being faster than C.

Per-loop breakdowns are shown in Table 4; the Power8's advantage is clear on the two direct loops, and a high bandwidth is achieved, especially in single precision, where data is in cache for save_soln. The indirect read/write loop (res) runs in the same time in both precisions, this kernel is likely to be bound by caching, branching and serialisation overheads. Finally, the computationally intensive kernel (adt) again runs in the same time in both precisions, suggesting a lower efficiency when executing division and square root operations. It is also worth noting that neither of the two kernels that define overall performance (adt and res) seem to be limited by bandwidth, and that significantly more time is spent in MPI, 10−15 %, likely due to load imbalance, compared to Intel platforms (3–5%).

The airfoil benchmark has sufficiently few kernels so that a one-off hand-written vectorisation is possible, extending our work presented in [7], where we discuss the pros and cons of our vectorisation approach, including our choice of data layouts. Converting all the kernels to use vectors doesn't make all of them faster, due to the need for of packing vectors and then unpacking them,

Table 5. Useful bandwidth (BW - GB/s) and computational (Comp - GFLOPS/s) throughput of hand-vectorised implementations on Airfoil

Kernel	Double precision			Single precision		
	Time	BW	Comp	Time	BW	Comp
save_soln	0.57	323	20.2	0.14	641	80
adt_calc	3.66	88	100.7	2.63	61	140
res_calc	16.04	43	52.4	11.1	31	75
bres_calc	0.02	132	41.1	0.01	57	56
update	5.74	136	17.1	3.06	128	32

Table 5 shows the breakdowns for each kernel when vectorised. Clearly, the save_soln kernel did not benefit, it only moves data, however the performance of adt_calc increased 2.29× in double and 2.84× in single precision - this kernel was clearly compute-bound in the scalar case. In the hand-vectorised case, reciprocals and square root operations use the fast estimates provided by the instruction set, and are corrected using one Newton-Raphson step. Unlike the first two kernels, res_calc is actually negatively affected by vectorisation, due to the overhead of packing and unpacking of vector registers and the relatively few number of operations. Finally, vectorisation only helps update in the single precision case, where the benefits of fast reciprocals outweigh vector packing/unpacking. For the overall best performance, where only those kernels are vectorised where there is a performance increase; the performance ratio between the single and double precision versions, 1.22×, is still far from the ideal 2×, mainly due to res_calc being latency limited.

In comparison, runtime on a pair of Xeon E5-2650 v3 CPUs with the Intel compiler, the adt_calc kernel does vectorize automatically, and the full benchmark takes 23.38 s in single and 30.27 s in double precision (a ratio of 1.3×). On a K40 GPU it runs in 10.5 s in single and 17.6 s in double precision.

7.2   BookLeaf and Hydra

BookLeaf is an unstructured mesh benchmark application from the Mantevo Suite - it solves a small hydrodynamics problem with a low order finite element method, and uses the arbitrary Lagrangian-Eulerian method. It is entirely written in Fortran 90, and is available at [1], and it has been converted to use the OP2 library (Fortran API) as well. BookLeaf has a large number of computational loops (51), structured across a number of different source files, with 12 indirect loops that have gather-scatter access patterns and 39 direct loops that only access data directly on the iteration set. We evaluate the SOD testcase on a 4 million element mesh with ALE enabled.

BookLeaf, with a large number of direct loops, exploits the large amount of bandwidth available on the Power8 platform, however, even so, in all testcases, over 60 % of time is spent in these critical indirect loops. Figure 9 shows performance of the two different implementations compiled with either GNU or XL: on the reference implementation, XL slightly outperforms GNU, and on the OP2 version, GNU is faster - particularly in the case of MPI+OpenMP (the reference version does not have an OpenMP implementation), and on kernels that have significant amounts of branching. Overall, a sustained bandwidth of 131 GB/s is achieved; while most computational loops achieve a bandwidth that is well over 200 GB/s, a handful of computationally expensive loops pull down the average. Best performance is achieved with the GNU compiler at an SMT4 setting (9.7 s).

In comparison, runtime on an Intel E5-2650 v3(Haswell) CPU with the intel compiler is 19.01 s (a ratio of 1.9×), and on a K80 GPU it is 5.3 s (a ratio of 0.49×).

Hydra is a production CFD application used at Rolls-Royce plc. for the simulation of design of turbomachinery, it is a highly complex code that can simulate various aspects of the design, including steady and unsteady flows that occur

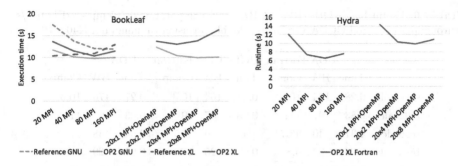

Fig. 9. Performance of the Power8 on BookLeaf and Hydra with different compilers and implementations.

around adjacent rows of rotating and stationary blades in the engine, the operation of compressors and turbines, and many others. Hydra solves the Reynolds-Averaged Navier-Stokes (RANS) equations, with a 5-step Runge-Kutta method for time-marching, accelerated by multi-grid and Jacobi preconditioning. Hydra has previously beed converted to use OP2 and tested on Intel CPUs and GPUs [8].

Benchmarking on a 2.4 million edge NASA Rotor 37 testcase gives results shown in Fig. 9; similarly to BookLeaf, best performance (6.48 s) is achieved at an SMT4 setting; the average bandwidth is 47 GB/s, with a few highly complex loops pulling down the average, while the rest achieve 150–250 GB/s. In comparison, runtime on the Intel E5-2650 v3 (Haswell) CPU is 9.2 s (1.4×) and on a K80 GPU runtime is 5.1 s (0.78×).

8 XL CUDA Fortran

Finally, we give some early results from the IBM XL CUDA Fortran compiler, currently in the 15.1.4 alpha version. Syntax is identical to the one used in the PGI CUDA Fortran compilers, although in the pre-release version only a restricted set of features are supported. Otherwise, using the compiler is simple; one either has to use the xlcuf compiler, or the regular xlf compiler with the -qcuda option. It uses the XL compiler's optimisations passes to apply transformations to both device and host code, before passing NVVM IR to the NVIDIA compiler.

We have managed to compile a version of the Airfoil CUDA Fortran code and show results here running on a K40 GPU in our Power8 system, comparing performance to CUDA C code compiled with nvcc on the same system and the CUDA Fortran code compiled with the PGI compilers on an x86 system, running on a different K40 card. Breakdowns are shown in Table 6; the XL compilers deliver very good performance, likely thanks to the optimisation passes done before passing the NVVM IR to the NVIDIA compilers. Scatter-gather type computations affect the performance of res_calc significantly. The number of registers used by the PGI and XL compilers are very close (31/79/63/48/61 for save_soln,adt_calc,res_calc,bres_calc,update respectively with XL), but still

Table 6. Useful bandwidth (BW - GB/s) and computational (Comp - GFLOPS/s) throughput of Airfoil CUDA versions in double precision running on a K40 GPU

Kernel	XL CUDA Fortran			PGI CUDA Fortran			CUDA C		
	Time	BW	Comp	Time	BW	Comp	Time	BW	Comp
save_soln	0.28	164	10.3	0.28	164	10.3	0.27	170	10.6
adt_calc	0.83	97	111	0.93	87	99	0.83	97	111
res_calc	4.31	40	48.7	4.4	39	47.7	3.64	48	57
bres_calc	0.06	33	6.8	0.08	25	5.1	0.07	29	5.8
update	1.28	152	19.1	1.38	142	17.7	1.19	164	20.6
total	6.75			7.07			6.0		

significantly more than for the C version (24/62/52/37/29). Notably, the XL version performs the same number of non-coherent cache loads for each kernel as the C version, whereas PGI's version uses less. This shows a good match between what performance one might expect from the Fortran variant and the C variant.

9   Conclusions

The POWER8 platform has very good computational power (900 GFLOPS/s in single and 500 GFLOPS/s in double precision) and exceptional bandwidth (up to 300 GB/s) available as clearly shown by the synthetic benchmarks; although it is crucial that thread pinning is used at every stage.

On more real-world benchmarks we can exploit the potential throughput to varying degree. On the computationally intensive one-factor Black-Scholes benchmark up to 50 % of the theoretical peak is achieved, albeit only with a manually vectorized (altivec) implementation, as the compiler does not yet auto-vectorize the loop being used. Performance is competitive with current Intel architectures. The three-factor Black-Scholes benchmark poses some further challenges to the compiler; manual vectorization with altivec is again necessary, but even then suboptimal code is generated when OpenMP is enabled, therefore we cannot achieve performance anywhere near the theoretical peak. This issue is currently under further investigation.

The structured mesh application, CloverLeaf 2D/3D, built on a domain specific active library (OPS) is a good test of the compiler's auto-vectorization capabilities; after examining the best way of organizing the loop nest, vectorization is achieved on most loops. Given this, a very high fraction of the peak bandwidth is achieved on most computational loops, save for a couple of computationally intensive ones, and overall performance is excellent, up to four times faster than on Intel CPUs, and 40 % faster than an NVIDIA K40 GPU.

In case of the unstructured mesh applications, such as Airfoil, BookLeaf, and Hydra, built on the OP2 domain specific library, the irregular scatter/gather memory access patterns introduce a lot of latency, and in some cases manual vectorization impedes overall performance. Even so performance is up to 1.9×higher than on Intel Xeon (Haswell) CPU, with most loops achieving a high fraction of peak memory bandwidth.

Tests show that the XL compilers outperform the GNU compilers in most cases, by up to 20 %, particularly when altivec vectors are used. Code vectorisation is still a challenge for both compilers, but we have shown that with appropriate loop structures and pointer decorations many structured-mesh computations do vectorise. MPI+OpenMP performance in Fortran matches pure MPI performance for both compilers, however, with C variants there is still a significant performance degradation.

As early results show, the XL compilers are extending support for hybrid CPU-GPU architectures, with CUDA Fortran support available in June 2016 and OpenMP 4 (device) subsequently. PGI is also releasing its compilers for the platform (currently in beta). Overall, the POWER8 platform is a very promising target for High Performance Computing applications, especially in bandwidth-intensive cases. It is already delivering good performance, which we expect to get even better with evolving compilers.

Acknowledgments. The OP2 project has been funded by the UK Technology Strategy Board and Rolls-Royce plc. through the Siloet project, the UK Engineering and Physical Sciences Research Council projects
EP/I006079/1, EP/I00677X/1 on "Multi-layered Abstractions for PDEs".

The OPS project is funded by the UK Engineering and Physical Sciences Research Council projects EP/K038494/1, EP/K038486/1, EP/K038451/1 and EP/K038567/1 on "Future-proof massively-parallel execution of multi-block applications" and EP/J010553/1 "Software for Emerging Architectures" (ASEArch) project. Cloverleaf development is supported by the Royal Society through their Industry Fellowship Scheme (IF090020/AM).

The authors would like to thank Chris Bowler, Carlo Bertolli, Wang Chen and Kelvin Li at IBM for their help in accessing expertise and software for the development of these experiments.

References

1. Bookleaf mini-app. https://github.com/UK-MAC/BookLeaf_ref. Accessed 4 Jan 2016
2. Adinetz, A.V., Baumeister, P.F., Böttiger, H., Hater, T., Maurer, T., Pleiter, D., Schenck, W., Schifano, S.F.: Performance evaluation of scientific applications on POWER8. In: Jarvis, S.A., Wright, S.A., Hammond, S.D. (eds.) PMBS 2014. LNCS, vol. 8966, pp. 24–45. Springer, Heidelberg (2015). doi:10.1007/978-3-319-17248-4_2
3. Giles, M., László, E., Reguly, I., Appleyard, J., Demouth, J.: GPU implementation of finite difference solvers. In: Proceedings of the 7th Workshop on High Performance Computational Finance, pp. 1–8. IEEE Press (2014)
4. Heroux, M., Barrett, R.: Mantevo project (2011)
5. McCalpin, J.D.: Memory bandwidth and machine balance in current high performance computers. In: IEEE Computer Society Technical Committee on Computer Architecture (TCCA) Newsletter, pp. 19–25, December 1995

6. Reguly, I.Z., Keita, A.-K., Giles, M.B.: Benchmarking the ibm power8 processor. In: Proceedings of the 25th Annual International Conference on Computer Science and Software Engineering, pp. 61–69. IBM Corp. (2015)
7. Reguly, I.Z., László, E., Mudalige, G.R., Giles, M.B.: Vectorizing unstructured mesh computations for many-core architectures. In: Proceedings of the Programming Models and Applications on Multicores and Manycores, PMAM 2014, pp. 39:39–39:50. ACM, New York (2007)
8. Reguly, I.Z., Mudalige, G.R., Bertolli, C., Giles, M.B., Betts, A., Kelly, P.H.J., Radford, D.: Acceleration of a full-scale industrial CFD application with OP 2. IEEE Trans. Parallel Distrib. Syst. **PP**(99), 1 (2015)
9. Reguly, I.Z., Mudalige, G.R., Giles, M.B., Curran, D., McIntosh-Smith, S.: The OPS domain specific abstraction for multi-block structured grid computations. In: Proceedings of the Fourth International Workshop on Domain-Specific Languages and High-Level Frameworks for High Performance Computing, pp. 58–67. IEEE Press (2014)

Measuring and Managing Energy in OpenPOWER

Todd Rosedahl[✉], Charles Lefurgy, and Martha Broyles

IBM, Armonk, USA
{rosedahl,lefurgy,mbroyles}@us.ibm.com

Abstract. This paper presents the design and implementation of energy measurement and management features found in OpenPOWER systems. The firmware and its ecosystem are open source to allow the community to extend the capabilities.

Keywords: Energy · Measurement · Management · OpenPOWER · Firmware · POWER8

1 Overview

The energy required to power and cool computers can be a significant cost to a business – reducing profit margins and consuming resources. In addition, the cost of creating power and cooling infrastructure can be prohibitive to business growth. In response to these challenges, IBM developed EnergyScale[TM] [5] technology for IBM Power systems.

Power8 systems implement EnergyScale in both hardware and firmware with a new device called the On-Chip Controller (OCC). The OCC firmware provides detailed measurement and management of component power and thermals. This enables better facility planning, provides energy and cost savings, enables peak energy usage control, and increases system availability. Administrators may leverage these capabilities to control the power consumption and performance of POWER processor-based systems to meet their particular data center needs.

Additionally, as part of the OpenPOWER initiative, IBM has released the OCC power management firmware as open source [1]. The first section of this paper describes the OCC hardware and firmware and how it provides system power/thermal management and measurement. With the open source code, system developers and researchers are free to create their own solutions to complicated power/performance issues.

In the second half of this paper, a tool called AMESTER [2] will be described. AMESTER, in conjunction with the OCC, provides deep performance/power profiling by enabling access to a rich set of sensor information as well as a set of controls. AMESTER also has been released as open source and now system developer and researchers have an additional power measurement tool at their disposal. In this paper, sample results using AMESTER will be shown including a new result that shows the power savings benefit of using Internal Voltage Regulator Modules on a per core basis.

© Springer International Publishing AG 2016
M. Taufer et al. (Eds.): ISC High Performance Workshops 2016, LNCS 9945, pp. 255–267, 2016.
DOI: 10.1007/978-3-319-46079-6_18

2 OCC Overview

The OCC is designed to measure and manage performance and energy consumption. It provides access to detailed chip temperature, power, and utilization data, as well as complete control of processor frequency and memory bandwidth. This enables customization for performance and energy management, or for maintaining system reliability and availability. Partners now have the flexibility to create innovative power, thermal, and performance solutions on POWER systems.

The OCC is a PowerPC 405 processor that is embedded directly on the POWER8 chip along with the main POWER processor cores. It has its own dedicated 512 K SRAM, access to main memory, and 2 dedicated General Purpose off-load Engines (called GPEs). Figure 1 shows how the OCC interacts with other hardware and firmware in Power8. The main OCC firmware runs a 250 μs loop that utilizes the GPEs to continuously collect system power data by domain, processor temperatures, memory temperatures, and processor utilization data. The firmware communicates with the open source OpenPOWER Abstraction Layer (OPAL) stack via main memory. In conjunction with the operating system, it uses the data collected to determine the proper processor frequency and memory bandwidth to enable the following functions.

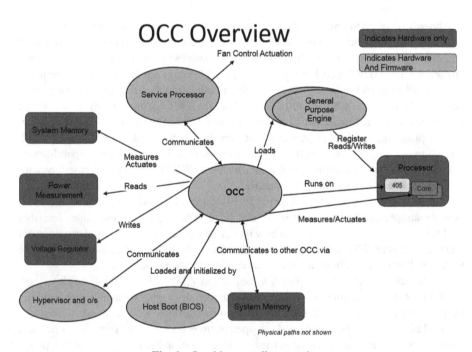

Fig. 1. On-chip controller overview

2.1   Functional Overview

Performance Boost. The POWER processors can be set to frequencies above nominal. The OCC monitors the system and controls the processor frequency and memory bandwidth to keep the system thermally safe and within acceptable power limits.

Power Capping. A system power limit can be set. The OCC will continually monitor the power consumption and will reduce the allowed processor frequency to maintain that power limit.

Energy Saving. When the system utilization is low, the OCC infrastructure can be used to put the system into a low power state. This function can be used to comply with various government idle power regulations and standards.

System Availability. OCC supports a Quick Power Drop signal that can be used to respond to power supply failures or other system events that require a rapid power reduction. This function enables systems to run through component or data center power and thermal failures without crashing.

System Reliability. The OCC can be used to keep component temperatures within reliability limits, extending device lifetime and limiting service costs.

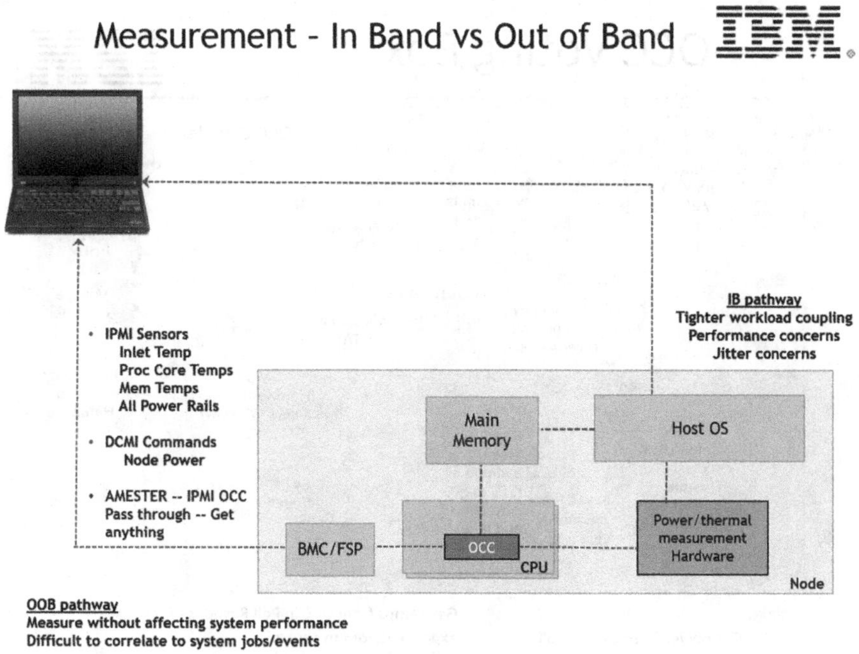

Fig. 2. Out-of-band measurement

Performance per Watt Tuning. As the system utilization varies, the OCC can provide monitoring information and frequency control that maximizes system performance per watt metrics.

Data Collection. There are a number of ways to get the data out from the system as shown in Fig. 2. Standard IPMI sensors are used to provide power readings from various power rails within the system. Processor and memory temperatures are also presented as IPMI sensors.

Additionally, there is a pass-through interface that provides direct access to the OCC. This has advantages over in-band collection as it does not use any system resources.

2.2 OCC Details

The OCC works in conjunction with the operating system to provide customized energy management solutions. The standard Linux governors allow users to select power management modes that made specific performance and power consumption trade-offs. For example, the "on demand" governor adjusts core clock frequency maintain a high level of core utilization for the running workload. The role of OCC is to keep the system within specified power/thermal limits. It does this by running power

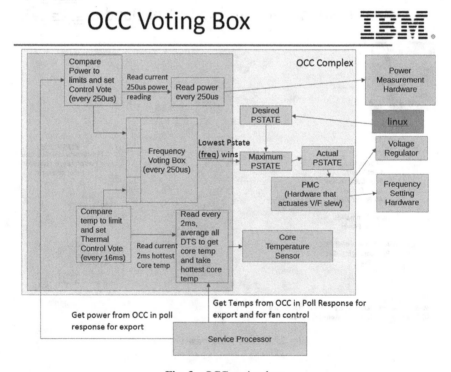

Fig. 3. OCC voting box

Further PSTATE Details

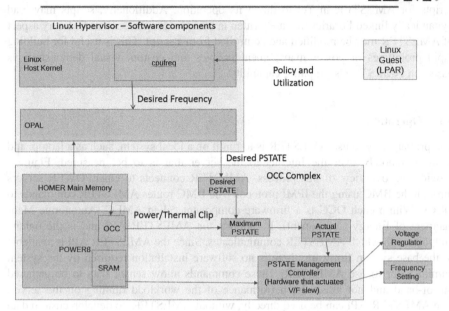

Fig. 4. PSTATE control details

and thermal control loops that monitor the following: node power, socket powers, DIMM temperature, processor core temperatures. When the operating system requests a frequency, this gets translate to a PSTATE by an open source software layer called OPAL (Open Power Abstraction Layer). OPAL uses data presented by the OCC via a shared main memory region (Shown by HOMER in Fig. 4) in order to translate from frequency to PSTATE. If the PSTATE selected by the OS will cause the system to exceed a power or thermal limit, the OCC complex will clip the frequency and only allow the PSTATE in the "maximum PSTATE" register to be realized in the hardware.

See Figs. 3 and 4 for details on the hardware/firmware paths and loop timings.

3   AMESTER

AMESTER (Automated Measurement of Systems for Temperature and Energy Reporting) is a tool for monitoring power consumption and performance metrics in IBM systems. Within IBM, AMESTER has been used since 2005 to develop and test the energy management features in EnergyScale. Several academic, government research labs, and IBM clients have used AMESTER to collect data for research publications and better understand IBM system power consumption. It has proven to be valuable for visualizing power measurements and prototyping new power management policies. In 2016, AMESTER became an open source project to make it broadly available to the OpenPOWER community.

AMESTER provides both a GUI for interactive use and a non-interactive mode for unattended data collection. AMESTER is written completely in Tcl/Tk. Users can write scripts for AMESTER in Tcl to direct its operation. Additionally, scripts may load dynamically linked libraries that are written in other languages, such as C. Every aspect of AMESTER may be modified and controlled from a script. This is useful for building rapid prototypes of power management policies and custom visual demonstrations based on AMESTER's graphing capability.

3.1 Operation

The primary way to use AMESTER is to run it on a local system, such as a laptop, and connect remotely over the Internet to the server that is to be measured. Figure 2 provides an overview of this process. AMESTER connects to OpenPOWER servers through the BMC using the IPMI protocol. The BMC routes AMESTER commands to OCCs. Within each OCC is a firmware component called AMEC (Autonomic Management of Energy Component). It supports the AMESTER API and is the unique endpoint with which AMESTER communicates. Since the AMESTER API is available in the base system firmware, there is no software installation required by the system administrator to use AMESTER. These commands allow sensor data to be gathered out-of-band and not affect the performance of the workload running on the server. The AMESTER API can be used directly, without AMESTER, to develop custom data collection programs for other environments [3].

Here is an example of using a script to attach AMESTER to an OpenPOWER system using a privileged IPMI account:

```
openpower myserver -addr 9.3.29.165
    -ipmi_user ADMIN -ipmi_passwd admin
```

This creates an object named **myserver** that represents the OpenPOWER system, as shown in Fig. 5. Screenshot of sensor data collection. AMESTER will automatically discover all available sensors and parameters available from the firmware and create corresponding objects for use by the user scripts. Objects are supported by the Itcl package for Tcl. Table 1 shows the object naming convention for POWER8 and provides example object names. The objects provide methods to invoke sensor data collection and return data values.

Table 1. Object name convention

Component	Object name convention	Example
System	*host*	myserver
OCC AMEC	*host*_node#_ame#	myserver_node0_ame0
Sensor	*host*_node#_ame#_*sname*	myserver_node0_ame0_PWR250US (System power consumption)
Parameter	*host*_node#_ame#_*pname*	myserver_node0_ame0_freq_or (Core frequency override)

The *node* designation in the object name is to support prior multi-node (multi-planar) POWER servers. AMESTER can attach to many servers simultaneously, which makes it useful for studying power management of clusters.

3.2 Sensors

The principal function of AMESTER is to collect power and performance metrics from the firmware. The user specifies a list of sensors for AMESTER to gather in the background as quickly as possible. As sensors arrive the GUI is updated and user provided callbacks are processed. Figure 5 shows a screenshot of data collection. An example of requesting sensor collection for the system power consumption (updated 250 ms) and average chip temperature (updated every 2 ms) follows:

```
myserver_node0_ame0 set_sensor_list
   {PWR250US TEMP2MSP0}
myserver_node0_ame0 sensor_window_raise
```

Sensor Description. In addition to the actual sensor value (e.g. CPU socket power), each sensor also has metadata fields, shown in Table 2, that are queried once from the

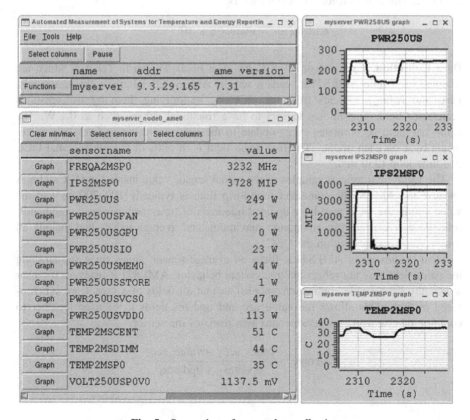

Fig. 5. Screenshot of sensor data collection

Table 2. Sensor metadata fields.

Field	Description
sensornum	The numeric sensor ID used in OCC commands
sensorname	A string name for use in AMESTER GUI and TCL commands
u_value	A string describing the sensor unit. For example, "W" for Watts
freq	The update rate (Hz) of the sensor in the OCC.
scalefactor	A floating-point multiplier used to interpret the 16-bit value field sent by the OCC

OCC during the initial connection phase. These fields, which are constants for a particular level of OCC firmware, describe how often the data is collected, the data units, etc. and are needed in order to use the data correctly.

Some sensors are updated on the shortest real-time control interval of the OCC, which is 250 microseconds in POWER8. Other sensors are updated at a slower rate. This internal update rate is reflected in the sensor's *sensorname* and *freq* fields.

Sensors may take on real values, even though the OCC does not support floating-point math. This is implemented by programming the OCC sensor with a *scalefactor*. The scalefactor is a floating-point value with a 48-bit signed mantissa and 8-bit signed exponent. It is used as a multiplier to interpret the raw sensor bits sent from the OCC. The equation for the scalefactor is:

$$scalefactor = mantissa \times 10^{exponent}$$

Data Collection. Each sensor in OCC has data fields, shown in Table 3, which are returned each time AMESTER reads a sensor. AMESTER interprets the *value, min, max,* and *value_acc* fields from the OCC by multiplying them by the sensors's scalefactor field. This allows sensors to have fractional values, such as 0.1 W. The *value_acc* field accumulates every update to the sensor and the *updates* field increments by 1 on each update. The *timestamp* field is in units of the fundamental OCC real-time loop (250 ms).

The *value* field reflects samples of the actual sensor value inside the OCC. This is because the AMESTER command round-trip time is typically 100–200 ms and the value within the OCC may have updated hundreds of times between read commands. Still the user can get true minimum, maximum, and average values that include all sensor value updates within the OCC.

Most studies using AMESTER focus on average sensor values since subsampling the value field may not reflect the true system behavior. AMESTER reads each sensor atomically (in a single command/response) so that all fields of a sensor are synchronized in time. This allows the value_acc and updates fields to be used together to compute precise averages between any two reads of the sensor.

$$average = \frac{value\_acc_2 - value\_acc_1}{updates_2 - updates_1}$$

Table 3. Sensor data fields

Field	Description	Size in OCC (bits)
value	The sensor's value	16
min, max	Minimum and maximum values since last reset	16
value_acc	Accumulates every write to value field	64
updates	Counts number of writes to value field	32
timestamp	OCC time of last update	32

Furthermore, multiple AMESTER instances simultaneously attached to a system can use this method to compute averages over timescales of interest without interference.

It is possible to tightly time-synchronize values across sensors, since read commands typically complete within 1 OCC control interval. In POWER8 OCC, up to 10 sensors may be received in one read command. This is limited only by the buffer size in the firmware implementation.

Triggers. A user-supplied callback procedure can be registered to run whenever sensor data is received. The callback is registered by setting the global variable *new_data_callback* with the procedure name. The callback receives the updated sensor object as an argument. The callback can inspect the updated sensor object and take appropriate action, such as writing a trace to a file. An example printing all sensor updates to the console is shown below:

```
proc my_callback {sensorobj} {
    puts "[$sensorobj cget -sensorname] =
        [$sensorobj cget -value]"
}

set ::new_data_callback my_callback
```

3.3 Trace Buffers

The AMESTER trace buffer interface makes it possible to study system behavior at small timescales. Since the sensor interface can take 100 s of milliseconds to poll sensor values, it is not sufficient for studying and debugging OCC control loops which often operate quicker than 1 ms. The trace buffers are implemented by reserving some of the OCC SRAM memory to capture runs of sensor values. Every sensor value change can be captured until the buffer fills. The AMESTER API provides a way to specify which sensors and parameters (described later) compose the trace record written into the trace buffer.

In POWER8, there are two trace buffers. One buffer, called *trace250us*, operates on a 250 μs period and the other buffer, called *trace2 ms*, operates on a 2 ms period. The periods correspond to real-time control intervals within the OCC. When the AMESTER command to begin recording is sent to the system, the primary OCC signals all

OCCs to begin tracing. This synchronizes both trace buffers across all POWER8 chips. During each trace interval, the OCC snapshots the programmed sensors and parameters into a trace record. Once the trace buffer is filled, AMESTER reads the raw buffer data, parses the trace records, and writes them to a file. The trace buffers are 8 KB each. Therefore, a single 16-bit sensor value can be recorded for 1024 ms into *trace250us* and for 8192 ms into *trace2 ms*.

3.4   Parameters

AMESTER's parameter interface was developed to allow OCC developers to debug new features. It gives the developer the ability to specify a section of the OCC SRAM memory, such as a global variable, and then read or write it from AMESTER to affect the behavior of the running system. Parameter values types include signed and unsigned integers of various sizes as well as hexadecimal strings for raw data. Additionally, parameters may be an array of values to simplify reading and writing from scripts. The parameter window, shown in Fig. 6, provides an easy way to inspect and change the parameter values.

Parameters speed the debug-compile-test cycle by allowing specific tests to be run without re-compiling the OCC firmware and loading it into the system. For example, it has been used to provide setpoints and thresholds for algorithm tuning. We have used the parameter feature in conjunction with trace buffers to observe the input and output of power capping and thermal feedback controllers over each control interval.

An OCC developer can create a new parameter simply by specifying a global variable and adding an entry to the parameter table in the OCC firmware. For example, the setpoint for the thermal controller resides in variable *g_amec_sys.thermalproc. setpoint* and the value is in units of 0.1 degrees Celsius. This is added to the parameter table in 1 line of code using a macro:

```
AMEC_PARM_UINT16(PARM_SYS_THRM_SP,"sys_thrm_sp",&g_am
ec_sys.thermalproc.setpoint)
```

The macro specifies the type and size of the parameter. The developer only needs to supply a unique number to identify the parameter (PARM_SYS_THRM_SP) in the low-level AMESTER API commands, a nice name for AMESTER to display, and the pointer to the value. From AMESTER, the parameter may be read into a variable by a user script:

```
set tempC [myserver_node0_ame0_sys_thrm_sp read]
```

It may also be written to control the OCC to use 85.0 degrees Celsius:

```
myserver_node0_ame0_sys_thrm_sp write 850
```

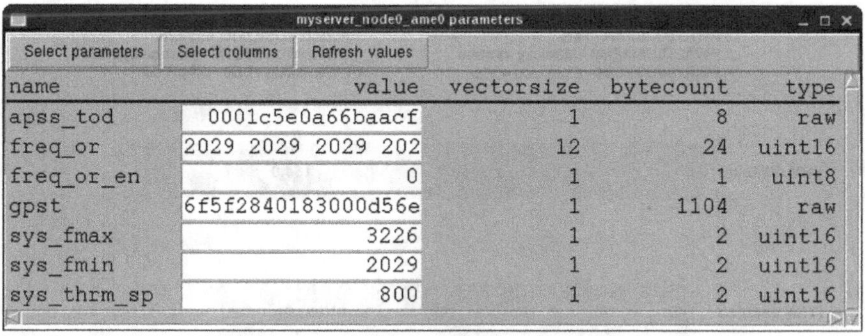

name	value	vectorsize	bytecount	type
apss_tod	0001c5e0a66baacf	1	8	raw
freq_or	2029 2029 2029 202	12	24	uint16
freq_or_en	0	1	1	uint8
gpst	6f5f2840183000d56e	1	1104	raw
sys_fmax	3226	1	2	uint16
sys_fmin	2029	1	2	uint16
sys_thrm_sp	800	1	2	uint16

myserver_node0_ame0 parameters — Select parameters | Select columns | Refresh values

Fig. 6. Screenshot of parameter window

3.5 Use Case

In this section we show how AMESTER can be used to measure the reduction in power due to the POWER8 internal voltage regulators. On POWER8, each core can be set to an independent voltage and frequency [4]. We consider the case where all 12 cores are running a heavy workload. The first 6 cores are running at the lowest frequency of 2066 MHz to represent a workload that is memory bounded and cannot use extra frequency to improve performance. The other 6 cores represent a CPU-bound workload running at the highest frequency of 3233 MHz. Previously, on POWER7, the voltage of all cores was driven by an external regulator that was set based on the highest frequency cores. In POWER8, each core has an internal voltage regulator module (iVRM) that sets the core voltage independently from other cores. In this case, the cores with lower clock frequency use the iVRM at a lower voltage, while the cores at higher clock frequency remain on the external voltage regulator at the usual high voltage. This reduces the overall power footprint of the chip.

To explore this particular power management strategy, we use the on demand linux governor to set a maximum frequency for the fast cores, but override the frequency for the slower cores using the *freq_or* AMESTER parameter, shown in Fig. 6. Then we use the watchsensor.tcl script provided with AMESTER to select the power sensors and voltage sensors for tracing to a CSV file.

The results for our scenario are shown in Fig. 7. When iVRM is disabled, all cores use external voltage regulation and the external voltage regulator is set to 1.1375 V. When iVRMs are enabled, the 6 low-frequency cores use a lower voltage of 0.850 V and the 6 high-frequency cores still run from the external regulator at 1.1375 V. With iVRMs enabled, the chip power reduces by 25 % (39 W) and the overall system power reduces by 13 % compared to no iVRMs enabled. The sensor data shows the entire power reduction is due to the POWER8 chip Vdd voltage rail alone and other subsystems are not affected. Additionally, AMESTER collected performance data for each core using the instruction-per-second sensors (not shown) to show that performance was not affected.

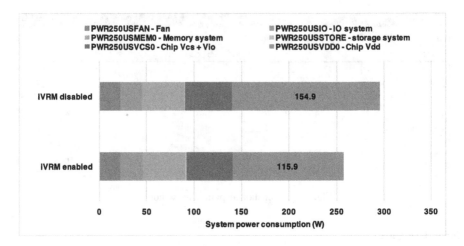

Fig. 7. Power consumption by subsystem

4 Related Work

Industry-standard protocols for reporting power in computers have been previously available. The IPMI protocol, which runs on the BMC, includes a Sensor Data Repository function that allows out-of-band measurements to be collected [6]. Today, IPMI is limited to reading 1 sensor record per read command and has 1 timestamp for the entire sensor repository. BMC firmware populates the IPMI sensors using I^2C-bus [7] and PMBus [9] protocols to gather measurements from system devices. Manufacturer specific command extensions to IPMI, such as Intel's Node Manager [9] and DCMI [10] also report power consumption metrics.

In contrast to the prior work, AMESTER commands were designed to allow a more flexible, user-specified set of sensors to be returned by a single read command in near real time (under 1 s). The AMESTER interface exposes the true sensor update rate for each sensor and allows each sensor to have a timestamp for its last update. This allows for measurements to be correctly time-aligned with respect to each other. AMESTER tracks an accumulator for each sensor, allowing precise averages to be calculated over arbitrary periods by multiple users. Furthermore, AMESTER's tracing capability allows it to keep up with sensor measurement generation for in-depth study over short time periods. Limitations of AMESTER today are that it cannot collect every sensor update for sub-second sensors due to bandwidth limitations of the BMC and network. Similar limitations exist for IPMI.

5 Conclusion

The POWER8 OCC delivers real-time power management features that improve the performance and reliability of OpenPOWER systems. The AMESTER tool provides insights on the power consumption and performance behavior of the system through time-synchronized visualization. Together, OCC and AMESTER provide the Open-POWER community with strong foundation for prototyping new power management capabilities.

References

1. OpenPOWER OCC: https://github.com/open-power/occ
2. AMESTER: https://github.com/open-power/amester
3. El-Essawy, W.: IPMItoolRaw Command Interface to OpenPOWER POWER8 On Chip Controller: Sensor reading commands, Version 0.4 (2016). https://github.com/open-power/docs/blob/master/occ/OCC_ipmitool_sensors.pdf
4. Zyuban, V., et al.: IBM POWER8 circuit design and energy optimization. IBM JR&D **59**(1), 1–16 (2015)
5. Broyles, M., et al.: IBM EnergyScale for POWER8 Processor-Based Systems, white paper, November 2015. http://public.dhe.ibm.com/common/ssi/ecm/po/en/pow03125usen/POW03 125USEN.PDF
6. Intel: Hewlett-Packard, NEC, and Dell, IPMI - Intelligent Platform Management Interface Specification Second Generation v2.0, Rev. 1.1, E7 Markup, 21 April 2015
7. NXP: I^{2}C-bus specification and user manual, Rev. 6, 4 April 2014
8. Intel, Intel Intelligent Power Node Manager 3.0 External Interface Specification Using IPMI, Document Number 332200-001US, March 2015
9. System Management Interface Forum: PMBus Power System Management Protocol Specification Part II – Command Language, Rev. 1.2, 6 September 2010
10. Intel, DCMI – Data Center Manageability Interface Specification, Version 1.5, Rev. 1.0, 23 August 2011

Performance Analysis of Spark/GraphX on POWER8 Cluster

Xinyu Que$^{(\boxtimes)}$, Lars Schneidenbach$^{(\boxtimes)}$, Fabio Checconi$^{(\boxtimes)}$,
Carlos H.Ã. Costa, and Daniele Buono

IBM TJ Watson, Yorktown Heights, NY 10598, USA
{xque,schneidenbach,fchecco,chcost,dbuono}@us.ibm.com

Abstract. POWER 8, the latest RISC (Reduced Instruction Set Computer) microprocessor of the IBM Power architecture family, was designed to significantly benefit emerging workloads, including Business Analytics, Cloud Computing and High Performance Computing. In this paper, we provide a thorough performance evaluation on a widely used large-scale graph processing framework, Spark/GraphX, on a POWER 8 cluster. Note that we use Spark and Java versions out of the box without any optimization. We examine the performance with several important graph kernels such as Breadth-First Search, Connected Components, and PageRank using both large real-world social graphs and synthetic graphs of billions of edges. We study the Spark/GraphX performance against some architectural aspects and perform the first Spark/GraphX scalability test with up to 16 POWER 8 nodes.

Keywords: POWER8 · Spark/GraphX · Graph algorithm

1 Introduction

As the amount of data generated and collected continues to grow at an exponential rate, large-scale graph processing frameworks, such as Pregel [22], PowerGraph [12], GraphX [13], and many others [25–27,29], have been developed. These frameworks are used to extract the desired information from Big Data for business and daily life as graphs are a natural representation for unstructured data.

GraphX is becoming more and more popular because it is a library that comes with Spark, a now widely used cluster computing engine for big data analytics. It is similar to Hadoop MapReduce [1]. While it performs several orders of magnitude faster than Hadoop MapReduce in many applications [35], Spark differentiates itself from MapReduce in several aspects which are important to GraphX. This includes novel in-memory storage abstractions, the Resilient Distributed Datasets (RDDs), support for general computation of Directed Acyclic Graphs (DAGs), lineage-based fault tolerance, and many more. These novelties allow Spark to support a wide range of big data analytics such as graph processing and machine learning, which normally require iterative steps and multiple

© Springer International Publishing AG 2016
M. Taufer et al. (Eds.): ISC High Performance Workshops 2016, LNCS 9945, pp. 268–285, 2016.
DOI: 10.1007/978-3-319-46079-6_19

data join operations. GraphX extends the Spark operators by introducing a few of it is own, specific to graph processing.

POWER 8 [4,30] is the first processor supporting OpenPOWER [2]. It is designed with high memory capacity and bandwidth, low latency access, and high thread density to deliver unprecedented performance for emerging workloads. It shows a great impact on the performance of SparkBench [3,19], a Spark benchmark developed by IBM Research, which covers a comprehensive set of applications such as machine learning and SQL queries as well as a diverse set of high performance computing applications [8,11,21]. Moreover, all the aforementioned research was conducted either on commodity X86 cluster or a single POWER 8 node. In this paper, we provide a comprehensive performance evaluation of Spark/GraphX from a system perspective on a POWER 8 cluster with 17 nodes (1 master + 16 slave nodes). While there's literature about Spark on previous generations of the POWER architecture [23], to the best of our knowledge, these are the first Spark/GraphX scalability results on a POWER 8 cluster in the literature.

Our main contributions are as follows:

1. We analyze the performance of Spark/GraphX on a set of graph kernels with both real-world graphs, such as Twitter [16] and Friendster [34], and synthetic RMAT graphs [10,10,18,28].
2. We provide a fresh look on performance of Spark/GraphX by targeting some POWER 8 architectural aspects such as Non-Uniform Memory Access (NUMA) and Simultaneous Multithreading (SMT)
3. We perform comprehensive scalability tests of Spark/GraphX on POWER 8 cluster from 2 nodes to 16 nodes.

The rest of the paper is organized as follows. Section 2 reviews the related work on POWER 8 and Spark/GraphX. After that, Sect. 3 provides a brief description of three important graph kernels we used in this research. Section 4 presents the comprehensive performance evaluation of the Spark/GraphX on POWER 8 cluster. Finally, Sect. 5 concludes our work.

2   Related Work

In this section we review the literature related to POWER 8 and Spark/GraphX performance analysis.

In [8], Brock, Liu, and Rajamani report record-setting performance for the STAC-A2 benchmark, a well-rounded HPC benchmark that stresses a system at scale. The paper presents solutions for a POWER 8 S824 server with different algorithmic optimizations. In [11], the performance of POWER 8 is evaluated in the context of a widely-used computational neuroscientific application modeling large-scale neuronal network using detailed morphologies. [9] describes a new methodology to design SpMV algorithms for POWER 8 systems which shows quasi-optimal scaling performance. [21] provides insight into the relevant characteristics of POWER 8 using both a set of microbenchmarks and a wide range of applications which are difficult to optimize on other processors and accelerators. [3] studies Spark performance on a single POWER 8 S882L system using SparkBench. All this valuable research is focused on a single POWER 8 machine. We provide a first look to Spark/GraphX performance on a cluster with 17 POWER 8 nodes.

Lim et al. [20] present an extensive empirical evaluation of three graph processing platforms including Pegasus, Spark/GraphX and Urika. The experiments with GraphX running on a 65 node cluster in a public Cloud environment show that GraphX outperforms Urika and Pegasus on iterative operations like connected components and PageRank. [7] addresses the problem of parallelizing the de Bruijn graph-based de novo genome sequence assembly on distributed memory systems by proposing a new tool, Spaler, based on Spark using the GraphX API, which scales better than existing tools. [14] proposes building a scalable hypergraph analysis framework based on GraphX and examines the programmability with two real-world datasets on a 6-node cluster. [17] analyzes Maximum Flow Algorithm on GraphX. The author finds that limiting the active set results in insignificant gains of performance. Caching of RDD results is reported to speed up performance by factors of 1.2 to 1.4 with the claim that the factor correlates with the runtime and/or number of iterations. While earlier studies on GraphX focus on different angles, none of them provides a thorough performance study of GraphX by considering architecture characteristics such as NUMA, and SMT.

3   Graph Analytics Building Blocks in GraphX

In this section, we describe a set of representative graph kernels, including Breadth-First Search (BFS), Page Rank (PR) and Connected Components (CC), which are heavily used as building blocks for big data analytics. We also present code snippets of these graph kernels within the GraphX implementation of Pregel. Our evaluation in Sect. 4 is based on these kernels.

3.1   Breadth-First Search

Graph traversals are often used as basic components of more sophisticated methods for big data analytics. For example, algorithms to calculate centrality measures, or heuristic search algorithms, such as A* [31,36] use graph traversal as a building block. Because of its importance, BFS has been chosen by Graph 500 (http://www.graph.500.org/) to rank supercomputer performance on data-intensive applications. Recursive MATrix (RMAT) scale-free graphs [10,18,28] have been chosen as the input data because of their similarity to graphs occurring in many real-world applications.

```
1   object PredShortestPathsPregel {
2     type SPMap = Map[VertexId, (VertexId, Int)]
3     private def makeMap(x: (VertexId, (VertexId, Int))*) = Map(x: _*)
4     private def incrementMap(spmap: SPMap, pred: VertexId): SPMap = spmap.map {
5       case (v, (p, d)) => v -> (pred, d + 1) }
6     private def addMaps(spmap1: SPMap, spmap2: SPMap): SPMap =
7       (spmap1.keySet ++ spmap2.keySet).map {
8         k => k -> {
9           val p1 = spmap1.getOrElse(k, (-1L, Int.MaxValue))
10          val p2 = spmap2.getOrElse(k, (-1L, Int.MaxValue))
11          if (p1._2 < p2._2)
12            p1
13          else
14            p2
15        }
16      }.toMap
17    def run[VD, ED: ClassTag](graph: Graph[VD, ED], landmarks: Seq[VertexId]): Graph[SPMap, ED] = {
18      val spGraph = graph.mapVertices { (vid, attr) =>
19        if (landmarks.contains(vid)) makeMap((vid, (vid, 0))) else makeMap()
20      }
21      val initialMessage = makeMap()
22      def vertexProgram(id: VertexId, attr: SPMap, msg: SPMap): SPMap = {
23        addMaps(attr, msg)
24      }
25      def sendMessage(edge: EdgeTriplet[SPMap, _]): Iterator[(VertexId, SPMap)] = {
26        val newAttr = incrementMap(edge.srcAttr, edge.srcId)
27        if (edge.dstAttr != addMaps(newAttr, edge.dstAttr) ) Iterator((edge.dstId, newAttr))
28        else Iterator.empty
29      }
30      Pregel(spGraph, initialMessage)(vertexProgram, sendMessage, addMaps)
31    }
32    private def unmap(spmap: SPMap, root: VertexId) : Int = {
33      val entry = spmap.getOrElse(root, (-1L, Int.MaxValue))
34      entry._2
35    }
36    def bfs[ED](graph: Graph[SPMap, ED], root: VertexId): VertexRDD[Int] = {
37      graph.vertices.mapValues( (vid, attr)=>unmap(attr, root) ).filter{ case(vid, attr)=>attr<Int.MaxValue }
38    }
39  }
```

Listing 1.1. Pregel-based BFS

Our BFS implementation in Listing 1.1. is performed in 2 stages. The first stage uses the Pregel API to annotate the graph in a similar way a shortest path algorithm would do. The second stage extracts the actual BFS result sets for each root. Listing 1.2 shows the 2 stages. Note that the measured times in Sect. 4 include the extraction and printing (not shown) of the size of the result to make Spark actually instantiate the result and force Spark to perform the operations. Otherwise, Spark might defer or skip the processing entirely and the measurements wouldn't represent the actual processing time due to lazy evaluation[1] [6,35].

```
1   val pspgraph = PredShortestPathsPregel.run(graph, Array(root)).cache
2   var bfsverts = Array(root).map{ r=>r->PredShortestPathsPregel.bfs(pspgraph, r).collect.toSet }.toMap
3   var spsshorten = bfsverts.mapValues( { d => (d.size, 0.0) } )
```

Listing 1.2. Calling Pregel-based BFS

---

[1] All transformations in Spark are lazy, in that they do not compute their results right away. Instead, they just remember the transformations applied to some base dataset (e.g. a file). The transformations are only computed when an action requires a result to be returned to the driver program.

3.2 Page Rank

PageRank is a very popular graph algorithm and is also frequently used for benchmarking and comparison. It ranks the importance for the vertices in a graph and the computation is performed in a iterative manner to update the ranking scores of each vertex [24]. GraphX comes with two implementations of PageRank, running with a fixed number of iterations and running until convergence. For simplicity, we are measuring the static page rank version using 5 iterations. Same as with the BFS result, we are adding another operation that touches the result to cause Spark to perform the requested activity within the measurement frame. In this case we just count the vertices in the result. Alternatively, retrieving the max or the average page rank result would work too. Since those operations may involve additional computation, we decided to stick to the counting.

```
1    val pr_graph = graph.ops.staticPageRank( options.pageRankIterLimit )
2    var res_verts = pr_graph.vertices.count()
```

Listing 1.3. Calling PageRank

3.3 Connected Components

For an undirected graph, this algorithm computes the connected component membership of each vertex. That is, within each connected component, all the vertices are reachable from each other. The parallel algorithms to find connected components is based on label propagation [15]. The algorithm initializes each vertex with an id and then iteratively updates minimum reachable vertex id of each vertex until it converges. At convergence, the vertices that belong to the same component have the same smallest *id* for each component. Similar to PageRank, we also use the GraphX implementations of Connected Components. Here too, we are counting the number of components in the result to instantiate the computation.

```
1    val cc_graph = graph.ops.connectedComponents()
2    val components = cc_graph.vertices.map { case (vid, data) => data }.distinct()
3    components.foreach{ v => println(v) }
4    cc_erts = components.count()
```

Listing 1.4. Calling ConnectedComponents

4 Experimental Results

In this section, we present the experimental analysis of the Spark/GraphX on a 17 nodes POWER 8 cluster. We begin by introducing the experimental environment and the input graphs. Then we present the results of the performance, scaling, and the profiling analysis.

4.1 Experimental Environment

The cluster used in this experimental evaluation is a 17 nodes POWER 8 cluster at IBM T.J. Watson Research Center. Each node is an IBM POWER 8 non-virtualized (PowerNV) S822LC server, an instantiation of POWER 8 Firestone architecture, which has a two-socket POWER 8 processor running at 3491 MHz clock. Each socket has 10 physical cores with 8-way simultaneous multithreading (SMT) per core. The node runs RedHat Enterprise Linux (RHEL) 7.2 with 512 GB physical memory and 1.2 TB Hitachi 10K RPM hard drive. All nodes are equipped with Mellanox ConnectX-4 EDR Host Channel Adapters.

We use Spark version 1.6.0 and IBM Java version ibm-java-ppc64le-80. Unless stated otherwise, we configure Spark with $SPARK\_WORKER\_CORES = 8$ to take advantage of SMT, and $SPARK\_WORKER\_MEMORY=24\ GB$. One node is designated as the master node and the slave nodes are launched with the configuration that utilizes the numactl to control Non-Uniform Memory Access (NUMA) policies for processes and shared memory allocation. In our experiments, we change the number of workers/executors via $spark.default.parallelism$ so that it's adjusted to match the total number of cores on all executor nodes [5].

4.2 Benchmarks and Metrics

In our evaluation, we used both real-world and synthetic graphs, as listed in Table 1. The real-world social graphs include Twitter follower links and Friendster online social network with over a billion edges. The synthetic RMAT graph is a popular family of scale-free graphs that has been adopted by many benchmarks. Note that for detailed profiling in Sects. 4.3 and 4.4 we use only RMAT graphs in this paper. All 3 graphs from Table 1 are used for scaling tests in Sect. 4.5.

Table 1. Graphs Used for Evaluation

Category	Name	Description	# Vertices	# Edges	Diameter	References
Real-world	Twitter	The entire Twitter follower links (Jul '09)	41.7M	1,470M	18	[16]
	Friendster	Friendster online social network	65.6M	1,806M	32	[34]
Synthetic	RMAT	Conforming to Graph500 Specifications	2^{SCALE}	$2^{SCALE+4}$	≈ 13	[10,10,18,28]

4.3 Effects of Non-Uniform Memory Access (NUMA)

We started the experiments by examining the Non-Uniform Memory Access (NUMA) effect on the graph kernels. We compared two Spark configurations, namely "With Numactl" and "No Numactl". For the "With Numactl" case, we

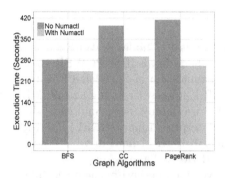
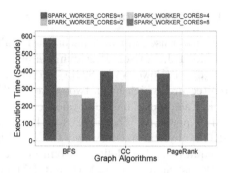

Fig. 1. NUMA effect.   **Fig. 2.** SMT effect.

bind the *SPARK_WORKER* to a set of specific CPU cores and have the worker
always allocate memory on the local memory controller. On the contrary, "No
Numactl" does not set an arbitrary CPU and memory affinity. We run Breadth-
First Search (BFS), PageRank (PR), and Connected Components (CC) using 4
slave nodes and we use RMAT graph scale 25 and edge factor 16, ≈ 33 million
vertices and 1 billion directed edges.

Figure 1 reports the execution time of BFS, Connected Components, and
PageRank on Spark with and without Numactl configured. Note that we use the
same number of *Spark_Worker, Spark_Executor* and *Executor_memory* for both
cases. As shown in the figure, in general, using Numactl shows significant performance improvements compared to the cases not using Numactl. To be specific,
we observed a 13.9 % performance improvement for BFS, 25.7 % performance
improvement for CC, and 36.7 % performance improvement for PR.

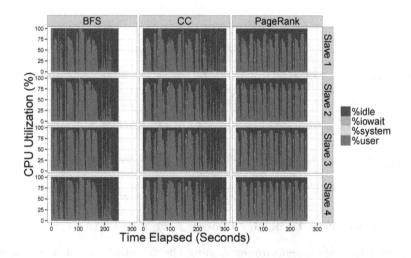

Fig. 3. CPU utilization profiling with Numactl.

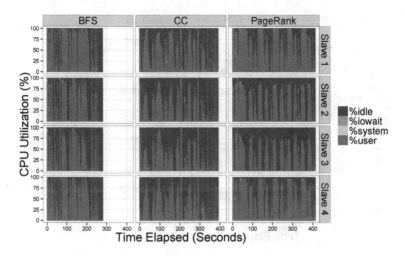

Fig. 4. CPU utilization profiling without Numactl.

To further understand the benefits of Numactl, we monitored the resource consumption using Linux System Activity Report (**SAR**[2]). Figures 3, 4, 5, 6, 7, 8, 9 and 10 report the CPU, memory, disk, and network utilization for each algorithm on all the slave nodes. In general, we observed well balanced resource activities across all the slave nodes.

For CPU utilization in Figs. 3 and 4, we report idle, iowait, system, and user (Spark tasks). Different algorithms have different demands of the CPU resource. Using Numactl achieves higher average CPU utilization with up to 11 % compared to not using Numactl. Breadth-First Search results show an average of 49 % and 48 % CPU utilization for With Numactl and No Numactl cases respectively. With Numactl, Connected Components has an average of 50 % CPU utilization, 10 % higher than the case without Numactl. For PageRank, the average CPU utilization is 61 % with Numactl and 50 % without Numactl.

In Figs. 5 and 6, we report the memory utilization of Spark tasks (kbmemused), memory used to cache data by the kernels (kbcached), and the amount of memory swapped (kbswpused). In GraphX, the graph algorithm is executed in a sequence of iterations which normally cache the vertex and edge RDDs in memory. And we observed a stable usage of memory for all these algorithms. Different algorithms show different memory usage. This is due to the different number of iterations and behaviors (e.g. communication pattern) in each iteration. The average memory usage is shown in Table 2

Figures 7 and 8 show disk activity including the blocks per second read from the devices (bread/s) and the blocks per second written to the devices (bwrite/s). Different algorithms shows different disk access behaviors. Breadth-First Search demands fewer disk access compared to Connected Components and PageRank. With Numactl, we observed an average of 50 MB/Second write for BFS,

---

[2] A system monitor command used to report on various system loads.

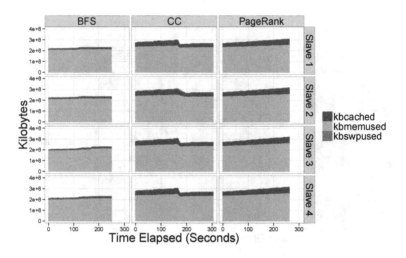

Fig. 5. Memory profiling with Numactl.

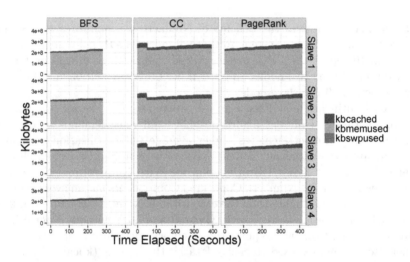

Fig. 6. Memory profiling without Numactl.

135 MB/Second write for CC, and 128 MB/Second write for PageRank. For the cases not using Numactl, the average write is lower than cases with Numactl, 44 MB/Second for BFS, 92 MB/Second for CC, and 101 MB/Second for PageRank. This mirrors the differences in CPU utilization in Figs. 3 and 4. Note that there are no disk read operations monitored by **SAR**. This is because the operating systems uses a lot of memory to cache the disk reads as we noticed in Figs. 5 and 6.

We also profiled the network IO activities for each slave node. As shown in Figs. 9 and 10, the total number of packets received per second (rxpck/s) and the

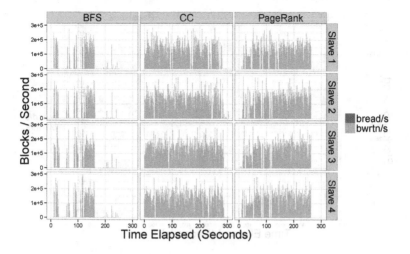

Fig. 7. Disk profiling with Numactl.

Table 2. Memory usage of graph kernels. Numbers in GB.

	With Numactl		No Numactl	
Kernel	kbcached	kbmemused	kbcached	kbmemused
BFS	12	210	13	212
CC	38	242	29	233
PR	44	248	26	229

total number of packets transmitted per second (txpck/s) are reported for different algorithms. The network activities reflect the iterations of the algorithms. Each iteration involves at least one sendMessage phase which is an all to all communication. In general, the average rxpck/s is similar to txpck/s. Similar to the disk activities, Numactl results in higher network rxpck/s or txpck/s for all the algorithms compared to the case not using Numactl. We observed an average of ≈ 2100 rxpck/s(txpck/s) for BFS, ≈ 2133 rxpck/s(txpck/s) for CC and ≈ 1400 rxpck/s(txpck/s) for PageRank with Numactl. For the case not using Numactl, ≈ 1800 rxpck/s(txpck/s) for BFS, ≈ 1770 rxpck/s(txpck/s) for CC, and ≈ 995 rxpck/s(txpck/s) for PageRank have been monitored.

4.4 Effects of Simultaneous Multithreading (SMT)

As we discussed earlier, the POWER 8 processor chip supports eight hardware threads per core. Applications normally gain benefits by using all the SMT threads of the processor cores [21]. In this experiment, we examine how SMT affects the GraphX applications. Spark is launched on 4 slave nodes and configured with *SPARK_WORKER_INSTANCES=20*, which will launch 20 JVMs per

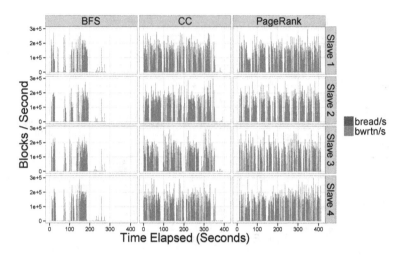

Fig. 8. Disk profiling without Numactl.

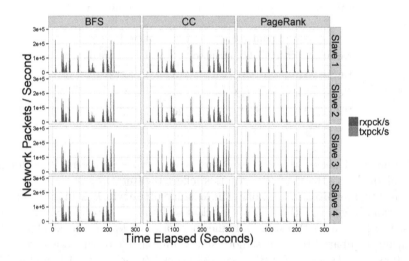

Fig. 9. Network profiling with Numactl.

node. We vary the *SPARK_WORKER_CORES* to 1, 2, 4, and 8 to allow each worker to use different number of hardware threads. Similar to the NUMA effect experiments, we use the same graph as the input and run Breadth-First Search, Connected Components, and PageRank on different SMT configurations. Note that Numactl has been used in all those configurations.

Figure 2 shows the performance comparison of using different values for *SPARK_WORKER_CORES*. Clearly using more hardware threads per core improves the performance for all these algorithms. We observed significant

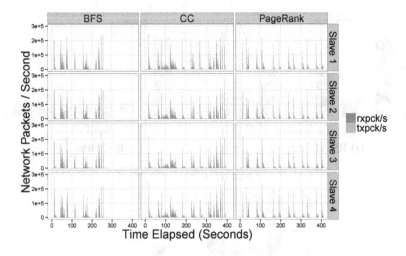

Fig. 10. Network profiling without Numactl.

improvement when increasing the number of used hardware threads from 1 to 8: 59 % performance improvement for Bread-First Search, 27 % performance improvement for Connected Components, and 32 % performance improvement for PageRank, which is a good indication that increasing the number of threads allows for better utilization of the bandwidth, thereby gaining benefits for the application performance.

4.5   Scalability Analysis

For the scalability experiments, we consider two cases, scaling with different number of *SPARK_WORKER_INSTANCES* and scaling with different number of slave nodes. The graphs used include both very large social graphs such as Twitter and Friendster and an RMAT graph with 2^{26} vertices and 2^{30} undirected edges. Note that in the scalability test we have Numactl configured for all the experiments and also configure each worker to use 8 hardware threads to take the advantage of the SMT.

Scalability with Different Number of Spark Workers. In this scalability test, we run Spark on 8 slave nodes but with different numbers of *SPARK_WORKER_INSTANCES* including 5, 10, and 20. As shown in Fig. 11, significant performance improvement is observed when increasing the number of *SPARK_WORKER_INSTANCES* for all the cases. We observed an average of 2–3X with up to 5.21X speedup of using 20 workers compared to using only 5 workers. This is mainly due to the more effective usage of the memory bandwidth. In addition, different algorithms seem to be sensitive to the different graphs because of the difference in the topology. RMAT graph shows a speedup of 4.36X for Breadth-First Search, 2.28X for PageRank, and 2.22X for Connected

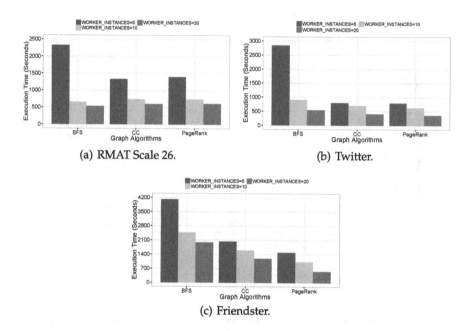

(a) RMAT Scale 26.

(b) Twitter.

(c) Friendster.

Fig. 11. Strong scaling with different spark workers.

Components. Twitter social graph demonstrates a speedup of 5.21X for Breadth-First Search, 2.2X for PageRank, 1.96X for Connected Components. Finally, the Friendster social graph exhibits a speedup of 2.07X for Breadth-First Search, 2.65X for PageRank, and 1.7X for Connected Components.

Scalability with Different Number of Slave Nodes. In order to analyze scalability with different numbers of slave nodes, we fix the number of workers per slave node and scale from 2 slave nodes all the way to 16 slave nodes running different algorithms with different graphs. In general, as shown in Fig. 12 (a), (c) and (e), noticeable performance improvement has been achieved when increasing the number of slave nodes. While different graphs behave differently, we observed up to 3.3X speedup for RMAT graph, 4.1X speedup for Twitter graph, and 5.2X speedup for Friendship graph when increasing the number of slave nodes from 2 to 16. However, the scaling tends to be sub-linear. For example, the PageRank algorithm on Friendster graph shows a speedup of 1.8X when moving from 2 slave nodes to 4 slave nodes (a factor of 2), and a speedup of 5.2X when moving from 2 slave nodes to 16 slave nodes (a factor of 8). Such sub-linear scaling behavior has also been observed by [13,32]. In addition, among those graph kernels, Breadth-First Search seems to be more vulnerable to the performance degradation, showing the worst scaling behavior, 2.9X speedup for RMAT, 2.5X speedup for Twitter, and 1.5X speedup for Friendster from 2 slave nodes to 16 slave nodes.

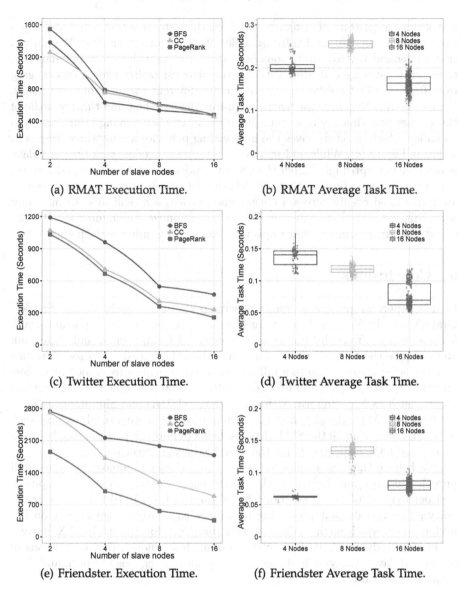

(a) RMAT Execution Time.

(b) RMAT Average Task Time.

(c) Twitter Execution Time.

(d) Twitter Average Task Time.

(e) Friendster. Execution Time.

(f) Friendster Average Task Time.

Fig. 12. Strong scaling with different nodes.

While the relative poor scaling performance of graph algorithms could be partially attributed to high communication overhead relative to computation characteristics [12,13], we provide a different angle to looking into the causes of the different scaling behavior of different graphs. Figure 12 (b), (d), and (f) shows the histogram of the average execution time per task of the executors for different graphs on different numbers of slave nodes. Note that these tasks include a full run of three algorithms. The figures give both the histogram (dots) and the *hinges* (first quartile, median, and third quartile) of the average task time. We noticed that in general the executors somehow show a certain degree of imbalance in terms of the average task time with a ratio (shortest task/longest task) ranging from 0.41 to 0.77 for different algorithms on different numbers of slave nodes. Figure 12 (d) is the only case where the mean, median, first and third quartile of the average task time are monotonically decreasing when moving from 4 nodes to 16 nodes, which in return gives the best scaling behavior among three graphs as shown in Fig. 12 (c). While, in Fig. 12 (b) and (e), the average task time of 4 slave nodes case is surprisingly higher than 8 slave nodes cases or 16 slave nodes cases, which may be an indication that the default partition strategy, vertex-cut (edges are partitioned evenly across a cluster and vertices are replicated to machines with adjacent edges) though it is claimed to minimize communication [12,33], can still incur imbalance, thus impacting the overall scaling performance.

5   Conclusions

In this paper, we present a comprehensive performance evaluation of Spark/-GraphX on a POWER 8 cluster with 17 nodes. We use a set of important graph kernels such as Breadth-First Search, Connected Components, and PageRank and examine the GraphX performance with both large real-world social graphs and synthetic graphs of up to a billion edges. We provide a fresh look at performance of Spark/GraphX on POWER 8, with focus on the impact of architectural aspects such as Non-Uniform Memory Access (NUMA) and Simultaneous Multithreading (SMT). Results show that configuring for architectural features such as NUMA and using all the SMT threads, helps to improve performance by up to 25.7 % and 58 % respectively, for the examined graph kernels.

We believe that the results we present and the methodology we show will provide guidance and insight to the practitioners working on the development and deployment of graph solutions based on Spark on POWER 8. The scalability study reveals that processing imbalance can have a huge impact on the performance, which might indicate future directions for Spark/GraphX study.

In this study, we limited ourselves to unmodified, non-optimized versions of Spark and Java. Applying and comparing optimized versions of Spark and Java is subject to future work.

References

1. Hadoop MapReduce. https://hadoop.apache.org/
2. OpenPOWER. http://openpowerfoundation.org/
3. Big Data and Analytics on IBM Power Systems (2015). https://www.ibm.com/developerworks/community/blogs/f0f3cd83-63c2-4744-9021-9ff31e7004a9/entry/Apache_Spark_Runs_2X_Faster_on_IBM_s_POWER8?lang=en
4. POWER8 - the first OpenPOWER processor (2015). http://openpowerfoundation.org/blogs/power8-the-first-openpower-processor/

5. Spark configuration (2016). http://spark.apache.org/docs/latest/configuration. html
6. Spark programming guid (2016). http://spark.apache.org/docs/latest/ programming-guide.html
7. Abu-Doleh, A., Catalyurek, U.V.: Spaler: Spark And GraphX based de novo genome assembler. In: 2015 IEEE International Conference on Big Data (Big Data), pp. 1013–1018. IEEE (2015)
8. Brock, B., Liu, F., Rajamani, K.: Stac-a2™ benchmark on POWER8. In: Proceedings of the 8th Workshop on High Performance Computational Finance, WHPCF 2015, p. 1:1–1:8. ACM, New York (2015)
9. Buono, D., Petrini, F., Checconi, F., Liu, X., Que, X., Long, C., Tuan, T.C.: Optimizing sparse matrix-vector multiplication for large-scale data analytics. In: Proceedings of the 30th ACM on International Conference on Supercomputing, ICS 2016. ACM (2016, to appear)
10. Chakrabarti, D., Zhan, Y., Faloutsos, C.: R-MAT: a recursive model for graph mining. In: Proceedings of the 4th ACM on International Conference on Data Mining (SDM 2004), Lake Buena Vista, pp. 442–446, April 2004
11. Ewart, T., Yates, S., Cremonesi, F., Kumbhar, P., Schürmann, F., Delalondre, F.: Performance evaluation of the IBM POWER8 architecture to support computational neuroscientific application using morphologically detailed neurons. In: Proceedings of the 6th International Workshop on Performance Modeling, Benchmarking, and Simulation of High Performance Computing Systems, PMBS 2015, p. 1:1–1:11. ACM, New York (2015)
12. Gonzalez, J.E., Low, Y., Gu, H., Bickson, D., Guestrin, C.: PowerGraph: distributed graph-parallel computation on natural graphs. In: Proceedings of the 10th USENIX Conference on Operating Systems Design and Implementation, OSDI 2012, pp. 17–30. USENIX Association, Berkeley (2012)
13. Gonzalez, J.E., Xin, R.S., Dave, A., Crankshaw, D., Franklin, M.J., Stoica, I.: GraphX: graph processing in a distributed dataflow framework. In: Proceedings of the 11th USENIX Conference on Operating Systems Design and Implementation, OSDI 2014, pp. 599–613. USENIX Association, Berkeley (2014)
14. Heintz, B., Chandra, A.: Enabling scalable social group analytics via hypergraph analysis systems. In: 7th USENIX Workshop on Hot Topics in Cloud Computing (HotCloud 2015). USENIX Association, Santa Clara, July 2015
15. Kang, U., Tsourakakis, C.E., Faloutsos, C.: Pegasus: a peta-scale graph mining system implementation and observations. In: Proceedings of the 2009 Ninth IEEE International Conference on Data Mining, ICDM 2009, pp. 229–238. IEEE Computer Society, Washington, DC (2009)
16. Kwak, H., Lee, C., Park, H., Moon, S.: What is Twitter, a social network or a news media? In: WWW, pp. 591–600. ACM, New York (2010)
17. Langewisch, R.: A performance study of an implementation of the push-relabel maximum flow algorithm in Apache Spark's GraphX (2015)
18. Leskovec, J., Chakrabarti, D., Kleinberg, J., Faloutsos, C., Ghahramani, Z.: Kronecker graphs: an approach to modeling networks. J. Mach. Learn. Res. **11**, 985–1042 (2010)
19. Li, M., Tan, J., Wang, Y., Zhang, L., Salapura, V.: SparkBench: a comprehensive benchmarking suite for in memory data analytic platform spark. In: Proceedings of the 12th ACM International Conference on Computing Frontiers, CF 2015, pp. 53:1–53:8. ACM, New York (2015)

20. Lim, S., Lee, S., Ganesh, G., Brown, T.C., Sukumar, S.R.: Graph processing platforms at scale: practices and experiences. In: 2015 IEEE International Symposium on Performance Analysis of Systems and Software, ISPASS 2015, 29–31 March 2015, Philadelphia, PA, USA, pp. 42–51 (2015)

21. Liu, X., Buono, D., Checconi, F., Choi, J.W., Que, X., Petrini, F., Gunnels, J., Stuecheli, J.: An early performance study of large-scale POWER8 SMP systems. In: Proceedings of the 2016 IEEE International Parallel and Distributed Processing Symposium. IPDPS 2015, IEEE Computer Society, Washington, DC (2016)

22. Malewicz, G., Austern, M.H., Bik, A.J., Dehnert, J.C., Horn, I., Leiser, N., Czajkowski, G.: Pregel: a system for large-scale graph processing. In: Proceedings of the 2010 ACM SIGMOD International Conference on Management of Data, SIGMOD 2010, pp. 135–146. ACM, New York (2010)

23. Mushtaq, H., Al-Ars, Z.: Cluster-based Apache Spark implementation of the GATK DNA analysis pipeline. In: IEEE International Conference on Bioinformatics and Biomedicine, pp. 1471–1477. IEEE Computer Society (2015)

24. Page, L., Brin, S., Motwani, R., Winograd, T.: The PageRank citation ranking: bringing order to the web. Technical report 1999–66, Stanford InfoLab, previous number=SIDL-WP-1999-0120, November 1999

25. Que, X., Checconi, F., Petrini, F., Liu, X., Buono, D.: Exploring network optimizations for large-scale graph analytics. In: Proceedings of the International Conference for High Performance Computing, Networking, Storage and Analysis, SC 2015, pp. 26:1–26:10. ACM, New York (2015)

26. Roy, A., Mihailovic, I., Zwaenepoel, W.: X-stream: Edge-centric graph processing using streaming partitions. In: Proceedings of the Twenty-Fourth ACM Symposium on Operating Systems Principles, SOSP 2013, pp. 472–488. ACM, New York (2013)

27. Salihoglu, S., Widom, J.: GPS: a graph processing system. In: Proceedings of the 25th International Conference on Scientific and Statistical Database Management, SSDBM 2013, pp. 22:1–22:12. ACM, New York (2013)

28. Seshadhri, C., Pinar, A., Kolda, T.G.: An in-depth study of stochastic Kronecker graphs. In: International Conference on Data Mining, pp. 587–596. IEEE Computer Society, Los Alamitos (2011)

29. Shun, J., Blelloch, G.E.: Ligra: a lightweight graph processing framework for shared memory. SIGPLAN Not. 48(8), 135–146 (2013)

30. Sinharoy, B., Norstrand, J.A.V., Eickemeyer, R.J., Le, H.Q., Leenstra, J., Nguyen, D.Q., Konigsburg, B., Ward, K., Brown, M.D., Moreira, J.E., Levitan, D., Tung, S., Hrusecky, D., Bishop, J.W., Gschwind, M., Boersma, M., Kroener, M., Kaltenbach, M., Karkhanis, T., Fernsler, K.M.: IBM POWER8 processor core microarchitecture. IBM J. Res. Dev. 59(1), 2:1–2:21 (2015)

31. Sud, A., Andersen, E., Curtis, S., Lin, M.C., Manocha, D.: Real-time path planning for virtual agents in dynamic environments. In: IEEE Virtual Reality, Charlotte, NC, March 2007

32. Wu, M., Yang, F., Xue, J., Xiao, W., Miao, Y., Wei, L., Lin, H., Dai, Y., Zhou, L.: GraM: scaling graph computation to the trillions. In: Proceedings of the Sixth ACM Symposium on Cloud Computing, SoCC 2015, pp. 408–421. ACM, New York (2015)

33. Xin, R.S., Gonzalez, J.E., Franklin, M.J., Stoica, I.: GraphX: a resilient distributed graph system on spark. In: First International Workshop on Graph Data Management Experiences and Systems, GRADES 2013, pp. 2:1–2:6. ACM, New York (2013)

34. Yang, J., Leskovec, J.: Defining and evaluating network communities based on ground-truth (2012). CoRR
35. Zaharia, M., Chowdhury, M., Franklin, M.J., Shenker, S., Stoica, I.: Spark: cluster computing with working sets. In: Proceedings of the 2nd USENIX Conference on Hot Topics in Cloud Computing, HotCloud 2010, p. 10. USENIX Association, Berkeley (2010)
36. Zhang, L., Kim, Y.J., Manocha, D.: A simple path non-existence algorithm using C-obstacle query. In: Proceedings of the International Workshop on the Algorithmic Foundations of Robotics (WAFR 2006), New York City, July 2006

Performance of the 3D Combustion Simulation Code RECOM®-AIOLOS on IBM® POWER8® Architecture

Alexander Berreth[1(✉)], Benedetto Risio[1], Markus Bühler[2],
Benedikt Anlauf[2], and Pascal Vezolle[3]

[1] RECOM® Services GmbH, Nobelstraße 15, 70569 Stuttgart, Germany
{A.Berreth,B.Risio}@recom-services.de
[2] IBM Deutschland Research and Development GmbH, Schönaicher Str. 220,
71032 Böblingen, Germany
Buehler@de.ibm.com
[3] IBM Systems France, Montpellier, France
Vezolle@fr.ibm.com

Abstract. The IBM POWER8 CPU is a high-performance multi-core hardware which targets the usage with computational intense numerical codes. Combustion modeling is among the most computational demanding mathematical problems. Therefore, in this paper we present a performance analysis of the 3D-combustion modeling software RECOM-AIOLOS on a POWER8 node. The analysis reveals the strengths of the POWER8 hardware being a NUMA system, but also the importance of a proper memory allocation when using OpenMP or a hybrid (OpenMP + MPI) parallelization approach on such a system.

1 Introduction

The 3D-combustion modeling software RECOM-AIOLOS [1, 2] is a tailored application for the mathematical modeling of industrial firing systems ranging from several hundred kW to more than 1000 MW. In-depth validation using measurements from industrial power plants, the extension of chemical reaction models and the rapid development of computer technology have made RECOM-AIOLOS a well proven and reliable tool for the prediction of industrial furnace efficiency. The software solves approx. 100 conservation equations (mass, momentum, energy, species concentrations, radiation) on a 20-30 million cells finite volume grid, leading to high computational demands. Originally being designed for high-performance computing on parallel vector-computers and massively parallel systems, the software has been ported to x86-based multi-core systems to expand the hardware base [3]. In the present work the software was further ported to IBMs POWER8 based multi-core systems. The performance achieved on the IBM POWER8 architecture was compared to the performance achieved on the latest Intel architecture.

Trademarks of IBM in USA and/or other countries

© Springer International Publishing AG 2016
M. Taufer et al. (Eds.): ISC High Performance Workshops 2016, LNCS 9945, pp. 286–292, 2016.
DOI: 10.1007/978-3-319-46079-6_20

2 Hardware

The following hardware was used in the present work:

2.1 IBM POWER8 Node

The POWER8 benchmarks were carried out on a two-socket IBM S824L [4] node of the PADC (POWER Acceleration and Design Center) Böblingen. The nodes consist of two 10-core POWER8 CPUs with a speed of 3.4 GHz and 230 GB/s memory bandwidth. The software was compiled using the IBM xlf Fortran compiler version 15.1.4 beta using the MPI library openmpi version 1.6.5.

2.2 Intel Haswell Node

The performance tests on the Intel architecture were performed on a two-socket Intel Haswell node using two 12-core Intel® Xeon® CPU E5-2680 v3 (30 M Cache, 2.50 GHz, 68 GB/s memory bandwidth). The software was compiled with the Cray Fortran Compiler version 8.4.3 using the MPI library craympich version 7.3.3.

3 Application Performance Achieved on IBM POWER8

The performance tests were performed with a 3D model of an existing combustion chamber. The total size of the numerical grid used for the tests is approx. 20 mio. cells. Due to the use of a domain decomposition method, the loop lengths vary between 75000 and 8.4 mio. elements. To evaluate the performance of the 3D combustion simulation code RECOM-AIOLOS the wall-clock time of 20 iterations was measured and averaged. Speedup was calculated in relation to the execution time of one process with 1 thread. The 3D combustion simulation code RECOM-AIOLOS uses a hybrid parallelization approach which allows the simultaneous use of OpenMP and MPI.

Figure 1 shows the performance achieved by the RECOM-AIOLOS code on the IBM POWER8 architecture for different parallelization settings (number of OpenMP threads and number of MPI ranks on a single node).

With pure OpenMP parallelization, a speedup of 10.1 was achieved when using 20 threads (SMT1) on the available 20 cores. No or only little performance gain was achieved when using more than 20 threads (SMT2, SMT4 or SMT8). Increasing the number of MPI processes and reducing the number of OpenMP threads showed a significant improvement of the performance, giving the best SMT1 speedup of 15.1 with 4 MPI processes and 5 threads per process.

Using 2 (SMT2) or 4 (SMT4) threads per core showed a further performance gain. The best performance with a speedup of 22.7 was achieved with 8 MPI processes and 10 threads per process (SMT4). No performance gain could be observed for SMT8.

The low OpenMP performance could be attributed to the small loop lengths in the test case. On NUMA systems, memory is allocated by a so-called first-touch policy,

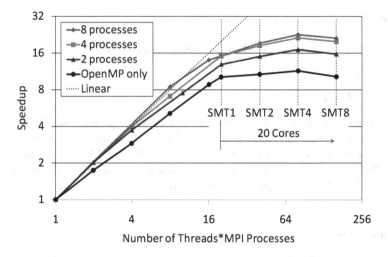

Fig. 1. RECOM-AIOLOS speedup on POWER8 using a hybrid parallelization approach.

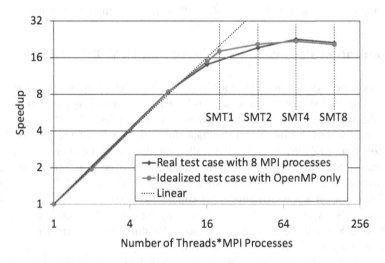

Fig. 2. RECOM-AIOLOS speedup: Hybrid vs. idealized OpenMP

where the physical memory is allocated by the first thread/core using the memory. As with the first touch not only single elements, but a whole memory page is allocated, it is likely, that many of the data elements of the small loops fit into one 64 kB memory page and are allocated by the first thread/core on the first NUMA node. Therefore the probability of a low performing distant memory access is high for the other OpenMP threads/cores.

In order to verify the performance dependence on the memory access pattern, an idealized test case with a loop size of 10 mio. elements was created. For this case a proper memory allocation was possible and the OpenMP threads were able to access local memory. The now achieved maximum performance with pure OpenMP (Speedup 21.9 on 80 Threads – SMT4, see Fig. 2) was very similar to the performance achieved with the best hybrid approach (Speedup 22.7 on 8 processes with 20 threads each – SMT4).

4   Application Performance on POWER8 Compared to Haswell

In Fig. 3 the performance achieved on an Intel Haswell node is shown. The speedup for the test case was significantly lower compared to the POWER8 node. But the speedup was much less dependent on the parallelization setting on Haswell. The ratio of the best hybrid performance compared to the best OpenMP performance was 1.12 for Haswell and 2.0 for POWER8. The best speedup achieved on Haswell was only 11.1 with 2 MPI processes and 12 OpenMP threads each and no performance gain was achieved with HyperThreading.

The higher sensitivity on the parallelization setting on the POWER8 system could be attributed to the higher number of NUMA nodes (4 instead of 2 on the Haswell node). Therefore more care is necessary on the POWER8 system to achieve a proper memory allocation, e.g. making it necessary to use hybrid parallelization with at least 4 MPI processes (one on each NUMA node).

We haven't yet fully investigated the root causes for the better scalability of POWER8 compared to Haswell on RECOM-AIOLOS. An obvious contributor is Haswell's throttling. It reduces the processors clock frequency when it gets too hot. An issue that is much as more likely the more cores are in use, such reducing the speedup.

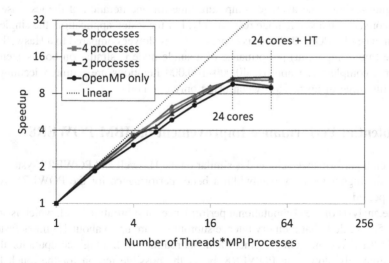

Fig. 3. RECOM-AIOLOS speedup on Haswell using a hybrid parallelization approach

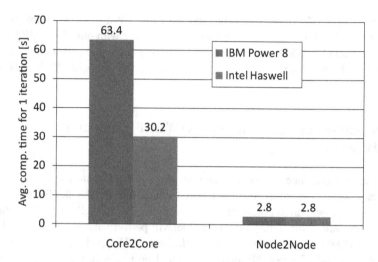

Fig. 4. Computing time (wall-clock time) on POWER8 vs. Haswell

Investigations of other memory bound codes, mainly from the CFD space, indicate that, as expected, further reasons are to be found in the memory subsystem.

We noticed, for instance, that the number of load and store LLC (last level cache) misses increase by factors of 6.5x and 650x on Haswell, respectively, while increasing only in the 20 % range on POWER8, when going from one core to 10 cores per socket.

This means, it is not only the raw memory bandwidth, but also the larger and partitioned L3 caches that support a better use of the cores. The buffering and prefetching capabilities of POWER8's L4 cache does also help to hide memory latencies and such improve scalability.

Figure 4 shows the average computing time for one iteration of the test case on a single core and on a single node respectively. For the tested application, the single core performance of a POWER8 core is approx. 2 times slower compared to a Haswell core. But the (more important) performance of a single node is similar on both systems.

For a complete run approx. 40.000–100.000 iterations are required leading to a computing time of up to 78 h when using only one node.

5 Potential Performance Improvement on IBM POWER8

The overall performance achieved is similar on the Haswell and POWER8 systems, but due to the higher memory bandwidth a better performance for the POWER8 system was expected.

The analysis of the computational performance on subroutine level, which is shown in Fig. 5, revealed, that memory intense subroutines are up to about 1.8 times faster on the POWER8 systems. On the other hand, subroutines with a high computational load are significantly slower on POWER8, being the possible reason for the much lower single core performance of the POWER8 core.

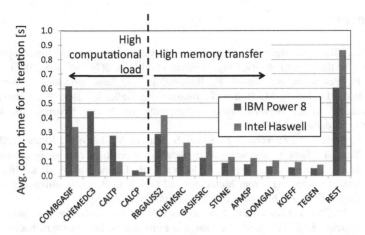

Fig. 5. Routine based computing time (wall-clock time) on POWER8 vs. Haswell

Further analysis (e.g. of compiler output) showed that the major loops in the compute intense routines are not vectorized being the reason for the low performance of these routines. The problem was addressed to the IBM compiler team, which was able to identify the reason for the missing vectorization. The team is currently working on a better vectorization support, which should be released with the next compiler version of the IBM xlf compiler.

Under the assumption that the compute-intense subroutines achieve the same computational speed as on Haswell, the performance on one POWER8 node should be approx. 30 % better compared to one Haswell node. This could be verified by manually vectorizing one of the most important kernels.

6   Summary

The 3D-combustion modeling software RECOM-AIOLOS was ported to the POWER8 hardware. With a proper NUMA memory allocation an excellent speedup on the available 20 cores was achieved when using OpenMP, MPI or a hybrid parallelization approach and a further significant performance gain was observed when using 4 threads per core (SMT4). At the time, the overall performance achieved on one 2-socket IBM POWER8 node was similar to the performance on a 2-socket Intel Haswell node. The lack of vectorization for the compute intense subroutines was identified as the major bottleneck that slowed down the performance on the POWER8 hardware. With an improved vectorization, a further performance gain could be expected on the POWER8 system.

References

1. Risio, B., Blum, F., Hetzer, J., Berreth, A.: Towards an innovative virtual optimisation machine for the power industry. Prog. Comput. Fluid Dyn. **5**(7), 398–405 (2005)
2. Risio, B., Passmann, N., Wessel, F., Reinartz, E.: 3D-flame modelling in power plant applications. In: Resch, M., Roller, S., Benkert, K., Galle, M., Bez, W., Kobayashi, H., Hirayama, T. (eds.) High-Performance-Computing on Vector Systems, pp. 101–110. Springer, Heidelberg (2008)
3. Risio, B., Berreth, A., Zuckerman, S., Koliai, S., Ivascot, M., Jalby, W., Krammer, B., Mohr, B., William, T.: How to accelerate an application: a practical case study in combustion modelling. In: Chapman, B., Desprez, F., Joubert, G.R., Lichnewsky, A., Peters, F., Priol, T. (eds.) Parallel Computing: From Multicores and GPU's to Petascale. Advances in Parallel Computing, vol. 19, pp. 661–668. IOS Press, Amsterdam (2010)
4. Caldeira, A., Cho, Y, Cruickshank, J., Grabowski, B., Haug, V., Laidlaw, A., Sung, S.: IBM Power System S824L Technical Overview and Introduction. http://www.redbooks.ibm.com/redpapers/pdfs/redp5139.pdf

Performance-Portable Many-Core Plasma Simulations: Porting PIConGPU to OpenPower and Beyond

Erik Zenker[1,2], René Widera[1], Axel Huebl[1,2(✉)], Guido Juckeland[1],
Andreas Knüpfer[2], Wolfgang E. Nagel[2], and Michael Bussmann[1(✉)]

[1] Helmholtz-Zentrum Dresden–Rossendorf, Dresden, Germany
{e.zenker,r.widera,a.huebl,g.juckeland,m.bussmann}@hzdr.de
[2] Technische Universität Dresden, Dresden, Germany
{andreas.knuepfer,wolfgang.nagel}@tu-dresden.de

Abstract. With the appearance of the heterogeneous platform Open-Power, many-core accelerator devices have been coupled with Power host processors for the first time. Towards utilizing their full potential, it is worth investigating performance portable algorithms that allow to choose the best-fitting hardware for each domain-specific compute task. Suiting even the high level of parallelism on modern GPGPUs, our presented approach relies heavily on abstract meta-programming techniques, which are essential to focus on fine-grained tuning rather than code porting. With this in mind, the CUDA-based open-source plasma simulation code PIConGPU is currently being abstracted to support the heterogeneous OpenPower platform using our fast porting interface cupla, which wraps the abstract parallel C++11 kernel acceleration library Alpaka.

We demonstrate how PIConGPU can benefit from the tunable kernel execution strategies of the Alpaka library, achieving portability and performance with single-source kernels on conventional CPUs, Power8 CPUs and NVIDIA GPUs.

Keywords: OpenPower · Heterogeneous computing · HPC · C++11 · CUDA · OpenMP · Particle-in-cell · Platform portability · Performance portability

1 Introduction

PIConGPU [2] is a fully-relativistic, multi-GPU, 3D3V particle-in-cell (PIC) code. As such it allows to model the mutual interaction between electromagnetic fields and charged particles, including effects of retardation in special relativity (SRT) and the collective motion of collisionless plasmas, by solving Maxwell's equations self-consistently for charged particles and electromagnetic fields. Besides the satisfied demand for large scales and high resolutions by computing the whole

This project has received funding from the European Unions Horizon 2020 research and innovation programme under grant agreement No 654220.

M. Taufer et al. (Eds.): ISC High Performance Workshops 2016, LNCS 9945, pp. 293–301, 2016.
DOI: 10.1007/978-3-319-46079-6_21

PIC cycle on GPUs, simulations of laser-ion acceleration from overdense targets [19] induce a further complexity in the dynamics of the plasma from collisional excitation and ionization processes. As the free electron density from ionization processes determines intrinsic observables such as the plasma wavelength, the modeling of underlying quantum processes needs to be taken into account and is not yet covered in the plain electrodynamics provided by PIC. Our approach to enhance the PIC algorithm is therefore to add a Monte Carlo step in the simulation with 0-D atom physics from SCFLY [4]. This method requires to calculate the transition rate matrix, representing the likelihood of change of the atomic configuration of each ion from one time step to the next. Each of the quantum processes has its own individual models, calibrated with experimental and theoretical estimates. Even when considering the reduction of possible transitions by using an effective number of states, removing physically forbidden and very unlikely transitions, the total number of transitions can grow quadratically with the number of considered configurations. In combination with the dependency of the transition matrix elements on local quantities, such as the energy distribution of neighboring electrons and photons of each individual ion in the plasma, the required amount of memory can easily grow into the size of several dozen gigabytes for a non-equilibrium system.

None of the accelerators that are currently available or announced for the near future fulfill these memory requirements. However, the accelerator's host system provides access to fast and large main memories and file systems. The host's CPUs are used as a first computing stage to reduce the full transition matrix to smaller lookup tables. CPUs excel at this task, since they typically provide better performance on trigonometric functions and implicit solvers. Accordingly, only relevant data needs to be streamed to the GPU.

The OpenPower platform couples various advanced hardware technologies on the same system [11] such as Power CPUs, NVIDIA GPUs, and fast CPU–GPU interconnect technology [7]. To fully utilize the compute power of this platform, it is currently necessary to use various programming models such as CUDA for GPU and OpenMP for CPU. However, this style of programming has the disadvantage that the code is difficult to maintain and it requires more work to switch algorithms between GPU and CPU implementations. A uniform programming model allows to selectively determine the kernel execution hardware depending on the algorithmic requirements. These requirements depend on the models of the individual physical process: some are memory bound, some compute bound, and the user chooses, based on domain knowledge and the relevance, on which hardware these processes should be executed.

Currently, widely utilized uniform parallel programming models such as OpenCL [17] do not fulfill all our requirements of a sustainable, open, maintainable, testable, optimizable, and single-source programming model. Loop and container based approaches such as RAJA [9], Kokkos [5], and OpenMP 4.0 [15] would require a complete redesign of the CUDA based PIConGPU code. With *Alpaka* [20], there exists an interface for parallel kernel acceleration which enables the programmer to compile single-source C++ kernels to various architectures, while providing all the requirements mentioned above. As a first step to selective kernel acceleration on the OpenPower platform, PIConGPU has been ported with the CUDA-like interface *cupla* [16] to Alpaka, which currently allows for an execution either on the CPU or on the GPU.

This paper is structured as follows. In Sect. 2, we give a brief overview on PIConGPU, Alpaka, and cupla. In Sect. 3, we provide our experiences on porting PIConGPU with cupla from CUDA to Alpaka. Finally, the ported prototype is evaluated on various architectures in Sect. 4.

2 Preliminaries

2.1 PIConGPU

PIConGPU is a multi-GPU particle-in-cell (PIC) code for three-dimensional field–particle interaction with high spatial resolution. The code decomposes its global simulation domains into a grid of cells. Cells are grouped into a cuboid volume called *super cell*, and multiple of these super cells are again grouped into a cuboid volume which defines the local simulation domain of a single GPU.

Additionally, there is a second, spatially continuous domain for finite size macro particles such as ions and electrons. They are able to move through the cells and interact with them, making PIC a particle mesh algorithm [3]. Macro particles are grouped in frames, where each frame contains as many macro particles as there are cells in a super cell. Frames are stored in a doubly linked list and correspond to a particular super cell.

Most of the operations on the cells are local stencils which include only a few neighboring cells and are therefore well suited to CUDA programming model of a multidimensional grid. PIConGPU is mapped to this model as follows: The local simulation domain is mapped to the grid of a single GPU. A super cell is mapped to a block that contains as many threads as there are cells — in our simulation this amounts usually to 256 cells. A thread calculates the field of a cell and its proportion of particles of its super cell.

2.2 Alpaka and cupla

Alpaka provides a uniform, abstract C++ interface to a range of parallel programming models. It can express multiple levels of parallelism and allows for generic programming of kernels either for a single accelerator device or a single address space with multiple CPU cores. The Alpaka abstraction of parallelization is influenced by and based on the groundbreaking CUDA abstraction of a multidimensional grid of blocks of threads. The four main execution hierarchies introduced by Alpaka are called *grid*, *block*, *thread*, and *element* level. The element level denotes an amount of work a thread needs to process sequentially. These levels describe an index space which is called *work division*. Other programming models call these levels differently e.g. OpenCL *work-groups* of *work-items*, OpenMP *teams* of *threads*, and OpenACC *gang, worker, and vector*.

Separating parallelization abstraction from specific hardware capabilities allows for an explicit mapping of these levels to hardware. The current implementation includes mappings to programming models, called back-ends, such as OpenMP, CUDA, C++ threads, and boost fibers [14]. Nevertheless, mapping implementations are not limited to these choices and can be extended or adapted for application-specific optimizations. Which back-end and work division to utilize is parameterized per kernel within the user code.

A fast approach to port CUDA code to Alpaka is provided by the CUDA-like Alpaka interface cupla [$q\chi ap'la$?]. Cupla leaves most CUDA API calls unchanged, yet performs Alpaka calls in the background. Thus, cupla provides a simple and fast porting approach by reducing the number of lines of the original CUDA code a programmer needs to modify.

3   Porting with cupla

In this section we discuss the steps necessary to port the CUDA accelerated code of PIConGPU from GPU to CPU hardware. Our approach is to replace CUDA by the CUDA-like interface cupla. Afterwards, we can utilize Alpaka's CUDA and OpenMP 2.0 back-ends to execute our kernels on both GPUs and CPUs.

Cupla leaves most parts of the CUDA code unchanged such as memory allocations, memory copies, stream handling, device handling, and index queries. The programmer is still required to handle three porting steps. Firstly, the cuda_runtime.hpp include has to be replaced by cuda_to_cupla.hpp and all .cu files renamed to .cpp. Secondly, The __host__, __device__, and __global__ keywords need to be replaced by equivalent cupla macros and CUDA global functions rewritten into parenthesis operators of C++ functors. The accelerator object of the accelerator template type has to be passed to these operators and the underlying device functions. Finally, each shared memory allocation has to be replaced by an equivalent cupla macro. Figure 1 shows equivalent CUDA and cupla code snippets of a kernel function initializing an array by a constant value. In contrast to the CUDA kernel, each thread of the cupla kernel loops over the x dimension of the element level.

The native PIC code consists of about forty thousand lines of code. This code is a mixture C++11 and platform-dependent CUDA code. R. Widera programmed about two days, applied the cupla porting steps mentioned above, touched most of our nine hundred device functions, forty kernels, amounting to two thousand lines of code, to provide the first Alpaka based prototype. Although this prototype did not utilize the *element* level, it was already executable on both a Power8 device using the OpenMP 2.0 back-end and on an NVIDIA device using the CUDA back-end. The number of threads in a block was left unchanged. Accordingly, the domain of a super cell is processed by a block consisting of 256 threads.

This block-size leads to inefficient communication between threads on the Power8 when the element level is omitted, resulting in more frequent cache misses and a decrease in performance. Accordingly, the integration of the element level

```
1  // CUDA Kernel
2  __global__ void kernel ( int * data )
3  {
4      int id = blockDim.x * blockIdx.x
5                  + threadIdx.x;
6      data[ id ] = 42;
7  }
```

```
1   // Alpaka Kernel
2   struct void kernel {
3     template < typename Acc >
4     ALPAKA_FN_ACC void operator () (
5       Acc const & acc,
6       int * data
7     ) const
8     {
9         int id = blockDim.x * blockIdx.x * elemDim.x
10                  + threadIdx.x * elemDim.x;
11        for( int elem = 0; elem < elemDim.x; ++elem)
12          data[ id + elem ] = 42
13    }
14  };
```

Fig. 1. CUDA and cupla kernels which initialize each element in the input array `data` by the value 42. The cupla kernel on the bottom was created through wrapping the CUDA kernel on the top within a C++ functor. Each thread of the cupla kernel processes multiple elements through looping over the dimensions of the additional element level. In the cupla kernel `blockDim`, `blockIdx`, `threadIdx`, and `elemDim` are pre-processor macros accessing the `acc` variable.

enables for a work division of blocks with a single thread and multiple elements to calculate the entire domain of a super cell. This provides a more efficient mapping of Alpaka-threads to hardware threads and, therefore, an improved vectorization and cache utilization by the compiler. The integration of the element level required to loop over the fixed-size element index space for each sequential kernel part. These sequential parts were wrapped in lambda functions. Furthermore, single element variables were expanded to multidimensional fixed-size arrays. This change, on three thousand lines of code, took our developer about ten days.

To sum up, our developer modified about five thousand lines of code in a matter of two weeks, after which the entire forty thousand lines PIConGPU code could be compiled and run efficiently on CPU and GPU devices. It was not necessary to modify the core data structures or algorithms of PIConGPU. The element level has been added to enable a single thread to process the domain of a super cell. In the following section we will evaluate the performance of our Alpaka-based PIC simulation on both architectures.

4 Evaluation

This section provides the evaluation of the PIConGPU code [18] that was ported to various compute architectures (see Table 1). We measured the runtime and performance of the memory-bound PIC algorithm as implemented in PIConGPU with a simulation of the Kelvin-Helmholtz instability [3] for one thousand time steps in double and single precision and compared these results between the various architectures. The simulation was parameterized with the Boris pusher, Esirkepov current solver, Yee field solver, trilinear interpolation in field gathering, three spatial dimensions (3D3V), 128 cells in each dimension, electron and ion species with each sixteen particles per cell, and quadratic-spline interpolation (TSC) [8]. On all CPU devices the OpenMP 2.0 back-end was used with a block consisting of a single thread with 256 elements. On NVIDIA GPUs the CUDA back-end is used with a block consisting of 256 threads with a single element. All GPU evaluations are compiled with nvcc[1] 7.0 and all CPU evaluations with gcc[2] 4.9.2.

Table 1. Compute nodes for evaluation (core counts in braces are HW threads).

Vendor	AMD	Intel	IBM	NVIDIA
Architecture	Interlagos [1]	Haswell [10]	Power8 [6]	Kepler [12]
Model	Opteron 6276	Xeon E5-2698v3	Power8 8247-42L	K80 GK210
Used devices per node	4	2	2	1
Cores per device	16	16 (32)	10 (80)	2496
Base clock frequency	2.3 GHz	2.3 GHz	2.1 GHz	0.56 GHz
Release date	Q4/2011	Q3/2014	Q1/2014	Q4/2014
Peak performance(sp)	960 GFLOPS	2354 GFLOPS	1120 GFLOPS	4350 GFLOPS
Peak performance(dp)	480 GFLOPS	1177 GFLOPS	560 GFLOPS	1450 GFLOPS

Figure 2 displays the measured runtime and efficiency of the evaluated simulation. On the NVIDIA K80, the differences in runtime between the native and the ported PIC code are about one percent for single precision. For double precision, the Alpaka based code is even faster, because Alpaka emulates double *atomicAdd* using *atomicCAS* instead of the slower *atomicExch* used by the native PIConGPU implementation. Nevertheless, this small optimization could have been introduced easily into the native PIConGPU code to achieve the same runtime results. According to these measurements, Alpaka can keep its promise of zero-overhead abstraction on the same architecture even for rather complex applications such as PIConGPU. The runtime between GPU and CPU implementations differ in one order of magnitude for single precision.

---

[1] --use_fast_math --ftz=false -g0 -O3 -m64.
[2] -g0 -O3 -m64 -funroll-loops -march=native --param max-unroll-times=512 -ffast-math.

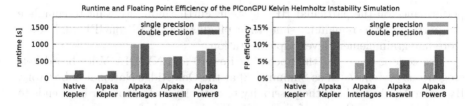

Fig. 2. As an example to evaluate a memory-bound PIC code, runtime and floating point efficiency of the PIConGPU Kelvin-Helmholtz instability simulation for single precision and for double precision was measured on various architectures (see Table 1).

However, the results need to be evaluated in relation to the theoretical peak performance of the particular architecture. This metric is denoted as floating point efficiency in Fig. 2. Regarding floating point efficiency, CPU and GPU vary by a factor of three to four on single precision and by a factor of two on double precision. Thus, Alpaka provides not just portability between GPU and CPU, but decent performance on both. All evaluated CPU architectures show similar runtime and efficiency characteristics. Nevertheless, the Intel architecture offers the lowest runtime and highest (theoretical) peak performance of all evaluated CPU devices. However, there still exists some potential to increase performance, as it only provides five percent floating point efficiency on double precision. While the IBM and AMD architectures fare slightly better with about eight percent double precision efficiency, there is still a lot of potential compared to the GPU efficiency. By refining the Alpaka back-ends and tuning the work division, this potential can be utilized to increase the performance of the CPU architectures even more.

5 Conclusion

We have presented the current progress in porting the particle-in-cell simulation PIConGPU onto the OpenPower platform through utilizing the CUDA-like Alpaka interface *cupla* . The core routines of the forty thousand lines mixed C++ and CUDA code have been ported from CUDA to Alpaka within two weeks. Through this abstraction, the ported PIConGPU implementation is executable on AMD, IBM, Intel, and NVIDIA architectures. The code was not just ported, but has been moved to a generic *single-source* multi-platform programming model. Thus, PIConGPU never needs to be ported again.

The native CUDA version and the Alpaka version show no significant differences in runtime or performance on the NVIDIA hardware, which demonstrates zero overhead abstraction capabilities of Alpaka. GPU and CPU devices differ in a factor of about two in efficiency on double precision, providing decent performance among the evaluated architectures.

Future work will focus on the evaluation of each kernel on CPU and GPU hardware separately. Based on these measurements, we want to provide a static mapping of kernels to heterogeneous hardware to achieve the best possible overall performance on the particular HPC system. Furthermore, we want to complete the porting of the remaining simulation plugins within PIConGPU and add a more fine-grain element level implementation.

The code is ready for the upcoming Power9 and NVIDIA Volta-based heterogeneous systems such as Summit [13] at the Oak Ridge National Laboratory. By using Alpaka we have the possibility to optimize and adapt our back-ends to these systems once they are fully specified and available for evaluation.

References

1. AMD: AMD Opteron 6200 Series Processor Quick Reference Guide. https://www.amd.com/Documents/Opteron_6000_QRG.pdf. Accessed 11 Apr 2016
2. Burau, H., Widera, R., Hönig, W., Juckeland, G., Debus, A., Kluge, T., Schramm, U., Cowan, T.E., Sauerbrey, R., Bussmann, M.: PIConGPU: a fully relativistic particle-incell code for a GPU cluster. IEEE Trans. Plasma Sci. **38**(10), 2831–2839 (2010)
3. Bussmann, M., Burau, H., Cowan, T.E., Debus, A., Huebl, A., Juckeland, G., Kluge, T., Nagel, W.E., Pausch, R., Schmitt, F., Schramm, U., Schuchart, J., Widera, R.: Radiative signatures of the relativistic Kelvin-Helmholtz instability. In: Proceedings of the International Conference on High Performance Computing, Networking, Storage and Analysis, p. 5. ACM (2013). doi:10.1145/2503210.2504564
4. Chung, H.-K., Chen, M.H., Lee, R.W.: Extension of atomic configuration sets of the Non-LTE model in the application to the Kα diagnostics of hot dense matter. High Energy Density Phys. **3**(1), 57–64 (2007)
5. Carter Edwards, H., Trott, C.R., Sunderland, D.: Kokkos: enabling manycore performance portability through polymorphic memory access patterns. J. Parallel Distrib. Comput. **74**(12), 3202–3216 (2014)
6. Fluhr, E.J., Friedrich, J., Dreps, D., Zyuban, V., Still, G., Gonzalez, C., Hall, A., Hogenmiller, D., Malgioglio, F., Nett, R., Paredes, J., Pille, J., Plass, D., Puri, R., Restle, P., Shan, D., Stawiasz, K., Deniz, Z.T., DieterWendel, M.Z.: 5.1 POWER8 TM: a 12-core server-class processor in 22nm SOI with 7.6 Tb/s off-chip bandwidth. In: 2014 IEEE International Solid-State Circuits Conference Digest of Technical Papers (ISSCC), pp. 96–97. IEEE (2014)
7. Foley, D.: DataNVLink, Pascal and Stacked Memory: Feeding the Appetite for Big Data. https://devblogs.nvidia.com/parallelforall/nvlink-pascal-stacked-memory-feeding-appetite-big-data/. Accessed 13 Jun 2016
8. Hockney, R.W., Eastwood, J.W.: Computer Simulation Using Particles. CRC Press, Boca Raton (1988). ISBN:0-85274-392-0
9. Hornung, R.D., Keasler, J.A.: The RAJA portability layer: overview and status. Lawrence Livermore National Laboratory, Livermore, USA, LLNL-TR-661403 (2014)
10. Intel: Intel Xeon Processor E5-2698 v3 Specification. http://ark.intel.com/de/products/81060/Intel-Xeon-Processor-E5-2698-v3-40M-Cache-2_30-GHz. Accessed 11 Apr 2016
11. de Oliveira, M.F.: NVIDIA on IBM POWER8: Technical overview, software installation, and application development (2015)
12. NVIDIA: Tesla K80 GPU Accelerator Board Specification. http://images.nvidia.com/content/pdf/kepler/Tesla-K80-BoardSpec-07317-001-v05.pdf. Accessed 11 Apr 2016

13. Oak Ridge National Laboratory: Summit. Scale new heights. Discover new solutions. Oak Ridge National Laboratory's next High Performance Supercomputer. https://www.olcf.ornl.gov/summit/. Accessed 10 Apr 2016
14. Kowalke, O.: Boost.Fiber. https://github.com/olk/boost-fiber. Accessed 12 Apr 2016
15. OpenMP: OpenMP application program interface version 4.0 (2013)
16. Widera, R.: cupla: C++ User interface for the Platform independent Library Alpaka. https://github.com/ComputationalRadiationPhysics/cupla. Accessed 14 Mar 2016
17. Stone, J.E., Gohara, D., Shi, G.: OpenCL: a parallel programming standard for heterogeneous computing systems. Comput. Sci. Eng. **12**(1–3), 66–73 (2010)
18. Widera, R., Worpitz, B., Zenker, E., Huebl, A., Juckeland, G., Knüpfer, A., Nagel, W.E., Bussmann, M.: PI- ConGPU, Alpaka, cupla software bundle for IWOPH 2016 submission, May 2016. doi:10.5281/zenodo.53761
19. Zeil, K., Metzkes, J., Kluge, T., Bussmann, M., Cowan, T.E., Kraft, S.D., Sauerbrey, R., Schramm, U.: Direct observation of prompt pre-thermal laser ion sheath acceleration. Nat. Commun. **3**, 874 (2012)
20. Zenker, E., Worpitz, B., Widera, R., Huebl, A., Juckeland, G., Knüpfer, A., Nagel, W.E., Bussmann, M.: Alpaka - an abstraction library for parallel kernel acceleration. In: International Parallel and Distributed Processing Symposium Workshops. IEEE (2016). doi:10.1109/IPDPSW.2016.50

Application Performance on Intel Xeon Phi – Being Prepared for KNL and Beyond

IXPUG

Application Performance on Intel Xeon Phi – Being Prepared for KNL and Beyond

Richard A. Gerber[1], Kent Milfeld[2], Chris J. Newburn[3],
and Thomas Steinke[4]

[1] National Energy Research Scientific Computing Center at Lawrence Berkeley
National Lab. (NERSC), Berkeley, USA
ragerber@lbl.gov
[2] Texas Advanced Computing Center (TACC), Austin, USA
milfeld@tacc.utexas.edu
[3] Intel Corporation, Santa Clara, USA
chris.newburn@intel.com
[4] Zuse Institute Berlin (ZIB), Berlin, Germany
steinke@zib.de

The ISC16 workshop "Application Performance on Intel Xeon Phi – Being Prepared for KNL and Beyond" brought together about 100 members of a world-wide community of application developers and technology experts working to prepare scientific application codes to run at high performance on high performance computing systems powered by the Intel Xeon Phi processor. Intel released details of the Xeon Phi processor codenamed "Knight's Landing" or "KNL" at ISC16 and this workshop featured the first public KNL application performance results, delivered through a series of peer-reviewed presentations, lightening talks, and keynotes from Intel's Chief Architect for KNL, Avinash Sodani, and John McCaplin from the Texas Advanced Computing Center (TACC). The first KNL-based supercomputers are arriving this year at the National Energy Research Scientific Computing Center at Lawrence Berkeley National Laboratory, Argonne National Laboratory, TACC, and Los Alamos National Laboratory. Smaller KNL-based systems will be available this year at other places, e.g. a Cray KNL evaluation system at the Zuse Institute Berlin.

The Intel Xeon Phi Users Group (IXPUG) organized the workshop, which followed a similar event at ISC15 and built upon recent longer workshops in Berkeley, CA; Ostrava, Czech Republic, and St. Petersburg, Russia and Birds of a Feather sessions at ISC15 and SC15. The next IXPUG event, IXPUG 2016, is scheduled to be held at Argonne National Laboratory outside Chicago in September 2016. IXPUG is an independent organization working to build an international community to share challenges, experiences and best-practice methods for the optimization of HPC workloads on the Intel Xeon Phi. IXPUG workshops cover topics in application performance and scalability challenges at all levels - from single processor, to moderately-scaled cluster, up to large HPC configurations with many Xeon Phi devices. IXPUG also provides an effective conduit for application developers to interact directly with Intel engineers and other experts. Further information about IXPUG can be found at the IXPUG website (http://ixpug.org).

The Xeon Phi has a number of architectural features that provide opportunities for large gains in performance using the manycore, power efficient processing cores But taking advantage of these features can present a number of challenges for programmers used to coding for traditional Xeon-type processors. Many if not most existing codes have to be refactored to take advantage of the Xeon Phi's on-chip High Bandwidth Memory (HBM), longer 512-bit vector units, and up to 72 cores on a single socket. The papers in this workshop cover optimization and scalability topics in real-world HPC applications, e.g. data layouts and code restructuring for efficient SIMD operation, work distribution and thread management. Aspects related to KNL features have considerable weight in the studies. The versatility and value of tools for development, debugging and performance analysis is also covered. The keynotes presented recent information about the KNL processor, and trends in HPC system performance; and Lightning Talks provide late-breaking work and experiences on Intel Xeon Phi systems. Keynotes and Lightning Talks are available at https://www.ixpug.org.

Call for Papers

Papers presented at the workshop were selected from submissions solicited from the community through a call for submissions issued in March 2016. Submissions were reviewed by the program committee (listed below) and accepted papers are scheduled to be published by Springer in post-workshop ISC'16 Workshop Proceedings.

A summary of the call follows:

The IXPUG workshop is about sharing ideas, implementations, and experiences that will help users take advantage of new technologies such as AVX512 operations, high-bandwidth memory (HBM) and OmniPath. These architectural advances in Vectorization, Memory, and Communications on the Intel Xeon Phi platform will help boost adoption of many-core architecture in HPC as well as other computational spaces.

In the workshop you will experience an open forum with fellow application programmers, Intel Phi architecture designers, and compiler and tool experts. In addition to the technical paper presentations, the program will include a morning keynote on Intel microprocessors and an afternoon presentation on HPC performance trends. There will also be two Lightning Talks sessions and the workshop will conclude with a discussion.

IXPUG welcomes paper submissions on innovative work from KNC and KNL users in academia, industry and government labs, describing original discoveries and experiences that will promote and prescribe efficient use of many-core and multicore systems.

Topics of interest are (but not limited to):

- Vectorization: Data layout in cache for efficient SIMD operations, SIMD directives and operations, and 2-core tiling with 2D interconnected mesh
- Memory: Data layout in memory for efficient access (data preconditioning), access latency concerns (prefetch, streams, costs for HBM), partitioning of DDR and HBM for applications (memory policies)
- Communication: including early experiences with OmniPath
- Thread and Process Management: Process and thread affinity issues, SMT (simultaneous multi-threading, in core), balancing processes and threads
- Programming Models: OpenMP 4.x, hStreams, using MPI 3 on Xeon Phi, hybrid programming (MPI/OpenMP, others)

- Algorithms and Methods: including scalable and vectorizable algorithms
- Software Environments and Tools
- Benchmarking & Profiling Tools
- Visualization

Program Committee

Damian Alvarez-Mallon	Forschungszentrum Jülich
Ryan Coleman	Sandia National Lab
Douglas Doerfler	NERSC/Berkeley Lab
Richard Gerber	NERSC/Berkeley Lab
Antonio Gomez	TACC
Simon Hammond	Sandia National Lab
Rahul Hardikar	Indian Institute of Science
Helen He	NERSC/Berkeley Lab
Dave M. Hiatt	big denominator
Michael Klemm	Intel Corp.
Lars Koesterke	TACC
Rakesh Krishnaiyer	Intel Corp.
Olli-Pekka Lehto	CSC - IT Center for Science Ltd.
John Linford	ParaTools, Inc.
Simon McIntosh-Smith	Bristol Univ.
John Michalakes	NREL
Kent Milfeld	TACC
Chris J. Newburn	Intel Corp.
Dmitry Prohorov	Intel Corp.
Karthik Raman	Intel Corp.
Carlos Rosales	TACC
Hideki Saito	Intel Corp.
Abhinav Sarje	Berkeley Lab
Thomas Steinke	Zuse Institute Berlin
Estela Suarez	Forschungszentrum Jülich
Srinath Vadlamani	Paratools, Inc.
Jerome Vienne	TACC

Workshop Organizers

Richard A. Gerber	National Energy Research Scientific Computing Center at Lawrence Berkeley National Lab. (NERSC)
Kent Milfeld	Texas Advanced Computing Center (TACC)
Chris J. Newburn	Intel Corporation
Thomas Steinke	Zuse Institute Berlin (ZIB)

A Comparative Study of Application Performance and Scalability on the Intel Knights Landing Processor

Carlos Rosales[✉], John Cazes, Kent Milfeld, Antonio Gómez-Iglesias,
Lars Koesterke, Lei Huang, and Jerome Vienne

Texas Advanced Computing Center, The University of Texas at Austin,
Austin, TX, USA
{carlos,cazes,milfeld,agomez,lars,huang,viennej}@tacc.utexas.edu

Abstract. Intel Knights Landing represents a qualitative change in the Many Integrated Core architecture. It represents a self-hosted option and includes a high speed integrated memory together with a two dimensional mesh used to interconnect the cores. This leads to a number of possible runtime configurations with different characteristics and implications in the performance of applications. This paper presents a study of the performance differences observed when using the three MCDRAM configurations available in combination with the three possible memory access or cluster modes. We analyze the effects that memory affinity and process pinning have on different applications. The Mantevo suite of mini applications and NAS Parallel Benchmarks are used to analyze the behavior of very different application kernels, from molecular dynamics to CFD mini-applications. Two full applications, the Weather Research and Forecast (WRF) application and a Lattice Boltzman Suite (LBS3D) are also analyzed in detail to complete the study and present scalability results of a variety of applications.

Keywords: KNL · MCDRAM · Scalability · MIC

1 Introduction

Over recent years one of the design criteria in HPC systems has been power efficiency. Efforts to save power have been applied to all levels, from megawatt savings in power conversion and cooling at the center level, to picojoule savings in logical units and data transfers [17]. The new designs will certainly benefit the effective carbon footprint of data centers; but moreover, these changes will benefit the efforts to create an HPC exaflop machine with reasonable power requirements.

A significant surge in Floating Point operation efficiency was realized when GPUs, which already had a significant single precision performance, included a CUDA paradigm [11] and microprocessor features for the HPC community to use these GPGPUs as floating point accelerator devices.

© Springer International Publishing AG 2016
M. Taufer et al. (Eds.): ISC High Performance Workshops 2016, LNCS 9945, pp. 307–318, 2016.
DOI: 10.1007/978-3-319-46079-6_22

Meanwhile, during the same period, core replication became the mode for increasing workload capacity, as power restraints restricted further increases in clock frequencies. Further parallelism was achieved by increasing the number of Vector Processing Units (VPU) per core, widening the registers from 128b to 512b, and making them FMA capable.

Even with all the efforts in core and VPU units (also known as SIMD units), Intel also directed their efforts into accelerator capabilities in a series of programs (Larrabee [12]) that culminated in the Many Integrated Core (MIC) Architecture [4]. The Phi product line of these many-core systems began with the Knights Corner (KNC) as a coprocessor board attached to a host through a PCI-e bus. The coprocessor interacts with the host through the PCI-e bus, similar to the way a GPGPU does.

Because of the characteristics previously described, there are currently many accelerated systems in the Top 500[1]. These systems present nodes with at least one GPGPU or one MIC, although it is possible to find systems in which each node has two or more accelerators. There are also systems that present both types of accelerators in different nodes.

Most HPC programmers realize that a major bottleneck of accelerated computing is in the speed of the PCI-e bus; and there is a limited memory capacity on the device since only GDDR (Graphics DDR) memory is used. While some applications perform well within these constrains, for other applications it is difficult to shoehorn their algorithms into a remote device with limited memory.

The 2nd generation Intel® Xeon Phi™ processor, code named Knights Landing (KNL), has architectural features that are designed to solve the shortcoming mentioned directly above, and address the power efficiency concerns at a microprocessor level [14].

The microprocessor architecture has features (southside bus, etc.) that allow the processor to run as a bonafide stand-alone system. Hence, there are no execution offloads through a PCI-e bus, as is required when using multiple KNCs. Also, chips with Omni-Path [2], the new Intel fabric, can bypass the PCI-e bus for external communication. There are two different types of memory in KNL: MCDRAM and DDR4. The on-module MCDRAM [14] provides the high-speed memory that accelerated applications have become accustomed to; and the usual DDR4 memory provides the capacity storage many HPC applications require.

KNL cores are organized as tiles, where each tile is comprised of two cores. While L1 cache is implemented at the core level, L2 cache is shared at the tile level. Tiles are interconnected using a mesh (as opposed to the bidirectional ring in the KNC). All the cores on the chip are cache coherent, so that the tile with a specific data can supply that data to another tile in the chip. This mesh can be clustered to achieve a higher performance for specific memory access patterns in applications. The three modes of operation are: All-to-All, Quadrant and Sub-NUMA clustering [14].

There will always be an ongoing effort in the HPC community to adapt to the new computing technologies that provide significant opportunities to

---

[1] http://www.top500.org/.

compute efficiently and faster. As stated, KNL systems provide new technologies in memory access, communication, and SIMD execution. In this article we explore these technologies with applications and benchmarks, and report programming concepts that will be useful in adapting applications to these new features.

The rest of the paper is organized as follows: Sect. 2 introduces the different applications that we use for our experiments as well as different configurations of the hardware, while the results of those experiments are presented in Sect. 3. Finally, Sect. 4 summarizes the paper and presents a set of ideas that will be explored in the future.

2   Background

We have selected a set of applications and miniapps to study the different configurations of Intel KNL regarding MCDRAM and cluster modes. The miniapps are representative of popular applications in HPC environments.

2.1   Mantevo

The Mantevo suite [5] provides a set of application proxies or miniapps that can be used to measure the performance of hardware. These are self-contained, stand-alone applications. They represent some of the most common scenarios in scientific computing and include numerical kernels that focus on specific aspects of the hardware. We focus on the following miniapps for the experiments presented in this paper:

1. **MiniFE**: a finite elements application. It solves a nonlinear system of equations. Like most of the codes that solve these functions, a large portion of the time is spent in a conjugate gradient solver. While it can be configured to study the repercussions of, for example, load imbalance in the execution, we will focus on well-balanced test cases. It is a memory-bound application, which makes it an optimal candidate to study the impact of the different memory configurations previously introduced. The operations performed by the application greatly depend on memory throughput and, when many cores are used within one processor, it often leads to CPU stalls. The application has received a lot of attention in the past and it is possible to find diverse implementations of MiniFE with different levels of optimization. It is a C++ code, parallelized with MPI and OpenMP. We use the reference OpenMP version.
2. **MiniMD**: molecular dynamics code. This is a small version of the well-known code LAMMPS. It implements spatial decomposition, where each processor works on subsets of the simulation box. MiniMD computes atoms movements in a 3D space using the Lennard-Jones pair interaction. It follows a stencil communication pattern where neighbors exchange information about atoms in

boundary regions. Because of these characteristics, it provides good weak scaling. It also presents different implementations in C++ (MPI+OpenMP, OpenSHMEM,...), and we will focus on the MPI+OpenMP version in this paper. A single MPI task was used for all the runs.

2.2   NAS Parallel Benchmarks

The well-documented NAS Parallel Benchmarks (NPB) [1,8,16] is a suite of parallel workloads designed to evaluate performance of various hardware and software components of a parallel computing system. These benchmarks span different problem sizes, called classes in NPB terminology and in this paper we use class C, which is standard for the analysis of single-node systems. Most of the NAS benchmarks are computational kernels. **IS** performs sorting of integer keys using a linear time Integer Sorting algorithm based on computation of the key histogram. **EP** evaluates an integral by means of pseudorandom trials. **FT** contains the computational kernel of a 3-D Fast Fourier Transform (FFT). **CG** uses a Conjugate Gradient method to compute approximations to the smallest eigenvalues of a sparse unstructured matrix. **MG** uses a V-cycle Multi Grid method to compute the solution of the 3-D scalar Poisson equation. **LU**, **SP**, and **BT** are simulated CFD mini-applications that solve the discretized compressible Navier-Stokes equations. **BT** and **SP** both apply variations of the Alternating Direction Implicit (ADI) approximate factorization technique to decouple solution in the x, y, and z-coordinate directions. The resulting systems are 5×5 block-tridiagonal and scalar pentadiagonal, respectively, which can be solved independently. **LU** applies the symmetric successive over-relaxation (SSOR) technique to an approximate factorization of the discretization matrix into block-lower and block-upper triangular matrices. **UA** evaluates unstructured computation, parallel I/O, and data movement using unstructured adaptive mesh with dynamic and irregular memory accesses.

2.3   WRF

The Weather Research and Forecasting(WRF) Model [13] is a widely used numerical weather prediction system used for both research and operational forecasts. WRF is primarily a Fortran code implemented using MPI and OpenMP for distributed computing. The problem space on each process is divided into tiles that are processed by OpenMP threads. Ideally, the best performance is achieved when the size of the tile (in terms of the problem in WRF) fits into the smallest cache. Having multiple application tiles allows WRF to obtain high levels of memory bandwidth utilization.

A substantial effort was made to optimize WRF for the first generation Xeon Phi, Knights Corner [7]. The current version of WRF, 3.7.1, supports a configuration option for the KNC. This configuration was modified to compile the KNL instruction set using the -xMIC-AVX512 option rather than the -mmic option. The source code was not modified for this study.

2.4   LBS3D

LBS3D is a multiphase Lattice Boltzmann Code based on the Free Energy method of Zheng, Shu and Chew [18]. This code simulates the flow of two immiscible, isothermal, incompressible fluids with great spatial and temporal detail. For details on the model we refer the interested reader to [9,15]. LBS3D is an optimized implementation of this model, originally developed for execution in the first generation Intel Xeon Phi [10]. While both OpenMP and hybrid MPI+OpenMP versions of the code are available, the results reported in this work are for the OpenMP version only.

2.5   MCDRAM Modes

The MCDRAM and the DDR4 can be configured in three different modes: Flat, Cache and Hybrid. This section describes each of them briefly.

- **Flat Mode** MCDRAM memory appears to the programmer as a continuation of the main memory. Allocation in the 16 GB MCDRAM area or the DDR4 area is determined by NUMA controls or specific allocation calls with the memkind library [3]. This mode should be optimal for applications with high memory bandwidth requirements but moderate memory footprint.
- **Cache Mode** MCDRAM is treated as an effective Level 3 cache between the KNL tiles and the main DDR4 memory on the node. Memory allocation and transfers are controlled automatically by the OS kernel. This mode should be optimal for applications with very large memory footprint, significant memory bandwidth requirements, and a regular memory access pattern.
- **Hybrid Mode** MCDRAM can be statically divided into 25/50/75 % blocks to be used as cache or flat memory. This mode may be best for advanced users wishing to fully optimize their code or workflow.

2.6   Memory Access Modes

On top of three basic configuration modes for MCDRAM, KNL offers multiple ways to group coherency across the many cores/tiles in the processor. The following access modes, among others that differ only slightly from these, are available:

- **All-to-All** Cache tag directory is distributed across all tiles.
- **Quadrant** Cache tag directory located in the same quadrant as the corresponding memory. Should improve latency with respect to All-to-All mode when most accesses are local.
- **Sub-NUMA Cluster 2/4** Each half or quadrant is exposed as a separate NUMA node by subdividing the tiles into clusters. This configuration may be of high interest to users of hybrid codes trying to balance the number of MPI tasks and OpenMP threads used during execution. Currently this seems to be available only for KNL processors with 36 active tiles, and we have been unable to test this particular configuration.

3   Evaluations

All the results presented in this work were obtained on a Knights Landing pre-production system, B0 stepping, 1.30 GHz, 64 cores (32 tiles), 16 GB MCDRAM, 96 GB DDR4 (16 × 6 DDR4 2133 DIMMs), run with multiple clustering and memory modes. At the time of submitting this paper we have been able to complete experiments with the following memory configurations for KNL: Flat Mode (All-to-All and Quadrant), Cache (All-to-All). In the case of the Flat Mode we used NUMA memory policy to determine where memory should reside (MCDRAM or main DDR4 memory). For example to run purely on the MCDRAM we used `numactl --membind=1 ./executable` and to run purely on the main memory we used `numactl --membind=0 ./executable`. No such control is available in Cache Mode, of course, since the MCDRAM is not exposed as a NUMA node in that case.

3.1   Memory Access Scaling

To begin, we created a simple saxpy-loop program to mimic the triad benchmark in STREAM [6], so that we could quickly determine a profile showing how the memory bandwidth scales with the thread count. The loop, consisting of 100,000,000 iterations with double precision data, is repeated 200 times (after data was initialized), and compiled with only -O3 and -xMIC-AVX2 optimizations. We present these results first, so that the reader has a clear picture of the bandwidth capability at different thread counts.

Four types of memory access are shown in Fig. 1. On a node configured with FLAT mode memory and All-to-All Clustering, three experiments were performed: scaling using DDR4 memory access, by simply invoking the executable; scaling using MCDRAM, by accessing MCDRAM through a NUMA command (MC-numa) at execution; and scaling using MCDRAM, through a memkind library call to hbw_malloc within the code (MC-hbw). The fourth experiment used a node configured with Cache mode memory and All-to-All clustering (MC-cache).

The simple-saxpy results show that a maximum DDR4 bandwidth of 82 GB/s is reached with 14 threads, while a maximum MCDRAM bandwidth of 419 GB/s is reached with 64 thread (for MC-numa). These profiles match the triad STREAM benchmarks that users can derive from the `micprun -k stream` command, preinstalled on the KNL. The micprun scan reports STREAM triad maximums of 82 GB/s and 428 GB/s for DDR4 and MCDRAM, respectively.

Note, the scaling profiles of MC-numa, MC-cache, and MC-hbw are all the same, with the same performance ordering throughout the whole range. NUMA controlled bandwidths are the highest, followed by cache accesses; and accesses through hbw_malloc have the worst performance. The difference between MC-numa and MC-hbw is about 12 % for the first and last 10 thread counts, and 7 % throughout the middle of the curve. While it does seem reasonable that MCDRAM access through cache (MC-cache) may have a performance hit (relative to a non-cached mode), one would expect no difference between the MC-numa and MC-hbw experiments.

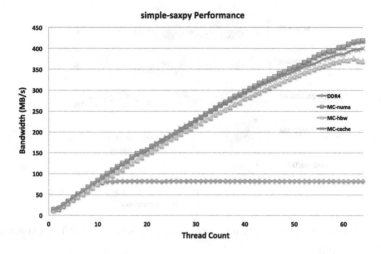

Fig. 1. Bandwidth scaling for DDR4 and MCDRAM memory.

3.2 Memory Configuration Effect on MCDRAM Contained Workloads

This section describes the effect of different memory configuration settings for workloads that can be fitted inside the MCDRAM memory footprint (MiniFE: problem size $256 \times 256 \times 256$ (approximately 6 GB footprint); MiniMD: 500K atoms and 1K iterations (300 MB); WRF: a standard CONUS 12 km benchmark case was used; LBS3D: size $256 \times 256 \times 256$, with a footprint of approximately 6 GB; NAS Class C with a memory footprint of approximately 6 GB). All results correspond to the average of multiple runs with no significant deviation in runtimes across the sample.

Figures 2 and 3 show the effect of memory configuration on all the applications studied. Performance has been normalized to that of running in the slower of the measured modes for each application individually, in order to be able to show all results in a single graph. Notice how MiniMD, which is highly insensitive to memory bandwidth, sees little difference from the change in configuration, while LBS3D, MiniFE and NAS BT, EP, FT MG and SP see an remarkable speedup when running inside MCDRAM. It can be explained by the fact that these applications are sensitive to the bandwidth.

While the performance of WRF is strongly correlated with memory bandwidth, it does have more computational overhead than LBS3D and MiniFE. Hence, the performance improvements for WRF are slightly less than those for the simpler LSB3D and MiniFE codes.

Keep in mind that all the workloads fit in MCDRAM in this case, which explains how closely Cache and Flat/MCDRAM modes are in all cases. In the Fig. 2, A2A refers to All-to-All mode, while Quad refers to Quadrant mode. NAS benchmarks presented in Fig. 3 were only executed in All-to-All mode.

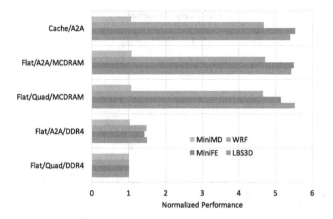

Fig. 2. Comparative effect of memory configuration on MCDRAM-contained workloads.

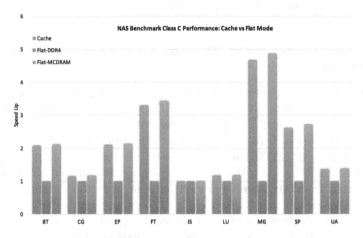

Fig. 3. Comparative effect of memory configuration on MCDRAM-contained workloads using NAS

3.3   Memory Configuration Effect on Non-MCDRAM Contained Workloads

We have compared the performance of several large data sets, from 6 GB to 48 GB memory footprints, when running in Cache Mode, and when running in Flat Mode and allocating to main DDR4 memory. Figure 4 shows that there is a significant improvement in performance across all executions, with a minimum improvement of almost 19 % for both LBS3D and miniFE. As expected, the benefit of using cache mode decreases as the workload grows beyond the cache size. The fact that an improvement of nearly 19 % is still present for workloads with memory footprints that triple the MCDRAM cache size is a good indicator of the benefit of running in this configuration mode.

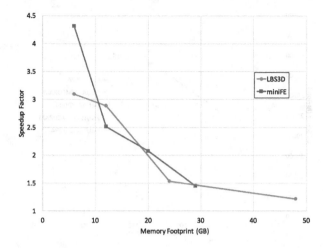

Fig. 4. Effect of Cache Mode for non-MCDRAM contained workload (LBS3D and MiniFE).

Our tests show that the benefit from using cache mode is not independent of the type of memory access and the number of threads used, which is expected. More work will be necessary in this area to fully characterize the benefits of using the cache mode, but the results obtained so far are encouraging.

3.4   Scalability and Memory Configuration

Performance for a fixed workload was measured for each of the applications in each of the previously mentioned memory configuration modes.

Figure 5 shows excellent scalability for MiniFE when using MCDRAM, with the code scaling very strongly throughout the range of 1 thread per core (up to 64 threads), and then speedup continues at a smaller rate beyond that. When allocating to DDR4 memory the scalability stalls between 16 and 32 threads, with the All-to-All clustering outperforming Quadrant cluster asymptotically. This is because the available memory bandwidth to main memory has been exhausted.

LBS3D behaves in a similar manner, as shown in Fig. 6, with very strong scalability up to 128 threads. The main difference between the results for LBS3D and MiniFE is that after 128 threads LBS3D actually starts to slow down even when running in MCDRAM. This is most likely due to the sheer number of streams in flight, which lowers prefetcher efficiency and increases the likelihood of conflicts. The LBS3D performance also seems to stall earlier, around 16 threads, when allocation is purposefully set in the main system DDR4 memory rather than the MCDRAM.

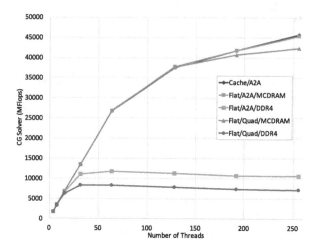

Fig. 5. Scalability of MiniFE on a single KNL processor using different memory configurations.

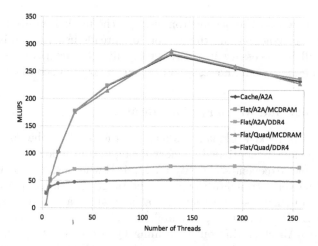

Fig. 6. Scalability of LBS3D on a single KNL processor using different memory configurations.

In the case of MiniMD we observe relatively less scalability all the way through the thread range, with no significant changes between different memory configuration modes (see Fig. 7). The similarity of results from different configurations is expected, since the code does not show a strong dependence on memory bandwidth as is typical for Molecular Dynamics codes. The overall scalability seems weak, but this could be a case where additional tests using multiple MPI tasks are required in order to obtain a higher performance. That work is currently being performed.

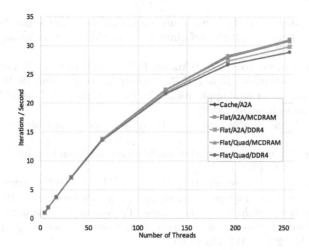

Fig. 7. Scalability of MiniMD on a single KNL processor using different memory configurations.

4   Conclusion and Outlook

This paper has presented a set of studies of the performance of representative applications and miniapps on Intel KNL.

The results show that Cache Mode operates very efficiently for MCDRAM-contained workloads, and that memory-bandwidth bound applications see a performance improvement commensurate with the bandwidth ratio between MCDRAM and main DDR4 memory. Initial scalability results show promise for all the applications considered.

As future work we consider detailed studies of the effect of Cache Mode in workloads that do not fit inside MCDRAM. We also plan on continuing these studies to further understand the implications of pining the different processes/threads to cores.

References

1. Bailey, D.H., Barszcz, E., Barton, J.T., Browning, D.S., Carter, R.L., Dagum, D., Fatoohi, R.A., Frederickson, P.O., Lasinski, T.A., Schreiber, R.S., Simon, H.D., Venkatakrishnan, V., Weeratunga, S.K.: The NAS parallel benchmarks. Int. J. Supercomputer Appl. **5**(3), 63–73 (1991)
2. Birrittella, M.S., Debbage, M., Huggahalli, R., Kunz, J., Lovett, T., Rimmer, T., Underwood, K.D., Zak, R.C.: Intel® omni-path architecture: enabling scalable, high performance fabrics. In: Hot Interconnects, pp. 1–9. IEEE (2015)
3. Cantalupo, C., Venkatesan, V., Hammond, J.R., Czuryło, K., Hammond, S.: User extensible heap manager for heterogeneous memory platforms and mixed memory policies (2015)

4. Duran, A., Klemm, M.: The Intel many integrated core architecture. In: 2012 International Conference on High Performance Computing and Simulation (HPCS), pp. 365–366, July 2012
5. Heroux, M.A., Doerfler, D.W., Crozier, P.S., Willenbring, J.M., Edwards, H.C., Williams, A., Rajan, M., Keiter, E.R., Thornquist, H.K., Numrich, R.W.: Improving performance via mini-applications. Technical report SAND2009-5574, Sandia National Laboratories, 3 (2009)
6. McCalpin, J.: Stream benchmark (1995). www.cs.virginia.edu/stream/ref.html #what
7. Michalakes, J.: Optimizing weather models for Intel Xeon Phi. Intel Theater Presentation SC 2013 (2013)
8. NASA Advanced Supercomputing Division: NAS parallel benchmarks (2016). http://www.nas.nasa.gov/publications/npb.html. Accessed Jun 2016
9. Nourgaliev, R.R., Dinh, T.N., Theofanous, T., Joseph, D.: The lattice Boltzmann equation method: theoretical interpretation, numerics and implications. Int. J. Multiph. Flow **29**(1), 117–169 (2003)
10. Rosales, C.: Porting to the Intel Xeon Phi: opportunities and challenges. In: Extreme Scaling Workshop (XSW 2013), pp. 1–7. IEEE (2013)
11. Sanders, J., Kandrot, E.: CUDA by Example: An Introduction to General-Purpose GPU Programming, Portable Documents. Addison-Wesley Professional, Reading (2010)
12. Seiler, L., Carmean, D., Sprangle, E., Forsyth, T., Abrash, M., Dubey, P., Junkins, S., Lake, A., Sugerman, J., Cavin, R., Espasa, R., Grochowski, E., Juan, T., Hanrahan, P.: Larrabee: A many-core x86 architecture for visual computing. In: ACM SIGGRAPH 2008 Papers, SIGGRAPH 2008, pp. 18:1–18:15. ACM, New York (2008). http://doi.acm.org/10.1145/1399504.1360617
13. Skamarock, W.C., Klemp, J.B., Dudhia, J., Gill, D.O., Barker, M., Duda, K.G., Huang, X.Y., Wang, W., Powers, J.G.: A description of the advanced research WRF version 3. Technical report, National Center for Atmospheric Research (2008)
14. Sodani, A., Gramunt, R., Corbal, J., Kim, H.S., Vinod, K., Chinthamani, S., Hutsell, S., Agarwal, R., Liu, Y.C.: Knights landing: second-generation Intel Xeon Phi product. IEEE Micro **36**(2), 34–46 (2016)
15. Succi, S.: The Lattice Boltzmann Equation: For Fluid Dynamics and Beyond. Oxford University Press, Oxford (2001)
16. Wong, F.C., Martin, R.P., Arpaci-Dusseau, R.H., Culler, D.E.: Architectural Requirements and scalability of the NAS parallel benchmarks. In: Proceedings of the 1999 ACM/IEEE Conference on Supercomputing (1999)
17. Wong, P.C., Shen, H.W., Johnson, C.R., Chen, C., Ross, R.B.: The top 10 challenges in extreme-scale visual analytics. IEEE Comput. Graph. Appl. **32**(4), 63 (2012)
18. Zheng, H., Shu, C., Chew, Y.T.: A lattice Boltzmann model for multiphase flows with large density ratio. J. Comput. Phys. **218**(1), 353–371 (2006)

Application Suitability Assessment for Many-Core Targets

Chris J. Newburn, Jim Sukha$^{(\boxtimes)}$, Ilya Sharapov, Anthony D. Nguyen, and Chyi-Chang Miao

Intel Corporation, Hudson, USA
{chris.newburn,jim.sukha,ilya.sharapov,anthony.d.nguyen,
chyi-chang.miao}@intel.com

Abstract. Many-core hardware platforms offer a tremendous opportunity for scaling up performance, but not all codes that run on these platforms have been modernized sufficiently to fully utilize the hardware. Assessing whether a code will effectively utilize a given platform can be challenging, particularly for new or potential future platforms where native execution on real hardware is not possible. In this case, one typically relies on architecture simulators and other workload characterization tools, which are often not user-friendly for developers who want to do a quick initial assessment of an application's suitability for a many-core architecture.

To help address this challenge, we present QMSprof, a tool and a set of analyses for an initial assessment of the suitability of a set of applications for a simulated extremely-parallel many-core target. QMSprof automates the process of running a suite of workload binaries through Intel® Software Development Emulator (SDE) and the Sniper multi-core simulator and extracting high-level summary statistics. The tool generates comparative plots summarizing key metrics across the workload suite, including the mix of vector and nonvector instructions, scalability with increasing thread count, memory bandwidth utilization, and statistics on cache misses and working set size. These summary metrics are designed to aid performance tuners in selecting promising codes for a many-core target and in pinpointing opportunities for additional tuning. To illustrate the utility of our tool, we also describe some sample results from characterizing applications on a hypothetical many-core architecture.

Keywords: Many-core · Performance · Characterization · Code modernization

1 Introduction

Not all applications are cut out for execution on extremely-parallel machines like those of the Intel® Xeon Phi™ Processor Family [9], also known as the

This research was, in part, funded by the U.S. Government and DOE. The views and conclusions contained in this document are those of the authors and should not be interpreted as representing the official policies, either expressed or implied, of the U.S. Government.

© Springer International Publishing AG 2016
M. Taufer et al. (Eds.): ISC High Performance Workshops 2016, LNCS 9945, pp. 319–338, 2016.
DOI: 10.1007/978-3-319-46079-6_23

"Knights" family. Such machines offer high levels of thread parallelism, vector parallelism and bandwidth. If an application fails to exploit these salient features, its performance will fall far short of the capabilities of these machines.

Those who seek to characterize applications on new architectures often lack the time for detailed analysis, or the expertise, or both. Application developers today typically rely on profiling and analysis tools, such as Intel® VTune™ Amplifier (or VTune™ for short)[8] or Intel® Advisor [6] to understand application behavior on existing hardware. When real hardware is not available however, e.g., because it is a future architecture under development, one typically must resort to using a combination of workload characterization and simulation tools. Unfortunately, since these tools are usually designed for hardware architects rather than application developers, they can overwhelm the uninitiated user with raw statistics, and are not user-friendly for a developer who is looking for a quick high-level profile of their application on a future architecture.

This paper describes *QMSprof*, a tool and set of analyses for assessing how well-suited an application is for extremely-parallel many-core targets, such as the Intel Xeon Phi product line. The name **QMSprof** stems from its implementation, because it derives its results from other **Q**uick **M**ultithreaded **S**imulation and **prof**iling tools. QMSprof runs a suite of workload binaries through two underlying tools, Intel® Software Development Emulator (Intel® SDE) [7] and the Sniper multi-core simulator [2,14], aggregates results, and produces high-level analysis and summary plots. This analysis is designed to provide a high-level summary of application characteristics, enabling users to more easily determine which workloads may be more suitable than others for a many-core architecture. The results produced from QMSprof are expected to be useful as part of an initial triage of applications being brought into tuning sessions, highlighting key characteristics that may warrant deeper analysis or additional optimization.

In this paper, we describe the application of QMSprof and analyses to regions of interest (ROIs) that are marked as important, from eight workloads of general interest to the HPC community, simulated on a hypothetical many-core architecture. The focus of the paper is to demonstrate the *kinds* of analyses supported by QMSprof and what the results may *look* like, not the specific numbers for any workload or architecture. Thus, one should **not** interpret any numerical results on our simulated architectural model in this paper as corresponding to absolute performance on any existing or future Intel silicon. However, we expect the *tools and methodology* to be of interest to those porting their applications to current and future Intel® Xeon Phi™ Processor many-core machines such as Knights Landing (KNL), as well as wide Intel® Xeon Processor machines.

2   Overview of Tool and Analysis

QMSprof streamlines the process of running a suite of workloads through the Intel Software Development Emulator (SDE) and the Sniper simulator, extracting high-level summary statistics, and generating comparative plots. This section describes the interface and operation of two components of QMSprof, namely the data collector which generates raw SDE and Sniper data for a particular experiment, and the data analyzer which extracts and summarizes the results.

2.1 Data Collector

The *data collector* is a Python module that generates run scripts for a set of SDE and Sniper runs, sweeping across a suite of workloads, Sniper configurations, and different thread counts. Users must provide the following inputs to the collector:

1. **Workload binaries and run parameters**: For each workload in the desired suite, a binary compiled with a special begin and end markers around a single region of interest, and any required input files and command-line arguments.
2. **Sniper Models**: Configuration files for different Sniper models to be run.
3. **Environment Setup**: Other configuration parameters specific to the user's desired run environment (e.g., paths to specific OpenMP runtime libraries or configuration for job managers in a cluster environment).
4. **Experiment Script**: The description of the particular subset of workloads, models, and thread counts to run in a particular experiment.

These four configuration inputs are separable and can be specified mostly independently by different area experts. Workload binaries, input files, and run parameters are typically provided by application experts who are familiar with regions of interest to profile. Sniper models can be provided by hardware architects familiar with specifying relevant architecture parameters in the simulator. The environment setup file can be specified by individuals familiar with details of the installed run environment. Finally, the experiment script is specified by the end user who wants to run particular experiments.

Users configure QMSprof by describing inputs as Python dictionaries and lists, a user interface that is both relatively human-readable and suitable for automation. A detailed example of the interface is illustrated in Appendix A.

Once all the inputs have been specified, the collector takes the list of runs specified in the experiment script and generates a shell script for each Sniper and/or SDE run. These shell scripts can be run directly at a command prompt, or fed into a job manager in a distributed compute environment. QMSprof generates shell scripts, rather than invoking Sniper and SDE directly, because this intermediate step facilitates debugging. When runs fail, one can simply manually edit a generated run script and debug an individual run, without trying to repeat an entire sweep of experiments. In our prototype, we set up QMSprof to run on Intel NetBatch, an internal distributed computing environment which has been used for many years for simulations and other compute-intensive jobs [1,13,21]. It is straightforward, however, to extend QMSprof to submit jobs to other publicly available job managers such as SLURM [19].

QMSprof uses the following Intel SDE and Sniper execution modes to collect raw statistics:

1. **SDE Instruction Mix.** SDE provides an instruction mix tool that produces statistics on the numbers and types of instructions executed.

2. **SDE Footprint Tool.** SDE also provides a tool that estimates the memory footprint of a profiled region in a program, both at cache-line and page granularity. More specifically, SDE tracks the distinct cache lines or pages accessed in a region of interest, and can classify them as either data or code.
3. **Sniper Simulation.** Sniper is an execution-driven high-speed x86 simulator which can be used to characterize a workload by executing the workload on a generic many-core configuration.

Sniper runs slower than SDE, but it collects additional raw statistics that are useful for our analysis. QMSprof adds two flags to each Sniper run to gather additional information: `--profile` to collect information on function calls, including a percentage breakdown of instructions and time spent inside and outside of the OpenMP library, and `--cheetah` to profile the working set of threads executing in the region of interest, using a known technique for efficient simulation of multiple cache sizes in a single run [15].

2.2 Data Analysis

The *data analyzer* in QMSprof is a set of scripts that extracts data from an experiment run by the collector, and generates various output summary plots. In particular, QMSprof can generate the following summary data:

1. **Vector Instruction Mix**: A breakdown of the types of vector instructions executed by each run.
2. **Thread Scalability**: Running time of benchmarks variants in the experiment as a function of thread count.
3. **Memory bandwidth**: A measure of the average memory bandwidth utilization of the application.
4. **Cache Miss Statistics**: A plot of the miss rates and misses per 1 K instructions for the last-level cache.
5. **Working set size**: An analysis of the last-level cache sizes needed to achieve a given miss rate.
6. **OpenMP overhead**: The fraction of total execution time spent in the OpenMP runtime, which can indicate overheads from fork/join and dynamic scheduling.
7. **Memory footprint**: A measure of the new number of distinct pages of memory required to execute each workload.

The analyzer produces two forms of output, namely (1) comma-separated value files amenable to import into a spreadsheet, or (2) data and plot files for gnuplot, version 4.6 [18]. In subsequent sections of this paper, we describe the summary plots generated by the analyzer in greater detail and explain why they are useful for understanding the suitability of a workload for a many-core architecture. We also performed an analysis of the granularity of OpenMP parallel regions, but since it is not fully automated, we do not show that here. Table 1 summarizes the execution mode of Sniper or SDE used for each analysis, and identifies comparable analyses from Advisor and VTune, if they exist.

In general, compared to Advisor and VTune, QMSprof is optimized for different purposes. Both Advisor and VTune are primarily designed for characterization of full-scale workloads, running natively on existing hardware, while QMSprof is designed to extract important high-level summary statistics from slower but more detailed simulations of targeted regions of interest in a workload. Native execution has a few limitations compared to a simulation-based approach, which include a lack of accurate FLOPS counting and a limited ability to estimate performance on future hardware that may have different characteristics. QMSprof is able to use Sniper to simulate models of hardware that do not exist today, or even models that are impractical to build but can provide interesting insights through limit studies and other hypothetical what-if scenarios. Similarly, its use of SDE allows for more detailed accounting of dynamically executed instructions which are difficult to do with current hardware. Additionally, although running workloads through Sniper or SDE is slower than native execution, the resulting statistics tend to be less affected by measurement noise and thus more amenable to comparison across workloads.

Table 1. Execution modes from SDE and Sniper used by the analyses in QMSprof. The table also indicates which analyses are supported by the Advisor and VTune tools. A ✓ and ~ indicate full and partial support, respectively.

Characterization	SDE		Sniper			Advisor	VTune
Mode	-mix	-footprint	Default	–profile	–cheetah		
Vector Instruction Mix	✓					~	~
Thread Scalability			✓			✓	
Memory Bandwidth Utilization			✓				✓
Cache Miss Statistics			✓			~	~
Working Set Size			✓		✓		
OpenMP Runtime Fraction			✓	✓			✓
Memory Footprint		✓				✓	

As indicated in Table 1, Advisor provides some analyses similar to QMSprof. Intel® Advisor 2016/2017 offers vectorization, FLOPS and roofline analysis capabilities, for both Xeon and Xeon Phi. These capabilities provide per-loop and optionally per-program information on the following data ingredients in ways that are similar to four of the numbered QMSprof features above: (1) static and limited dynamic instruction mixes, (2) thread scalability, (4) memory bandwidth and (7) memory footprint. Advisor analysis is targeted towards end-user complex code modernization, offering insight at the loop/function granularity, with low runtime overhead and multiple data representations and data sources, such as compiler opt-reports, the access pattern profiler, or trip count/FLOPS analysis. Unlike QMSprof, Advisor does not focus on contrasting aggregated program-level characteristics across workloads or platforms. Also, with the exception of Thread Scalability and AVX-512 codepath projection features, it does not model platforms other than currently-available silicon. Instruction mix and footprint data is currently not a first class citizen information in Advisor; it is not always exposed in detail and is sometimes provided with lower accuracy to minimize runtime overhead.

VTune supports many detailed analyses of a single workload, and is generally optimized for a deep dive into the behavior of a few workloads on real silicon, rather than QMSprof which is optimized for a quick initial comparison of select statistics across a large set of workloads. VTune provides information on code performance through several predefined analysis types. For example, VTune includes algorithmic analysis types, such as hotspot analysis and threading concurrency analysis with locks and waits profiling to find synchronization bottlenecks. It also includes microarchitecture analysis types, such as general exploration analysis with a hierarchical organization of event-based metrics for identifying the dominant performance bottlenecks in an application, memory access analysis showing processor stalls by memory hierarchy, memory bandwidth information, and a correlation of memory objects with memory performance metrics. VTune's statistic collection methods include hardware performance monitoring, binary instrumentation, instrumented threading runtimes, and static analysis. VTune covers the following analyses in QMSprof listed above: (1) vector instruction mix based on KNL's limited hardware profiling that are mitigated by static analysis, (3) memory bandwidth including DRAM, MCDRAM and QPI bandwidth types, (4) cache miss statistics, (6) OpenMP serial time, imbalance and overhead with cause, and MPI time spent spinning in active waiting for hybrid MPI + OpenMP applications. VTune is evolving to offer a combination of thread scalability, memory and FPU utilization aspects in one analysis type called HPC Performance Characterization.

2.3   Prototype Implementation

We have implemented a prototype of QMSprof that works with SDE and an Intel-internal version of Sniper. We use an internal version of Sniper primarily because it supports execution of binaries compiled for the AVX512 instruction set, a feature currently not available in the public version of Sniper. Currently, there exists a formal process for developers with appropriate restricted-secret NDA approvals to access the Intel-internal version of Sniper, and our scripts and configuration files can be made available to those who have access to the Intel-internal version of Sniper.

For the empirical results presented in the rest of this paper, since SDE is publicly available, the analyses in QMSprof that are based on SDE can be reproduced by all users. The analysis based on Sniper could also be repeated using the public version of Sniper, using only AVX128 vectors, but this change in Sniper versions would affect the instruction mix and potentially the interactions with the memory system.

3 A Case Study

In the remainder of this paper, we demonstrate QMSprof by applying it to a case study that evaluates 8 HPC workloads on a generic many-core micro-architecture model. This section describes the workloads and the Sniper model used for our case study. Although detailed simulation results are not the focus of this paper, we describe our experimental methodology to provide some context for understanding QMSprof's output.

We tested regions of interest (ROIs) chosen from eight representative HPC workloads: BlackScholes [10], Himeno [4], LULESH [3], miniFE [3], Simple-MOC kernel [16], SNAP [3], SMC [17,20], and WSM5 [5]. We also tested two microbenchmarks: PeakFLOPS, a synthetic kernel created to achieve near maximal performance on floating-point computations, and STREAM [11,12], a synthetic kernel designed to achieve maximal memory bandwidth usage. BlackScholes, Himeno, and SimpleMOC (kernel), are relatively simple kernels, while the remaining codes are regions taken from more complex proxy apps. All codes are strong-scaled with OpenMP.

We spent little or no effort tuning these workloads, instead taking the binaries generated by the compiler mostly as-is. Frankly, scenarios with poorly-tuned workloads are more common than those with extensive tuning and optimization. *The condition of the workloads and the actual conclusions based on the data are not the focus of the paper; instead, the analysis methodology and tools are.* This usage model matches a typical work flow for a performance modeling expert or an architecture expert, who can experiment with changes in architecture, but is often not in a position to optimize workloads.

For each workload, we chose an ROI which executes on a scaled data set for somewhere between 100 to 500 million instructions. This choice is driven in part by the simulation speed of Sniper, which simulated on roughly 0.1 to 1 million instructions per second in our study. This speed is obviously too slow to estimate the performance of a multicore applications on a full production-size input. We believe it is sufficient, however, for understanding the impact of changes in architectural parameters such as cache sizes, prefetchers, out-of-order execution width, etc., provided that workload experts can provide representative scaled-down inputs. The analyses that are based on SDE and Sniper share the same binaries and hence have the same ROI markers. The binaries were compiled with the -xMIC-AVX512 flag using version 16.0 of the Intel compiler.

The SDE-based analyses are target independent. For Sniper, we model a many-core micro-architecture with 16 3-wide, out-of-order cores. Each core has a 32 K L1-D cache, a 32 K L1-I cache, and a vector unit capable of executing AVX512 instructions. Hardware prefetchers are enabled. Each pair of cores share an 1 MB L2. Sixteen cores can access up to 512 MB of in-package memory through a single memory controller, with a bandwidth limit of 48 GB/s. Note that this configuration models only a fraction (e.g., 1/4) of a full many-core die. Although this model does not capture any sharing or contention effects that would exist in an application that requires shared-memory communication between the fractions of the die, it is reasonable for modeling a single rank of an MPI application that uses OpenMP threads to populate 16 cores.

Finally, although we believe our model has many of the salient features of a many-core architecture and is useful for some relative comparisons between workloads, it is important to note that its architectural parameters **intentionally do not match any known product** on the Intel Xeon Phi roadmap. Thus, our model or results **should not be used as estimate of absolute performance on Knights Landing or any other Intel silicon.**

4   Output from the Data Analyzer

In this section, we discuss each QMSprof output for the case study described in Sect. 3, explaining how each analysis can be used to determine the relative suitability of a workload for a many-core architecture.

4.1   Vector Instruction Mix

The first analysis one would typically run is an instruction mix, which shows the vector instructions executed in a workload, expressed as a fraction of the total instructions executed. To get maximal benefit from a many-core architecture like Xeon Phi, we generally want the fraction of vector instructions to be as close to 100 % as possible. Moreover, we ideally prefer to have full-length vector instructions, i.e., AVX512 packed SIMD instructions, rather than shorter-vector or SIMD scalar instructions. We also prefer fewer masked vector instructions, since 0-valued mask bits imply unused vector lanes. If the fraction of vector instructions is low, this is an alert that some vectorization enabling may be required for compiler-generated code, or that vector-enabled libraries may not be in use. If the ratio of scalar SIMD to packed SIMD is high, significant time may being spent in unvectorized outer loops, suggesting a possible need for placing vectorization directives on outer loops. Excessive masking may be mitigated by eliminating conditionals, which is sometimes possible by inlining functions to enable constant propagation by the compiler.

QMSprof automatically generates plots from SDE that reveal packed vs. scalar SIMD, and non-scalar AVX type, as shown in Fig. 1. This analysis is run first because it runs faster on the SDE emulator than on the Sniper simulator. In our case study, we see that only BlackScholes and PeakFLOPS are getting close to having 100 % of vector instructions. Other workloads have a noticeable fraction of shorter vectors (e.g., LULESH, at 70 % short vectors), or non-vector instructions, even though we compiled the workloads targeting AVX512. Finally, there appears to be little use of masking (reported separately from the plot shown) in these workloads, with the highest fraction of 14 % of all instructions for WSM5. Reporting of data types, e.g. single-precision, double-precision and bit-wise SIMD, has also been demonstrated, but is not shown here. This instruction mix analysis is useful in correlating performance differences with and without vectorization (e.g., for the Intel compiler, code compiled

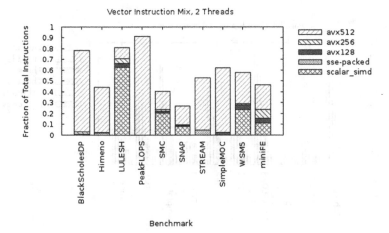

Fig. 1. Instruction mix of workloads, classifying percentages of vector instructions executed. This data was collected using SDE for runs with two OpenMP worker threads.

with the -no-simd -no-vec -no-openmp-simd flags). Since the direct evaluation of that silicon performance is not part of QMSprof, we do not show those results.

4.2 Thread Scalability

Thread scalability analysis can provide guidance on how to balance parallelism between MPI ranks and threads: more MPI ranks may be better when OpenMP thread scaling trails off. Thread serialization may not be noticed, but it tends to kill scalability. The thread scaling efficiency can be inferred from QMSprof's plot of Sniper-based parallel speedups as a function of **thread count** P.

Figure 2 shows a parallel speedup plot produced by QMSprof for our case study. For our workloads, we see that SimpleMOC, SNAP, BlackScholes, and WSM5 are the 4 workloads (ignoring PeakFLOPS) that scale reasonably well by adding more threads, while the others appear to have other limits to scalability. QMSprof can be configured to test scalability on a few different Sniper models with different parameters (e.g., different cache size, bandwidth, etc.). It also produces additional summary plots which help users understand other scalability limiters in greater detail.

Memory Bandwidth and Cache Behavior. Memory bandwidth and cache misses can become bottlenecks that limit thread scaling, and QMSprof produces summary plots for each, as shown in Fig. 3. The lack of thread scaling for Himeno, STREAM and miniFE correlate with the high memory bandwidth that does not scale with threads. High bandwidth is not necessarily an indication of high cache miss rates. BlackScholes has a low cache miss rate, but bandwidth that scales with threads; this is an indication of effective prefetching. We focus on last-level

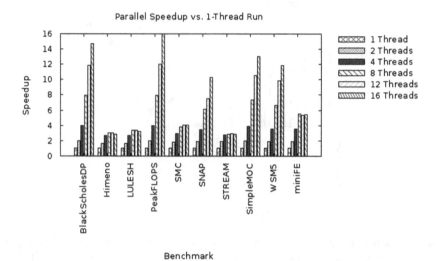

Fig. 2. Parallel speedup of workloads. This plot shows speedup for various numbers of threads from P=1 to P=16, on a simulated 16-core architecture with each pair of cores sharing an L2.

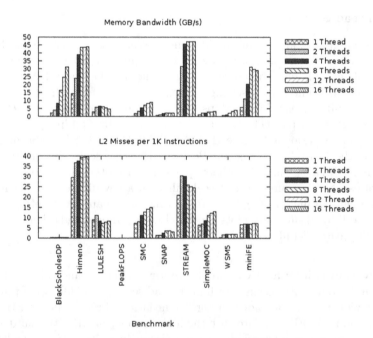

Fig. 3. Average memory bandwidth (top) and demand L2 misses per 1K instructions (bottom) for various thread counts, aligned to the same set of workloads.

cache misses per 1 K instructions executed as a metric instead of absolute miss rates, since it tends to be a better indicator of performance impact.

OpenMP Runtime Overheads. Another thread scaling inhibitor is overheads in both serial and parallel sections in a program. Serial sections, which can come from both an application or a parallel runtime such as OpenMP, do not speed up as more threads are added, and thus naturally limit scalability. Similarly, other OpenMP overheads in a parallel region will not be amortized away if there is too little work within a parallel region and the number of threads is large. QMSprof aggregates profiling data from Sniper to help users estimate such overheads.

Figure 4 shows that LULESH, miniFE, and SimpleMOC are the only workloads which spend more than 5 % of their total execution time in the OpenMP runtime. The implementations of LULESH and miniFE we used are known to have many fine-grained parallel regions, which contribute to fork-join overheads. SimpleMOC had many dynamically-scheduled loops, which contributes to the runtime overhead. In particular, for SimpleMOC, Sniper's profile output indicated that most of the time spent in the OpenMP runtime was in methods for lock acquisition, even for the single-thread runs. The current QMSprof prototype does not distinguish between overheads in serial and parallel sections, although we observed through other analysis that serial sections in the chosen ROIs of these workloads were generally negligible.

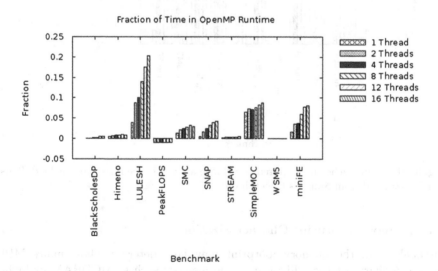

Fig. 4. Fraction of execution time that is overhead in the OpenMP runtime. A negative fraction (e.g., for PeakFLOPS) indicates that OpenMP was not detected at all, which usually means the workload was parallelized using some other approach.

4.3 Working Set Analysis

Thread scaling, analyzed in Sect. 4.2, is impacted by whether there is constructive interference across threads, and what cache capacity is needed per thread to keep cache miss rates low. Decisions about the number of threads to use per core, or per L2, or per set of L2s, or per in-package memory, may be based on the working set per thread and the kind of interference there is across threads. We use Sniper's 'Cheetah' functionality [15] to estimate the working set sizes for the applications, providing a more direct measure of the effect of changing cache sizes than the analysis in Sect. 4.2. Sniper allows us to estimate the cache miss rate for the outer-level cache as a function of cache size, at power-of-2 cache sizes, using a single simulation run. We extracted the minimum cache sizes needed to achieve a given cache miss rate (ranging from 1 % to 20 %), as shown in Fig. 5. This kind of exploratory analysis is not generally available with hardware-based profiling.

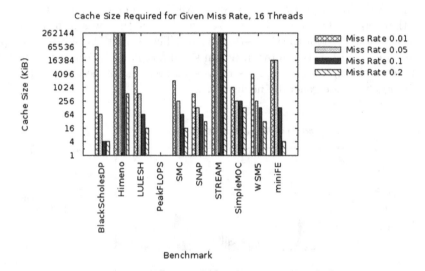

Fig. 5. Minimum cache size required to achieve a given cache miss rate (or less). This plot is extracted from Sniper's Cheetah data.

4.4 Memory Footprint Characterization

An analysis of the memory footprint may help determine how many MPI ranks can share resources like in-package memory such as MCDRAM or high-bandwidth memory (HBM). Large memory footprints cause a capacity issue, which can turn into a performance issue. We use the footprint tool from SDE to count the *total* number of pages accessed at a 2 MB page size in Fig. 6, regardless of caching effects. From this data, we observe that most of the workloads in our study access a total number of pages which is unlikely to fit into a typical L2 cache, and some would fit in a modest amount of in-package memory.

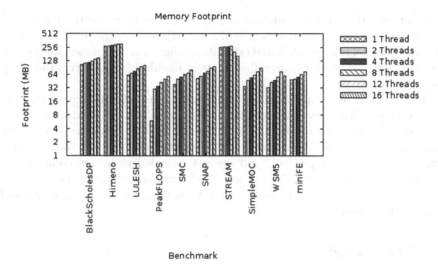

Fig. 6. Memory footprint of workloads, as measured by total memory covered (MB) and estimated using SDE, for accesses at the granularity of 2 MB pages.

Although we observed some correlation between working sets size and memory footprint for the workloads in this study, in general a large memory footprint, as measured above by SDE, does not necessarily indicate a large working set for the workload, since memory that is only accessed once still contributes to the number of new pages. This analysis does not give any good measure of data sharing between threads, since at any fixed value of memory footprint, the partitioning of data between the threads could be arbitrary. For example, we could have complete sharing, with all threads accessing all the data, or complete partitioning, with each thread accessing its own private data.

5 Conclusions

Harvesting thread and vector parallelism are critical to reaching peak performance on extreme-scale execution targets. Yet many applications do not approach peak performance on many-core targets because they lack effective parallelization for threaded and vector architectures, and they lack effective memory tuning. The QMSprof infrastructure provides an initial but broad-ranging analysis that give an indication of how well suited an application is for making good use of a many-core target, how well it can be scaled within that target with respect to memory capacity, MPI rank vs. OpenMP threading trade-offs, threads per core and per L2, whether additional memory blocking may be required, and how well vectorized it is.

While QMSprof does not offer all of the characterization that one could ever ask for, we've demonstrated that it provides a useful beginning. Based on feedback on the perceived utility of this tool and on what additional characterizations might provide the greatest benefit, more features may be added to QMSprof as they are brought to a sufficient degree of automation. Since the primary motivation for QMSprof is for quick initial estimates rather than comprehensive studies, however, some selectivity is desirable to avoid inundating users with too many statistics.

This analysis of suitability could either be used to prioritize codes that are already more suitable over others that are not (yet) suitable, and/or they can be used to focus optimization efforts on making applications more suitable for highly-parallel targets. While the absolute results presented here are not specific to a given target product, and are not intended to be representative of Knights Landing or other such products, the trends and "shape of the curves" is expected to provide some actionable insights to those assessing suitability and doing optimization.

6   Future Work

One characterization that could form an interesting complement to what has been done here is to analyze the effectiveness in trading off number of threads for number of MPI ranks, especially with respect to its impact on the memory system. Another, which is of particular interest for offload, is an analysis of the volume of data that must be communicated between the sequential parts of the program that might be executed on an Intel Xeon with low latency, and the highly-parallel parts that might be executed on a high-throughput Intel Xeon Phi Processor.

Workload statistics, like execution time and cache misses, could be reported for each serial section and OpenMP parallel region by compiling some additional instrumentation markers into the OpenMP runtime. This could help to highlight the significant serial sections and their characteristics.

One might also add silicon-based data collection, and possibly automate the correlation of simulation results with real silicon measurements. Runs on real silicon may enable us to analyze larger problem sizes. One challenge however, is that for the relatively small problems we typically run through simulation using QMSprof, real silicon measurements may be much more noisy. One benefit of using Sniper and SDE to collect raw data is that these tools have relatively little to no sensitivity to the runtime environment, which tends to make their results much more repeatable.

A   Appendix: Interface for QMSprof

This appendix demonstrates the interface for QMSprof. We first present an example of configuring the collector to run simulations, and then describe how to run the analyzer to extract summary statistics and generate plots.

A.1   Collector Interface

The collector interface for QMSprof is divided into four major parts, namely configuration for (1) workload binaries and run arguments, (2) Sniper models, (3) environment setup, and (4) experiment script.

For part (1), binaries and run arguments are configured by specifying a **Benchmarks** dictionary, which maps a key for each benchmark to a per-benchmark dictionary with additional information. When running an experiment, the collector uses information from a per-benchmark dictionary to *stage* each simulation run, i.e., creating a separate run folder for each simulation run in a staging area, and copying and/or renaming any necessary binaries and input files into that folder. This staging step is needed because workloads are not always built to support concurrent executions from the same run folder.

The per-benchmark dictionary is built to support benchmark *variants*, i.e., different versions of the same workload, with possibly different binaries or run arguments. This dictionary has several expected fields:

1. **bindir**: This string lists the subdirectory of the root benchmark directory containing the files for this benchmark. The root benchmark directory is a global variable specified separately in the top-level of the configuration file.
2. **files**: This dictionary maps a variant of the benchmark to a list of files needed to run each variant. Each file is itself a pair, with the first value being the name of the file in the source binary directory, and the second value being the name of the target file in the staging area. This pair allows an input file to be renamed in the staging area before it is run.
3. **runargs**: This dictionary maps a variant of a benchmark to the command-line arguments needed to run the variant.
4. **gen_inputs**: This dictionary maps a variant to a list of shell commands to execute in **bindir** to generate any input files that are needed for a run.
5. **requires_MPI**: This flag is set if this particular binary requires the use of an MPI library to execute. Our current prototype assumes one MPI rank per program, but in principle this assumption could be relaxed.

For the **files**, **runargs**, and **gen_inputs** dictionaries, if no exact match to a particular variant name is found in the dictionary, QMSprof will map to the key that matches the longest prefix.

As an example, Fig. 7 shows part of a configuration file specifying binaries and arguments for two benchmarks: LULESH and SNAP. In this configuration, running the **sim_vec** variant of the LULESH, uses the source file **lulesh2.0_vec** from the subdirectory **LULESH/binaries**. The staging process will copy and rename (or link) to a file named **LULESH_sim_vec** in a each simulation run directory. This staging allows QMSprof to use a consistent naming convention for its implementation, without requiring users to duplicate or change input file names in the

source directory. To run the `sim_vec` variant of LULESH, QMSprof will use the
`sim` argument of `-s 27 -i 6 -p`, since `sim` is the longest matching prefix of
`sim_vec`.

SNAP has a slightly more complicated description, with a script command
list in its `gen_inputs` parameter. This command list indicates that before staging
any files in the `files` list, the collector should run the script `genFile` from the
`SNAP/binaries` directory to generate extra input files. The strings `<P>` is a
special pattern in arguments and commands that the collector replaces with the
thread count for a particular run. Similarly, `<RunDir>` is a special pattern that
gets represents the run directory used to store and run the binary.

Configuration of parts (2) and (3) are relatively straightforward, as illustrated
in Fig. 8. The `SniperConfigs` dictionary describes the Sniper models that can be
used in an experiment. The key `16C_2wide` is a descriptive (usually short) string

```
Benchmarks = {
    "LULESH" : {
        "bindir"    :   "LULESH/binaries",
        "files" : {
            "test_vec"   : [ ("lulesh2.0_vec",   "LULESH_test_vec")  ],
            "test_novec" : [ ("lulesh2.0_novec", "LULESH_test_novec")],
            "sim_vec"    : [ ("lulesh2.0_vec",   "LULESH_sim_vec")   ],
            "sim_novec"  : [ ("lulesh2.0_novec", "LULESH_sim_novec") ],
        },
        "runargs" : {
            "test"    : "-s 4 -i 1",
            "sim"     : "-s 27 -i 6 -p",
            "full"    : "-s 36 -i 4 -p",
        }
    },
    "SNAP" : {
        "bindir"      : "SNAP/binaries",
        "gen_inputs" : {
            "test" : [ "genFile 1 1 <P> 4 4 4 8 8  1 <RunDir> fin_test_P<P>" ],
            "sim"  : [ "genFile 1 1 <P> 4 4 4 8 64 3 <RunDir> fin_sim_P<P>" ],
        },
        "files" : {
            "test_vec"  : [ ("snap_test_vec",  "SNAP_test_vec")  ],
            "sim_vec"   : [ ("snap_sim_vec",   "SNAP_sim_vec")   ],
        },
        "runargs" : {
            "test" : "fin_test_P<P> fout_test_P<P>",
            "sim"  : "fin_sim_P<P> fout_sim_P<P>",
        },
        requires_MPI = True
}
```

Fig. 7. Example **Benchmarks** dictionary for configuring workloads in QMSprof.

```
# Sniper configurations
SniperConfigs = {
    "16C_2wide"      : "Manycore_16c_2wide.cfg",
    "16C_3wide"      : "Manycore_16c_3wide.cfg",
}

# Environment setup
EnvFiles = {
    "DefaultOpenMP"  : "ICCDefaultOpenMP.sh"
}

# Configure job manager
import collector.Netbatch
BatchJobModule = collector.NetBatch
BatchJobManager = BatchJobModule.JobManager()
```

Fig. 8. Example configuration for QMSprof for Sniper configurations and environment setup.

that the user provides for the Sniper configuration file `Manycore_16c_2wide.cfg`. Similarly, in the `EnvFiles` dictionary, `DefaultOpenMP` is a description of the environment file `ICCDefaultOpenMP.sh`. Each run script created by QMSprof sources a particular environment file before each run, passing in the thread count of the run as its argument. Thus, the user should use the environment file to setup any necessary runtime libraries or tools (e.g., compiler libraries, Sniper and SDE), and any other environment variables such as `OMP_NUM_THREADS`. Finally, Fig. 8 also specifies the job manager (e.g., Intel NetBatch) to use to run jobs in the desired compute environment.

Finally, for part (4), Fig. 9 shows an example experiment script that specifies the runs in the experiment. Each run (e.g., `Run0`) is specified as a tuple with 5 entries:

1. **Sniper configuration**: The Sniper configuration for the run, as defined by the keys in the input `SniperConfigs` dictionary. For example, `Run0` runs the `16C_2_wide` config.
2. **Thread Set**: The thread counts to run. For example, `Run0` uses the thread counts of 1, 2, 4, 8, 12, and 16.
3. **Experiment File**: The environment file for the run, as defined by the keys in the input `EnvFiles` dictionary. For example, `Run0` uses the `DefaultOpenMP` environment file.
4. **Program list**: The workload variants to run. The example in Fig. 9 executes both the `sim_vec` and `sim_novec` variants of LULESH and SNAP.
5. **Experiment Knobs**: An object that captures all the other configuration knobs for a particular run. This example uses default values for all the knobs, but additional customization is possible.

```
import collector.config    # Import collector module
import SampleConfig        # Import user's configuration file
# Get default simulation knobs
knobs = collector.config.Knobs(SampleConfig)

my_prog_list = ["LULESH_sim_vec", "LULESH_sim_novec",
                "SNAP_test_vec", "SNAP_sim_vec"]

experiment_map = {
   "Run0" : ("16C_2wide",
            [1, 2, 4, 8, 12, 16],
            "DefaultOpenMP",
            my_prog_list,
            knobs),
   "Run1" : ("16C_3wide",
            [1, 2, 4, 8, 12, 16],
            "DefaultOpenMP",
            my_prog_list,
            knobs),
}

# Name of directory to store simulation output.
output_directory = "SimOutput"
collector.experiment.GenScripts("ExperimentDescription",
                        experiment_map,
                        SampleConfig.BatchJobManager,
                        output_directory)
```

Fig. 9. Example experiment script for QMSprof.

A.2 Analyzer Interface

The analyzer for QMSprof is a separate script that takes a single input directory as its argument, scans the input directory for SDE and Sniper simulation output, parses the relevant raw statistics output files, and then generates summary plots. Our prototype for QMSprof has the specific plots demonstrated in Sect. 4 hard-coded as output, but in principle one could implement a more complex interface that would allow for some customization in the generated plots. The analyzer generates Gnuplot scripts and data files as output, which can be manually edited (e.g., to change titles, labels, or legends), and rerun manually to recreate plots.

Our prototype analyzer assumes that simulation output for each simulation run is placed in a separate folder, with the thread count appearing in the folder name. The analyzer uses the names of output folders to group different thread counts for a benchmark together in summary plots, and eliminates the common suffix across all runs to shorten legends in generated plots. These assumptions are designed for processing the output from the QMSprof collector, but one can also use the analyzer to generate summary plots from other simulation runs if the output directories follow a compatible naming convention.

References

1. Bentley, B.: Validating the Intel® Pentium® 4 microprocessor. In: Proceedings of the 38th Annual Design Automation Conference, DAC 2001, pp. 244–248. ACM, New York (2001). http://doi.acm.org/10.1145/378239.378473
2. Carlson, T.E., Heirman, W., Eeckhout, L.: Sniper: exploring the level of abstraction for scalable and accurate parallel multi-core simulation. In: International Conference for High Performance Computing, Networking, Storage and Analysis (2011)
3. CORAL Collaboration: Oak Ridge, Argonne, Livermore. Benchmark codes. https://asc.llnl.gov/CORAL-benchmarks/
4. Himeno, R.: Himeno benchmark (2016). http://accc.riken.jp/en/supercom/himenobmt/
5. Hong, S.Y., Lim, J.O.J.: The WRF single-moment 6-class microphysics scheme (WSM 2006). J. Korean Meteorol. Soc. 42(2), 129–151 (2006)
6. Intel® Advisor (2016). https://software.intel.com/en-us/intel-advisor-xe
7. Intel® Software Development Emulator (2016). https://software.intel.com/en-us/articles/intel-software-development-emulator
8. Intel® VTune™ Amplifier (2016). https://software.intel.com/en-us/intel-vtune-amplifier-xe
9. Intel® Xeon Phi™ Product Family (2016). http://www.intel.com/content/www/us/en/processors/xeon/xeon-phi-detail.html
10. Li, S.: Case study: computing black-scholes with Intel® advanced vector extensions (2012). https://software.intel.com/en-us/articles/case-study-computing-black-scholes-with-intel-advanced-vector-extensions
11. McCalpin, J.D.: Memory bandwidth and machine balance in current high performance computers. IEEE Comput. Soc. Techn. Committee Comput. Archit. (TCCA) Newsl. 19–25 (1995)
12. McCalpin, J.D.: STREAM: sustainable memory bandwidth in high performance computers (2016). https://www.cs.virginia.edu/stream/
13. Shai, O., Shmueli, E., Feitelson, D.G.: Heuristics for resource matching in intel's compute farm. In: Desai, N., Cirne, W. (eds.) JSSPP 2013. LNCS, vol. 8429, pp. 116–135. Springer, Heidelberg (2014). doi:10.1007/978-3-662-43779-7_7
14. The Sniper Multi-Core Simulator (2016). http://snipersim.org
15. Sugumar, R.A., Abraham, S.G.: Efficient simulation of caches under opt replacement with applications to miss characterization. In: Proceedings of the ACM SIGMETRICS Conference (1993)
16. Tramm, J., Gunow, G.: SimpleMOC-kernel, version 2.0 (2015). https://github.com/ANL-CESAR/SimpleMOC-kernel
17. Valles, A., Zhang, W.: Optimizing for reacting Navier-Stokes equations. In: Reinders, J., Jeffers, J. (eds.) High Performance Parallelism Pearls, pp. 69–85. Morgan Kaufmann, Boston (2015). http://www.sciencedirect.com/science/article/pii/B9780128021187000042
18. Williams, T., Kelley, C.: gnuplot 4.6 (2014). http://www.gnuplot.info/docs_4.6/gnuplot.pdf
19. Yoo, A.B., Jette, M.A., Grondona, M.: SLURM: simple linux utility for resource management. In: Feitelson, D., Rudolph, L., Schwiegelshohn, U. (eds.) JSSPP 2003. LNCS, vol. 2862, pp. 44–60. Springer, Heidelberg (2003). doi:10.1007/10968987_3

20. Zhang, W.: miniSMC Benchmark (2014). https://github.com/WeiqunZhang/miniSMC
21. Zhang, Z., Phan, L.T.X., Tan, G., Jain, S., Duong, H., Loo, B.T., Lee, I.: On the feasibility of dynamic rescheduling on the Intel distributed computing platform. In: Proceedings of the 11th International Middleware Conference Industrial Track, Middleware Industrial Track 2010, pp. 4–10. ACM, New York (2010). http://doi.acm.org/10.1145/1891719.1891720

Applying the Roofline Performance Model
to the Intel Xeon Phi Knights Landing Processor

Douglas Doerfler$^{(\boxtimes)}$, Jack Deslippe, Samuel Williams, Leonid Oliker,
Brandon Cook, Thorsten Kurth, Mathieu Lobet, Tareq Malas, Jean-Luc Vay,
and Henri Vincenti

Lawrence Berkeley National Laboratory, Berkeley, USA
{dwdoerf,jrdeslippe,swwilliams,
loliker,bgcook,tkurth,mlobet,tmalas,jlvay,hvincenti}@lbl.gov

Abstract. The Roofline Performance Model is a visually intuitive
method used to bound the sustained peak floating-point performance of
any given arithmetic kernel on any given processor architecture. In the
Roofline, performance is nominally measured in floating-point operations
per second as a function of arithmetic intensity (operations per byte of
data). In this study we determine the Roofline for the Intel Knights Landing (KNL) processor, determining the sustained peak memory bandwidth
and floating-point performance for all levels of the memory hierarchy, in
all the different KNL cluster modes. We then determine arithmetic intensity and performance for a suite of application kernels being targeted for
the KNL based supercomputer Cori, and make comparisons to current
Intel Xeon processors. Cori is the National Energy Research Scientific
Computing Center's (NERSC) next generation supercomputer. Scheduled for deployment mid-2016, it will be one of the earliest and largest
KNL deployments in the world.

1 Introduction

Moving an application to a new architecture is a challenge, not only in porting of
the code, but in tuning and extracting maximum performance. This is especially
true with the introduction of the latest manycore and GPU-accelerated architectures, as they expose much finer levels of parallelism that can be a challenge for
applications to exploit in their current form. To address this challenge, NERSC
has established a collaborative partnership with code teams porting their codes
to Cori and its Intel Knights Landing (KNL) processors. Called NESAP (NERSC
Exascale Science Applications Program), this collaborative will partner the code
teams with key personal from NERSC, Cray, and Intel [13,15].

One method being used within NESAP to identify and better understand
the fundamental architectural bottlenecks, and hence providing a path to better
understand where to focus optimization efforts, is to develop a Roofline Performance Model (Roofline) for KNL [23]. We find that the roofline model provides
an important framework for the optimization conversation with code teams. The
KNL hardware provides many new features like dual 512-bit vector units, up to

© Springer International Publishing AG 2016
M. Taufer et al. (Eds.): ISC High Performance Workshops 2016, LNCS 9945, pp. 339–353, 2016.
DOI: 10.1007/978-3-319-46079-6_24

288 hardware threads and the addition of on-package high-bandwidth memory. The roofline model enables a code team to determine which of these new hardware features they should target. For example, in a memory bandwidth bound code optimizations targeting better vectorization would be fruitless until other optimizations targeting data-reuse are considered.

In this paper, we will present an overview of the Roofline Model, describe the methodology and tools that were used to characterize code performance, and briefly describe some of the optimizations that were made to improve performance.

2   The Roofline Model and Arithmetic Intensity

Bottlenecks associated with in-core computation (as opposed to network communication or I/O) are often characterized by instruction- or data-level parallelism within a loop nest as derived from instruction latencies, throughputs, and vector widths of the target processor [3]. Unfortunately, today, it is far more common that performance bottlenecks are associated with the movement of data through the deep cache/memory hierarchy. In an ideal architecture, cache and memory latencies are effectively hidden through a variety of techniques (out-of-order execution, prefetching, multithreading, DMA, etc.) leaving bandwidth as the ultimate constraint. Thus, loop nest (kernel) execution time can be bound by the volume of data movement and the bandwidth to the level of memory capable of containing that data. This bound can be refined by the instruction- and data-level parallelism inherent in the kernel and demanded by the architecture. Although this bound is specific to a particular problem size, one can transform the relationship in order to bound the performance a processor can attain for a given computation. The resultant Roofline Bound [21,22] is shown in Eq. 1 where the *Arithmetic Intensity* (AI) represents the total number of floating-point operations performed by the kernel divided by the total resultant data movement after being filtered by the cache.

$$\text{GFLOP/s} = \min \begin{cases} \text{Peak GFLOP/s} \\ \text{Peak GB/s} \times \text{Arithmetic Intensity} \end{cases} \quad (1)$$

Consider the canonical STREAM TRIAD kernel x[i] = a[i] + alpha * b[i];: We observe each iteration of this kernel reads two doubles, performs one FMA, write allocates one double, and writes back one double. This provides an arithmetic intensity of 0.0625 FLOPs per byte. On a system with 10 GB/s of memory bandwidth and 100 GFlop/s of peak performance, the Roofline model will bound performance at 0.625 GFlop/s or less than 1 % of peak.

Although the STREAM TRIAD kernel has no data locality, stencils like a canonical 7-point constant coefficient stencil do. Although such a kernel presents 7 reads and one write to the cache subsystem, in an ideal execution, all but one read and one write allocate/writeback should be filtered by the cache. As such, the ultimate arithmetic intensity for such a kernel is 0.291 FLOPs per byte.

Failure to attain this arithmetic intensity (as measured by memory controller performance counters) is indicative of a discrepancy between the cache requirements as presented by the code and the cache capacity provided by the processor, and strongly motivates effective cache blocking (loop tiling).

Although the 7-point stencil performs 7 floating-point operations, they are actually a mix of 6 adds and 1 multiply. For architectures that execute multiplies and adds in different pipelines, peak performance may only be attained if the dynamic instruction mix is balanced. In this example, the effective peak is only 58 % of the peak on a machine that implements FMA or separate multiple and add pipelines. Although, the bandwidth-intensive nature of the 7-point stencil precludes it from being compute-limited, other kernels may be sensitive to this imbalance.

We may similarly refine the "Peak GFlop/s" of Eq. 1 into a function of the instruction-, data-level parallelism within the kernel. Whereas the former is often attributed to a lack of loop unrolling, the latter is often associated with an inability to vectorize the kernel in order to target 128-, 256-, or 512-bit vector instructions. Regardless, the penalty on the performance bounds can be severe — up to 80× on an Intel Knights Landing processor.

Figure 1a presents a generic Roofline model in which performance is plotted as a function of arithmetic intensity. Additional "ceilings" denote restricted performance bounds derived from the lack of parallelism. For each kernel, a series of "walls" can be constructed based on the difference in total data movement (compulsory, capacity, conflict) and the theoretical data movement lower bound (compulsory cache misses) [8]. For working sets that fit in main memory, performance is initially bound by memory bandwidth. Cache blocking will increase arithmetic intensity, but will require some degree of vectorization to improve performance.

3   Target Hardware Architecture

Cori is a Cray XC40 [5] based supercomputer and is being deployed in two phases. Phase 1 uses Intel Haswell multi-core processors and was deployed late-2015.

- Cray XC40 architecture with the Aries Dragonfly topology high speed network
- 1,630 compute nodes, where each node contains 2, 16-core, 2.3 GHz Haswell processors and 128 GB DDR4 2133 MHz memory
- 1.92 PFLOP/s (theoretical peak)
- 203 TB aggregate memory
- 30 PB scratch storage with a peak bandwidth of > 700 GB/sec

Phase 2, scheduled for deployment mid-2016, will be an expansion of Cori and add over 9,300 Intel Knights Landing based nodes. Since Cori's KNL based partition is still to be deployed, the KNL results were collected using standalone Intel white boxes with pre-production KNL processors.

- KNL preproduction, B0 stepping
- 64 cores @ 1.3 GHz with 4 hyper-threads per core (256 total threads)

- 16 GB MCDRAM, >460 GB/sec peak bandwidth
- 96 GB (6 × 16 GB) DDR4 @ 2133 GHz, 102 GB/sec peak

For this study, all results are collected with a single Cori Haswell based node and then compared to a single KNL white box. Multi-node analysis will be the subject of future studies. We used MPI and at least one rank per socket to avoid NUMA effects in Cori's dual-socket Haswell node. In addition, for most applications we used the Linux *numactl* utility to control memory affinity on the KNL, targeting MCDRAM only (*numactl -m 1*) or DDR4 only (*numactl -m 0, or without numactl*) in our tests. All applications use double-precision floating-point unless stated otherwise.

4   Tools and Methods

Using the Empirical Roofline Toolkit (ERT) [10,23], we measured the maximum sustained bandwidth at each level of the cache hierarchy and the maximum sustained floating-point rate for the KNL processor. We configured the toolkit with the following parameters:

- ERT_CC mpiicc
- ERT_CFLAGS -O3 -xMIC-AVX512 -fno-alias -fno-fnalias -DERT_INTEL
- ERT_FLOPS 1,2,4,8,16,32,64,128
- ERT_ALIGN 64
- ERT_MPI_PROCS 1,2,4,8,16
- ERT_PROCS_THREADS 256
- ERT_OPENMP_THREADS 1-256
- ERT_NUM_EXPERIMENTS 3
- ERT_MEMORY_MAX 8589934592

ERT performs a sweep of all the specified MPI rank combinations specified by ERT_MPI_PROCS. For each MPI sweep it executes a computational kernel with ERT_FLOPS operations per loop iteration. ERT keeps the total concurrency (ERT_PROCS_THREADS) fixed for each sweep, so as the number of MPI ranks increases, the number of threads per rank decreases an equal amount. We used the toolkit's nominal *driver1* and *kernel1*[1]. The toolkit then searches all results and uses the maximum values found for the L1, L2 and DRAM interfaces. The results are shown in Fig. 1b. The Linux utility *numactl* was used to target MCDRAM (flag *-m 1*) or DDR4 (flag *-m 0*) respectively.

The KNL is capable of being configured in multiple different MCDRAM and sub-NUMA modes. An explanation of all the possible configurations is beyond the scope of this paper, but can be found in Sodani's Hot Chips presentation [18]. The ERT was applied using Quad-Cache, Quad-Flat, Sub-NUMA Cluster 2 (SNC2) and Sub-NUMA Cluster 4 (SNC4) modes to determine if there was a significant difference in performance. All four modes provided equivalent floating-point performance, which is expected with the ERT as the peak floating-point rates are achieved with a working set that fits in L1 cache. The MCDRAM

---

[1] We added a *#pragma unroll (8)* around the inner loop to enable vectorization.

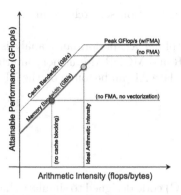

(a) Generic Roofline Performance

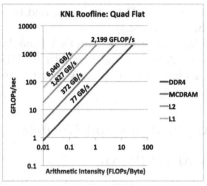

(b) KNL ERT Performance

Fig. 1. 1a) Generic Roofline representation showing the ultimate bounds on performance, bandwidth, and arithmetic intensity, with ceilings to denote limitations from a lack of various forms of parallelism. 1b) Applying the Roofline Toolkit, we estimate KNL maximum sustained memory bandwidth for the L1 and L2 caches, the MCDRAM and DDR4 bandwidth, and the maximum sustained performance in GFLOP/s.

Table 1. ERT performance for different KNL memory modes

	Quad cache	Quad flat	Sub-NUMA cluster 2	Sub-NUMA cluster 4
GFLOP/s	2,205	2,199	2,224	2,212
MCDRAM GB/s	345	372	381	415
DDR4 GB/s	-	77	77	77

performance does vary, with Quad-Cache mode giving the lowest performance, Quad-Flat and SNC2 providing near equal bandwidths, and SNC4 giving the best performance, 20 % higher than Quad-Cache. The results of the ERT are used to form the roofline for the applications and kernels in Sect. 5 (Table 1).

Unless otherwise noted, *all application results presented in the following sections are for Quad-Flat mode* as at time of this study it was the most mature from a software and firmware perspective. In addition, we did collect application data for SNC2, SNC4 and in some cases Quad-Cache but did not see performance differences greater than 20 % from that obtained with Quad-Flat and we feel Quad-Flat is representative of all modes except Quad-Cache. We will do a more extensive and detailed comparison in future studies.

We used Intel's Software Development Emulator (SDE) [17,19] to count the number of floating-point operations. SDE is capable of dynamic instruction tracing, and we use this capability to obtain total instructions executed, the instruction type (e.g. read, read width, single-precision, double-precision, fused multiply-add, SIMD width, etc.), and the instruction set architecture grouping (e.g. SSE, AVX, etc.).

For this study, we use Intel's VTune Amplifier XE performance analysis tool to measure data movement at both the DDR and MCDRAM memory interfaces. A tutorial for using SDE and VTune to calculate AI can be found on the NERSC web site [7,14].

5   Applications and Kernels

5.1   WARP-PICSAR

WARP is an open-source particle-in-cell (PIC) code designed to simulate charged particle beams and laser-matter interaction [9]. To aid in preparing for Cori, the library PICSAR has been developed. This library contains a Fortran kernel based on WARP with optimized subroutines. These high-performance subroutines are interfaced with a python class that can be imported and used in WARP scripts. It also contains a stand-alone Fortran code that is used as a test bed for optimization and profiling. The typical PIC kernel is composed of a time loop with four intermediate steps: the Maxwell solver, the field gathering, the particle pusher and the current deposition [4]. For many cases, interpolation processes such as the current deposition and the field gathering represents the most costly steps and are weakly vectorized in their common form.

A first optimization is the implementation of a hybrid threaded parallelization. PIC codes usually use a domain decomposition with one MPI process per subdomain. OpenMP provides a second level of parallelization inside subdomains. The subdomains are then divided into tiles, i.e. small portion of the subdomain having their own particle property arrays. Tiling improves memory locality and significantly diminishes RAM memory access (cache reuse). With more tiles than OpenMP threads, tiles computation is automatically load balanced with the OpenMP scheduler. On Haswell, field grid arrays can be fully contained in L2 when tile dimension is sufficiently small (below $8 \times 8x8$). On KNL, tile field arrays can be in L2 (512 KB) whereas all the problem is contained in the HBM.

Direct current deposition and field gathering interpolation steps were rewritten to enable more efficient vectorization than the classical form [20]. Vectorization is done by adding !$OMP SIMD directives. In addition, a particle cell sorting process has been added. Performed on every given time step in each tile, it further improves cache reuse and memory locality while accessing particle properties, especially during the current deposition and field gathering.

As a test case, we consider a Maxwellian homogeneous plasma with initial thermal velocity of 0.1c. The domain discretization is of $100 \times 100 \times 100$ cells with 20 super-particles per cell. The simulations are performed on a node of Haswell with 2 MPI tasks and 16 OpenMP threads, and on Intel Xeon Phi KNL with 4 MPI tasks and 32 OpenMP threads. Performance can be slightly better when hyper-threading is used on KNL: we use 2 threads per core. Tile dimension is of $8 \times 8x8$ cells. The tile size is 250 KB for internal temporary current grids

Table 2. PICSAR arithmetic intensity and performance

Optimization	Haswell		KNL MCDRAM		KNL DDR		KNL/HSW speedup
	AI	GFLOP/s	AI	GFLOP/s	AI	GFLOP/s	
Original	0.57	16.7	0.13	5.6	0.13	5.4	0.34
Tiling	1.10	32.0	0.56	20.0	0.56	19.2	0.63
Tiling+Vectorization	1.50	67.5	0.81	60.4	0.81	49.4	0.89

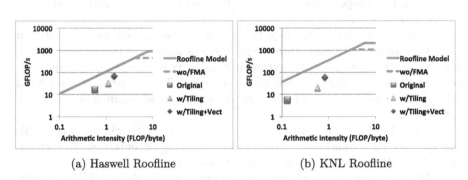

(a) Haswell Roofline   (b) KNL Roofline

Fig. 2. The tiling optimization increases AI and moves the data point to the right. Applying the vectorization optimization allows PICSAR to take advantage of the additional effective memory bandwidth and increases the overall performance for both architectures.

(used for vectorization), 31 KB for local current grid and 640 KB for particle properties. On Haswell, the global field arrays (27 Mb) fit in L3 and the local tile field arrays fit in L2. On KNL, the problem is fully contained in the HBM. Local tile field arrays fit in L2. Memory management is still under study.

Arithmetic intensities for each of the optimization steps is shown in Table 2. Figure 2 illustrates applying the results to the Roofline Model, demonstrating how tiling and vectorization improve AI and increase overall performance, reaching a higher memory bandwidth ceiling.

After tiling and vectorization optimizations, memory locality is improved, resulting in an overall performance improvement for both architectures. Performance relative to the original code improves by a factor of 4.0 for Haswell and 10.8 for KNL MCDRAM. Although final KNL performance is 0.89 times that of Haswell, it is important to note that both architectures benefited from the optimizations with KNL demonstrating the largest individual gain. For KNL, the speedup seen by using MCDRAM vs. DDR is 1.2, demonstrating that to some degree PICSAR is memory bandwidth bound.

5.2   EMGeo

In geophysical-imaging, medium properties can be studied by performing scattering experiments using electromagnetic or seismic waves. Quantities such as densities, elasticities, stress etc. of the medium can be obtained from fitting the observed measurements to the results predicted by a simulation. The code EMGeo performs these simulations and solves the inverse scattering problem in the Laplace-Fourier domain [16]. We focus only on the Seismic part and forward step of the inverse scattering problem, which involves inverting a large sparse matrix. For this purpose, EMGeo uses an Induced Dimensional Reduction (IDR) Krylov subspace solver.

The Sparse Matrix Vector (SpMV) product is responsible for two thirds of the total runtime. EMGeo performs SpMV operations using two low-bandwidth matrices (with maximum of 12 nonzero per row). We use the larger matrix in our benchmark. The production code evaluates about 256 independent right hand sides (RHS) in column major format. All the arrays are stored in double-complex data format.

We use Sliced ELLPack (SELL) sparse matrix format, Spatial Blocking (SB), and multiple right hand sides (nRHS) cache blocking optimizations to increase AI and thus the performance in the SpMV operations.

Table 3 summarizes our optimization improvements in the SpMV benchmark. For EMGeo, we only used a single socket on the Cori Haswell node to avoid NUMA issues and aid in analyzing the code characteristics. With full optimization, the GFLOP/s rate increases by a factor of 4.1 on Haswell and 3.9 on KNL. The KNL rate is 3.6× better than in a single Haswell socket, mainly due to the high memory bandwidth in KNL, where the benchmark is memory bandwidth bound. The SELLPack format reduces the FLOP count and data movement, so the AI and GFLOP/s values do not reflect the actual improvement in execution time where we see a 5.0× speedup in Haswell, a 4.8× speedup on KNL and a 3.6× speedup of KNL relative to Haswell.

Although the SB optimization improves the performance in Haswell, it degrades the performance in KNL, even after tuning the cache blocks size. We believe that the SB technique is effective when a large shared cache memory

Table 3. EMGeo arithmetic intensity and performance. "Best" referts to SB in Haswell and loop reordering in KNL

Optimization	Haswell (1 Sckt)		KNL MCDRAM		KNL DDR		KNL/HSW speedup
	AI	GFLOP/s	AI	GFLOP/s	AI	GFLOP/s	
Original	0.31	19.2	0.27	71.1	0.27	23.5	3.7
SELL	0.27	16.9	0.24	71.0	0.24	21.2	4.2
SB	0.34	20.2	0.28	62.3	0.28	20.9	3.1
SELL+SB	0.31	19.2	0.26	63.9	0.26	19.6	3.3
nRHS+SELL+Best	1.29	77.7	0.76	278.5	0.76	65.8	3.6

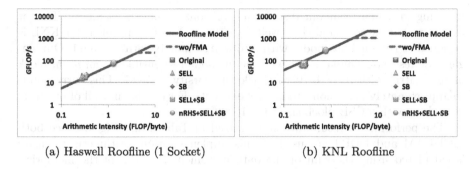

(a) Haswell Roofline (1 Socket)   (b) KNL Roofline

Fig. 3. The EMGeo roofline analysis shows that on Haswell and KNL the code is memory bound, and despite the optimizations performed on the code only modest improvements in performance are made. However, adding multiple right hand sides improves memory locality and hence improves AI, with a corresponding improvement in performance.

is available, which is the case for Haswell, but not KNL. We replace the SB in KNL's code in the last row of Table 3 with loop reordering, which is equivalent to SB of size one. Our roofline analysis shows that our optimizations improved the arithmetic intensity from 0.3 to 1.3 in Haswell and from 0.3 to 0.8 in KNL, as shown in Figure 3. The SpMV optimization translates into an overall speedup of 1.8× in Haswell and 3.3× in KNL for the forward step of the full application, using a grid of size $100 \times 50 \times 50$. The Details of this study are available in [11].

5.3 MFDn

The Many-body Fermion Dynamics for nuclei (MFDn) code is a nuclear physics code in which the lowest few eigenvalues and eigenvectors of a very large real sparse symmetric matrix are found though iterative means [12]. Sparse matrix vector and and sparse matrix transpose vector products are key kernels in the iterative eigensolver. The sparse matrix is stored in a compressed sparse block coordinate (CSB_COO) [1,2] format which allows efficient linear algebra operations on the large sparse matrix. The sparse matrix elements and corresponding indices account for 64 GB of the memory and the input/output vectors account for up to 16 GB depending on the specific problem.

Improving data reuse, allowing vectorization and effectively using as much aggregate bandwidth as possible are key challenges. We therefore replaced sparse matrix vector (SpMV) with sparse matrix-matrix (SpMM) operations on blocks of vectors. To better utilize memory bandwidth we explicitly place the input/output vectors in MCDRAM and the rest of the code and data reside in DDR4. Generally the larger the block of vector operations that can be done simultaneously (the number of right hand sides (nRHS)) the better the performance, however the number of vectors is limited by the available MCDRAM.

Our test problem consists of 2 protons and 6 neutrons. The sparsity structure is determined by the many body basis states and quantum selection rules resulting in a quasi-random distribution of nonzero matrix elements. That it is, the matrix is not banded or well structured. The test problem for KNL is designed to run on 4,560 nodes with a total nxn matrix with $n = 3e11$. Our single node test case simulates the work of one node responsible for an mxm block of the matrix with $m = 1e10$ with a local sparsity of 5e−7. This corresponds to approximately 7.5e9 nonzero matrix elements. For consistency all of our tests were done with a CSB block size, $\beta = 16000$.

The performance results are summarized in Table 4 and Fig. 4. Since both MCDRAM and DDR4 are used in this implementation, arithmetic intensity is calculated using the sum of the data movement for both of the memories. All floating-point calculations are single precision and the Roofline model in Fig. 4 is adjusted accordingly, although current performance is no where close to GFLOP/s ceiling. Using 8 RHS improves performance by a factor of 2.9 for Haswell and 6.4 for KNL. KNL performance is 1.6 times that of Haswell, and 3.6 times better than using DDR only, the latter demonstrating MFDn is memory bandwidth bound.

Table 4. MFDn arithmetic intensity and performance

nRHS	Haswell		KNL MCDRAM		KNL DDR		KNL/HSW speedup
	AI	GFLOP/s	AI	GFLOP/s	AI	GFLOP/s	
1	0.23	23.2	0.13	17.1	0.13	13.5	0.74
4	0.62	56.8	0.25	62.4	0.25	27.8	1.1
8	0.80	67.5	0.30	109.1	0.30	30.7	1.6

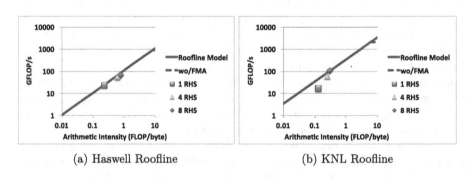

(a) Haswell Roofline   (b) KNL Roofline

Fig. 4. MFDn clearly meets the bandwidth bound portion of the roofline model (single precision FP only). By increasing the number of simultaneous vectors (RHS), performance improves as arithmetic intensity increases. However, the number of RHS is limited by available MCDRAM capacity.

5.4   BerkeleyGW

BerkeleyGW is a materials science application for computing excited state properties of materials - those associated with electrons populating orbitals beyond the quantum ground state [6]. BerkeleyGW takes as input the ground-state data computed from a number of DFT codes like Quantum ESPRESSO, SIESTA, PARATEC. The code is dominated by dense linear algebra (Matrix Multiply (GEMM), Diagonalization and Inversion), FFTs and hand tuned code representing tensor contraction like operations expressed as large array reductions. We predominantly focus on the hand-tuned routines in our KNL preparation, which in recent years has become a more significant amount of the runtime of a GW calculations due to changing use cases. The performance of the FFTs and linear algebra steps will be discussed in a separate article on BGW performance.

Following our optimization process, we show the following data points for the baseline MPI-only code. in Table 5 and Fig. 5.

- We refactor primarily to support OpenMP threads and improved data-locality. The code at this point has a three loop structure, with an outer loop targeted at MPI, and nested inner-loops with large trip counts targeting threads and AVX parallelization.
- We factor the code to support compiler auto-vectorization by moving a innermost trip-count 3 loop outwards, remove cycle statements and conditionals.
- We add a layer of cache-blocking to effectively reuse the L2. We reordered loops to improve vectorization (moving a loop of trip count 3 outwards), improving AI. We introduce cache blocking around the trip-count 3 loop. On Haswell, we are able to effectively use L3 and so no again in AI is seen.
- We replace the complex divide with a manual divide over the real absolute value of the complex number in order to avoid x87 instruction generation.
- We put back in the explicitly complex divide but utilize the compiler flag *-fp-model fast = 2* which avoids x87 instructions by assuming there is no overflow concern. Additionally, we run with 2 threads per core, which is where most of the speedup occurs.

In summary, a few key lessons stand out from BerkeleyGW. For a code with an AI between 1–10 (i.e. near the roofline cusp), good performance requires, good data reuse out of L2 cache to reach the highest AI (KNL's lack of L3 can make it more punishing), placement of data in HBM, and good use of the vector processing units are all essential for good performance. The current limiting factor is the latency in the divides, lack of multiply add balance and remaining conditionals. After all the optimizations, performance relative to the original code improves by a factor of 11.8 for Haswell and 25.8 for KNL MCDRAM. The KNL demostrated a 1.35 times improvement over Haswell. Comparing KNL MCDRAM to KNL DDR, using MCDRAM allows for a performance improvement factor of 1.75.

Table 5. BerkeleyGW arithmetic intensity and performance

Optimization	Haswell		KNL MCDRAM		KNL DDR		KNL/HSW speedup
	AI	GFLOP/s	AI	GFLOP/s	AI	GFLOP/s	
Refactored	2.64	38.7	1.93	9.80	1.93	9.80	0.25
+Vectorized	3.68	100.3	0.66	143.4	0.66	55.1	1.43
+Blocked	3.77	100.3	1.79	153.2	1.79	140.8	1.53
+Improved Vect	3.78	142.6	1.80	178.4	1.80	142.1	1.25
+Hyperthreads	3.27	186.9	1.76	252.6	1.76	144.0	1.35

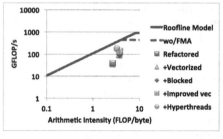

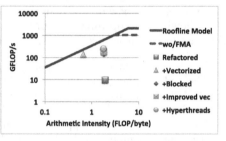

(a) Haswell Roofline   (b) KNL Roofline

Fig. 5. BerkeleyGW is a good example of an application that benefited from blocking, threading and vectorization improvements. For Haswell, *+Blocked* provides no further improvement over *+Vectorized*, due to the fact that the working set fits within the Haswell L3 cache. For KNL, *+Vectorized* performance is limited by MCDRAM BW (due to its low AI) and *+Blocked* is necessary to see improvements in further optimizations.

5.5   Performance Summary and Observations

Table 6 shows the fully optimized performance for each application or kernel. They all demonstrated significant performance gains over the baseline code for both Haswell and KNL architectures. The KNL architecture showed overall better performance than Haswell with the exception of PICSAR, however both architectures benefited significantly from the optimization process.

Applying results to the Roofline Model, no application or kernel had an AI that put it in the regime of being computational bound, all were in a region in which memory bandwidth was the limiting factor to performance. EMGeo and MFDn were clearly bandwidth bound, while PICSAR and BerkeleyGW showed there is headroom for further optimization.

We observe that Haswell consistently attains a higher AI than KNL. As all applications perform the same number of floating point operations, we conclude that KNL generally moves more data to/from main memory than Haswell. As a result, the theoretical performance benefits of higher MCDRAM bandwidth are not fully realized. Exploration of the performance tradeoffs between larger

Table 6. Performance summary

	GFLOP/s			Speedup	
	Haswell	KNL MCDRAM	KNL DDR	KNL/HSW	MCDRAM/DDR
PICSAR	67.5	60.4	49.4	0.89	1.2
EMGeo (SpMV)	77.7[a]	181.0	43.6	2.33[a]	4.2
MFDn	67.5	109.1	30.7	1.62	3.6
BerkeleyGW	186.9	252.6	144.0	1.35	1.75

a EMGeo Haswell performance is for a single socket.

on-chip L2/L3 caches (reduced data movement) and reduced computational performance (fewer cores for constant chip area) are in order.

6 Conclusion and Outlook

In this study we have developed a Roofline Model for the Intel Knights Landing processor and have estimated upper bounds for L1, L2, MCDRAM and DDR4. We then measured the performance of a suite of NESAP applications (or proxy kernels) and used the Roofline Model to determine to what degree they were compute- or memory-bound. Each application developer then explored a variety of optimizations to improve both arithmetic intensity and overall performance. We then re-evaluated the impact of those optimizations relative to the Roofline ceilings. All of the evaluated applications were able to substantially improve their overall performance on both Haswell and KNL processors, often by increasing the computational arithmetic intensity and improving memory bandwidth utilization. Having a visual representation of the performance ceiling helps guide application experts to appropriately focus their optimization efforts.

Acknowledgments. This research used resources of the National Energy Research Scientific Computing Center, a DOE Office of Science User Facility supported by the Office of Science of the U.S. Department of Energy under Contract No. DE-AC02-05CH11231.

This material is based upon work supported by the Advanced Scientific Computing Research Program in the U.S. Department of Energy, Office of Science, under Award Number DE-AC02-05CH11231.

J.D. was supported by the SciDAC Program on Excited State Phenomena in Energy Materials funded by the U. S. Department of Energy, Office of Basic Energy Sciences and of Advanced Scientific Computing Research, under Contract No. DE-AC02-05CH11231 at Lawrence Berkeley National Laboratory

References

1. Aktulga, H.M., Buluc, A., Williams, S., Yang, C.: Optimizing sparse matrix-multiple vector multiplication for nuclear configuration interaction calculations. In: International Parallel and Distributed Processing Symposium (IPDPS 2014), May 2014

2. Aktulga, H.M., Yang, C., Ng, E.G., Maris, P., Vary, J.P.: Improving the scalability of a symmetric iterative eigensolver for multi-core platforms. Concurrency Comput. Pract. Exp. **26**(16), 2631–2651 (2014). doi:10.1002/cpe.3129
3. Carr, S., Kennedy, K.: Improving the ratio of memory operations to floating-point operations in loops. ACM Trans. Program. Lang. Syst. **16**(6), 1768–1810 (1994). http://doi.acm.org/10.1145/197320.197366
4. Birdsall, C.K., Langdon, A.B.: Plasma Physics Via Computer Simulation. Series in Plasma Physics. CRC Press, Boca Raton (2005)
5. Cray xc series supercomputers. http://www.cray.com/products/computing/xc-series
6. Deslippe, J., Samsonidze, G., Strubbe, D.A., Jain, M., Cohen, M.L., Louie, S.G.: Berkeleygw: a massively parallel computer package for the calculation of the quasiparticle and optical properties of materials and nanostructures. Comput. Phys. Commun. **183**(6), 1269–1289 (2012). http://www.sciencedirect.com/science/article/pii/S0010465511003912
7. Doerfler, D.: Understanding application data movement characteristics using intel vtune amplifier and software development emulator tools. In: IXPUG 2015, Berkeley, CA, September 28 - October 2 2015
8. Hill, M.D., Smith, A.J.: Evaluating associativity in CPU caches. IEEE Trans. Comput. **38**(12), 1612–1630 (1989)
9. Lawrence Berkeley National Laboratory.: Warp website. http://warp.lbl.gov
10. Ligocki, T.: Roofline toolkit. https://bitbucket.org/berkeleylab/cs-roofline-toolkit
11. Malas, T., Kurth, T., Deslippe, J.: Optimization of the sparse matrix-vector products of an idr krylov iterative solver for the intel knl manycore processor (in preparation)
12. Maris, P., Aktulga, H.M., Caprio, M.A., Çatalyürek, Ü.V., Ng, E.G., Oryspayev, D., Potter, H., Saule, E., Sosonkina, M., Vary, J.P., Yang, C., Zhou, Z.: Large-scale ab initio configuration interaction calculations for light nuclei. J. Phys. Conf. Ser. **403**(1), 012019 (2012). http://stacks.iop.org/1742-6596/403/i=1/a=012019
13. NERSC: Cori. https://www.nersc.gov/systems/cori/
14. NERSC: Measuring arithmetic intensity. https://www.nersc.gov/users/application-performance/measuring-arithmetic-intensity
15. Nesap. http://www.nersc.gov/users/computational-systems/cori/nesap/
16. Petrov, P.V., Newman, G.A.: 3d finite-difference modeling of elasticwave propagation in the laplace-fourier domain. Geophysics **77**(4), T137–T155 (2012). doi:10.1190/geo2011-0238.1
17. Raman, K.: Calculating "flop" using intel software developmentemulator (intelsde) (March 2015). https://software.intel.com/en-us/articles/calculating-flop-using-intel-software-development-emulator-intel-sde
18. Sodani, A.: Knights landing (knl): 2nd generation intel xeon phiprocessor. In: Hot Chips 27. Flint Center, Cupertino, August 23rd-25th 2015. http://www.hotchips.org/wp-content/uploads/hc_archives/hc27/HC27.25-Tuesday-Epub/HC27.25.70-Processors-Epub/HC27.25.710-Knights-Landing-Sodani-Intel.pdf
19. Tal, A.: Intel software development emulator. https://software.intel.com/en-us/articles/intel-software-development-emulator
20. Vincenti, H., Lehe, R., Sasanka, R., Vay, J.: An efficient and portable SIMD algorithm for charge/current deposition in Particle-In-Cell codes. ArXiv e-prints, January 2016
21. Williams, S.: Auto-tuning Performance on Multicore Computers. Ph.D. thesis, EECS Department, University of California, Berkeley, December 2008

22. Williams, S., Watterman, A., Patterson, D.: Roofline: an insightful visual performance model for floating-point programs and multicore architectures. Commun. ACM **52**(4), 65–76 (2009)
23. Williams, S., Stralen, B.V., Ligocki, T., Oliker, L., Cordery, M., Lo, L.: Roofline performance model. http://crd.lbl.gov/departments/computer-science/PAR/research/roofline/

Dynamic SIMD Vector Lane Scheduling

Olaf Krzikalla[1]([⊠]), Florian Wende[2], and Markus Höhnerbach[3]

[1] Technische Universität, Dresden, Germany
olaf.krzikalla@tu-dresden.de
[2] Zuse Institute, Berlin, Germany
wende@zib.de
[3] RWTH University, Aachen, Germany
hoehnerbach@aices.rwth-aachen.de

Abstract. A classical technique to vectorize code that contains control flow is a control-flow to data-flow conversion. In that approach statements are augmented with masks that denote whether a given vector lane participates in the statement's execution or idles. If the scheduling of work to vector lanes is performed statically, then some of the vector lanes will run idle in case of control flow divergences or varying work intensities across the loop iterations. With an increasing number of vector lanes, the likelihood of divergences or heavily unbalanced work assignments increases and static scheduling leads to a poor resource utilization. In this paper, we investigate different approaches to dynamic SIMD vector lane scheduling using the Mandelbrot set algorithm as a test case. To overcome the limitations of static scheduling, idle vector lanes are assigned work items dynamically, thereby minimizing per-lane idle cycles. Our evaluation on the Knights Corner and Knights Landing platform shows, that our approaches can lead to considerable performance gains over a static work assignment. By using the AVX-512 vector compress and expand instruction, we are able to further improve the scheduling.

Keywords: SIMD vectorization · Dynamic scheduling · Intel Xeon Phi

1 Introduction

Programming for modern manycore processors, like Intel's Xeon Phi Knights Corner and upcoming Knights Landing, involves SIMD parallelism as a key mechanism to performance. Unlike multi-processing and -threading, the Single-Instruction Multiple-Data execution model poses the difficulty to orchestrate an increasingly large number of tightly coupled execution streams for which there is only one program state. The latter means that the achievable (overall) performance gain with VL SIMD vector lanes can be close to VL if the program contains only simple loop structures with no control flow divergences—which for many scientific codes is not the case. Straightforward single loop vectorization with a static assignment of loop iterations to SIMD lanes hence will not work when aiming at an efficient utilization of the respective compute resources.

© Springer International Publishing AG 2016
M. Taufer et al. (Eds.): ISC High Performance Workshops 2016, LNCS 9945, pp. 354–365, 2016.
DOI: 10.1007/978-3-319-46079-6_25

Recent compiler development as well as the introduction of the OpenMP 4.x SIMD constructs constitute massive improvements in compiler vectorization capabilities. While irregular control flow and function call hierarchy within SIMD contexts can be handled effectively by current compilers, they do not handle the inherent issue of idle vector lanes when loads are unbalanced, yet.

Dynamic SIMD vector lane scheduling approaches this issue by scheduling loop iterations to SIMD lanes at runtime, depending on load imbalances across the lanes. The goal is that all SIMD lanes consistently perform meaningful calculations instead of—in the case of static scheduling—waiting for a single lane to complete before moving on to the next set of iterations. As a non-trivial user-level optimization, dynamic scheduling, however, is code invasive and requires user assistance that is beyond the capability of current compiler directives.

The Mandelbrot algorithm is a well known representative of unbalanced workloads. In this paper, we describe different ways to implement dynamic SIMD vector lane scheduling for the Mandelbrot algorithm. Particularly, we

- contrast using low-level SIMD intrinsics coding with high-level approaches using either OpenMP 4.x compiler directives or array notation.
- discuss for the different implementations their portability with respect to code adaptations and performance on different target platforms.
- host our SIMD versions of the Mandelbrot algorithm as open source code [2].

Related Work: On GPUs, under-utilization of available SIMD resources has already been identified as an performance issue for some time. Consequently, dynamic scheduling has been explored on such architectures [4,6]. For traditional SIMD machines the problem of under-utilization has only recently shifted into focus due to increases in vector width and the necessity to exploit it [10]. Some automatic tools have explored the possibility for dynamic scheduling [7,8] for a limited selection of loop patterns.

2   Mandelbrot Set

The Mandelbrot set is the set of complex numbers c, such that the sequence $z_0 = 0, z_{k+1} = z_k^2 + c$, stays bounded. In practice, this condition is checked by iterating through the sequence, until $|z_k|$ exceeds a certain bound, or "sufficiently many" elements in the sequence have been considered. For visualization purposes, the index k, at which one of these conditions is fulfilled, is used. This is known as the *escape time algorithm*, given in Listing 1. In the images that it computes, each pixel corresponds to a value c, and the pixel value is the escape time.

Figure 1 visualizes the kind of images produced by Listing 1. Each image has a resolution of 1920 by 1200 pixels, each pixel being colored according to the escape time k. The first setup (*full*) produces the most popular image of the Mandelbrot set by varying c between $-2 - 1i$ and $1 + 1i$ with an iteration limit of 100. The second setup (*zoomed*) magnifies a section of the Mandelbrot set from $c = -0.74544 - 0.113225i$ to $c = -0.74514 - 0.112925i$ with an iteration limit 10000. As the picture is zoomed in, the iteration limit has to be increased

(a) *full* image.

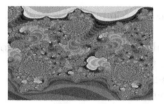

(b) *zoomed* image.

Fig. 1. Images of the Mandelbrot set used for assessing the algorithm performance.

in order to visualize details. Consequently, the potential for load unbalance is higher in the second image, as evident by the large, noisy sections within it.

SIMD Vectorization: Computing an image of the Mandelbrot set using the escape time algorithm is a typical example of an embarrassingly parallel problem. Every pixel of the image can be computed independently. A vectorization of the pixel loop requires a transformation of the control flow to a data flow model, where a block of VL pixels is processed at once. Listing 1 demonstrates a possible approach using wrapper classes for Intel Cilk Plus Array Notation [3,9]. The approach exploits the fact, that once a complex number meets the escape criteria ($|z| \geq 2$), then also all following numbers will meet that criteria. Thus a vectorized iteration is executed for all vector lanes until either all numbers have escaped or the maximum iteration count is reached. The number of iterations needed to compute a block of pixels is equal to the pixel requiring the largest number of iterations.

```
1   void Mandelbrot(float c_re,          void Mandelbrot_SIMD(float c_re[VL],
2                   float c_im,                                float c_im[VL],
3                   int maxIter,                               int maxIter,
4                   int& out){                                 int out[VL]){
5     complex<float>                        complex<float_array>
6       c(c_re,c_im),                         c(c_re[0:VL],c_im[0:VL]),
7       z(0.0f,0.0f);                         z(0.0f,0.0f);
8     int n=0;                              int n=0;
9                                           int_array n_array(0),mask;
10    for(n=0; n<maxIter; n++){            for(n=0; n<maxIter; n++){
11                                           mask=(norm(z)<2.0f);
12      if(norm(z)>=2.0f)                    if(all_zero(mask))
13        break;                               break;
14      z=z*z+c;                             z=z*z+c;
15                                           n_array+=mask;
16    }                                    }
17    out=n;                              out[0:VL]=n_array[0:VL];
18  }                                    }
```

Listing 1. Scalar and SIMD version of the Mandelbrot set escape time algorithm.

Figure 2 depicts this execution scheme for two blocks of 4 pixels on $VL = 4$ SIMD lanes. Solid gray boxes represent per-vector-lane iterations for which the

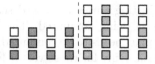

Fig. 2. A sample workload distribution across vector lanes.

escape criteria is not met, whereas for unfilled boxes it is. The first block of 4 pixels needs 3, and the second block 5 iterations, respectively. Computing all 8 pixels thus requires a total of 8 iterations, giving a speedup of 2.5 over executing all 20 pixels one after another in scalar fashion. Since some computation slots (unfilled boxes) are not used for meaningful computation, the parallel efficiency for $VL = 4$ is at most 0.625. Executing the same distribution of iterations on $VL = 8$ SIMD lanes requires 5 iterations, and gives a maximum parallel efficiency of 0.5, and even lower values for VL larger than 8.

Table 1 confirms this observation for the two Mandelbrot images shown in Fig. 1. We have calculated the expected maximum *Speedups* and parallel *Efficiencies* based on the count distribution in the images. For this purpose, we have summed up the maximum iteration counts for $VL = 4, 8, 16$. The column *Iterations* represents the number of times the statement z=z*z+c is executed. As one can see, $VL = 4$ gives always reasonable speedups. However, for an architecture providing 16 SIMD vector lanes, the insufficient utilization of computation slots becomes the major performance road block for compute intense images.

Table 1. Achievable speedups using static vector lane scheduling.

Image	VL	Iterations	Speedup	Efficiency
full	scalar	69877898		
maxIter = 100	4	17898739	3.9	0.98
$x = -0.5 \pm 1.5$	8	9129166	7.65	0.96
$y = 0 \pm 1$	16	4692441	14.89	0.93
zoomed	scalar	370027284		
maxIter = 10000	4	119251980	3.1	0.78
$x = -0.74529 \pm 1.5e^{-4}$	8	71485539	5.18	0.65
$y = 0.113075 \pm 1.5e^{-4}$	16	43958870	8.42	0.53

3   Array as Value (AAV)

We have solved the problem of under-utilized SIMD vector lanes by scheduling the computation of pixels to SIMD vector lanes as soon as they finish their current computation. We have investigated two scheduling schemes that differ in their efficiency and programmability.

The program given in Listing 2 uses a *blocked* scheme. The vector `pixel` contains the indices of pixels being computed. The loop condition at line 5 checks whether at least one pixel needs to be computed. The condition inside the loop checks the escape criteria. Only for those vector lanes matching the escape criteria the condition body is executed. Inside the condition body the results of just escaped vector lanes are stored. Then these vector lanes are immediately initialized with the indices of the next pixels to be computed (line 9) and the start values for the actual computation (lines 10–12). Pixels are statically assigned to vector lanes—the index of a pixel modulo the vector length is the vector lane. Figure 3a depicts this scheduling scheme for the distribution of iterations from Fig. 2 across 4 vector lanes. This approach does not need any horizontal vector operations and is easily programmable using array notation. Due to the immediate reinitialization of escaped vector lanes the computation at line 15 nearly always utilizes all vector lanes. Only at the end of the computation some computation slots will remain unused. A vector lane might run out of work, even if there is still work left for other vector lanes.

```
1   void Mandelbrot(float c_re[N],float c_im[N],int maxIter,int out[N]){
2       complex<float_array> c(c_re[0:VL],c_im[0:VL]),z(0, 0);
3       int_array pixel(0,1,..,VL);
4       int_array count_array(0);
5       while(reduce_min(pixel)<N) {
6           int_array mask=(norm(z)<2.0f);
7           if((mask[:]==0 || count_array[:]==maxIter) && pixel[:]<N){
8               out[pixel[:]]=count_array[:];
9               pixel[:]+=VL;
10              count_array[:]=0; z.real[:]=z.imag[:]=0.0f;
11              if(pixel[:]<N){
12                  c.real[:]=c_re[pixel[:]]; c.imag[:]=c_im[pixel[:]];
13          } }
14          count_array+=1;
15          z=z*z+c;
16  } }
```

Listing 2. Mandelbrot kernel using dynamic blocked SIMD vector lane scheduling.

```
1   __m512i next={VL,VL+1,..,2*VL-1};
2   while(..){
3       __mmask16 mask=.. // test escape condition
4       if(escape_mask!=0){
5           _mm512_mask_i32scatter_epi32(image,mask,pixel,count_array,4);
6           pixel=_mm512_mask_expand_epi32(pixel,mask,next);
7           next=_mm512_add_epi32(next,_mm512_set1_epi32(_popcnt32(mask)));
8           // reinitialize masked lanes according to pixel
9   } }
```

Listing 3. Condition body using smoothed dynamic vector lane scheduling.

Therefore we have also investigated a *smoothed* scheme. In this scheme pixels are sequentially assigned to just finished vector lanes (Fig. 3b). This reduces the number of unused computation slots even further. The scheduling of the pixel numbers to vector lanes can be done using the expand instruction, which is available in the AVX-512 instruction set [1]. Since this instruction currently cannot be expressed using array notation, Listing 3 shows a possible implementation of the condition body using intrinsics: lines 6 and 7 replace the line 9 of Listing 2.

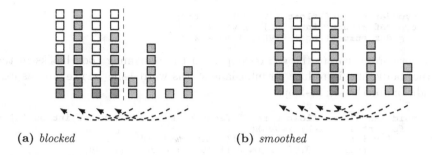

(a) *blocked*   (b) *smoothed*

Fig. 3. Dynamic scheduling of a workload distribution across SIMD vector lanes.

Table 2. Achievable speedups using blocked/smoothed dyn. vector lane scheduling.

Image	VL	Blocked dynamic			Smoothed dynamic		
		Iterations	Speedup	Efficiency	Iterations	Speedup	Efficiency
full	scalar	69877898			69877898		
	4	17548608	3.98	0.99	17470398	3.9997	1
	8	8828655	7.91	0.99	8735818	7.999	1
	16	4467240	15.64	0.98	4368581	15.996	1
zoomed	scalar	370027284			370027284		
	4	94491326	3.92	0.98	92609380	3.995	0.999
	8	48393462	7.65	0.96	46411004	7.97	0.996
	16	25215795	14.67	0.92	23385660	15.82	0.989

Table 2 presents the effectiveness of dynamic vector lane scheduling using the same method as for Table 1. It should be noted that the efficiency numbers in these tables consider only the inner loop computation. For the static scheduling approach SIMD vector lanes in the outer loop computations are fully utilized, whereas for dynamic scheduling approaches vector lanes in the inner loop computations are fully utilized. The outer loop of the Mandelbrot algorithm contains only the initialization of z and c. Additionally, the inner loop body will be executed much more often. Thus, the under-utilization in the outer loop becomes negligible, as confirmed by our experimental results in Sect. 6.

4   Enhanced Explicit Vectorization (EEV)

The "enhanced explicit vectorization" coding scheme is based on a combination of loop blocking with high-level vectors and compiler directives to process these vectors. We propose for the Mandelbrot kernel the following code transformation:

Step 1: Operate on blocks of pixels of size VL, and replace scalar data types by high-level vector data types, e.g. ($\#defineVL = 16$ for Xeon Phi):

```
typedef struct{ float x[VL]; } vec_f32;
typedef struct{ int x[VL]; } vec_i32;
typedef struct{ bool x[VL]; } mask_x32;
```

Furthermore, separate the while-loop from the remaining code blocks in the kernel body, and introduce an inter-lane status word lane_alife_any as exit condition for the while-loops:

```
1   void Mandelbrot(float c_re[N],float c_im[N],int maxIter,int out[N]){
2     for(int i=0; i<N; i+=VL){
3       for(int ii=0; ii<VL; ii++){ // data initialization
4         z_re.x[ii]=0.0f; z_im.x[ii]=0.0f; count.x[ii]=0;
5         lane_alife.x[ii]=((i+ii)<N ? true : false);
6       }
7       bool lane_alife_any=true;
8       while(lane_alife_any){ // compute: moved the innermost loop into the while loop
9         for(int ii=0; ii<VL; ii++){
10          if(lane_alife.x[ii]){
11            if(count.x[ii]<maxIter && (z_re.x[ii]*..)<4.0f){
12              count.x[ii]++; z_im.x[ii]=..; z_re.x[ii]=..;
13            } else lane_alife.x[ii]=false; // this lane is done
14        } }
15        lane_alife_any=false;
16        for(int ii=0; ii<VL; ii++)
17          if(lane_alife.x[ii]) // exit condition: does any lane continue the loop execution?
18            lane_alife_any=true;
19      }
20      for(int ii=0; ii<VL; ii++)
21        if((i+ii)<N) out[i+ii]=count.x[ii]; // unpack results into the output array
22  } }
```

Each SIMD lane stores its activity status in the vector lane_alife. Only if for none of the active lanes the predicate count.x[ii]<maxIter&&..<4.0f evaluates to true, the while-loop stop.

Step 2: Replace the "for(int i=0;..)"-loop by an index vector vi which for each SIMD lane holds the loop iteration that is currently processed. Every time the current iteration is done, the index is moved forward (by VL in the code below). In addition to the lane_alife status vector, we introduce a vector lane_acquire_work to signal the lanes' idle state:

```
1   void Mandelbrot(float c_re[N],float c_im[N],int maxIter,int out[N]){
2     for(int ii=0; ii<VL; ii++){ // Prologue: data initialization
3       ............ // same as in step 2
4       vi.x[ii]=ii; lane_alife.x[ii]=(vi.x[ii]<N ? true : false);
5       lane_acquire_work.x[ii]=false;
6     }
7     bool lane_alife_any=true;
8     while(lane_alife_any){ // Compute: process current loop iterations
9       for(int ii=0; ii<VL; ii++){
10        if(lane_alife.x[ii]){
11          if(count.x[ii]<maxIter && (z_re.x[ii]*..)<4.0f){
12            ............ // same as in step 2
13          } else lane_acquire_work.x[ii]=true; // replaces lane_alife.x[ii]=false
14      } }
15      lane_alife_any=false;
16      for(int ii=0; ii<VL; ii++){ // pre-scheduling of loop iterations
17        if(lane_acquire_work.x[ii]){
18          out[vi.x[ii]]=count.x[ii]; // store result of current iteration
19          vi.x[ii]+=VL; // move to the next set of loop iteration
20          ............ // initialize c_re, z_re, z_im, count as above
21          if(vi.x[ii]>=N) lane_alife.x[ii]=false; // this lane is done
```

```
22            lane_acquire_work.x[ii]=false;
23          }
24        if(lane_alife.x[ii])  // exit condition: are there lanes that continue the loop execution?
25          lane_alife_any=true;
26  } } }
```

All `for`-loops in Step 2 are candidates for vectorization, e.g., via the OpenMP 4.x compiler directive `#pragma omp simd simdlen(VL)`. In this way, the code is portable across different platforms (see Table 3) and compilers. However, the EEV approach is code invasive in that it might require to not just apply the scalar-to-vector replacement, but additionally to introduce some control logic around the code blocks to allow for efficient SIMD code generation.

The dynamic scheduling in Step 2 uses the *block* scheme where the index `vi` is moved forward by VL, thereby partitioning the total number N of loop iterations into disjoint sets $I_s = \{i = s + n\,\text{VL} \mid n = 0, \ldots, N/\text{VL} - 1\}$, s=0,...,VL-1. The implicit assumption is that $|I_s| \approx |I_{s'}|$ for all s, s'. The latter, however, is not always satisfied. Alternatively, we implement the *smoothed* scheduling scheme as described in Sect. 3. For that purpose, we initialize `vi` as above, and introduce a scalar variable `current_i=VL`. When pre-scheduling loop iterations, we create a vector `vi_next` whose entries on SIMD lanes that need to acquire new work follow from incrementing `current_i` serially. The respective loop is separated from the subsequent assignment `vi.x[ii]=vi_next.x[ii]` in line 20.

Optimization 1: Execute the pre-scheduling loop just if at least one SIMD lane needs to acquire new work. For that purpose we introduce an additional status word `lane_acquire_work_any`, which is initialized to `false` at the beginning of the `while`-loop body, and is set to `true` if any of the lanes sets its `lane_acquire_work` status flag. The pre-scheduling loop then is placed within a conditional block `if(lane_acquire_work_any) { <pre-scheduling loop> }`.

Optimization 2: Kernels that are not compute-intensive can benefit from not pre-scheduling successive loop iterations immediately when a SIMD lane becomes idle, but after a fixed number of `while`-loop iterations at earliest.

5 Low-Level Optimizations Using SIMD (INTR)insics

The previous techniques relied on the compiler's vectorization capabilities. Without changing the fundamental approach, the implementation can be formulated in terms of SIMD intrinsics. Such an implementation eliminates the majority of overheads that arise when mandating vectorization. While an intrinsics approach provides some cross-compiler portability, it is fundamentally hardware dependent—in our case targeting IMCI and AVX-512 devices. In contrast, other implementation techniques can run on CPUs as well. Vector classes [5] might lead to more maintainable and portable code while preserving low overheads.

The implementation using intrinsics (INTR) follows the same principles as the EEV implementation. Particular, it also supports the various optimizations that were applied there. For example, the intrinsics algorithm can be "widened" to compute any multiple of VL pixels at once, and can be "unrolled" to perform multiple iterations before checking if more work needs to be acquired.

One common source of overhead is spilling data from registers into memory where not necessary. Both the AAV and EEV approaches are prone to this issue, as the compiler needs to optimize out loads and stores in them. This issue does not arise when directly operating on register values with intrinsics. Intel SDE, an emulator that can target KNL, reports the number of reads and writes to stack memory: According to these counts, the EEV code accesses the stack six times more frequently than the intrinsics variant.

The intrinsics code also has a different instruction mix, where more fused-multiple-add (FMA) operations are generated by the compiler during optimization. According to SDE, the number of executed math vector instructions is roughly equal among EEV and INTR, but INTR executes three times as many FMAs. This might be due to the lower spilling rate of the intrinsics code, leaving more intermediate values in registers to be incorporated into FMAs.

Additional, but less impactful differences include manual unrolling, aiding the branch prediction using __builtin_expect and explicitly taking advantage of the expand instruction. However, the compiler seems to be keen on applying some of these tricks itself in the EEV version, too.

6   Measurements

We have conducted the experimental evaluation on three Intel systems:

- Xeon E5-2680v3, **Haswell** generation, 2.5GHz, 12 cores.
- Xeon Phi 5110P, **Knights Corner** generation, 1.053 GHz, 60 cores.
- **Knights Landing** preproduction system, B0 stepping, 1.3 GHz, 64 cores.

The programs were compiled using the Intel compiler version 16.0.2. The compilation option set used was: icc -O3 -std=c++11 [-mmic, -AVX512] Our performance metric is cycles (taken with rdtsc). Other than in the listings given in this paper the values for the complex variable c are computed on the fly.

Table 3 presents a collection of performance data for the presented approaches. For the *full* image, dynamic scheduling decreases performance. In that case, the iteration limit is low, and the image has large, uniform regions, resulting in little opportunity to exploit dynamic scheduling, and the overhead associated with it can not be amortized. Nevertheless, it is apparent that the three variants AAV, EEVS and INTS, which fundamentally use the same approach, all attain similar performance across all platforms. The additional optimizations in EEV and INTR lead to another significant speedup. Indeed, the performance gap between EEV and INTR decreases to just 20 % as optimizations are applied.

In the *zoom* image, the advantage of dynamic scheduling becomes apparent, being roughly 50 % faster (as opposed to 30 % slower) as the static scheduling for the AAV, EEVS and INTR, and leading to even higher speedups for EEV and INTR. Note that again the intrinsics and the portable solutions are close-by in terms of performance.

Table 3. Experimental comparison of scheduling vectorization approaches. $C = 10^6$ cycles, S = Speedup w.r.t. scalar, E = Efficiency = S/VL. EEVS = EEV without unrolling or widening, INTS = Intrinsics without unrolling or widening.

Image	Method	Knights landing			Knights corner			Haswell		
		C	S	E	C	S	E	C	S	E
full	scalar	1273			1908			748		
	AAV (static)	113	11.2	0.70	265	7.2	0.45	126	5.9	0.74
	INTS (static)	75	17.0	1.06	121	15.8	0.99	–		
	EEV (static)	64	19.9	1.24	139	13.7	0.86	82	9.1	1.14
	AAV (block)	191	6.7	0.42	289	6.6	0.41	241	3.1	0.39
	EEVS (block)	205	6.2	0.39	268	7.1	0.44	218	3.4	0.42
	EEVS (smooth)	200	6.4	0.40	290	6.6	0.41	225	3.3	0.41
	INTS (block)	141	9.1	0.57	204	9.3	0.58	–		
	INTS (smooth)	135	9.4	0.59	196	9.7	0.61	–		
	EEV (block)	61	21.0	1.31	161	11.8	0.74	137	5.5	0.69
	EEV (smooth)	63	20.1	1.26	161	11.8	0.74	144	5.2	0.65
	INTR (block)	51	24.8	1.55	140	13.6	0.85	–		
	INTR (smooth)	47	26.9	1.68	130	14.6	0.91	–		
zoomed	scalar	6824			9666			4310		
	AAV (static)	1021	6.7	0.42	2514	3.8	0.24	1021	4.2	0.53
	INTS (static)	662	10.3	0.64	1020	9.5	0.59	–		
	EEV (static)	666	10.2	0.64	1198	8.1	0.51	857	5.0	0.63
	AAV (block)	849	8.0	0.50	1305	7.4	0.46	1110	3.9	0.49
	EEVS (block)	884	7.7	0.48	1164	8.3	0.52	843	5.1	0.64
	EEVS (smooth)	833	8.2	0.51	1152	8.4	0.53	830	5.2	0.65
	INTS (block)	664	10.3	0.64	949	10.2	0.64	–		
	INTS (smooth)	609	11.2	0.70	881	11.0	0.69	–		
	EEV (block)	304	22.4	1.40	753	12.8	0.80	653	6.6	0.82
	EEV (smooth)	294	23.2	1.45	697	13.9	0.87	671	6.4	0.80
	INTR (block)	287	23.8	1.49	724	13.3	0.83	–		
	INTR (smooth)	241	28.3	1.77	612	15.8	0.99	–		

7   Conclusion

The investigation in this paper has shown, that traditional vectorization techniques like control-flow to data-flow conversion need to be conceptually reconsidered for contemporary SIMD architectures with their wide vector registers. Under-utilization of SIMD vector lanes can cause a severe efficiency degradation. Our concept of dynamic vector lane scheduling breaks with the paradigm, that a block of iterations is executed synchronously in a vectorized loop. In our approach, loop iterations are assigned to vector lanes on the fly, leading to a much better utilization of available compute resources. By refining the Mandelbrot algorithm accordingly, we are able to double the computation speed for compute-intense images.

We have developed two different scheduling schemes. The *blocked* scheme is easily programmable and can be expressed using existing high-level language constructs like Cilk Plus array notation. The more elaborated *smoothed* scheme leads to an even better utilization of vector lanes. We have implemented these schemes using three different programming approaches (AAV, EEV and INTR). Both AAV and EEV use high-level SIMD vector operations to enable code portability, whereas INTR draws on low-level vector coding with SIMD intrinsics. Our implementations of the Mandelbrot algorithm show that with EEV code and performance portability can be achieved at the same time. However, the portable methods could further profit from additional compiler improvements that simplify and support the implementation of dynamic scheduling.

We believe that dynamic vector lane scheduling will become an important vectorization technique for a wide range of algorithms. Loops with diverging control flows as well as loops containing inner loops with a varying number of iterations can benefit from our approach. E.g. the transformation of the Mandelbrot algorithm can be generalized as shown in Listing 4. The for-loop on the left side shall be vectorized. The *condition* terminating the inner loop is variant to the enclosing loop. A traditional vectorization would utilize all vector lanes in the *initialization* and in the *store result* steps. The *computation* step would be masked depending on which vector lanes already have met *condition*. The vectorized code outlined on the right side uses dynamic vector lane scheduling. There the utilization of vector lanes is interchanged: *initialization* and *store result* are masked, while *computation* now utilize all vector lanes. Our results suggest that such an interchange should be considered as a part of the SIMD vector optimization strategy. However, while further research is needed in order to obtain an automatic transformation of such codes, it remains a programmer task to rate the meaningfulness of that transformation.

```
1                                          schedule first n[vect]
2                                          initialization[vect]
3    for(n=0;n<maxIter;n++) {              while(n[any]<maxIter) {
4      initialization                        if(condition[vect]) {
5      while(!condition)                        store result[masked]
6      {                                        schedule next n[masked]
7        computation                            initialization[masked]
8      }                                      }
9      store result                          computation[vect]
10   }                                      }
```

Listing 4. Generalized transformation scheme.

Acknowledgements. This work has been funded by *SAXonPHI – Intel Parallel Computing Center Dresden* at the Center for Information Services and High Performance Computing, TU Dresden, by the *Research Center for Many-core HPC* (IPCC) at Zuse Institute Berlin, and by the Intel Parallel Computing Center at RWTH Aachen University.

References

1. Intel Intrinsics Guide: _mm512_mask_expand_epi32. Website. https://software. intel.com/sites/landingpage/IntrinsicsGuide/#text=_mm512_mask_expand_ epi32&techs=AVX_512&expand=2162,2162
2. Mandelbrot Algorithms with Dynamic SIMD Vector Lane Scheduling. https:// github.com/IXPUG/WG_Vectorization/tree/master/dynamic-simd-scheduling
3. Outer Loop Vectorization via Intel Cilk Plus Array Notations. https://software.int el.com/en-us/articles/outer-loop-vectorization-via-intel-cilk-plus-array-notations
4. Cheng, Y., An, H., Chen, Z., Li, F., Wang, Z., Jiang, X., Peng, Y.: Understanding the SIMD efficiency of graph traversal on GPU. In: Sun, X., Qu, W., Stojmenovic, I., Zhou, W., Li, Z., Guo, H., Min, G., Yang, T., Wu, Y., Liu, L. (eds.) ICA3PP 2014. LNCS, vol. 8630, pp. 42–56. Springer, Heidelberg (2014). doi:10.1007/ 978-3-319-11197-1_4
5. Fog, A.: VCL C++ vector class library. http://www.agner.org/optimize/vector class.pdf
6. Fung, W.W.L., Sham, I., Yuan, G., Aamodt, T.M.: Dynamic warp formation and scheduling for efficient GPU control flow. In: Proceedings of the 40th Annual IEEE/ACM International Symposium on Microarchitecture, MICRO 40, pp. 407– 420. IEEE Computer Society, Washington, D.C., USA (2007)
7. Krzikalla, O., Feldhoff, K., Müller-Pfefferkorn, R., Nagel, W.E.: Scout: a source-to-source transformator for SIMD-Optimizations. In: Alexander, M., et al. (eds.) Euro-Par 2011. LNCS, vol. 7156, pp. 137–145. Springer, Heidelberg (2012). doi:10. 1007/978-3-642-29740-3_17
8. Krzikalla, O., Feldhoff, K., Müller-Pfefferkorn, R., Nagel, W.: Auto-vectorization techniques for modern SIMD architectures. In: 16th International Workshop on Compilers for Parallel Computing (CPC 2012), Padova, Italy, January 2012
9. Krzikalla, O., Zitzlsberger, G.: Code vectorization using intel array notation. In: Proceedings of the 3rd Workshop on Programming Models for SIMD/Vector Processing, WPMVP 2016, p. 6 (2011). Observation of strains. Infect Dis Ther. 3(1), 35–43.: 1–6: 8, New York, NY, USA, ACM (2016)
10. Satish, N., Kim, C., Chhugani, J., Saito, H., Krishnaiyer, R., Smelyanskiy, M., Girkar, M., Dubey, P.: Can traditional programming bridge the ninja performance gap for parallel computing applications? In: Proceedings of the 39th Annual International Symposium on Computer Architecture, ISCA 2012, pp. 440–451. IEEE Computer Society, Washington, D.C., USA (2012)

High Performance Optimizations for Nuclear Physics Code MFDn on KNL

Brandon Cook[1]($\boxtimes$), Pieter Maris[2], Meiyue Shao[1], Nathan Wichmann[3],
Marcus Wagner[3], John O'Neill[4], Thanh Phung[4], and Gaurav Bansal[4]

[1] Lawrence Berkeley National Laboratory, Berkeley, CA 94720, USA
{bgcook,myshao}@lbl.gov
[2] Department of Physics and Astronomy,
Iowa State University, Ames, IA 50011, USA
[3] Cray Inc., Seattle, USA
[4] Software and Services Group, Intel Corporation, Santa Clara, USA

Abstract. Initial optimization strategies and results on MFDn, a large-scale nuclear physics application code, running on a single KNL node are presented. This code consists of the construction of a very large sparse real symmetric matrix and computing a few lowest eigenvalues and eigenvectors of this matrix through iterative methods. Challenges addressed include effectively utilizing MCDRAM with representative input data for production runs on 5,000 KNL nodes that require over 80 GB of memory per node, using OpenMP 4 to parallelize functions in the construction phase of the sparse matrices, and vectorizing those functions in spite of while-loops, conditionals, and lookup tables with indirect indexing. Moreover, hybrid MPI/OpenMP is employed not only to maximize the total problem size that can be solved per node, but also to eventually minimize parallel scaling overhead through the best scaling combination of MPI ranks per node with OpenMP threads. We describe a vectorized version of a popcount operation to avoid serialization on intrinsic popcnt which only operates on scalar registers. Additionally we leverage SSE 4.2 string comparison instructions to determine nonzero matrix elements. By utilizing MCDRAM, we achieve excellent Sparse Matrix–Matrix multiplication performance; in particular, using blocks of 8 vectors lead to a speedup of 6.4× on KNL and 2.9× on Haswell compared to the performance of repeated SpMV's. This optimization was essential in achieving a 1.6× improvement on KNL over Haswell.

Keywords: Vectorization · MCDRAM · KNL · MFDn · Sparse matrix · SpMV

1 Introduction

Many-Fermion Dynamics—nuclear, or MFDn, is a configuration interaction (CI) code for nuclear structure calculations. It is a platform independent Fortran 90 code using a hybrid MPI/OpenMP programming model, and is being used on

© Springer International Publishing AG 2016
M. Taufer et al. (Eds.): ISC High Performance Workshops 2016, LNCS 9945, pp. 366–377, 2016.
DOI: 10.1007/978-3-319-46079-6_26

current supercomputers such as Edison at NERSC, Mira at ALCF, and Titan at OLCF for ab initio calculations of atomic nuclei using realistic nucleon–nucleon and three-nucleon forces [3,7–9]. A calculation consists of generating a many-body basis space, constructing the many-body Hamiltonian matrix in this basis, obtaining the lowest eigenpairs, and calculating a set of observables from those eigenpairs. Key computational challenges for MFDn include effectively using the available aggregate memory, efficient construction of the matrix, and efficient sparse matrix–vector products used in the solution of the eigenvalue problem.

In principle an infinite-dimensional basis space is needed for an exact representation of the many-body wavefuctions. However, in practice the basis space is truncated and observables are studied as a function of the truncation parameters. Typical basis space dimensions for large-scale production runs are of the order of several billion. The corresponding many-body matrix is extremely sparse, with tens of trillion nonzero matrix elements, which are stored in core. This defines one of the key computational challenges for this code—effectively using the aggregate memory available in a cluster.

To accurately capture this need we developed a test code which uses representative data for production calculations on 5,000 Knights Landing (KNL) nodes (approximately half the size of Cori at NERSC) using over 80 GB of memory per node. In such a production run, half of the symmetric matrix is distributed in a two-dimensional fashion over the available MPI ranks. Each MPI rank constructs and stores its own sparse submatrix. The test code performs nearly all the computational work a single node would do in the production run but with the communication removed.

2   Target Architecture

The optimizations on MFDn presented in this work target the Cori supercomputer at the National Energy Research Scientific Computing Center (NERSC). Cori is a Cray XC40 based supercomputer deployed in two phases.

Phase 1

- 1,630 compute nodes with 128 GB DDR4@2133 MHz per node and 2 16-core 2.3 GHz Intel Haswell processors
- 1.92 PFLOPs theoretical peak
- 203 TB aggregate memory
- Aries Dragonfly topology network
- Deployed late-2015

Phase 2

- Scheduled deployment mid-2016
- Over 9,300 self-hosted Knights Landing (KNL) compute nodes
- Over 1 PB aggregate memory (DDR4 and MCDRAM combined)
- Aries Dragonfly topology network

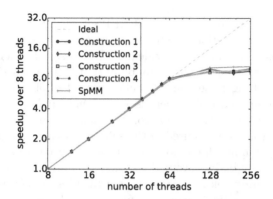

Fig. 1. OpenMP thread scaling of kernels on KNL B0 with 64 physical cores and up to 4 logical threads per core. Speedup is measured against wall time with 8 threads.

As Cori Phase 2 is not available at the time of writing, we perform our tests using the following platform:

- B0 stepping KNL preproduction white boxes
- 64-cores @ 1.3 GHz and 4 logical threads per core
- 16 GB MCDRAM
- 96 GB DDR4 @ 2133 MHz

On Haswell we achieved the best performance with one MPI rank per socket (i.e., two MPI ranks per node, and avoiding NUMA issues) and 16 threads per rank resulting in one thread per physical core. Our initial tests on KNL showed that hyperthreading was beneficial and that 4 threads per core was best, see Fig. 1. Furthermore, one MPI rank with 256 threads was more efficient than two MPI ranks with 128 threads or four MPI ranks with 64 threads. In addition to being most efficient, using one MPI rank per node avoids memory overhead from data replicated across MPI ranks and facilitates addressing large blocks of MCDRAM. Hence, unless otherwise noted, all tests reported below on KNL were done in quadrant+flat mode with one MPI rank and 256 threads. For allocations to MCDRAM we used the memkind [4] library and **FASTMEM** directives.

3 Optimization of SpMV/SpMM Kernel

The lowest few eigenvalues and eigenvectors of the very large real sparse symmetric Hamiltonian matrix are found with iterative solvers Lanczos [6] or LOBPCG [5]. The key kernels in the iterative eigensolver are Sparse Matrix–Vector (SpMV) and Sparse transposed Matrix–Vector (SpMVT) products, as only half of the symmetric matrix is stored in order to save memory. The sparse matrix is stored in a CSB_Coo format [1,2], which allows for efficient linear algebra operations on very sparse matrices, improved cache reuse on multicore architectures and thread scaling even when the same structure is used for both

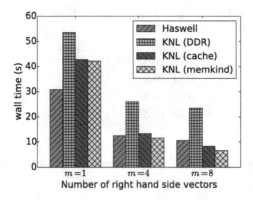

Fig. 2. Wall time for SpMM kernel on Haswell and KNL. KNL (DDR) means no MCDRAM was utilized. KNL (cache) indicates that cache mode was used. KNL (memkind) indicates that input/output vectors were explicitly kept in MCDRAM using directives.

SpMV and SpMVT (as is the case in this application). The thread scalability of this kernel is shown in Fig. 1; it scales ideally with the number of physical cores and additional hyperthreads provide some small additional benefit. The figure was generated with 8 simultaneous vectors allocated to MCDRAM and different numbers of vectors (not shown) display the same behavior.

In a production run on 5,000 KNL nodes over 80 GB of memory per node is required for a calculation. The nonzero matrix elements and corresponding indices account for 64 GB of the memory and the input/output vectors account for up to 16 GB depending on the specific problem and on the eigensolver that is used. Improving data reuse, utilizing vectorization, and effectively using as much aggregate bandwidth as possible are key challenges for computing sparse matrix-vector products in MFDn. To improve data reuse and allow for vectorization, in LOBPCG we replace SpMV with SpMM (i.e., SpMV operations on a block of vectors). To fully utilize AVX-512 instructions on KNL up to 16 single-precision vectors could be used, but we limit our study to 8 vectors due to memory requirements and the need to balance simultaneous data use from each memory system. To access more memory bandwidth we explicitly place the input/output vectors in MCDRAM using the memkind [4] library and FASTMEM directives.

To analyze the performance we measure the arithmetic intensity (AI, the ratio of FLOPs to data movement) of the SpMM operation. We used the dynamic instruction tracing capabilities of Intel's Software Development Emulator (SDE) to count the number of floating point operations. Due to the size of the matrices and vectors the most relevant measure for data movement are the main memory counters. To access the data movement at DDR and MCDRAM controllers we use Intel's VTune Amplifier XE. In our experiments we used a fixed CSB_Coo block size $\beta = 16,000$ to maintain consistency, though this value should be

Table 1. Performance data for SpMM on m vectors for 2 socket Haswell with 2 MPI ranks and 16 OpenMP threads.

m	AI	GFLOPs	DDR GB/s
1	0.23	23.2	122–125
4	0.62	56.8	125
8	0.80	67.5	122–125

Table 2. Performance data for SpMM on m vectors for B0 KNL with 64 cores with 256 OpenMP threads.

m	AI_{DDR}	AI_{MCDRAM}	AI_{total}	GFLOPs	DDR GB/s	MCDRAM GB/s
1	0.20	0.33	0.13	17.1	83	55
4	0.80	0.36	0.25	62.4	80	170–190
8	1.57	0.37	0.30	109.1	71	290–310

adjusted to match the cache sizes of the current hardware and matrix sparsity of a given Hamiltonian.

On Haswell operating on blocks of vectors with SPMM operations resulted in a speedup of 2.9× over operating on a single vector at a time. Due to the low value of AI for SPMM operations memory bandwidth is the limiting factor in performance. Sustained memory bandwidth on Haswell was measured to be $B_{DDR}^{HSW} = 128\,GB/s$. Performance measurements are summarized in Tables 1 and 2. The theoretical peak performance in GFLOP/s is $P(m) = B_{DDR}^{HSW} \cdot AI(m)$, where B is bandwidth and AI is arithmetic intensity. Our measurements show we achieve a large fraction of theoretical maximum performance and that we are utilizing nearly all of the available memory bandwidth. However, as m increases we achieve a lower fraction of theoretical peak performance. This is a result of the larger working set resulting in increased cache pressure. Tuning of the CSB_Coo block size, β, could mitigate this effect, but is outside the scope of this work as the optimal choice depends on the specific hardware and the specific sparsity structure and physics of each problem.

On KNL we will use data from both DDR and MCDRAM. In this case two factors, the total data movement and the ratio of data movement on MCDRAM to DDR, are important. The measured peak sustained bandwidth was $B_{DDR}^{KNL} = 83\,GB/s$ for DRR and $B_{MCDRAM}^{KNL} = 390\,GB/s$ for MCDRAM on our KNL white boxes. For optimal performance the ratio of data moved on each controller should match the ratio of available bandwidth ($R_{max} = B_{MCDRAM}^{KNL}/B_{DDR}^{KNL} \approx 4.7$) in order to fully utilize each memory system. For $m = 1, 4, 8$ the ratio of data moved on each controller is $R = 0.6, 2.2, 4.2$, respectively. We estimate that if enough MCDRAM was available the ratio for $m = 16$ would be $R \approx 8$, which would result in the DDR being under-utilized. Increasing m reduces the traffic on DDR and reduces the total data moved on both controllers, resulting in

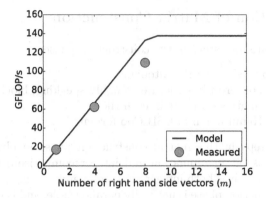

Fig. 3. Performance model for utilizing data from MCDRAM and DDR simultaneously on KNL. The dots are measurements taken with 256 threads on B0.

increased total arithmetic intensity. Assuming that it is possible to simultaneously utilize both memory systems fully the expected performance in GFLOP/s is given by $P(m) = \min\{B_{\mathrm{DDR}}^{\mathrm{KNL}} \cdot AI_{\mathrm{DDR}}(m), B_{\mathrm{MCDRAM}}^{\mathrm{KNL}} \cdot AI_{\mathrm{MCDRAM}}(m)\}$. The peak performance predicted by this model (the curve) and measured data points (the dots) for $m = 1, 4, 8$ are shown in Fig. 3. In this model the data movement on DDR is inversely proportional to the m since we reduce the number of times the full matrix must be read by m. However, the data movement on the MCDRAM is nearly constant as the same amount of matrix vector products must be computed. At low values of m the DDR bandwidth is the limiting factor, but as more traffic is shifted to MCDRAM it becomes the limiting factor, where the crossover point is defined by the ratio of data movement on each set of controllers in the kernel.

On Haswell and KNL machines we find $m = 8$ simultaneous vectors to be the most efficient given constraints on memory capacity and bandwidth. Analysis suggests that further improvements in performance for $m > 8$ are not likely on KNL given the ratio of available DRR and MCDRAM bandwidth. In the case of $m = 8$ we achieve a 1.6× increase in performance over a dual socket Haswell node with a single KNL. We also find that increasing m from 1 to 8 increases performance by 6.4× on KNL and 2.9× on Haswell. For completeness we also include timing data from a KNL configured in quadrant+cache mode in Fig. 2. We omit detailed analysis as this mode consistently has lower performance than explicitly managing the memory and reduces the total addressable memory of a node. The SNC modes were not analyzed due to the memory overhead associated with additional MPI ranks, lower efficiency, and complications of allocating the large vectors across NUMA domains.

4   Optimization of Matrix Construction

In MFDn, there are four steps in the construction phase:

1. Count nonzero tiles in the Hamiltonian;
2. Construct the nonzero tile structure (roughly speaking, block structure);
3. Count nonzero matrix elements in each tile;
4. Construct the Hamiltonian in CSB_Coo format.

The first three steps in this matrix construction phase involves only integer arithmetic, such as bit manipulation and integer comparison; the actual construction (step 4) involves both integer arithmetic and floating point operations. The matrix construction phase is naturally parallelizable, and is performed without any MPI communication (even for a production run). However, efficient implementation of the construction phase is challenging due to conditionals and use of lookup tables with indirect indexing. The matrix construction phase is not bound by memory bandwidth and is primarily sensitive to integer compute performance and random indirect access to lookup tables. In our tests cache mode had no benefit for the construction. In the following we discuss several optimization techniques we have applied to the matrix construction phase.

Typical Loop Structure. The (i, j)th entry of the many-body Hamiltonian with a d-body interaction, $H(i, j) = \langle \Phi_i | H | \Phi_j \rangle$, is nonzero only when the many-body basis states Φ_i and Φ_j differ by at most d single particle states. A typical loop structure in the matrix construction phase (steps 3–4) is shown in Fig. 4.

---

1. Loop over column states (Φ_j)
2.   Loop over row states (Φ_i)
3.   Quickly estimate the number of different states between Φ_i and Φ_j
4.   Carefully check whether $H(i, j) \neq 0$ if the quick test passed
5.   (optional) Compute the nonzero matrix entry
6.   End Loop
7. End Loop

Fig. 4. A typical loop structure in the matrix construction phase (steps 3–4).

In MFDn a many-body basis state Φ_i can be represented by a sequence of integers, denoted by BIN(Φ_i). Each binary bit of BIN(Φ_i) indicates whether a single particle state is occupied (each single particle state can either be occupied or not occupied). Information regarding all differently-occupied single particle states between Φ_i and Φ_j is encoded by BIN(Φ_i) $\oplus$ BIN(Φ_j), where $\oplus$ denotes the bitwise exclusive or operation. The number of differently-occupied single particle states is then obtained by counting the number of 1's in BIN(Φ_i) $\oplus$ BIN(Φ_j), i.e., the popcount of BIN(Φ_i) $\oplus$ BIN(Φ_j). In the 3rd line of the loop above, we only compute the popcount of the first integer of BIN(Φ_i) $\oplus$ BIN(Φ_j), representing

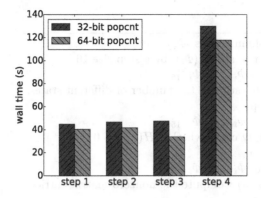

Fig. 5. Timings on B0 KNL for the four matrix construction phases.

the lowest 32 single particle states, to quickly identify most of the zero entries. The 4th and 5th lines of the loop are more complicated, and are accomplished by subroutine calls.

Promoting 32-bit Integers to 64-bit. The first optimization we made is to use 64-bit integers to encode $BIN(\Phi_i)$ instead of 32-bit integers. Consequently, computing the popcount of the first integer of $BIN(\Phi_i)$ now checks the lowest 64 single particle states. Compared to the original 32-bit version, the 64-bit version quickly identifies more zero entries and reduces the subsequent calls to expensive subroutines (4th line in Fig. 4), while the additional cost in popcount is negligible. Such a change leads to about 15 % improvement in the first three steps in the construction phase; see Fig. 5.

Loop Unrolling. To optimize the loop in Fig. 4 we manually unroll the inner loop, for instance, by a step size 16.[1] Then lines 3–5 in the loop becomes three independent loops of size 16, as shown in Fig. 6.

The first innermost loop (lines 3–5) in Fig. 6 can potentially be vectorized. The subroutine calls in lines 7 and 10 can also be adjusted so that the subroutines accepts arrays of inputs and outputs. By doing so increases data reuse, and allows the compiler to generate vectorized instructions.

Vectorizing Popcount. Unfortunately, the Fortran intrinsic `popcnt` does not vectorize, preventing any loop involving `popcnt` from being vectorized. This is due the hardware instruction only operating on integer registers. To bypass this obstacle, we replace `popcnt` by a hand coded popcount implementation. A simple implementation of popcount shown in Fig. 7 already vectorizes. Another implementation shown in Fig. 8 also vectorizes and is in general faster than that in Fig. 7 by a small margin. Table 3 shows timing results of step 3 in the construction phase on KNL.

---

[1] The optimal choice of this number is certainly architecture dependent.

1. Loop over column states (Φ_j)
2.   Loop over row states (Φ_i), by a step size 16
3.   Loop over $\Phi_i, \ldots, \Phi_{i+15}$
4.   Quickly estimate the number of different states.
5.   End Loop
6.   Loop over $\Phi_i, \ldots, \Phi_{i+15}$
7.   Carefully check whether $H(i,j) \neq 0$
8.   End Loop
9.   Loop over $\Phi_i, \ldots, \Phi_{i+15}$
10.   (optional) Compute the nonzero matrix entries
11.   End Loop
12.   End Loop
13. End Loop

Fig. 6. Unroll the inner loop in Fig. 4 by a step size 16.

```
popcount = 0
do i = 0, 63
    if (btest(x, i)) popcount = popcount + 1
end do
```

Fig. 7. A simple implementation of popcount for 64-bit integers.

```
y = x - iand(ishft(x, -1), Z'5555555555555555')
y = iand(y, Z'3333333333333333') + iand(ishft(y, -2), Z'3333333333333333')
y = iand(y + ishft(y, -4), Z'0F0F0F0F0F0F0F0F')
popcount = ishft(y * Z'0101010101010101', -56)
```

Fig. 8. An optimized implementation of popcount for 64-bit integers.

Table 3. Timings (sec) for different versions of popcount.

	ifort v. 16.0.2	ifort v. 17 beta
Fortran intrinsic popcnt	34.05	34.01
popcount in Fig. 7	34.26	103.43
popcount in Fig. 8	33.90	32.46

```
#include "nmmintrin.h"

int nzcount(short *colstates, short *rowstates, int ncol, int nrow, int oprank) {
    const int mode = _SIDD_SWORD_OPS | _SIDD_CMP_EQUAL_ANY |
                     _SIDD_BIT_MASK | _SIDD_MASKED_NEGATIVE_POLARITY;
    int i, j, ii = 0, jj = 0, count = 0;
    for (j = 0; j < ncol; j++) {
        __m128i v_col = _mm_load_si128((__m128i*) &colstates[ii]);
        ii += 8; jj = 0;
        for (i = 0; i < nrow; i++) {
            __m128i v_row = _mm_load_si128((__m128i*) &rowstates[jj]);
            jj += 8;
            __m128i res_v = _mm_cmpistrm(v_row, v_col, mode);
            count += (_mm_popcnt_u32(_mm_extract_epi32(res_v, 0)) <= oprank);
        }
    }
    return count;
}
```

Fig. 9. An implementation of detailed state comparison using SSE 4.2 intrinsics.

State Comparison with SSE 4.2 Intrinsics. In MFDn, in addition to the bit representation, there is also an index-based representation of the occupied single particle states in Φ_i. This representation is used in the detailed tests for the states (4th line Fig. 4). The detailed test counts the number of differently occupied states, or the symmetric difference of the two sets of indices describing which states are occupied. Depending on the number of different states occupied and the n-body interactions a quantum selection rule is then applied.

On machines which support the SSE 4.2 instruction set the __cmpistrm intrinsic function can be used to perform an all-to-all comparison of eight 16-bit integers in a single instruction. In this function a and b are __m128i and can hold eight 16-bit integers. By appropriately setting the control bits with mode the result will be a bit mask which is 1 if the element in that position in a does not have a matching value in b. The count of differences is obtained by extracting the relevant part of the resulting mask and calculating the popcount. Our implementation is shown in Fig. 9. In our test case the number of occupied single particle states is 8 which perfectly matches the register size. For cases with less than 8 one can pad the integer representation with zeros. Additional logic is required for cases with more than 8 occupied states, but the generalization is straightforward. Unfortunately there are not corresponding AVX-512 instructions, but techniques based on rotations, shuffles and comparisons are interesting possibilities for future work.

The efficiency of the SSE 4.2 approach is shown in Fig. 10. For comparison we show the timings for the 32-bit and 64-bit popcount tests (using the machine instructions) followed by the original scalar detailed comparison test. In addition we include the timing for when only the detailed comparisons were done. The SSE 4.2 approach demonstrates very promising efficiency over the popcount ones, though completely skipping quick tests does not seem wise. This suggests that

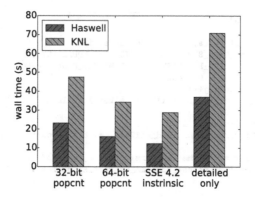

Fig. 10. Timings for the 3rd matrix construction phases where the number of nonzero matrix elements are counted. Timings taken with 256 threads on B0 KNL with 64 cores in quadrant+flat mode and on 2 Haswell sockets with 16 threads each.

a well-tuned implementation on the target architecture should identify a good balance between quick tests and detailed comparisons.

5   Conclusion and Outlook

We found that improved data reuse and vectorization were essential for improving the performance of MFDn on KNL over Haswell. Especially in the SpMM kernel where we achieved a 1.6× speedup over Haswell by operating on $m = 8$ simultaneously. In this kernel we also show that by utilizing directives and the memkind library effective use of both DDR and MCDRAM memories can be achieved at the same time, along with the importance of balancing the load on each memory system. Our optimizations for the matrix construction benefit both Haswell and KNL architectures, by reducing branching and enabling use of vector registers. OpenMP 4 directives we used to implement vectorized popcount functions and simd intrinsic functions are shown to provide excellent performance in detailed comparisons of quantum many-body states. Future efforts to explore the application of AVX-512 instructions in the matrix construction phases will prove key in obtaining further improvements in the matrix construction phases of MFDn.

Acknowledgments. This work is supported in part by U.S. DOE Grant Number DESC0008485 (SciDAC/NUCLEI). This research used resources of the National Energy Research Scientific Computing Center (NERSC), a DOE Office of Science User Facility supported by the Office of Science of the U.S. Department of Energy under Contract No. DE-AC02-05CH11231.

References

1. Aktulga, H.M., Buluç, A., Williams, S., Yang, C.: Optimizing sparse matrix-multiple vectors multiplication for nuclear configuration interaction calculations. In: 2014 IEEE 28th International on Parallel and Distributed Processing Symposium, pp. 1213–1222. IEEE (2014)
2. Aktulga, H.M., Yang, C., Ng, E.G., Maris, P., Vary, J.P.: Improving the scalability of a symmetric iterative eigensolver for multi-core platforms. Concurr. Comput. Pract. Exper. **26**(16), 2631–2651 (2014)
3. Binder, S., Calci, A., Epelbaum, E., Furnstahl, R.J., Golak, J., Hebeler, K., Kamada, H., Krebs, H., Langhammer, J., Liebig, S., Maris, P., Meißner, U.G., Minossi, D., Nogga, A., Potter, H., Roth, R., Skiniński, R., Topolnicki, K., Vary, J.P., Witała, H.: Few-nucleon systems with state-of-the-art chiral nucleon-nucleon forces. Phys. Rev. C **93**(4), 044002 (2016)
4. Cantalupo, C., Venkatesan, V., Hammond, J.R., Hammond, S.: User extensible heap manager for heterogeneous memory platforms and mixed memory policies (2015)
5. Knyazev, A.V.: Toward the optimal preconditioned eigensolver: locally optimal block preconditioned conjugate gradient method. SIAM J. Sci. Comput. **23**(2), 517–541 (2001)
6. Lanczos, C.: An iteration method for the solution of the eigenvalue problem of linear differential and integral operators. J. Res. Natl. Bur. Std. B Math. Sci. **45**(4), 255–282 (1950)
7. Maris, P., Caprio, M.A., Vary, J.P.: Emergence of rotational bands in ab initio no-core configuration interaction calculations of the Be isotopes. Phys. Rev. C **91**(1), 014310 (2015)
8. Maris, P., Vary, J.P., Navratil, P., Ormand, W.E., Nam, H., Dean, D.J.: Origin of the anomalous long lifetime of 14C. Phys. Rev. Lett. **106**(20), 202502 (2011)
9. Maris, P., Vary, J.P., Gandolfi, S., Carlson, J., Pieper, S.C.: Properties of trapped neutrons interacting with realistic nuclear Hamiltonians. Phys. Rev. C **87**(5), 054318 (2013)

Optimization of the Sparse Matrix-Vector Products of an IDR Krylov Iterative Solver in EMGeo for the Intel KNL Manycore Processor

Tareq Malas[(✉)], Thorsten Kurth, and Jack Deslippe

National Energy Research Scientific Computing Center,
Lawrence Berkeley National Laboratory, Berkeley, USA
tmalas@lbl.gov

Abstract. In geophysical-imaging, medium properties can be studied by performing scattering experiments using electromagnetic or seismic waves. Quantities such as densities, elasticities, stress etc. can be obtained from fitting the observed measurements to the results predicted by a simulation. The EMGeo software performs these simulations and solves the inverse scattering problem in the Laplace-Fourier domain. In this paper, we focus on the Seismic part and forward step of the inverse scattering problem, which involves inverting a large sparse matrix. For this purpose, EMGeo uses an Induced Dimensional Reduction (IDR) Krylov subspace solver. The Sparse Matrix Vector (SpMV) product is responsible for more than half of the total runtime. We demonstrate how we use spatial and multiple Right Hand Side (RHS) blocking cache optimizations to increase arithmetic intensity and thus the performance, as SpMV product is memory bandwidth-bound. Our optimizations achieve 5.0× and 4.8× speedup in the SpMV product in Haswell and KNL processors, respectively. We also achieve 1.8× and 3.3× speedup in the overall IDR solver in Haswell and KNL processors, respectively. We also give an outlook over possible future optimizations.

Keywords: Intel knights landing optimization · Matrix vector product optimization · IDR Krylov solver optimization · Multiple right-hand side blocking · Spatial blocking

1 Introduction

Problem Description: EMGeo is a seismic tomography software which infers the composition of the ground using electromagnetic (EM) and seismic scattering information. It is a 3D full waveform inversion scheme for elastic wave propagation in the Fourier domain. The EM and seismic parts are very similar as the system has the same number of unknowns. However, the latter is more involved as the propagating waves have longitudinal as well as transversal polarized components which are tightly coupled through properties of the medium. In this presentation, we are going to present improvements for the seismic problem in the

© Springer International Publishing AG 2016
M. Taufer et al. (Eds.): ISC High Performance Workshops 2016, LNCS 9945, pp. 378–389, 2016.
DOI: 10.1007/978-3-319-46079-6_27

forward step of the computation. This step requires solving large-scale implicit linear systems in the frequency domain. EMGeo mitigates that by avoiding performing a brute-force forward inversion of the transfer matrix which describes the medium, but instead inverting on a set of representative vectors using Krylov iterative solvers. The workflow is as follows: the general objective of EMGeo is to minimize the cost functional

$$\phi(\mathbf{m}) = \frac{1}{2} \sum_{s_k} \sum_q \left\| \mathbf{E} \left[\mathbf{d}_q^{\mathrm{obs}}(s_k) - \mathbf{d}_q^{\mathrm{sim}}(\mathbf{m}, s_k) \right] \right\|^2 + \frac{\lambda}{2} \left\| \mathbf{W} \mathbf{m} \right\|^2. \tag{1}$$

Here, $\mathbf{d}_q^{\mathrm{obs}}(s_k), \mathbf{d}_q^{\mathrm{sim}}(\mathbf{m}, s_k)$ are observed and predicted signals at position q, $\mathbf{W}$ a regularization matrix, λ a Lagrange parameter to avoid overfitting, $\mathbf{E}$ is a (diagonal) error matrix which includes uncertainties in the measured data and $\mathbf{m}$ are the model parameters. Furthermore, s_k denotes a 'frequency' along with a dampening term, i.e. $s_k = \sigma_k + i\,\omega_k$, used in the Laplace transformation of the time-dependent fields $\mathbf{d}_q^{\mathrm{obs}}(t)$. The expensive part in expression (1) is the computation of the simulated response, i.e. $\mathbf{d}_q^{\mathrm{sim}}(\mathbf{m}, s_k)$. It is obtained by interpolating the velocity field $\mathbf{v}$ of the seismic waves propagating through the medium, i.e. $\mathbf{d}_q^{\mathrm{sim}}(\mathbf{m}, s_k) = \hat{\mathbf{G}} \mathbf{v}_q(\mathbf{m}, s_k)$. The velocities are in turn computed by solving a sparse linear system which can be discretized with finite differences (FD) on a staggered grid (c.f. [8,9] for more details):

$$\left[1 - \langle \mathbf{b} \rangle \mathbf{D}_\tau \cdot \left(\langle \mathbf{k}\mu \rangle \circ \mathbf{D}_v \right) \right] \mathbf{v}_q = \mathbf{f}_q, \tag{2}$$

where $\circ$ denotes the Hadamard product, $\langle \mathbf{k}\mu \rangle$ and $\langle \mathbf{b} \rangle$ are block matrices of averaged elastic parameters which describe the medium and $\mathbf{D}_\tau, \mathbf{D}_v$ are block-matrices of FD operators. Furthermore, $\mathbf{v}_q$ is the velocity vector of interest and $\mathbf{f}_q$ the source vector in the Laplace-Fourier domain. Both (super-)vectors are in structure-of-array form, i.e. $\mathbf{g} = (\mathbf{g}_x, \mathbf{g}_y, \mathbf{g}_z)^T$ for $\mathbf{g} = \mathbf{v}$ or $\mathbf{g} = \mathbf{f}$ respectively. The components $\mathbf{g}_i$ contain all i-components of the respective field for all grid points in x, y, z-major order.

The matrices in (2) can then be written as follows [9]:

$$\mathbf{D}_\tau = \begin{pmatrix} \tilde{D}_x & D_y & D_z & \tilde{D}_x & 0 & \tilde{D}_x \\ \tilde{D}_y & D_x & 0 & \tilde{D}_y & D_z & \tilde{D}_y \\ \tilde{D}_z & 0 & D_x & \tilde{D}_z & D_y & \tilde{D}_z \end{pmatrix}^T \; ; \quad \mathbf{D}_v = \begin{pmatrix} D_x & \tilde{D}_y & \tilde{D}_z & 0 & 0 & 0 \\ 0 & \tilde{D}_x & 0 & D_y & \tilde{D}_z & 0 \\ 0 & 0 & \tilde{D}_x & 0 & \tilde{D}_y & D_z \end{pmatrix}. \tag{3}$$

Here, D_i and $\tilde{D}_i$ denote FD operators for direction i. In the following, we will denote $\langle \mathbf{b} \rangle \mathbf{D}_\tau$ by D_τ and $\langle \mathbf{k}\mu \rangle \circ \mathbf{D}_v$ by D_v. This is just for brevity as multiplying the medium dependent factors do not change the sparsity pattern of these matrices as long as they are not zero (which is usually true). Figure 1 depicts the sparsity pattern of these two matrices, where N is the number of total grid points.

Challenges: There are two challenging aspect in this calculations. First, the SpMV product in (2) needs to be optimized, as it amounts to two thirds of the time spent in the linear solver. However, SpMV operation is notoriously memory bandwidth-bound as its arithmetic intensity is low. In Sect. 2, we explain how we address this

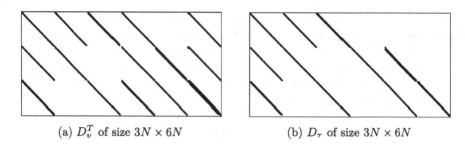

(a) D_v^T of size $3N \times 6N$ (b) D_τ of size $3N \times 6N$

Fig. 1. The sparsity pattern of D_v and D_τ matrices

issue with cache blocking. Second, global reductions and halo exchanges need to be optimized in order to improve strong scaling of our code. This can in part be done by solving (2) for multiple right hand sides and overlapping communication and computation in a clever way, which is left for future work.

Hardware: We use two systems for our performance measurements. The first one is the HPC system Cori Phase I at NERSC, which features 1630 nodes with 128 GiB DDR memory, Cray Aries interconnect and two Xeon® E5 CPUs per node. The Intel Xeon® E5, also termed Haswell, micro-architecture is a 22 nm fabric with support for AVX2. The NERSC Cori Phase I system uses revision E5-2698, which is comprised of 16 physical cores which can host up to 2 threads per core. It achieves 2.3 GHz in sustained and 3.6 GHz in turbo mode. It is further equipped with 3 cache levels, where L1 and L2 caches are of size 64 kiB and 256 kiB respectively. The L3 cache is shared between all cores on a physical CPU and of 40 MiB in size. The theoretical peak DDR memory bandwidth of this architecture is 68 GB/s per socket. The sockets are connected via Intel Quickpath Interconnect® with 9.6 GT/s, which translates to an effective memory bandwidth of ∼19.6 GB/s.

The second system we are considering is the new Intel Knights Landing (KNL) CPU, which is a second generation processor from the Intel Xeon Phi® family. We are using B0 stepping in revision 7210, which features 64 improved Silvermont® cores with 1.3 GHz clock rate, improved out-of-order processing as well as up to four hyperthreads per core. The cores are connected in a two-dimensional mesh of tiles, where each tile is comprised of two cores with 1 MiB L2 cache and two AVX512-enabled vector units each. Furthermore, KNL features 16 GiB MCDRAM, which is a high-bandwidth on-package memory with transfer-rates of up to 430 GB/s. The additional DDR memory, of which there are 96 GB in our setup, can be accessed at about 90 GB/s. The KNL processor mesh as well as the memory can be configured in different ways: the processor can be partitioned into 1, 2 or 4 partitions referred to as *Quadrant*, *SNC2* and *SNC4* mode respectively. The *SNC2* and *SNC4* abbreviations stand for *sub-NUMA clustering* and allow for fine-grained control over thread binding and thus possibly to a mitigation of memory access latency. The different memory configuration options are referred to as *Cache*, *flat* and *hybrid*. In *Cache* mode,

MCDRAM acts as a huge L3 cache and thus cannot be addressed manually by the user. In the *flat* model case, MCDRAM and DDR work side by side and the user has to manually allocate memory in either one. The *hybrid* mode allows for mixing the first two options, i.e. by assigning 50 % or 75 % of the MCDRAM to work as DDR cache, and the remaining fractions can be addressed manually by the user.

2   Approach

We apply techniques to reduce the memory traffic and increase the in-cache data reuse in the SpMV product of EMGeo code. We replace the ELLPack sparse matrix format, which is used in EMGeo code, with Sliced ELLPack (SELLPack) format to reduce the FLOPS and memory transfers. We also apply cache blocking techniques to increase the SpMV product operation *Arithmetic Intensity* (AI). Namely, we use Spatial Blocking (SB) and multiple Right Hand Side (mRHS) cache blocking.

EMGeo uses ELLPack data format because the maximum number of Non-Zero (NNZ) elements in each row is 12. ELLPack allocates a rectangular matrix, setting the width to the largest row width and pads smaller rows with zeroes. Most of the rows in D_r matrix contain 12 NNZ/row, so the padding overhead of the rows is minimal. However, half of the rows in D_v matrix contain 8 NNZ/row, so we use the SELLPack format proposed in [6]. SELLPack format allows defining different number of NNZ/row in different sections of the same matrix. We reorder D_v matrix, as shown in Fig. 2a, to have 12 NNZ/row in the first half of the matrix and 8 NNZ/row in the second half of the matrix. The reordering does not impact the performance, as the code performs it once. This effectively saves 17 % of D_v SpMV product operations.

We apply SB techniques [1,4] to reduce the main memory data traffic of the multiplied vector. In the regular update order of the SpMV product, the elements of the multiplied vector are accessed several times. As the vectors are larger than the cache memory, the vector elements are brought from main memory several times. SB changes the operation order in the matrix, such that blocks of matrix rows touching the same vector elements are updated together, while these vector elements are in the cache memory. This idea is illustrated in Fig. 2b. First the SpMV product of the dark red rows of the matrix is performed, while keeping the dark red part of the vector in the cache memory. Then the bright blue part is updated similarly, etc. As long as the block size fits in the cache memory, each element of the vector is brought once from the main memory. We show in Sect. 3 that combining SB and mRHS blocking can be inefficient in KNL due to the small cache memory size. Therefore, we reorder the loop over the Matrix components (i.e., row blocks of size N) with the loop over the rows of one component, which effectively reduces the SB block size to one row. As a result, the first row of each matrix component is evaluated first, then the next row, etc.

EMGeo solves Eq. (2) for multiple independent sources (RHS). In the RHS cache blocking approach we perform the SpMV product over several RHS's while

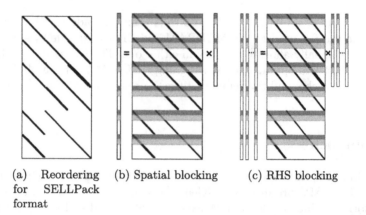

(a)   Reordering   (b) Spatial blocking   (c) RHS blocking
for   SELLPack
format

Fig. 2. Showing the reordered D_v matrix for SELLPack format in (a). Also, showing spatial (b) and RHS blocking (c) update order (Color figure online)

a block of the matrix is in the cache memory, which is relevant to [2,3]. RHS blocking amortizes the cost of loading the matrix from main memory, which is the dominant contributor of the main memory data traffic. We use row-major ordering in the RHS matrix to provide contiguous and vectorization-friendly data access pattern. The RHS blocking update order, combined with SB, is illustrated in Fig. 2c. First, each dark red block of the matrix performs the SpMV product over all the RHS, while the block is in the cache memory, then the bright blue blocks are updated, etc.

3   Analysis and Modeling SpMV Product Optimization

We analyze the FLOPS and memory data transfer requirement of the base case (i.e., the unoptimized code) and our improvements. Modeling the performance provides bounds of the expected performance improvement. We use the cache block size model to reduce the cache block size tuning parameter search space. In the following, we analyze the matrix and vector requirements separately then combine the total requirements together to estimate the AI of different setups.

Matrix data transfer and FLOPS requirement: The matrix is loaded once from main memory per SpMV product. Each element of the matrix requires loading 16 Bytes for the double complex number and 4 Bytes for the index. Moreover, the SpMV product requires 6 FLOPS to perform each complex number multiplication as well as twice the matrix bandwidth minus one FLOPS per matrix row for the reduction. Table 1.a. summarizes the total FLOPS and bytes requirement of D_v and D_τ. We notice that SELLPack format saves 20 % and 21 % in the data and the FLOPS compared to ELLPack data format, respectively.

Vectors data transfer requirement: In the "naïve" SpMV product update order, the vectors are loaded multiple times from main memory because they cannot fit

Table 1. Improvements of D_v and D_t (a,b) and their combined effects (c). N is the number of total grid points

Matrix	Format	Data (Bytes)		FLOPS	
D_v	ELLPack	**1440N**	$=12*(16+4)*6N$	**564N**	$=(12*6 + 11*2)*6N$
	SELL	**1200N**	$=10*(16+4)*6N$	**468N**	$=(10*6 + 9*2)*6N$
D_τ	ELLPack	**720N**	$=12*(16+4)*3N$	**282N**	$=(12*6 + 11*2)*3N$

(a) D_v and D_τ Matrices data transfer and FLOPS requirement

Approach	D_v		D_τ		Total transferred elements
Naïve	**27N**	$=3N*5+6N*2$	**15N**	$=6N*1.5+3N*2$	42N
SB	**15N**	$=3N+6N*2$	**12N**	$=6N+3N*2$	27N
Improvement	1.8×		1.25×		1.6×

(b) Naïve and spatial blocking data transfer requirement

Approach	Flops	Bytes	AI	Transfer improvement
Naïve	846N	2832N	0.30	–
SELL	750N	2592N	0.29	1.09×
SB	846N	2592N	0.33	1.09×
SELL + SB	750N	2352N	0.32	1.20×

(c) Combined improvement

in the cache memory. Each nonzero $N \times N$ block of the matrix, requires loading N numbers of the multiplied vector. Hence, D_v SpMV product requires loading 15 N numbers (loading the multiplied vector 5 times) and D_τ SpMV product requires loading 9 N numbers (loading the multiplied vector 1.5 times). SB can ideally load the multiplied vector once during the SpMV product by reusing each vector element completely while in the cache memory. The results vector requires two data transfers per number between the cache and the main memory, assuming no streaming stores operations. In Table 1.b, we show the vectors data transfer model of D_v and D_τ SpMV products using the naïve and SB approaches. The total data transfer requirement of the vectors is insignificant compared to the matrices in the SpMV products. However, the vector data transfer becomes significant in the RHS cache blocking optimization.

Total data transfer and arithmetic intensity: We show the AI model, the total FLOPS, and data transfer requirement of the SpMV product in Table 1.c, when using SELLPack format and SB techniques. Although the SELLPack optimization does not improve the AI, it reduces the total FLOPS and data transfer, thus it improves the performance. We use the data transfer reduction factor as an indication to the performance improvements, as the SpMV product is memory bound. We model the RHS blocking improvements factor by considering the memory data transfer reduction as the ratio in the following equation:

$$\text{Improvement factor} = \frac{M_{RHS} \times (M_b + V_b)}{M_b + V_b \times M_{RHS}} \quad (4)$$

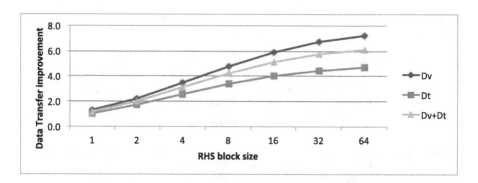

Fig. 3. Spatial and RHS blocking estimated data transfer improvement factor, as calculated in Eq. (4)

where M_{RHS} is the number of blocked RHS, M_b and V_b are the required matrix and vector main memory loads, respectively. Here we divide the required data transfer of separate SpMV products by the required data transfer of loading the matrix once with M_{RHS} vectors. In Fig. 3, we show the model data transfer improvement factor of the RHS blocking with SELLPack and SB, using the naïve implementation as the baseline. We observe significant improvement by the RHS blocking compared to other techniques, as it amortizes the matrix data transfer, which is the significant part. As the RHS block size increases we notice less improvement, for example, from 32 to 64 RHS.

3.1   Cache Block Size Model

Increasing the RHS block size reduces the number of matrix rows that fit in the cache memory. We construct a cache block size model to estimate the number of rows that fit in the cache memory from the parameters setup. The number of rows that fit in a given Cache memory is

$$
C \left/ \left(\frac{V_e}{\text{row}} \times M_{RHS} \times 16 + 2 \times \frac{NNZ}{\text{row}} \times (16 + 4) \right) \right. \tag{5}
$$

where C is the cache memory block size in bytes. V_e/row is the number of loaded vector elements per matrix row, for example, $V_e/\text{row} = 4$ in D_v SpMV product, as we need to store one element of the result vector and read three elements of the multiplied vector. We show examples of the expected block size of various RHS block sizes and relevant cache sizes for the D_v and D_τ SpMV products in Fig. 4. Each core in Haswell has 2.5 MiB L3 cache memory per core. We use the rule-of-thumb that half of this value is usable for blocking [5,10], i.e., 1.25 MiB. Similarly we consider that KNL has 128 kiB L2 cache per thread when using two-threads per core. We observe that the block size decreases significantly in KNL when the RHS block is >16, which results in a significant control flow overhead. Therefore, we replace the SB with loop reordering in KNL to reduce the cache block size requirements.

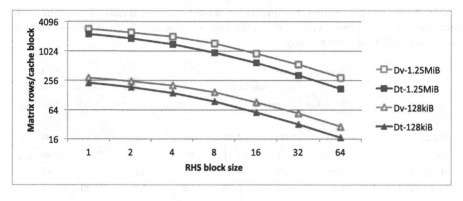

Fig. 4. RHS cache block size model at various setups. The legend refers to matrix–"cache memory size".

4   Performance Results

We study the impact of the D_v SpMV product optimization techniques in a separate benchmark to understand their characteristics. We also observe the impact of our OpenMP parallelization of the code and using our SpMV product optimization techniques in the EMGeo application.

4.1   SpMV Product Benchmark

We use a benchmark code for the D_v SpMV product in the EMGeo application, as the SpMV products consume significant portion of the code runtime, as we show in Sect. 4.2. Table 2 shows the performance improvements and the transferred memory volumes improvements model prediction and measurement, using different optimization combinations. We show results for a single socket Haswell and KNL processors, using a grid of size $110 \times 110 \times 105$. The results in the last row in Table 2 use SB and loop reordering in Haswell and KNL, respectively, in addition to the SELL and mRHS optimizations. We do not use SB in KNL optimizations because it results in less performance than the naïve code. In the RHS blocking optimization, we use 32 and 64 RHS block size in Haswell and KNL, respectively. The SpMV operation is repeated 100 times, where every 10 repetitions are timed together. We report the median time of the experiments.

KNL results are reported in SNC2-flat mode using MCDRAM only, as the data fits in the MCDRAM in the production code. We observe similar performance in all KNL modes. Using the MCDRAM memory, compared to using the DDR4, increases the performance in KNL by a factor of 3.0× and 4.2× in the naïve and optimized codes, respectively. KNL is faster than a single socket Haswell processor by over a factor of 3×, which is mainly attributed to the higher memory bandwidth.

We make several observations regarding the transferred memory volume improvement model and measurements in Table 2. The measurements are closer

Table 2. D_v SpMV product benchmark measurements and model of different optimizations in shared memory. "Best" in the last row refers to SB and loop reordering in Haswell and KNL, respectively

Processor	Haswell (1 socket)			KNL			KNL/
	Perf.	Mem vol. improv.		Perf.	Mem vol. improv.		Haswell
Approach	Speedup	Measured	Model	Speedup	Measured	Model	Speedup
Naïve	-	-	-	-	-	-	3.71
SELL	1.05	1.06	1.15	1.19	1.09	1.15	4.20
SB	1.05	1.11	1.11	0.88	1.06	1.11	3.08
SELL+SB	1.26	1.28	1.30	1.13	1.23	1.30	3.33
Best+SELL+mRHS	4.97	5.36	6.75	4.79	3.50	7.20	3.58

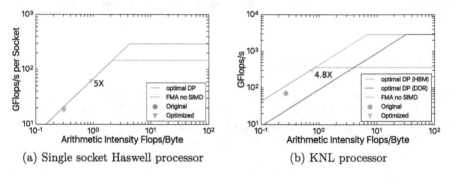

(a) Single socket Haswell processor   (b) KNL processor

Fig. 5. The roofline results of different optimization techniques over the D_v SpMV product benchmark

to the model in Haswell, especially the "SB" and "SELL+SB" results, which may be attributed to its larger cache memory per core. The optimizations in the last row result in large gap between the memory measurements and model. We observed that the gap increases as we use larger RHS block size. Consequently, the KNL result has larger gap as it uses double the RHS block size.

The roofline analysis [12–14] of the D_v benchmark results is shown in Fig. 5, where we used the techniques described in [7] and using Intel Software Development Emulator [11] to prepare these results. The roofline model shows that our RHS blocking technique significantly improves the AI. The code is still memory bandwidth-bound, so it cannot benefit from vectorization optimizations.

4.2 EMGeo Performace

We measure the time in the major components of EMGeo code. The time is mainly dominated by the IDR solve, which is in turn is dominated by the SpMV products and the MPI communication. Our experiments consist of single Cori node, single KNL processor, and 16 Cori nodes results.

Table 3. Single node (a) and multi-node performance (b) of EMGeo code. Note that SpMV product and communication time are parts of the IDR solve time

	IDR solve	SpMV		Communication		MPI topology			Threads/
	Time	Time	%	Time	%	X	Y	Z	process
				Haswell					
Original	208	147	71%	30	14%	2	4	4	1
Optimized	118.5	40	34%	14	12%	1	1	2	16
Speedup	1.76x	3.68x	-	2.14x	-	-	-	-	-
				KNL					
Original	151.7	79	52%	53	35%	4	8	4	1
Optimized	45.6	19.25	42%	14	31%	4	4	4	2
Speedup	3.33x	4.10x	-	3.79x	-	-	-	-	-

(a) Single node performance

	IDR solve	SpMV		Communication		MPI topology			Threads/
	Time	Time	%	Time	%	X	Y	Z	process
Original	342	122	36%	216	63%	4	8	16	1
Optimized	174	38	22%	64	37%	2	4	4	16
Speedup	1.97x	3.21x	-	3.38x	-	-	-	-	-

(b) performance on 16 Haswell nodes

We summarize the single node results in Table 3.a. The experiment evaluates 32 RHS with 500 Krylov solver iterations, using a $100 \times 50 \times 50$ grid size, which is comparable to the subdomain size in productions scenarios. The original code does not have shared memory parallelization, so it uses one MPI rank per core. The optimized code uses 32 RHS block size and uses single MPI rank per socket in Haswell experiment. We observe that the SpMV product takes over half of the runtime in the original IDR solver implementation. Our SpMV product optimizations result a speedup of 3.7× in Haswell and 4.1× in KNL, which is different than D_v SpMV product improvements in the benchmark. In addition to the difference in the grid size, D_τ SpMV product has less benefit from our optimization because it does not utilize the SELLPack format. Moreover, several SpMV product kernels in the application are fused with other kernels to improve the data locality. The reduction in the MPI ranks by a factor of 16× has significant impact in speeding up the code, as less ranks are involved in the reductions and halo exchange operations.

We show results for KNL in Quad flat mode, as we obtain the same performance in the other modes. The whole application data fits in the MCDRAM memory, so we run the code using the MCDRAM only. The best performance in KNL is observed at two threads per core. We tuned the MPI ranks vs. the OpenMP threads manually in the optimized code. We observe 3.3× speedup in the code, where the SpMV and communication operations run about 4.1× and 3.8× faster, respectively. Using the MCDRAM memory, compared to using the DDR4 only, increases the performance in KNL by a factor of 4.2× in the optimized code.

We summarize the results of a 16 Cori nodes experiment in Table 3.b. The experiment evaluates 32 RHS with 2500 Krylov solver iterations limit, using a grid of size 100^3. The SpMV product optimizations result in less improvement in this code, mostly, because smaller subdomains are evaluated in shared memory. The MPI communication consumes about half the runtime due to the increased surface-to-volume ratio of the subdomains. Again, by reducing the number of MPI processes by a factor of 16×, our optimized version achieves about 3.4× speedup in the communication time. We discuss further ideas to handle this issue in the future work section.

5   Conclusion and Outlook

In this paper, we present optimization techniques in Intel Haswell and KNL processors for EMGeo software. In particular, we optimize the SpMV product in the IDR Krylov solver part, where most of the application time is spent. We obtain performance improvements by reducing the data traffic to the main memory in the SpMV products and reducing the MPI communication time by using hybrid MPI+OpenMP parallelization. We use SB, SELLPack sparse matrix format, and most importantly a RHS cache blocking technique. We deploy performance modeling to identify relevant optimizations and to understand the optimization quality and issues.

Our optimizations improved the performance of the D_v SpMV product by a factor of 5.0× in Haswell and 4.8× in KNL. We improve the performance of the forward step of EMGeo application by incorporating our SpMV optimizations and using OpenMP parallelization. As a result, The application runs 1.8× and 3.3× faster in Haswell and KNL, respectively.

In general, KNL achieves better performance than Haswell due to the higher available memory bandwidth. SB did not improve the KNL performance, but we gained the desired improvement by reordering the loops to access the matrix rows in an array-of-structures pattern.

RHS blocking provides significant performance improvements and prepares the code to use block IDR algorithm and overlap computations with communication in the solver. We plan to implement and validate the Block IDR method, which is expected to significantly reduce the required iteration count to convergence. We also plan to overlap the computations and communication of independent RHS to obtain better strong scaling performance.

Acknowledgments. This research used resources of the National Energy Research Scientific Computing Center, a DOE Office of Science User Facility supported by the Office of Science of the U.S. Department of Energy under Contract No. DE-AC02-05CH11231.

References

1. Datta, K.: Auto-tuning stencil codes for cache-based multicore platforms. Ph.D. thesis, EECS Department, University of California, Berkeley. http://www.eecs. berkeley.edu/Pubs/TechRpts/2009/EECS-2009-177.html
2. Gropp, W., Kaushik, D., Keyes, D., Smith, B.: Toward realistic performance bounds for implicit CFD codes. In: Proceedings of parallel CFD, vol. 99, pp. 233–240. Citeseer (1999)
3. Kreutzer, M., Thies, J., Röhrig-Zöllner, M., Pieper, A., Shahzad, F., Galgon, M., Basermann, A., Fehske, H., Hager, G., Wellein, G.: GHOST: building blocks for high performance sparse linear algebra on heterogeneous systems abs/1507.08101 (2015). http://arxiv.org/abs/1507.08101
4. Malas, T., Hager, G., Ltaief, H., Stengel, H., Wellein, G., Keyes, D.: Multicore-optimized wavefront diamond blocking for optimizing stencil updates. SIAM J. Sci. Comput. **37**(4), C439–C464 (2015). doi:10.1137/140991133
5. Malas, T.M.: Tiling and asynchronous communication optimizations for stencil computations. Ph.D. thesis, King Abdullah University of Science and Technology, December 2015
6. Monakov, A., Lokhmotov, A., Avetisyan, A.: Automatically tuning sparse matrix-vector multiplication for GPU architectures. In: Patt, Y.N., Foglia, P., Duesterwald, E., Faraboschi, P., Martorell, X. (eds.) HiPEAC 2010. LNCS, vol. 5952, pp. 111–125. Springer, Heidelberg (2010). doi:10.1007/978-3-642-11515-8_10
7. NERSC: Measuring arithmetic intensity. https://www.nersc.gov/users/application-performance/measuring-arithmetic-intensity
8. Petrov, P.V., Newman, G.A.: Three-dimensional inverse modelling of damped elastic wave propagation in the fourier domain. Geophys. J. Int. **198**(3), 1599–1617 (2014)
9. Petrov, P.V., Newman, G.A.: 3d finite-difference modeling of elastic wave propagation in the laplace-fourier domain. Geophysics **77**(4), T137–T155 (2012). doi:10. 1190/geo2011-0238.1
10. Stengel, H., Treibig, J., Hager, G., Wellein, G.: Quantifying performance bottlenecks of stencil computations using the execution-cache-memory model. In: Proceedings of the 29th ACM on International Conference on Supercomputing, pp. 207–216. ACM (2015)
11. Tal, A.: Intel software development emulator. https://software.intel.com/en-us/articles/intel-software-development-emulator
12. Williams, S.: Auto-tuning performance on multicore computers. Ph.D. thesis, EECS Department, University of California, Berkeley, December 2008
13. Williams, S., Watterman, A., Patterson, D.: Roofline: an insightful visual performance model for floating-point programs and multicore architectures. Commun. ACM. **52**(4), 65–76 (2009)
14. Williams, S., Stralen, B.V., Ligocki, T., Oliker, L., Cordery, M., Lo, L.: Roofline performance model. http://crd.lbl.gov/departments/computer-science/PAR/rese arch/roofline/

Optimizing a Multiple Right-Hand Side Dslash Kernel for Intel Knights Corner

Aaron Walden[1(✉)], Sabbir Khan[1], Bálint Joó[2], Desh Ranjan[1],
and Mohammad Zubair[1]

[1] Department of Computer Science, Old Dominion University,
Norfolk, VA 23529, USA
{awalden,skhan,dranjan,zubair}@cs.odu.edu
[2] Thomas Jefferson National Accelerator Facility,
Newport News, VA 23606, USA
bjoo@jlab.org

Abstract. There is a significant interest in the computational physics community to perform lattice quantum chromodynamics (LQCD) simulations, which can run into the trillions of operations. LQCD computations solve a sparse linear system using a Wilson Dslash kernel, which has an arithmetic intensity of 0.88–2.29. This makes Dslash memory bandwidth-bound on most architectures, including Intel Xeon Phi Knights Corner (KNC). Most research optimizing the Dslash operator has been focused on single right-hand side (SRHS) linear solvers. There is a class of LQCD computations which aims to solve systems with multiple right-hand sides (MRHS), presenting additional opportunities for data reuse and vectorization. We present two approaches to MRHS Dslash: a vector register blocking approach and one using the software package QPhiX with a custom code generator for low-level intrinsics. We observed significant speedups using our approaches, with sustained performance of over 700 GFLOPS (single precision) in one instance. We achieved up to 29 % of theoretical peak performance compared to a maximum of 13 % obtained by the previous SRHS method using QPhiX.

Keywords: LQCD · Optimization · Performance · Wilson-Dslash · Code generator · Parallel programming · Vectorization · Xeon Phi Knights Corner

1 Introduction

Lattice quantum chromodynamics (LQCD) is a uniquely important computational technique for the simulation of the strong nuclear force, which governs

Notice: Authored by Jefferson Science Associates, LLC under U.S. DOE Contract No. DE-AC05-06OR23177. The U.S. Government retains a non-exclusive, paid-up, irrevocable, world-wide license to publish or reproduce this manuscript for U.S. Government purposes.

© Springer International Publishing AG 2016
M. Taufer et al. (Eds.): ISC High Performance Workshops 2016, LNCS 9945, pp. 390–401, 2016.
DOI: 10.1007/978-3-319-46079-6_28

quark and gluon interaction in the nucleon. LQCD is to date the only non-perturbative, model-independent, quantum field theory in use for the calculation of quark-gluon interactions. LQCD simulations are thus needed for areas of research at the frontiers of physics, including understanding of the allowed states and structure of hadronic and nuclear matter. To facilitate numerical computation, LQCD discretizes space-time as a 4-dimensional hypercubic lattice. To simulate larger lattices with shorter lattice spacing, ever-increasing computing power is required. The computational core of LQCD with Wilson fermions is the Wilson Dslash operator (henceforth Dslash), a nearest neighbor stencil operator summing matrix-vector multiplications over lattice points, whose performance is bandwidth-bound on most architectures [7]. Reportedly, up to 90 % of LQCD running time may be spent applying Dslash [6]. Clearly, optimization of Dslash is paramount in the performance of LQCD simulations.

We approach the optimization of Dslash by designing two different kernels for Intel Xeon Phi Knights Corner (KNC). Significant research has been devoted to exploring KNC's potential to drive LQCD simulations [5,7,8,10,14]. The bulk of this research in the area of Dslash has involved single right-hand side (SRHS) solvers, though [10,12] use multiple right-hand sides (MRHS). We describe Dslash kernels applied to MRHS in parallel on a single node. For our approaches, we have written kernels which use 8 and 16 right-hand sides (RHS). The intuition behind a MRHS approach is that each RHS can make use of the same gauge field configuration (see Sect. 2.1), which can increase the arithmetic intensity of the Dslash operator from 0.92 (SRHS) to 1.47 (16 RHS) in an otherwise unoptimized scenario.

In the first of our two approaches, we hand code a kernel using KNC vector *intrinsics* (see Sect. 2.2) which uses a register blocking (RegBlk) technique to minimize the pressure register spills would put on the L1 cache. We reduce register pressure by specifying a certain order to the matrix-vector multiplications and by holding accumulated sums in vector registers. This is straightforward in a kernel with 8 RHS, but requires some tricks to eliminate spills in a 16 RHS kernel, due to the limited number of vector registers. We also explain our approach to vectorization for KNC's powerful vector processing unit (VPU). In contrast to RegBlk, vectorization is simple for 16 RHS and challenging for 8 RHS.

Our second approach optimizes a kernel using the *QPhiX* LQCD framework [4] and its custom code generator [3], which generates SIMD intrinsics for modern architectures. The goal of QPhiX is to provide a high level module which handles threading, cache-blocking, and MPI communication and a module which provides an abstraction into which the code generator can plug SIMD intrinsics for various architectures. QPhiX and its code generator also provide multiple configurations (blocking, vector length, precision) and approaches to vectorization. We modified the code generator to provide a new configuration option for 16 RHS and to support prefetching on KNC. We also modified QPhiX to support MRHS (for example, a new memory layout is necessary) and our own site traversal strategies (see Sect. 6). To implement 8 RHS, we modified the 16 RHS code produced by the code generator.

The remainder of this paper is structured as follows. In Sect. 2 we describe the Dslash operator at a high level as well as the target hardware, KNC. In Sect. 3 we detail our RegBlk implementations. In Sect. 4 we describe the QPhiX and code generator (QPhiX-CoGen) approach. Finally, we discuss our results and compare them to a SRHS QPhiX-CoGen kernel.

2   Background

2.1   Dslash

LQCD's Dslash operator is applied over a finite space-time discretized as a 4-dimensional hypercubic lattice. One may imagine the lattice as a set of linked points. In LQCD, quark fields are represented by lattice points and gluon fields by the links. The lattice has some length in a direction $\mu \in \{x, y, z, t\}, L_\mu$. The number of sites on a lattice is given by $VOL = L_x \times L_y \times L_z \times L_t$. Each site (with coordinates $<x, y, z, t>$) has 2 neighbors for each direction, forward and backward, which correspond to the positive and negative directions on that axis. For neighbor site determination, the lattice has periodic boundary conditions.

We can think of Ψ and $\mathbf{U}$ as the input to Dslash. Ψ defines ψ for every site, a 4×3 matrix of complex numbers called a *spinor*. $\mathbf{U}$ defines U for every site, a 3×3 matrix of complex numbers called a gauge field or gauge matrix. Since U are members of the group $SU(3)$, they can be stored in several representations. A particular trick is to store only two rows of a 3×3 unitary matrix representation, and to reconstruct the 3rd row by appealing to unitarity (i.e. that $\det(U) = 1$) from the complex conjugate of the vector product of the first two rows.

Dslash computes χ for all of the even or odd (based on sum of coordinates) sites on the lattice. χ is also a spinor of the same dimensions as ψ, and in a full solver will be used as the input to another iteration of the computation.

We can employ a spin projection trick, reducing $\psi \in \mathbb{C}^{4 \times 3}$ to $\psi' \in \mathbb{C}^{2 \times 3}$, which increases the arithmetic intensity of the operator. Applying Dslash to a site will calculate χ by summing $U\psi'$ for each neighbor of the site in question into what we'll call χ^u, the upper sum. Simultaneously, the lower sum χ^l will be computed as a permutation of the result of $U\psi'$ for each neighbor. These two sums together form χ. For more information about Dslash, please see [9].

2.2   Intel Xeon Phi Knights Corner

Knights Corner is a line of many-core PCIe coprocessor cards in the Intel Xeon Phi family. KNC cards are massively parallel chips with high memory bandwidth suited for scientific computing applications. They feature up to 61 cores running at up to 1.238 GHz. A key feature of KNC is its VPU. KNC boasts 512-bit vector registers, capable of SIMD operations on 16 single precision numbers simultaneously. Individual cores can support up to 4 hardware threads, each with a full context of registers, including vector registers, of which there are 32. Intel provides a set of C-style functions called intrinsics, which act directly on vector registers in an assembly-like way. For further KNC details, please see [1].

3   Multiple Right-hand Side Performance Model

The approach of solving for MRHS is an established technique in LQCD research [10,13]. We create a new operator with lower bandwidth needs than N applications of the original operator. Application of Dslash to a single site performs 1320 FLOPs. Because we assume the operator is bandwidth-bound [7], we can analyze the expected speedup for different numbers of right-hand sides if we take the performance to be equal to: $\frac{\text{FLOPs}}{\text{byte}} \times$ bandwidth. Then, we need only divide the MRHS FLOPs/byte by the SRHS FLOPs/byte to compute speedup. We begin by defining variables. N is the number of right hand sides. Let G be the number of components in a gauge matrix and let $F = \texttt{sizeof(float)}$. In this model, we will not consider architectural details like cache line size. For each site's Dslash computation, we need to load $8GF$ bytes. Let S be the number of components in a spinor (24). Let us define a SRHS *neighbor spinor reuse factor* R_1 and similarly R_N for MRHS. This is the number of neighbor spinors already present in cache when processed. For each site in SRHS, then, we need to load $(8 - R_1)$ neighbor spinors plus one unavoidable spinor to write the output. In total, this is $SF((8 - R_1) + 1)$ bytes in spinors. For MRHS, we replace R_1 with R_N and multiply the neighbor spinors and FLOPs by N. That gives us MRHS FLOPs/byte of $\frac{1320N}{8GF+NSF((8-R_N)+1)}$ and SRHS FLOPs/byte of $\frac{1320}{8GF+SF((8-R_1)+1)}$. Then, to compute speedup, we divide MRHS by SRHS:

$$\text{speedup} = \frac{8NGF + NSF(9 - R_1)}{8GF + NSF(9 - R_N)}$$

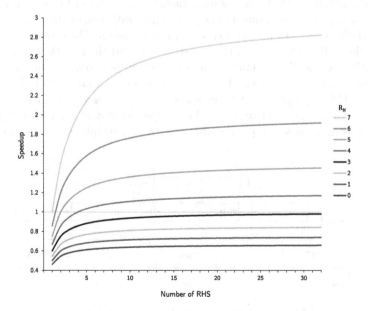

Fig. 1. MRHS scaling for values of N and R_N.

To visualize our speedup as values of N and R_N vary, we can assume values of the other variables. We can take R_1 to be 7, which is borne out in practice for at least lattices up to 32^4, though it requires substantial effort to achieve [14]. Single precision ($F = 4$), a spinor size of $S = 24$, and 12-compression of U meaning $G = 12$ (see Sect. 6), yields the graph of speedup versus N shown in Fig. 1. A separate curve is shown for each value of parameter $R_N \in \{0, 1, \dots, 7\}$, which is not necessarily restricted to integers. Notice we require $R_N > 3$ to achieve any speedup, which will limit our performance gains for lattices of medium to large size, as spinor data scales by N and cache size remains fixed.

4   Register Blocking Approaches

8 RHS. We must compute $U\psi'$ for a single U and 8 different ψ'. This suggests a simple vectorization – broadcast a component of U to fill a register then fill another register with whatever will be multiplied by that component of U. That will be a row of ψ'. Happily, because there are 2 (real or imaginary) components in a row of ψ' and 8 RHS, we can fill a vector register with a row of ψ' by treating the real and imaginary components separately. We cannot store rows of ψ' in memory directly, however, as they are a projection (see Sect. 2.1) of some ψ, meaning the components of ψ' are formed by computing the sum or difference of two components of ψ. Thus, we must store components of ψ in pairs of 8 (for each RHS) which interact with other pairs to form a row of the projected ψ'. With such a layout, we fully vectorize both the projections and the matrix-vector multiplications.

In the projection of ψ, when row 0 interacts with row 2, row 1 interacts with row 3. For a given μ, real components always interact with real or imaginary components and vice versa. All interactions occur intra-column. The direction of μ only changes signs. Bearing in mind these restrictions and the fact that KNC allows permutation across 256-bit lanes, it is clear we can pair components by column and realness, and these pairs and the general data layout are given in Fig. 2.

For 8 RHS, the upper and lower sums occupy 12 vector registers (24 components, 2 components per register). The projected matrix occupies 6 registers. We can project a single component of U at a time, multiplying by the rows of ψ'

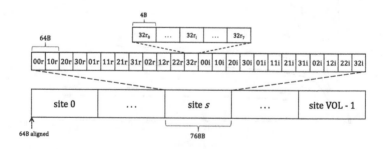

Fig. 2. Layout of 8 RHS RegBlk in memory.

and storing the result in two accumulator registers, one for the real and imaginary components of the row of the result. We then proceed across a row of U, computing the dot product of the first row and column of U and ψ', respectively. Once a component of $U\psi'$ has been computed, it can be added directly to the upper sum and some component of the lower sum. his requires only an additional 3 registers, bringing the total to 21, well short of the limit of 32.

16 RHS. KNC's vector length is 64 bytes or 16 4-byte floats. This simplifies the vectorization scheme for 16 RHS. Each component of ψ fills one vector register, so there is no need to worry about how different components will interact during projection and multiplication. Thus, all of the difficulties of the 8 RHS scheme vanish, and we simply place each component of ψ in its own register.

16 RHS register blocking requires a different approach than the one we use for 8 RHS. We must necessarily keep the upper and lower sums in registers (to avoid spills) and this requires 24, leaving only 8 for calculations. Since our 8 RHS algorithm requires loading all projections, that would require $24 + 12$ registers for 16 RHS, so we must use a different approach.

The problem lies in the temporary accumulation of sums. What we can do to solve this is propagate the sign changes required by the lower sum down to the lower level multiplies, changing `fmadds` to `fnmadds` where appropriate. Then we no longer require any intermediate accumulation registers. We can add directly to the upper and lower sums when computing $U\psi'$. We offer a practical example to aid in understanding. For each direction, we add to χ_{00r}^u (upper sum, component 00r) the real part of the complex dot product of the first row and column of U and ψ', respectively.

$$\chi_{00r}^u \leftarrow \chi_{00r}^u + u_{00r}\psi'_{00r} - u_{00i}\psi'_{00i} + u_{01r}\psi'_{10r} - u_{01i}\psi'_{10i} + u_{02r}\psi'_{20r} - u_{02i}\psi'_{20i}$$

This is straightforward. Let us assume we are computing for the first direction backward. Then, we subtract the same dot product used to add to χ_{00r}^u from 01i of the lower:

$$\chi_{01i}^l \leftarrow \chi_{01i}^l + -(u_{00r}\psi'_{00r} - u_{00i}\psi'_{00i} + u_{01r}\psi'_{10r} - u_{01i}\psi'_{10i} + u_{02r}\psi'_{20r} - u_{02i}\psi'_{20i})$$

This is how we go about *unrolling* the multiplication to eschew intermediate sums. We simply compute the dot product twice, using `fmadd` and `fnmadd` where appropriate to account for the sign changes. Unrolling allows us to carry out the computation using only 5 registers (a row of ψ' and a component of U) in addition to the sums.

This approach results in approximately 23 % more cycles spent on vector arithmetic instructions compared to the 8 RHS approach, but these may be hidden behind load latencies.

5 QPhiX and Code Generator Based Approach

QPhiX and its code generator provide an approach to vectorization over multiple sites, but no MRHS option. We have modified both QPhiX and its code generator to compute the Dslash operator using 16 RHS. To do so, we modified QPhiX's memory layout to add an extra dimension for each site, over which we vectorize. We also customized the threaded loop over sites in order to experiment with our own site traversal strategies (see Sect. 6).

In typical SRHS Wilson Dslash, vectorization is done over sites. Thus, each vector register holds multiple sites' worth of data. The unmodified code generator generates intrinsics according to this requirement. We have modified the code generator for our MRHS implementation to generate intrinsics to vectorize our code on the number of RHS. We also modified the broadcast of elements of U to only broadcast from a single site's U. Finally, we modified the code generator to produce prefetch instructions of gauge field data for the current site and spinor data for the current and next sites.

For 8 RHS, the approach (pairing, memory layout, etc.) is the same as Reg-Blk, the only difference is that the code generator based approach lacks register blocking.

6   Results

Experimental Setup. To optimize our different approaches to Dslash implementation, we test every combination of the following options: number of RHS (8/16), lattice size ($8^4/16^4/24^4/32^4$), software prefetching (L1/L2/both/none), thread interleaving (interleaving/default), gauge compression (12/16/default), and cache-controlling traversal (CCT/default).

We discuss additional optimization experiments in [2]. In total, we experiment with over 192 different parameter combinations. In this section we will briefly describe the novel experimental techniques. Please see the referenced thesis for full details.

Thread interleaving divides a chunk of sites among the threads of a single core instead of allocating $\frac{1}{\text{threads\_per\_core}}$ of that chunk of contiguous sites to a single thread (the default allocation). In the former chunk, threads *step over* one another in an interleaved pattern. For example, with 4 threads per core, thread 0 would process sites 0, 4, etc., thread 1 would process sites 1, 5, and so on. See Fig. 3. *Compression* refers to the size of stored gauge matrices, as mentioned in Sect. 2.1. *Cache-controlling traversal* (CCT) is a method of lattice traversal (order sites are processed by threads) that aims to increase the effective size of L2 by performing controlled evictions using the _mm_clevict intrinsic. By traversing slices of the t dimension one a time, we can use controlled evictions to *make room* for new data by explicitly evicting data which we know will not be reused. LRU evictions may result in eviction of data which could be reused by Dslash. Our t slice traversal makes it possible to perform controlled evictions in this way.

All kernels were compiled by the Intel C++ compiler version 16.0.0 and run in native mode on a Xeon Phi 7120P card using 60 cores and 4 threads per core. All experiments were run in single precision. Unless otherwise noted, results are given in GFLOPS.

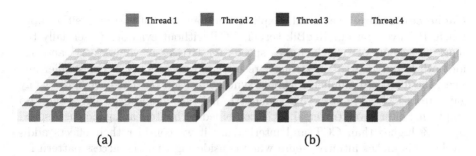

Fig. 3. (a) Default chunking. Threads process their chunks lexicographically. (b) Interleaved traversal. Threads in a core alternate sites in a lexicographical manner. To divide the sites thusly, take the plane shown to be the entire lattice.

6.1   Optimization Results

We begin by discussing the results of our optimization experiments on our kernel implementations. For a full treatment of these results for RegBlk, please see [2].

Prefetching. As expected, both L1 and L2 prefetching increase performance in almost all cases. L1 prefetches increase speeds by roughly 20 %. L2 prefetches increase speeds by 40–60 % with higher increases for larger lattices. The exception is that L2 prefetches decrease speed by 15 % in the case of lattices of volume 8^4 for both 8 and 16 RHS, but only for our RegBlk approach and only when 2 MB memory pages are enabled. At 8^4, for a given core, all processed sites fit in L2, eliminating the need for these prefetches. Why there is no such performance change for QPhiX+CoGen is unknown.

Interleaving. Thread interleaving results show consistency for number of RHS but are inconsistent across lattice volumes. Results show a strong increase for 8^4, strong decrease for 16^4, little change for 24^4, and strong increase for 32^4. The number of RHS does not strongly influence this pattern. Results are amplified for our RegBlk approach. We hypothesize that interleaving results are sensitive to the access pattern of site data, which is consistent for a given lattice volume.

Compression. Gauge compression results are as expected. In most cases, compression to 16 numbers gives superior performance due to increased arithmetic intensity. The reason that 12-compression fails is that backward U are not stored contiguously. U are associated with the forward links of one site and those matrices are stored contiguously in memory, indexed by the linearized index of the site. Backward U are loaded as the (Hermitian conjugate of the) forward link of the backward neighbor. These U are thus stored in 4 noncontiguous locations. Because 12 floats is smaller than the cache line size of KNC (64B), an unused 16B are loaded for every backward 12-compressed U. This results in the same amount of data being loaded for 12 and 16 compression, but 12-compression performs extra integer operations. For very small lattices (8 RHS 8^4), the default (uncompressed) option is superior because there is an excess of memory bandwidth.

Cache-controlling traversal. Explicit evictions were of no use in either approach. However, for our RegBlk kernel, CCT without evictions (essentially the blocking scheme of [11]) increases speeds for lattices of volumes 24^4 and 32^4 for both 8 and 16 RHS. A stronger result is observed for 32^4. For smaller lattices, the increased number of thread synchronization barriers overshadows any gains from CCT. We observe a synergistic increase in speed for 32^4 when also employing interleaved traversal. CCT combined with interleaving increases speed by 32 % higher than CCT and interleaving if we consider their effects additively. This makes intuitive sense when considering that the access pattern for CCT+interleaving differs from using either alone. Though we observe improvement using CCT for 24^4, a different combination of results is superior. We do not observe the synergistic effect of interleaving and CCT for 24^4, which is consistent with interleaving's ineffectiveness for 24^4. Again, in the QPhiX+CoGen approach, we see a similar pattern of results but they are dampened.

Table 1 shows the (condensed) results of our optimization experiments on our kernels. For the full results of all 192+ combinations of experimental parameters, see [2]. The relative difference in performance for 8 RHS versus 16 RHS is what we would expect due to the higher arithmetic intensity of 16 RHS.

Table 1. Optimization results (GFLOPS). Highest results in bold. *Def* refers to the unoptimized base RegBlk or QPhiX+CoGen MRHS implementation. *Opt* refers to the highest result achieved using some combination of our optimization techniques.

	RegBlk				QPhiX+CoGen			
	8 RHS		16 RHS		8 RHS		16 RHS	
VOL	Def	Opt	Def	Opt	Def	Opt	Def	Opt
8^4	579	651	640	**708**	306	343	385	411
16^4	405	419	463	**473**	399	440	392	425
24^4	300	337	326	**375**	302	346	289	320
32^4	255	346	235	**387**	263	301	243	304

We should note here that we performed an additional experiment to verify the soundness of our 16 RHS RegBlk approach. We compared our unrolled approach to a modification using accumulator registers in place of extra dot products, ignoring spills. Our unrolled approach performed some 25 % better or more in all test cases.

6.2 Results Comparison

RegBlk vs. QPhiX+CoGen. In all cases, the best results are obtained by our 16 RHS RegBlk approach. For lattices of size 8^4 and 16^4, QPhiX+CoGen 16 RHS performs nearly as well as the RegBlk approach, if we discount several factors. In the RegBlk approach, the OpenMP thread spawn is placed outside of the iteration loop, but QPhiX+CoGen pays the cost of spawning threads

Table 2. Comparison of highest results by lattice size, MRHS vs. SRHS (GFLOPS).

VOL	MRHS	SRHS	Speedup
8^4	708	–	–
16^4	473	251	1.88
24^4	375	255	1.47
32^4	387	315	1.23

on every iteration, which accounts for approximately 150 GFLOPS lost at 8^4. The remaining difference is accounted for by the L2 prefetching issue from the previous section. For 32^4, RegBlk gains a significant amount of performance from thread interleaving and cache-controlling traversal. QPhiX+CoGen does not show nearly the same level of performance gain from these options. Because the implementations only differ meaningfully in the inclusion of register blocking, we surmise the differences observed, especially in situations with higher cache use (CCT+interleaving at 32^4), are due to increased cache pressure caused by register spilling, which is avoided by RegBlk.

MRHS vs. SRHS. In Table 2 we compare the best results from our MRHS kernels to the results of a SRHS kernel using unmodified QPhiX+CoGen which has been tested on the same hardware setup. We observe a set of speedups consistent with the performance model we introduced in Sect. 3. In this model, speedup is dependent on the parameter R_N, the MRHS spinor reuse factor, which is not possible to measure directly. We note that at maximum reuse (which we estimate to be 7 out of 8 neighbors reused), the achievable speedup is approximately 2.8. Though we do not have a result for SRHS 8^4, if we estimate that number at 251, the speedup for MRHS at 8^4 would be 2.8. This follows from the lattice size: at this size, R_N is very high because nearly the entire lattice fits into L2. For further evidence validating our model, consider 16 RHS 16^4, which has neighbor (read) data equal to SRHS 32^4. Considering that the write data also scales with N, we would expect a somewhat smaller reuse factor for 16 RHS 16^4. Given the speedup of 1.88, we calculate a reuse factor of approximately 6 for 16 RHS 16^4, which is very close to the 7 we assume for SRHS 32^4.

As the amount of MRHS spinor data scales with N, the reuse factor and speedup drop quickly. Looking at Table 1, we see that without optimization, speedup for 16 RHS 32^4 is below 1.0. Measuring bandwidth at 140 GB/s, we can calculate, using our model, that our optimizations for RegBlk 16 RHS 32^4 must have increased R_N by a factor of 3.8 in order to achieve the speedup we did over the default RegBlk 16 RHS implementation.

7   Conclusions and Future Work

We have presented the optimization of a single precision Dslash kernel for KNC using a dual approach which included a register blocking hand-coded kernel and a kernel customized from QPhiX and its code generator. We achieved 29 % of peak performance on our target architecture, KNC, compared to 13 % achieved by the previous SRHS kernel. We observed speedups of 23 % and greater in all tested regimes, showing that our kernel is effective on real world problem sizes. We have shown with a direct comparison that register blocking for KNC's VPU may be a critical component of high-performance kernels, as the non-blocked approach showed dampened ability to gain speedup from advanced cache-blocking techniques that are required to achieve the kind of spinor reuse necessary for MRHS implementations to be worthwhile [2].

In our future work, we will continue to optimize our highest performing kernel. We plan to investigate controlled spilling of registers to test the feasibility of implementing a RegBlk approach similar to that of 8 RHS for 16 RHS by using strategic stores to L1 to avoid having to compute extra dot products. We will attempt to increase data reuse in our kernel by testing more advanced lattice traversal techniques. In the area of QPhiX+CoGen, we will give the code generator the ability to generate 8 RHS code as it currently does 16 RHS. After optimization is complete, we will integrate our kernel into a full multi-node LQCD solver.

Acknowledgments. This work was partially supported by a grant from Jefferson Lab. Aaron Walden and Sabbir Khan were also partially supported by the Old Dominion University Modeling and Simulation Fellowship Program and gratefully acknowledge this support. This material is based upon work supported by the U.S. Department of Energy, Office of Science, Office of Nuclear Physics under contract DE-AC05-06OR23177.

References

1. Intel® XeonPhi™ Coprocessor: Software developers guide. Technical report, Intel Corporation, March 2014
2. Walden, A.: An optimized multiple right-hand side Dslash Kernel for Intel® Xeon Phi™. Master's thesis, Old Dominion University, Norfolk, VA (2016). http://www.cs.odu.edu/~awalden/walden_ms_thesis.pdf
3. Joó, B., et. al: Code generator for the QPhiX library, Wilson fermions. https://github.com/JeffersonLab/qphix-codegen
4. Joó, B., et. al: QPhiX: QCD for Intel Xeon Phi and Xeon processors. https://github.com/JeffersonLab/qphix
5. Diavastos, A., Stylianou, G., Koutsou, G.: Exploring parallelism on the Intel® Xeon Phi™ with lattice-QCD kernels. http://clusterware.cyi.ac.cy/data/paper.pdf
6. Gupta, R.: Introduction to lattice QCD. arXiv:hep-lat/9807028. http://arxiv.org/abs/hep-lat/9807028
7. Heybrock, S., Joó, B., Kalamkar, D.D., Smelyanskiy, M.,Vaidyanathan, K., Wettig, T., Dubey, P.: Lattice QCD with domain decomposition on Intel® Xeon Phi™ co-processors. In: Proceedings of the International Conference for High Performance Computing, Networking, Storageand Analysis, SC 2014, pp. 69–80. IEEE Press, Piscataway (2014). http://dx.doi.org/10.1109/SC.2014.11

8. Joó, B., Kalamkar, D.D., Vaidyanathan, K., Smelyanskiy, M., Pamnany, K., Lee, V.W., Dubey, P., Watson, W.: Lattice QCD on Intel® Xeon Phi^{TM} coprocessors. In: Kunkel, J.M., Ludwig, T., Meuer, H.W. (eds.) Supercomputing. LNCS, vol. 7905, pp. 40–54. Springer, Heidelberg (2013)
9. Joó, B., Smelyanskiy, M., Kalamkar, D.D., Vaidyanathan, K.: Chapter 9-Wilson Dslash kernel from lattice QCD optimization. In: Reinders, J., Jeffers, J. (eds.) High Performance Parallelism Pearls Volume Two: Multicore and Many-Core Programming Approaches, vol. 2, pp. 139–170. Morgan Kaufmann, Boston (2015). http://www.sciencedirect.com/science/article/pii/B9780128038192000239
10. Kaczmarek, O., Schmidt, C., Steinbrecher, P., Mukherjee, S., Wagner, M.: HISQ inverter on Intel Xeon Phi and NVIDIA GPUs. CoRR abs/1409.1510 (2014). http://arxiv.org/abs/1409.1510
11. Nguyen, A., Satish, N., Chhugani, J., Kim, C., Dubey, P.: 3.5D blocking optimization for stencil computations on modern CPUs and GPUs. In: Proceedings of the 2010 ACM/IEEE International Conference for High Performance Computing, Networking, Storage and Analysis, SC 2010, pp. 1–13. IEEE Computer Society, Washington, DC (2010). http://dx.doi.org/10.1109/SC.2010.2
12. Richtmann, D., Heybrock, S., Wettig, T.: Multiple right-hand-sidesetup for the DD-αAMG. In: Proceedings of the 33rd International Symposium on Lattice Field Theory, July 2015. http://arxiv.org/abs/1601.03184
13. Sakurai, T., Tadano, H., Kuramashi, Y.: Application of block Krylovsubspace algorithms to the Wilson-Dirac equation with multiple right-hand sides inlattice QCD. Comput. Phys. Commun. **181**(1), 113–117 (2010). http://www.sciencedirect.com/science/article/pii/S0010465509002859
14. Smelyanskiy, M., Vaidyanathan, K., Choi, J., Joó, B., Chhugani,J., Clark, M.A., Dubey, P.: High-performance lattice QCD for multi-core based parallelsystems using a cache-friendly hybrid threaded-MPI approach. In: 2011 International Conference for High Performance Computing, Networking, Storage and Analysis (SC), pp. 1–10, November 2011

Optimizing Excited-State Electronic-Structure Codes for Intel Knights Landing: A Case Study on the BerkeleyGW Software

Jack Deslippe[1]([✉]), Felipe H. da Jornada[2], Derek Vigil-Fowler[3],
Taylor Barnes[1], Nathan Wichmann[4], Karthik Raman[5],
Ruchira Sasanka[5], and Steven G. Louie[2]

[1] NERSC, Lawrence Berkeley National Laboratory, Berkeley, USA
jrdeslippe@lbl.gov
[2] Department of Physics, University of California at Berkeley,
and Materials Sciences Division, Lawrence Berkeley National Laboratory,
Berkeley, USA
[3] National Renewable Energy Laboratory, Golden, USA
[4] Cray, Saint Paul, USA
[5] Intel, Hillsboro, USA

Abstract. We profile and optimize calculations performed with the
BerkeleyGW [2,3] code on the Xeon-Phi architecture. BerkeleyGW
depends both on hand-tuned critical kernels as well as on BLAS and
FFT libraries. We describe the optimization process and performance
improvements achieved. We discuss a layered parallelization strategy to
take advantage of vector, thread and node-level parallelism. We discuss
locality changes (including the consequence of the lack of L3 cache) and
effective use of the on-package high-bandwidth memory. We show preliminary results on Knights-Landing including a roofline study of code
performance before and after a number of optimizations. We find that
the GW method is particularly well-suited for many-core architectures
due to the ability to exploit a large amount of parallelism over plane-wave
components, band-pairs, and frequencies.

1 Introduction to GW

The *ab initio* GW approximation is a theoretical framework that allows one to
compute excited-state properties of materials without any adjustable parameters. Properties such as bandstructures and the optical absorption spectra of a
variety of systems can be computed with this approach, which are of great importance in energy applications like solar cells, batteries, LEDs etc. The GW name
derives from the approximation to the electron-electron interaction in materials where the electron self-energy (similar to correlation energy) is written as
$\Sigma = iGW$, where G stands for the electron Green's function and W for the elec-
trically screened Coulomb interaction. GW calculations are based on the framework of many-body perturbation theory; so they require approximate electron

© Springer International Publishing AG 2016
M. Taufer et al. (Eds.): ISC High Performance Workshops 2016, LNCS 9945, pp. 402–414, 2016.
DOI: 10.1007/978-3-319-46079-6_29

orbitals and energies produced at a mean-field level as input, which are commonly generated with density-functional theory (DFT) codes such as PARSEC [9], PARATEC [13], Quantum ESPRESSO [5], and SIESTA [15].

The GW approximation can be cast into a Schrödinger-like equation with the form [6,7]

$$\left[-\frac{1}{2}\nabla^2 + V_{\text{loc}} + \Sigma(E_n) \right] \phi_n = E_n \phi_n, \qquad (1)$$

where V_{loc} is the combined electron-ion and electron-electron electrostatic attraction, Σ is the electron self-energy operator within the GW approximation (which depends on the DFT orbitals and energies), and E_n and ϕ_n are the electron energies and orbitals. The orbitals can be described in real space as $\phi_n(\mathbf{r})$ or in Fourier space as $\phi_n(\mathbf{G})$, and are represented by complex double precision arrays in the most general case.

GW applications are becoming increasingly used at US Department of Energy (DOE) HPC facilities such as NERSC [10] – the production HPC center in Berkeley. In the summer of 2016, NERSC will field a new HPC system, named Cori, with more than 9000 nodes powered by Intel's Knights Landing (KNL) processors, which are based on Intel's new Many Integrated Core (MIC) architecture. The GW methodology is particularly primed for many-core systems like this because it has many layers of parallelism available to exploit, which include k/q-point, band/orbital-pair, basis-set, and energy parallelism. This is typically multiple orders of magnitude more parallelism than is available in a DFT calculation.

GW calculations can be quite efficiently computed with the BerkeleyGW [2,3] software package, which is able to efficiently take advantage of all the levels of parallelization mentioned. BerkeleyGW is a production GW code written in FORTRAN 2003 and originally optimized for massive distributed-memory HPC systems via MPI parallelization. It is natural to extend the parallelization and optimization in BerkeleyGW to target new MIC architectures.

A typical calculation with BerkeleyGW contains several distinguishable time-consuming steps. In order to optimize these steps on the KNL architecture, we create representative kernels that represent each step, which are described at the end of this section. In Sect. 2, we discuss the performance and optimization strategy for these kernels, as well as work to optimize the Quantum ESPRESSO [5] DFT package (commonly used as input to BerkeleyGW).

1.1 Kernel A Description: Computation of Orbital Transition Probabilities

In this kernel, we construct transition probabilities (referred to as "matrix elements") between electron orbitals under a plane-wave-like perturbation as

$$M_{nn'}(\mathbf{G}) = \langle n | e^{i\mathbf{G}\cdot\mathbf{r}} | n' \rangle. \qquad (2)$$

Here, $\mathbf{G}$ is a plane-wave coefficient in Fourier space, and $\langle n |$ are the input mean-field electronic orbitals, which can also be denoted by ϕ_n. These matrix elements are computed in BerkeleyGW by performing many FFTs:

$$M_{nn'}(\{\mathbf{G}\}) = \mathrm{FFT}^{-1}\left(\phi_n(\mathbf{r})\phi_{n'}^*(\mathbf{r})\right). \tag{3}$$

One can see that a 3D (complex double precision) FFT needs to be performed for each pair of orbitals. Since the number of orbitals scales with the number of atoms, N, the complexity of this calculation is $O(N^3 \log N)$.

1.2   Kernel B Description: Construction of the Electronic Polarizability

In this kernel, the previously-computed "matrix elements" are combined to compute the polarizability of the system, one of the main ingredients of the self-energy

$$\chi_{\mathbf{GG'}}(E) = \sum_n^{occ}\sum_{n'}^{emp} M_{nn'}^*(\mathbf{G})M_{nn'}(\mathbf{G'})\frac{1}{E_n - E_{n'} - E}, \tag{4}$$

where E_n are the mean-field electronic energies and E is the response energy typically computed on a grid of around 50 values. This expressions has a computational complexity of $O(N^4)$ with number of atoms N, and it is evaluated as a large parallel (complex double precision) matrix-matrix multiplication

$$\chi_{\mathbf{GG'}}(E) = \mathbf{M}^*(\mathbf{G}, (n, n'), E) \cdot \mathbf{M}^{\mathrm{T}}(\mathbf{G'}, (n, n'), E), \tag{5}$$

for each E, where (n, n') represents a single composite index that is summed over as the inner dimension in the matrix-matrix product. The matrices $\mathbf{M}$ can be expressed in terms of the matrix elements M as

$$\mathbf{M}(\mathbf{G}, (n, n'), E) = M_{nn'}(\mathbf{G}) \cdot \frac{1}{\sqrt{E_n - E_{n'} - E}}. \tag{6}$$

1.3   Kernel C Description: Computation of Electron Self-Energy

We often approximate the self-energy operator, Σ, to be diagonal in the DFT orbital basis, and also often employ the Hybertsen-Louie generalized plasmon-pole (GPP) approximation [6,7], which models the energy dependence of χ and simplifies the energy integrals needed to compute Σ. Then, Σ takes the form

$$\Sigma_n = \sum_{n'}\sum_{\mathbf{GG'}} M_{n'n}^*(-\mathbf{G})M_{n'n}(-\mathbf{G'})\frac{\Omega_{\mathbf{GG'}}^2}{\tilde{\omega}_{\mathbf{GG'}}(E - E_{n'} - \tilde{\omega}_{\mathbf{GG'}})}v(\mathbf{G'}), \tag{7}$$

where Ω and $\tilde{\omega}$ are precomputed complex double-precision arrays derived from $\chi_{\mathbf{GG'}}(0)$, $v = 1/\mathbf{G}^2$ is the electronic Coulomb interaction, and E is a parameter which sets the desired energy at which to evaluate the material response. The above represents an array reduction (tensor contraction) type of operation, which typically relies on high memory-bandwidth for performance. However, as we will see below, some data reuse is possible if we consider multiple E values (by default we consider 3). For each orbital n computed, the complexity of evaluating Σ is therefore $O(N^3)$. If all n orbitals are considered, the complexity is $O(N^4)$.

2   Optimization Process for KNL

We now describe the optimization of the 3 BerkeleyGW micro kernels described in Sect. 1 for KNL, and also present an optimization for the prerequisite DFT step, illustrated with the Quantum ESPRESSO software. Each kernel has unique challenges, varying arithmetic intensity, [12] and relies either on effective use of the KNL VPUs, MCDRAM, or both. Kernels A and B rely on math libraries (FFT and BLAS) while kernel C is hand-tuned.

Unless otherwise stated, KNL results in this paper are based on the KNL 7210 (64 core, bin 3) part with 16 GB on-package high-bandwidth memory (HBM) MCDRAM and 96 GB of traditional DDR memory. We run with the KNL in the "quadrant" NUMA mode with MCDRAM configured as a flat memory except with specified. In most cases, we assume the ability to strong scale to a sufficient number of nodes to run entirely out of MCDRAM - however, we discuss the use of fastmem directives where appropriate, and find equivalent performance can be generally achieved by targeting only a few arrays for MCDRAM. Intel Haswell architecture numbers are based on a single node of the Cori-Phase 1 system with dual-socket 16 core Xeon E5-2698 processors per node, Ivy Bridge numbers are based on a NERSC Edison node with dual socket 12 core E5-2695 processors per node, and Sandy Bridge numbers are based on a dual socket 8 core E5-2670 processor node. Comparisons are based on the highest SSE or AVX level supported by each architecture. Finally, we use the 2016 update 2 suite of Intel compilers and MKL unless otherwise specified.

2.1   Kernel A Optimization

The $O(N^2)$ FFTs are distributed over the MPI tasks in BerkeleyGW such that each MPI task owns a subset of the FFTs to perform, however each individual FFT is done on a single MPI rank. This distribution of work is favorable for many-core systems, KNL in particular, because it reduces inter-node communication while maintaining a large amount of on-node work left to exploit with on-node parallelization (threads and vectors). Contrast this to a typical DFT calculation where a fewer amount of FFTs are each typically performed in parallel across the MPI tasks in the calculations – leaving a challenge to exploit more parallelism on node.

Targeting KNL, we maintained the MPI distribution of the $O(N^2)$ 3D FFTs but utilize threaded FFT library implementations to handle the thread and vector level performance. To test performance on KNL, we created a kernel that performs a threaded fftw_many [4] call on complex double-precision arrays. We tested this on various architectures using the MKL fftw backend. In Fig. 1 (left), we show the limit of a single very large (6 GB) complex 3D FFT - on the dual-socket Xeon-System we estimate throughput by computing two such FFTs (one on each socket). In Fig. 1 (right), we show many (400) 135^3 FFTs. In this case, on both Xeon and Xeon-Phi we use use both MPI and OpenMP to distribute out the work - 2 MPI tasks on the dual-socket Xeon nodes and 4 MPI tasks on the Xeon-Phi nodes. For the larger FFT, one can clearly see a 2x advantage

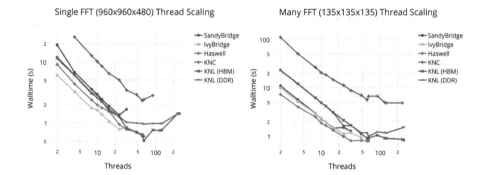

Fig. 1. (Left) Thread scaling (including hyperthreads) of the large complex 3D FFT limit on different architectures. (Right) Thread scaling for 400 135^3 FFTs on various architectures. We compare one Xeon-Phi processor to 2 sockets of Xeon, with threads spread across 2 MPI ranks. DDR/HBM refer to running the calculation out of DDR or MCDRAM with the MCDRAM configured as a flat memory.

streaming data out of MCDRAM vs DDR; however, this advantage is mostly lost when performing many small FFTs – where we likely see more reuse out of cache. The larger FFTs on the bin 3 KNL outperform Haswell by about 20 % while the many smaller FFTs perform at near the same performance between Haswell and bin 3 KNL. Note, if we force the dual-socket Xeon systems to perform a single FFT across both sockets (instead of 1 each), the KNL performance advantage nearly doubles - significant if MPI rank reduction is desirable.

Hybrid Functional Optimization in Quantum ESPRESSO. Quantum ESPRESSO calculations are often used as the mean-field starting point for BerkeleyGW, and often employ exact-exchange based functionals. In analogy to the BerkeleyGW Kernel A problem, exact-exchange requires the computation of $O(N^2)$ FFTs, with a minimum of two FFTs per band/orbital pair. However, unlike BerkeleyGW, Quantum ESPRESSO by default parallelizes these $O(N^2)$ FFTs individually over the MPI tasks in the calculations. A level of band parallelism was previously implemented, but with a number of limitations: (1) it parallelized over only one of the band indices; and (2) if the band parallelization was utilized (i.e., multiple FFTs were performed at once), the parallelization of the remainder of the calculation would be negatively impacted. Both of these issues limit performance on many-core systems. In order to improve the FLOP density on node, we add an additional level of MPI parallelism for band-pairs inspired by the band-pair parallelization in BerkeleyGW, and we enable simultaneous parallelism of the $O(N^2)$ FFT problem and the remainder of the computation. The FFTs can then be done on-node with the expected performance above on KNL. As illustrated by Fig. 2, these modifications substantially improve the overall strong scaling of the code through both on-node and inter-node improvements.

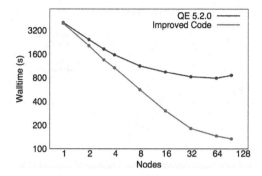

Fig. 2. Strong-scaling of an exact-exchange calculation on a simulation of 64 water molecules on the NERSC Edison (dual-socket Ivy-Bridge) system. The blue curve corresponds to the timings of Quantum ESPRESSO version 5.2.0, while the red curve provides the results of the improvements described in text. (Color figure online)

2.2   Kernel B Optimization

Kernel B contains two computationally intensive steps. The first is the evaluation of Eq. 6 which involves multiplying every element of array M by a pre-computed energy denominator. This is a stream like operation. The second major step is the matrix-matrix multiply itself performed in parallel via many ZGEMMs. Our runs emulate periodic systems with 4000 planewaves, 2000 bands/orbitals and 20 energies (simulated across 50 nodes) leading to matrices of size (565×4800).

We found initially that the performance on KNL suffered due to poor thread scaling of array initialization and the stream-like step described above. For example, the code contained FORTRAN vector statements like:

```
myarray(:,:) = 0D0
```

which are vectorized but not threaded by the compiler. The relatively low bandwidth driven by a single thread, leads such statements to particularly suffer. Secondly we found significantly worse performance on KNL for the stream step described above. This was due to poor data reuse by explicitly calculating the arrays M for each energy E. By instead computing this on the fly immediately before the ZGEMM for each E, we can reuse data efficiently out of L2 cache across the tiles. In Fig. 3, you can see that the optimal performance on bin 3 KNL is about 33 % better than our dual-socket Haswell node. About 80 % of the runtime is ZGEMM - a ratio that increases with problem size.

It is additionally interesting to note that this kernel performs best when run in pure OpenMP mode on the Xeon-Phi. The performance is roughly 30 % slower when using 2 MPI tasks and spreading the OpenMP threads between them, and the separation worsen as more MPI tasks are added. The difference stems primarily from the ZGEMM step, suggesting it is optimal to have a single large threaded ZGEMM on the node rather than multiple simultaneous MPI driven ZGEMMs. The behavior is similar in both quadrant and SNC4 NUMA modes.

Kernel B Thread Scaling

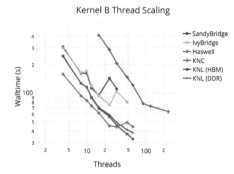

Fig. 3. Thread scaling (including hyperthreads) of optimized kernel B on various architectures. Threads are spread across 2 MPI tasks (one per socket) on Xeon. We run with pure OpenMP on Xeon-Phi in quadrant mode with MCDRAM configured as flat memory.

The performance also does not benefit from hyperthreading on KNL as evident by the sharp upturn in walltime in Fig. 3.

2.3 Kernel C Optimization

As described in Sect. 1, Kernel C is comprised of hand-tuned array reduction-like operations. Since this kernel doesn't rely on math libraries like kernels A and B, a greater amount of work was required to tune this kernel. In recent years, this kernel has represented a growing fraction of the BerkeleyGW runtime, primarily due to use-cases where solutions for many electronic states are required. We describe the multi-step optimization process below:

1. The original code was an MPI-only application where little effort had been spent to analyze or optimize the performance.
2. We refactor the code to have a multi-loop structure appropriate for expressing layered parallelism in terms of MPI, OpenMP and vectors.

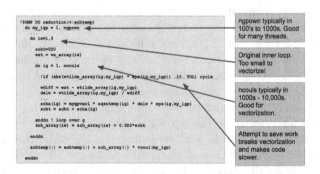

Fig. 4. Code changes to enable compiler auto-vectorization and efficient use of VPU lanes. See description in the text.

3. We refactor the code to enable compiler auto-vectorization. Figure 4 illustrates some of the code changes made to enable vectorization. In particular, we remove cycle statements originally intended to save unnecessary work when thinking serially, we move an inner loop with a trip count of 3 outwards and replace it with a new inner loop with a trip count on the order 1000 or greater. This large inner loop enables us to ignore impacts of alignment and peel/remainder loops.

4. From VTune [8], we determine that we have poor reuse of L2 on both Xeon and Xeon-Phi because accessed rows of arrays `wtilde_array`, `aqsntemp`, `eps` combine to require 1.5 MB (3-5x larger than L2 per core). However, we do get good reuse of the shared 40 MB L3 on Xeon. To improve the situation on Xeon-Phi, we add a level of cache blocking for effective reuse of the L2 cache on both Xeon and Xeon-Phi architectures. In particular, we modify the following (simplified) block of code from

```
do my_igp = 1, ngpown ! OpenMP
  do iw = 1 , 3
    do ig = 1, igmax
      load wtilde_array(ig,my_igp) !512KB per row
      load aqsntemp(ig,n1) !512KB per row
      load eps(ig,my_igp) !512KB per row
```

to

```
do my_igp = 1, ngpown ! OpenMP
  do igbeg = 1, igmax, igblk
    do iw = 1 , 3
      do ig = 1, igmax
        do ig = igbeg, min(igbeg + igblk,igmax)
          load wtilde_array(ig,my_igp) !512KB per row
          load aqsntemp(ig,n1) !512KB per row
          load eps(ig,my_igp) !512KB per row
```

While this only improves reuse by a factor of 3, it is enough to prevent the code from being bandwidth-bound on KNL when using MCDRAM (see roofline figure). The speedup is significantly greater on the Xeon-Phi architecture due the lack of L3. We see negligible speedup on Haswell.

5. We eliminate some conditionals in vector regions to improve vector performance.

6. We utilize > 1 thread per physical core - up to 2 threads per core on Haswell and 4 threads per core on KNL.

Figure 5 shows the optimization process plotted on a roofline [1,19] curve where the x-axis is the arithmetic-intensity (FLOP/bytes-from-memory) computed with Intel's VTune (bytes from memory read) [8] and SDE tools (FLOP/s) [16]. On Haswell, one can see an overall trend towards higher arithmetic intensity and higher performance. We have a final peak performance of

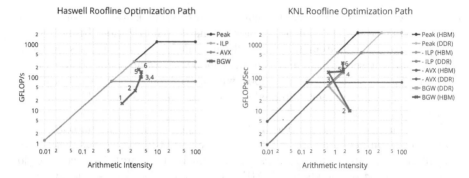

Fig. 5. Optimization process of kernel C on the roofline [17–19] model for Haswell and KNL. The two slopes on the KNL roofline represent running out of DDR or MCDRAM in flat mode. The three ceilings correspond to peak, peak minus Instruction Level Parallelism from FMA and dual VPUs, and the additional loss of vector parallelism (a factor of 4 for Haswell and a factor of 8 for KNL). Arithmetic intensity is measured as the FLOP per byte read+written to memory. See text for more details.

170 GFLOP/s from a final arithmetic intensity of around 3. The performance doesn't quite hit the roofline due to a number of limitations: there is a divide in the final loop that has a multi-cycle latency, there is not a perfect balance between multiplies and adds – a complex multiply involves 4 multiplies and 2 adds, for example – and there are additional conditionals left in the code:

```
do ig = igbeg, min(igend,igmax)
  wdiff = wxt - wtilde_array(ig,my_igp)
  delw = wtilde_array(ig,my_igp) / wdiff
  ...
  scha(ig) = aqsntemp(ig,n1) * delw * eps(ig,my_igp)
  if (wdiffr.gt.limittwo .and. delwr.lt.limitone) then
    scht = scht + scha(ig)
  ...
```

On KNL, the optimization path is not as straightforward: the vectorization step 3, while improving the performance, actually reduces the arithmetic intensity. This is due to the fact that we moved the iw loop (trip count 3) outwards to enable compiler auto-vectorization. This loop provided a reuse factor of 3 for streamed arrays. The issue is rectified by the cache-blocking enabled in step 4. A take-home lesson is that the lack of L3 cache on KNL makes data locality even more important in some situations, as the MCDRAM on KNL is generally out-performed by L3 on Xeon.

The overall walltime for the example problem considered is shown in Fig. 6. For the optimized case, we obtained runtimes of 11.5 s, 21.8 s, and 18.6 s on KNL (MCDRAM), KNL (DDR) and dual-socket Haswell respectively. We observe that vectorization and cache blocking improve the performance on KNL significantly more than on Haswell. Additionally, the performance on KNL with DDR is worse

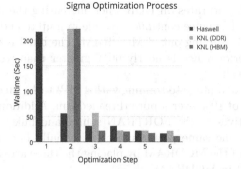

Fig. 6. Walltime for example runs of kernel C used in Fig. 5 for different optimization steps described in the text. Here one Xeon-Phi processor is compared against 2 Xeon sockets. Optimal MPI/OpenMP ratios are used.

than MCDRAM due to fact we are bandwidth limited in the DDR case – points 3,4,5,6 are pinned to the DDR roofline in Fig. 5.

From Figs. 5 and 6, we observe as high as 30 % speedups with hyperthreads on Haswell and KNL utilizing MCDRAM. We see no speedups on KNL when running out of DDR since we have already saturated the available memory bandwidth. This stems from both the ability of multiple threads to drive more bandwidth on KNL and the likelihood of latency hiding in the divides.

We show in Fig. 7 a comparison of pure thread scaling for the optimized code on various Xeon and Xeon-Phi architectures. For low concurrencies, we observe that performance out of DDR and MCDRAM on the KNL is similar. However,

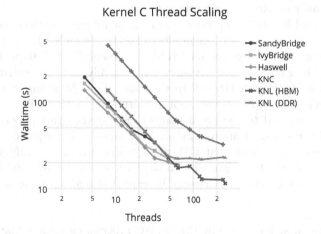

Fig. 7. Thread scaling (including hyperthreads) of optimized kernel C on various architectures. Comparison shows one Xeon-Phi processor against 2 sockets of Xeon. Threads are spread across 2 MPI tasks in the Xeon case.

performance quickly saturates on DDR when increasing the number of threads beyond 40. KNL performance continues to scale well up to and beyond the physical core count when running out of MCDRAM. The bin 3 KNL (when running out MCDRAM) performance is nearly 60 % greater than we what achieve on two sockets of Haswell.

We find a slight advantage to running with 4 MPI tasks (in either SNC4 mode or quadrant mode) of $\tilde{1}0\%$ over a pure threaded run. Additionally, we explicitly add FASTMEM directives to the FORTRAN source and link with memkind and find we can obtain the same performance (marginally better) as running the entire problem out of the MCDRAM by placing the three arrays (wtilde_array, aqsntemp, and eps) in MCDRAM.

Kernel C shows that, for a hand-tuned code with an arithmetic intensity near the roofline vertex (between 1–10), a rich optimization arena exists for improving performance on KNL.

3   Conclusions and Outlook

We have optimized several kernels in BerkeleyGW as well as in the Quantum ESPRESSO DFT code (used as input to BerkeleyGW) targeting the NERSC Cori system. In some cases, math libraries provide an efficient path towards optimal code. However, in some cases, for example kernel C, it took a significant effort to produce optimized code. Performant runs on KNL require effective use of the dual VPUs, MCDRAM, and L2 caches, and efficient thread scaling. For codes with arithmetic intensities near the roofline vertex ($\sim$5 for KNL with MCDRAM), one must essentially consider all optimization avenues on the hardware. One clear trend when optimizing this material science workload for KNL is that optimizations originally targeting the Xeon-Phi architecture improve the code significantly on Xeon architectures as well.

Kernel B and Kernel C represent the most significant bottlenecks in a GW calculations (both scaling with the number of atoms as $O(N^4)$). Both see significant performance advantage on bin 3 KNL over Haswell, 33 %–60 %. For Kernel A, dominated by FFTS, we see advantages for bin 3 KNL in the extremely large limit but near parity with Haswell in the small limit. It is important to note that we expect about a 10 % increase in performance on bin 1 KNL (which will power Cori) compared to the bin 3 numbers reported in this paper due to an addition of 4 cores and an approximately 10 % increase in frequency.

Finally, our work shows that GW applications are particularly well-suited for many-core architectures like that in the Cori system at NERSC because of the many layers of parallelism that can be exploited both on-node and between nodes.

Acknowledgments. Supported by the SciDAC Program on Excited State Phenomena in Energy Materials funded by the U.S. Department of Energy, Office of Basic Energy Sciences and of Advanced Scientific Computing Research, under Contract No. DE-AC02-05CH11231 at Lawrence Berkeley National Laboratory. Derek Vigil-Fowler is support by NREL's LDRD Director's Postdoctoral Fellowship. This research used resources of the National Energy Research Scientific Computing Center, a DOE Office of Science User Facility supported by the Office of Science of the U.S. Department of Energy under Contract No. DE-AC02-05CH11231.

We acknowledge helpful conversations with Mike Greenfield, Paul Kent, David Prendergast and Pierre Carrier.

References

1. Cs roofline toolkit. https://bitbucket.org/berkeleylab/cs-roofline-toolkit
2. Deslippe, J., Samsonidze, G., Strubbe, D.A., Jain, M., Cohen, M.L., Louie, S.G.: BerkeleyGW: a massively parallel computer package for the calculation of the quasiparticle and optical properties of materials and nanostructures. Comput. Phys. Commun. **183**(6), 1269–1289 (2012)
3. http://www.berkeleygw.org
4. Frigo, M., Steven, G.J.: FFTW: an adaptive software architecture for the FFT. In: Proceedings of the 1998 IEEE International Conference on Acoustics, Speech and Signal Processing, vol. 3, pp. 1381–1384. IEEE (1998)
5. Giannozzi, P., Baroni, S., Bonini, N., Calandra, M., Car, R., Cavazzoni, C., Ceresoli, D., Chiarotti, G.L., Cococcioni, M., Dabo, I., Dal Corso, A., Fabris, S., Fratesi, G., de Gironcoli, S., Gebauer, R., Gerstmann, U., Gougoussis, C., Kokalj, A., Lazzeri, M., Martin-Samos, L., Marzari, N., Mauri, F., Mazzarello, R., Paolini, S., Pasquarello, A., Paulatto, L., Sbraccia, C., Scandolo, S., Sclauzero, G., Seitsonen, A.P., Smogunov, A., Umari, P., Wentzcovitch, R.M.: J. Phys.: Condens. Matter **21**, 395502 (2009). http://dx.doi.org/10.1088/0953-8984/21/39/395502
6. Hybertsen, M.S., Louie, S.G.: Electron correlation in semiconductors and insulators: band gaps and quasiparticle energies. Phys. Rev. B **34**(8), 5390 (1986)
7. Hybertsen, M.S., Louie, S.G.: First-principles theory of quasiparticles: calculation of band gaps in semiconductors and insulators. Phys. Rev. Lett. **55**(13), 1418 (1985)
8. Intel vtune. https://software.intel.com/en-us/intel-vtune-amplifier-xe
9. Kronik, L., Makmal, A., Tiago, M.L., Alemany, M.M.G., Jain, M., Huang, X., Saad, Y., Chelikowsky, J.R.: PARSEC the pseudopotential algorithm for realspace electronic structure calculations: recent advances and novel applications to nanostructures. Phys. Status Solidi (b) **243**(5), 1063–1079 (2006)
10. NERSC. http://www.nersc.gov
11. NERSC: Cori. http://www.nersc.gov/systems/cori/
12. NERSC: Measuring arithmetic intensity. http://www.nersc.gov/users/application-performance/measuring-arithmetic-intensity
13. Pfrommer, B., Raczkowski, D., Canning, A., Louie. S.G.: PARATEC (PARAllel Total Energy Code), Lawrence Berkeley National Laboratory (with contributions from Mauri, F., Cote, M., Yoon, Y., Pickard, C., Heynes, P.). For more information see www.nersc.gov/projects/paratec. There is no corresponding record for this reference
14. Raman, K.: Calculating "flop" using intel software development emulator (intel sde), March 2015. https://software.intel.com/en-us/articles/calculating-flop-using-intel-software-development-emulator-intel-sde
15. Soler, J.M., Artacho, E., Gale, J.D., Garca, A., Junquera, J., Ordejn, P., Snchez-Portal, D.: The SIESTA method for ab initio order-N materials simulation. J. Phys. Condens. Matter **14**(11), 2745 (2002)

16. Tal, A.: Intel software development emulator. https://software.intel.com/en-us/articles/intel-software-development-emulator
17. Williams, S.: Auto-tuning Performance on Multicore Computers. Ph.D. thesis, EECS Department, University of California, Berkeley, December 2008
18. Williams, S., Watterman, A., Patterson, D.: Roofline: An insightful visual performance model for floating-point programs and multicore architectures. Commun. ACM **52**(4), April 2009
19. Williams, S.: Roofline performance model. http://crd.lbl.gov/departments/computer-science/PAR/research/roofline/

Optimizing Wilson-Dirac Operator and Linear Solvers for Intel® KNL

Bálint Joó[1](✉), Dhiraj D. Kalamkar[2], Thorsten Kurth[3](✉), Karthikeyan Vaidyanathan[2](✉), and Aaron Walden[3,4]

[1] US DOE Jefferson Lab, Newport News, VA, USA
bjoo@jlab.org
[2] Intel Parallel Computing Labs, Bangalore, India
karthikeyan.vaidyanathan@intel.com
[3] National Energy Research Scientific Computing Center, Berkeley, CA, USA
tkurth@lbl.gov
[4] Old Dominion University, Norfolk, VA, USA

Abstract. Lattice Quantumchromodynamics (QCD) is a powerful tool to numerically access the low energy regime of QCD in a straightforward way with quantifyable uncertainties. In this approach, QCD is discretized on a four dimensional, Euclidean space-time grid with millions of degrees of freedom. In modern lattice calculations, most of the work is still spent in solving large, sparse linear systems. This part has two challenges, i.e. optimizing the sparse matrix application as well as BLAS-like kernels used in the linear solver. We are going to present performance optimizations of the Dirac operator (dslash) with and without clover term for recent Intel® architectures, i.e. Haswell and Knights Landing (KNL). We were able to achieve a good fraction of peak performance for the Wilson-Dslash kernel, and Conjugate Gradients and Stabilized BiConjugate Gradients solvers. We will also present a series of experiments we performed on KNL, i.e. running MCDRAM in different modes, enabling or disabling hardware prefetching as well as using different SoA lengths. Furthermore, we will present a weak scaling study up to 16 KNL nodes.

1 Introduction

Quantum Chromodynamics (QCD) is the theory of the strong nuclear force and interactions, and is responsible for binding quarks into protons and neutrons through the exchange of gluons. Further, residual strong force interactions are responsible for binding protons and neutrons into nuclei which make up atoms and ultimately most of the visible matter in the universe. QCD is also one of the theories making up the Standard Model of elementary particles and interactions. Lattice QCD (LQCD) [4,14,16] is a discretized version of QCD where Euclidean

---

B. Joó—Notice: Authored by Jefferson Science Associates, LLC under U.S. DOE Contract No. DE-AC05-06OR23177. The U.S. Government retains a non-exclusive, paid-up, irrevocable, world-wide license to publish or reproduce this manuscript for U.S. Government purposes.

© Springer International Publishing AG 2016
M. Taufer et al. (Eds.): ISC High Performance Workshops 2016, LNCS 9945, pp. 415–427, 2016.
DOI: 10.1007/978-3-319-46079-6_30

space time is replaced by a 4-dimensional hypercubic lattice. LQCD is itself a fully renormalizable quantum field theory, where the quark matter fields of QCD (so called spinors) are ascribed to lattice sites and gluons fields (so called gauge fields) are ascribed to the lattice links. As LQCD is the only known, model independent, methodology to carry out QCD calculations in the *non-perturbative* regime, it is of vital importance to Nuclear and High Energy physics research and is a major user of supercomputing cycles at HPC centers around the world. A key component of LQCD calculations is the solution of the lattice Dirac equation which encodes the interactions of the quarks and gluons. For reasons, which are beyond the scope of this contribution, various formulations of the Dirac equation exist. In this contribution we will focus on the so called Wilson [21] and Sheikholeslami-Wohlert [17] (colloquially known as Wilson-Clover) formulations.

Intel® Xeon Phi Knights Landing (KNL) is the second generation of the Intel® Xeon Phi architecture products. The CPU studied in this paper is B0 hardware in two configurations: 7250 parts which feature 68 cores (referred to as configuration A) and 7210 parts which feature 64 cores (referred to as configuration B). In both cases, the cores are connected in a 2-dimensional mesh of tiles, with each tile containing 2 cores. The cores are based on the Intel® *Silvermont* architecture running at 1.4 Ghz and augmented by two 512-bit vector units. The cores on a tile share 32 Kb L1 and 1 Mb L2 data cache. The KNL chip also features up to 16 Gb of on package High Speed memory (known as MCDRAM), with a STREAMS bandwidth of ~450 Gb/sec. KNL processors can be partitioned in several ways, for example as a flat mesh, or in quadrant mode with or without sub-NUMA clustering (SNC). In quadrant more, the chip is logically split into 4 quadrants and in SNC mode, each quadrant constitutes a separate NUMA domain, with each quadrant containing one memory controller. Thus the SNC mode enables slightly reduced latencies when communicating between cores, due to restricting coherency traffic to a quadrant.[1] The MCDRAM can be configured in three different ways: in flat-mode used as directly addressable memory, in a cache mode, where it appears as a transparent cache and in a hybrid mode, where one portion is used as cache, and the remainder is used as directly addressable memory.

In this paper we report on the performance of the Wilson and Wilson Clover components on Knight's Landing. We use the publicly available *QPhiX* code [9–11] which implements the techniques reported in [8] for the Wilson dslash operator. In addition we have also implemented various forms of the *Clover* operator and Conjugate Gradients [6] and BiCGStab [18]. The code supports multi-node decomposition and we illustrate weak scaling results in this contribution.

2   Background and Implementation Details

We now turn to discuss the Dirac operator and some implementation details that are relevant to the discussion of our performance results. Most of these details

---

[1] Due to the page limitation, we can not include numbers from SNC studies in this presentation.

are discussed in great detail in [8,9] and we will restrict ourselves to the salient points here.

The Wilson Dirac Operator and Clover Term: Our fields are defined on a hypercubic 4-dimensional lattice of dimensions L_x, L_y, L_z and L_t in the X, Y, Z and T spacetime dimensions respectively. We also label our sites as even or odd, depending on whether the sum of their 4-dimensional space-time coordinates, is even or odd. This implements a checkerboarding of the sites and we store the data for even and odd sites in separate arrays. Each such array has dimensions $(L_x/2) \times L_y \times L_z \times L_t$ sites. Our gauge fields are $SU(3)$ matrices ascribed to directed lattice links, which are 3×3 complex matrices. In our implementation we can employ 2-row compression [3], reducing the data to a 2×3 complex matrix where the third row can be reconstructed on the fly. For each site, we keep the link matrices pointing in the forward and backward directions (to enable unit stride access) resulting in the gauge field being stored as 8 link matrices emanating from each site. Our spinor data is comprised of 12 complex numbers per lattice site, corresponding to 4 *spin* components, each of which is a 3-vector of complex numbers, where the factor 3 is the number of *colors*.

The Wilson Dslash operator is defined as

$$D_{x,y} = \sum_{\mu=0}^{3} U_{2\mu}(x)\left(1 - \gamma_\mu\right)\delta_{x+\mu,y} + U_{2\mu+1}^{\dagger}(x - \mu)\left(1 + \gamma_\mu\right)\delta_{x-\mu,y} \qquad (1)$$

where $\mu \in [0..3]$ is the dimension index, $U_{2\mu}(x)$ $(U_{2\mu+1}^{\dagger})$ are the forward (backward) pointing gauge links emanating from site x respectively. The Kronecker factors $\delta_{x\pm\mu,y}$ couple neighboring spinors in forward/backward $\pm\mu$-direction. Finally the γ-matrices are generators of the Clifford algebra $C\ell_{1,3}(\mathbb{R})$. They can be represented by sparse 4×4 complex matrices acting only on spin components. To apply the Wilson Clover operator, we also need to store the so called *clover term* A for each site. In our case, this term is defined as:

$$A = (N_d + m) - i\frac{1}{8}c_{sw}\sigma_{\mu\nu}F_{\mu\nu} \qquad (2)$$

where N_d is the number of dimensions, m is the quark mass and $\sigma_{\mu,\nu} \equiv [\gamma_\mu, \gamma_\nu]$. The coefficient c_{sw} is the so called *clover coefficient* and $F_{\mu\nu}$ is the QCD field strength tensor. In general, A is a 12×12 complex matrix. With an appropriate choice of γ matrices however, it reduces to a block diagonal form comprised of 2 blocks of 6×6 complex numbers. Furthermore, each block is hermitian and allows for an $L^{\dagger}dL$ decomposition into a diagonal matrix of 6 real numbers d and L being a strictly lower triangular matrix of 15 complex components. The total storage per site thus reduces to 12 real and 30 complex numbers. We also need the inverse clover term A^{-1} which has a similar structure. Both A and A^{-1} are precomputed and supplied by the users to QPhiX.

Our solvers employ the even-odd Schur-complement preconditioned Dirac operators, which are generically of the form: $M_{oo} = A_{oo} - D_{oe}A_{ee}^{-1}D_{eo}$, where the indices e and o refer to even and odd lattice sites. Since D is a nearest neighbor stencil, it takes even sites to odd sites or vice versa. A is local, hence it takes sites even sites to even and odd sites to odd. In the case of $c_{sw} = 0$ we recover an operator known as the preconditioned Wilson Dirac operator, whereas for $c_{sw} \neq 0$ we call the operator preconditioned Clover-Dirac operator. We implement the operators with two kernels: for the Clover case, one evaluates $y_e = A_{ee}^{-1} D_{eo} x_o$ and the second one computes $z_o = A_{oo} x_o - b D_{oe} y_e$. In the Wilson case we specialize these as $y_e = D_{eo} x_o$ and $z_o = a x_o - b D y_e$ where a and b are user supplied real values.

Data Layout in QPhiX: We rearrange the degrees of freedom described above to target vectorization. We adopt an array of structures of arrays (AOSOA) layout where we split the lattice site dimension of our arrays into chunks of SOA sites and make this our fastest running dimension. We notionally split the X and Y plane into tiles. These tiles have dimensions SOA in the X direction and ngy in the Y direction. The constraint is that $SOA \times ngy = V$, with V the hardware vector length. The idea is that we fill vector registers with data from SOA sites along the X dimension, drawn from ngy separate values of the coordinate in the Y direction. For Xeon Phi architectures, convenient values of SOA in single precision are 4, 8 and 16. The case of $SOA = V = 16$ allows straightforward load/stores with aligned packed loads/stores. In the cases of $SOA = 4, 8$ we use load-unpack and pack store, which is faster on this architecture than general gathers. For Xeon systems with $V = 8$ good choices for SOA are 4, and 8. Hence our spinor data is stored as `float spinor[ nvec ][3][4][2][ SOA ]` where nvec is the number of SOA length blocks $nvec = (L_x/2) \times L_y \times L_z \times L_t/SOA$. For our gauge and clover fields which are *read only data* to facilitate single stride reading we can pregather the the ngy strips resulting in an array of the shape `float gauge[ nvec/ ngy ][8][3][3][2][ SOA*ngy ]`. Finally our nvec vectors are laid out with the X dimension going fastest. If the X dimension can be split into N_{xvec} SOA length chunks ($N_{xvec} = (L_x/2)/SOA$), then indexing notionally runs as $vec = x_v + N_{xvec}(y + L_y(z + L_z t))$. In practice this may be complicated slightly by padding in the XY and XYZ dimensions, please see [8] for details.

Cache Blocking And Load Balancing: QPhiX implements the 3.5D blocking strategy of [15]. This involves, vectorizing over the X and Y directions, blocking in the Y and Z dimensions and streaming through the T dimensions. In practice this is done by specifying block sizes B_y and B_z in the Y and Z dimensions. The lattice is then split into strips of size $\frac{L_x}{2} \times \frac{L_y}{B_y} \times \frac{L_z}{B_z} \times L_t$. These blocks are assigned to cores and are processed concurrently by the SIMT threads on that core. Further, to cope with multiple NUMA domains, the T direction can be split by the number of NUMA domains. One needs to arrange that the cores processing a chunk of strips belonging to a particular domain, are actually in that domain physically so that first touch after allocation is effective. This is done by core affinity mechanisms outside of QPhiX, e.g. using the `KMP_AFFINITY` and `KMP_PLACE_THREADS`, mechanisms for the Intel Compiler. Generally this process can result in a number of strips in a NUMA domain which may not be divided equally by the number of cores in that domain. To cope with this the T dimension can be split further, to increase the number of strips. An algorithm for doing so while taking advantage of all cores is discussed in detail in [8]. The initial split factor for NUMA domains is denoted by the parameter *minct*. In our tests when running on dual socket Haswell systems we used $minct = 2$ when running a single executable on both sockets. When running one task per socket, and on KNL in quadrant/flat mode or in multi-node runs with 1 process per socket, we used $minct = 1$.

Code Generator and Prefetching: The kernels for performing the calculations on a block of $SOA \times ngy$ sites, are generated by a small code-generator. This code generator allows us to abstract our vector operations, and can generate intrinsics code for SSE, AVX, AVX2-FMA, AVX512, KNC and BlueGene/Q QPX architectures. Further it allowed us to insert software prefetching, both for L1 and L2 caches. This was very important for the Knight's Corner (KNC) architecture. For KNL, preceding work in [13] suggested that software prefetching may be less effective and actually lead to slight performance loss in the presence of the hardware prefetcher, and work in a microbenchmark suggested that it may be beneficial to turn off hardware prefetching and use software prefetching only. The code generator allowed us to easily check this in QPhiX, and we report results in Sect. 4.2.

BLAS Like Kernel fusion: Linear solvers like Conjugate Gradients (CG) and BiCGStab rely on Level 1 BLAS like vector vector routines. These have a low arithmetic intensity individually, and occasionally it is possible to reuse fields temporally amongst successive kernels, for example when computing residua. The kernels here are: $r = b - t$ where $t = Mx$, followed immediately by $n2 = ||r||^2$. In other words one can reuse r immediately. In QPhiX we fuse such kernels to increase arithmetic intensity due to reduced memory traffic. Our implementation relies on combining a generic parallel loop over spinors with C++ functors (also known as function objects) implementing the BLAS operation over a block of SOA spinors, similar in style to Kokkos kernels [5].

3 Related Work

The majority of the techniques behind the Wilson-Dslash operator in QPhiX have been discussed in [8] and a thorough description of QPhiX is given in [9], however, these papers discussed Xeon and KNC results. In this contribution we consider KNL which has several different features from KNC that are relevant from a performance point of view including improved hardware prefetching, out of order execution, three different modes for the MCDRAM and a variety of on chip clustering modes. Using code generators to write high performance code is relatively common, a classic example being the BAGEL [2] code generator. There are alternatives to the tiled data layout that we have used in QPhiX for vector-ization, examples are the 'virtual node layout' described in [1] and for a case of domain decomposition with fixed sized domains one can use the techiques in [7]. The techniques for utilizing compression for $SU(3)$ matrices; both the 2-row for-mat used in QPhiX, and also an 8-real number compression; were first discussed in the context of reducing memory bandwidth pressure in QCD kernels in [3], for GPUs. There are also different techniques in the community for registerizing complex numbers for vectorization, for example, in [12]. The QPhiX infrastructure has been retargeted also to applying Wilson Dslash to multiple vectors at the same time, and to the highly improved staggered quark formulation, with results presented at this workshop [19].

4   Single Node Performance Measurements

We now discuss performance numbers we obtained from running QPhiX on a single KNL node. We focus on memory bandwidth measurements and sustained Gflops.

4.1   Setup

Hardware: We performed our tests on a single node of the Endeavor cluster, where every node is equipped with one KNL B0 chip of configuration A (c.f. Sect. 1). Furthermore, each node has 96 Gb of DDR memory with peak bandwidth of 90 Gb/s. We have tested our code in quadrant mode chip configuration and in both, flat and cache mode MCDRAM configurations. Since our code fits entirely into MCDRAM, we can just use numactl to bind the executable to MCDRAM or DDR respectively. Therefore, we can use MCDRAM without code changes.

Software Environment: For compiling our QPhiX test code, we used the Intel® C++ compiler 2016, update 2.[2] This compiler supports OpenMP 4.5 and we make heavy use of the OpenMP SIMD directives.

QPhiX parameters: We test problems with a local volume of size 32^4 with a block sizes of $By = Bz = 4$ on KNL, and applied padding factors of 1 in both the XY plane and the XYZ volume, to reduce associativity misses. We time the application of the Wilson Dslash operator as well as the CG and BiCGStab solvers. To determine floating point operation rates (FLOPS) we counted the number of *useful floating point operations* executed in our benchmarks, and divided them by measured wallclock time. We did not include any operations resulting from overhead such as recreation of the 3rd row of our gauge fields.

4.2   Results and Discussion

We ran performance measurements on configuration A. For all our tests, we employed 64 cores and ran 1,2 or 4 threads on each of these cores. This was achieved by setting KMP_AFFINITY=compact,granularity=threads, and KMP_PLACE_THREADS=1s,Cc,Nt with C the number of cores and N = 1, 2 or 4. The

---

[2] we have also tested a beta of ICC 2017, but we found no significant differences in performance.

number of OMP threads was set during runtime using `omp_set_num_threads()` based on the number of cores and SMT threads chosen via command line parameters. Since our code is mostly memory bandwidth bound, we aimed at estimating the possible gains by using MCDRAM over DDR. For that purpose, we ran QPhiX solely in DDR and then solely in MCDRAM mode. Assuming an arithmetic complexity of 2.29 (based on optimal cache reuse), we can estimate the effective bandwidth using the roofline model [20]. Using a measured maximum performance of 191 GFLOPS/s for DDR and 505 GFLOPS/s for MCDRAM, we obtain effective bandwidths of 83 Gb/s and 221 Gb/s for DDR and MCDRAM respectively. We do not see a significant difference when running in cache mode compared to running from MCDRAM in flat mode. This is expected, as our problem fits into the total available MCDRAM. We note that these effective bandwidths suggest that we close to saturating the bandwidth of DDR, but are less effective at exhausting the bandwidth of MCDRAM with Dslash. The reason for this is still under investigation. We observe however, that the streaming-like kernels in our code do better, i.e. the STREAM-like `aypx` obtains 393 Gb/s, which is ~87 % of the total available bandwidth when running from MCDRAM. Nonetheless, we do not yet hit the STREAMS bandwidths in our code.[3] In order to test if this is attributed to hardware prefetching deficiencies, we assisted the compiler by adding prefetch statements to our code. We tested three different modes, i.e. full hardware prefetching, software assisted hardware prefetching (denoted by +Sfw+HW in Fig. 1) and pure software prefetching (denoted by +Sfw-HW in Fig. 1). The chart in Fig. 1 shows that there are no consistent and significant differences between these different prefetching modes. We further observe that there is a significant difference between one, two or four threads per core in terms of total performance. When running from MCDRAM, the performance is always better when running with two or 4 threads, than a single thread, as a single thread cannot saturate the MCDRAM bandwidth. In case of DDR however, single thread performance is highest. This might be attributed to lower DDR latency and the fact that a single thread is able to saturate the DDR bandwidth. We can also see that for the more memory bound kernels (BiCGStab and also CG, not shown), a dual socket Haswell systems performs better than a KNL run from DDR. This is mainly because of the memory bandwidth differences: a dual socket Haswell system provides about 130 Gb/s peak, whereas the KNL only provides 90 Gb/s peak from DDR. Comparing SOA lengths, we find that 4 performs consistently worse than 8 and 16, whereas we do not observe a huge performance gain switching from 8 to 16. The pattern an SOA length of half the vector length seems to perform best is in line with earlier findings of [8] on the KNC architecture.

In terms of thread scaling, DDR performance is best for one, whereas MCDRAM performance is best for 2 threads. This might be explained by bandwidth and latency: for MCDRAM, two threads are needed to saturate

---

[3] Similar measurements for DDR yield a similar result, i.e. ~70 GB/s which corresponds to about 77 % of DDR bandwidth peak performance. Remarkably, this value is lower as the computed effective bandwidth for the Dslash kernel.

bandwidth, whereas for runs from DDR, latency might be the most limiting factor and thus one thread does not overwhelm the prefetcher.

We further inspected the performance benefit of using AVX512 in favor of AVX2 by compiling QPhiX with either set of intrinsics and SOA 8 and measured the best performance in either case. Figure 2 demonstrates that the performance improvements from AVX512 are consistently around 20 %.

5   Multi-node Scaling Study

We now turn to weak scaling experiments of QPhiX on multiple Haswell and KNL nodes. We applied some small scaling improvements to the code, i.e. the use of message queues which allow for *out-of-order* receives. Weak scaling is the relevant metric for high capacity, e.g. for data post-processing workflows.

5.1   Setup

Hardware: We performed the Haswell scaling study on the NERSC Cori Phase I system. This is a Cray XC system comprised of 1630 compute nodes. The nodes are equipped with two 2.3 Ghz 16-core Intel® Haswell CPUs with L1 and L2 caches sizes of 64 Kb, 256 Kb per core respectively as well as a shared 40 Mb L3 cache per socket. Each node has 128 Gb of DDR. For communication, the high-bandwidth, low-latency Cray Aries interconnect with dragonfly topology is used. The KNL study was performed on up to 16 single socket configuration B KNL nodes, equipped with Intel® Omni-Path Architecture featuring Intel® OPA Host Fabric Interface, Series 100 ASIC (B0 silicon). The network switches used are Intel® OPA Switch: Series 100 Edge Switch - 48 port (B0 silicon).

Software Environment: For the Haswell study We use Intel® ICC in version 2016, update 2 for compiling the code. We further use the MPI provided by Cray, i.e. cray-mpich v7.3.1, which is a proprietary implementation of MPICH2. Since Haswell does not support AVX512, the maximal SOA length we can use is 8, and to generate our kernels we used AVX2 including FMA instructions, generated by our code-generator. We performed a single socket test run and observed that SOA length 8 performed about 11 % better than SOA 4, so we used the former for the scaling study. For the KNL runs, we have used Intel® ICC 2016 with AVX512 optimizations and SOA 16 as well as Intel® MPI 5.1.2.

QPhiX Parameters: As mentioned above, we are going to target capacity workloads and thus maximize the local volume. Local means in this context, that we ran one MPI rank per socket and the volume local to the socket was set to 32^4 for both architectures. Note that the optimal size for Haswell is 16^4, whereas the optimal size for KNL is about 32^4 but larger local volumes are preferable and more important for (pre-)exa-scale applications. We use cache block sizes of 8^2 and 4^2 for Haswell and KNL respectively. In the former case, we employ two hyperthreads in z-direction and one in y-direction, whereas in the latter one we employ 4 hyperthreads in z and one in y-direction. In these tests we did not

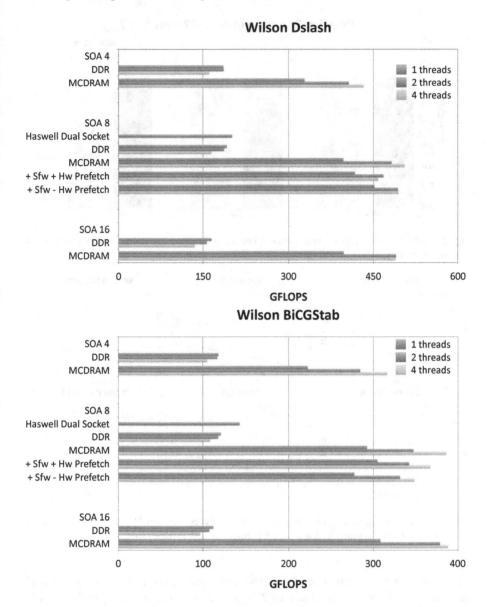

Fig. 1. Single node KNL performance for Wilson Dslash operator (top), BiCGStab solver (bottom). We compare the performance of our kernels for SOA-lengths of 4,8 and 16, various memories and prefetching modes. The different colored bars denote runs with one, two and four hyperthreads respectively.

use any array padding. In our weak scaling runs, we increased our global volume along with the number of ranks, by a factor of two at every step. Our strategy was to first increase the t-direction up to a global size of 256, then to continue

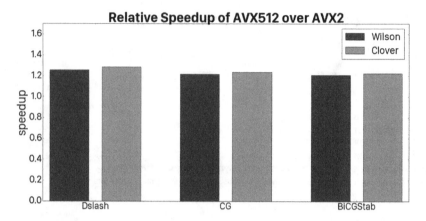

Fig. 2. Relative speedup of our various kernels obtained by using AVX512 intrinsics instead of AVX2 intrinsics.

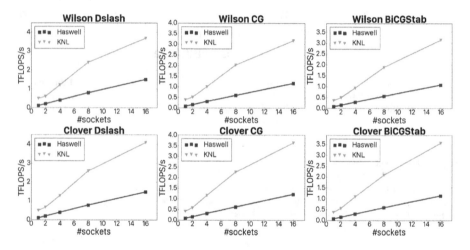

Fig. 3. Weak scaling of the Dslash kernels and solvers on Cori Phase 1 (squares) and KNL+Omni-Path (triangles) for a local volume of 32^4 lattice sites.

with doubling the z-direction up to the same value, then we scale in y-s and then in x. Note that a global size of 256^4 is a reasonable size for (pre-)exa-scale lattice calculations and thus it is reasonable to stop doubling a dimension once it's extent has reached that value. We time the Wilson Dslash and Clover operators for application to a vector and the runtime of CG and BiCGStab solvers using these kernels. The FLOPs are estimated as described in Sect. 4.1.

5.2 Results and Discussion

The results of our weak scaling runs are displayed in Fig. 3. The square and triangular markers and lines correspond to Haswell and KNL respectively.

The panels on the top show the plain Wilson operator, whereas the results on the bottom include the clover term. Note that for 16 sockets, another communication direction is introduced and the corresponding overhead can explain the dip after 8 sockets for KNL. Similar things can be observed for the smaller local volume of 16^4 sites on Haswell as well, but it is not significant for the large volume used in this study. The results in Fig. 3 exhibit good weak scaling performance for all the kernels we have investigated. The scaling is better for KNL, reaching 3.5-4 Teraflops on 16 sockets, which is a factor 4 better than Haswell.

6   Conclusions

We have discussed performance results for the Wilson-Dslash operator, Conjugate Gradients, and BiCGStab solvers on Knight's Landing and have compared them with the performances seen on Haswell nodes on Cori. We have chosen relatively large problem sizes per node as in this initial exploration we are focused on the capacity/throughput regime of calculations. We achieve sustained performance of about 500 GFLOPS/s for Wilson-Dslash, and slightly lower values of 417 GFLOPS/s and 387 GFLOPS/s for CG and BiCGStab respectively. The latter two kernels are significantly more memory bound and we do not fully utilize the available bandwidth yet. We are investigating restructuring the code to sustain more bandwidth in the future. The weak scaling study shows good scaling up to 16 sockets of Haswell using the Cray Aries fabric, and 16 KNL nodes using an Intel OmniPath architecture fabric, where, where scaling on KNL is significantly better, reaching a factor of 3.5-4 speedup compared to Haswell at 16 sockets.

Acknowledgments. The majority of this work was carried out during a NERSC Exascale Scientific Application Program (NESAP) deep dive known as a *Dungeon Session* at the offices of Intel in Portland, Oregon. We thank NERSC and Intel for organizing this session. We also like to thank Jack Deslippe for insightful discussions. Performance results were measured on the Intel Endeavor cluster and on the Cori Phase I system at NERSC with additional development work carried out on systems at Jefferson Lab. B. Joó gratefully acknowledges funding from the U.S. Department of Energy, Office of Science, Office of Advanced Scientific Computing Research, Office of Nuclear Physics and Office of High Energy Physics under the SciDAC program (USQCD). This material is based upon work supported by the U.S. Department of Energy, Office of Science, Office of Nuclear Physics under contract DE-AC05-06OR23177. The National Energy Research Scientific Computing Center (NERSC) is a DOE Office of Science User Facility supported by the Office of Science of the U.S. Department of Energy under Contract No. DE-AC02-05CH11231.

References

1. Boyle, P.: The BlueGene/Q supercomputer. In: PoS LATTICE 2012, vol. 20 (2012). http://pos.sissa.it/archive/conferences/164/020/Lattice%202012_020.pdf
2. Boyle, P.A.: The bagel assembler generation library. Comput. Phys. Commun. 180(12), 2739–2748 (2009). http://www.sciencedirect.com/science/article/B6TJ5-4X378GD-2/2/34878900f618e4e37cb7f051b6218436, 40 YEARS OF CPC: A celebratory issue focused on quality software for highperformance, grid and novel computing architectures
3. Clark, M.A., Babich, R., Barros, K., Brower, R.C., Rebbi, C.: Solving Lattice QCD systems of equations using mixed precision solvers on GPUs. Comput. Phys. Commun. 181, 1517–1528 (2010)
4. Creutz, M.: Quarks, Gluons and Lattices. Cambridge Monographs on Mathematical Physics, 169 p. Univ. Pr., Cambridge (1983)
5. Edwards, H.C., Sunderland, D.: Kokkos array performance-portable manycore programming model. In: Proceedings of the 2012 International Workshop on Programming Models and Applications for Multicores and Manycores, PMAM 2012, pp. 1–10. ACM, New York (2012). http://doi.acm.org/10.1145/2141702.2141703
6. Hestenes, M.R., Stiefel, E.: Methods of conjugate gradients for solving linear systems. J. Res. Nat. Bureau Stand. 49(6), 409–436 (1952)
7. Heybrock, S., Joó, B., Kalamkar, D.D., Smelyanskiy, M., Vaidyanathan, K., Wettig, T., Dubey, P.: Lattice QCD with domain decomposition on intel® xeon phi™ co-processors. In: Proceedings of the International Conference for High Performance Computing, Networking, Storage and Analysis, SC 2014, pp. 69–80. IEEE Press, Piscataway (2014). http://dx.doi.org/10.1109/SC.2014.11
8. Joó, B., Kalamkar, D., Vaidyanathan, K., Smelyanskiy, M., Pamnany, K., Lee, V., Dubey, P., Watson, W.: Lattice QCD on Intel(R) XeonPhi(TM) Coprocessors. In: Kunkel, J., Ludwig, T., Meuer, H. (eds.) ISC 2013. LNCS, vol. 7905, pp. 40–54. Springer, Heidelberg (2013). http://dx.doi.org/10.1007/978-3-642-38750-0_4
9. Joó, B., Smelyanskiy, M., Kalamkar, D.D., Vaidyanathan, K.: Chapter 9 - Wilson dslash kernel from lattice QCD optimization. In: Reinders, J., Jeffers, J. (eds.) High Performance Parallelism Pearls Volume Two: Multicore and Many-core Programming Approaches, vol. 2, pp. 139–170. Morgan Kaufmann, Boston (2015). http://www.sciencedirect.com/science/article/pii/B9780128038192000239
10. Joó, B.: qphix package web page. http://jeffersonlab.github.io/qphix
11. Joó, B.: qphix-codegen package web page. http://jeffersonlab.github.io/qphix-codegen
12. Kaczmarek, O., Schmidt, C., Steinbrecher, P., Mukherjee, S., Wagner, M.: HISQ inverter on intel xeon phi and NVIDIA gpus. CoRR abs/1409.1510 (2014). http://arxiv.org/abs/1409.1510
13. Kalamkar, D.D., Smelyanskiy, M., Farber, R., Vaidyanathan, K.: Chapter 26 - quantum chromodynamics (QCD). In: Reinders, J., Jeffers, J., Sodani, A. (eds.) Intel Xeon Phi Processor High Performance Programming Knights Landing Edition. Morgan Kaufmann, Boston (2016)
14. Montvay, I., Munster, G.: Quantum Fields on a Lattice. Cambridge Monographs on Mathematical Physics, 491 p. Univ. Pr., Cambridge (1994)
15. Nguyen, A.D., Satish, N., Chhugani, J., Kim, C., Dubey, P.: 3.5-D blocking optimization for stencil computations on modern CPUs and GPUs. In: SC, pp. 1–13 (2010)

16. Rothe, H.J.: Lattice Gauge theories: an Introduction. World Sci. Lect. Notes Phys. **74**, 1–605 (2005)
17. Sheikholeslami, B., Wohlert, R.: Improved continuum limit lattice action for QCD with Wilson Fermions. Nucl. Phys. B **259**, 572 (1985)
18. van der Vorst, H.A.: Bi-CGSTAB: a fast and smoothly converging variant of Bi-CG for the solution of nonsymmetric linear systems. SIAM J. Sci. Stat. Comput. **13**(2), 631–644 (1992)
19. Walden, A., Khan, S., Joó, B., Ranjan, D., Zubair, M.: Optimizing a multiple right-hand side Dslash kernel for intel knights corner. In: Taufer, M., Mohr, B., Kunkel, J.M. (eds.) High Performance Computing. LNCS, vol. 9945, pp. 1–12. Springer International Publishing, Switzerland (2016)
20. Williams, S., Waterman, A., Patterson, D.: Roofline: an insightful visual performance model for floating-point programs and multicore architectures. Commun. ACM **52**, 65–76 (2009)
21. Wilson, K.G.: Quarks and strings on a lattice. In: Zichichi, A. (ed.) New Phenomena in Subnuclear Physics, p. 69. Plenum Press, New York (1975)

P^3MA

First International Workshop on Performance Portable Programming Models for Accelerators (P^3MA)

http://www.csm.ornl.gov/workshops/p3ma2016/
June 23, 2016 co-located with ISC 2016

Summary of the Workshop's CFP Process

First International Workshop on Performance Portable Programming Models for Accelerators (P^3MA) co-located with ISC 2016 was held at Frankfurt, Germany on June 23. The workshop solicited papers on topics covering feature sets of programming models (including but not limited to directives-based programming models), their implementations, and experiences with their deployment in HPC applications on multiple architectures, performance modeling and evaluation tools, asynchronous task and event-driven execution/scheduling. We received 13 submissions in total. All submitted manuscripts were peer reviewed. The review process was not double blind, i.e., authors were known to reviewers. Submissions were judged on correctness, originality, technical strength, and significance, quality of presentation, and interest and relevance to the conference scope. We chose 8 papers to be published in the workshop proceedings, Springer-Verlag Lecture Notes in Computer Science (LNCS) volumes.

Workshop Summary

The workshop was held on June 23 at ISC and brought together researchers, vendors, users and developers to brainstorm aspects of heterogeneous computing and its various tools and techniques. Around 50 attendees were present to see Dr. Si Hammond from Sandia National Laboratories, USA, give a keynote on Balancing Productivity, Portability and Performance - The Challenge for Programming Models at Exascale. All of the 8 accepted papers were presented at the workshop with topics ranging from using low-level to high-level programming models for heterogeneous systems, experiences porting legacy code to accelerators, addressing memory requirements, and creating translations from one standard to the other.

Prof. Haohuan Fu, Deputy Head of the National Supercomputing Center in Wuxi and Associate Professor at the Center for Earth System Science, Tsinghua University, China, gave an invited talk on preparing the Community Atmospheric Model climate application to run and scale on Sunway TaihuLight, announced at ISC'16 as the new number one HPC system on the Top500 list. His talk included their experiences with custom loop transformation tools for code refactoring, using OpenACC to program the heterogeneous architecture of TaihuLight, and extensions to the OpenACC standard that were implemented to enable various optimizations in the application.

NVIDIA generously offered to sponsor the 'Best Paper Award' with NVIDIA's newest PASCAL compute capable card. This award was presented to "Task-Based Cholesky Decomposition on Knights Corner using OpenMP" from UTK. The award was determined by the Technical Program Committee and the Program Chairs from viewpoints of the technical and scientific merits, impact on the science and engineering of the research work and the clarity of presentation of the research contents in the paper.

Organizing Committee

Steering Committee

Matthias Muller	RWTH Aachen University, Germany
Barbara Chapman	Stony Brook University, USA
Oscar Hernandez	ORNL, USA
Duncan Poole	OpenACC, USA
Torsten Hoefler	ETH, Zurich
Michael Wong	OpenMP, Canada
Mitsuhisa Sato	University of Tsukuba, Japan

Program Chair(s)

Sunita Chandrasekaran	University of Delaware, USA
Graham Lopez	ORNL, USA

Program Committee

Samuel Thibault	INRIA, University of Bordeaux, France
James Beyer	NVIDIA, USA
Wei Ding	AMD, USA
Saber Feki	King Abdullah University, Saudi Arabia
Robert Henschel	Indiana University, USA
Michael Klemm	Intel, USA
Eric Stotzer	Texas Instruments, USA
Amit Amritkar	University of Houston, USA
Guido Juckeland	HZDR, Germany
Will Sawyer	ETH, Zurich
Sameer Shende	University of Oregon, USA
Costas Bekas	IBM, Zurich
Toni Collis	University of Edinburgh, Scotland
Adrian Jackson	University of Edinburgh, Scotland
Henri Jin	NASA, USA

Andreas Knuepfer   TU Dresden, Germany
Steven Olivier   Sandia National Laboratory, USA
Suraj Prabhakaran   TU Darmstadt, Germany
Bora Ucar   ENS De Lyon, France
Sandra Wienke   Aachen University, Germany

A C++ Programming Model for Heterogeneous System Architecture

Ralph Potter[1]([⊠]), Russell Bradford[1], Alastair Murray[2], and Uwe Dolinsky[2]

[1] Department of Computer Science, University of Bath, Bath, UK
{r.potter,r.j.bradford}@bath.ac.uk
[2] Codeplay Software Ltd., Edinburgh, UK
{alastair.murray,uwe}@codeplay.com

Abstract. This paper describes a shared-source programming model and compiler for Heterogeneous System Architecture, based on C++14.

Heterogeneous System Architecture provides hardware specifications, a runtime API and a virtual instruction set to enable heterogeneous processors to interoperate through a unified virtual address space. However, it does not define a high-level kernel language such as OpenCL C or CUDA. This lack of a high-level kernel language presents a barrier to the exploitation of the capabilities of these heterogeneous systems.

Through the use of automatic call-graph duplication in the compiler, we enable code reuse and sharing of data structures between host processor and accelerator devices with fewer annotations than CUDA or C++AMP. We utilize the unified virtual address space to enable sharing data between devices via pointers, rather than requiring copies. We show that through the use of address space inference, existing standard C++ code such as the standard template library can be utilized with minimal modifications on accelerators.

Keywords: C++ · Programming models · Heterogeneous system architecture · GPU

1 Introduction

Heterogeneous System Architecture (HSA) is an architecture that integrates heterogeneous processors such as CPUs, GPUs and DSPs via a shared memory system. The HSA specifications [1–3] define hardware requirements, a runtime API and virtual instruction set. Unlike other standards for programming heterogeneous accelerators, such as OpenCL [4], CUDA [5] or C++AMP [6], HSA does not provide a high-level kernel language. Instead, it provides HSAIL, a virtual instruction set for targeting HSA-compliant devices. This makes it impractical to develop non-trivial applications targeting this architecture without a compiler.

Little work has been published exploring the properties of HSA-based systems. We believe this is in part due to the limited availability of languages and tools. Other authors have opted to target existing programming languages and

© Springer International Publishing AG 2016
M. Taufer et al. (Eds.): ISC High Performance Workshops 2016, LNCS 9945, pp. 433–450, 2016.
DOI: 10.1007/978-3-319-46079-6_31

models, such as OpenMP[1], C++AMP[2] and OpenCL[3] at HSA. We opted for a different approach, choosing to develop a shared-source C++ programming model for HSA that closely mirrors the underlying capabilities of HSA.

Previous approaches to C++ on heterogeneous devices have typically wrapped pointers to memory allocations in some form of additional data structure, such as the `array` and `array_view` classes in C++AMP, or the `buffer` and `accessor` classes in SYCL [7]. These container types cannot be trivially integrated with existing code without modification. Due to HSA's unified virtual address space we are able to relax this constraint. In our model, we are able to share pointers directly between host and accelerator code without the need for container classes. CUDA also supports unified virtual memory, but requires additional annotations on all device functions. By eliminating this restriction and minimizing the use of non-standard keywords within our model, we are able to compile and execute a wide variety of existing C++ code without the need for intrusive modifications.

Our contributions are:

- A shared-source C++ programming model for Heterogeneous System Architecture. We map the complex segmented virtual address space of HSA onto the single address space model of C++.
- We demonstrate that this can be achieved by using only minor annotations, which can often be hidden by the API. This enables the programmer to compile complex, pre-existing code, such as code using the C++ standard template library *without modification*.

```
// A multi-producer, multi-consumer ring buffer on the host processor.
mpmc_ring_buffer<float> buf;

// A C++11 atomic, shared by both the host processor and the kernel agent.
std::atomic<bool> run = true;

// Start the kernel on a throughput processor (GPU, DSP) to continually
// dequeue items from the buffer and process.
auto future = queue->parallel_for<class dequeue>(SIZE, [&](){
  // Poll the std::atomic for termination status.
  while (run) {
    // If the ring buffer is not empty, dequeue an item and process.
    float entry;
    if (buf.try_dequeue(entry))
      ...;
  }
});

// On host CPU: loop continually, pushing items into the buffer.
```

---

[1] https://github.com/HSAFoundation/HSA-OpenMP-GCC-AMD.

[2] https://bitbucket.org/multicoreware/cppamp-driver-ng-35.

[3] https://github.com/HSAFoundation/CLOC.

```
while (run) {
  float entry = ...;
  buf.enqueue(entry);
}

// Wait for kernel completion.
future.wait();
```
Listing 1. Shared Ring Buffer.

We motivate this paper with an example that cannot presently be achieved in OpenCL, SYCL, CUDA, or C++AMP. Listing 1 demonstrates a multi-producer, multi-consumer ring buffer that is simultaneously accessed by both a host processor and a throughput coprocessor such as a graphics processing unit (GPU) or digital signal processor (DSP). This ring buffer is implemented entirely in standard C++14, utilizing `std::atomic` to provide synchronization. A number of issues arise when attempting to implement this example using existing programming models. OpenCL 1.2, SYCL and C++AMP lack the capability for concurrent access to a shared data structure from the host processor and an accelerator, completely preventing the implementation of this example. OpenCL 2.0 devices may optionally provide the required hardware features to enable the utilization of atomic operations to ensure a consistent view of shared virtual memory. However, OpenCL has a C-based kernel language, requiring separate implementations of the `mpmc_ring_buffer` class for host and accelerator devices. CUDA uses a C++ dialect for both host and kernel languages, but requires the explicit annotation of accelerator functions (`__device__`) and the use of differing data types and synchronization primitives between host and accelerator, effectively requiring two separate implementations.

2 Heterogeneous System Architecture

A HSA system consists of a number of *agents* communicating through a unified virtual memory system. An *agent* may be either a hardware or software component which interacts with the HSA memory model. Agents schedule work to be processed by other agents in a system by writing Architected Queuing Language (AQL) packets into a queue associated with the target agent. A subset of agents are able to consume kernel dispatch packets. We refer to these agents as *kernel agents*. These agents are capable of executing kernels lowered from HSA's virtual instruction set.

For example, an AMD Kaveri CPU exposes two HSA agents, one for the CPU, and one for the integrated GPU. However, only the integrated GPU is currently capable of consuming kernel dispatch packets.

HSAIL and BRIG

As discussed previously, the HSA specifications do not define a high-level kernel language. Instead HSA defines an intermediate language, Heterogeneous System Architecture Intermediate Language (HSAIL) and a binary representation,

BRIG. HSA uses a split compilation model, where high-level languages such as C++ or Java can be compiled to HSAIL or BRIG offline. At run-time, a finalizer provided as part of a HSA implementation can be used to lower this HSAIL to target machine code for a specific kernel agent. For the remainder of this paper, any references to HSAIL can be assumed to apply equally to both HSAIL and BRIG, while explicit references to BRIG will refer to the binary form.

HSAIL supports two machine models, referred to as large and small. These machine models define the size of certain data types, most notably pointer types, and the size of operands for certain instructions, e.g. the small machine model does not support 64-bit atomics.

Listing 2 illustrates a simple vector addition kernel expressed in OpenCL C, while Listing 3 demonstrates a translation of the corresponding kernel to HSAIL.

```
kernel void vec\_add(global float* a, global float* b, global float* c) {
  int i = get\_global\_id(0);
  a[i] = b[i] + c[i];
}
```

Listing 2. OpenCL vector addition kernel.

Memory Model

Agents within a HSA system access shared system memory through a unified virtual address space. This unified address space ensures that an address passed between agents will remain valid, subject to some constraints that will be discussed later in this section. Enabling agents to exchange data by passing pointers, rather than requiring copies, can greatly reduce memory bandwidth requirements when transferring work between agents when compared to models such as OpenCL 1.2, which lacks similar guarantees.

```
prog kernel &vector_add(kernarg_u64 %a, kernarg_u64 %b, kernarg_u64 %c)
{
  ld_kernarg_align(8)_width(all)_u64 $d1, [%a]; // Load pointer args.
  ld_kernarg_align(8)_width(all)_u64 $d2, [%b];
  ld_kernarg_align(8)_width(all)_u64 $d3, [%c];
  workitemabsid_u32 $s0, 0;        // Get the 1D work-item index.
  cvt_u64_u32 $d0, $s0;            // Convert index to byte-offset.
  shl_u64 $d0, $d0, 2;
  add_u64 $d1, $d1, $d0;          // Add offset to base pointers.
  add_u64 $d2, $d2, $d0;
  add_u64 $d3, $d3, $d0;
  ld_global_align(4)_f32 $s0, [$d2]; // Load floating point inputs.
  ld_global_align(4)_f32 $s1, [$d3];
  add_ftz_f32 $s0, $s1, $s0;      // Add inputs.
  st_global_align(4)_f32 $s0, [$d1]; // Store the result.
  ret;
};
```

Listing 3. HSAIL vector addition kernel.

Table 1. Characteristics of HSA memory segments

Segment	Granularity	Persistence	Host Access	Pointer size Small/Large	Flat Addressable
Private	Work-Item	Work-Item	None	32-bit	Yes
Group	Work-Group	Work-Group	None	32-bit	Yes
Global	System/Agent	Application	Read/Write	32/64-bit	Yes
Read-Only	Agent	Application	API	32/64-bit	No
Kernarg	Grid	Kernel Dispatch	Write	32/64-bit	No
Arg	Work-Item	Arg Block	None	32-bit	No
Spill	Work-Item	Work-Item	None	32-bit	No

The unified virtual address space is further subdivided into *segments*. HSA defines 7 segments which have differing lifetimes, addressability, access rights and visibility of updates. These segments are disjoint regions of the virtual address space.

The *private* segment holds variables that are local to a single work-item while the *group* segment provides storage for variables shared by work-items within a single work-group. The *global* segment represents shared system memory and is used to hold data that is accessible to all agents in the system. Addresses in the global segment may be read from or written to by all agents in the system, including the host processor. On systems implementing the full HSA profile, the stack and heap used by the host processor fall within the global segment. The *readonly* segment can be used to hold variables that remain constant during the duration of a kernel execution. The *kernarg* segment holds kernel arguments, and is read-only only from within a kernel dispatch (Table 1).

The *arg* segment is used to pass arguments to and from functions. Unlike the kernarg segment, variables is the arg segment are non-uniform across work-items and are only visible from the work-item with which they are associated. HSAIL defines a finite number of virtual registers. The *spill* segment can be used where necessary to handle register spills.

Instructions which transfer data between registers and memory, such as loads, stores and atomic instructions, encode the segment of their operands within the instruction. For example, `ld_global_u32` is a load of a 32-bit integer from an address in the global segment. We can see this in Listing 3, where loading the kernel arguments from the kernarg segment into registers requires the use of `ld_kernarg` instructions, while loading the floating point operands for the addition from the global segment requires the use of `ld_global`.

Addresses may be associated with a particular segment, or they may be flat addresses. A flat address can be considered an address in a virtual segment that encompasses the private, group and global segments. Unfortunately, flat addresses cannot address data in the readonly segment. A model that operates entirely on flat addresses would therefore have to choose to eliminate the use of the readonly segment, which has potential performance implications.

Secondly, flat addresses require a 64-bit representation under HSA's large machine model, increasing register pressure and potentially decreasing compute density compared to the 32-bit private and group segment addresses. Finally, using explicitly specified segment addresses provides the HSAIL finalizer with additional information which may enable further optimization or more efficient scheduling.

The visibility of writes to shared virtual memory allocations in HSA is modified by a property referred to as *granularity*. HSA does not guarantee a consistent view of memory for every load or store instruction. Instead, the HSA memory model guarantees that each work-item or agent receives a consistent view with respect to a set of synchronization points. Memory allocated through the use of system allocators such as `malloc` or `new` is *fine-grained*. For these allocations, memory fences, atomic or signal operations, and kernel boundaries may all act as synchronization points. Some regions of the virtual address space may only support *coarse-grained* allocation. Memory from these regions is allocated through the `hsa_memory_allocate` API function. At any point in time, only a single agent may hold ownership of a coarse-grained allocation, and ownership is transferred via the `hsa_assign_agent` API function. HSA guarantees that the virtual address of a coarse-grained allocation remains constant when ownership is transferred between agents. However, the physical location backing an allocation may change in this case.

3   Programming Model

We adopt a shared-source model, where code for execution on both the host processor and kernel agents may be contained in the same translation unit. Each translation unit that contains code for execution on a HSA kernel agent is compiled twice. One compilation pass generates host code, emitting an ELF object in the ISA of the host processor (typically x86_64). A second compilation pass selectively identifies and compiles the subset of functions that are required for execution on the kernel agents. These functions are compiled into BRIG, and the BRIG binary is embedded into specially named section of an ELF object. These object files can then be linked into a final executable. The BRIG objects are loaded from the executable at runtime, linked to resolve cross translation unit function calls, and then finalized into the native ISA of each kernel agent in the system.

This shared-source model is similar to that adopted by existing C++-based programming models for GPUs and other accelerators such as CUDA, SYCL and C++AMP. The unified virtual memory system in HSA allows our approach to relax some of the constraints that we find in models intended for use with discrete accelerators and disjoint address spaces. Most notably, we are able to pass data structures between agents by address, rather than relying on container types such as OpenCL's buffers. Addresses in the global segment will remain valid and consistent across agents, allowing us to make use of data structures that contain pointers as members. This enables the implementation of important data structures such as trees and linked lists without the need to make intrusive changes to accommodate API specific container types.

In general we only require kernel functions to be annotated with an attribute [[hsa::kernel]] analogous to CUDA requiring the __global__ attribute. Unlike CUDA though, which requires device functions to be annotated with __device__, or C++AMP which requires the restrict(amp) clause for them, we do not require annotations of device functions, enabling standard C++ code to be called from a kernel. However, an [[hsa::function]] attribute is provided to explicitly declare/define (non-kernel) device functions to enable linking them from device code in other translation units. Like the C++AMP restrict(amp) the [[hsa::function]] attribute also enables explicit overloading of host functions with device functions that have the same signatures.

```
[[hsa::kernel]]
void vec_add(float* a, float* b, float* c) {
  uint32_t i = rt::builtin::workitemabsid(0);
  a[i] = b[i] + c[i];
}
```

Listing 4. A minimal kernel.

Listing 4 demonstrates a minimal vector addition kernel under our model. The segment-unqualified pointer arguments are treated as global segment addresses. This example is equivalent to the OpenCL implementation shown in Listing 2 and the HSAIL implementation in Listing 3.

The programming models adopted by OpenCL 1.2, SYCL and C++AMP typically require that data required for processing on an accelerator be copied into some form of device accessible buffer.

In contrast to this, the unified virtual address space in HSA allows us to reason that a valid CPU pointer is equivalent to a pointer in the global segment. This enables us to pass host pointers directly as kernel arguments and dereference them on kernel agent without the need for an intermediate copy. This allows us to eliminate the overhead of populating device buffers and copying them from host to device. CUDA and OpenCL 2 also support shared virtual memory, albeit requiring specialized allocators in some cases.

```
float* a, b, c;
auto future = queue->parallel_for(grid_size, vec_add, a, b, c);
future.wait();
```

Listing 5. Enqueuing a kernel.

Listing 5 demonstrates enqueuing a kernel function using our model. The parallel_for method enqueues a kernel by writing an AQL packet to the corresponding queue. The arguments are the grid extents, a function pointer corresponding to the kernel function, and a variadic set of arguments to be passed as kernel arguments. The parallel_for function returns a future. The future is returned immediately after a kernel has been enqueued, and before kernel execution has completed. Calling the wait member function on the future will cause execution to block until the kernel has completed execution.

Lambda functions may also be used to represent kernels, as shown in Listing 6. When using lambdas to represent kernels, we require the use of an additional template parameter to provide a name for the kernel. This requirement is due to the need for consistent name mangling between host and kernel compilation.

```
std::vector<float> a{count};
std::vector<float> b{count};
std::vector<float> c{count};

queue->parallel_for<class vector_add>(count, [&](){
  uint32_t i = rt::builtin::workitemabsid(0);
  a[i] = b[i] + c[i];
});
```

Listing 6. Using lambda functions as kernels.

Memory Segments

As discussed in Sect. 2, HSA subdivides its virtual address space into a number of segments. The arg, kernarg and spill segments can be entirely handled by the compiler backend without the need to express them in the programming model.

We map segment-unqualified pointers and references to the global segment. This encompasses the majority of addresses, including stack and heap variables on the host CPU, and unannotated global variables. This is motivated by the desire to share unmodified data structures containing pointers between the host and kernel agents.

Automatic variables declared within the scope of a kernel function, or any function within the call-graph of a kernel function are implicitly treated as part of the private segment. As such, it is not necessary to annotate declarations of private variables. Despite this, we provide a generalized attribute, `[[hsa::private]]`, to enable the annotation of pointers and references to variables in the private address space. Call-graph duplication and `auto`/`decltype` make this rarely necessary in our experiments.

For group and readonly segments, we provide generalized attributes to annotate allocations, pointers and references.

Variables in the group segment can be allocated as either program scope global variables, or as static storage duration variables. Unlike OpenCL, we allow the declaration of group segment variables in any function within the call-graph of a kernel function, rather than restricting declarations to kernel function scope. Variables in the group segment are uninitialized by default, and constructors for class variables will not be called. Where the calling of constructors is required, it can be accomplished through the use of placement `new`.

Call-graph Duplication

The memory segment on which load, store and atomic instructions operate is encoded as part of the instruction representation in HSAIL. Consequently several different implementations of a function may be required for any function with pointer or reference arguments. One approach to this is to require the programmer to manually define such alternative implementations. Indeed, our model allows for this approach. A programmer may choose to overload a function based on the segment to which any pointer or reference argument belongs.

However, this approach rapidly becomes onerous. Given a function with N pointer or reference declarations in its parameters, and M possible segments, an upper-bound of M^N additional implementations of a function may be required. These pointer or reference parameters may be explicit, or implicit, e.g. the *this* pointer on non-static member functions, or the implicit pointer added to return structures. Furthermore, we cannot resolve this issue simply through the use of flat addresses throughout the application. Whilst the flat segment is defined as a superset of the private, group and global segments, it does not encompass the readonly segment, and so the issue persists[4].

We resolve these issues through the use of automatic call-graph duplication, as described by Cooper et al. [8] This triggers in cases where a function call cannot be resolved due solely to a mismatch between the segments of the parameters declared in the callee signature and the arguments of the call expression. In this case, the callee function is duplicated and its parameters are modified to correspond to the segments of the arguments of the triggering call expression. The compiler-internal representation of the duplicated function is then traversed and updated in order to correctly propagate the modified parameters throughout the duplicated function. This may require the recursive application of call-graph duplication to function calls located within the duplicated function.

```
// A standard C++ function accepting a pointer argument.
void f(int *i) { *i = 0; }

// An integer allocated in the group segment.
[[hsa::group]] int g;

[[hsa::kernel]] void k() {
  // An integer implicitly allocated in the private
  // segment.
  int p;
  // Neither call matches the declaration:
  //   void f(int *)
  // Our compiler creates duplicates:
  //   void f(int[[hsa::private]] *)
  //   void f(int[[hsa::group]] *)
  f(&p);
  f(&g);
}
```

Listing 7. Call-graph duplication.

---

[4] The HSA 1.0.3 runtime for AMD devices also lacks support for flat addresses on the private segment.

Listing 7 provides an example of this duplication process. Here we define a function, f, with a single unqualified integer pointer parameter. Within the kernel function, k, we find 2 calls to f. The argument to the first function call is the address of a local variable within the scope of a kernel function (&p), and is implicitly a member of the private segment. The argument for the second function call (&g) is the address of a variable allocated in the group segment. Due to the segments of the pointer arguments, neither call expression matches the original declaration of f. Therefore, our compiler creates 2 duplicates of f and modifies the signature of each duplicate to match the arguments found in the call expression. It will then rebuild the body of each duplicate taking into account the modified signature to ensure correctness. Finally, the call expressions are updated to reference the duplicated functions.

Sharing Data-Structures

The strength of our model comes from combining the features previously described. The combination of HSA's cache-coherent virtual memory, call-graph duplication within the compiler and the mapping of segment-unqualified pointers to the global segment allows fine-grained coherent sharing of data structures between the host processor and kernel agents in a manner that is not possible under existing GPGPU programming models due to either language or hardware limitations.

```
// Declare an unordered map and populate it with data.
std::unordered_map<uint32_t, float> map;
populate_map(map);

// Declare a vector to receive results.
std::vector<float> output(SIZE);

// Run a kernel to perform the map lookup in parallel.
auto future = queue->parallel_for<class parallel_map>(SIZE, [&](){
  // For simplicity, we use the work-item ID as the search key.
  uint32_t i = rt::builtin::workitemabsid(0);

  // Perform lookup on map, captured by reference from outer scope.
  auto iter = map.find(i);
  output[i] = iter->second;
});

future.wait();
// output is now populated with the results of the lookup.
```

Listing 8. Standard template library classes used within a kernel lambda function.

Listing 8 illustrates this using a parallel map lookup as an example. A kernel is defined using a lambda function which captures a std::unordered_map object (map) and a std::vector (output) by reference. Each work-item then queries its unique ID, and uses that ID as a key to perform a lookup on the map and storing the result into the vector, output. We made *no modifications* to the implementations of std::vector or std::unordered_map to accomplish this.

The references to map and output within the lambda function correspond to addresses in the global segment. Our compiler will then create duplicates of any functions called directly or indirectly from the kernel, in this case the find member function of std::unordered_map, the subscript operator of std::vector and any further functions referenced by them.

This sharing of unmodified standard C++ classes between the host processor and kernel agents is one of the strengths of our approach. This is only possible due to the ability of our model to operate directly on pointers without container types and only minimal need for non-standard attributes, which can often be hidden by the API. Indeed, all of the user code in Listing 8 is standard C++.

Dynamic memory allocation cannot be performed within a kernel dispatch. However, kernels are able to submit AQL packets to queues serviced by other agents, including the CPU. malloc and free can therefore be implemented by submitting an AQL agent dispatch packet to the CPU and blocking the kernel until the packet has been processed. This enables the implementation of functionality requiring dynamic memory allocation, such as vector resizing, albeit at high synchronization cost.

There are some limitations to what we can currently accomplish. We do not currently support virtual function calls or exception handling. Whilst the HSA specifications define support for indirect function calls through a function pointer, the only HSA runtime implementation currently available does not support this feature.

4   Compiler Implementation

We implement the functionality described within this section as extensions to Clang [9] and LLVM [10]. The compiler backend used in this work is derived from the HSAIL LLVM backend published by the HSA Foundation[5], with additional modifications to support the functionality described in the paper.

Clang has been extended with new targets to support both 32 and 64-bit HSAIL. HSA-specific functionality such as querying work-item IDs is exposed through the addition of target specific built-in functions.

Only a subset of the complete program source needs to be compiled for HSA. In order to extract this subset, we identify functions marked with the [[hsa::kernel]] and [[hsa::functions]] attributes. We then recursively traverse the internal representation of these functions, identifying any function call expressions and marking these functions as also requiring code generation for HSA. This same traversal is used to provide the automatic call-graph duplication described in the preceding section.

These manipulations could be performed at a later stage within the compiler through LLVM IR transformations. However, performing them as abstract

---

[5] https://github.com/HSAFoundation/HLC-HSAIL-Development-LLVM.

syntax tree manipulations enables interaction with the C++ type system, in particular the template system, enabling developers to utilize function overloading and template specialization based on memory segments.

5   Evaluation

We evaluate the performance of a number of benchmarks on OpenCL and our HSA-based model. Due to a lack of existing benchmarks for either our model or HSA, we port a number of OpenCL samples for use as benchmarks. All of the following benchmarks ran on an AMD A10-7850K processor, with 16 GB of DDR3-1600 RAM. We measure execution time in terms of synchronous execution as observed by the host processor. This means that queueing overhead is included in all results for both OpenCL and our model. All results are the mean of 1000 iterations unless otherwise noted.

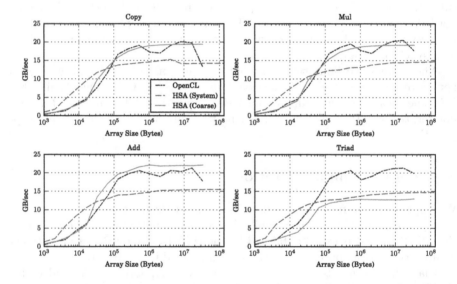

Fig. 1. GPU-STREAM: Memory bandwidth

Stream

In order to illustrate the performance characteristics of the memory on our test system, we use a modified implementation of the STREAM benchmark [11]. The STREAM benchmarks measure sustained memory bandwidth over 4 simple kernels. We extend GPU-STREAM[6] to make use of our compiler and runtime. GPU-STREAM measures the time required to enqueue a kernel and synchronize back to the host processor. The cost of copying the input and output arrays between the host processor and the GPU are excluded from the measurements.

---

[6] https://github.com/UoB-HPC/GPU-STREAM.

From Fig. 1 we observe that coarse-grained memory in HSA and OpenCL buffers produce similar performance for the Copy, Mul and Add kernels, although coarse-grained memory produces a more predictable performance curve. We also observe that using fine-grained system memory appears to have a lower overhead when dispatching kernels, and so results in improved performance for buffers below approximately 64 KB. However, fine-grained memory results in significantly reduced bandwidth on larger data sets. The OpenCL and HSA runtimes have a maximum size of 256 MB for OpenCL buffers and coarse-grained allocations respectively, while fine-grained allocations are only constrained by available RAM.

The coarse and fine-grained measurements were performed using the same kernel. The only difference in these cases is the manner in which the memory was allocated. As such, it is unclear why the performance of coarse-grained allocations in the Triad example differs from the pattern observed in the preceding examples. In this case, coarse-grained memory fails to achieve the throughput of fine-grained system memory, and performs significantly worse than OpenCL buffers.

Bitonic Sort

We evaluated an implementation of Batcher's bitonic mergesort [12] from the AMD APP SDK, and provide a comparison across a range of array sizes. Additionally, we provide results for `std::sort` from the C++ standard library. Bitonic sorting requires multiple kernel executions to completely sort a dataset, and so we reduce our sample size to 100 iterations of the full sorting algorithm. The results can be found in Fig. 2. None of the results include the initial cost of populating the input buffer. We also note that the bitonic sort sample found in the AMD APP SDK, and consequently our port, is implemented for clarity and not optimized for maximum performance.

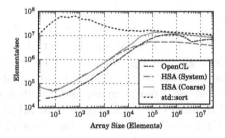

Fig. 2. Bitonic sort

For small array sizes, both HSA implementations outperform the OpenCL implementation. However, these small workloads are the least appropriate to processing on the GPU, and the throughput of the CPU implementation outclasses all three GPU variants. For larger datasets($> 10^5$ elements), we observe that a GPU-based sort using our HSA-based model and coarse-grained memory becomes competitive with `std::sort`. The coarse-grained HSA-based sort outperforms the OpenCL sort both in terms of throughput and consistency. However, we note that in the majority of cases, it appears that simply using std::sort may be both the simplest and more performant option here.

Black-Scholes

We provide a comparison of the Black-Scholes sample from the AMD APP SDK to a version ported to run on our HSA-based compiler and runtime. The Black-Scholes kernel relies upon the OpenCL built-in functions for exponential and logarithmic functions. Whilst HSAIL does provide equivalent instructions to many of the OpenCL built-in functions, it does not provide base e exponentials or logarithms. In order to resolve this, we provided our own implementations of `exp` and `log`, adhering to the same precision requirements as described in the OpenCL specification ($\leqslant 4$ ULP). Beyond providing the necessary implementations of `exp` and `log`, the port makes no algorithmic changes to the kernel being profiled.

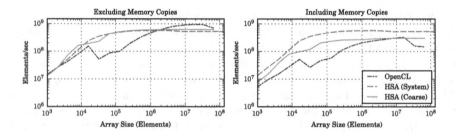

Fig. 3. Black-Scholes

We measure execution time, both inclusive and exclusive of memory copies. Our results can be seen in Fig. 3. Ignoring the cost of memory transfers, the OpenCL kernel achieves higher peak performance on large datasets. We attribute this to a more mature compiler in the AMD OpenCL implementation, when compared to the combination of our compiler and the finalizer in the HSA runtime. Our HSA-based runtime benefits from faster kernel dispatchs resulting in improved performance for small datasets, and also demonstrates a more stable and predictable performance curve throughout.

When the cost of memory transfers is considered, the fine-grained results are unchanged due to not requiring copies. However, throughput for both OpenCL and coarse-grained allocations is reduced. The net result is that whilst fine-grained allocations produce the highest kernel execution times, the elimination of copying still leads to the greatest total throughput.

SVM Binary Tree Search

The SVMBinaryTreeSearch sample from the AMD APP SDK serves to highlight one of the key advantages of our approach. This sample uses the support for coarse-grained shared virtual memory introduced in OpenCL 2.0 to implement a binary tree that is manipulated on both the CPU and GPU. Due to differing languages used for host code (C++) and device code (OpenCL C) in the sample, the data structures for representing the tree nodes and representing search keys are defined twice, in two different source files, but must maintain compatible binary layouts. Under our model, a single-source language and a single definition of data types can be used.

For the evaluation, a set of 64 K random numbers are generated and a binary search tree is constructed from them. We then generate 1 million random search keys, and perform a parallel search, matching nodes to corresponding search keys. The results of this evaluation can be found in Fig. 4 and Table 2.

Fine-grained (system allocated) memory performs poorly for this use case. The fine-grained allocation results in low cache hit rates (34 %) coupled with a smaller quantity of data fetched from memory. The coarse-grained allocation achieves much a higher hit rate (80 %), along with a greater quantity of data fetched. These two examples execute identical kernels, and so we can conclude that these performance discrepancies are attributable to differing cache and memory management strategies for coarse and fine-grained allocations. The OpenCL implementation results in similar behaviour to the coarse-grained example, with our HSA-based runtime achieving a modest speedup whilst also demonstrating reduced performance variance.

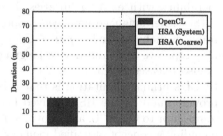

Fig. 4. SVM binary tree search

Table 2. SVM binary tree search

Runtime	Execution Time (ms)	Std. Dev.	Fetch size (KB)	Cache Hit Rate (%)
OpenCL	19.13	0.34	276000	79.8 %
HSA (System)	69.84	0.82	12000	33.6 %
HSA (Coarse)	17.32	0.17	278000	79.5 %

6   Related Work

Research into high-level programming of parallel and heterogeneous hardware is expanding rapidly. Given that HSA is relatively new, however, only a small portion of research has targeted it. Initial support for programming HSA platforms came in the form of tools such as CLOC [13] that do not provide a cohesive programming model but rather provide a method to compile and run code on HSA platforms. In the case of CLOC it gives the programmer the tools to compile OpenCL kernels to HSAIL offline, and a library to allow the programmer to execute the kernels. POCL [14] is an open-source OpenCL implementation that has been used for HSA development [15]. However, the results on HSA were generally poor compared to native OpenCL, and the publicly available code only supports OpenCL 1.2. Others have also started to exploit the benefits of HSA to enable more advanced functionality. The HCC compiler [16] can compile C++AMP to HSA. This compiler also provides support for a more compact, C++ AMP derived, model: HC. HC removes some of the limitations of C++AMP while providing a simpler syntax. More traditionally, the directive-based OpenMP 4.0 allows the programmer to mark regions of code to "offload", although the programmer must also provide a description of how to map data to the device. The GCC compiler has support for targeting HSA devices with these "offload" regions.

Generic C++AMP can use OpenCL to provide heterogeneous functionality, but loses the benefits of HSA. There have been various other proposals for C++ models to wrap OpenCL functionality. A version of OpenCL C++ [17] has been proposed. This still requires separate host and device languages, and although a unified pointer type is provided it is separate from native pointers and thus does not allow interoperability with existing libraries. Distinct from this, an official OpenCL C++ [18] kernel language has been proposed by the Khronos group. Although this provides many of the benefits of C++, such as classes and templates it still requires separate host and device languages. To address this the Khronos group has also released SYCL [7], a C++ shared-source OpenCL programming model. SYCL's primary limitation is that it is based on OpenCL 1.2 and thus cannot provide many of the HSA derived benefits of our model. CUDA [5], a primary competitor to OpenCL, also provides a C++ shared-source programming model, including a concept of unified memory. It is, however, vendor specific and requires custom keywords and syntax to exploit heterogeneous functionality. CUDA is API driven, similarly to OpenCL, and thus programs written in CUDA tend to be far more verbose than in our model.

Finally, there are several library-based solutions for heterogeneous programming, most prominently the Parallel STL and Boost.Compute. The Parallel STL [19] is strongly influenced by a variety of vendor-specific C++ implementation efforts. It describes parallel execution policies for STL algorithms, such as `std::sort` or `std::for_each`. This provides the programmer with seamless high-level access to standard parallel functionality, and the ability to compose their own functionality. Boost.Compute [20] provides a wider range of functionality than the Parallel STL, but it is explicitly built on OpenCL concepts and thus exposes details such as buffers and queues to the programmer – something that neither the Parallel STL nor the environment described in this paper require. The primary limitation of all library-based approaches is what can be constructed out of the provided building blocks. Language-based approaches, such as the one described in this paper, allow the programmer more freedom in what they construct, at the cost of requiring compiler functionality to implement some features.

7   Conclusions and Future Work

We have described a shared-source C++14 based programming model for HSA, supported by an enhanced compiler and runtime, mapping the highly segmented memory model onto the single-address space memory model found in C++. We do this whilst requiring only limited source code annotations. This enables the rapid reuse of existing standard C++ code on heterogeneous accelerators. We demonstrate the fine-grained sharing of data structures between the host processor and kernel agents, without the need for copies or container types. We have demonstrated similar performance to OpenCL across a range of benchmarks.

Limitations with the current HSA runtime prevent the implementation of a number of C++ features. Most notably, the runtime lacks support for indirect function calls and exceptions. Future work will include support for calling functions through pointers (which also enables calls to virtual methods), the compiler support for this is described in previous work [8].

References

1. HSA Foundation: HSA Platform System Architecture Specification. HSA (2015a)
2. HSA Foundation: HSA Runtime Programmers Reference Manual. HSA (2015c)
3. HSA Foundation: HSA Programmers Reference Manual. HSA (2015b)
4. Khronos OpenCL Working Group: The OpenCL Specification. Khronos (2015b)
5. NVIDIA Corporation: CUDA Programming Guide. NVIDIA (2008)
6. Microsoft: C++ AMP: Language and Programming Model. Microsoft (2013)
7. Khronos OpenCL Working Group – SYCL subgroup: SYCL Specification. Khronos (2015)
8. Cooper, P., Dolinsky, U., Donaldson, A.F., Richards, A., Riley, C., Russell, G.: Offload – automating code migration to heterogeneous multicore systems. In: Patt, Y.N., Foglia, P., Duesterwald, E., Faraboschi, P., Martorell, X. (eds.) HiPEAC 2010. LNCS, vol. 5952, pp. 337–352. Springer, Heidelberg (2010). doi:10.1007/978-3-642-11515-8_25
9. Clang: a C language family frontend for LLVM (2015). http://clang.llvm.org/. Accessed 24 Nov 2015
10. Lattner, C., Adve, V.S.: LLVM: a compilation framework for lifelong program analysis & transformation. In: 2nd IEEE/ACM International Symposium on Code Generation and Optimization, pp. 75–88. IEEE Computer Society (2004)
11. McCalpin, J.D.: Memory bandwidth and machine balance in current high performance computers. In: IEEE Computer Society Technical Committee on Computer Architecture Newsletter (1995)

12. Batcher, K.E.: Sorting networks and their applications. In: AFIPS Conference Proceedings: 1968 Spring Joint Computer Conference. AFIPS Conference Proceedings, vol. 32, pp. 307–314. Thomson Book Company, Washington, D.C. (1968)
13. Rodgers, G.: CLOC compiler and sample SDK (2015). https://github.com/HSAFoundation/CLOC. Accessed 29 Nov 2015
14. Jääskeläinen, P., de La Lama, C.S., Schnetter, E., Raiskila, K., Takala, J., Berg, H.: pocl: a performance-portable opencl implementation. Int. J. Parallel Prog. **43**(5), 752–785 (2015)
15. Yang, C.C., Wang, S.C., Chen, C.C., Lee, J.K.: The support of an experimental OpenCL compiler on HSA environments. In: Proceedings of the 21st International Conference on Parallel and Distributed Processing Techniques and Applications, pp. 184–190 (2015)
16. Sander, B., Stoner, G., chi Chan, S., Chung, W.H.: HCC: a C++ compiler for heterogeneous computing. Technical report, ISO/IEC JTC1 SC22 WG21 (2015)
17. Gaster, B.R., Howes, L.W.: OpenCL C++. In: Cavazos, J., Gong, X., Kaeli, D.R. (eds.) Proceedings of the 6th Workshop on General Purpose Processor Using Graphics Processing Units, GPGPU-6, pp. 86–95. ACM (2013)
18. Khronos OpenCL Working Group: The OpenCL C++ Specification. Khronos (2015a)
19. Hoberock, J.: Technical specification for C++ extensions for parallelism. Technical report, ISO/IEC JTC1 SC22 WG21 (2015)
20. Lutz, K.: Boost. Compute (2015). https://boostorg.github.io/compute/. Accessed 29 Nov 2015

Battling Memory Requirements of Array Programming Through Streaming

Mads R.B. Kristensen[1]($\boxtimes$), James Avery[2]($\boxtimes$), Troels Blum[1],
Simon Andreas Frimann Lund[1], and Brian Vinter[1]

[1] Niels Bohr Institute, University of Copenhagen, Copenhagen, Denmark
madsbk@nbi.ku.dk
[2] Department of Computer Science, University of Copenhagen,
Copenhagen, Denmark
avery@diku.dk

Abstract. A barrier to efficient array programming, for example in
Python/NumPy, is that algorithms written as pure array operations
completely without loops, while most efficient on small input, can lead
to explosions in memory use. The present paper presents a solution to
this problem using *array streaming*, implemented in the automatic parallelization high-performance framework *Bohrium*. This makes it possible
to use array programming in Python/NumPy code directly, even when
the apparent memory requirement exceeds the machine capacity, since
the automatic streaming eliminates the temporary memory overhead by
performing calculations in per-thread registers.

Using Bohrium, we automatically fuse, JIT-compile, and execute
NumPy array operations on GPGPUs without modification to the user
programs. We present performance evaluations of three benchmarks, all
of which show dramatic reductions in memory use from streaming, yielding corresponding improvements in speed and utilization of GPGPU-
cores. The streaming-enabled Bohrium effortlessly runs programs on
input sizes much beyond sizes that crash on pure NumPy due to exhausting system memory.

1 Introduction

High-productivity programming languages are very popular in the scientific community. They enable rapid prototyping of new ideas, which is essential for timely
scientific discovery; and the shorter, clearer code makes it much easier to verify
correctness. The Python programming language is an example of such a language. It provides rapid prototyping [2,30], it can act as glue between library
calls [8,14,33], and it can stand alone with good scalable performance [19,20].
The performance of Python itself[1], can be hundreds of times slower than equivalent programs in C, but when NumPy [32] is programmed idiomatically using
array programming, it is possible to achieve reasonable performance. In array
programming, loops are not written explicitly, but instead expressed as operations on arrays. The Bohrium project [18] takes Python/NumPy performance to

---

[1] The standard interpreter, CPython, implemented in C.

© Springer International Publishing AG 2016
M. Taufer et al. (Eds.): ISC High Performance Workshops 2016, LNCS 9945, pp. 451–469, 2016.
DOI: 10.1007/978-3-319-46079-6_32

<table>
<tr><td>

```
1  import numpy as np
2  def pi(N):
3    t = 0
4    for _ in xrange(N):
5      x = np.random.random(1)
6      y = np.random.random(1)
7      t += np.sqrt(x*x+y*y)<=1.0
8    pi = t * 4.0 / N
9  print pi(10**8)
```

(a) Loop

</td><td>

```
1  RANDOM a1
2  RANDOM a2
3  MUL a3 a1 a1
4  MUL a4 a2 a2
5  ADD a5 a3 a4
6  DEL a3
7  DEL a4
8  SQRT a6 a5
9  DEL a5
10 LEQUAL a7 a6 1.0
11 DEL a6
12 SUM a8 a7
13 MUL a9 a8 4.0
14 DEL a8
15 DIV a10 a9 N
16 DEL a9
17 DEL a1
18 DEL a2
19 DEL a7
20 SYNC a10
```

</td></tr>
</table>

```
1  import numpy as np
2  def pi(N):
3    x = np.random.random(N)
4    y = np.random.random(N)
5    t = np.sqrt(x*x+y*y) <= 1.0
6    return np.sum(t) * 4.0 / N
7  print pi(10**8)
```

(b) Array programming

(c) Bohrium

Fig. 1. Monte Carlo Pi implemented in Python 2.7 and NumPy 1.8 using: (a) for-loop, (b) array-programming, and (c) Bohrium bytecode (simplified).

the next level and through JIT-compilation provides sequential performance on par with hand tuned C code and parallel performance on par with hand tuned OpenMP (SMP), OpenCL (GPU), and MPI (cluster) code. The only requirement of the user is that she use the array programming model.

But while array programming is both convenient and facilitates efficient execution, it introduces its own problems compared to the otherwise low-performance loops in high-productivity languages such as Python/NumPy, Matlab [24], and R [11]. Consider Fig. 1, which shows two Python/NumPy programs that approximate π using the Monte Carlo method. In Fig. 1a, a for-loop calculates a single random coordinate in each iteration whereas in Fig. 1b, all N random coordinates are calculated independently. The Fig. 1b version is how every teacher and every book will tell you to use array programming in order to achieve good performance in Python. Indeed, the Fig. 1b version will in most cases outperform Fig. 1a with *two orders of magnitude*. However, the memory requirement of Fig. 1b grows linearly in N. Thus, for large N, the Fig. 1b version will run out of memory, in contrast to Fig. 1a, which has a constant memory use. For programs that are written fully as array programs, i.e. when all loops are formulated as array operations, memory consumption is often asymptotically the same as its time complexity. In the example of Monte Carlo Pi, this is manageable as the time complexity is only linear but, as we shall see later, array programming can quickly lead to high polynomial memory requirements, causing memory to run out even for small problem sizes.

The present work uses automatic array streaming to address the explosion in memory requirements of array programming in Python/NumPy programs. For the example of Monte Carlo π, instead of allocating the random value arrays in memory, the idea is to *stream* the arrays such that only one element per computing thread is instantiated at any given time. This streaming technique is only applicable to temporary arrays, requiring us to detect temporary NumPy arrays at runtime and stream them. Furthermore, since the whole point of Python/NumPy is high-productivity, we have to apply this streaming technique seamlessly so that no change to the original Python/NumPy code is needed.

In compiler terminology, array streaming is also known as loop fusion when combined with array contraction (or scalar replacement). It is a well-studied optimization technique that both improves cache utilization and memory use. It is NP-hard to do optimally [7], but with the theoretical fusion framework of [15], it is possible to find solutions that are good enough in practice.

The present work brings this compiler optimization technique to the Python language by combining three projects: the fusion framework of [15], the OpenCL kernel generations of [5], and the Bohrium runtime system [18].

2 Array Programming

As an example illustrating the methods used in array programming, consider the following different implementations of matrix multiplication in Python/NumPy.

```
1  import numpy as np
2  def matmul(A,B):
3     nrow = A.shape[0]
4     ncol = B.shape[1]
5     C = np.zeros((nrow, ncol))
6     for i in xrange(nrow):
7        for j in xrange(ncol):
8           for k in xrange(A.shape[1]):
9              C[i,j] += A[i,k] * B[k,j]
10    return C
```

(a) **Loop**, space complexity: $\mathcal{O}\left(n^2\right)$

```
1  import numpy as np
2  def matmul(A,B):
3     nrow = A.shape[0]
4     ncol = B.shape[1]
5     C = np.zeros((nrow, ncol))
6     for i in xrange(nrow):
7        for j in xrange(ncol):
8           C[i,j] += np.sum(A[i,:]*B[:,j])
9     return C
```

(b) **Hybrid**, space complexity: $\mathcal{O}\left(n^2\right)$

```
1  import numpy as np
2  def matmul(A,B):
3     Bt = np.transpose(B)
4     T  = A[:,np.newaxis,:]*Bt[np.newaxis,:,:]
5     return np.sum(T,axis=2)
```

(c) **Array Programming**, space complexity: $\mathcal{O}\left(n^3\right)$

Fig. 2. Three matrix multiplication implementations in Python/NumPy. Inputs A and B are NumPy arrays of same size and compatible shape.

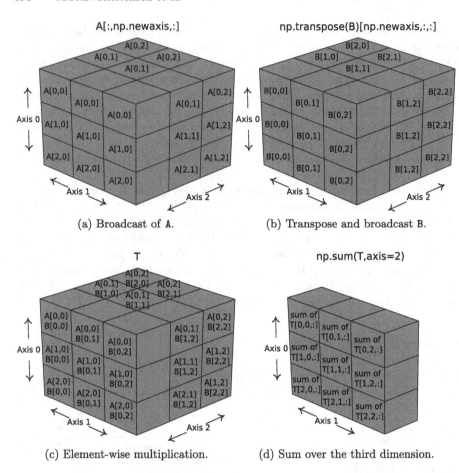

(a) Broadcast of A.

(b) Transpose and broadcast B.

(c) Element-wise multiplication.

(d) Sum over the third dimension.

Fig. 3. An illustration of the NumPy broadcast technique, which we use to implement matrix multiplication (Fig. 2c).

For the sake of the example, assume that matrix multiplication did not exist in NumPy and we had to implement it using basic Python/NumPy primitives.

A straightforward approach is to use three nested for-loops (Fig. 2a), which has a time complexity of $O(n^3)$ and requires no extra memory beyond the $n \times n$ input and output matrices, for a total space complexity of $O(n^2)$ (for simplicity, we assume square matrices). However, the implementation is verbose and the performance is horrible: multiplying two arrays of size 200^2 has an execution time of 5.0 s (Sect. 6 for hardware specifics). This is because all calculations are done in pure Python.

We can improve performance by implementing the loop over k as an array operation and a sum (Fig. 2b). The implementation now uses a temporary vector of length n that it sums over (line 8) but the space complexity is still $O(n^2)$. The code is more readable and outperforms the previous version by an order of magnitude: an execution of 0.3 s. Since the multiplication and sum are now NumPy array operations, a for-loop within the C implementation of NumPy does the calculation. Still, the implementation calls the NumPy array operations n^2 times, which incurs a significant CPython overhead.

In order to improve the performance even further, we can replace all three loops with array operations (Fig. 2c). Now, the implementation calculates all scalar multiplications in one operation and writes the result to the temporary array T of size n^3. It uses a NumPy technique known as *broadcast*, which basically means to increase the number of an array's dimensions by repeating the data of the original array into the this new dimension (Fig. 3). Due to this broadcast, the space complexity is now $O(n^3)$. However, with a small problem size of 200^2 this implementation improves the performance by another order of magnitude: an execution of 0.02 s. This is the preferred implementation approach in array programming languages such as Python/NumPy but it is often not possible because of the memory usage, a simple $10,000 \times 10,000$ matrix multiplication would require more than 7 TB of memory with this approach.

3   Related Work

The primary contribution of the present work is automatic, seamless streaming of array operations on parallel hardware. Although numerous projects strive to improve the efficiency of Python applications, the streaming introduced in this paper is to the authors knowledge new.

Efforts such as Cython [3], IronPython [9], Jython [29], and Pythran [10] facilitate static source-to-source translation to C, .NET, Java, and C++, respectively. These projects provide interoperability features with the respective languages and runtimes. Dynamic approaches based on JIT-compilation is demonstrated by Weave [12], Numexpr [6], and Numba [28]. Weave lets the user inline C and C++ code, Numexpr compiles strings containing Python expressions, and Python code is delegated to Numba by annotating functions.

Compiling Python programs, either statically or dynamically, to representations closer to the hardware, and thereby bypassing the standard Python interpreter upon execution, effectively improves application throughput. However, none of these approaches fully exploit array semantics for optimization which is the focus of the work described in this paper.

Several projects target parallel hardware from Python, such as GPG-PUs, via a multi-dimensional array abstraction. Projects include CudaNdarray/Theano [4], GPUArray/PyOpenCL/PyCUDA [13], Cudamat [25], and Gnumpy [31]. However, these are either explicit in the sense that the user must control data movement and write OpenCL [26]/CUDA [27] kernels or limited in their support for array notation. None address the issue of maintaining the array programming abstraction and the associated memory requirements.

The work presented in this paper is in contrast compatible with the NumPy array abstraction and manages all concerns of mapping array operations to the hardware.

A key distinguishing feature of the work described in this paper, in contrast to the projects mentioned above, is the focus on treating Python as an array language. That is, maintaining the high-level abstractions and exploiting array semantics to extract data-parallelism, analyze dependencies between array operations to stream operations and utilize the parallel hardware.

Domain specific programming languages and libraries exist for tensor contraction that make use of array streaming (called loop fusion and memory minimization) [1, 21] but they are very domain specific. Other projects expose the streaming model explicitly to the user in languages such as NESL [23] and Haskell [22].

4   The Bohrium Runtime System

The open-source project Bohrium[2] is a runtime system for high-performance high-productivity development [17,18]. Bohrium provides the mechanics to couple an array-programming language or library with an architecture-specific implementation seamlessly. Bohrium lazily records array operations, such as NumPy array operations, compiles them into architecture-specific binaries, e.g. GPGPU kernels, and executes them.

Bohrium consists of a number of components that operate on a hardware agnostic array bytecode. Components can be architecture-specific but they all use the same bytecode and communication protocol and can be interchanged. This design makes it possible to combine components in a setup that match a specific execution environment without changing the user applications.

Frontend. Figure 4 illustrates the different components that make up the Bohrium runtime system and how they are connected. At the highest level, we have the frontend programming language; Bohrium supports Python/NumPy, C++, and Microsoft .NET. For the examples in this paper, we will only use the Python/NumPy frontend, but the mechanics of array streaming is unaffected by the choice of frontend language.

Bridge. Connected to the frontend is a *Bridge* component, whose job is to translate the frontend language into Bohrium array bytecode. In the case of Python/NumPy, the Python array operations and the Bohrium array bytecode are almost in one-to-one correspondence. Figure 1c shows the list of array bytecode that the bridge generates when given the Python code in Fig. 1b. The first bytecode operand is the output array and the remaining operands are either input arrays or input literals. Since there is no scope in the bytecode, Bohrium uses DEL to destroy arrays and SYNC to move array data into the address space of the frontend language – in this case triggered by the Python `print` statement (Fig. 1c, line 7). There is no explicit bytecode for constructing arrays; on first encounter, Bohrium constructs them implicitly.

Note that Bohrium needs no modifications to the Python code – with the Python command line option `python -m bohrium`, it is possible to use Bohrium

---

[2] Available at http://www.bh107.org.

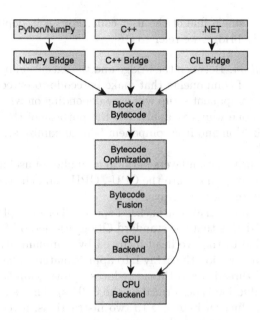

Fig. 4. Component overview

```
1  #pragma OPENCL EXTENSION cl_khr_fp64 : enable
2  #include <ocl_random.h>
3  #define ds2 3125
4  #define ds1 32000
5  __kernel __attribute__((work_group_size_hint(128, 1, 1)))\
6      void kernel1(__global ulong* a9, const ulong N){
7      const size_t idd1 = get_global_id(0);
8      if (idd1 >= ds1)
9          return;
10     ulong v9 = 0ul;
11     for (int idd2 = 0; idd2 < ds2; ++idd2){
12         double v1 = random(N, idd2 + idd1*ds1);
13         double v2 = random(N, idd2 + idd1*ds1);
14         double v3 = v1 * v1;
15         double v4 = v2 * v2;
16         double v5 = v3 + v4;
17         double v6 = sqrt(v5);
18         uchar v7 = v6 <= 1.0;
19         ulong v8 = v7;
20         v9 = v9 + v8;
21     }
22     size_t v9idx = idd1;
23     a9[v9idx] = v9;
24 }
```

Fig. 5. The C++/OpenCL source code of the Monte Carlo Pi example (Fig. 1c) that the GPU backend generates (simplified).

without changing a single line of the user code. For an in-depth description of the Python/NumPy bridge, we refer to [16].

Bytecode Optimization. Between the bridge and the execution backend, Bohrium supports a number of components that make bytecode-to-bytecode transformations. The specific component setup will vary depending on which optimizations and fuse strategies one wants to apply. For the purpose of this paper, the goal of both the optimization and fuse component is to maximize array streaming for the GPU backend.

The bytecode optimization layers perform a number of useful tasks, the most important of which are common to the CPU-, GPU-, and cluster vector engines, such as eliminating temporary arrays.

Optimization-layers can also be backend-specific. For example, an obstacle for streaming on the GPU is that the standard $\mathcal{O}(\log_2 n)$-method for 1D reduction[3] performs poorly due to the overhead incurred by communication. For GPU, a faster method is to partition the array into approximately equally sized chunks, one for each GPU thread. Each thread reduces its own chunk, after which the usual $\mathcal{O}(\log_2 n)$-reduction is performed by the CPU(s). This is handled by transforming each 1D-reduction bytecode to two instructions, a reduction over one axis on a 2D reshaped array, and a second reduction over the resulting vector. If the shape of the 2D arrays is such that the size of first dimension equals the number of GPU hardware threads, the first reduction on the GPU will have perfect utilization and the second reduction on the CPU will be small, improving the performance of the overall reduction.

Looking at the Monte Carlo Pi example (Fig. 1c), the change to the bytecode is straightforward. We represent the arrays, $a_1, \ldots, a_8$, with two dimensions instead of one, where the size of the first dimension approximates the number of GPU hardware threads, and add another SUM after line 12 that will reduce the now 1D output from the SUM from line 12 to a scalar.

Connected to the optimization component, we have the fuser component, which fuses array operations that can be executed in a single kernel. The partition of operations into kernels of fused operations is determined by (approximately) optimizing a cost function designed to maximize the number of streamed arrays. In the next section, we will describe this process, but for now just assume that the fuse component fuses array operations into kernels that the GPU backend can execute as is.

GPU Backend. After the bytecode has been fused into kernels, the GPU backend is ready to execute them[4].

For each fused bytecode kernel, the GPU backend generates OpenCL source code, compiles the code, and executes it. For an in-depth discussion of this

---

[3] A *reduction* performs an associative binary operation on all elements along an axis. The prototypical reductions are *sum* and *product*, but any associative binary operation can be used.

[4] When no GPU is available, the bytecode kernels will be send directly to the CPU backend.

code generation, we refer to [5]. Here, we will simply show how the generated C/OpenCL implementation of the Monte Carlo example (Fig. 5). The mapping from the bytecode to the OpenCL code is straightforward: each hardware thread generates some random numbers, apply some arithmetic, and accumulates the result into v9. Finally, each thread writes the result into an index of the output array a9, making it possible for the CPU backend to reduce v9 into the final scalar. Note that beside v9, all the variables are scalars rather than arrays, *streaming* the arrays v1–v8.

The GPU backend uses a cache to store previously generated OpenCL kernels, amortizing the compilation overhead.

5   Streaming of Arrays

Streaming of array operations can improve cache utilization and reduce the memory requirement of the overall program. It is possible to stream an array when only a single operation reads or writes to that said array – we say that the array is a temporary array. In order to maximize the number of temporary arrays in a program, we will combine (or fuse) individual array operation to be executed together in a single kernel, increasing the number of streamable arrays.

Consider the two for-loops in Fig. 6a, which are fused into one for-loop, Fig. 6c, with the result of much improved cache utilization since array T and A are only traversed once instead of two times. For the next level of improvement, the for-loop in Fig. 6d does not allocate the array T at all. Instead, it uses the scalar t to stream the intermediate result of B[i] * A[i], which is possible because T is only used within the for-loop – it is a temporary array local to the for-loop.

Not all fusion of array operations are allowed. Consider the two loops in Fig. 6b: the second loop traverses the result from the first loop in reverse, we must compute the complete result of the first loop before continuing to the second loop. This prevents fusion of the two for-loops and streaming of T, since it is not temporary to any one for-loop. Additional analysis sometimes allows transforming the program into a form that is amenable to fusion and streaming, but this is outside the scope of the present paper. In the remainder of the text, we will assume that any such transformation has already been performed.

5.1   Fusibility

Array streaming depend on fusing array operations, so it is necessary to determine which operations we can legally fuse, and which we can profit from fusing. Generally, it is useful to fuse two array operations when the result of each output array element can be calculated independently without any communication between threads or processors:

Definition 1 (Fusibility). *A Bohrium array operation, f, is* data-parallel, *i.e., each output element can be calculated independently, when the following*

```
#define N 1000
double A[N], B[N], T[N];
for(int i=0; i<N; ++i)
    T[i] = B[i] * A[i];
for(int i=0; i<N; ++i)
    A[i] += T[i];
```

(a) Two forward iterating loops.

```
#define N 1000
double A[N], B[N], T[N];
int j = N;
for(int i=0; i<N; ++i)
    T[i] = B[i] * A[i];
for(int i=0; i<N; ++i)
    A[i] += T[--j];
```

(b) A forward and a reverse iterating loop.

```
for(int i=0; i<N; ++i){
    T[i] = B[i] * A[i];
    A[i] += T[i];
}
```

(c) Loop fusion: the two loops from Fig. 6a fused into one.

```
for(int i=0; i<N; ++i){
    double t = B[i] * A[i];
    A[i] += t;
}
```

(d) Array contraction: the temporary array T from Fig. 6c is contracted into the scalar t.

Fig. 6. Loop fusion and array contraction in C.

holds: *If an input and an output or two output arrays overlap, they must be identical. We define* fusible *operations to be those that can be executed together without losing data-parallelism.*

5.2   Fusion of Array Operations

Reference [15] describes methods for finding a partition of operations such that a cost function is optimized, or near-optimized using a fast approximation heuristic. In the present work, we apply the methods from Ref. [15] to generate kernels that optimize for array streaming. For completeness, we summarize the method in this subsection, and a streamlined greedy algorithm is given in Sect. 5.3.

The problem of finding the optimal operation partitions is called the *Fusion of Array Operations Problem* (FAO problem), and is defined as follows:

Definition 2. *Given a set of array operations, A, equipped with a strict partial order imposed by the data dependencies between them, $(A, \overset{d}{<})$, find a partition, P, of A for which:*

1. *All operations within a block in P are fusible (Definition 1).*
2. *For all blocks, $B \in P$, if $a_1 \overset{d}{<} a_2 \overset{d}{<} a_3$ and $a_1, a_3 \in B$ then $a_2 \in B$. (I.e. the partition obeys dependency order).*
3. *The cost of the partition is minimal.*

A key feature of the FAO problem is the ability to specify an arbitrary cost function that defines the cost of a partition. The only requirement is that the cost must be monotonic decreasing on fusion, i.e. fusing two array operations must not increase the cost. In our case, the object is to maximize the number of streamed arrays thus an appropriate cost is the number of Bohrium arrays that are **not** streamed, but could have been.

A partition of the operations is represented by a *WSP-state* ("Weighted Subroutine Partition" [15], Sect. 6), which makes it possible to solve the problem of finding an optimal partition using graph methods.

Definition 3 (WSP-state). *Given a sequence of array operations, a WSP-state is a quadruple $G = (V, E_d, E_f, E_w)$ that describes a partition of the operations.*

Blocks *Each vertex in V represent a sequence of fused array operations that the Bohrium backend will execute as one binary kernel.*

Dependency Edges *(V, E_d) is a directed acyclic graph describing dependency order between blocks i.e. there is an edge $(u, v) \in E_d$ if and only if an array operation in u must precede an array operations in v.*

Fuse-preventing Edges *(V, E_f) is a undirected graph describing non-fusibility between blocks, i.e. there is an edge $(u, v) \in E_f$ if and only if an array operation in u is non-fusible with an array operation in v.*

Weight Edges *(V, E_w) is a weighted graph such that the weight of edge (u, v) is the difference in cost from the present partition to the one where u and v are merged.*

To optimize for streaming, the present work uses the *Max Contract* cost function from [15], for which the weight of an edge $(u, v) \in E_w$ is the number of arrays created in u and at the same time destroyed in v.

Not all WSP-states are legal:

Definition 4 (Legality). *A WSP-state, $G = (V, E_d, E_f, E_w)$, is **legal** if and only if:*

1. *The digraph (V, E_d) is acyclic (i.e. no cyclic dependency between operations).*
2. *All array operations represented by a vertex, $v \in V$, must be fusible.*

It follows directly from Definitions 3 and 4 that any topological ordering of the vertices in a WSP-state is a correct execution order of the fused array operations.

A WSP-state supports edge contraction:

MERGE(G, e)

Given a WSP-state, $G = (V, E_d, E_f, E_w)$, and an edge $e \in E_d$, the function $G' \leftarrow$ MERGE(G, e) contracts the edge e, i.e. the endpoint vertices, (u, v), of e, are merged into one new vertex $x \in G'$. We avoid parallel edges in E_w by collapsing them into one and accumulate their weights.

Bottom and *top* WSP states correspond to the bottom and top partition, where all instructions are in separate, respectively, the same kernel. Given a sequence of array operations, we start from the bottom WSP-state in which each array operation is a vertex, and the edges in E_d, E_f, and E_w are the pair-wise dependencies, fusibility, and streaming potential between all vertices. The bottom WSP-state is trivially legal (Definition 4).

```
1: function TRANSITIVE((V, E_d), (u, v))
2:     l ← length of longest path from u to v in E_d
3:     if l = 1 then
4:         return true
5:     else
6:         return false
```

Fig. 7. Function to determine transitive redundancy.

```
1: function GREEDY((V, E_d, E_f, E_w))
2:     while E_w ≠ ∅ do
3:         e ← HEAVIEST(E_w)
4:         if TRANSITIVE((V, E_d), e) or e ∈ E_f then
5:             Remove edge e from E_w
6:         else
7:             (V, E_d, E_f, E_w) ← MERGE((V, E_d, E_f, E_w), e)
8:     return (V, E_d, E_f, E_w)
```

Fig. 8. Function to merge vertices greedily.

5.3   Greedy Algorithm

The *Reachability through legal merges* proposition (proof in [15]) states that there exist a sequence of legal merges, starting from the bottom WSP-state, and ending with a WSP-state that optimizes the cost function.

However, it turns out that finding an optimal WSP-state is NP-hard, hence not practical. Instead, we will use a greedy approximation algorithm, which repeatedly fuses the two vertices connected by the heaviest streaming edge while maintaining legality of the WSP-state.

Let us define some functions from [15]:

TRANSITIVE(G, e) (see pseudo code Fig. 7)
    Given a digraph, $G = (V, E_d)$, and an edge $e \in E_d$, the function TRANSITIVE(G, e) returns *true* if and only if e is *redundant by transitivity*. An edge, $(u, v) \in E_d$, is redundant when there exist an alternative path in (V, E_d) from u to v. This is important since merging over a redundant edge introduces cycles.

HEAVIEST(E_w)
    Given set of edges, E_w, the function $e \leftarrow$ HEAVIEST(E_w) returns the edge $e \in E_w$ with the heaviest weight. The implemention is a simply linear search through the set with a complexity of $\mathcal{O}(E_w)$.

GREEDY$((V, E_d, E_f, E_w))$
    Given a WSP-state, G=(V, E_d, E_f, E_w), the function $G' \leftarrow$ GREEDY(G) repeatedly merges over edges, $(u, v) \in E_w$, with the heaviest weight.
    Figure 8 shows the implementation that uses the function HEAVIEST to find

the edge in $(u, v) \in E_w$ with the greatest weight. If (u, v) is redundant by transitivity, we cannot merge over it since it will introduce cycles and make the WSP-state illegal (Definition 4(1)). However, since (u, v) is redundant we can remove it without changing the dependency order between vertices. Similarly, if (u, v) is in E_f, a merge will fuse non-fusible array operations and make the WSP-state illegal (Definition 4(2)). Because of these conditions, each merger returns a new legal WSP-state, which makes the final returned WSP-state, G', legal as well.

The number of iterations in the while loop (line 2) is bounded by $\mathcal{O}(E_w)$ since at least one edge, $e \in E_w$, is removed in each iteration either explicitly (line 5) or implicitly by MERGE (line 7).

The Bohrium fuse component uses the greedy algorithm to find a legal partition of the array operations that comes close to maximizing the number of arrays streamed. It can be shown that the complexity of the greedy algorithm is $\mathcal{O}(E_w(V + E_d + E_w))$.

6   Evaluation

In this section, we will evaluate the performance of the streaming ability of Bohrium by comparing it with Native NumPy. We run three different scientific Python programs and report their execution time, which is the mean of 5 identical executions. We also include an error bar that shows two standard deviations from the mean in the results. Before each execution, we remove any cache files written by Bohrium or Nvidia/CUDA, so as to make sure we measure the overhead of compilation. We run on an Intel Core i7-4790k machine with 8 CPU-cores, 8 GB DDR3 of main memory and a Nvidia GeForce GTX 980 GPU with 4 GB DDR5 of memory. It is a standard installation of Ubuntu Linux 14.04.2 with GCC v4.8.4, Python v2.7.10, NumPy 1.8.2, and OpenCL v1.1.

The three scientific Python program is part of an open source benchmark tool and suite named Benchpress[5]:

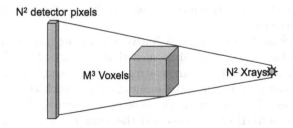

Fig. 9. The X-ray simulation in vectorized form traces all rays from the detector pixels through the model to the source and calculates the total absorption from the source to the detector.

---

[5] Available at http://benchpress.readthedocs.org/.

Monte Carlo Pi. A calculation of π using the Monte Carlo method (Fig. 1b). The time complexity is $O(n)$ where n is the number of random samples, which we vary from 10^8 to 10^{11} throughout the benchmark. The execution uses six one dimensional arrays of length n. As previously discussed, it is possible for Bohrium to stream these six arrays such that only an element per GPU-core is instantiated at a given time.

X-ray simulator. Given a 3D scene represented as voxels, which specifies an X-ray source, an X-ray detector, and an object, the X-ray simulator calculates the resulting image on the sensor (Fig. 9). The algorithm uses the AxisAlignedBoundingBox algorithm to calculate distances traveled within a voxel of each ray. The simulation calculates the distance from the X-ray source to each voxel, as well as the distance from each detector pixel to each voxel. Where both distances are not infinite, i.e. the ray intersects the voxel, the absorption coefficient of the voxel is then added to an absorption tensor. Finally, a reduction of the absorption tensor, which reduces it down to a 2D array, sums all absorptions along an X-ray, which is the final simulated image. The algorithm uses a 5-fold product of 3D scene resolutions and 2D detector resolutions. The time complexity is $O(m^3n^2)$ where m^3 is the number of grid points in the model and n^2 is the number of pixels in the detector. We fixed the size of the scene to 50^3 but varied the detector size from 20^2 to 633^2 in the benchmark.

Magnetic Field Extrapolation. This program performs a reconstruction of the Sun's magnetic field in 3D extrapolated from 2D data. The time complexity is $O(n^5)$ where n^2 is the number of pixels in the input data, which we varied from 40^2 to 159^2 in the benchmark.

All three benchmarks exclusively use array programming. Thus, when not streaming any arrays, the space complexity equals the time complexity.

We perform two kinds of benchmarks – one where we compare Bohrium with itself and one where we compare Bohrium with Native NumPy. When comparing Bohrium against itself, we run two executions for each benchmark: one with streaming enabled and one with streaming disabled thus we evaluate the direct effect of array streaming. We use the largest possible data sizes that no streaming permits.

When comparing Bohrium against Native NumPy, we run for a range of input data sizes. We have chosen the sizes such that the size of the first execution can fit in memory without any array streaming, i.e. using Native NumPy. In each following runs, we increase the input data size such that the number of processed elements increases with an order of magnitude. E.g., in Fig. 11 the first run processes 3 GB of elements and the second run processes 30 GB etc. Since Native NumPy runs on the CPU and the Bohrium runs on the GPU, we do not evaluate the streaming performance in isolation. However, it indicates the performance boost a user can expect when using Bohrium on a GPU-enabled system.

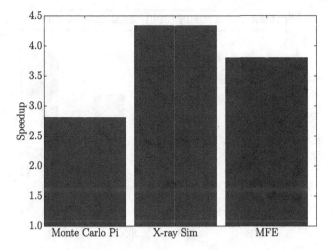

Fig. 10. Speedup of Bohrium with array streaming compared to Bohrium without array streaming. Both executions runs on the GPU.

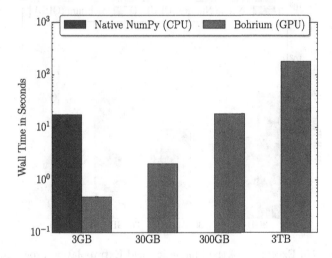

Fig. 11. Execution time of the Monte Carlo Pi program.

Finally, we point out that we do not change a single line of NumPy code before using Bohrium. For example, in order to use Bohrium when running the Monte Carlo Pi code in Fig. 1b, we simply run the command `python -m bohrium MonteCarloPi.py`.

Discussion. Figure 10 shows the performance benefit of array streaming – all three benchmarks achieve significant speedup when using array streaming.

Figures 11, 12, and 13 show the result of the three benchmarks. In all three benchmarks, the Bohrium execution outperforms the Native NumPy execution

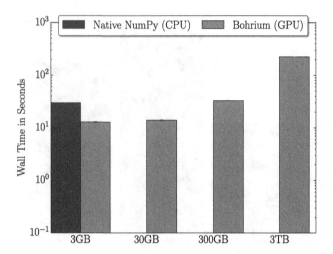

Fig. 12. Execution time of the X-ray simulator program.

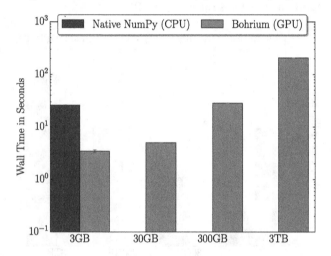

Fig. 13. Execution of the Magnetic Field Extrapolation program.

significantly – Bohrium with GPU target handles a problem size of two orders of magnitude greater than Native NumPy, which is restricted to CPU, in approximately the same time. Array streaming in Bohrium not only enables much larger problems, it also significantly improves the performance.

In the Monte Carlo Pi benchmark (Fig. 11), the execution time increases close to linearly with the memory use. This is because the initial problem size is large enough to utilize most of the GPU-cores, hide the memory latency, and amortize the JIT compilation overhead.

This is not the case in the X-ray simulator (Fig. 12) and the Magnetic Field Extrapolation (Fig. 13) benchmark where the execution time between the first and the second execution is very small. Here, the initial problem size is not large enough to utilize the GPU fully, so we see faster-than-linear scaling early on. The GPU only reaches full utilization (and linear scaling) at around 300 GB processed elements. This indicates that streaming is absolutely necessary for making proper use of the GPU in array programming.

7   Conclusion

In this paper, we demonstrate that by combining the theoretical work of array operation fusion [15] and the automatic parallelization framework Bohrium [18], it is possible to automatically stream temporary arrays in Python/NumPy programs without any modification to the code.

Array streaming solves the counterintuitive problem, that fully utilization of array programming, which improves productivity and performance, also makes it impossible to run on a machine with a realistic amount of memory. With our work, we can keep encouraging the scientific community to use array programming in Python/NumPy without having to insert for-loops just to avoid an explosion in memory usage.

Acknowledgement. James Avery was partially supported by the Danish Council for Independent Research *Sapere Aude* grant "Complexity through Logic and Algebra" (COLA).

References

1. Auer, A.A., Baumgartner, G., Bernholdt, D.E., Bibireata, A., Choppella, V., Cociorva, D., Gao, X., Harrison, R., Krishnamoorthy, S., Krishnan, S., et al.: Automatic code generation for many-body electronic structure methods: the tensor contraction engine. Mol. Phy. **104**(2), 211–228 (2006)
2. Ayer, V.M., Miguez, S., Toby, B.H.: Why scientists should learn to program in python. Powder Diffr. **29**, S48–S64 (2014)
3. Behnel, S., Bradshaw, R., Citro, C., Dalcin, L., Seljebotn, D.S., Smith, K.: Cython: the best of both worlds. Comput. Sci. Eng. **13**(2), 31–39 (2011)
4. Bergstra, J., Breuleux, O., Bastien, F., Lamblin, P., Pascanu, R., Desjardins, G., Turian, J., Warde-Farley, D., Bengio, Y.: Theano: a CPU and GPU math expression compiler. In: Proceedings of the Python for Scientific Computing Conference (SciPy), June 2010. Oral Presentation
5. Blum, T., Kristensen, M.R.B., Vinter, B.: Transparent GPU execution of NumPy applications. In: 2014 IEEE 28th International Parallel and Distributed Processing Symposium Workshops & PhD Forum (IPDPSW). IEEE (2014)
6. Cooke, D., Hochberg, T.: Numexpr. Fast evaluation of array expressions by using a vector-based virtual machine
7. Darte, A., Huard, G.: New results on array contraction [memory optimization]. In: Proceedings of the IEEE International Conference on Application-Specific Systems, Architectures and Processors, pp. 359–370. IEEE (2002)
8. Enkovaara, J., Romero, N.A., Shende, S., Mortensen, J.J.: Gpaw-massively parallel electronic structure calculations with python-based software. Procedia Comput. Sci. **4**, 17–25 (2011)

9. Foord, M., Muirhead, C.: IronPython in Action. Manning Publications Co., Greenwich (2009)
10. Guelton, S., Brunet, P., Amini, M., Merlini, A., Corbillon, X., Raynaud, A.: Pythran: enabling static optimization of scientific python programs. Comput. Sci. Discov. **8**(1), 014001 (2015)
11. Ihaka, R., Gentleman, R.: R: a language for data analysis and graphics. J. Comput. Graph. Stat. **5**(3), 299–314 (1996)
12. Jones, E., Miller, P.J.: Weaveinlining C/C++ in Python. OReilly Open Source Convention (2002)
13. Klckner, A., Pinto, N., Lee, Y., Catanzaro, B., Ivanov, P., Fasih, A.: PyCUDA and PyOpenCL: a scripting-based approach to GPU run-time code generation. Parallel Comput. **38**(3), 157–174 (2012)
14. Kristensen, M.R.B., Happe, H., Vinter, B.: GPAW optimized for Blue Gene/P using hybrid programming. In: IEEE International Symposium on Parallel Distributed Processing, IPDPS 2009, pp. 1–6 (2009)
15. Kristensen, M.R.B., Lund, S.A.F., Blum, T., Avery, J.: Fusion of array operations at runtime. In: Proceedings of the 25th International Conference on Parallel Architectures and Compilation Techniques (PACT 2016). ACM (2016)
16. Kristensen, M.R.B., Lund, S.A.F., Blum, T., Skovhede, K.: Separating NumPy API from implementation. In: 5th Workshop on Python for High Performance and Scientific Computing (PyHPC 2014) (2014)
17. Kristensen, M.R.B., Lund, S.A.F., Blum, T., Skovhede, K., Vinter, B.: Bohrium: unmodified NumPy code on CPU, GPU, and cluster. In: 4th Workshop on Python for High Performance and Scientific Computing (PyHPC 2013) (2013)
18. Kristensen, M.R.B., Lund, S.A.F., Blum, T., Skovhede, K., Vinter, B.: Bohrium: a virtual machine approach to portable parallelism. In: 2014 IEEE International Parallel and Distributed Processing Symposium Workshops (IPDPSW), pp. 312–321. IEEE (2014)
19. Kristensen, M.R.B., Vinter, B.: Numerical python for scalable architectures. In: Proceedings of the Fourth Conference on Partitioned Global Address Space Programming Model, PGAS 2010, pp. 15:1–15:9. ACM, New York (2010)
20. Kristensen, M.R.B., Zheng, Y., Vinter, B.: PGAS for distributed numerical python targeting multi-core clusters. In: International Parallel and Distributed Processing Symposium, pp. 680–690 (2012)
21. Lam, C.-C., Cociorva, D., Baumgartner, G., Sadayappan, P.: Optimization of memory usage requirement for a class of loops implementing multi-dimensional integrals. In: Carter, L., Ferrante, J. (eds.) LCPC 1999. LNCS, vol. 1863, pp. 350–364. Springer, Heidelberg (2000). doi:10.1007/3-540-44905-1_22
22. Madsen, F.M., Clifton-Everest, R., Chakravarty, M.M.T., Keller, G.: Functional array streams. In: Proceedings of the 4th ACM SIGPLAN Workshop on FunctionalHigh-Performance Computing, FHPC 2015, pp. 23–34. ACM, New York (2015)
23. Madsen, F.M., Filinski, A.: Towards a streaming model for nested data parallelism. In: Proceedings of the 2nd ACM SIGPLAN Workshop on Functional High-Performance Computing, pp. 13–24. ACM (2013)
24. MATLAB. version 7.10.0 (R2010a). The MathWorks Inc., Natick, Massachusetts (2010)
25. Mnih, V.: Cudamat: a cuda-based matrix class for python. Department of Computer Science, University of Toronto, Technical report, UTML TR, 4 (2009)
26. Munshi, A., et al.: The OpenCL specification. Khronos OpenCL Working Group **1**, 11–15 (2009)

27. NVIDIA Corporation. NVIDIA CUDA Programming Guide 2.0 (2008)
28. Oliphant, T.: Numba python bytecode to llvm translator. In: Proceedings of the Python for Scientific Computing Conference (SciPy) (2012)
29. Pedroni, S., Rappin, N.: Jython Essentials: Rapid Scripting in Java, 1st edn. O'Reilly & Associates Inc., Sebastopol (2002)
30. Rickett, C.D., Choi, S.-E., Rasmussen, C.E., Sottile, M.J.: Rapid prototyping frameworks for developing scientific applications: a case study. J. Supercomput. **36**(2), 123–134 (2006)
31. Tieleman, T.: Gnumpy: an easy way to use gpu boards in python (2010)
32. Van Der Walt, S., Colbert, S., Varoquaux, G.: The numpy array: a structure for efficient numerical computation. Comput. Sci. Eng. **13**(2), 22–30 (2011)
33. van Rossum, G.: Glue it all together with python. In: Workshop on Compositional Software Architectures, Workshop Report, Monterey, California (1998)

From Describing to Prescribing Parallelism: Translating the SPEC ACCEL OpenACC Suite to OpenMP Target Directives

Guido Juckeland[1,2]($\boxtimes$), Oscar Hernandez[1,3], Arpith C. Jacob[1,4],
Daniel Neilson[1,5], Verónica G. Vergara Larrea[1,3], Sandra Wienke[1,6],
Alexander Bobyr[1,7], William C. Brantley[1,8], Sunita Chandrasekaran[1,9],
Mathew Colgrove[1,10], Alexander Grund[1,2], Robert Henschel[1,11],
Wayne Joubert[1,3], Matthias S. Müller[1,6], Dave Raddatz[1,12],
Pavel Shelepugin[1,7], Brian Whitney[1,13], Bo Wang[1,6], and Kalyan Kumaran[1,14]

[1] SPEC High Performance Group (HPG), Gainesville, USA
info@spec.org
[2] Helmholtz-Zentrum Dresden-Rossendorf (HZDR), Dresden, Germany
g.juckeland@hzdr.de
[3] Oak Ridge National Laboratory, Oak Ridge, TN, USA
[4] IBM T. J. Watson Research Center, Yorktown Heights, NY, USA
[5] IBM, Markham, ON, Canada
[6] RWTH Aachen University, Aachen, Germany
[7] Intel, Nizhny Novgorod, Russia
[8] AMD, Austin, TX, USA
[9] University of Delaware, Newark, DE, USA
[10] NVIDIA, Santa Clara, CA, USA
[11] Indiana University, Bloomington, IN, USA
[12] SGI, Milpitas, CA, USA
[13] Oracle, Redwood Shores, CA, USA
[14] Argonne National Laboratory, Lemont, IL, USA
http://www.spec.org/hpg

Abstract. Current and next generation HPC systems will exploit accelerators and self-hosting devices within their compute nodes to accelerate applications. This comes at a time when programmer productivity and the ability to produce portable code has been recognized as a major concern. One of the goals of OpenMP and OpenACC is to allow the user to specify parallelism via directives so that compilers can generate device specific code and optimizations. However, the challenge of porting codes becomes more complex because of the different types of parallelism and memory hierarchies available on different architectures. In this paper we discuss our experience with porting the SPEC ACCEL benchmarks from OpenACC to OpenMP 4.5 using a performance portable style that lets the compiler make platform-specific optimizations to achieve good performance on a variety of systems. The ported SPEC ACCEL OpenMP benchmarks were validated on different platforms including Xeon Phi, GPUs and CPUs. We believe that this experience can help the community and compiler vendors understand how users plan to write OpenMP 4.5 applications in a performance portable style.

© Springer International Publishing AG 2016
M. Taufer et al. (Eds.): ISC High Performance Workshops 2016, LNCS 9945, pp. 470–488, 2016.
DOI: 10.1007/978-3-319-46079-6_33

Keywords: SPEC · SPEC ACCEL · OpenMP · OpenACC · Offloading

1   Introduction

Architecture-specific programming is not an option for performance portability, specially for a large scientific application with hundreds of functions and hundreds of thousands to millions of lines of code. It is often unrealistic to use these approaches to port the whole application to GPUs, Intel Xeon Phis and CPUs since this may require a substantial rewrite of the code base in the target APIs. Although currently over 20 % of supercomputers on the TOP500 list (based on the number of systems or over 30 % based on the achieved FLOPs) [26] are equipped with GPUs, Intel Xeon Phis and multicore accelerators, many users and applications on these systems have not yet taken advantage of their performance benefits on account of these programming challenges. An effective higher-level programming model is desperately needed for applications to take advantage of the power of these accelerators.

One of the goals of directive-based programming is to allow the user to specify parallelism via directives so that compilers can generate device specific code and optimizations. However, the task of porting codes with directives is still challenging because it relies on compilers and users to map different types of parallelism and memory hierarchies available on different architectures. The programmer faces the trade-off of tuning their code for a specific platform versus keeping the code at a higher abstraction with patterns that a compiler can understand and optimize.

OpenACC is a relatively new directive based solution to program an accelerator which describes the parallelism of an application and relies on the compiler to generate efficient code. This gives the compiler the flexibility to generate optimized code that works on multiple platforms. It works well on GPUs and multicore architectures, however, OpenACC is relatively young and not supported on all platforms. Having a descriptive model is good, but there is no guarantee that the compiler can generate the most efficient code for a given architecture because of its limited analysis.

OpenMP, on the other hand, is a more mature and widely used approach for shared-memory programming. It has been widely supported by industry and academia. Traditionally, OpenMP uses a prescriptive approach where the user explicitly specifies the parallel execution strategy and maps it to the underlying architecture. This is good for performance, as the programmer has more control over the optimizations, but it affects performance portability across heterogeneous architectures (e.g. GPUs, FPGAS). Starting with OpenMP 4.0, the specification provides new features to make it possible to run codes on both general-purpose multicore CPUs and accelerators in a work-sharing fashion under a single programming paradigm. These capabilities have been further improved in the progress towards the latest release of the specification, namely, OpenMP 4.5. Despite the prescriptive nature of OpenMP, by using a "performance portable" programming style it is possible to provide the compiler the necessary flexibility to generate efficient code for a variety of underlying target architectures.

The SPEC ACCEL Benchmark [12] is developed by the SPEC High Performance Group (HPG). It is targeted to measure the performance of applications using hardware accelerated offloading and, thus, complements the existing SPEC MPI2007 [18] and SPEC OMP2012 [17] benchmarks. The latest release of SPEC ACCEL is version 1.1 which contains an OpenCL and an OpenACC suite. The OpenACC suite consists of 15 applications written in C or Fortran. Since OpenACC implementations cannot (yet) cover all acceleration platforms and to contrast it with the newly available OpenMP target offloading, the SPEC HPG members decided to translate this suite to OpenMP. The group aimed at the most direct translation possible in order provide a semantic equivalence which enables researchers to compare both platforms. It must be noted that the SPEC Fair Use Policy forbids a direct comparison of a result from one suite with a result from another suite, especially using SPEC metrics.[1] Nevertheless, it is obvious that such a comparison is of academic interest which is allowed when meeting certain requirements.[2] The primary goal of this paper is, however, not to compare the two programming models, but rather report on the difficulties of the porting process and to provide guidance on how to translate between them or implement parallelism with them. Unfortunately, we cannot (yet) report actual performance results since a number of OpenMP compilers and runtimes used by the various vendors are still in development.

This paper first presents previous work on comparing OpenACC and OpenMP in Sect. 2. Afterwards the current version of the OpenACC standard and the OpenMP specification are compared side by side in Sect. 3 to derive a translation strategy from one to the other. SPEC HPG decided on a fixed OpenMP "style" for tightly and loosely nested loops based on the feedback from the OpenMP language committee which is shown in Sect. 4. Section 5 explains why and how special attention needs to be paid to team synchronization in order to prevent race conditions. In Sect. 6 the challenges of different interpretations of the specification by the OpenMP runtime implementors, which can lead to dramatically different program behavior, are discussed. Finally, Sect. 7 provides a summary and an outlook into the release plans for the final suite.

2   Related Work

Since the release of the OpenMP 4.0 specification in 2013 [20], compiler implementations of the incorporated OpenMP Accelerator Model finally get more mature and support more accelerator architectures. Today, Intel provides offload

---

[1] https://www.spec.org/fairuse.html#Comparisons.
[2] https://www.spec.org/fairuse.html#Academic.

capabilities for its Xeon Phis [10, 19] and Cray for NVIDIA GPUs [6]. Oracle also understands OpenMP 4.0, but runs device constructs on the host [22]. GCC supports OpenMP 4.0 since its version 4.9.1, but has ignored the offloading features until April 2015. Its version 5 introduces firstly offloading to Intel's Xeon Phi Knights Landing architectures [8] and version 6 adds support for AMD's Heterogeneous System Architectures (HSA) [7]. The clang/ LLVM community is also actively working on implementing OpenMP offload capabilities for x86, PowerPC and NVIDIA GPUs [3,4] and they actually planned to add support in its 3.8 release [28]. Instead, current corresponding patches [1] are still reviewed and integrated into Clang's trunk. PathScale recently introduced OpenMP 4.0 support for CPUs, AMD and NVIDIA GPUs [23]. Texas Instruments (TI) implements the OpenMP Accelerator Model for its TI Keystone II architecture comprising of ARMs and DSPs [16]. Finally, two research compilers have been developed: HOMP builds upon the ROSE OpenMP implementation and generates CUDA code for NVIDIA GPUs [13], whereas Agathos et al. [2] build upon the OMPI OpenMP compiler and target boards that contain ARM processors and an embedded accelerator called Epiphany.

The growing compiler support of the OpenMP Accelerator Model raises the question on the performance portability across vendors and architectures. While performance portability across accelerators has been already discussed in the context of OpenCL [5,24] and OpenACC [9,25], little work has covered it with respect to the OpenMP Accelerator Model. Wienke et al. [27] compare the offload capabilities of OpenACC and OpenMP 4.0 using structured patterns but do not include any performance evaluations. Juckeland et al. [11] present challenges from porting SPEC ACCEL OpenACC benchmarks to OpenMP 4.0. However, they specifically target their OpenMP offload code at Intel Xeon Phi architectures and do not discuss design choices across different vendors and architectures. A broader coverage of architectures and programming models is investigated by Martineau et al. [15]. They only focus on one application, i.e. the mini-app TeaLeaf, and compare performance of code versions written in Kokkos, RAJA, OpenACC, OpenMP 4.0, CUDA and OpenCL across a CPU architecture, an NVIDIA Kepler GPU and an Intel Xeon Phi (where applicable). Although they discuss the tradeoff of having a low vs. high number of OpenMP 4.0 target regions, they do not elaborate on further issues that impact performance portability of OpenMP 4.0 codes. Lin et al. [14] port two stencil applications using the OpenMP Accelerator Model. They concentrate on NVIDIA GPUs using the HOMP compiler and describe arising challenges like complex data types, collapsing, third-party libraries and usage of caches.

In contrast to previous work, this paper covers a comprehensive discussion of design choices for performance-portable code using the OpenMP Accelerator Model across 15 different applications. Since SPEC believes in one code for all compiler vendors and architectures, this is of particular importance.

3 Porting OpenACC 2.5 to OpenMP 4.5

Since OpenMP 4.5 and OpenACC 2.5 are differing standards, it is important for users to understand their differences to be able to make informed decisions about use of each API for a given application to be deployed to attached accelerators.

OpenACC provides constructs that are used to perform computations on an accelerator device. The *acc parallel* construct is used to create a parallel region. Code within this region is offloaded to an attached device for computation. The similar *acc kernels* construct creates a program region to be compiled into a sequence of kernels for execution on the device.

The directive clauses *copy*, *copyin* and *copyout* control the data movement between host and attached device. To optimize data traffic between host and device, OpenACC also allows users to create a data region containing one or more parallel regions, enabling the parallel regions to share the data while it is resident in device memory.

OpenACC expresses the levels of parallelism via *gang*, *worker* and *vector* constructs. Each gang contains one or more workers. Users specify the size of gangs, workers and vectors or allow the compiler to select them automatically.

To support heterogeneous computer architectures, the OpenMP 4.0/4.5 programming model changed substantially from previous versions of the API. The OpenMP "fork-join" model was extended with the introduction of device constructs for programming accelerators. These allow compute-intensive code regions to be offloaded to accelerator devices. OpenMP 4.5 uses the *target* construct to create a data environment on the device and then execute the code region on that device. Users specify *device(device_id)* to select which accelerator to use if multiple accelerators are attached to the host.

In OpenMP 4.5, the *map* clause associates the current data environment on the host with the device data environment. Data attributes *to*, *from*, *tofrom* and *alloc* control data creation and movement for a targeted device. To minimize unneeded data movement between device and host, OpenMP 4.0 provides the *target data* construct for creating a device data environment that is persistent across multiple contained target execution regions.

To specify the execution configuration for parallel computation on the device, OpenMP 4.5 uses the *teams* construct to create a league of thread teams, with the master thread of each team beginning execution at the onset of the region. The *distribute* construct specifies that the workload of one or more loops will be distributed to thread teams, for which each team will be assigned a chunk of the workload. The chunk size is determined by current runtime settings. Vectorization can be enabled by use of the *simd* construct.

Side by Side Comparison

What follows is a comparison of OpenMP 4.5 and OpenACC 2.5 constructs. We assume that the C language is used; comparisons for Fortran are similar. In each comparison, code fragments are given which have similar or identical behavior

Table 1. OpenACC 2.5 and OpenMP 4.5 accelerator programming comparison

OpenMP 4.5	OpenACC 2.5
target data	data
target {enter, exit} data	{enter, exit} data
use_device_ptr()	host data
target update	update
target	parallel
teams	gang
-	kernels
distribute / parallel for / simd	loop [gang / worker / vector]
declare target	routine & declare
-	cache
atomic	atomic
taskwait	wait
task	-
target nowait	async
target depend	-
is_device_ptr	device_ptr
private / firstprivate	private / firstprivate
declare target link	declare link

Table 2. Directives to specify execution on accelerator device

OpenMP 4.5	OpenACC 2.5
	acc_set_device_num(n)
#pragma omp target device(n)	#pragma acc parallel
{	{
...	...
}	}

in OpenMP and OpenACC. Since the relationship between the two APIs is not entirely isomorphic, comments on differences are given when appropriate.

Table 1 presents in summary form a comparison of OpenMP 4.5 and OpenACC 2.5 syntax. Specifics regarding how corresponding constructs compare are detailed below.

Executing on the Device. In OpenMP, the *target* directive begins a region of code to be executed on the accelerator device. In OpenACC, the *parallel* directive opens a device execution region (Table 2). In either case, optional syntax can be used to specify the desired device if multiple devices are present. Both forms allow optional clauses to specify data transfers to support device code execution; data regions can also be specified independently, as will be described later.

Table 3. OpenACC and OpenMP clauses that specify gangs and teams

OpenMP 4.5	OpenACC 2.5

`#pragma omp target teams \`
  `num\_teams(n)`
`{`
  `...`
`}`
	`#pragma acc parallel \`
	  `num\_gangs(n) ...—`
	`{`
	  `...`
	`}`

It should be noted that OpenACC also has a *kernels* directive which can be used to specify multiple device kernels in sequence, whereas the *parallel* directive specifies only a single kernel that runs on the device. OpenACC currently allows asynchronous device operations which are supported in OpenMP 4.5 via the *target nowait* clause.

Specifying Teams/Gangs. In OpenACC and OpenMP, the concept of *gangs* or *teams* denotes a collection of thread groups satisfying certain properties: for example, it is not possible to synchronize across different gangs or teams over the lifetime of their existence.

In OpenMP, the *teams* directive creates a league of thread teams that execute in the region. For convenience, this directive can be combined with the *target* construct; adjacent directives can also be combined for convenience in some other contexts in OpenMP and OpenACC. In OpenACC, a *num_gangs* clause for a *parallel* directive specifies a number of work units that is equivalent to the OpenMP teams concept.

Table 3 shows how to specify teams and gangs in OpenMP and OpenACC. In OpenMP a single master thread from each team is active in the structured block, whereas in OpenACC in the absence of further directives the structured block executes in "gang-redundant" mode. These directives are generally not used in this manner in isolation but are combined with additional parallelism at the thread and vector level.

Similarly to teams and gangs, other levels exist in OpenMP and OpenACC which we describe on the following sections.

Distributing Loop Iterations to Teams/Gangs. The OpenMP *distribute* directive specifies that the iterations of one or more loops will be executed by the active thread teams. In the absence of further specifications, elements of the iteration space are each assigned to the master thread of each team and only these master threads are deployed. The equivalent construct in OpenACC is a *loop* directive with distribution of iterations to gangs while still in worker-single and vector-single mode (Table 4).

For OpenACC and OpenMP, it is possible in some cases to apply loop directives to multiple nested loops via flattening the iteration space by use of the

Table 4. Loop directives for distributing loops iterations to teams/gangs

OpenMP 4.5	OpenACC 2.5

`#pragma omp distribute`
`for (i=0; i<N; ++i)`
`{`
`    ...`
`}`
	`#pragma acc loop gang`
	`for (i=0; i<N; ++i)`
	`{`
	`    ...`
	`}`

Table 5. Loop directives for distributing to teams/gangs and threads

OpenMP 4.5	OpenACC 2.5

`#pragma omp target teams \`
`    num_teams(n) \`
`    thread_limit(m)`
`{`
`    #pragma omp distribute \`
`        parallel for`
`    for (i=0; i<N; ++i) {`
`        ...`
`    }`
`}`
	`#pragma acc parallel \`
	`    num_gangs(n) num_workers(m) \`
	`    vector_length(1)`
	`{`
	`    #pragma acc loop \`
	`        gang worker`
	`    for (i=0; i<N; ++i) {`
	`        ...`
	`    }`
	`}`

collapse clause. Also, the OpenMP *dist_schedule* clause and the OpenACC *tile* clause can be used to control how loop indices are mapped to teams or gangs.

Distributing Loop Iterations to Teams/Gangs and Threads. The *distribute parallel loop* directive instructs OpenMP to distribute iterations of a loop to threads and teams. The corresponding OpenACC *loop* directive that activates gang and worker parallelism has similar effects.

Distributing Loop Indices to Teams/Gangs, Threads and Vector Lanes. In OpenMP the *simd* directive indicates that a loop should be vectorized for the targeted platform. When used in conjunction with the distribute and parallel loop directive, this has behavior similar to the OpenACC *loop* directive with gang, worker and vector parallelism activated. As pointed out in [29], for OpenACC in some situations it may be possible to specify only gang and vector parallelism and obtain equivalent behavior, based on optimization decisions made by the compiler (Tables 5 and 6).

Setting Function Attributes. In OpenACC and OpenMP, a function can be given attributes to enable it to be executed on an accelerator device. In OpenMP, the *declare target* directive specifies that the function can be executed on the default accelerator device. Similarly, In OpenACC the *routine* directive

Table 6. Loop directives for distributing to teams/gangs, threads and vector lanes

OpenMP 4.5	OpenACC 2.5
```#pragma omp target teams \ num_teams(n) \ thread_limit(m) { #pragma omp distribute \ parallel for simd simdlen(k) for (i=0; i<N; ++i) { ... } }```	```#pragma acc parallel \ num_gangs(n) num_workers(m) \ vector_length(k) { #pragma acc loop \ gang worker vector for (i=0; i<N; ++i) { ... } }```

Table 7. Directives to set function attributes

OpenMP 4.5	OpenACC 2.5
```#pragma omp declare target void sub(...) {...} #pragma omp end declare target```	```#pragma acc routine void sub(...) {...}```

allows the function to be called in a parallel execution region, with an optional *device_type* clause used to specify the device(s) allowed. See Table 7

To support nested levels of parallelism spanning multiple layers of subroutine calls, OpenACC also permits the *gang*, *worker* and *vector* clauses. The *gang* clause, for example, denotes that the function or one of its callees can contain a loop with gang, worker or vector parallelism; likewise, *worker* for worker or vector parallelism and *vector* for vector parallelism. Use of the *seq* clause indicates that the function and callees do not specify any parallelism and thus can be called at any parallelism level.

The OpenMP *declare simd* directive specifies that a function, when called in a *simd* region, will execute by using *simd* instructions when appropriate.

Creating a Data Region. OpenMP and OpenACC also have a mechanism for specifying a data region, which is a period of execution time with distinct beginning and end for which the residence of a data object on the device can be defined. This region can be identical to the parallel execution region or can be specified independently as described here. The relevant operations that can be selected are to allocate memory for the object on the device and copy the host data object to the device on region entry and to copy the data object back to the host and delete the device object on exit.

The OpenMP *target data* directive is used to specify data transfers between host and accelerator within a code region. The same behavior in OpenACC can

Table 8. Directives for specifying a data region

OpenMP 4.5	OpenACC 2.5

`#pragma omp target data device(n) \`
`  if(expr) \`
`  map(to:a[0:n]) \`
`  map(tofrom:b[0:n]) \`
`  map(from:c[0:n]) \`
`  map(alloc:d[0:n])`
`{`
`  ...`
`}`
	`acc_set_device_num(n)`
	`#pragma acc data \`
	`  if(expr) \`
	`  copyin(a[0:n] \`
	`  copy(b[0:n]) \`
	`  copyout(c[0:n]) \`
	`  create(d[0:n])`
	`{`
	`  ...`
	`}`

be effected using the *data* directive. Table 8 shows the corresponding clauses for the two directives. The same effects can be obtained for a parallel execution region by using these clauses to control data behavior on entry to and exit from the parallel region. It should be noted that OpenACC also provides the *enter data* and *exit data* clauses which allow more flexible specification of data regions not associated with a single code block.

Updating Data Objects. Within the data region it may be necessary to refresh the host data object with the corresponding data on the device or vice versa (Table 9). The OpenMP *target update* directive is an executable directive which performs a refresh of a host data item from the device copy of the item with the *from* clause or vice versa with the *to* clause. In OpenACC this is accomplished with the *update* directive using the *host* clause or *device* clause, respectively. It should be pointed out that in OpenMP the *device* keyword has a different meaning from OpenACC: it specifies which of multiple devices to use for a device operation.

Defining Device Data Objects. In OpenACC and OpenMP it is possible to specify that a data item is associated with an implicit data region for the lifetime of the item (Table 10). This can be done with the OpenMP *declare target* directive or the OpenACC *declare* directive. The OpenACC version allows greater control over the data region by allowing the transfer clauses such as "copy", and "copyin" to specify transfers.

Table 9. Directives for updating a data object

OpenMP 4.5	OpenACC 2.5

`double a[n], b[n];`
`#pragma omp target update from(a[0:n])`
`#pragma omp target update to(b[0:n])`
	`double a[n], b[n];`
	`#pragma acc update host(a[0:n])`
	`#pragma acc update device(b[0:n])`

Table 10. Directives for defining device data objects

OpenMP 4.5	OpenACC 2.5
`#pragma omp declare target`	
`double target[n];`	`double target[n];`
`#pragma omp end declare target`	`#pragma acc declare copy(z[0:n])`

4 Translating the Parallelization of Nested Loops

Nested loops, i.e. two or more loops can be grouped into tightly or loosely nested loops. Their parallelization strategy is similar and discussed in the following.

Tightly Nested Loops are two or more loop constructs that have no intermediate program statements. They are common when iterating over the elements of a multi-dimensional data structures where each loop represents a running index for one dimension. Such loops also offer a number of code optimization options, e.g. loop fusion or blocking. At the same time they can also be parallelized—at least for all loops that have no loop carried data dependencies.

The OpenACC suite of the SPEC ACCEL uses both the *parallel loop* and the *kernels* construct to parallelize tightly nested loops as shown in the exemplary code below. The main difference between the two is that the *parallel loop* guarantees a parallizable loop while the *kernels* construct places the burden of identifying parallelism by data dependency analysis on the compiler.

```
1 #pragma acc parallel loop \
       collapse(3)
3 for (i=0;i<L;i++) {
     for (j=0;j<M;j++) {
5      for (k=0;k<N;k++) {
         a[i][j][k]=...
7      }
     }
9 }
```

```
1 #pragma acc kernels
  for (i=0;i<L;i++) {
3   for (j=0;j<M;j++) {
      for (k=0;k<N;k++) {
5       a[i][j][k]=...
      }
7   }
  }
```

The OpenACC compiler can map both statements in the same fashion to the underlying parallelization target using both block and thread level parallelism as well as vectorization. Translating such a construct to OpenMP target directives requires a manual mapping of these two different strategies due to the prescriptive nature of OpenMP. The following translation was applied to all tightly nested loops to maintain the "spirit" of the OpenACC version and to allow for the largest possible platform portable parallelization. It must be noted that the collapse level was reduced by one in order to make room for the *simd* clause on the innermost loop to enable vectorization of this loop level. The innermost loop was not collapsed with the rest to avoid the performance penalties that the *simd* directive can experience due to array index recalculation.

```
 1  #pragma omp target teams
 2  #pragma omp distribute parallel for collapse(2)
 3  for (i=0;i<L;i++) {
 4    for (j=0;j<M;j++) {
 5      #pragma omp simd
 6      for (k=0;k<N;k++) {
 7        a[i][j][k]=...
 8      }
 9    }
10  }
```

Loops with data dependencies are moved to the innermost level to prevent unnecessary thread synchronization.

Loosely Nested Loops are two or more loops constructs that have intermediate code in between. They typically occur when one outer (or inner) loop is used to iterate over something other than the elements of the current data structure, e.g. an outer loop the counts the overall simulation time steps of the iteration. An example OpenACC implementation of such a construct could be as shown below (left side). The OpenMP implementation (right side) uses a similar approach as previously: It moves the *target team* region as far outside as possible and then creates *distribute parallel for* and simd regions for each inner loop construct.

```
 1  #pragma acc kernels
 2  for (i=0;i<L;i++) {
 3    // initialization
 4    #pragma acc loop
 5    for (j=0;j<M;j++) {
 6      b[j]=...
 7    }
 8    // some more stuff
 9    #pragma acc loop \
10            collapse(2)
11    for (j=0;j<M;j++) {
12      for (k=0;k<N;k++) {
13        a[j][k]=...
14      }
15    }
16  }
```

```
 1  #pragma omp target teams
 2  for (i=0;i<L;i++) {
 3    // initialization
 4    #pragma omp distribute \
 5            parallel for simd
 6    for (j=0;j<M;j++) {
 7      b[j]=...
 8    }
 9    // some more stuff
10    #pragma omp distribute \
11            parallel for
12    for (j=0;j<M;j++) {
13      #pragma omp simd
14      for (k=0;k<N;k++) {
15        a[j][k]=...
16      }
17    }
18  }
```

This approach is, however, only valid when there is no data dependency between the inner parallel regions, as is discussed in the following section.

5   Multiple Parallel Regions and Team Synchronization

A *team* in OpenMP is a group of one or more threads that cooperatively execute a region. To fully exploit hardware resources of an accelerator it is often necessary to distribute work across a league of teams. For instance, on a CUDA-enabled GPU a team is equivalent to a block, and a league of teams is simply a grid; executing a CUDA kernel with only a single block generally does not make effective use of the GPU hardware.

Consider the following example:

```
#pragma omp target teams
{
    #pragma omp distribute
    #pragma omp parallel for
    for (i = 0; i <= gp21; i++) {
        a[i] = ...
    }
}
```

Iterations of the parallel loop are chunked and distributed across teams. Each team, in turn, partitions its chunk of iterations across its threads.

The teams in a league may run concurrently, though not all teams in the league are required to do so. For instance, a conforming implementation is free to have a subset of the teams running concurrently to completion while the remainder of the teams in the league wait their turn to be scheduled for execution. This flexibility in implementation means that OpenMP can be implemented on many accelerators architectures, but also that it is not possible to synchronize the teams in a league with each other while they are running. Thus, barriers only synchronize the threads within a team, and do not synchronize across teams in a league.

While the OpenMP standard defines an implicit barrier across all threads within a team after the *parallel* construct, there can be no such barrier across teams after the *distribute* directive. This may lead to race conditions if the user incorrectly assumes an implied barrier after the *distribute* directive.

Consider the following code snippet where the iterations of two consecutive loops are distributed across one or more teams and then parallelized across threads in a team. Elements of array 'a' are modified in the first loop and read from in the second.

```
1  #pragma omp target teams
2  {
3      #pragma omp distribute parallel for
4      for (i = 0; i <= gp21; i++) {
5          a[i] = ...
6      }
7      #pragma omp distribute parallel for
8      for (i = 0; i <= gp21; i++) {
9          ... = a[i+1]
10     }
11 }
```

Suppose only one team is launched at runtime. Due to the implied barrier at the end of the *parallel* construct of the first loop, all threads in the team wait until all elements of array 'a' are flushed to storage before proceeding to the second.

If, instead, two or more teams are launched at runtime, it is possible for some teams to be executing the first loop while other teams have proceeded to the second, or even for some teams to have fully completed the entire *target* region before others have started. Since there is no implied barrier after the *distribute* construct, a thread in one team executing the first loop may be in a data race with a thread in another team executing the second.

The only way to synchronize work distributed across a team is through the implicit synchronization point at the end of the *target* construct; execution of a *target* region is not considered complete until all teams in the league that is executing the region have completed. Thus, to avoid a data race we must split the above into two separate *target* constructs as shown below:

```
1  #pragma omp target teams distribute parallel for
2  for (i = 0; i <= gp21; i++) {
3      a[i] = ...
4  }
5  #pragma omp target teams distribute parallel for
6  for (i = 0; i <= gp21; i++) {
7      ... = a[i+1]
8  }
```

6   OpenMP 4.5 and the Different Implementations

The OpenMP 4.0 specification [20] released in July 2013 introduced the OpenMP Accelerator Model. In the specification, the OpenMP API was extended to support accelerator and SIMD programming, allowing the user to specify regions of code that can be offloaded to one or more target devices. More recently, with the release of the OpenMP 4.5 specification [21], support for the Accelerator Model was further extended. Several major changes in OpenMP 4.5 affect the accelerator model including: new default data-mapping attributes, unstructured data mapping support and asynchronous execution, as well as runtime routines for memory management, extended attributes for SIMD loops, among others.

New Default Data-Mapping Attributes. Scalar and pointers variables now are *firstprivate* by default. In the previous version of the specification, these variables were implicitly *map(tofrom:)*. Variables other than scalars are by default declared as *map(tofrom:)*, such as arrays or the contents of shaped pointers. As a result, scalar variables in reduction clauses must be explicitly scoped with *map(tofrom:)*, otherwise the final value is not propagated from the device to the host. This new default behavior improves the performance to the target region as it avoids unnecessary data transfers from the accelerator.

Unstructured Data Mapping. The changes to default data-mapping attributes, in combination with the newly introduced *target enter data* and *target exit data* constructs, provide better support for unstructured data mapping on devices. The programmer now has greater flexibility to specify target data regions with dynamic extents that may go over several call chains or across files.

Asynchronous Execution. The *nowait* and *depend* clauses are added as options to the *target* construct and improve support for asynchronous execution of target tasks on accelerator devices. These two clauses provide a greater degree of flexibility for task execution. The *nowait* clause, for example, allows for execution of the target region to be asynchronous, and the depend clause specifies the data flow dependences of the implicit task of target region.

Device Memory Management. Several runtime routines are introduced to better manage memory on target devices, including routines to allocate, copy, and free device memory via *omp_target_alloc*, *omp_target_memcpy*, and *omp_target_free*, respectively. In addition, routines to control the mapping of device pointers to host pointers are added via the *omp_target_associate_ptr* and *omp_target_disassociate_ptr* constructs. Furthermore, the *omp_target_is_present* routine can be used to determine if a pointer in the host is associated with an allocated area on the device.

SIMD Width. The *simd* clause is extended to allow the programmer to specify the preferred number of concurrent iterations to execute per SIMD chunk via the *simdlen* clause. The actual number of iterations executed, however, is implementation dependent.

Certain behaviors of the OpenMP 4.5 accelerator model execution are implementation defined, and as such, are left for compiler implementors to optimize for specific architectures. For example, when a *teams* construct is executed, a league of threads is created, where the total number of teams is implementation defined but must be less than or equal to the number of teams specified by the *num_teams* clause. If the user does not specify the *num_teams* clause, then the number of teams is left completely to the implementation.

Similarly, the maximum number of threads created per team is implementation defined. The user has the option to specify a *thread_limit* clause that gives an upper bound to the implementation defined value for the number of threads per team. The purpose of this implementation defined behavior is to allow the compiler or runtime to pick the best value for a given target region on a given architecture. If a parallel region is nested within a *teams* construct, the number of threads in a parallel region will be determined based on Algorithm 2.1 of the OpenMP 4.5 specification [21]. A user can request a given number of threads for a parallel region via the *num_threads* clause.

For work-sharing constructs such as *distribute* and *parallel for/do*, if no *dist_schedule* or *schedule* clauses are specified, the schedule type is implementation defined. For a SIMD loop, the number of iterations executed concurrently at any given time is implementation defined, as well. The preferred number of iterations to be executed concurrently and/or its safe values for SIMD can be specified via the *simdlen* and *safelen* clauses, respectively.

The Intel 16.2 compiler, for example, sets the default value for *num_teams* to one and attempts to use all the number of threads available on the host. When using an Intel Xeon Phi as an accelerator in offload mode, the Intel compiler reserves one core on the coprocessor to manage the offloading, and uses all the remaining threads available on the Intel Xeon Phi (Knights Corner) for execution. On the other hand, the Cray 8.4.2 compiler, by default, uses one team and one thread when running on the host. When running on the GPU, however, if there is a nested parallel region within a team, it defaults to one thread per parallel region. Another example of an implementation dependent behavior can be observed in the LLVM compiler, which defaults to *schedule(static,1)* for the parallel loops when executed inside a target region that is offloaded to a GPU. Due to the slightly different interpretations of the OpenMP specification, it is crucial to understand how the specific compiler being used implements a particular feature.

7   Summary and Outlook

Moving from one directive based offloading scheme to another proved more challenging than anticipated—and suggested by initial publications comparing OpenACC and OpenMP 4.0. Finding a way of translating the described parallelism of the SPEC ACCEL OpenACC applications in a platform and performance portable way to the prescriptive format of OpenMP 4.5 required multiple iterations as well as feedback from all HPG members that had (early) access to various OpenMP 4.5 compilers and runtimes. In the end, the group decided on the rather straightforward mapping for trivial conversions as described in Sect. 3 and chose the approach from Sect. 4 to translate nested loops. Using this approach, we were able to write OpenMP 4.5 in a "performance portable" style, that is, the group was able to produce a version of the OpenMP target suite that runs on all tested platforms without any significant performance penalties. We believe that this style of OpenMP programming gives the compiler and runtime significant amount of flexibility to optimize OpenMP 4.5 to a variety of platforms.

SPEC HPG acknowledges that, while the group tried for the most platform compatible style for OpenMP directives, different targets can achieve an even better performance with platform specific optimizations to the OpenMP directives. These optimizations could include a specific thread scheduling, workload distribution, different collapse levels, or even the removal of directives. In order to allow targets and platforms to showcase this "better" use of directives, SPEC HPG intends to allow code modifications to all directives for submissions using the *peak* metric.

The SPEC High Performance Group is currently reviewing all benchmark suite applications with the goal of freezing their code one after another. Once this is accomplished, the suite will go into the release cycle which includes a blind submissions phase to populate first officially published results. It is the declared goal to release the suite well within 2016.

Acknowledgments. The authors thank Cloyce Spradling for his work on the SPEC harness as well as the SPEC POWER group for their work on enabling the integration of power measurements into other SPEC suites.

SPEC®, SPEC ACCEL™, SPEC CPU™, SPEC MPI®, and SPEC OMP® are registered trademarks of the Standard Performance Evaluation Corporation (SPEC).

References

1. Github repository for the extended Clang implementation supporting OpenMP 4.0 (2016). https://github.com/clang-omp/clang_trunk
2. Agathos, S.N., Papadogiannakis, A., Dimakopoulos, V.V.: Targeting the parallella. In: Träff, J.L., Hunold, S., Versaci, F. (eds.) Euro-Par 2015. LNCS, vol. 9233, pp. 662–674. Springer, Heidelberg (2015). doi:10.1007/978-3-662-48096-0_51
3. Bertolli, C., Antao, S.F., Bercea, G.T., Jacob, A.C., Eichenberger, A.E., Chen, T., Sura, Z., Sung, H., Rokos, G., Appelhans, D., O'Brien, K.: Integrating GPU support for OpenMP offloading directives into clang. In: Proceedings of 2nd Workshop on the LLVM Compiler Infrastructure in HPC, LLVM 2015, NY, USA, pp. 5:1–5:11. ACM, New York (2015). http://doi.acm.org/10.1145/2833157.2833161
4. Bertolli, C., Antao, S.F., Eichenberger, A.E., O'Brien, K., Sura, Z., Jacob, A.C., Chen, T., Sallenave, O.: Coordinating GPU threads for OpenMP 4.0 in LLVM (2014)
5. Calore, E., Schifano, S.F., Tripiccione, R.: On portability, performance and scalability of an MPI OpenCL lattice Boltzmann code. In: Lopes, L., et al. (eds.) Euro-Par 2014. LNCS, vol. 8806, pp. 438–449. Springer, Heidelberg (2014). doi:10. 1007/978-3-319-14313-2_37
6. Cray: Cray Compiling Environment Release: Overview and Installation Guide (Document: S-5212-84) (2015)
7. Foundation, F.S.: GCC 6 Release Series: Changes, New Features, and Fixes (2016). https://gcc.gnu.org/gcc-6/changes.html

8. GCC Wiki: Offloading Support in GCC. https://gcc.gnu.org/wiki/Offloading
9. Herdman, J.A., Gaudin, W.P., Perks, O., Beckingsale, D.A., Mallinson, A.C., Jarvis, S.A.: Achieving portability and performance through OpenACC. In: Proceedings of 1st Workshop on Accelerator Programming Using Directives, WACCPD 2014, pp. 19–26. IEEE Press, Piscataway (2014). http://dx.doi.org/10.1109/WACCPD.2014.10
10. Intel Corporation: Intel® C++ Compiler 16.0 User and Reference Guide: OpenMP* Support (2015)
11. Juckeland, G., Grund, A., Nagel, W.E.: Performance portable applications for hardware accelerators: lessons learned from SPEC ACCEL. In: 2015 IEEE International Parallel and Distributed Processing Symposium Workshop (IPDPSW), pp. 689–698, May 2015
12. Juckeland, G., et al.: SPEC ACCEL: a standard application suite for measuring hardware accelerator performance. In: Jarvis, S.A., Wright, S.A., Hammond, S.D. (eds.) PMBS 2014. LNCS, vol. 8966, pp. 46–67. Springer, Heidelberg (2015). http://dx.doi.org/10.1007/978-3-319-17248-4_3
13. Liao, C., Yan, Y., Supinski, B.R., Quinlan, D.J., Chapman, B.: Early experiences with the OpenMP accelerator model. In: Rendell, A.P., Chapman, B.M., Müller, M.S. (eds.) IWOMP 2013. LNCS, vol. 8122, pp. 84–98. Springer, Heidelberg (2013). http://dx.doi.org/10.1007/978-3-642-40698-0_7
14. Lin, P.H., Liao, C., Quinlan, D.J., Guzik, S.: Experiences of using the OpenMP accelerator model to port DOE stencil applications. In: Terboven, C., de Supinski, B.R., Reble, P., Chapman, B.M., Müller, M.S. (eds.) IWOMP 2015. LNCS, vol. 9342, pp. 45–59. Springer, Berlin (2015)
15. Martineau, M., McIntosh-Smith, S., Boulton, M., Gaudin, W.: An evaluation of emerging many-core parallel programming models. In: Proceedings of 7th International Workshop on Programming Models and Applications for Multicores and Manycores, PMAM 2016, NY, USA pp. 1–10 (2016)
16. Mitra, G., Stotzer, E., Jayaraj, A., Rendell, A.P.: Implementation and optimization of the OpenMP accelerator model for the TI Keystone II architecture. In: DeRose, L., Supinski, B.R., Olivier, S.L., Chapman, B.M., Müller, M.S. (eds.) IWOMP 2014. LNCS, vol. 8766, pp. 202–214. Springer, Heidelberg (2014)
17. Müller, M.S., et al.: SPEC OMP2012 — an application benchmark suite for parallel systems using OpenMP. In: Chapman, B.M., Massaioli, F., Müller, M.S., Rorro, M. (eds.) IWOMP 2012. LNCS, vol. 7312, pp. 223–236. Springer, Heidelberg (2012). http://dx.doi.org/10.1007/978-3-642-30961-8_17
18. Müller, M.S., van Waveren, M., Lieberman, R., Whitney, B., Saito, H., Kumaran, K., Baron, J., Brantley, W.C., Parrott, C., Elken, T., Feng, H., Ponder, C.: SPEC MPI2007 - an application benchmark suite for parallel systems using MPI. Concurr. Comput.: Pract. Exper. **22**(2), 191–205 (2010). http://dx.doi.org/10.1002/cpe.v22:2
19. Newburn, C.J., Dmitriev, S., Narayanaswamy, R., Wiegert, J., Murty, R., Chinchilla, F., Deodhar, R., McGuire, R.: Offload compiler runtime for the Intel Xeon Phi™ coprocessor. In: 2013 IEEE 27th International Parallel and Distributed Processing Symposium Workshops and Ph.D. Forum (IPDPSW), pp. 1213–1225 (2013)
20. OpenMP Architecture Review Board: OpenMP Application Program Interface. Version 4.0, July 2013. http://www.openmp.org/mp-documents/OpenMP4.0.0.pdf

21. OpenMP Architecture Review Board: OpenMP Application Program Interface. Version 4.5, November 2015. http://www.openmp.org/mp-documents/openmp-4.5.pdf
22. Oracle: Oracle® Solaris Studio 12.4: OpenMP API User's Guide (2014). http://docs.oracle.com/cd/E37069_01/pdf/E37081.pdf
23. PathScale: PathScale ENZO 2015 (2015). http://www.pathscale.com/enzo
24. Pennycook, S.J., Jarvis, S.A.: Developing Performance-Portable Molecular Dynamics Kernels in OpenCL. In: 2012 SC Companion: High Performance Computing, Networking, Storage and Analysis (SCC), pp. 386–395 (2012)
25. Sabne, A., Sakdhnagool, P., Lee, S., Vetter, J.S.: Evaluating performance portability of OpenACC. In: Brodman, J., Tu, P. (eds.) LCPC 2014. LNCS, vol. 8967, pp. 51–66. Springer, Heidelberg (2015). http://dx.doi.org/10.1007/978-3-319-17473-0_4
26. Strohmeier, E., Simon, H., Dongarra, J., Meurer, M.: The 46th top. 500 list, November 2015. http://top500.org/list/2015/11/
27. Wienke, S., Terboven, C., Beyer, J.C., Müller, M.S.: A pattern-based comparison of OpenACC and OpenMP for accelerator computing. In: Silva, F., Dutra, I., Santos Costa, V. (eds.) Euro-Par 2014 Parallel Processing. LNCS, vol. 8632, pp. 812–823. Springer, Heidelberg (2014). http://dx.doi.org/10.1007/978-3-319-09873-9_68
28. Wong, M.: The future of GPU/accelerator programming models. In: Keynote at the 2nd Workshop on the LLVM Compiler Infrastructure in HPC (2015). https://llvm-hpc2-workshop.github.io/slides/Wong.pdf
29. Woolley, C.: Profiling and tuning OpenACC code. http://on-demand.gputechconf.com/gtc/2012/presentations/S0517B-Monday-Programming-GPUs-OpenACC.pdf

GPU-STREAM v2.0: Benchmarking the Achievable Memory Bandwidth of Many-Core Processors Across Diverse Parallel Programming Models

Tom Deakin[(✉)], James Price, Matt Martineau, and Simon McIntosh-Smith

Department of Computer Science, University of Bristol, Bristol, UK
tom.deakin@bristol.ac.uk

Abstract. Many scientific codes consist of memory bandwidth bound kernels — the dominating factor of the runtime is the speed at which data can be loaded from memory into the Arithmetic Logic Units, before results are written back to memory. One major advantage of many-core devices such as General Purpose Graphics Processing Units (GPGPUs) and the Intel Xeon Phi is their focus on providing increased memory bandwidth over traditional CPU architectures. However, as with CPUs, this peak memory bandwidth is usually unachievable in practice and so benchmarks are required to measure a practical upper bound on expected performance.

The choice of one programming model over another should ideally not limit the performance that can be achieved on a device. GPU-STREAM has been updated to incorporate a wide variety of the latest parallel programming models, all implementing the same parallel scheme. As such this tool can be used as a kind of *Rosetta Stone* which provides both a cross-platform and cross-programming model array of results of achievable memory bandwidth.

1 Introduction

The number of programming models for parallel programming has grown rapidly in recent years. Given that they in general aim to both achieve high performance and run across a range of hardware (i.e. are portable), the programmer may hope they are abstract enough that they enable some degree of *performance portability*. In principle therefore, one might expect that, when writing or porting a new code, the choice of parallel programming language should largely be a matter of preference. In reality there are often significant differences between the results delivered by different parallel programming models, and thus benchmarks play an important role in objectively comparing across not just different hardware, but also the programming models. This study aims to explore this space and highlight these differences.

Many scientific codes are memory bandwidth bound, and thus are commonly compared against the STREAM benchmark, itself a simple achievable memory

© Springer International Publishing AG 2016
M. Taufer et al. (Eds.): ISC High Performance Workshops 2016, LNCS 9945, pp. 489–507, 2016.
DOI: 10.1007/978-3-319-46079-6_34

bandwidth measure [10]. In this work we implemented the STREAM benchmark in a wide variety of parallel programming models and across a diverse range of CPU and GPU devices, comparing the percentage of theoretical peak that was achieved.

Specifically, we make the following contributions:

1. We port the STREAM memory bandwidth benchmark to seven parallel programming models, all of which support many-core processors: Kokkos, RAJA, OpenMP 4.x, OpenACC, SYCL, OpenCL and CUDA.
2. We present performance portability results for these seven parallel programming models on a variety of GPUs from two vendors and on several generations of Intel CPU along with IBM's Power 8 and Intel's Xeon Phi (Knights Landing).
3. We update the GPU-STREAM benchmark to provide a 'Rosetta Stone', a simple example code which can assist in understanding how to program in the different programming models. This will also enable testing of future programming models in a simple way.

The paper is structured as follows: in Sect. 2 we introduce the STREAM benchmark and explain the basic structure. In Sect. 3 we describe the key features of the programmings models we use in this paper, before presenting performance results in Sect. 4. Finally we conclude in Sect. 5.

2   Measuring Memory Bandwidth

The STREAM Benchmark [10] measures the time taken for each of four simple operators (kernels) applied to three large arrays (a, b and c), where α is a scalar constant:

1. Copy: $c[i] = a[i]$
2. Multiply: $b[i] = \alpha c[i]$
3. Add: $c[i] = a[i] + b[i]$
4. Triad: $a[i] = b[i] + \alpha c[i]$

These kernels have been demonstrated to be *memory bandwidth bound*. The number of bytes read from and written to memory can be modelled by visual inspection of the source code. We let β be the size in bytes of an element — for double precision floating point $\beta = 8$. For an array containing N elements, the copy and multiply kernels read $N\beta$ bytes and write $N\beta$ bytes, totalling $2N\beta$ bytes. The add and triad kernels both read $2N\beta$ bytes and write $N\beta$ bytes, totalling $3N\beta$ bytes. Running the kernels in the order enumerated above ensures that any caches are invalidated between kernel calls; N is chosen to be large enough to require the data to be moved from main memory — see [10] for the rules of running STREAM. The achieved sustained memory bandwidth can be found as the ratio of bytes moved and the execution time of the kernel. A typical modern CPU can achieve a STREAM result equivalent to 80 % or more of its peak memory bandwidth.

GPU-STREAM is a complementary benchmark to the standard CPU version of STREAM. GPU-STREAM enables the measurement of achievable memory bandwidth across a wide range of multi- and many-core devices [4]. The first version of GPU-STREAM implemented the four STREAM kernels in OpenCL and CUDA, allowing the benchmark to be used across a diverse set of hardware from a wide range of vendors. As a tool it allows an application developer to know how well a memory bandwidth bound kernel is performing. GPU-STREAM is Open Source and available on GitHub at github.com/UoB-HPC/GPU-STREAM. The webpage maintains a repository of all our results and we encourage submission of additional measurements. In this paper we expand GPU-STREAM to consider a second dimension to this reference point, namely the programming model.

2.1 Related Work

The *deviceMemory* benchmark from the Scalable HeterOgeneous Computing (SHOC) Benchmark Suite is an implementation of the triad STREAM kernel [3]. However, this also includes the PCIe transfer time in the bandwidth measurement. Including this factor hides the bandwidth to device memory itself. In a large scale application consisting of many kernels the transfer of memory to the GPU would be performed upfront and data would not be transferred at each kernel execution. As such comparing performance "relative to STREAM" is not possible with the SHOC benchmark.

The *clpeak* benchmark, whilst measuring device memory bandwidth implements a reduction so is not a direct comparison to STREAM [1].

The Standard Parallel Evaluation Corporation (SPEC) ACCEL benchmark suite whilst containing many memory bandwidth bound kernels does not include a STREAM kernel [16].

To the authors knowledge, the only study that has compared the same simple benchmark in all the programming models of interest across a wide range of devices is one they themselves performed, where the TeaLeaf heat diffusion mini-app from the Mantevo benchmark suite was used in a similar manner to measure performance portability [6,9].

3 Programming Models

A parallel programming model along with an implementation of that model provides programmers a way to write code to run on multiple physical execution units. A common way of providing this functionality is via an Application Programming Interface (API) which may be through function calls, compiler directives or an extension to a programming language.

We briefly introduce each of the programming models used in this paper. Due to the simplicity of the STREAM kernels, we also include the triad kernel in each model to enable the reader to make a look-and-feel comparison. A similar approach was taken with the TeaLeaf mini-app in. This approach also helps to demonstrate the similarities and differences between these parallel programming

```
template <class T>
void triad()
{
  const T scalar = 3.0;
  for (int i = 0; i < array_size; i++)
    a[i] = b[i] + scalar * c[i];
}
```

Fig. 1. STREAM triad baseline kernel in C++

models, exposing how intrusive or otherwise the models may be for existing code. We take the standard STREAM triad kernel written in a baseline of C++ running on a CPU in serial, as shown in Fig. 1.

The update to the GPU-STREAM benchmark [4] presented in this paper has been designed in a plug-and-play fashion; each programming model plugs into a common framework by providing an implementation of an abstract C++ class. This means that the "host code" is identical between different models. Note that an independent binary is built per parallel programming model, avoiding any possibility of interference between them. Further programming models are simple to add using this approach.

In considering the memory bandwidth of kernels alone, the transfer of memory between the host and device is not included as in our previous work. Therefore timings are of the kernel execution time and measure the movement of memory on the device alone. The framework developed ensures that all data transfer between host and device is completed before the timing of the kernels are recorded. This therefore requires that each kernel call is *blocking* so that the host may measure the total execution time of the kernels in turn. This is consistent with the approach in the original STREAM benchmark.

Additionally our framework has memory movement routines to ensure that data is valid on the device a priori to the kernel execution.

3.1   OpenCL

OpenCL is an open standard, royalty-free API specified by Khronos [11]. The model is structured such that a host program co-ordinates one or more attached accelerator devices; this is a fairly explicit approach as the API gives control over selecting devices from a variety of vendors within a single host program. Because OpenCL is designed to offload to generic devices, vendor support is widespread from manufactures of CPUs, GPUs, FPGAs and DSPs.

Each OpenCL device has its own memory address space, which must be explicitly controlled by the programmer; memory is not shared between the host and device. OpenCL 2.0 introduced a Shared Virtual Memory concept which allows the host and device to share an address space, although explicit synchronisation for discrete devices is still required via the host to ensure memory consistency.

Kernels are typically stored as plain text and are compiled at run time. The kernels are then run on the device by issuing them to a command queue. Data movement between host and device is also coordinated via a command queue.

The host API is provided via C function calls, and a standard C++ interface is also provided. Kernels are written in a subset of C99; OpenCL 2.2 provisionally allows kernels to be written in C++. The GPU-STREAM triad kernel in OpenCL C99 is shown in Fig. 2.

```
std::string kernels{R"CLC(
  constant TYPE scalar = 3.0;

  kernel void triad(
    global TYPE * restrict a,
    global const TYPE * restrict b,
    global const TYPE * restrict c)
  {
    const size_t i = get_global_id(0);
    a[i] = b[i] + scalar * c[i];
  }
)CLC"};

template <class T>
void OCLStream<T>::triad()
{
  (*triad_kernel)(
    cl::EnqueueArgs(queue, cl::NDRange(array_size)),
    d_a, d_b, d_c
  );
  queue.finish();
}
```

Fig. 2. OpenCL triad kernel

3.2 CUDA

CUDA is a proprietary API from NVIDIA for targeting their GPU devices [12]. CUDA kernels are written in a subset of C++ and are included as function calls in the host source files. They are compiled offline.

The API is simplified so that no explicit code is required to acquire a GPU device; additional routines are provided to allow greater control if required by the programmer.

In the more recent versions of CUDA the memory address space is shared between the host and the GPU so that pointers are valid on both. Synchronisation of memory access is still left to the programmer. CUDA also introduces Managed memory which allows a more automatic sharing of memory between host and device. With upcoming Pascal GPUs, the GPU is allowed to cache data accessed from the host memory; previously it was zero copy.

The GPU-STREAM triad kernel is shown in Fig. 3. Note that CUDA requires specification of the number of threads per thread-block, therefore the size of the arrays must be divisible by 1024 in our implementation.

```
template <typename T>
__global__ void triad_kernel(T * a, const T * b, const T * c)
{
  const T scalar = 3.0;
  const int i = blockDim.x * blockIdx.x + threadIdx.x;
  a[i] = b[i] + scalar * c[i];
}

template <class T>
void CUDAStream<T>::triad()
{
  triad_kernel<<<array_size/1024, 1024>>>(d_a, d_b, d_c);
  cudaDeviceSynchronize();
}
```

Fig. 3. CUDA triad kernel

3.3   OpenACC

The OpenACC Committee, consisting of members including NVIDIA/PGI, Cray and AMD, partitioned from the OpenMP standard to provide a directive-based solution for offloading to accelerators [13]. The accelerator is programmed by adding compiler directives (pragmas or sentinels) to standard CPU source code. A few API calls are also provided to query the runtime and offer some basic device control and selection.

There are two different options for specifying the parallelism in offloaded code. The OpenACC **parallel** construct starts parallel execution on the device, redundantly if no other clauses are present. The **loop** construct is applied to the loop to describe that the loop iterations are to be shared amongst 'workers' on the device. The **kernels** pragma indicates that the region will be offloaded to the device as a series of 'kernels' and any loops encountered will be executed as a kernel in parallel. The **kernels** construct allows the compiler to make decisions about the parallelism, whereas the **parallel** construct gives the programmer control to define the parallelism. The parts of the code which are run on the accelerator are compiled offline, and can be tuned for particular accelerators via compiler flags.

Current implementations of OpenACC can target devices including AMD and NVIDIA GPUs, IBM Power CPUs and x86 multi-core CPUs. Current OpenACC compilers that are available include GCC 6.1, Cray and PGI (NVIDIA).

The GPU-STREAM triad kernel is shown in Fig. 4. Note that a `wait` clause is required for the offload to be blocking as is required by our framework to ensure timing is correct. The `present` clause specifies that the memory is already available on the device and ensures a host/device copy is not initiated.

```
template <class T>
void ACCStream<T>::triad()
{
  const T scalar = 3.0;

  unsigned int array_size = this->array_size;
  T * restrict a = this->a;
  T * restrict b = this->b;
  T * restrict c = this->c;
  #pragma acc kernels present(a[0:array_size], b[0:array_size],
  ↪ c[0:array_size]) wait
  for (int i = 0; i < array_size; i++)
  {
    a[i] = b[i] + scalar * c[i];
  }
}
```

Fig. 4. OpenACC triad kernel

3.4   OpenMP

The OpenMP specification from the OpenMP Architecture Review Board has traditionally allowed thread based parallelism in the fork-join model on CPUs [14]. The parallelism is described using a directive approach (with pragmas or sentinels) defining regions of code to operate (redundantly) in parallel on multiple threads. Work-sharing constructs allow loops in a parallel region to be split across the threads. The shared memory model allows data to be accessed by all threads. An OpenMP 3 version of the triad kernel, suitable for running only on CPUs is shown in Fig. 5.

The OpenMP 4.0 specification introduced the ability to offload regions of code to a target device. The approach has later been improved in the OpenMP 4.5 specification. Structured blocks of code marked with a `target` directive are executed on the accelerator, whilst by default the host waits for completion of the offloaded region before continuing. The usual work-sharing constructs allow loops in the `target` region and further directives allow finer grained control of work distribution.

Memory management in general (shallow copies) is automatically handled by the implementation; the host memory is copied to the device on entry to the offloaded region by natural extensions to the familiar implicit scoping rules in the OpenMP model. Finer grained control of memory movement between the

```
template <class T>
void OMP3Stream<T>::triad()
{
  const T scalar = 3.0;
  #pragma omp parallel for
  for (int i = 0; i < array_size; i++)
  {
    a[i] = b[i] + scalar * c[i];
  }
}
```

Fig. 5. OpenMP triad kernel

```
template <class T>
void OMP45Stream<T>::triad()
{
  const T scalar = 0.3;

  unsigned int array_size = this->array_size;
  T *a = this->a;
  T *b = this->b;
  T *c = this->c;
  #pragma omp target teams distribute parallel for simd map(to:
  ↪  a[0:array_size], b[0:array_size], c[0:array_size])
  for (int i = 0; i < array_size; i++)
  {
    a[i] = b[i] + scalar * c[i];
  }
}
```

Fig. 6. OpenMP v4 triad kernel

host and device is controlled via target data regions and memory movement clauses; in particular arrays must be mapped explicitly.

The unstructured target data regions in OpenMP 4.5 allow simple integration with our framework. The scoping rules of OpenMP 4.0 require the memory movement to the device must be written in our driver code, breaking the separation of implementation from driver code in our testing framework; OpenMP 4.5 fixes this issue.

The OpenMP 4 version of the GPU-STREAM triad kernel is shown in Fig. 6.

3.5 Kokkos

Kokkos is an open source C++ abstraction layer developed by Sandia National Laboratories that allows users to target multiple architectures using OpenMP, Pthreads, and CUDA [5]. The programming model requires developers to wrap up application data structures in abstract data types called Views in order to distinguish between host and device memory spaces. Developers have two options when writing Kokkos kernels: (1) the functor approach, where a templated C++ class is written that has an overloaded function operator containing the kernel logic; and (2) the lambda approach, where a simple parallel dispatch function such as `parallel_for` is combined with an anonymous function containing the kernel logic. It is also possible to nest the parallel dispatch functions and achieve nested parallelism, which can be used to express multiple levels of parallelism within a kernel.

The Kokkos version of the GPU-STREAM triad kernel is shown in Fig. 7.

```
template <class T>
void KOKKOSStream<T>::triad()
{
  View<double*, Kokkos::Cuda> a(*d_a);
  View<double*, Kokkos::Cuda> b(*d_b);
  View<double*, Kokkos::Cuda> c(*d_c);

  const T scalar = 3.0;
  parallel_for(array_size, KOKKOS_LAMBDA (const int index)
  {
    a[index] = b[index] + scalar*c[index];
  });

  Kokkos::fence();
}
```

Fig. 7. Kokkos triad kernel

3.6 RAJA

RAJA is a recently released C++ abstraction layer developed by Lawrence Livermore National Laboratories that can target OpenMP and CUDA [7]. RAJA adopts a novel approach of precomputing the iteration space for each kernel, abstracting them into some number of Segments, which are aggregated into a container called an IndexSet. By decoupling the kernel logic and iteration space it is possible to optimise data access patterns, easily adjust domain decompositions and perform tiling. The developer is required to write a lambda function containing each kernel's logic that will be called by some parallel dispatch function, such as `forall`. The dispatch functions are driven by execution policies, which describe how the iteration space will be executed on a particular target architecture, for instance executing the elements of each Segment in parallel on a GPU.

The RAJA version of the GPU-STREAM triad kernel is shown in Fig. 8.

```
template <class T>
void RAJAStream<T>::triad()
{
  T* a = d_a;
  T* b = d_b;
  T* c = d_c;
  const T scalar = 3.0;
  forall<policy>(index_set, [=] RAJA_DEVICE (int index)
  {
    a[index] = b[index] + scalar*c[index];
  });
}
```

Fig. 8. RAJA triad kernel

3.7 SYCL

SYCL is a royalty-free, cross-platform C++ abstraction layer from Khronos that
builds on the OpenCL programming model (see Sect. 3.1) [8]. It is designed to
be programmed as single-source C++, where code offloaded to the device is
expressed as a lambda function or functor; template functions are supported.

SYCL aims to be as close to standard C++14 as possible, in so far as a standard C++14 compiler can compile the SYCL source code and run on a CPU via

```
template <class T>
void SYCLStream<T>::triad()
{
  const T scalar = 3.0;
  queue.submit([&](handler &cgh)
  {
    auto ka = d_a->template get_access<access::mode::write>(cgh);
    auto kb = d_b->template get_access<access::mode::read>(cgh);
    auto kc = d_c->template get_access<access::mode::read>(cgh);
    cgh.parallel_for<class triad>(nd_range<1>{array_size,
    ↪  WGSIZE}, [=](nd_item<1> item)
    {
    ka[item.get_global()] = kb[item.get_global()] + scalar *
    ↪  kc[item.get_global()];
    });
  });
  queue.wait();
}
```

Fig. 9. SYCL triad kernel

a header-only implementation. A SYCL device compiler has to be used to offload the kernels onto an accelerator, typically via OpenCL. The approach taken in SYCL 1.2 compilers available today is to generate SPIR, a portable intermediate representation for OpenCL kernels. The provisional SYCL 2.2 specification will require OpenCL 2.2 compatibility.

The SYCL version of the GPU-STREAM triad kernel is shown in Fig. 9.

4 Results

Table 1 lists the many-core devices that we used in our experiment. Given the breadth of devices and programming models we had to use a number of platforms and compilers to collect results. Intel do not formally publish peak MCDRAM bandwidth results for the Xeon Phi, so the presented figure is based on published claims that MCDRAM's peak memory bandwidth is five times that of KNL's DDR.

The HPC GPUs from NVIDIA were attached to a Cray XC40 supercomputer 'Swan' (K20X) and a Cray CS cluster 'Falcon' (K40 and K80). We used the GNU compilers (5.3 on Swan, 4.9 on Falcon) for Kokkos and RAJA results and the Cray compiler (8.5 on Swan, 8.4 on Falcon) for OpenMP and OpenACC results. The codes were built with CUDA 7.5.

The AMD GPUs were attached to an experimental cluster at the University of Bristol. We used the ComputeCpp compiler (2016.05 pre-release) from Codeplay [2] along with the AMD-APP OpenCL 1.2 (1912.5) drivers for SYCL results. We used the PGI Accelerator 16.4 for OpenACC on the AMD S9150 GPU.

The NVIDIA GTX 980 Ti is also attached to the University of Bristol experimental cluster (the "Zoo"). We used the clang-ykt fork of Clang for OpenMP[1]; note that the Clang OpenMP 4.x implementation is still under development and is not a stable release. We used PGI Accelerator 16.4 for OpenACC. We used CUDA 7.5 drivers for CUDA and OpenCL.

The Sandy Bridge CPUs are part of BlueCrystal Phase 3, part of the Advanced Computing Research Centre at the University of Bristol. Here we used the Intel 16.0 compiler for original STREAM and our C++ OpenMP implementation. RAJA and Kokkos were compiled using the GNU compilers. We used the PGI Accelerator 16.4 compiler for OpenACC and CUDA-x86. We used the Intel OpenCL Runtime 15.1 for OpenCL.

The Ivy Bridge CPUs are part of the experimental cluster at the University of Bristol. We used the GNU 4.8 compilers for RAJA and Kokkos and the Intel 16.0 compiler for original STREAM and our C++ OpenMP version. We used the ComputeCpp compiler from Codeplay along with the Intel OpenCL Runtime 15.1 for SYCL. We used the same OpenCL driver for OpenCL. We used the PGI Accelerator 16.4 compiler for OpenACC and CUDA-x86.

---

[1] https://github.com/clang-ykt.

The Haswell and Broadwell CPUs are part of a Cray XC40 supercomputer. We used the Cray compiler for original STREAM and our C++ OpenMP implementation. RAJA and Kokkos used the GNU compilers. We used the PGI 16.3 compiler for OpenACC for CUDA-x86.

The Intel Xeon Phi (Knights Landing) are part of the experimental cluster in Bristol. We used the Intel 2016 compiler for all results except OpenACC where we used the PGI compiler. Because the device in binary compatible with AVX2 architectures we specified Haswell as a target architecture for OpenACC.

We used the XL 13.1 compiler for all results on the Power 8.

Table 1. List of devices

Name	Class	Vendor	Peak memory BW (GB/s)
K20X	GPU	NVIDIA	250
K40	GPU	NVIDIA	288
K80 (1 GPU)	GPU	NVIDIA	240
GTX 980 Ti	GPU	NVIDIA	224
S9150	GPU	AMD	320
Fury X	GPU	AMD	512
E5-2670 (Sandy Bridge)	CPU	Intel	$2 \times 51.2 = 102.4$
E5-2697 v2 (Ivy Bridge)	CPU	Intel	$2 \times 59.7 = 119.4$
E5-2698 v3 (Haswell)	CPU	Intel	$2 \times 68 = 136$
E5-2699 v4 (Broadwell)	CPU	Intel	$2 \times 76.8 = 153.6$
Xeon Phi (Knights Landing) 7210	MIC	Intel	$\sim 5 \times 102 = 510$
Power 8	CPU	IBM	$2 \times 192 = 384$

In the next few sections we describe our experiences in porting the GPU-STREAM kernels to the seven different parallel programming models in our study, before describing the performance we were able to achieve when running these implementations on a diverse range of many-core devices.

4.1   Code Changes and Experiences

The C++ solutions of SYCL, RAJA and Kokkos all provide a similar syntax for describing the parallel work. A for-loop is replaced by an equivalent statement with the loop body expressed as a lambda function. The directive based approaches of OpenMP and OpenACC both annotate for-loops with compiler directives which describe the parallelism of the loop. OpenCL and CUDA require the loop body to be written in a separate function which is then instantiated on the device with an API call which defines the number of iterations; the iteration is no longer is expressed as a loop. Table 2 gives an idea of how much code was required to implement this benchmark in each of the programming models. The number of lines of code in the specific implementation in each of the programming models of our virtual class was counted and is shown in the first column. For each version we also include the change in the number of lines of code compared to our baseline OpenMP version in C++ implemented in our framework.

Table 2. Lines of code to implement class

Implementation	Lines of code in class	Difference
OpenMP 3 (baseline)	113	0
CUDA	183	+70
OpenCL	229	+116
OpenACC	138	+25
OpenMP 4.5	138	+25
Kokkos	150	+37
RAJA	144	+31
SYCL	145	+32

Whilst the authors found that writing this simple benchmark in each of the programming models was a simple task, getting them to build on a variety of platforms for a variety of devices was a significant challenge in many cases. Additionally, major changes to the code were required in order for specific platform and compiler combinations to be performant, or in some cases to work at all.

The OpenMP 4.0 programming model does not allow for control of the data on the target device in an unstructured way. The data on the device is controlled by scoping rules in the code, and as such an OpenMP 4.0 implementation required an invasive procedure to add this to our code, breaking our abstraction of model from control and timing code. OpenMP 4.5 addresses this issue with `target data enter` and `exit` regions, however OpenMP 4.5 compilers were not available on all platforms at the time of writing so we had to use both 4.0 and 4.5 versions to collect the range of results.

We had to remove the `simd` clause from the OpenMP directives to achieve good performance with Clang, and use a static schedule with a chunk size of one (which can be specified via an environment variable). These changes render the code non-portable, however once OpenMP offload support becomes mature these will not be required.

Our experience of the disruption of OpenMP 4 is more related to availability of tools over issues with the model itself.

OpenACC using the PGI compiler targeting host CPUs, the AMD GPUs and the NVIDIA GTX 980 Ti, all required specifying the pointers as `restrict` in order for the loop to be parallelised, although this is not standard C++. Using `parallel loop independent` does parallelise the loop without specifying `restrict`. This was a relatively simple change, in a simple benchmark case, but there may be larger codes where the reason the automatic parallelism fails may not be evident. This would result in the programmer changing the *way* they express the same parallelism when using a particular programming model by altering the code for a different architecture or compiler, the code itself is no longer performance portable — you require one implementation per device.

However, all compilers supporting OpenMP 4 and OpenACC would not correctly offload the kernel without re-declaring the arrays as local scope variables. These variables are declared inside the class, but the compilers were unable to recognise them in the directives (Cray), or else crash at runtime (PGI targeting GPUs). The authors have found this is also the case with using structure members in C. It is the opinion of the authors that these local variables should not be required for correct behaviour.

The PGI compiler has support for CUDA-x86 whereby CUDA code can target host CPUs. All kernel calls are considered blocking unlike the CUDA API itself, and the `cudaSynchronizeDevice()` call is not supported; as such we had to remove this from the code, reducing the portability of the CUDA code. Additionally the compiler failed to build the code with templated classes.

In SYCL, explicitly choosing the size of a work-group was required to achieve good performance. As the programming model does not stipulate that this size must be set, this requirement is likely to disappear with future updates to the compiler. This is similar to OpenCL's ability to leave the choice of work-group size up to the run-time.

In addition to these code changes, despite trying to use a unified build system (CMake), many of the data points required specific compiler invocations.

4.2   Performance

We display the fraction of peak memory bandwidth we were able to achieve for a variety of devices against each programming model in Fig. 10. We used 100 iterations with an array size of 2^{25} double precision elements (268 MB).

When writing code targeting NVIDIA GPUs, the results with all the programming models are similar. Both the high-level models, such as RAJA and Kokkos, and the directives based approaches, such as OpenMP and OpenACC, demonstrate equivalent performance to CUDA and OpenCL on these devices, which is a very encouraging result.

When targeting AMD GPUs however, we are unable to collect a full set of data points because neither RAJA nor Kokkos provide GPU implementations of their model to run on non-NVIDIA GPUs. This is currently a weakness of the RAJA and Kokkos implementations, which could be addressed when proper OpenMP 4.5 support becomes more widely available; note that RAJA and Kokkos use OpenMP for their CPU implementation and CUDA for the NVIDIA GPU implementation. It should be noted that the data points that we were able to collect for AMD's GPUs achieved the highest fractions of peak for all GPUs (83–86 %).

We use the original 'McCalpin' STREAM benchmark written in C and OpenMP as a baseline comparison for the CPU results. Thread binding is used

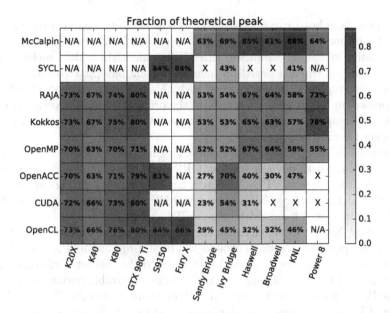

Fig. 10. Performance relative to theoretical peak of GPU-STREAM on 10 devices

via the OpenMP implementation selecting a compact affinity. We did not experiment with streaming stores. Figure 10 shows that there is some loss of performance when using C++ and OpenMP 3 for running on CPUs compared to the much simpler C language version. For example, on Broadwell CPUs the C++ version achieves 64 % of peak memory bandwidth, compared to 83 % when using the C version; both these codes use the standard OpenMP 3 programming model.

We used PGI's implementation of OpenACC for multi-core CPUs. On the Sandy Bridge and Ivy Bridge system we used the `numactl` tool for thread pinning and specified the `ACC_NUM_CORES` environment variable to the total number of cores in our dual-socket CPU systems. The Haswell and Broadwell CPUs are in a Cray system so were required to use the options within `aprun` to run the binary. Despite this however it does not demonstrate good peak performance on the CPUs in general. For the Xeon Phi we needed to use `MP_BLIST` to pin the OpenACC threads as `numactl` did not pin these threads correctly.

Both RAJA and Kokkos use the OpenMP programming model to implement parallel execution on CPUs. The performance results on all four CPUs tested show that RAJA and Kokkos performance matches that of hand-written OpenMP for GPU-STREAM. This result shows that both RAJA and Kokkos provide little overhead over writing OpenMP code directly, at least for GPU-STREAM. As such they may provide a viable alternative to OpenMP for writing code in a parallel C++-style programming model compared to the directive based approach in OpenMP. However as noted above, C++ compiler implementations of OpenMP may suffer from a performance loss compared to a C with OpenMP implementation.

OpenCL is able to run on the CPU as well, and we tested using the Intel OpenCL runtime. This is implemented on top of Intel's Thread Building Blocks, which results in non-deterministic thread placement. In a dual-socket system the placement of threads based on memory allocations (first touch) is important in achieving good bandwidth; as such this programming model suffers in performance on Intel CPUs compared to the original STREAM code. The PGI CUDA-x86 compiler gets similar performance to OpenCL, but they are both lower than OpenMP.

Figure 11 shows the raw sustained memory bandwidth of the triad kernel in each case. Many-core devices such as GPUs and Xeon Phi offer an increased memory bandwidth over CPUs, although the latest CPU offerings are competitive with GDDR memory GPUs. The AMD HPC GPU from AMD, the S9150, provides an increased bandwidth over NVIDIA's HPC offerings.

The Intel Xeon Phi (KNL) had the highest achieved memory bandwidth, however this performance was not achieved in all programming models. In general we ran one thread per core and this achieved the highest performance, but Kokkos needed two threads per core to achieve comparable performance.

The Power 8 results were collected with one thread per core. The bandwidth presented is using the same problem size as all the other results; a high bandwidth is possible with a large problem. It has been previously observed that performance can decrease with smaller problems [15].

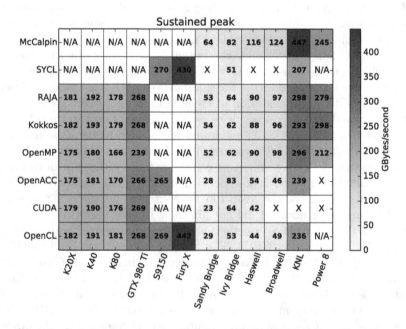

Fig. 11. Sustained memory bandwidth of GPU-STREAM on 10 devices

All of the parallel programming models explored in this paper are designed to be portable; at the very least this should enable running on a variety of devices across a variety of vendors. However, as can be seen in Figs. 10 and 11 there are a surprising number of results that are not possible to obtain. We mark those that are impossible to collect due to missing implementations from the vendors as 'N/A', and those we were unable to obtain due to difficulties with combinations of installed libraries and platforms with an 'X'. Note that the original STREAM benchmark from McCalpin was written in C with OpenMP 3 and so cannot run on GPUs.

For SYCL, ComputeCpp generates SPIR to be consumed by an OpenCL runtime. NVIDIA's OpenCL implementation does not currently support SPIR. ComputeCpp is not currently compatible with the systems which housed the Sandy Bridge, Haswell, and Broadwell CPUs.

OpenMP and OpenACC are supported by a variety of compilers to varying degrees. It is therefore simpler to discuss the available options for devices. For AMD GPUs, GCC 6.1 introduces OpenMP 4.5 support, but only for integrated graphics in the APU devices, not for the discrete GPUs used in this paper. The PGI Accelerator compiler supports AMD GPUs up to Hawaii so we used this for the S9150, but the Fury X's newer Fiji architecture is not yet supported.

The Cray compiler supports OpenMP targeting NVIDIA GPUs, with version 8.5 supporting OpenMP 4.5 and version 8.4 supporting OpenMP 4.0. We were able to use version 8.5 to collect results for the NVIDIA K20X with OpenMP 4.5 code, and had to resort to our OpenMP 4.0 code with Cray compiler version 8.4 for the K40 and K80 GPUs. The GTX 980 Ti GPU was not on a Cray system so we could not collect a result for it using the Cray compiler. However, Clang supports OpenMP 4.5 targeting NVIDIA GPUs, and so the result was obtained using this compiler.

The PGI CUDA-x86 compiler did compile the code for Broadwell and KNL but failed at runtime due to the number of available threads being unsupported. The PGI compiler was also unavailable on the Power 8 system so we were unable to collect OpenACC and CUDA results.

5   Conclusion

What is evident from Fig. 10 is that, in general, the more mature of these programming models provide better performance across the range of architectures. None of the programming models is currently available to run a single code across all devices that we tested. Whatever definition of 'performance portability' one might wish, a performance portable code must also at least be functionally portable across different devices.

The directive based approaches of OpenMP and OpenACC look to provide a good trade off between performance and code complexity. OpenACC demonstrates good GPU performance on products from both NVIDIA and AMD, however the CPU performance is poor. This limits OpenACC's relevance to CPUs due to implementations of the model at the time of writing.

With the directive based approaches of OpenMP and OpenACC the number of lines of code to add to an existing piece of C or Fortran code is minimal. If code is already in C++, then SYCL, RAJA and Kokkos provided a similar level of minimal disruption for performance.

Acknowledgements. We would like to thank Cray Inc. for providing access to the Cray XC40 supercomputer, Swan, and the Cray CS cluster, Falcon. Our thanks to Codeplay for access to the ComputeCpp SYCL compiler and to Douglas Miles at PGI (NVIDIA) for access to the PGI compiler. We would also like to that the University of Bristol Intel Parallel Computing Center (IPCC). This work was carried out using the computational facilities of the Advanced Computing Research Centre, University of Bristol - http://www.bris.ac.uk/acrc/. Thanks also go to the University of Oxford for access to the Power 8 system.

References

1. Bhat, K.: clpeak (2015). https://github.com/krrishnarraj/clpeak
2. Codeplay: ComputeCpp. https://www.codeplay.com/products/computecpp
3. Danalis, A., Marin, G., McCurdy, C., Meredith, J.S., Roth, P.C., Spafford, K., Tipparaju, V., Vetter, J.S.: The scalable heterogeneous computing (SHOC) benchmark suite. In: Proceedings of the 3rd Workshop on General-Purpose Computation on Graphics Processing Units, GPGPU-3, pp. 63–74. ACM, New York (2010). http://doi.acm.org/10.1145/1735688.1735702
4. Deakin, T., McIntosh-Smith, S.: GPU-STREAM: benchmarking the achievable memory bandwidth of graphics processing units (poster). In: Supercomputing, Austin, Texas (2015)
5. Edwards, H.C., Sunderland, D.: Kokkos array performance-portable manycore programming model. In: Proceedings of the 2012 International Workshop on Programming Models and Applications for Multicores and Manycores (PMAM 2012), pp. 1–10. ACM (2012)
6. Heroux, M., Doerfler, D., et al.: Improving performance via mini-applications. Technical report, SAND2009-5574, Sandia National Laboratories (2009)
7. Hornung, R.D., Keasler, J.A.: The RAJA Portability Layer: Overview and Status (2014)
8. Khronos OpenCL Working Group SYCL subgroup: SYCL Provisional Specification (2016)
9. Martineau, M., McIntosh-Smith, S., Boulton, M., Gaudin, W.: An evaluation of emerging many-core parallel programming models. In: Proceedings of the 7th International Workshop on Programming Models and Applications for Multicores and Manycore, PMAM 2016, pp. 1–10. ACM, New York (2016). http://doi.acm.org/10.1145/2883404.2883420
10. McCalpin, J.D.: Memory bandwidth and machine balance in current high performance computers. IEEE Comput. Soc. Tech. Comm. Comput. Archit. (TCCA) Newslett. 19–25 (1995)
11. Munshi, A.: The OpenCL Specification, Version 1.1 (2011)
12. NVIDIA: CUDA Toolkit 7.5
13. OpenACC-Standard.org: The OpenACC Application Programming Interface - Version 2.5 (2015)

14. OpenMP Architecture Review Board: OpenMP Application Program Interface, Version 4.5 (2015)
15. Reguly, I.Z., Keita, A.K., Giles, M.B.: Benchmarking the IBM Power8 processor. In: Proceedings of the 25th Annual International Conference on Computer Science and Software Engineering, pp. 61–69. IBM Corporation, Riverton (2015)
16. Standard Performance Evaluation Corporation: SPEC Accel (2016). https://www.spec.org/accel/

Porting the MPI Parallelized LES Model PALM to Multi-GPU Systems – An Experience Report

Helge Knoop[1](✉), Tobias Gronemeier[1], Christoph Knigge[1],
and Peter Steinbach[2]

[1] Institute of Meteorology and Climatology, Leibniz Universität Hannover,
Hannover, Germany
knoop@muk.uni-hannover.de
[2] Max Planck Institute of Molecular Cell Biology and Genetics, Dresden, Germany
https://palm.muk.uni-hannover.de

Abstract. The computational power of graphics processing units (GPUs) and their availability on high performance computing (HPC) systems is rapidly evolving. However, HPC applications need to be ported to be executable on such hardware. This paper is a report on our experience of porting the MPI + OpenMP parallelized large-eddy simulation model (PALM) to a multi-GPU environment using the directive based high level programming paradigm OpenACC. PALM is a Fortran-based computational fluid dynamics software package, used for the simulation of atmospheric and oceanic boundary layers to answer questions linked to fundamental atmospheric turbulence research, urban climate, wind energy and cloud physics. Development on PALM started in 1997, the project currently entails 140 kLOC and is used on HPC farms of up to 43200 cores. The porting took place during the GPU Hackathon TU Dresden/Forschungszentrum Jülich in Dresden, Germany, in 2016. The main challenges we faced are the legacy code base of PALM and its size. We report the methods used to disentangle performance effects from logical code defects as well as our experiences with state-of-the-art profiling tools. We present detailed performance tests showing an overall performance on one GPU that can easily compete with up to ten CPU cores.

Keywords: CFD · GPU · HPC · LES · MPI · OpenACC · PGI · Porting

1 Introduction

High performance computing (HPC) systems for scientific applications are rapidly gaining size, complexity and adoption in various fields of academia and industry. Recently, an increasing number of these systems provide access to graphics processing units (GPU) [1], adding additional computational power to the available CPU based system performance. Equipping small clusters or even workstations with multiple GPUs enables access to considerable computational power, even for, e.g., small businesses without access to HPC installations.

© Springer International Publishing AG 2016
M. Taufer et al. (Eds.): ISC High Performance Workshops 2016, LNCS 9945, pp. 508–523, 2016.
DOI: 10.1007/978-3-319-46079-6_35

Applications running on such equipped systems need to be capable of dealing with the GPU architecture in order to benefit. Examples of affected applications are machine learning applications [11], molecular dynamics simulations [18] and (besides many others) large-eddy simulation (LES) models. The LES method is a computational fluid dynamics (CFD) simulation technique which is computational expensive and thus its effective use is currently still limited to HPC systems. However, GPUs are a potential enabler for the operational application of this technique in smaller businesses and institutions e.g., for urban planning or wind-energy site assessment. In order to exploit the power of GPUs with existing LES models, they need to be ported to such a computer architecture.

This paper summarizes our experiences during the porting process of the parallelized large-eddy simulation model (PALM) for atmospheric and oceanic flows to a GPU environment. In order to minimize portability loss and porting workload, the directive-based high-level programming model OpenACC [17] was chosen. The porting took place during the one-week GPU Hackathon TU Dresden/Forschungszentrum Jülich in Dresden, Germany, in 2016. During the Hackathon, we were supported by three experienced mentors. With this report we intend to provide aid and guidance for other GPU porting endeavors on code bases similar to the LES technique.

The article itself is structured in four parts: First, PALM and its state-of-art prior to the Hackathon is described. Second, a chronological report is given on the efforts at the OpenACC Hackathon 2016 and afterwards. This is followed by a detailed performance analysis and at the end, we reflect on the progress we made during the Hackathon, discuss technical aspects and draw conclusions for their influence on our future code development.

2   PALM

PALM is an atmospheric CFD application and in particular an LES model to simulate the turbulent flows of atmosphere and ocean. PALM has been applied to answer questions linked to a variety of topics including fundamental atmospheric turbulence research (e.g., [8,14]), urban climate modeling (e.g., [5,12]), wind energy [7] and cloud physics [6]. PALM solves the Boussinesq-approximated Navier-Stokes equations on a discrete three-dimensional (3D) grid for a time dependent flow. A detailed description of the physics used in PALM can be found in [13].

PALM is written in Fortran95 [2] with some Fortran 2003 [20] extensions. It is optimized for running on massively parallel computer architectures. In order to distribute data and work across multiple cores and nodes the message passing interface (MPI) and the directive-based high level programming paradigm OpenMP are used. Parallelization is realized by a two-dimensional (2D) domain decomposition of the underlying Cartesian grid. The computational domain, which consists of a large cuboid representing a portion of the atmosphere, is divided into small vertical columns and each core solves the equations inside one of these vertical columns. After each time step, data situated at the borders of the columns are exchanged with the neighboring cores using MPI. The work flow of PALM is illustrated in Fig. 1 and can be paraphrased as follows: First, the model is initialized by setting up all relevant 3D arrays and distributing necessary data to each core (initialize). Second, the time dependent loop is executed (time loop), in which the prognostic equations are solved for wind-velocity components, temperature, kinetic energy, humidity and others. Following the prognostic equations, a Poisson equation for the perturbation pressure needs to be solved (pressure solver) during each iteration of the time loop. To do this, the data arrays have to be transformed via a fast Fourier transformation (FFT), which requires several calls of MPI routines due to the domain decomposition. At the end of each loop cycle data output is done by calling the output routines. After the time loop is finished the simulation gets finalized and additional output is done.

PALM has basic integrated profiling capabilities that are helpful for analysis during porting as well as for monitoring performance regressions between releases. The compute time consumed by each individual routine is measured using a built-in function named cpulog. It measures the execution time between two positions in the code by using the intrinsic Fortran function SYSTEM_CLOCK. At the end of a simulation, a list of time measurements and calling counts containing the most time-consuming routines is saved.

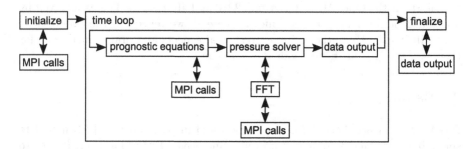

Fig. 1. Schematic work flow of PALM showing the most important parts of the model.

3   Porting PALM

3.1   Preparations

Optimizing an existing production-ready HPC source code base for performance should not be underestimated with regard to a high number of influential parameters (social, technical and design based) and time-consuming subtasks. Thus, automating a majority of the necessary steps to validate or falsify optimization hypotheses is crucial. The common work flow for this can be modeled as:

1. compile,
2. run or profile,

3. validate results,
4. interpret runtime,
5. update code and return to 1. If needed.

As the first three points do not require human intervention, automation of compilation, execution and validation yields a high return-on-investment. The automation does not only allow individual developers or developer groups to move forward autonomously, but it also ensures that the application logic is retained throughout the process. In order to achieve this, a set of shell scripts was created for building PALM, executing it with predefined parameter sets, and validating the results thereof.

To automate the compilation step, a build script was designed to flexibly and transparently adapt to the HPC environment of Taurus at the Center for Information Services and High Performance Computing (ZIH) Dresden, where the porting work took place. It allows to switch compilers and their parameters, switch between available MPI libraries and enable or disable profiling and debugging tools. The actual translation of source code to the PALM binary (using GNU make [21]) is performed in a setup-specific build directory to allow parallel testing of different setups. All these customizing options are available through the aforementioned build setup and each setup is labeled individually. The different build setups can then be chosen by providing the label as an argument to the build script, e.g.:

```
$ ./COMPILE palm_setup_pgi161_openmpi_scorep
```

where PALM is built using the PGI compiler [19] using the OpenMPI library and instrumenting the code with Score-P [16] markers. While we are aware that alternative multi-purpose build engines [3] are available, such as cmake [15] and others, this lightweight and custom approach allowed us to rapidly adapt and identify improvements to code translation and to be flexible in terms of the profiling tool-chain to be used. Given the time constraints of the Hackathon, no incentive urged us to invest resources in refactoring this build mechanism.

Our execution script is designed in a similar manner and based on the same keywords as the build script. Execution setups can be defined and customized for all possible steering parameters of the batch system. It is essential to have an execution setup available that allows a rapid testing of all parts of the LES model which are relevant to the profiling and code optimization process. The build and run script provided a common reference for the team. These scripts can be considered as an essential building block of the optimization process. Also, the PALM integrated automatic runtime measurements of all time-consuming routines (cpulog) are in line with this idea of receiving feedback quickly.

Further, a set of execution setups was created to test PALM regarding memory size and execution time. We found that a good execution setup during the porting process should complete in a fairly small walltime envelope but has a computational complexity that utilizes most of the available resources on the targeted GPU in terms of memory usage and occupancy. In other words, a balance has to be maintained between obtaining a representative sample of profiling data and yet retain a quick turn-around of optimization feedback to all developers involved. We thus agreed on two setups: a *small* one that would complete within one minute of walltime and yet force PALM to perform four iterations; and a *large* configuration that would complete within 5 min of walltime to allow a more global view on the impact of code optimization.

Finally, a lightweight automated testing process of the simulation results in terms of their correctness was introduced. For convenience, the evaluation result is summarized to check whether the execution was successful or not by textually comparing the ASCII output files produced in a given PALM run. PALM is neither equipped with a unit test suite nor are integration tests available so far. Any ambitious performance tuning of PALM should consider providing a comprehensive unit test suite commonly referred to as *test harness* [4]. This does not only ensure correct simulation results after optimizations were applied, but also exerts a high pressure to modularize the application even more, so that autonomous code modules can be extracted from the code base and be optimized independently.

3.2   Starting Position

The model PALM is optimized to run on computer architectures exposing a multi-tier cache hierarchy as well as on vector-based hardware [13]. Depending on the architecture used different branches of the code are executed to gain the best performance.

Before joining the Hackathon, PALM already contained GPU targeted code which based on the vector-optimized branch. This was mainly done by placing a data region around the whole program and adding OpenACC directives to single loops. GPU architectures are based on the parallelization paradigm "Single instruction, multiple threads" (SIMT). In hardware, this relates to the GPU executing one instruction by a group of threads at a single point in time (the hardware used for the Hackathon exposed a minimum group size of 32 threads). The more iterations a loop has, the more it benefits from SIMT architecture. In nature, a GPU is therefore much closer to a vector computer architecture than it is to a cache-optimized computer architecture. Hence, the GPU-optimized branch of PALM based on the vector-optimized branch of PALM with some slight changes to the vector-optimized branch. The GPU-optimized branch was maintained in parallel to the two already existing CPU targeted branches. However, the OpenACC-enabled code was only able to run on a single core while operating on a GPU. The goal for the Hackathon was to continue porting every routine of the program and get a fully functional version of PALM running on a multi-node multi-GPU system.

3.3   The First Unsuccessful Attempt

At the beginning of the Hackathon, it turned out that the GPU targeted routines did not produce the same results as the CPU-only routines. Therefore, during the first two days, the GPU routines were searched for source code defects (bugs) related to the existing GPU code base. This was a very time-consuming process, because the former porting turned out to be unstructured and poorly documented. Having three separate code bases made code debugging even more complicated. Also the size of PALM itself, with its 140 kLOC distributed over 472 routines made the debugging challenging. After two days trying to get the correct results within the GPU branch using the former implemented OpenACC directives, the results still differed from the CPU-only version.

Due to the difficulties regarding the partly ported code base mentioned above, it was decided to do a fresh start. All existing OpenACC directives were commented out to disable their functionality while still having them available during the upcoming second porting attempt. This helped to avoid recoding of already correctly ported parts of the code.

3.4   Starting a Structured Porting Attempt

Our porting effort from scratch focused on the GPU-optimized branch of PALM with all former OpenACC directives commented out.

The first step in a successful porting attempt is an extensive application run-time analysis using a sophisticated profiling tool. During the porting of PALM we used the Score-P measurement infrastructure, which is a highly scalable tool suite for profiling, event tracing, and online analysis of HPC applications [10]. We started several runs with different setups on multiple CPU cores using MPI in order to identify the top subroutines that consumed the most run time during the simulation. Score-P instrumentation and Vampir visualization [9] were applied. In Fig. 2, a Vampir visualization of the evolution of the PALM call stack during one cycle of the time loop is shown. It enables an easy identification of the hot-spot subroutines (marked in blue). The visualized run was performed on a single CPU core. The `time_integration` subroutine contains the whole time loop and is called directly from the main routine `palm`. During a time-loop cycle `time_integration` calls the subroutines `prognostic_equations` and `pres`. The subroutine `prognostic_equations` (marked in red) contains calls to several subroutines dealing with different terms of all required prognostic equations and the subroutine `pres` calls the pressure solver of choice. The chosen pressure solver, which is `poisfft` (marked in yellow) in our case, contains multiple FFT calls (`fft_x` and `fft_y`) and 3D array transpositions with heavy MPI communication. At the end of a time-loop cycle, the data output and other optional parts of the model, e.g., a soil model, are called.

We started this porting attempt by adding `!$acc kernels` directives to the hot-spot subroutines and kept profiling to see how the performance of the code evolved. We quickly realized that this work-flow cycle is quite time-consuming as some of the traces took 5–10 min to load in Vampir. This was mostly due to the fact that the hot-spot subroutines were called at a very high frequency on the used CPU cores and thus the number of traces exceeded an acceptable size for an undisturbed execution of Vampir.

The PGI compiler translates the OpenACC code to CUDA internally and emits CUDA PTX binary objects, which allows us to use the CUDA profiler as

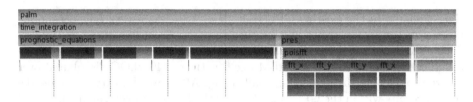

Fig. 2. Vampir screen-shot with the call-stack analysis of one cycle of the time loop in the PALM simulation. The prognostic equations (red) with their most time consuming subroutines (blue) are followed by the pressure solver (yellow). (Color figure online)

an alternative profiling tool. To realize this, the code was compiled using the options -acc and -ta=tesla to allow OpenACC interpretation, -Minfo=acc for OpenACC related compiler logging and -fastsse to enable fast SSE instructions for CPU based code.

Before profiling the application, the environment needs to be equipped with the following variables:

```
$ export COMPUTE_PROFILE=1        # 1 is on, 0 is off
$ export PGI_ACC_TIME=0           # 1 is on, 0 is off
$ export CUDA_PROFILE_LOG=./cuda_profile_out
$ export CUDA_PROFILE_CONFIG=${HOME}/cuda_prof.config
```

where COMPUTE_PROFILE enables the profiling (setting PGI_ACC_TIME would print a sum of the time needed for data movement between CPU and GPU and the time needed for computation on the GPU to the terminal). Once the application runs, it will store all relevant profiling output in cuda_profile_out inside the current working directory. The variable CUDA_PROFILE_CONFIG points to a configuration file that controls what metric is to be included in the profiling output (for more options see the online CUDA profiler documentation[1]). In our case, we added regperthread to the configuration file to extend the default output by the number of registers used per kernel.

For our large execution setup, which ran for 60 s on one node with one rank and one GPU, this produced a 210 MB ASCII text file. Amongst others, it contains the following information:

```
method=[ advec_u_ws_acc_2234_gpu ]
gputime=[ 1557.472 ]
regperthread=[ 160 ]
occupancy=[ 0.375 ]
```

The metrics in the above list give information about the name of the kernel which was profiled (method) and the time measured in microseconds spent on the GPU device during execution (gputime). Also the number of registers required by a kernel is given by regperthread, and occupancy gives the occupancy of the

---

[1] http://docs.nvidia.com/cuda/profiler-users-guide/#command-line-profiler-control.

GPU, which is used to determine how much of the computational capacity of the GPU is used by this single kernel. All of this information helped us to have a rapid turn-around frequency while doing GPU dedicated optimizations. So, rather than applying a sophisticated profiler like Score-P and Vampir, we had a very quick feedback to the changes we just made to our code. However, as the command-line based CUDA profiler can be difficult to use, one has to know exactly how to extract the needed information. Otherwise, using the NVIDIA Visual Profiler is inevitable as it contains very helpful visualizations, occupancy calculation, automatic kernel runtime analysis, etc.

Our porting approach was to add OpenACC directives to the hot-spot subroutines and wrap them into data regions. Inside a data region data are kept on the GPU and data transfer is limited to the beginning and the end of the data region as long as it is not explicitly initiated by, e.g., !$acc update. As porting progressed, the data regions grew and were pushed upward in the call stack, and as soon as the boundaries of two data regions collided, they were joined into one bigger data region. The code parts containing the OpenACC directives look mostly as follows:

```
!$acc data copyin( temp, u, v, w )
[...]
!$acc kernels present( temp, u, v, w )
DO  i = i_left, i_right
   DO  j = j_south, j_north
      DO  k = 1, nzt
         temp(k,j,i) = u(k,j,i) + v(k,j,i) + w(k,j,i)   !some work
      ENDDO
   ENDDO
ENDDO
!$acc end kernels

CALL completely_ported_subroutine
[...]
!$acc end data
```

where !$acc data copyin(temp, u, v, w) initiates the data region and copies the arrays temp, u, v, and w onto the GPU. The loops are surrounded by a kernel construct using !$acc kernels and !$acc end kernels. This enables the compiler to optimize the loop for the GPU. Additionally, present(temp, u, v, w) informs the compiler which variables are already present on the GPU to avoid unnecessary data transfer from the CPU to the GPU.

Organizing the data regions efficiently is essential to gain additional speedup, as the data transfer between the CPU and the GPU can impose a bottleneck. This means that data transfer should be limited to a minimum and as much data as possible should be kept on the GPU. This, however, is not always feasible. Especially data output or MPI communication requires some sort of data transfer between CPU and GPU. Therefore, particular attention was needed as the data regions arrived at the MPI calls. In order to utilize GPUs on a multiple-node setup while minimizing performance loss due to the data-transfer bottleneck, it was necessary to implement CUDA-aware MPI. CUDA-aware MPI can be realized by employing the OpenACC directive !$acc host_data. It essentially makes the address of data located on the GPU available on the CPU. For a MPI_SENDRECV call the directive can be used as follows:

```
!$acc host_data use_device( ar )
CALL MPI_SENDRECV( ar, size, MPI_REAL, left,  0,          &
                   ar, size, MPI_REAL, right, 0,          &
                   comm2d, status, ierr )
!$acc end host_data
```

The directive !$acc host_data use_device(ar) followed by an MPI call involving the array ar enables data transfer of ar directly between GPUs without a detour via their related host CPUs. The MPI call shown above, however, is a fairly simple example. PALM utilizes many different MPI functions in several parts of the code. MPI derived data types are heavily used in order to transfer slices of 2D and 3D arrays. These data types usually represent data that is non-contiguous in memory. We found that current MPI implementation releases like Open MPI v1.10.3 are showing a severe loss of performance as soon as non-contiguous derived data types are used in CUDA aware MPI calls. In case of 3D array slices this even resulted in a termination of the program due to a segmentation fault. Therefore we were not able to port these MPI calls to become CUDA aware. Instead we were forced to employ the OpenACC directive !$acc update in order to transfer the respective data to the CPU in advance of the MPI calls and back to the GPU thereafter.

```
!$acc update host( ar )
CALL MPI_SENDRECV(                                           &
    ar(nzb,nys-nbgp_local,nxl),   1, type_yz(grid_level),   &
                                  pleft,  0,                 &
    ar(nzb,nys-nbgp_local,nxr+1), 1, type_yz(grid_level),   &
                                  pright, 0,                 &
    comm2d, status, ierr )
!$acc update device( ar )
```

The penalty imposed by the data-transfer bottleneck greatly reduced our expected final speedup.

Finally, the FFT operations had to be ported to utilize the CUDA FFT library (cuFFT). As cuFFT functions are not available in Fortran, a C interface is required. We used the Fortran 2003 bind feature and the intrinsic module ISO_C_BINDING to make the cuFFT library available. After that work was limited to calling the cufftPlan1D routine to generate all required cuFFT plans which were then used in the subsequent calls of cufftExecD2Z and cufftExecZ2D for forward and backward transformation, respectively. At the end, the cufftDestroy function is called to release the resources allocated for the plans.

As soon as a routine was running entirely on a GPU, replacing the directives !$acc kernels with proper !$acc loop constructs enabled advanced loop tuning options. Assigning and varying the gang and vector size, we quickly realized that most of the times a simple !$acc kernels directive does the porting job quite well. On occasion, the data independency of loops was not detected correctly by the compiler. This is shown by the output, which is generated by using the $ -Minfo=acc flag of the PGI Fortran compiler. Adding some !$acc loop independent directives quickly solved this issue.

4 Performance Tests

With every check-in, PALM was getting faster on the GPU. In the end, the code ran and produced correct results. Within one week, we were able to port almost all the major routines of PALM to the GPU. Unfortunately, we were not able to finish all the porting work during the Hackathon. Back home we had to invest another couple of days in order to push the data region out of the main time loop.

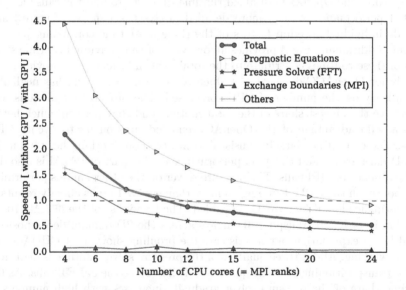

Fig. 3. The speedup factor (OpenACC-disabled runtime divided by OpenACC-enabled runtime) depending on the number of CPU cores (MPI ranks). The total speedup, the individual speedup of the tree most time consuming PALM routines and the combined speedup of the rest of the PALM routines are shown. Values greater than one (dashed line) indicate a performance gain and values smaller than one indicate a performance loss.

Finally we conducted performance tests based on a setup that filled most of the GPU memory and required a runtime of about 300 s on twenty-four CPU cores. We performed tests with the number of CPU cores ranging from four to twenty-four. Four is the minimum number of CPU cores required for the ported MPI code parts and twenty-four is the maximum allowed number of CPU cores for the setup, which still fits on one node. Each test is repeated with one GPU (OpenACC enabled) and without GPU (OpenACC disabled). The tests were conducted on a Cray XC30 at the North-German Supercomputing Alliance (HLRN). The compute node was a symmetric multiprocessing (SMP) node with four Intel Xeon 8-core SandyBridge Processors and one NVidia Tesla K40 attached. The node was exclusively used for the test and each test was repeated ten times in order to level out performance fluctuation. The tests were performed using the double precision floating point format. The results are presented in Fig. 3. The speedup factor calculated by comparing the runtime of the OpenACC-enabled tests and the OpenACC-disabled tests is shown depending on the number of CPU cores (MPI ranks). In total a solid advantage of the OpenACC-enabled runs on up to ten CPU cores can be observed. Increasing the number of CPU cores further resulted in a speedup factor of less than one which is a performance loss induced by utilizing the GPU. Using twenty-four CPU cores resulted in an OpenACC-enabled runtime that was almost doubled compared to the OpenACC-disabled runtime. In order to find the cause for this limited performance gain, a more detailed analysis is required. Figure 3 also provide individual speedup factors of the three most time consuming parts of PALM. Additionally Fig. 4 provides an overview of the individual runtime share each of these routines contribute to the total. This information is provided separately for OpenACC-disabled and OpenACC-enabled runs and has negligible dependency on the number of CPU cores used. The prognostic equations routines have the biggest share of the total runtime and they perform much better with a solid advantage of the OpenACC-enabled runs on up to twenty CPU cores. Theses routines largely consist of 3 nested loops working heavily on the big 3D data arrays and the good performance of this part of PALM is also due to the absence of MPI calls. The pressure solver on the other hand is performing very poorly on the GPU. Running on more than six MPI ranks already results in a performance loss if OpenACC is enabled. The heavy use of the MPI_ALLTOALL function in order to transpose 3D arrays across the 2D domain decomposition could be an explanation but in this case the profiling shows that CUDA-aware MPI is working. About three quarters of the pressure solver runtime is dedicated to the transpositioning and one quarter is dedicated to the cuFFT calls. As the runtime share of the pressure solver gradually increases with high numbers of MPI ranks, the impact of the observed performance loss with OpenACC enabled could be lethal in production runs (more than thousand MPI ranks). By far the worst performance loss, however, can be observed during the exchange of the horizontal boundaries between the MPI ranks. This routine only consists of a series of MPI calls that utilize non-contiguous derived data types with 3D arrays (see previous section). As we were not able to make these MPI calls CUDA aware, the loss can completely be blamed to the data-transfer bottleneck between host and device. We are aware that this issue could potentially be solved by wrapping the data array slices into separate buffers and unrolling the complex MPI calls into a series of simple MPI calls with MPI derived data types that are contiguous in memory. The complex data types however are deeply integrated into the software and any unrolling or change related to them entails a lot of effort. We therefore refrained from investing time into this approach. As MPI implementations gain capability in handling non-contiguous derived data types, we hope to see further speed improvements on the GPU. Finally it should be noted that the runtime of the OpenACC-enabled tests were not depending on the number of CPU cores used. The runtime variations between four CPU cores and one GPU versus twenty-four CPU cores and one GPU was around one percent. This shows that nearly the entire program is executed on the GPU. Brief tests comparing one node using twenty-four CPU cores and one GPU to two nodes using twelve CPU cores and one GPU on each node were conducted as well. As expected the runtime of the OpenACC-enabled tests were nearly cut in half as available GPU resources are doubled.

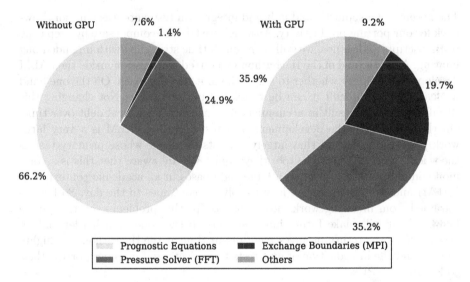

Fig. 4. Pie chart of the share the three most time consuming parts of PALM contribute to the total runtime for OpenACC-disabled tests (left) and openAcc-enabled tests (right). The share of all other routine runtimes is combined under "Others".

5 Summary

5.1 Porting Experience

We started our porting endeavor at the GPU Hackathon in Dresden with a partly and not correctly ported version of the computational fluid dynamics model PALM. During the Hackathon, which lasted for one week, we were able to port most of the routines of PALM to the GPU. We learned to use advanced profiling tools as a guide through such a porting process and we highly recommend their use for this purpose. The problems we faced taught us an important lesson about the significance of sophisticated testing capabilities in any software project similar in size and complexity to PALM. Also maintaining several mostly redundant branches of a code base in order to port or optimize for different computer architectures significantly reduced our productivity. Due to the difficulties we faced, we were unable to finish all the porting work during the Hackathon. However, the extensive and very helpful mentoring during the entire week gave us all the necessary knowledge and tooling to finish the leftover action items within a short time frame. The practical orientation of the Hackathon was responsible for an effective and valuable first-hand knowledge transfer. A deeper understanding of the OpenACC based porting concept and the architecture of GPUs in general was our reward.

5.2   Technical Conclusions

The absence of a sophisticated unit and integration test suite was a major drawback for our porting productivity. Although we tried to compensate by preparing testing scripts and setups, we still spent much time struggling with unguided bug hunting. After the end of the Hachathon we started a discussion inside the PALM developer community whether to adapt the unit test approach. On the one hand we learned how difficult it can be to extend untested code. Not changing this situation will only result in accumulation of more technological debt over time. On the other hand the development of a test suite for PALM is a very large work package for a team that largely consists of people whose primary task is the science and PALM is the tool they apply. We are aware that this is a common conundrum in projects with large code bases in an academic context (like PALM) and the discussion on how to solve it continues to the day. So far, we refrained from investing work into a solution to this problem even though we know that it will make future improvements to the code even harder and on top, decrease the return-on-investment of our time at the Hackathon. We highly recommend the introduction of unit tests to projects that consider porting their code-base to GPUs.

Our suggestion to institutions that are aiming to provide help for code-development teams like us would be to increase funding for manpower especially dedicated to code development and training therein. We suggest more research on how to make the introduction of unit and integration testing easier for existing scientific code bases especially in an academic and/or performance critical context (e.g., [4]). Additionally, a more detailed documentation of all the available OpenACC features could improve the effectiveness of any GPU porting work (e.g., online documentation including simple examples similar to the C++ reference[2]). With such a documentation at hand our first porting attempt might have been successful and reduced the time-expensive bug hunting. Especially the latest status of compiler implementation(s) and current limitations

---

[2] The C++ reference is available online at http://en.cppreference.com/w/.

are a valuable information and should be provided on a central website. For us this shortcoming, however, was greatly reduced by the extensive mentoring at the Hackathon. Therefore, we would like to encourage all involved institutions to continue organizing similar events. Their potential for first-hand knowledge transfer should not be underestimated.

5.3 Performance

The completely ported code was tested regarding its performance on one GPU and showed a solid speed improvement compared to the performance on up to ten CPU cores. Even though parts of the code are showing solid speed improvements compared to up to twenty CPU cores, the MPI heavy routines consume this advantage. We would like to emphasize our strong demand for a MPI implementation that is capable of handling non-contiguous derived data types in CUDA-aware MPI calls correctly and efficiently. Without such a capability the utilization of GPUs for large production runs of PALM and probably many other similar CFD applications will not be profitable.

Acknowledgments. We would like to thank the Oak Ridge National Laboratory (US), Nvidia Corporation Inc. (US), the Portland Group Inc. (US), the standards OpenACC committee as well as the Center for Information Services and High Performance Computing (ZIH) at Technische Universität Dresden and the Forschungszentrum Jülich for organizing the OpenACC Hackathon in March 2016. We would like to thank personally Fernanda Foertter, Guido Juckeland and Dirk Pleiter for organizing the Hackathon in Dresden. Further, we express our deep gratitude to Dave Norton (Portland Group) and Alexander Grund (HZDR; Rossendorf) for their instrumental contribution as members of the mentoring team during the Hackathon. The author team consists of three PALM developers (Knoop, Gronemeier, and Knigge) and one mentor of the Hackathon (Steinbach).

References

1. TOP500 Supercomputer Site. http://www.top500.org/list/2015/11/
2. Adams, J.C., Brainerd, W.S., Martin, J.T., Smith, B.T., Wagener, J.L.: Fortran 95 Handbook: Complete ISO/ANSI Reference. MIT Press, Cambridge (1998)
3. Doar, M.B.: Practical Development Environments. O'Reilly Media Inc., Sebastopol (2005)
4. Feathers, M.C.: Working effectively with legacy code. In: Zannier, C., Erdogmus, H., Lindstrom, L. (eds.) XP/Agile Universe 2004. LNCS, vol. 3134, p. 217. Springer, Heidelberg (2004). http://dx.doi.org/10.1007/978-3-540-27777-4_42
5. Gronemeier, T., Inagaki, A., Gryschka, M., Kanda, M.: Large-eddy simulation of an urban canopy using a synthetic turbulence inflow generation method. JJSCE B1 **71**(4), I_43–I_48 (2015). http://dx.doi.org/10.2208/jscejhe.71.i_43
6. Hoffmann, F., Raasch, S., Noh, Y.: Entrainment of aerosols and their activation in a shallow cumulus cloud studied with a coupled LCM-LES approach. Atmos. Res. **156**, 43–57 (2015). http://dx.doi.org/10.1016/j.atmosres.2014.12.008

7. Knigge, C., Raasch, S.: Improvement and development of one- and two-dimensional discrete gust models using a large-eddy simulation model. J. Wind Eng. Ind. Aerodyn. **153**, 46–59 (2016). http://dx.doi.org/10.1016/j.jweia.2016.03.004

8. Knigge, C., Auerswald, T., Raasch, S., Bange, J.: Comparison of two methods simulating highly resolved atmospheric turbulence data for study of stall effects. Comput. Fluids **108**, 57–66 (2015). http://dx.doi.org/10.1016/j.compfluid.2014.11.005

9. Knüpfer, A., Brunst, H., Doleschal, J., Jurenz, M., Lieber, M., Mickler, H., Müller, M.S., Nagel, W.E.: The Vampir performance analysis tool-set. In: Resch, M., Keller, R., Himmler, V., Krammer, B., Schulz, A. (eds.) Tools for High Performance Computing, pp. 139–155. Springer, Heidelberg (2008). http://dx.doi.org/10.1007/978-3-540-68564-7_9

10. Knüpfer, A., Rössel, C., an Mey, D., Biersdorff, S., Diethelm, K., Eschweiler, D., Geimer, M., Gerndt, M., Lorenz, D., Malony, A., Nagel, W.E., Oleynik, Y., Philippen, P., Saviankou, P., Schmidl, D., Shende, S., Tschüter, R., Wagner, M., Wesarg, B., Wolf, F.: Score-P: a joint performance measurement run-time infrastructure for Periscope, Scalasca, TAU, and Vampir. In: Brunst, H., Müller, M.S., Nagel, W.E., Resch, M.M. (eds.) Tools for High Performance Computing 2011, pp. 79–91. Springer, Heidelberg (2012). http://dx.doi.org/10.1007/978-3-642-31476-6_7

11. Krizhevsky, A., Sutskever, I., Hinton, G.E.: ImageNet classification with deep convolutional neural networks. In: Pereira, F., Burges, C.J.C., Bottou, L., Weinberger, K.Q. (eds.) Advances in Neural Information Processing Systems, vol. 25, pp. 1097–1105. Curran Associates, Inc. (2012). http://papers.nips.cc/paper/4824-imagenet-classification-with-deep-convolutional-neural-networks.pdf

12. Letzel, M.O., Helmke, C., Ng, E., An, X., Lai, A., Raasch, S.: LES case study on pedestrian level ventilation in two neighbourhoods in Hong Kong. Meteorol. Z. **21**(6), 575–589 (2012). http://dx.doi.org/10.1127/0941-2948/2012/0356

13. Maronga, B., Gryschka, M., Heinze, R., Hoffmann, F., Kanani-Sühring, F., Keck, M., Ketelsen, K., Letzel, M.O., Sühring, M., Raasch, S.: The Parallelized Large-Eddy Simulation Model (PALM) version 4.0 for atmospheric and oceanic flows: model formulation recent developments, and future perspectives. Geosci. Model Dev. **8**(8), 2515–2551 (2015). http://dx.doi.org/10.5194/gmd-8-2515-2015

14. Maronga, B., Hartogensis, O.K., Raasch, S., Beyrich, F.: The effect of surface heterogeneity on the structure parameters of temperature and specific humidity: a large-eddy simulation case study for the LITFASS-2003 experiment. Bound. Layer Meteorol. **153**(3), 441–470 (2014). http://dx.doi.org/10.1007/s10546-014-9955-x

15. Martin, K., Hoffman, B.: Mastering CMake, 4th edn. Kitware Inc., New York (2008)

16. an Mey, D., Biersdorff, S., Bischof, C., Diethelm, K., Eschweiler, D., Gerndt, M., Knüpfer, A., Lorenz, D., Malony, A.D., Nagel, W.E., Oleynik, Y., Rössel, C., Saviankou, P., Schmidl, D., Shende, S.S., Wagner, M., Wesarg, B., Wolf, F.: Score-P: a unified performance measurement system for petascale applications. In: Bischof, C., Hegering, H.-G., Nagel, W.E., Wittum, G. (eds.) Competence in High Performance Computing 2010, pp. 85–97. Springer, Heidelberg (2012). http://www.springerlink.com/content/t041605372024474/?MUD=MP

17. OpenACC-Standard.org: The OpenACC Application Programming Interface, 2.5 edn. (2015). http://www.openacc.org/sites/default/files/OpenACC_2pt5.pdf

18. Páll, S., Abraham, M.J., Kutzner, C., Hess, B., Lindahl, E.: Tackling exascale software challenges in molecular dynamics simulations with GROMACS. In: Markidis, S., Laure, E. (eds.) EASC 2014. LNCS, vol. 8759, pp. 3–27. Springer, Heidelberg (2015). http://dx.doi.org/10.1007/978-3-319-15976-8_1

19. PGI: PGI CUDA Fortran Compiler. http://www.pgroup.com/resources/cudafor tran.htm
20. Reid, J.: The new features of Fortran 2003. SIGPLAN Fortran Forum **26**(1), 10–33 (2007). http://dx.doi.org/10.1145/1243413.1243415
21. Stallman, R.M., McGrath, R., Smith, P.D.: GNU make: a program for directing recompilation, for version 3.81. Free Software Foundation (2004)

Software Cost Analysis of GPU-Accelerated Aeroacoustics Simulations in C++ with OpenACC

Marco Nicolini[1], Julian Miller[1(✉)], Sandra Wienke[1,2],
Michael Schlottke-Lakemper[2,3], Matthias Meinke[3], and Matthias S. Müller[1,2]

[1] IT Center, RWTH Aachen University, Aachen, Germany
{marco.nicolini,julian.miller}@rwth-aachen.de,
{wienke,mueller}@itc.rwth-aachen.de
[2] JARA – High-Performance Computing, Aachen, Germany
[3] Institute of Aerodynamics, RWTH Aachen University, Aachen, Germany
{m.schlottke-lakemper,m.meinke}@aia.rwth-aachen.de

Abstract. Aeroacoustics simulations leverage the tremendous computational power of today's supercomputers, e.g., to predict the noise emissions of airplanes. The emergence of GPUs that are usable through directive-based programming models like OpenACC promises a cost-efficient solution for flow-induced noise simulations with respect to hardware expenditure and development time. However, OpenACC's capabilities for real-world C++ codes have been scarcely investigated so far and software costs are rarely evaluated and modeled for this kind of high-performance projects. In this paper, we present our OpenACC parallelization of ZFS, an aeroacoustics simulation framework written in C++, and its early performance results. From our implementation work, we derive common pitfalls and lessons-learned for real-world C++ codes using OpenACC. Furthermore, we borrow software cost estimation techniques from software engineering to evaluate the development efforts needed in a directive-based HPC environment. We discuss applicability and challenges of the popular COCOMO II model applied to the parallelization of ZFS.

1 Introduction

Aeroacoustics simulations play an important role in today's aircraft development to meet the challenge of reduced noise emissions. The C++ multiphysics framework ZFS [23,27,29] simulates aeroacoustics phenomena by typically leveraging up to 30,000 cores of traditional HPC systems for several days. Adding GPU support to ZFS promises an improved performance per Watt ratio [31]. However, low-level GPU integration for large frameworks like ZFS is tedious and requires considerable effort. The directive-based programming model OpenACC offers a cost-efficient solution while also enabling an incremental acceleration process. OpenACC has been applied to accelerate numerous Fortran and C codes in the

© Springer International Publishing AG 2016
M. Taufer et al. (Eds.): ISC High Performance Workshops 2016, LNCS 9945, pp. 524–543, 2016.
DOI: 10.1007/978-3-319-46079-6_36

last years [22,35,39], however, its C++ capabilities have been rarely evaluated for real-world applications.

In this paper, we investigate the interaction of OpenACC and C++ through our parallelization of the discontinuous Galerkin (DG) solver for aeroacoustics problems in ZFS. From our implementation, we derive major challenges and lessons-learned for real-world C++ frameworks. Furthermore, the application of the incremental acceleration process allows us to present performance results from the current development status. These performance results do not only include execution times on NVIDIA Kepler GPUs, but also show PGI's new feature to run OpenACC code in parallel on host CPUs [37].

While OpenACC's ease-of-use is often highlighted [24,39], the analysis of its actual software costs is outside the scope of most works. In software engineering (SE), software cost analysis and estimation is a widely-used technique, but only few studies also consider this technique for HPC environments. Here, we also analyze the software costs of our OpenACC parallelization by examining the popular COCOMO II model from SE. We discuss applicability and challenges of COCOMO II for directive-based HPC programming by comparing modeled human efforts with actual efforts as recorded in a developer diary.

For both the OpenACC parallelization and the software cost analysis, we build upon a typical use case in HPC: domain scientists, here engineers, have developed a code base comprising the algorithmic functionality. HPC experts then port this application to OpenACC by parallelizing time-consuming kernels and data structures. We will concentrate on this additional HPC implementation work and the corresponding effort needed.

This paper is structured as follows: Sect. 2 covers related work. In Sect. 3, the multiphysics framework ZFS is introduced. We describe our OpenACC parallelization, performance results and lessons-learned in Sect. 4. The software cost analysis of this parallelization using COCOMO II is carried out in Sect. 5 and is compared to real development efforts in HPC. Finally, we conclude in Sect. 6.

2   Related Work

Directive-based accelerator programming models like OpenACC have become more popular for GPU programming in the last years. Lee and Vetter [21] review some of them. Accelerating traditional C or Fortran codes with OpenACC is well investigated [22,35,39]. In comparison, OpenACC offloading of C++ codes to a GPU is less researched and Hwu et al. [16] even state that approaches like OpenACC are not well-suited for object-oriented programming. Peng et al. [25] parallelize a C++ Particle-in-Cell simulation code (iPIC3D) with OpenACC. They found manual deep copies and non-working atomic capture directives in an early PGI compiler version as main issues. The MPI Lattice Boltzmann code Numeric Fluid Channel (NFC) is ported to OpenACC by Blair et al. [1]. They see difficulties in class data members or anything behind the hidden C++ `this` pointer used within parallel regions and apply copies to local scope to fix these problems. We present lessons-learned from a DG parallelization with C++ and OpenACC.

Similar to our work, Xia et al. [38] parallelize a DG method with OpenACC. However, they base their study on a Fortran code with unstructured grid topology, and present two contention-free vectorization strategies to avoid corresponding race conditions. Finally, the C++ *finite-volume* solver of ZFS has already been successfully accelerated with OpenACC in a previous work by Kraus et al. [20].

Advances for exascale computing yield more complex large-scale hardware environments. Thus, effort required for developing and maintaining codes for this hardware is continuously increasing. An estimation of these implementation efforts enables increasingly-important cost evaluations and strategic project management beforehand. For SE projects, a variety of methods to estimate the needed effort has been studied and extensively applied [4,17,30]. However, only few works cover software cost and productivity analysis in HPC in general [11]. Most of these methods were evaluated during DARPA's HPCS program [8] from 2002 to 2006. Kepner [19] provide a corresponding overview of HPC productivity and differentiate common HPC workflows to the ones found in general SE. Wienke et al. [33] cover HPC productivity as costs per program run of OpenACC and other parallel real-world code versions. Here, we focus on the Constructive Cost Model II (COCOMO II) [6] that is widely-accepted in SE but little researched for HPC cost estimations. In our previous work [32], we linked an adapted COCOMO II to a Pareto distribution for modeling development efforts. Kepner [18] also looked at an HPC effort estimation with COCOMO II for a comparison of effort for OpenMP and MPI. In this work, we analyze all COCOMO II parameters for our case study and compare the estimated effort to real effort needed for a first parallel OpenACC version. In contrast to other works that evaluate efforts in classroom experiments [9,14,40], we investigate software cost for parallelizing ZFS for an HPC expert while keeping the user's perspective.

3   Aeroacoustics Simulation Application ZFS

ZFS is a multiphysics framework developed by the Institute of Aerodynamics of RWTH Aachen University [23,27,29]. We apply OpenACC parallelization to its aeroacoustics simulation component, which solves the acoustic perturbation equations (APE) [10,28] with a DG method. By solving the APE, the acoustic pressure field for flow-induced noise is predicted, e.g., the noise produced by an airplane. The DG solver has been parallelized using a hybrid parallelization scheme (MPI and OpenMP) and scales efficiently to more than 400,000 cores[1].

The DG method used in ZFS is presented in detail by Schlottke et al. [28] and is based on the discontinuous Galerkin spectral element method (DGSEM) [13]. First, the computational domain is hierarchically split into disjoint elements that contain, e.g., integration node coordinates and conservative variables in underlying flat data arrays that are accessed by pointers. Then, the elements are mapped to a reference element and the weak formulation of the system of equations is

---

[1] The High-Q Club, http://www.fz-juelich.de/ias/jsc/EN/Expertise/High-Q-Club/ ZFS/_node.html.

Table 1. Sequence of events for the DG implementation in ZFS including the top 5 hotspots with their absolute runtime t and their relative runtime p compared to the main loop.

Line	Sequence of events	Hotspot	t	p
1	main loop over time steps	main loop	14.20 s	100 %
2	calculate time step length			
3	integrate with Runge-Kutta			
4	calculate derivative with DG method			
5	prolong from elements to their surfaces	4. prolongToSurfaces	1.34 s	9.4 %
6	calculate volume integral	2. calcVolumeIntegral	2.74 s	19.3 %
7	calculate flux on surfaces	1. fluxCalculation	6.63 s	46.7 %
8	innner surfaces flux			
9	boundary surfaces flux			
10	calculate surface integral	5. surfaceIntegral	1.19 s	8.4 %
11	apply Jacobian			
12	calculate source terms			
13	integrate with DG solution	3. timeIntegration	1.38 s	9.7 %

developed. Within each element, the solution and the fluxes are approximated by Lagrange polynomials, which may be discontinuous across element interfaces. For the fluxes on the element surfaces, a numerical flux formulation based on a Riemann solver is used. The integrals of the weak formulation are approximated using Gauss quadrature, yielding the time derivative at each node inside the elements. A five-stage fourth-order Runge-Kutta method [7] finally calculates the solution state at the next time step. Table 1 gives an overview of the sequence of events for the DG implementation in ZFS. Most kernels, such as the prolong step (line 5), the flux calculation (line 7), and the integral evaluations (lines 6 and 10), consist of a loop over all elements or surfaces. Simulation size and accuracy are controlled by the maximum grid refinement level, i.e., the number of hierarchical cell refinements, and the polynomial degree of the DG approximation.

To test our implementation during the development phase, a convergence test based on a manufactured solution was used. Since it is very sensitive to errors, even small inaccuracies have a large impact on selected integral error indicators. In addition, a more realistic setup with a pressure pulse reflected at a wall is used. The corresponding computational domain is a cube with a solid wall at the face in z-direction, and it is initialized with a single, Gaussian-shaped pressure pulse in close proximity to the wall. It is then simulated how the pulse spreads through the domain. By changing the grid resolution, the runtime for each setup can vary from a few seconds to several minutes on one CPU node.

Program-internal timers in ZFS measure the execution time for the different parts of the algorithm. They create an event-driven profile that summarizes the runtime behavior of ZFS for the respective simulation. We use these profiles to identify the compute-intensive kernels before we start offloading them to the GPU. For the hotspot analysis, the solid wall case was simulated with a maximum grid refinement level $l_{\max} = 4$ and polynomial degree $p = 3$. We use *GCC*'s g++ 4.9.2 for the best-effort performance results compared to other tested compilers (Clang, Intel, and PGI). The hotspot simulation runs serially

Table 2. Excerpt from the development diary.

Duration	Kernel	Description
5 h	calcVolumeIntegral	parallelized outer loop over all elements [...]
3 h	calcVolumeIntegral	calculate flux on GPU [...]
13 h	calcVolumeIntegral	fix the data movement [...]
10 min	resetRHS	fully offloaded, data movement [...]
8 h	prolongToSurface	offloaded kernel and subroutine `prolongToFaceGauss`

on a Sandy Bridge EP E5-2650 at 2 GHz. Section 4.2 reveals more information about hardware and compilers test setups. Table 1 shows the five most compute-intensive kernels (hotspots) in the main loop. In total, 93.5 % of the main loop runtime is spent in these hotspots.

Information about the needed development time for parallelizing a specific kernel of ZFS's DG solver is logged with a manual diary (see excerpt in Table 2) and extended with a descriptive text on applied changes. Other development efforts like understanding the code base, arranging the development environment, tuning and benchmarking are excluded from the diary.

4   OpenACC and C++

Until now, OpenACC has been mostly used to parallelize C and Fortran codes and rarely in the context of C++. Offloading C++ code with OpenACC raises additional complexity due to its object-oriented nature. In the following, we describe our challenges encountered during the implementation of the C++ DG solver of ZFS with OpenACC for GPUs and present lessons-learned. Our intermediate performance results are compared to the existing CPU-parallel implementation.

Using OpenACC allows to incrementally offload compute-intensive kernels to the GPU. We reflect this approach by parallelizing the kernels independently. We started with the top hotspots from Table 1, added `parallel loop` directives to the corresponding loops over ZFS elements or surfaces, and optimized the data transfer for each kernel using various OpenACC `data` clauses.

The next step was to transform the code, such that the program compiles and the test result remains correct. While we follow a straightforward approach for parallelization with OpenACC in general, such code transformations for OpenACC with C++ were especially challenging. A detailed description of these transformations can be found in the following section. After all kernels in the main loop were successfully offloaded to the GPU, we minimized the overall data movement. During the whole implementation, we ensured that the simulation produces correct results for our test cases.

Listing 1.1. Code snippet of the `calcVolumeIntegral` kernel used on the CPU.

```
1  // Create temporary storage for flux values
2  const ZFSId noNodesXD = ipow(noNodes1D, nDim);
3  vector<ZFSFloat> flux(noNodesXD * noVars * nDim);
4  for (ZFSId elementId = 0; elementId < noElements; elementId++) {
5      ...
6      // Calculate flux
7      m_sysEqn.calcFlux(elements[elementId].m_variables, polyDeg, &flux[0]);
8      // Copy flux to time derivative
9      ZFSFloatTensor f(&flux[0], noNodes1D, noNodes1D, nDim, noVars);
10     ZFSFloat* ut = m_rightHandSide[elementId];
11     for (ZFSId i = 0; i < noNodes1D; i++) {
12         ...
13             ut[index] += dhat[i * noNodes1D + l] * f(l, j, 0, n)
14                        + dhat[j * noNodes1D + l] * f(i, l, 1, n);
15         ...
16     }
17 }
```

Listing 1.2. Working directly on the underlying flat data arrays.

```
1  // Get chunk size and pointers for variables and right hand side
2  const ZFSId noVariables = maxNoNodesXD*noVars;
3  ZFSFloat* restrict variables = elements[0].m_variables;
4  ZFSFloat* restrict rightHandSide = m_rightHandSide[0];
5  #pragma acc parallel loop present(variables,rightHandSide,...)
6  for (ZFSId elementId = 0; elementId < noElements; elementId++) {
7      ...
8      // Calculate flux; compute pointer to first variable for this element
9      m_sysEqn.calcFlux(&variables[elementId*noVariables], polyDeg, &flux[0]);
10     ...
11     // Compute pointer to correct subarray of the right hand side
12     ZFSFloat* ut = &rightHandSide[elementId*noVariables];
13     ...
14 }
```

4.1   Challenges and Lessons-Learned

The major challenges and implementation efforts of the ZFS port cover code transformations needed to apply OpenACC to C++ code. We present these code transformations and lessons learned during this parallelization.

Numerous of the following code transformations are necessary to offload the `calcVolumeIntegral` kernel to the GPU. We present them as examples and in the order they were encountered. Listing 1.1 summarizes the relevant parts of the original code for calculating the volume integral on the CPU.

Data Structures. Parallelization of the outer loop in Listing 1.1 (line 4) by adding **parallel loop** raises the problem of preventing the compiler from creating accelerator code for this kernel because it cannot resolve the pointers from the element class (line 7) to the underlying data array in this compute region. Instead, we had to work directly on the underlying flat data arrays to port this kernel to the GPU. Our corresponding solution is shown in Listing 1.2 in lines 3 and 9 and requires the following data structure of the underlying array: Storage

Listing 1.3. Access the system of equations by reference to avoid calling its copy constructor.

```
1  SysEqn* sysEqn = &m_sysEqn;   // Create reference to m_sysEqn
2  #pragma acc parallel loop present(variables,sysEqn,...)
3  for (ZFSId elementId = 0; elementId < noElements; elementId++) {
4      ...
5      // Calculate flux; use reference to system of equations
6      sysEqn->calcFlux(&variables[elementId*noVariables], polyDeg, &flux[0]);
7      ...
8  }
```

order, access pattern and size of the variable sub-arrays must be the same as for the parent element array. Data structures in ZFS already fulfilled these constraints and no further changes were necessary. Thus, we used this approach for all occurrences of element or surface data in OpenACC kernels. However, having to transform the code in this way results in less readability of the code and thus in higher complexity to detect errors.

Two-Dimensional Arrays. The volume integral calculation further accesses the member variable rightHandSide (Listing 1.1, line 10), which stores the DG solution that is later used for the integration of the Runge-Kutta method. This variable is represented as two-dimensional array with the element index as first dimension and the variable index as second. Two-dimensional arrays typically consist of an array of pointers to an underlying flat array that holds the data. However, this data layout hinders the compiler to resolve the pointers in the outer array to the underlying data. Again, direct access to the array data solves this issue (see lines 4 and 12 in Listing 1.2).

Copy Constructors. Due to persisting errors in line 7 of Listing 1.1, the compiler is still not able to generate GPU code. The function call to calcFlux seems to be the obvious problem. However, detailed investigations show that the object for the system of equations (m_sysEqn) in the compute region prevents the offloading. As typical C++ feature, the compiler implicitly calls the copy constructor of SysEqn – or its inheriting classes – to create a copy of the object for the GPU memory. The compiler further implicitly tries to generate GPU code for the copy constructor function and may encounter code that is not easily portable. In our case, calls to a system function in the copy constructor prevent the offloading and we recommend to move the object explicitly to GPU memory without calling the constructor. Listing 1.3 shows how we use a reference to the object in the compute region and copy it as one-element array to the GPU.

Data Races in Compute Regions. The flux for each element that is calculated by the function calcFlux of the system of equations in line 7 of Listing 1.1 is temporarily stored in array flux. The serial ZFS version uses the same memory for the flux of all elements in the loop. To avoid data races, the MPI version has a copy of this array for each rank. For the OpenMP version, the array is marked

Listing 1.4. Large array for the flux of all elements.

```
1  // Create temporary storage for flux values
2  const ZFSId noNodesXD = ipow(noNodes1D, nDim);
3  // Get sub-array size and pointer to array for temporary data
4  const ZFSId noFlux = noNodesXD * noVars * nDim;
5  ZFSFloat* fluxAll = m_temp; // array size: noElements * noFlux
6  #pragma acc parallel loop present(variables,sysEqn,fluxAll,...)
7  for (ZFSId elementId = 0; elementId < noElements; elementId++) {
8     ...
9     // Get pointer to flux sub-array of this element
10    ZFSFloat* restrict flux = &fluxAll[elementId*noFlux];
11    // Calculate flux
12    sysEqn->calcFlux(&variables[elementId*noVariables], polyDeg, &flux[0]);
13    ...
14 }
```

Listing 1.5. Indexing multi-dimensional tensors

```
1  #pragma acc parallel loop present(fluxAll,sysEqn,variables,rightHandSide,dhat)
2  for (ZFSId elementId = 0; elementId < noElements; elementId++) {
3     ...
4     for (ZFSId i = 0; i < noNodes1D; i++) {
5        ...
6           // do no use tensor class, compute indices instead
7           ut[index] += dhat[i * noNodes1D + l]
8                      * flux[l*noNodes1D*nDim*noVars + j*nDim*noVars + n]
9                      + dhat[j * noNodes1D + l]
10                     * flux[i*noNodes1D*nDim*noVars + l*nDim*noVars + noVars + n];
11       ...
12    }
13 }
```

as `firstprivate`, such that each thread has its own copy. For the OpenACC implementation, we created an array that can hold the flux for all elements (see Listing 1.4). We preferred working on this large array over privatization of the data due to the reduced cost of creating it only once as class member instead of creating local copies at each kernel start.

Indexing Multi-dimensional Tensors. The ZFS conservative variables for one element are multi-dimensional tensors and must be accessed like that. A dedicated class simplifies the tensor-like access to the data. It stores the pointer to the underlying flat array and the dimension sizes. Lines 9 and 13f. in Listing 1.1 show the usage of this class. However, this tensor class is limited in use for OpenACC offloading because the compiler automatically shares the variable, i.e., the object and pointer to the data array, among threads inside a compute region. Thus, the volume integral calculation uses incorrectly the conservative variables of a single element for calculating all elements' volume integral. To tackle this problem, we directly index the `flux` data array (cf. Listing 1.5, lines 8 and 10). Unfortunately, with that, we lose the tensor class' ease of use and the redundant code for the index calculation is more difficult to maintain.

Summarizing, using C++ classes did not raise any unsolvable problems itself. However, calling constructors and destructors in compute regions must be taken special care of. For some use cases, calling the copy constructor should be avoided by calling the constructor outside the compute region and moving the object explicitly to the GPU. Furthermore, deep copies of dynamically-allocated object data must be performed manually by the programmer. Sometimes it is better to work directly on the data arrays instead of using the object for referencing this array. Template classes and functions as used in ZFS did not lead to any problems.

4.2 Performance Results

We present early performance results of the OpenACC code version described above. Note that performance tuning has not yet been focus of our porting activities and will be tackled in the near future. We compare our OpenACC version to the already existing CPU-parallel implementations with MPI and OpenMP. In addition, we test the new PGI OpenACC multicore feature [37] that enables running OpenACC accelerator code in parallel on host CPUs.

We run all CPU performance tests on a single node that contains two Sandy Bridge EP E5-2650 @ 2 GHz with combined 16 cores and 64 GB main memory. We activate process/thread binding and use 16 ranks for MPI and 16 threads for OpenMP and OpenACC multicore. We compile all CPU-parallel versions with GCC's g++ 5.3 and PGI's pgc++ 16.4. The GPU version is tested on the same host node with an attached NVIDIA Kepler K20x GPU containing 6 GB memory. The OpenACC GPU version is also compiled with PGI's pgc++ 16.4 and -O1 flag. Higher optimization levels introduced instability in compilation and, thus, could not be employed. The test simulates the solid wall setup (see Sect. 3) with a maximum grid refinement level $l_{max} = 4$ to 6 and polynomial degree $p = 3$ and 5. We omit the combination $l_{max} = 6$ and $p = 5$ because the size of the GPU memory is insufficient to run this simulation setup. We will tackle handling bigger data sets in future. The performance results are illustrated in Fig. 1. They present the average runtime over ten runs on a logarithmic scale. Standard deviation is below 6.9 % for most test runs, except for the GCC MPI version on the smallest test setup (with 23.9 %) and for the PGI OpenMP version on the smallest grid with higher polynomial degree (with 12.0 %).

Meeting our expectations, the performance of the MPI and OpenMP versions is roughly comparable since they both exploit parallelism on the level of elements and surfaces. In contrast, results do not meet our expectations for the PGI's OpenMP and OpenACC multicore version: Their performance is not supposed to differ greatly (here a factor of 2.0 to 2.8) since both rely on the same threading implementation. A detailed analysis reveals that our manual code transformations in the OpenACC version, which were necessary for the GPU offloading as mentioned above, improves the CPU performance as well. The performance difference is especially noticeable for the modified indexing of multi-dimensional tensors (see Sect. 4.1) in the `calcVolumeIntegral` kernel. Instead, the original and base OpenMP code uses a tensor class whose constructor and destructor

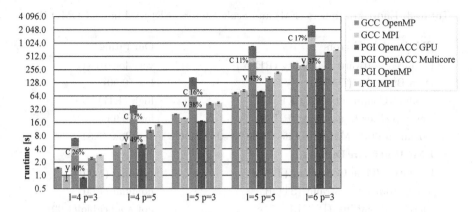

Fig. 1. Performance results and standard deviation of the parallel version runs of the ZFS DG solver.

are called for each element inside the loop (about 250 thousand times per kernel call for our largest test setup) and whose indexing operator [] is called multiple times for each element (up to 15 thousand times per element). Eliminating solely these expensive calls in the OpenMP version decreases the runtime difference of PGI's OpenMP and OpenACC multicore version to a factor of 1.7 to 2.2. The remaining performance difference is due to further transformations in the OpenACC version of the code. Comparing PGI's and GCC's OpenMP runtimes, we see a difference of 1.7× up to 2.2×. One reason are better C++ compiler optimizations with GCC. For example, interprocedural optimizations could be applied (in contrast to PGI) that seemingly resulted in similar code transformations as explained above. Finally, our current non-tuned OpenACC GPU-parallel version is 2.9× to 5.3× slower than PGI's OpenMP version. In comparison to the best-effort GCC versions, it is 7.1× to 10.2× slower than the MPI version and 4.7× to 11.5× slower than the OpenMP version. The runtime distribution across the two main GPU kernels is represented by the differently-colored bar shares in Fig. 1 (remember logarithmic scale). In comparison to Table 1, we see that the share for the `fluxCalculation` (C in Fig. 1) decreases from 46.7 % to between 17.0 % and 26.0 % while the `calcVolumeIntegral` kernel share (V in Fig. 1) increases from 19.3 % to between 37.3 % and 48.8 %.

Overall, our current OpenACC GPU version cannot yet compete with the highly-tuned MPI version of ZFS's DG solver, but tuning activities to leverage the full potential of GPUs are examined in the future. These optimizations include improvements to the data access patterns to better fit GPU architectures and further exploit potential parallelism. Nevertheless, we can see that an OpenACC-parallel code can also easily be tested in parallel on the CPU.

Table 3. Effort Multipliers (EM) and Scale Factors (SF) used in COCOMO II.

EM: Product Factors	Our rating
Required Software Reliability (RELY)	very low (0.81)
Data Base Size (DATA)	low (0.90)
Product Complexity (CPLX)	high (1.17)
Developed for Reusability (RUSE)	low (0.95)
Documentation Match to Life-Cycle Needs (DOCU)	very low (0.81)
EM: Platform Factors	
Execution Time Constraint (TIME)	nominal (1.00)
Main Storage Constraint (STOR)	nominal (1.00)
Platform Volatility (PVOL)	not applicable (1.00)
EM: Personnel Factors	
Analyst Capability (ACAP)	not applicable (1.00)
Programmer Capability (PCAP)	not applicable (1.00)
Applications Experience (APEX)	nominal (1.00)
Platform Experience (PLEX)	nominal (1.00)
Language & Tool Experience (LTEX)	high (0.91)
Personnel Continuity (PCON)	very high (0.81)
EM: Project Factors	
Use of Software Tools (TOOL)	very low (1.17)
Multisite Development (SITE)	nominal (1.00)
Required Development Schedule (SCED)	high (1.00)
Scale Factors	**Our rating**
Precedentedness (PREC)	norm (3.72)
Development Flexibility (FLEX)	high (2.03)
Architecture/Risk Resolution (RESL)	norm (4.24)
Team Cohesion (TEAM)	extra high (0.00)
Process Maturity (PMAT)	norm (4.68)

5   Software Cost Analysis

COCOMO II guides investment decisions for software projects in SE by estimating their needed development effort [6]. This effort estimate and corresponding development costs can be incorporated, e.g., into a total cost of ownership calculation (compare [33]) for HPC projects or centers. In the following, we summarize COCOMO II's Post-Architecture Model and how we apply it to the OpenACC-parallelization of ZFS. For that, we include a parameter analysis and highlight those with particular meaning in an HPC context. We compare our results of the cost estimation to the manual HPC developer logs of ZFS.

5.1 Overview of COCOMO II

COCOMO II is a parametric model [6] that is based on a regression analysis of historical software projects and measures the size of projects in thousands of source lines of code ($KSLOC$). The size of a software is estimated at the beginning of a project and is then refined with ratings of various factors influencing the cost of a project. These are, e.g., the quantity of reused code or documentation and they are rated from very low to extra high. These parameters are grouped into two categories: Effort multipliers (EM) are cost drivers which influence the size of a project in a linear way, whereas scale factors (SF) describe "the relative economies or diseconomies of scale encountered for software projects of different sizes" [3] (Table 3).

The effort model is divided into two main models depending on the state of the project. In the beginning of a project, the Early Design model provides an initial estimate. When reaching the Life Cycle Architecture (LCA) milestone [2], the Post-Architecture Model is applied instead. Key features for the LCA milestone are the identification of architecture drivers, like the required software reliability, which lead to the "definition of the software and architecture itself" [2]. Since ZFS' life-cycle architecture (cf. [5]) has been developed, the Post-Architecture model is used for all cost estimations. The main focus of this model is on the development and maintenance of a product and features the most detailed effort estimation.

COCOMO II estimates effort by

$$PM = A \cdot SIZE^B \cdot \prod_{i=1}^{17} EM_i \quad \text{with} \quad B = \beta_0 + \beta_1 \cdot \sum_{j=1}^{5} SF_j, \tag{1}$$

where PM is the resulting effort estimate in person months ($1\,PM \cong 152\,\text{h}$), A is a calibration constant of 2.94, and $SIZE$ is the estimated size of the software in $KSLOC$ with two calibration constants $\beta_0 = 0.91$ and $\beta_1 = 0.01$ [6].

An additional reuse model takes an existing code base into account. It models the effort for adapting the code base (re-engineering) to be reused for the current project at hand. It is calculated by

$$PM_{reuse} = \frac{ASLOC \cdot \frac{AT}{100}}{ATPROD}, \tag{2}$$

where PM_{reuse} is the effort estimate for the re-engineering in person months, $ASLOC$ is the estimated $SLOC$ which need to be adapted, AT is the percentage of code which is automatically re-engineered, and $ATPROD$ is the automatic translation productivity in $ASLOC$ per person month. The total estimated development cost of a project is the sum of PM and PM_{reuse}.

5.2 Methodology

COCOMO II estimates development time through $SLOC$, whose counting rules are defined by the COCOMO II Model Definition Manual [3]. The count of

$SLOC$ for ZFS was obtained by evaluating the relevant changes committed in a version control system. All $SLOC$ deleted to re-write the kernels (cf. Table 1) for the GPU are assumed to be adapted code ($ASLOC$).

The second type of input for COCOMO II are the parameters grouped in EM and SF. These are rated on a six-step scale from very low to extra high. In contrast to the well-defined rules of counting $SLOC$, the scaling parameters are subjective for many factors. Only about one fourth of the questions are defined by numerical values and almost all of the SF are based on the assessment of a person very familiar with the project. One example would be the required software reliability denoting "slight inconveniences" in case of a software failure as low values whereas "risk to human life" is rated high. COCOMO II parameters with particular meaning for the ZFS parallelization are discussed in the next section. All remaining or inapplicable parameters are set to the nominal value, which is 1.0 for all EM and between 3.04 and 4.68 for the SF [3]. To gather sufficient data for this rating, we conducted a detailed interview according to [12] with the OpenACC developer of ZFS, who is one of the authors. We then matched the answers to the rating scale from very low to extra high. After translating these ratings to numerical values as intended by the model, the total effort was calculated by (1).

In the next step, the estimation from COCOMO II was compared to data collected during the development. This data was obtained with a manual developer diary (cf. Table 2) and acts as the reference cost of the project.

We compute two estimations using the model: The estimation for counting all added $SLOC$ and a lower estimate for the added directives only. The latter accounts for an ideal case of a directive-only parallelization. This is, however, a theoretical approach since there were other changes needed to the base code for a numerically-correct execution on a GPU. Moreover, the effort is also estimated by setting all EM and SF to their respective nominal values. This nominal estimation is for comparison of this HPC project with an average software project.

5.3   Parameter Analysis for ZFS

At the beginning of the analysis, we focus on the model's complexity metric $SLOC$ and the different ways to count it for ZFS. First, the base code of ZFS according to COCOMO II is the total number of $SLOC$ of ZFS right before starting the OpenACC parallelization and accounts for 265 $KSLOC$. The effort needed to develop this base code is not evaluated since we are interested in the parallelization effort only. Second, the actual number of $SLOC$ of the porting to OpenACC was 563 added and 191 adapted $SLOC$. Third, we added only 54 $SLOC$ of pure OpenACC directives, i.e., about 10 % of all needed changes like code transformations.

Next, we analyze noticeable parameters of COCOMO II regarding the parallelization of ZFS. Refer to [3] to get a full description of these parameters. Our ratings can be found in Table 3. The required reliability ($RELY$) of ZFS is very low since a worst-case failure in the simulation software would require only a re-computation with a correct version of the software. Further, ZFS does not make use of a database ($DATA$) resulting also in our rating of very low. Product Complexity ($CPLX$) is a subjective rating of five distinct parameters which are combined in a weighted average: (1) Control Operations are rated very high due to the highly parallel nature of ZFS. (2) Computational Operations are rated extra high due the ZFS's complex numerical development. (3) We rate Device-dependent Operations high since ZFS executes operations at physical I/O level. (4) Data Management Operations is rated high because ZFS utilizes complex data restructuring and grid refinement methods. (5) ZFS uses very simple input forms and hard-coded output to log files which leads to the lowest rating (very low) for User Interface Management Operations. Combining the numerical values of all five ratings yields a total rating of high for $CPLX$. Documentation match to life-cycle needs ($DOCU$) is set to very low since the OpenACC parallelization of ZFS was not documented. The aim in HPC is to leverage all available resources, i.e., an extra-high rating of 95 % of the available resources for the Execution Time Constraint ($TIME$). As we did not tune the parallelization of ZFS yet, we use the GPU occupancy of the five hotspots of ZFS (cf. Table 1) as indicator for this parameter. A profiler reveals an averaged occupancy of approx. 15.5 %. Therefore, we set $TIME$ to the nominal rating (50 % or less usage of the available resources). Another method for estimating TIME is the roofline model [36]. Further, we rate $PCON$ very high since this project had no changes in personnel. The Use of Software Tools ($TOOL$) is rated very low since we used a repeating sequence of editing, coding and debugging. We delayed the deadline of the project by four weeks, i.e., roughly 25 % of the initial schedule, due to various obstacles in the set-up of the development environment for ZFS so that the Required Development Schedule ($SCED$) is rated high.

COCOMO II's reuse model bases its effort estimation on $ASLOC$ and on two parameters describing the automation of the adaption. The percentage of automatic translated (AT) code is set to 50 % since we adapted all code interactively. Automatic translation productivity ($ATPROD$) denotes the ratio of automatic translated source statements per person month. Since we did not use any form of automatic translation, $ATPROD$ is discarded from the calculations which yields a value of 1.

We also found several parameters to be not applicable to this project (see Table 3). For example, due to the small size of the parallelization, no analysts ($ACAP$) and teams of developers ($PCAP$) were involved.

5.4 Results and Discussion

The reference effort obtained through the developer's diary adds up to 65 h of porting time. It is split up into 22 distinct entries ranging from 10 min of porting to 13 h. The porting effort of each kernel was logged after successfully porting the respective kernel. However, this approach introduced inaccuracies of the development time due to the wide range in the time resolution.

Using the setup described above, the effort estimated by COCOMO II for parallelization and optimization of all $SLOC$ and $ASLOC$ is about 150 h of

Table 4. Results of the COCOMO II cost estimation.

Abbr	Settings	$SIZE$	$ASLOC$	Development time [hours]
RF	Reference cost	563	191	65.5
AC	All changes	563	191	150.4
DI	Directives only	54	–	10.2
NV	Nominal values of EM and SF	563	191	252.1
TU	Tuned ($TIME > 95\%$)	563	191	235.9

development (listed as AC in Table 4). Looking at the reuse model (2) only, the effort for adapting the 191 $ASLOC$ is estimated to about 14 h out of the total 150.4 h. The model's estimation is about 3× higher than the reference value (listed as RF in Table 4). One reason for the high estimation with COCOMO II may lay in the reference data of a manual development diary that can introduce inconsistent or incomplete data [15,26]. Assuming a self-overestimation in productivity of 13 % (taken from [15]), i.e., the actual effort is 13 % higher than the logged effort, would raise the reference cost to 74 h. Additionally, the diary excluded several development activities like tuning and set-up and focused instead on the main porting effort of ZFS's computational kernels and ended at a first parallel version. COCOMO, in contrast, accounts for the whole life cycle of a software project, which includes set-up and tuning efforts. In retrospective, we estimate the effort for our set-up in a new HPC environment to 20 h. Further, minimal tuning activities like data transfer optimizations have already been conducted and account for 6.5 h in the developer diary. Adding these two efforts would lead to a reference cost of 85 h (97 h with 13 % difference in the logging).

The estimation of COCOMO II's reuse model for adapting code shows to be inaccurate in terms of estimated effort for adapting $SLOC$. Our experience shows that a lot of the needed code changes were due to incompatible data structures on the GPU and could be reused only at parts of the code. Each unique adaption for the GPU required time for understanding the underlying problem. This development time is estimated very low compared to the total effort. One reason for the low estimate is COCOMO being based on large software projects with a lot of automatic translation of code with very little effort. Moreover, COCOMO's reuse model accounts for various techniques in object-oriented programming, like modularization and encapsulation, which ease the re-engineering process. In contrast, our adapted code parts were mostly specific to a kernel on the GPU. The low effort estimate for automated re-engineering can be observed in COCOMO II when applying the proposed default value of $ATPROD = 2400$ (cf. [3]). The reuse model is then almost omitted with an estimated effort of less than a minute.

Another estimation relies on counting the added OpenACC directives and statements only. This would be an ideal case, where no changes to the base code are needed except for OpenACC statements, and acts as the lowest estimation.

The size of 54 *SLOC* and the above settings result in an effort of only 10 h for parallelization (see DI in Table 4). This estimation of a directive-only parallelization is by a factor of six lower than the actual parallelization effort (RF) and by an order of magnitude smaller than the estimation of all *SLOC* and *ASLOC* (AC). This estimation is unrealistic for ZFS since the added directives and statements account for only approx. 10 % of the total size of the project. Moreover, COCOMO II was calibrated with large projects (several *KSLOC*) and might be inaccurate for small projects such as the porting of the DG part of ZFS to GPUs, especially for the directives-only estimation. This is, however, only an assumption since we could not record the effort for the directives without recording the majority of other changes as well.

For comparison, a nominal effort estimation was conducted by setting all *EM* and *SF* parameters to their respective nominal values. The result of this average software project estimate was even higher than the first estimate of our HPC project with about 238 h of development time (cf. NV in Table 4). This is especially surprising considering our initial assumption of HPC projects being more complex than general software projects because of high efforts of performance optimizations.

In the future, the parallel version of ZFS will be tuned to fully leverage the computational performance of GPUs. Since we only developed a first parallel version, the needed tuning effort can only be estimated by applying COCOMO II with a higher rating of *TIME*. When aiming for an close-to-optimal parallel version with an usage of more than 95 % of the available resources (*TIME* = extra high), the estimated development effort is raised to 236 h (additional 85 h for tuning) (listed as TU in Table 4). However, several HPC projects experience a tuning effort according to a Pareto distribution [32]. The distribution describes the effort needed to reach a percentage of the theoretical maximum performance of the underlying hardware. Accordingly, to reach the last 20 % of the maximal performance, 80 % of the total tuning effort is needed. This would result in approx. 54.4 h of tuning compared to the 6.5 h for this first-parallel-version. COCOMO II's estimation is therefore similar to the 80-20-rule mentioned above.

In conclusion, COCOMO II is not directly applicable to our ZFS case study. COCOMO II's complexity metric of *SLOC* did not fit our parallelization well and would have been infeasible or inaccurate to predict at the starting point of the project: We had only few added directives, but each required considerable time for analyzing and debugging, and numerous other complex code transformations on the base code were needed. Furthermore, the difference in effort varied across added and adapted *SLOC*: Correct parallelization needs usually a lot of development effort, other *SLOC* could be reused or can optimized with little effort through, e.g., compiler optimizations. This inaccuracy could be improved if more HPC projects similar in its size, programming model (OpenACC/C++), and use case were documented and analyzed according to the needed development effort. Additionally, an alternative base metric to *SLOC* could improve the accuracy of the cost model. A method for adapting COCOMO II to better fit the

HPC domain is proposed in Wienke et al. [34], which is based on a performance life-cycle instead of *SLOC*.

Finally, we also experienced several missing factors in COCOMO II that might be added to a cost model to better fit HPC projects: In general, adding directive-based parallelization to existing projects requires additional effort to understand the base code, to think about parallelism and to communicate with the domain scientist which is not captured by COCOMO II. Efforts to set-up the development environment, such as compilers, tools and needed libraries, can be very high and are also not included in COCOMO II. Further parameters of influence in HPC projects are delays due to scheduling processes and possible energy savings.

6   Conclusion

In this paper, we present the OpenACC parallelization of the aeroacoustics simulation software ZFS on a GPU and its software cost analysis with COCOMO II. We describe the incremental offloading of compute-intensive kernels and highlight code transformations needed to integrate OpenACC into a real-world C++ code. Lessons-learned include dealing with calls to constructors in compute regions, object-oriented data accesses, and data races. A comparison of early performance results of the OpenACC-parallelized code with PGI OpenMP simulations on the CPU shows 2.9× to 5.3× performance slowdowns. However, applied code transformations to OpenACC GPU code also pay off on the CPU: PGI's OpenACC multicore runs are up to 2.8× faster than respective OpenMP runs with PGI. Nevertheless, the performance of the highly-tuned CPU-only version built with GCC could not yet be reached.

Furthermore, we carried out a detailed parameter analysis for the cost model COCOMO II applied to the parallelization of ZFS and identified parameters not well-fitting or missing for HPC environments. We estimate lower and upper cost limits by investigating different parallelization scenarios and compare these with manually-tracked development efforts. Our analysis shows that COCOMO II is not suitable for our HPC project by overestimating the needed effort of the parallelization by a factor of 2.3.

In the future, we will tune the first parallel OpenACC version of ZFS and integrate a hybrid MPI/OpenACC parallelization to scale to large GPU clusters. We will also continue to log parallelization efforts for these activities to further investigate software cost estimation models in the HPC domain. In addition, we will extend our software cost analysis of COCOMO II by examining its sensitivity to inaccuracies in the input parameters.

References

1. Blair, S., Albing, C., Grund, A., Jocksch, A.: Accelerating an MPI lattice Boltzmann code using OpenACC. In: Proceedings of the Second Workshop on Accelerator Programming Using Directives, WACCPD 2015, pp. 3:1–3:9. ACM, New York (2015)

2. Boehm, B.: Anchoring the software process. IEEE Softw. **13**(4), 73–82 (1996)
3. Boehm, B., Abts, C., Brown, A.W., Chulani, S., Clark, B., Horowitz, E., Madachy, R., Reifer, D., Steece, B.: COCOMO II model definition manual, version 2.1. Technical report, University of Southern California (2000)
4. Boehm, B., Abts, C., Chulani, S.: Software development cost estimation approaches – a survey. Ann. Softw. Eng. **10**(1), 177–205 (2000)
5. Boehm, B., Clark, B., Horowitz, E., Westland, C., Madachy, R., Selby, R.: Cost models for future software life cycle processes: COCOMO 2.0. Ann. Softw. Eng. **1**(1), 57–94 (1995)
6. Boehm, B.W., Madachy, R., Steece, B., et al.: Software Cost Estimation with Cocomo II with CDROM. Prentice Hall PTR, Englewood Cliffs (2000)
7. Carpenter, M., Kennedy, C.: Fourth-order 2n-storage Runge-Kutta schemes. NASA Technical Memorandum 109112, pp. 871–885 (1994)
8. Dongarra, J., Graybill, R., Harrod, W., Lucas, R., Lusk, E., Luszczek, P., Mcmahon, J., Snavely, A., Vetter, J., Yelick, K., Alam, S., Campbell, R., Carrington, L., Chen, T.Y., Khalili, O., Meredith, J., Tikir, M.: DARPA's HPCS program: history, models, tools, languages. In: Advances in COMPUTERS High Performance Computing, Advances in Computers, vol. 72, pp. 1–100. Elsevier, Amsterdam (2008)
9. Ebcioglu, K., Sarkar, V., El-Ghazawi, T., Urbanic, J., Center, P.: An experiment in measuring the productivity of three parallel programming languages. In: Workshop on Productivity and Performance in High-End Computing (P-PHEC), pp. 30–36 (2006)
10. Ewert, R., Schröder, W.: Acoustic perturbation equations based on flow decomposition via source filtering. J. Comput. Phys. **188**(2), 365–398 (2003)
11. Funk, A., Basili, V., Hochstein, L., Kepner, J.: Application of a development time productivity metric to parallel software development. In: Proceedings of the Second International Workshop on Software Engineering for High Performance Computing System Applications, pp. 8–12. ACM (2005)
12. German Science Foundation (DFG): COCOMO II Cost Estimation Questionnaire (2000)
13. Hindenlang, F., Gassner, G., Altmann, C., Beck, A., Staudenmaier, M., Munz, C.D.: Explicit discontinuous Galerkin methods for unsteady problems. Comput. Fluids **61**, 86–93 (2012)
14. Hochstein, L., Carver, J., Shull, F., Asgari, S., Basili, V., Hollingsworth, J.K., Zelkowitz, M.V.: Parallel programmer productivity: a case study of novice parallel programmers. In: Proceedings of the ACM/IEEE SC 2005 Conference on Supercomputing, pp. 35–35 (2005)
15. Hochstein, L., Basili, V.R., Zelkowitz, M.V., Hollingsworth, J.K., Carver, J.: Combining self-reported and automatic data to improve programming effort measurement. In: Proceedings of the 10th European Software Engineering Conference Held Jointly with 13th ACM SIGSOFT International Symposium on Foundations of Software Engineering, ESEC/FSE-13, pp. 356–365. ACM, New York (2005)
16. Hwu, W.M., Chang, L.W., Kim, H.S., Dakkak, A., Hajj, I.E.: Transitioning HPC software to exascale heterogeneous computing. In: Computational Electromagnetics International Workshop (CEM), 2015, pp. 1–2 (2015)
17. Jorgensen, M., Shepperd, M.: A systematic review of software development cost estimation studies. IEEE Trans. Softw. Eng. **33**(1), 33–53 (2007)
18. Kepner, J.: High performance computing productivity model synthesis. Int. J. High Perform. Comput. Appl. **18**(4), 505–516 (2004)
19. Kepner, J.: HPC productivity: an overarching view. Int. J. High Perform. Comput. Appl. **18**(4), 393–397 (2004)

20. Kraus, J., Schlottke, M., Adinetz, A., Pleiter, D.: Accelerating a C++ CFD code with OpenACC. In: Proceedings of the First Workshop on Accelerator Programming Using Directives, pp. 47–54. IEEE Press (2014)
21. Lee, S., Vetter, J.S.: Early evaluation of directive-based GPU programming models for productive exascale computing. In: Proceedings of the International Conference on High Performance Computing, Networking, Storage and Analysis, SC 2012, pp. 23:1–23:11. IEEE Computer Society Press, Los Alamitos (2012)
22. Levesque, J.M., Sankaran, R., Grout, R.: Hybridizing s3d into an exascale application using OpenACC: an approach for moving to multi-petaflops and beyond. In: 2012 International Conference for High Performance Computing, Networking, Storage and Analysis (SC), pp. 1–11 (2012)
23. Lintermann, A., Meinke, M., Schröder, W.: Fluid mechanics based classification of the respiratory efficiency of several nasal cavities. Comput. Biol. Med. **43**(11), 1833–1852 (2013)
24. NVIDIA: Parallel Forall - OpenACC: Directives for GPUs (2012). https://devblogs.nvidia.com/parallelforall/openacc-directives-gpus/
25. Peng, I.B., Markidis, S., Vaivads, A., Vencels, J., Deca, J., Lapenta, G., Hart, A., Laure, E.: Acceleration of a particle-in-cell code for space plasma simulations with OpenACC. In: EGU General Assembly Conference Abstracts, vol. 17, p. 1276 (2015)
26. Perry, D.E., Staudenmayer, N.A., Votta, L.G.: Understanding and improving time usage in software development. In: Trends in Software: Software Process, vol. 5, pp. 111–135. Wiley, New York (1996)
27. Pogorelov, A., Meinke, M., Schröder, W.: Cut-cell method based large-eddy simulation of tip-leakage flow. Phys. Fluids **27**(7), 075106 (2015)
28. Schlottke, M., Cheng, H.J., Lintermann, A., Meinke, M., Schröder, W.: A direct-hybrid method for computational aeroacoustics. AIAA Paper 2015-3133 (2015)
29. Schneiders, L., Günther, C., Meinke, M., Schröder, W.: An efficient conservative cut-cell method for rigid bodies interacting with viscous compressible flows. J. Comput. Phys. **311**, 62–86 (2016)
30. Sharma, N., Bajpai, A., Litoriya, R.: A comparison of software cost estimation methods: a survey. Int. J. Comput. Sci. Appl. **1**(3), 121–127 (2012)
31. The Green 500: The Green500 List - November 2015 (2015). http://www.green500.org/lists/green201511
32. Wienke, S., Iliev, H., an Mey, D., Müller, M.S.: Modeling the productivity of HPC systems on a computing center scale. In: Kunkel, J.M., Ludwig, T. (eds.) ISC High Performance 2015. LNCS, vol. 9137, pp. 358–375. Springer, Heidelberg (2015)
33. Wienke, S., an Mey, D., Müller, M.S.: Accelerators for technical computing: is it worth the pain? A TCO perspective. In: Kunkel, J.M., Ludwig, T., Meuer, H.W. (eds.) ISC 2013. LNCS, vol. 7905, pp. 330–342. Springer, Heidelberg (2013)
34. Wienke, S., Miller, J., Schulz, M., Müller, M.S.: Development effort estimation in HPC. In: SC 2016: Proceedings of the International Conference for High Performance Computing, Networking, Storage and Analysis. IEEE Computer Society (2016)
35. Wienke, S., Springer, P., Terboven, C., an Mey, D.: OpenACC — first experiences with real-world applications. In: Kaklamanis, C., Papatheodorou, T., Spirakis, P.G. (eds.) Euro-Par 2012. LNCS, vol. 7484, pp. 859–870. Springer, Heidelberg (2012)
36. Williams, S., Waterman, A., Patterson, D.: Roofline: an insightful visual performance model for multicore architectures. Commun. ACM **52**(4), 65–76 (2009)
37. Wolfe, M.: OpenACC for Multicore CPUs (2015). http://www.pgroup.com/lit/articles/insider/v6n3a1.htm

38. Xia, Y., Lou, J., Luo, H., Edwards, J., Mueller, F.: OpenACC acceleration of an unstructured CFD solver based on a reconstructed discontinuous Galerkin method for compressible flows. Int. J. Numer. Meth. Fluids **78**(3), 123–139 (2015)
39. Xu, R., Chandrasekaran, S., Chapman, B.: Exploring programming multi-GPUs using OpenMP and OpenACC-based hybrid model. In: 2013 IEEE 27th International Parallel and Distributed Processing Symposium Workshops PhD Forum (IPDPSW), pp. 1169–1176 (2013)
40. Zelkowitz, M., Basili, V., Asgari, S., Hochstein, L., Hollingsworth, J., Nakamura, T.: Measuring productivity on high performance computers. In: IEEE International Symposium on Software Metrics 2005, p. 6 (2005)

Task-Based Cholesky Decomposition
on Knights Corner Using OpenMP

Joseph Dorris$^{(\boxtimes)}$, Jakub Kurzak, Piotr Luszczek, Asim YarKhan,
and Jack Dongarra

Innovative Computing Laboratory, Knoxville, TN 37996, USA
jdorris7@vols.utk.edu, {kurzak,luszczek,yarkhan,dongarra}@icl.utk.edu

Abstract. The growing popularity of the Intel Xeon Phi coprocessors
and the continued development of this new many-core architecture have
created the need for an open-source, scalable, and cross-platform task-
based dense linear algebra package that can efficiently use this type of
hardware. In this paper, we examined the design modifications necessary when porting PLASMA, a task-based dense linear algebra library,
to run effectively on Intel's Knights Corner Xeon Phi coprocessor. First,
we modified PLASMA's tiled Cholesky decomposition to use OpenMP
for its scheduling mechanism to enable Xeon Phi compatibility. We then
compared the performance of our modified code to that of the original dynamic scheduler running on an Intel Xeon Sandy Bridge CPU.
Finally, we looked at the performance of the new OpenMP tiled Cholesky
decomposition on a Knights Corner coprocessor. We found that desirable
performance for this architecture was attainable with the right code optimizations; these changes were necessary to account for differences in the
runtimes and in the hardware itself.

Keywords: Cholesky decomposition · Linear algebra · OpenMP ·
PLASMA · Task-based programming · Tile algorithms · Xeon Phi

1 Introduction

Linear systems of equations and eigenvalue problems are integral parts of many
different scientific and engineering applications. These codes can be very computationally intensive and much effort has been dedicated to increasing the speed
and efficiency of these codes. New accelerator and coprocessor architectures such
as GPUs and the Intel Xeon Phi offer the potential for increased performance,
but due to major architecture design differences (traditional CPU vs. accelerator), accelerators/coprocessors also have substantial overhead in terms of
optimizing old code to achieve the potential performance benefit of the new
architecture.

Developers of linear algebra libraries who want to utilize the Xeon Phi have
previously used techniques that offloaded the specific Basic Linear Algebra Sub-
program (BLAS) routines to the Xeon Phi, or used a hybrid approach that
offloaded some of the work, such as in Matrix Algebra on GPU and Multicore

© Springer International Publishing AG 2016
M. Taufer et al. (Eds.): ISC High Performance Workshops 2016, LNCS 9945, pp. 544–562, 2016.
DOI: 10.1007/978-3-319-46079-6_37

Architectures (MAGMA) [8]. This approach is designed based on the assumption that the controlling thread needs to be run on a separate primary processor such as is required for a GPU. However, the Xeon Phi architecture differs from a GPU in that it allows more complex threads than GPUs, which makes it more similar to a traditional CPU. This architecture, which has been referred to as "many-core," seems to be reverting back to a traditional multi-core lineage, and Intel announced that the next generation architecture (Intel Knights Landing) will work as a primary processor [17].

There are fewer options available for dense linear algebra when using the currently available Xeon Phi (Knights Corner) as a primary processor. Intel's Math Kernel Library (MKL) provides dense linear algebra routines on Intel architectures including the Xeon Phi. However, it is not open-source. Open-source software would allow developers to better understand the execution behavior of these routines and have the ability to customize parameters to tailor to their specific application. Also, MKL is not available for other non-Intel architectures that require effective and scalable dense linear algebra libraries.

One method for performing dense linear algebra on multi-core architectures is to use a task-based model for computations. This is the approach taken by PLASMA (Parallel Linear Algebra Software for Multicore Architectures), which has shown good performance on many different machines [1,4], but has yet to target the Xeon Phi due to differences in architectures. However, the implementation of task-dependencies in OpenMP 4.0 provides an opportunity to port this library to the Xeon Phi as well as decrease the size of the code base.

1.1 Contributions

The contributions of this paper are:

- We implemented a task-based tile Cholesky decomposition using OpenMP 4.0 directives based on the PLASMA linear algebra library.
- We compared the performance of using OpenMP's tasking dependencies with the previous dynamic scheduling mechanism.
- We measured the performance of this task-based tile Cholesky algorithm on Knights Corner.
- We investigated the execution behavior of this algorithm and discovered various ways of improving performance.

These contributions show the viability of task-based algorithms on the Xeon Phi architecture.

2 Background

2.1 Intel Xeon Phi Coprocessor

Intel developed the Xeon Phi coprocessor in response to the growing demand for accelerators to provide high performance and efficiency. The Xeon Phi's high performance is obtained by using a large number of cores, wide vector units, and multiple threads per core [10]. While code can be compiled for this architecture without major changes, reaching peak performance still depends on careful distribution of work across the threads and cores, as well as consideration of the vector units. Also, the Xeon Phi relies heavily on effective usage of the caches, and it can be difficult to use the caches in a way that does not incur cache consistency penalties with this many cores.

The most recent model of Xeon Phi is called Knights Corner (KNC) and has 61 cores operating at 1.238 GHz. Knights Corner has a 512-bit instruction set and 8 double precision wide vector processing units. It also supports fused multiply add, so it is capable of 16 double precision floating point operations per cycle [5]. This gives Knights Corner a theoretical double precision peak performance of 1,208.29 GFLOPS.

Knights Corner acts as a *coprocessor*. It is connected to a primary processor through a PCI Express bus and has its own embedded Linux operating system that handles all of the scheduling functionality and process and thread management. The operating system stack allows for a secure shell interface, through which code can be executed natively; heterogeneous code is also possible using the compiler offload capabilities [10].

Threads. The main difference between the Xeon Phi and other Intel multi-core architectures is its use of up to 4 hardware threads on each core with a short in-order pipeline. These are different from *hyperthreads*, which can be found on a Xeon CPU, in that hyperthreads are hardware threads on an out-of-order execution engine. In a Xeon CPU, the full floating point potential can be reached using a single thread and the out-of-order execution allows it to tolerate latency. Additional threads are only helpful for more latency tolerance, but often put more pressure on the memory. For this reason, typically only 1 thread is used per core for dense linear algebra codes on CPUs.

The Xeon Phi, on the other hand, schedules using a simple round-robin scheme with its 4 threads, and is able to execute 2 vector instructions in parallel, but they must come from different threads [15]. This means that peak performance is likely only possible with at least 2 threads per core. However, providing 4 threads per core provides more latency tolerance and is what is typically recommended. Drawbacks to adding additional threads can occur, however, in that they can negatively affect caching behaviors which could be especially detrimental in codes that are not compute bound.

2.2   PLASMA

The Parallel Linear Algebra Software for Multicore Architectures (PLASMA) project was developed at the Innovative Computing Laboratory (ICL) starting in 2007 to provide high performance dense linear algebra routines for multiple socket and multiple core architectures [4]. PLASMA contains many different linear algebra algorithms and supports single, double, single complex, and double complex precision. PLASMA is able to efficiently use the hardware by leveraging algorithms that can distribute the workload, and a system of dynamic scheduling in which work is assigned based on data and core availability. Thus, this is a system of asynchronous, out-of-order scheduling of task-structured operations.

Tiling. The benefit of PLASMA comes from its ability to effectively distribute the computation to multiple cores that can operate simultaneously on their contiguous memory blocks. This maximizes the operations performed on the data cached by each core prior to eviction, while also limiting synchronization issues. It accomplishes this feat using tiling algorithms.

Tile algorithms work by first separating the matrix into memory contiguous tiles. Thus, a matrix of size N by N will be divided into tiles of size NB by NB, producing $(N/NB)^2$ tiles of the matrix. Operations are performed between individual tiles and then combined to produce the overall desired computation. The tile operations can then be performed in parallel, when there are no dependencies between them, with minimized synchronization points and without the risk of cache consistency problems.

Deciding tile size is necessary to obtain good performance, since overall performance is affected by tile size and number of tiles, but the process is not always straightforward. Because of factors like memory latency and throughput of a given architecture, tiles can become increasingly memory-bound with smaller tiles, and thus can have reduced performance. However, if the tiles are too large then there may not be enough parallel work to be effectively distributed to all cores.

All of the separate tile operations are self-contained tasks that have memory dependencies associated with the data to be operated on, and some dependency-based order of operations specified by the tiled algorithm. This can be viewed as a graph where nodes represent tasks and edges represent dependencies between them. This forms a directed acyclic graph (DAG), and a DAG representation can help discover work that can be run in parallel because there are no remaining dependencies. Ideally, a scheduler would be able to identify some of this parallel work and distribute the work in a way that would allow for the fastest computation. The ability to transform linear algebra algorithms into a task-based model provides a representation that helps simplify parallelization.

Scheduling. PLASMA has two types of scheduling available: static and dynamic. The static scheduling mechanism will assign tasks to cores before execution and the tasks will wait to begin execution until all of their dependencies are met. Task dependencies and completions are then tracked by a global progress table. Performance then depends on using the static pipeline [12]. However, this method lacks the ability to schedule all tasks whose dependencies have been met as quickly as possibly because the scheduling is performed beforehand and will not be able to account for variations in task execution times. Artificial synchronization points expose serial sections of code, and this can leave some cores idle. Static scheduling also cannot distribute the tasks as well across a large number of cores, and lacks generality in that the pipeline must be considered when designing the algorithm.

PLASMA is designed to achieve the best performance when using a dynamic scheduling mechanism. This is different from static scheduling in that as cores finish tasks they can be assigned any tasks whose dependencies have been met at runtime. This is considered "data-driven" scheduling. This allows better work distribution and less idle time on all cores.

The dynamic scheduling was previously controlled by an internal runtime called QUARK (Queueing And Runtime for Kernels). This scheduler was shown to perform very well for previous PLASMA work distribution on other architectures. However, when we compiled PLASMA using QUARK on the Xeon Phi, initial tests showed that QUARK did not produce sufficient performance because multiple Xeon Phi threads were necessary per core. While only slight modifications to the code could have fixed this problem, another solution presented itself when the PLASMA project decided to transition to a new dynamic scheduling mechanism... OpenMP.

2.3   OpenMP

OpenMP [6] was created in October 1997 to provide an easy method for exploiting shared memory parallelism. OpenMP is an API that uses a collection of compiler directives, library routines, and environment variables to control underlying implementation. It is now an option provided by most compilers including Intel, which allows it be a viable option for parallel programming on the Xeon Phi. It was designed in a way that focused on ease of use but still allows a wide variety of features. It has continued to add to this list of features over the years, one of the most recent being tasking.

In 2009, the release of OpenMP 3.0 added support for the tasking model of parallelism which added the ability for parallelization of irregular problems, which have recursive, unbounded loops. In 2013, the release of OpenMP 4.0 added new capabilities to allow tasks to specify data dependencies. This provides support for a task-based model for programs in which each task can depend on data which may be manipulated by earlier tasks. The program can then be represented as a DAG of tasks, and these tasks are made to execute on available hardware as their dependencies are met.

GNU and Intel currently support OpenMP 4.0. This new support for tasks with dependencies provides the necessary abstraction to allow PLASMA to easily replace its internal dynamic scheduler with OpenMP task directives, and thus be able to run on a Xeon Phi coprocessor.

2.4   Cholesky Decomposition

Algorithm. Cholesky decomposition is the decomposition of a symmetric positive definite matrix A into a lower triangular matrix and its conjugate transpose (Eq. 2). Cholesky decomposition is used for solving linear systems of equations, which is common in many science and engineering applications. The formula for calculating each matrix entry can be seen in Eqs. 4 and 5. As the matrix grows in size, this algorithm for solving the matrix will depend on accessing increasingly distant memory locations which can make the work difficult to parallelize and lead to memory thrashing.

$$A = \begin{pmatrix} a_{11} & a_{12} & a_{13} \\ a_{21} & a_{22} & a_{23} \\ a_{31} & a_{32} & a_{33} \end{pmatrix} \tag{1}$$

$$A = LL^T = \begin{pmatrix} l_{11} & 0 & 0 \\ l_{21} & l_{22} & 0 \\ l_{31} & l_{32} & l_{33} \end{pmatrix} \begin{pmatrix} l_{11} & l_{21} & l_{31} \\ 0 & l_{22} & l_{32} \\ 0 & 0 & l_{33} \end{pmatrix} \tag{2}$$

$$= \begin{pmatrix} l_{11}^2 & l_{21}l_{11} & l_{31}l_{11} \\ l_{21}l_{11} & l_{21}^2 + l_{22}^2 & l_{31}l_{21} + l_{32}l_{22} \\ l_{31}l_{11} & l_{31}l_{21} + l_{32}l_{22} & l_{31}^2 + l_{32}^2 + l_{33}^2 \end{pmatrix} \tag{3}$$

$$l_{i,i} = \sqrt[2]{a_{i,i} - \sum_{k=1}^{i-1} l_{i,k}^2} \tag{4}$$

$$l_{i,j} = \frac{1}{l_{j,j}} \left(a_{i,j} - \sum_{k=1}^{j-1} l_{i,k}l_{j,k} \right), \quad i > j \tag{5}$$

Tiled Cholesky Decomposition. PLASMA uses a tiled version of Cholesky decomposition. The premise of this method is to separate the operations that are taking place in the above algorithm to allow effective parallelization. The creation of this algorithm can be seen in the LAPACK User's Guide [2]. It is composed of the BLAS tile operations: matrix-matrix multiplications (GEMM), solving the triangular matrix equation (TRSM), symmetric rank-k update (SYRK), and Cholesky decomposition (POTRF). All of these are Level 3 BLAS, which means that they are no longer memory bound and the peak theoretical performance will increase as the tile size increases.

There are three common variations for scheduling the tile operations necessary to complete the whole computation. They all have the same tasks and dependencies, as they are performing the same computation. However, the order in which these operations are scheduled can vary, and these variations can drastically affect the view of the tasks presented to the scheduler, and thus the order of completion of tasks.

Scheduling Variations. The three variations of tiled Cholesky decomposition are: right-looking (Fig. 1), left-looking (Fig. 2), and top-looking (Fig. 3). The availability of work as seen by the scheduler can be seen in the task dependency DAGs in Fig. 4.

The right-looking version can be considered the most aggressive and offers the most parallelization with its breadth first task exploration. This is why right-looking was previously selected for PLASMA dynamic scheduling. The top-looking version can then be described as the "lazy" version because it is using depth first exploration of the task graph, which limits the number of tasks

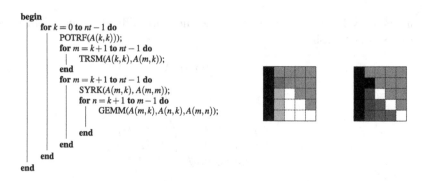

begin
 for $k = 0$ **to** $nt - 1$ **do**
  POTRF($A(k,k)$));
  for $m = k+1$ **to** $nt - 1$ **do**
   TRSM($A(k,k),A(m,k)$);
  end
  for $m = k+1$ **to** $nt - 1$ **do**
   SYRK($A(m,k), A(m,m)$);
   for $n = k+1$ **to** $m - 1$ **do**
    GEMM($A(m,k),A(n,k),A(m,n)$);
   end
  end
 end
end

Fig. 1. Right-looking variation of the tiled Cholesky decomposition (green = GEMM, red = POTRF, orange = TRSM, and purple = SYRK) (Color figure online)

that are immediately able to be run. The PLASMA static scheduler uses left-looking Cholesky decomposition because it was determined to be the best for the static pipeline [12].

3   Related Work

This paper is building off of previous work that took place to create PLASMA at the Innovative Computing Laboratory [4] in order to broaden the scope of the library to include Xeon Phi coprocessors. Virouleau et al. [18] evaluated replacing QUARK calls with OpenMP tasks with dependencies on Intel and AMD multi-core machines, but they did not measure performance on the Intel Xeon Phi and also did not compare to the performance when using the Intel OpenMP runtime.

LibFLAME [14] is a dense linear algebra library developed at the University of Texas at Austin. Dolz et al. [7] tested running libFLAME on a Xeon Phi while attempting to balance task and data parallelism to maximize performance and energy efficiency. However, they did not consider algorithm specific effects or the possibility of different BLAS routines being optimal with varying numbers of threads (to be discussed later). OmpSs [9] and XKaapi [13] provide OpenMP tasking-like alternatives for task implementations of Cholesky decomposition on a Xeon Phi.

Knights Corner has been available since 2012, allowing ample time for analysis. Schmidl et al. [16] studied the performance of OpenMP programs as compared to an Intel Xeon Sandy Bridge in terms of memory bandwidth and overhead of OpenMP constructs when utilizing the dynamic scheduler. However, the authors were not looking at tasks with dependencies and the degraded performance with a large number of tasks (likely because it was written before tasks with dependencies were implemented). Fang et al. [11] studied the Xeon Phi Architecture and performance, but was not focused on optimizations to increase performance.

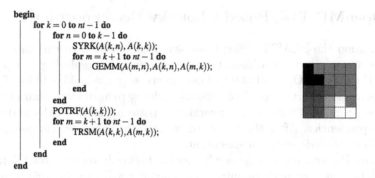

Fig. 2. Left-looking variation of the tiled Cholesky decomposition (green = GEMM, red = POTRF, orange = TRSM, and purple = SYRK) (Color figure online)

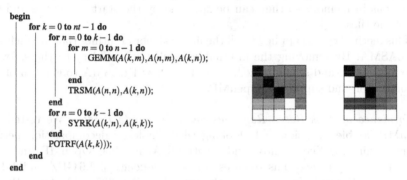

Fig. 3. Top-looking variation of the tiled Cholesky decomposition (green = GEMM, red = POTRF, orange = TRSM, and purple = SYRK) (Color figure online)

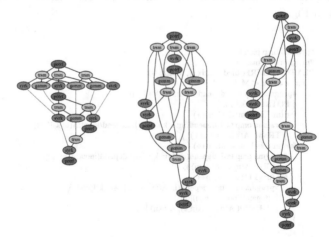

Fig. 4. DAGs for 3 variations of tiled Cholesky decomposition (from left to right): right-looking, left-looking, and top-looking. These show how the order in which tasks are presented to the scheduler affect the available parallelization (green = GEMM, red = POTRF, orange = TRSM, and purple = SYRK). (Color figure online)

4   OpenMP Task-Based Cholesky Decomposition

To transition the PLASMA tiled Cholesky decomposition to run on the Xeon Phi, we wrote the three different tiled versions in C, replacing the previous QUARK calls with OpenMP 4.0 tasking directives (right-looking in Fig. 5). This implementation starts a pool of threads with "**#pragma** omp parallel," and then uses a master thread to sequentially create all of the tasks and specify their dependencies. After the tasks are created, the scheduler can assign them to available threads/cores for execution.

OpenMP allows for specifying whether the task only needs to read data (in:), write data (out:), or both (inout:). The scheduler will then be able to use this information to safely start tasks when data dependencies are met. Specifying the dependencies is straightforward with the tile layout because each tile is contiguous in memory so they can be specified by the start of the tile and the size of the tiles.

This method can be applied to all the linear algebra routines that are included in PLASMA. By removing the internal scheduler, it would make the software more minimalist and standardized, as well as allow PLASMA to gain all of the customization and support of OpenMP.

Performance of Task-Based Runtimes on Xeon Sandy Bridge. We tested the OpenMP double precision right-looking tiled Cholesky decomposition performance on an Intel Xeon Sandy Bridge with QUARK, GCC OpenMP, and Intel OpenMP. This processor has 16 cores, a clock frequency of 2.6 GHz, and 8 double precision FLOPS/clock to give a theoretical peak of 332.8 GFLOPS. We set the outer blocking size to be 128 and varied N from 128 to 14080 to see how the scheduling mechanisms behaved as the number of tasks increased. The results can be seen in Fig. 6.

```
#pragma omp parallel
#pragma omp master
PLASMA POTRF( tiled_matrix A, tilesize ts) {
    for (k = 0; k < M; k++) {
        #pragma omp task depend(inout:A(k,k)[0:ts])
        { POTRF( A(k,k) ); }
        for (m = k+1; m < M; m++)
            #pragma omp task depend(in:A(k,k)[0:ts]) depend(inout:A(m,k)[0:ts])
            { TRSM( A(k,k), A(m,k) ); }
        for (m = k+1; m < M; m++) {
            #pragma omp task depend(in:A(m,k)[0:ts]) depend(inout:A(m,m)[0:ts])
            { SYRK( A(m,k), A(m,m) ); }
            for (n = k+1; n < m; n++)
                #pragma omp task depend(in:A(m,k)[0:ts], A(n,k)[0:ts]) \
                    depend(inout:A(m,n)[0:ts])
                { GEMM( A(m,k), A(n,k), A(m,n) ); }
        }
    }
}
```

Fig. 5. Right-looking tiled Cholesky decomposition with OpenMP tasks. This code segment shows how PLASMA-style tile algorithms can be expressed using OpenMP pragmas.

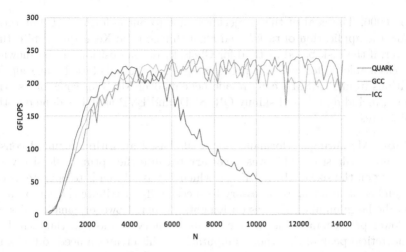

Fig. 6. Performance of double precision, right-looking, tiled Cholesky decomposition with different scheduler implementations on Xeon Sandy Bridge (QUARK runtime, GCC OpenMP, Intel OpenMP)

Based on the results, we can see that the GCC OpenMP implementation behaves similarly to the internally developed task-based runtime QUARK, which shows that OpenMP has the potential to be a complete replacement for our dynamic scheduler. However, the Intel OpenMP implementation has severely decreased performance when the matrix size N exceeds 4000, likely due to the large number of tasks. The Intel implementation of the OpenMP runtime is the only option available to the Xeon Phi, so this must be considered when optimizing for performance.

5   Task-Based Cholesky Decomposition on a Xeon Phi

5.1   Experimental Setup

Hardware. We ran all tests on a 61 core MIC 7120 (Knights Corner). We compiled our proof of concept code for this architecture using the Intel compiler and the "-mmic" flag. We launched every run using "micnativeloadex" which required 1 core for operating system functions and communication, leaving the other 60 cores available for the Cholesky decomposition. This left a theoretical maximum of 1,188.48 double precision GFLOPS, assuming each core was able to make full use of its vector instructions, use fused multiply add, and properly use multiple threads to perform 16 double precision FLOPS per cycle.

MKL Performance. To give a baseline for the possible performance of Cholesky decomposition on Knights Corner, we ran the MKL version 11.3.1 double precision Cholesky decomposition (DPOTRF) on matrices of varying sizes. The points tested for MKL performance were multiples of 200 and multiples of 256 up to 16000. The goal of this project was not to outperform MKL but rather to show the application of task-based algorithms on the Xeon Phi architecture. However, if the task-based method for Cholesky decomposition can be shown to have reasonable performance, it provides evidence that tile-based linear algebra algorithms from PLASMA can provide benefits over MKL for some of its other routines, including tall-and-skinny QR, SVD, and EVP as it has done on other architectures.

Tile Size. Measuring performance for a tile-based algorithm required considering various tile sizes. This was necessary because the optimal tile size varies depending on the size of the matrix on which the user intends to operate. A certain number of tiles will be necessary to successfully distribute the computation across the large number of cores on Knights Corner. However, smaller tiles will have lower performance due to being more memory bound and thus will limit the theoretical peak of the whole computation. This creates a need to find a tile size that balances these two considerations optimally for the overall matrix size. PLASMA intends to have desirable performance for all ranges of matrix sizes, so extensive testing on a wide range of tile sizes was required.

BLAS Library. We used the Intel multi-threaded MKL math library for the individual tile kernels (GEMM, POTRF, TRSM, and SYRK), which is optimized for Xeon Phi cores. This means that the computation used nested levels of threading. The top level distributed the work across the many cores and the second level provided multiple hardware threads for MKL. MKL could easily be replaced with other libraries as they become available or if they are necessary for another architecture.

Warmup. The first time we run an MKL routine, we incur some overhead from loading the libraries. When used in practice, it is likely that many calls will be made to these linear algebra routines, so this overhead can be ignored when timing for performance measurement. To account for this extra overhead, the PLASMA library timing examples provide a command line option to do a dry run of the algorithm once before running a computation for timing. This option must be used for all timings, and a warmup method was also used before the MKL performance measurement in Fig. 16.

Traces. To help understand the flow of execution and the scheduling of work on cores, traces were used (Figs. 7, 8, 13, and 14). These are figures that show the compute cores on the y axis and time along the x axis. This is a helpful tool for viewing how the computation progresses and how tasks are scheduled on the cores. These figures can also provide insight into factors that affect performance. Creating this visualization involved keeping track of which core the kernels ran on and the start and completion times for each. We recompiled the code separately with these function calls when tracing, and these runs were not used for measuring performance. The colored blocks on the trace represent the kernel that is running: green = GEMM, red = POTRF, orange = TRSM, and purple = SYRK.

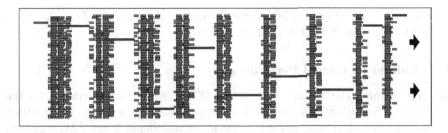

Fig. 7. PLASMA OpenMP Cholesky decomposition trace: all kernels use 4 threads (incomplete) (Color figure online)

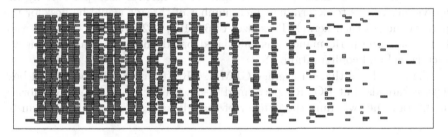

Fig. 8. PLASMA OpenMP Cholesky decomposition trace: DGEMM, DSYRK, and DTRSM use 4 threads, and DPOTRF uses 1 thread (Color figure online)

5.2 Execution Environment

Running a program using OpenMP on a Xeon Phi can be controlled by a large number of environment variables. These variables communicate to the Xeon Phi operating system and OpenMP about what hardware to use, how to schedule work on that hardware, the available threads, and many other customizations. We discovered, through investigation and testing, that the desired behavior of tiled OpenMP Cholesky required setting the following variables:

- KMP_PLACE_THREADS = 60t, 4c - use 60 cores and 4 hardware threads on each
- KMP_HOT_TEAMS_MODE = 1 - allows OpenMP threads to stay alive
- KMP_HOT_TEAMS_MAX_LEVEL = 2 - keeps nested level OpenMP threads alive
- OMP_NESTED = TRUE - allows multiple levels of parallelism
- OMP_NUM_THREADS = 60, 4 - a hierarchy of 60 threads and 4 subthreads
- OMP_PROC_BIND = spread, close - specifies how threads are bound to resources
- MKL_DYNAMIC = FALSE - disable MKL dynamic adjustment of threads
- MKL_DOMAIN_NUM_THREADS = MKL_DOMAIN_BLAS = 4 - suggests number of threads for a particular function domain

After we set these environment variables, we created an initial trace for the right-looking Cholesky decomposition on the Xeon Phi to discover what factors affected performance, and to gain insight into how the performance of the

Cholesky decomposition can be improved. A trace for a matrix of size N = 5120 and with a tile size NB = 256 is shown in Fig. 7.

5.3   Individual Kernel Performance

When examining the initial trace, the DPOTRF kernel, which consists of the fewest FLOPS of all of the kernels [3], is taking considerably longer to execute than all the other kernels. One can also see that in the task dependency DAG representation the DPOTRF kernels are a common path and a bottleneck for execution. These two observations make this kernel a prime target for optimization.

As a test, we decided to vary the number of threads used per core by the individual kernels to determine which number of threads would be best for the performance of each kernel. Tiles sizes of 64, 128, 192, 256, 384, and 512 were tested, and the performance was calculated based on the median runtime for each kernel and configuration.

Figure 9 shows that on average GEMM, TRSM, and SYRK performed best with 4 threads, but POTRF performed best with 1 thread. The MKL library allows runtime switching the number of threads used for a kernel, so it can be

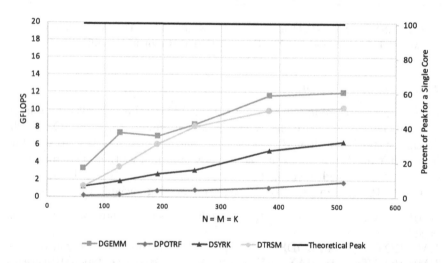

DGEMM Performance (GFLOPS)							DSYRK Performance (GFLOPS)					
threads	NB=64	NB=128	NB=192	NB=256	NB=384	NB=512	threads	NB=64	NB=128	NB=192	NB=256	NB=384	NB=512
1	2.963	3.486	3.104	3.404	6.384	6.570	1	1.133	1.875	1.970	1.971	2.295	3.003
2	2.805	3.998	3.807	4.635	6.583	7.674	2	1.057	1.794	1.726	1.711	2.145	2.834
3	2.675	3.478	4.530	4.244	6.705	7.869	3	0.993	1.659	1.470	1.527	1.947	2.682
4	3.297	7.321	6.925	8.331	11.592	12.036	4	1.199	1.830	2.665	3.121	5.295	6.367

DPOTRF Performance (GFLOPS)							DTRSM Performance (GFLOPS)					
threads	NB=64	NB=128	NB=192	NB=256	NB=384	NB=512	threads	NB=64	NB=128	NB=192	NB=256	NB=384	NB=512
1	0.137	0.220	0.748	0.792	1.088	1.724	1	1.304	3.262	3.960	4.176	5.395	5.323
2	0.100	0.062	0.426	0.544	0.944	1.627	2	1.331	3.623	5.420	6.828	9.092	9.272
3	0.091	0.036	0.339	0.480	0.826	1.402	3	1.267	3.350	6.096	7.457	8.164	8.478
4	0.081	0.134	0.323	0.333	0.802	0.884	4	1.214	3.427	6.050	8.061	9.894	10.199

Fig. 9. MKL v11.3.1 kernel performance on a single Knights Corner core

switched to 1 thread whenever the core is going to perform a POTRF, and then set back to 4 when the POTRF is completed to allow maximum performance for the other kernels. This decreased runtime and its effect on the trace can be seen in Fig. 8. The DPOTRF kernels complete much more quickly and therefore do not stall the execution of the other tasks to the same extent, which leads to increased overall performance.

This was an unexpected result, as it is commonly suggested to use 2–4 threads for peak performance. It was also very poor performance even with the best configuration which becomes obvious when one realizes that this scenario results in performance of less than 10 % of peak for a single core, with a tile of size 512 by 512. This result seems to suggest that an improved implementation of this kernel might be possible for small tile sizes, which would drastically improve performance of this algorithm, but is beyond the scope of this paper.

5.4 Scheduling Variations

The next test was to see which variations of tiled Cholesky decomposition (right-looking, left-looking, and top-looking) would perform the best on Knights Corner. Tiles of size 128, 256, and 512 were tested to observe the behavior of the different algorithms at different granularities.

The results are shown in Figs. 10, 11, and 12. For all tile sizes, the top-looking Cholesky implementation performed the best or equal to the other variations. While the right-looking implementation seemed to offer the most parallelism, and hence the hypothesized best performance on Knights Corner, this was not the case. Also, it can be seen that even when switching to the top-looking algorithm, using a tile size of 128 does not benefit from using a dynamic scheduler because of the immense load on the scheduler to manage the increased number of very small tasks.

The fact that the top-looking implementation, which was supposed to be the least aggressive, performed the best raised some questions as to why this was occurring. We obtained traces of a right-looking and a top-looking Cholesky decomposition at N = 5120, NB = 128 when the performance of each had diverged

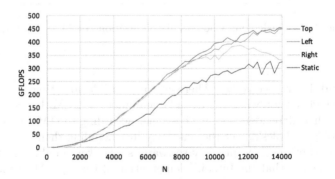

Fig. 10. Tiled Cholesky decomposition variations, NB = 256

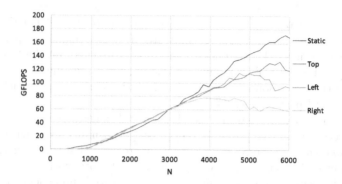

Fig. 11. Tiled Cholesky decomposition variations, NB = 128

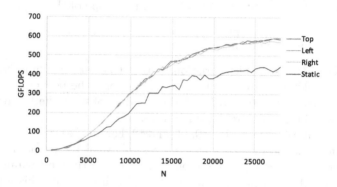

Fig. 12. Tiled Cholesky decomposition variations, NB = 512

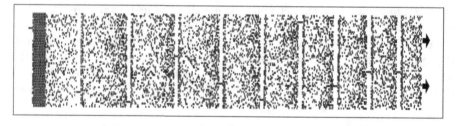

Fig. 13. OpenMP right-looking Cholesky decomposition-N = 5120, NB = 128 (incomplete)

(Figs. 13 and 14, respectively). There is considerable idle time on the right-looking implementation when there is a large number of GEMMs that need to be completed. Their dependencies have been met according to DAG representation for right-looking Cholesky, yet there is delay in scheduling them.

The Intel runtime is proprietary software, so we were unable to investigate further. We believe that the Intel implementation of the OpenMP runtime does not handle a large number of tasks well because of its method of maintaining the

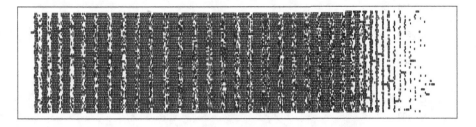

Fig. 14. OpenMP top-looking Cholesky decomposition-N = 5120, NB = 128

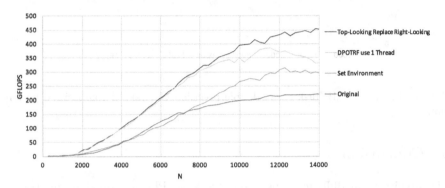

Fig. 15. OpenMP Cholesky decomposition incremental performance improvement (NB = 256)

tasks and the overhead associated with them. The top-looking version unrolls the DAG slower, so the runtime has less work when updating dependencies after the completion of tasks, and is better able to handle it.

5.5   Comparison and Final Performance

The combination of correctly setting environment variables, modifying the number of threads for DPOTRF, and using top-looking Cholesky decomposition—as opposed to the original right-looking Cholesky—offered the best performance. The incremental benefits of each modification, while using tiles of size 256, are shown in Fig. 15.

After these optimizations, the curves for different tile sizes can be compared to a standard LAPACK-style implementation in MKL. Tile sizes of 192, 256, and 384 are shown in Fig. 16 as they were found to have the best performance curves after sweeping through various tile sizes with all of the combined optimizations. In fact, as matrix size increases, the optimal tile size will also increase. This is caused by balancing individual kernel performance and work distribution. However, if set correctly by the user, tiled Cholesky decomposition can obtain performance comparable to MKL and can reach around 50 % of peak.

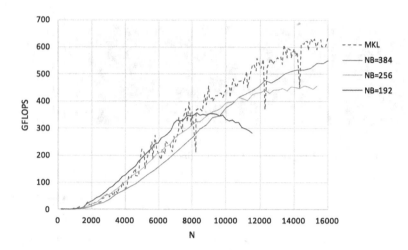

Fig. 16. Final OpenMP task-based double precision Cholesky decomposition performance

6 Conclusion

The architectural differences between the Xeon Phi and previous multi-core processors provided many challenges that had to be addressed to achieve good performance. This performance was only possible with multiple threads per core, which created hierarchical levels of parallelism that were not previously considered with PLASMA. Additionally, the optimal number of threads in this parallelism was not consistent between different kernels. This created issues like having to dynamically set the number of threads for MKL calls depending on the kernel.

The Intel OpenMP runtime had difficulty handling a large number of tasks, which added to the challenge. The improved performance of GCC OpenMP runtime implementation on a traditional CPU gives credence to the idea that this method of runtime could also provide improved performance on the Xeon Phi. However, until the Intel implementation is improved, we demonstrated that a method for mitigating these runtime issues is to use algorithms that limit the parallelism presented to the scheduler.

The PLASMA OpenMP framework can produce good performance for Cholesky decomposition on a Knights Corner after making only minor modifications. This proved that a port of PLASMA to the Xeon Phi will be straightforward and has potential for high performance.

7 Future Work

Many of the parameter configurations for optimal performance, such as using one thread for POTRF and choosing top-looking tiled Cholesky decomposition as opposed to right-looking, were based on underlying kernel and scheduler implementation issues that we believe may be changed in the future. The process outlined in this paper will need to be repeated for the Knights Landing processor to see if these decisions are still applicable. Also, PLASMA contains many other routines. Extensive testing is required for the other remaining algorithms to determine if any other kernels perform better with one thread, or if there are other factors that affect the performance. There is more work to be done before a Xeon Phi PLASMA release, but the applicability of this task-based approach to an order of magnitude more cores and the next generation of architectures is becoming evident.

Acknowledgements. This work has been funded by the National Science Foundation through the Sustained Innovation for Linear Algebra Software project (grant #1339822) and the Empirical Autotuning of Parallel Computation for Scalable Hybrid Systems project (grant #1527706).

References

1. Agullo, E., Demmel, J., Dongarra, J., Hadri, B., Kurzak, J., Langou, J., Ltaief, H., Luszczek, P., Tomov, S.: Numerical linear algebra on emerging architectures: the PLASMA and MAGMA projects. J. Phys. Conf. Ser. **180**, 012037 (2009). IOP Publishing
2. Anderson, E., Bai, Z., Bischof, C., Blackford, S.L., Demmel, J.W., Dongarra, J.J., Croz, J.D., Greenbaum, A., Hammarling, S., McKenney, A., Sorensen, D.C.: LAPACK User's Guide, 3rd edn. Society for Industrial and Applied Mathematics, Philadelphia (1999)
3. Blackford, S., Dongarra, J.J.: Installation guide for LAPACK. Technical report 41, LAPACK Working Note, June 1999 (originally released March 1992)
4. Buttari, A., Langou, J., Kurzak, J., Dongarra, J.: A class of parallel tiled linear algebra algorithms for multicore architectures. Parallel Comput. **35**(1), 38–53 (2009)
5. Chrysos, G.: Intel® Xeon Phi coprocessor-the architecture. Intel Whitepaper (2014)
6. Dagnum, L., Menon, R.: OpenMP: an industry-standard API for shared memory programming. IEEE Comput. Sci. Eng. **5**(1), 46–55 (1998)
7. Dolz, M.F., Igual, F.D., Ludwig, T., Piñuel, L., Quintana-Ortí, E.S.: Balancing task-and data-level parallelism to improve performance and energy consumption of matrix computations on the Intel Xeon Phi. Comput. Electr. Eng. **46**, 95–111 (2015)
8. Dongarra, J., Gates, M., Haidar, A., Jia, Y., Kabir, K., Luszczek, P., Tomov, S.: Portable HPC programming on Intel many-integrated-core hardware with MAGMA port to Xeon Phi. In: Wyrzykowski, R., Dongarra, J., Karczewski, K., Waśniewski, J. (eds.) PPAM 2013, Part I. LNCS, vol. 8384, pp. 571–581. Springer, Heidelberg (2014)
9. Duran, A., Ayguadé, E., Badia, R.M., Labarta, J., Martinell, L., Martorell, X., Planas, J.: OmpSs: a proposal for programming heterogeneous multi-core architectures. Parallel Process. Lett. **21**(02), 173–193 (2011)

10. Duran, A., Klemm, M.: The Intel many integrated core architecture. In: 2012 International Conference on High Performance Computing and Simulation (HPCS), pp. 365–366. IEEE (2012)
11. Fang, J., Varbanescu, A.L., Sips, H., Zhang, L., Che, Y., Xu, C.: An empirical study of Intel Xeon Phi (2013). arXiv preprint: arXiv:1310.5842
12. Kurzak, J., Ltaief, H., Dongarra, J., Badia, R.: Scheduling linear algebra operations on multicore processors. Concurr. Comput. Pract. Exp. **22**, 15–44 (2010)
13. Lima, J.V., Broquedis, F., Gautier, T., Raffin, B.: Preliminary experiments with XKaapi on Intel Xeon Phi coprocessor. In: 2013 25th International Symposium on Computer Architecture and High Performance Computing (SBAC-PAD), pp. 105–112. IEEE (2013)
14. Quintana-Ortí, G., Quintana-Ortí, E.S., Geijn, R.A., Zee, F.G.V., Chan, E.: Programming matrix algorithms-by-blocks for thread-level parallelism. ACM Trans. Math. Softw. (TOMS) **36**(3), 14 (2009)
15. Reinders, J.: In response to a forum post on 'what is the relation between "hardware thread" and "hyperthread"?', May 2014. https://software.intel.com/en-us/forums/intel-many-integrated-core/topic/515522
16. Schmidl, D., Cramer, T., Wienke, S., Terboven, C., Müller, M.S.: Assessing the performance of OpenMP programs on the Intel Xeon Phi. In: Mohr, B., Mey, D., Wolf, F. (eds.) Euro-Par 2013. LNCS, vol. 8097, pp. 547–558. Springer, Heidelberg (2013)
17. Trader, T.: Intel Debuts 'Knights Landing' Ninja Developer Platform. HPCwire, April 2016
18. Virouleau, P., Brunet, P., Broquedis, F., Furmento, N., Thibault, S., Aumage, O., Gautier, T.: Evaluation of OpenMP dependent tasks with the KASTORS benchmark suite. In: DeRose, L., Supinski, B.R., Olivier, S.L., Chapman, B.M., Müller, M.S. (eds.) IWOMP 2014. LNCS, vol. 8766, pp. 16–29. Springer, Heidelberg (2014)

Using C++ AMP to Accelerate HPC Applications on Multiple Platforms

M. Graham Lopez[1][(✉)], Christopher Bergstrom[2], Ying Wai Li[3], Wael Elwasif[1], and Oscar Hernandez[1]

[1] Computer Science and Mathematics Division,
Oak Ridge National Laboratory, Oak Ridge, TN, USA
{lopezmg,elwasifwr,oscar}@ornl.gov
[2] Pathscale Inc., Wilmington, DE, USA
cbergstrom@pathscale.com
[3] National Center for Computational Sciences,
Oak Ridge National Laboratory, Oak Ridge, TN, USA
yingwaili@ornl.gov

Abstract. Many high-end HPC systems support accelerators in their compute nodes to target a variety of workloads including high-performance computing simulations, big data / data analytics codes and visualization. To program both the CPU cores and attached accelerators, users now have multiple programming models available such as CUDA, OpenMP 4, OpenACC, C++14, etc., but some of these models fall short in their support for C++ on accelerators because they can have difficulty supporting advanced C++ features e.g. templating, class members, loops with iterators, lambdas, deep copy, etc. Usually, they either rely on unified memory, or the programming language is not aware of accelerators (e.g. C++14). In this paper, we explore a base-language solution called C++ Accelerated Massive Parallelism (AMP), which was developed by Microsoft and implemented by the PathScale ENZO compiler to program GPUs on a variety of HPC architectures including OpenPOWER and Intel Xeon. We report some prelminary in-progress results using C++ AMP to accelerate a matrix multiplication and quantum Monte Carlo application kernel, examining its expressiveness and performance using NVIDIA GPUs and the PathScale ENZO compiler. We hope that this preliminary report will provide a data point that will inform the

This manuscript has been authored by UT-Battelle, LLC under Contract No. DE-AC05-00OR22725 with the U.S. Department of Energy. The United States Government retains and the publisher, by accepting the article for publication, acknowledges that the United States Government retains a non-exclusive, paid-up, irrevocable, world-wide license to publish or reproduce the published form of this manuscript, or allow others to do so, for United States Government purposes. The Department of Energy will provide public access to these results of federally sponsored research in accordance with the DOE Public Access Plan (http://energy.gov/downloads/doe-public-access-plan). This paper is authored by an employee(s) of the United States Government and is in the public domain. Non-exclusive copying or redistribution is allowed, provided that the article citation is given and the authors and agency are clearly identified as its source.

© Springer International Publishing AG 2016
M. Taufer et al. (Eds.): ISC High Performance Workshops 2016, LNCS 9945, pp. 563–576, 2016.
DOI: 10.1007/978-3-319-46079-6_38

functionality needed for future C++ standards to support accelerators with discrete memory spaces.

Keywords: HPC · C++ for Accelerators · C++ AMP · Accelerator programming

1 Introduction and Background

With various accelerator architectures emerging in the HPC space, there have been renewed concerns about available programming models and their ability to provide performance portability for applications across platforms. To address these issues, there are a few efforts in development that, like C++ Accelerated Massive Parallelism (AMP), make heavy use of C++ language features. Kokkos [1] and RAJA [2] are template-based library solutions that attempt to hide low-level implementation details from the application developer to achieve good performance on multiple architectures. Unlike Kokkos/RAJA, AMP attempts to extend the C++ language directly to deal with accelerator programming and non-contiguous memories. There is slow progress being made in the C++ language standard as well, with a conservative proposal [3] to include preliminary support for generic parallelism in the upcoming C++17 standard. However, the present proposal lacks sufficient expressiveness to deal with the multiple memory address spaces and complex compute and memory hierarchies found in today's accelerator platforms. OpenMP [4,5] 4 and OpenACC [6] provide directive-based approaches to program C++ on accelerators but fall short on supporting many advanced C++ features (deep copy, STLs, etc.) and alternative approaches need to be explored. Perhaps the most similar programming model to AMP is NVIDIA's CUDA. Both allow the programmer to specify arbitrary compute kernels in the (slightly extended) native language, as well as directly managing the data transfer between host and device or relying on implicit transfer features of the runtime. The main differences are that CUDA is a single-vendor defined model optimized for a specific architecture, while AMP is an open standard that can be implemented by any compiler to target various accelerators. AMP also hides the low-level details a little bit more by discarding the concepts of threads, grid blocks, etc. that are usually specified in the CUDA programming model.

While C++ AMP is not widely implemented at present, it does attempt to offer a complete and open language-based solution for programming GPUs with discrete memory spaces while allowing the application to continue to use advanced features of C++. In this paper, we first give a brief overview of the main syntactic and semantic features of C++ AMP which provide the context for a preliminary evaluation of C++ AMP using both a well-understood and compute-bound kernel, matrix-matrix multiplication (GEMM), as well as an "in-the-wild" kernel from a quantum Monte Carlo application called QMCPACK. We then show the code transformations involved when using this model for each kernel and present some preliminary performance impressions using an experimental compiler-based implementation. Finally, we discuss our experiences with AMP in the context of new and upcoming C++ language standards as they apply to accelerator programming.

1.1   C++ AMP

C++ AMP is an open specification [7] based on a namespace that provides accelerator programming extensions to the C++ programming language. It is published by Microsoft Corporation, with input from PathScale Inc, NVIDIA Corporation, and Advanced Micro Devices Inc. (AMD). It supports offload of data-parallel algorithms to discrete accelerators like GPUs. The first implementation for C++ AMP was introduced in Microsoft Visual Studio 2012 [8], and experimental support has emerged in the PathScale [9] and LLVM/Clang [10,11] compilers as well.

When using C++ AMP, the programmer describes the computation to be performed on the accelerator by specifying the iteration space and the kernel to be applied over that space. The `parallel_for_each()` routine provides the mechanism for iterating through a domain. The computational kernel to execute on the accelerator is given by a lambda with the `restrict(amp)` keyword which indicates that the kernel contains the restricted subset of the C++ language that AMP is able to accelerate. The set of threads used for parallel execution on the accelerator is specified by creating `extent` or `tiled_extent` objects. Additionally, double-precision precise math and fast math libraries are provided for use on the accelerator, as well as several common numerical libraries that have been released for the C++ AMP programming model under the open-source Apache License, including random number generation (RNG), fast Fourier transform (FFT), basic linear algebra subroutines (BLAS), and linear algebra package (LAPACK).

The primary way to transfer data to the accelerator is by using the C++ AMP `array` and/or `array_view` objects. These objects need four pieces of information to describe the data: the rank (logical shape) of the data and the datatype of the elements are passed as type parameters, while the data itself and the physical shape of the array in memory are specified using constructor parameters. The `array` class causes a deep copy of the data when the object is constructed with a pointer to the original data set. The accelerator is able to access and modify its copy of the data, and after computation, the data must be copied out of the object to the source data structure. `array_view` objects can be constructed and accessed similarly, but instead of explicit data transfer happening upon construction, data is transferred implicitly to the accelerator on-demand at kernel execution time. After kernel execution, the data can be directly accessed on the host, and synchronization can be guaranteed using a provided method. For both `array` and `array_view` objects, shapes must be rectangular (in N dimensions), and can either be specified manually for each dimension or by using the C++ AMP `extent` class.

2   Preliminary Results

We have prototyped the use of C++ AMP for both a benchmark GEMM and a QMCPACK application kernel using the Pathscale ENZO 6.0.9 compiler. This work illustrates the use of the basic C++ AMP building blocks to parallelize the execution of nested loops used in both GEMM and QMCPACK. For a preliminary evaluation, we used two HPC platforms that are of significant relevance to the INCITE [12] and CORAL [13] programs of which QMCPACK is a part: one based on a representative node of Titan [14] containing a 16-core AMD Opteron 6274 CPU attached to an NVIDIA Tesla K20X GPU via PCIe v2, and the second a Summit [15] test node containing a Power8E CPU @ 2.61GHz processor with a NVIDIA Tesla K40m connected via PCIe v3.

2.1   Benchmark Kernels

Matrix Multiplication. To evaluate C++ AMP functionality, programmability and baseline performance, we wrote a simple matrix multiplication kernel. Below is the code snippet [16] that was used:

Listing 1.1. Matrix Multiplication Kernel in C++ AMP

```
1 double *ha, *hb, *hc;
  // allocate and initiliaze host data
  void MatrixMultiply(ha, hb, hc) {

    array_view<double, 2> a(SIZE, SIZE, ha);
6   array_view<double, 2> b(SIZE, SIZE, hb);
    array_view<double, 2> product(SIZE, SIZE, hc);

    parallel_for_each(product.extent,
       [=](index<2> idx) restrict(amp) {
11          int row = idx[0];
            int col = idx[1];
            for (int inner = 0; inner < SIZE; inner++) {
               product[idx] += a(row, inner) * b(inner, col);
            }
16   });
    product.synchronize();
  }
```

First, the 1-D host-memory arrays **ha**, **hb**, and **hc** are allocated and initialized to size **SIZE*SIZE*sizeof(double)**. Then these arrays are associated with the **array_view** objects **a**, **b**, and **product**. The **array_view** can only be initialized with 1-D arrays or rectangular blocks of memory. Next, the **parallel_for_each()** construct is used to parallelize the kernel over the row and columns of the matrix multiplication. After the computation completes, the **array_view** object on the host and accelerator are synchronized to ensure data coherency. We compiled and ran the C++ AMP matrix multiplication kernel on the Titan and test Summit nodes using the Pathscale ENZO 6.0.9 compiler that supports C++ AMP on multiple GPUs. For comparing the results in Fig. 1, we show the code listing for the tiled GEMM implementation in listing 1.2, but omit detailed discussion as this is available in other materials [16]:

Listing 1.2. Matrix Multiplication Kernel in C++ AMP with Tiling

```
   double *ha, *hb, *hc;
2  // allocate and initiliaze host data
   void MatrixMultiply(ha, hb, hc) {

       array_view<double, 2> a(n, n, A);
       array_view<double, 2> b(n, n, B);
7      array_view<double, 2> product(n, n, C);

       // Call parallel_for_each by using 2x2 tiles.
       parallel_for_each(product.extent.tile< TS, TS >(),
           [=] (tiled_index< TS, TS> t_idx) restrict(amp)
12         {
               int row = t_idx.local[0];
               int col = t_idx.local[1];
               int rowGlobal = t_idx.global[0];
               int colGlobal = t_idx.global[1];
17             int sum = 0;

               for (int i = 0; i < n; i += TS) {
                   tile_static int locA[TS][TS];
                   tile_static int locB[TS][TS];
22                 locA[row][col] = a(rowGlobal, col + i);
                   locB[row][col] = b(row + i, colGlobal);
                   t_idx.barrier.wait();

                   for (int k = 0; k < TS; k++) {
27                     sum += locA[row][k] * locB[k][col];
                   }

                   t_idx.barrier.wait();
               }
32
               product[t_idx.global] = sum;
           });
           product.synchronize();

37 }
```

QMCPACK - three-body Jastrow factor QMCPACK [17,18] is an open-source software package that enables quantum Monte Carlo (QMC) simulations of realistic materials on large parallel computers. It is implemented using C++ object-oriented and generic programming design patterns, and achieves efficient parallelism through the hybrid use of MPI/OpenMP and inlined specializations to use SIMD intrinsics. Additionally, a port to CUDA for NVIDIA GPU acceleration was done, but some of the data structures and algorithms needed refactoring for efficient execution on the accelerator. QMCPACK is one of the applications participating in the CORAL [13] application readiness program (CAAR) for the POWER-based Summit [15] system to be deployed as the next leadership-class machine at Oak Ridge National Lab (ORNL).

Quantum Monte Carlo methods are a class of stochastic-based, ab initio electronic structure calculations to solve the time-independent Schrödinger equation in quantum mechanics for the ground state energy and its corresponding physical state, or the so-called wavefunction. Regardless of the algorithm employed, the code takes a trial wavefunction as an initial input. It then employs an iterative Monte Carlo procedure to optimize the wavefunction and obtains the ground state.

One commonly used type of wavefunction is composed of a product of Slater determinants and Jastrow factors. The Slater determinants encapsulate the electrons' distribution, whereas the Jastrow factors capture the Coulombic interactions among the electrons or ions. The kernel that we are porting here to C++ AMP is a prototype of the evaluation of the three-body Jastrow factor, which accounts for the interactions among any two electrons and an ion for the entire system. Thus, there are three nested for loops in the kernel, two of which loop over the number of electron-ion pairs, and one which loops over the number of electron-electron pairs in the physical system. It is for this reason the calculation of the three-body Jastrow is computationally intensive, as the number of electrons in a typical calculation could be few hundred up to thousands.

Listing 1.3 shows the original version of the QMCPACK Jastrow kernel. The code uses several custom linear vector and tensor classes TinyVector, Tensor, and MyVector. The result of the kernel is captured in the grad and hess arguments.

Listing 1.3. Original QMCPACK Kernel

```
inline
real_type evaluate(real_type r_12, real_type r_1I,
             real_type r_2I, TinyVector<real_type,3> &grad,
             Tensor<real_type,3> &hess,
             MyVector &gamma){
  real_type val = 0.0;  grad = 0.0;  hess = 0.0;
  real_type r2l(1.0), r2l_1(0.0), r2l_2(0.0), lf(0.0);
  for (int l=0; l<=N_eI; l++) {
    real_type r2m(1.0), r2m_1(0.0), r2m_2(0.0), mf(0.0);
    for (int m=0; m<=N_eI; m++) {
      real_type r2n(1.0), r2n_1(0.0), r2n_2(0.0), nf(0.0);
      for (int n=0; n<=N_ee; n++) {
        real_type g = gamma(l,m,n);
        val += g*r2l*r2m*r2n;
        grad[0] += nf * g *r2l * r2m * r2n_1;
        // Omit code for grd[1] and grd[2]
        hess(0,0) += nf*(nf-1.0) * g * r2l   * r2m * r2n_2;
        // Omit code for calculating other hess() entries
```

```
              r2n_2 = r2n_1; r2n_1 = r2n; r2n *= r_12; nf += 1.0;
            }
            r2m_2 = r2m_1; r2m_1 = r2m; r2m *= r_2I; mf += 1.0;
          }
23        r2l_2 = r2l_1; r2l_1 = r2l; r2l *= r_1I; lf += 1.0;
        }
        for (int i=0; i<C; i++){
          hess(0,0)=(r_1I - L)*(r_2I - L)*hess(0,0);
          // Omit code for updating other hess() entries
28        grad[0] = (r_1I - L)*(r_2I - L)*grad[0];
          // Omit code for updating other grad() entries
          val *= (r_1I - L)*(r_2I - L);
        }
        hess(1,0) = hess(0,1);
33      hess(2,0) = hess(0,2);
        hess(2,1) = hess(1,2);
        return val;
      }
```

The motivation to explore the use of C++ AMP for this kernel came from the fact that it had not been ported to CUDA yet, and initial attempts to use directives for accelerator offload were not satisfactory, requiring reduced usage of custom C++ classes and data structures needed in the application. Furthermore, developer investment in CUDA is being reduced for this application for portability reasons. Using C++ AMP to parallelize the two loops requires capturing the main data structures into **array<>** objects for access on the accelerator inside the **parallel_for_each** looping construct. Listing 1.4 shows the C++ AMP code corresponding to the three nested **for** loops making up the first part of the QMCPACK kernel. Note that we omit some of the common code elements and present primarily the parts that illustrate the modifications needed to adapt the kernel to the C++ AMP interface.

Listing 1.4. QMCPACK Kernel Using C++ AMP

```
      real_type grd_acc[3] = {0.0, 0.0, 0.0};
      real_type hess_acc[6] = {0.0, 0.0, 0.0, 0.0, 0.0, 0.0};
4     // local for grad
      real_type grd0, grd1, grd2;
      grd0 = grd1 = grd2 = 0.0;
      // local for gamma (need to be changed to a 1D array)
      int g_size = (N_eI+1) * (N_eI+1) * (N_ee+1);
9     real_type gmm[g_size];
      for (int l=0; l<=N_eI; l++)
        for (int m=0; m<=N_eI; m++)
          for (int n=0; n<=N_ee; n++)
            gmm[l*N_eI*N_eI + m*N_eI + n] = 1.0;
14
      real_type _r2l[N_eI], _r2l_1[N_eI], _r2l_2[N_eI];
      _r2l[0] = 1.0; _r2l_1[0] = _r2l_2[0] = 0.0;
      for (int l=0; l<N_eI-1; l++){
        _r2l_2[l] = _r2l_1[l-1];
19      _r2l_1[l] = _r2l[l-1];
        _r2l[l] = _r2l[l-1] * r_1I;
      }
```

```
  {
        extent<2> e(N_eI, N_eI);
24      array_view<real_type, 1> av_gmm(g_size, gmm);
        array_view<real_type, 1> av_r2l(N_eI, _r2l);
        array_view<real_type, 1> av_r2l_1(N_eI, _r2l_1);
        array_view<real_type, 1> av_r2l_2(N_eI, _r2l_2);
        array<real_type, 2> value(e);
29      array<real_type[3], 2> grd(e);
        array<real_type[6], 2> hss(e);
        parallel_for_each(e,
            [=, &value, &grd, &hss](index<2> idx) restrict(amp) {
            int l = idx[0]; int m = idx[1];
34          real_type r2n(1.0), r2n_1(0.0), r2n_2(0.0), nf(0.0);
            real_type mf = (real_type)m;      real_type lf = (real_type)l;
            real_type r2l = av_r2l[l];        real_type r2l_1 = av_r2l_1[l];
            real_type r2l_2 = av_r2l_2[l];    real_type r2m = av_r2l[m];
            real_type r2m_1 = av_r2l_1[m];    real_type r2m_2 = av_r2l_2[m];
39          for (int n=0; n<=N_ee; n++){
                const real_type g = av_gmm[l *N_eI * N_eI + m * N_eI + n];
                value[idx] += g*r2l*r2m*r2n;
                grd[idx][0] += nf * g *r2l    * r2m    * r2n_1;
                // Omit code for other grd[] entries
44              hss[idx][0] += nf*(nf-1.0) * g * r2l    * r2m    * r2n_2;
                // Omit code for other hss[] entries
                r2n_2 = r2n_1; r2n_1 = r2n;   r2n *= r_12;
                nf += 1.0;
            } // end for n
49      } // end parallel_for lambda function
        ); //end parallel_for
  }
```

The code illustrates the general approach for porting an existing application to the C++ AMP programming model. Since the C++ AMP data model is implemented primarily using the **array<>** and **array_view<>** classes, existing data generally needs to go through a copy-in/copy-out process to the corresponding C++ AMP data structure. The overhead for creating and accessing data through the C++ AMP data structures will depend on how compatible the underlying memory layout is with the layout supported by C++ AMP (**array_view**ss can be created using raw pointers as shown in Listing 1.4).

The listing also shows an example of creating and using *accelerator-only* data structures to control data movement into and out of an accelerator with disjoint memory. The variables **value, grd** and **hss** are used in the listed part of the kernel. Their lifetime extends to the rest of the kernel (not shown above) where the reduction operation is performed. They are then explicitly copied over to their host counterparts at the end of the kernel function execution.

2.2 Preliminary Performance Evaluation

The first panel of Fig. 1 shows the performance achieved using different matrix sizes on the test Summit node, and second panel of Fig. 1 shows the performance achieved using different matrix sizes on the Titan node. The execution times shown include the data transfer time between host and device. Each GEMM experiment uses double-precision data and compares the C++ AMP code represented by listing 1.1 to a more optimized C++ AMP implementation using a tiled algorithm as well as the highly-tuned NVIDIA CUBLAS DGEMM routine. While this kernel realizes the expected performance improvement when moving

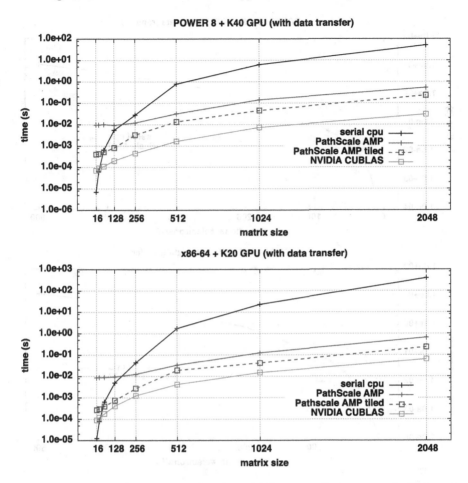

Fig. 1. Matrix multiplication Kernel in C++ AMP on a preliminary test Summit node (Power8E CPU @ 2.61GHz processor with a NVIDIA Tesla K40 m connected via PCIe v3) and a Titan node (16-core AMD Opteron 6274 CPU attached to an NVIDIA Tesla K20X GPU via PCIe v2).

from the K20 to the K40, the relatively basic AMP implementations do not see quite the amount of improvement of the hyper-tuned CUBLAS implementation. Also, as this is a compute-bound kernel, we do not expect the improved PCIe bandwidth of the POWER8 node to play a significant role in this case.

Figure 2 shows the performance speedup of the Jastrow QMC application kernel on our two HPC node types as described in Sect. 2. These timings include the time required for data transfer between host and device, as well as the manually-implemented reduction operation as explained below. The performance gain for large particle numbers is about an order of magnitude, and while the kernel involves a triply-nested loop, the computation to memory bandwidth density isn't quite as high as the GEMM algorithm. While we were able to run the kernel and accelerate it on the GPUs, C++ AMP currently lacks a reduction

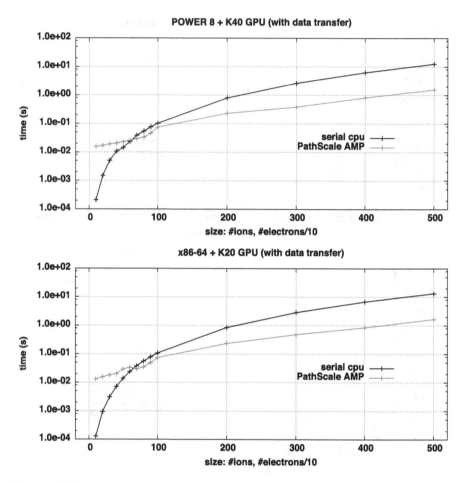

Fig. 2. QMC 3-body Jastrow kernel implemented in C++ AMP on a preliminary test Summit node (Power8E CPU @ 2.61 GHz processor with a NVIDIA Tesla K40m connected via PCIe v3) and a Titan node (16-core AMD Opteron 6274 CPU attached to an NVIDIA Tesla K20X GPU via PCIe v2).

construct. This led us to implement the reduction manually in the application. This is an area where C++ AMP needs improvement. The reduction was implemented using local arrays of type `tile_static` in order to share work among compute elements during the reduction operation. Listing 1.5 shows the implementation for the reduction for the calculated value, gradient, and Hessian of the Jastrow terms. We believe that the performance gain by moving from the CPU implementation to the accelerated AMP implementation could be further improved by having natively supported and well-optimized constructs for reduction operations. This would also increase the programmer productivity and code brevity regarding this kernel.

Listing 1.5. QMCPACK Kernel Using C++ AMP

```
extent<1> e2((N_eI+1)*(N_eI+1));
parallel_for_each(e2.tile<N_eI+1>(),
    [&](tiled_index<1> idx) restrict(amp) {
4        int l = idx.tile[0];
         int m = idx.local[0];
         tile_static real_type v[N_eI+1];

         v[m] = value[l][m];
9        idx.barrier.wait();
         if (m == 0) {
             for (int i=1; i<=N_eI; ++i) {
                 v[0] += v[i];
             }
14           value[l][0] = v[0];
         }
         for (int i=0; i<3; ++i) {
             v[m] = grd[l][m][i];
             idx.barrier.wait();
19           if(m == 0) {
                 for (int j=1; j<=N_eI; ++j) {
                     v[0] += v[j];
                 }
                 grd[l][0][i] = v[0];
24           }
         }
         for (int i=0; i<6; ++i) {
             v[m] = hss[l][m][i];
             idx.barrier.wait();
29           if(m == 0) {
                 for (int j=1; j<=N_eI; ++j) {
                     v[0] += v[j];
                 }
                 hss[l][0][i] = v[0];
34           }
         }
    });

    for (int i=0; i<=N_eI; ++i) {
39      val += value[i][0];
        for (int j=0; j<3; ++j) grd_acc[j] += grd[i][0][j];
        for (int j=0; j<6; ++j) hess_acc[j] += hss[i][0][j];
    }
```

3   Discussion

The C++ AMP programming model could be attractive for some C++ application developers because it offers a language-based solution for discrete accelerator offload, yet works well with native language features. Ideally, HPC applications would be well-supported by features in the C++ language standard itself, and indeed progress is being made in this direction. NVIDIA, Microsoft, and Intel independently proposed library approaches for standardized C++ parallelism, and these authors were eventually asked to submit a joint proposal to the committee, which was then refined over two years and informed along the way by experimental implementations. The result of this effort can be found in the parallelism technical specification (TS) N4507 which was subsequently included into the C++17 standard.

The parallelism features that have been included in C++17 show some similarities to the AMP model, defining execution policies and methods to specify computational kernels. It even includes exception handling, which is not covered by the AMP specification. However, the main feature set missing from C++17 that may prevent its wide adoption among HPC applications is the lack of data handling facilities. For heterogeneous systems with accelerators that have discrete memory address spaces, there is currently no way to specify which data should be moved between memory spaces and when the movement should take place. However, the concurrency and parallelism subgroup of the C++ language committee is working on followups to both technical specifications that will further augment the features that are included in the C++17 standard. Features are being considered [19,20] from HPX [21] and OpenCL [22] because, even though they include an HPC domain view-point, they are modeled after the existing parallel and concurrency TSs and so retain appropriateness for the consumer domain as well.

4   Early Conclusions and Future Work

In this paper we describe how C++ AMP works and can potentially be used on different platforms including x86-64 and OpenPOWER systems with NVIDIA GPUs. We describe the language constructs that C++ AMP provides to accelerate applications written in C++. We were able to use C++ AMP to accelerate a matrix multiplication kernel and important computational regions from the QMCPACK application. The success from AMP is its ability to use parallel primitives and data constructs that fit the native C++ programing model. Evaluating the C++ AMP programming model is a step toward a C++ solution to program accelerators. One of the differences with C++ AMP and the upcoming C++17 draft is that C++ AMP is aware of the different memory spaces between the accelerator and host; the language provides namespaces and objects to manage and synchronize shared data objects between the host and the accelerator. Upcoming explorations will include immediate concerns such as a more generalized yet performant way to handle data reductions within AMP parallel regions and exploring more target accelerator and multicore architectures. Longer-term studies in which we are interested include more detailed comparisons with the newly released C++17 concurrency and parallelism features which are only recently emerging in compiler implementations.

Acknowledgements. This material is based upon work supported by the U.S. Department of Energy, Office of science, and this research used resources of the Oak Ridge Leadership Computing Facility at the Oak Ridge National Laboratory, which is supported by the Office of Science of the U.S. Department of Energy under Contract No. DE-AC05-00OR22725.

References

1. Edwards, H.C., Trott, C.R., Sunderland, D.: Kokkos: Enabling manycore performance portability through polymorphic memory access patterns. J. Parallel Distrib. Comput. **74**(12), 3202–3216 (2014). Domain-Specific Languages and High-Level Frameworks High-Performance Computing. http://www.sciencedirect.com/science/article/pii/S0743731514001257

2. Hornung, R.D., Keasler, J.A.: The RAJA portability layer: Overview and status (2014). https://e-reports-ext.llnl.gov/pdf/782261.pdf

3. Hoberock, J.: Working draft, technical specification for C++ extensions for paralllelism (2014). http://www.open-std.org/jtc1/sc22/wg21/docs/papers/2014/n4071.htm

4. Beyer, J.C., Stotzer, E.J., Hart, A., de Supinski, B.R.: OpenMP for accelerators. In: Chapman, B.M., Gropp, W.D., Kumaran, K., Müller, M.S. (eds.) IWOMP 2011. LNCS, vol. 6665, pp. 108–121. Springer, Heidelberg (2011)

5. Liao, C., Yan, Y., de Supinski, B.R., Quinlan, D.J., Chapman, B.: Early experiences with the OpenMP accelerator model. In: Rendell, A.P., Chapman, B.M., Müller, M.S. (eds.) IWOMP 2013. LNCS, vol. 8122, pp. 84–98. Springer, Heidelberg (2013)

6. CAPS, CRAY and NVIDIA, PGI: The OpenACC application programming interface (2013). http://openacc.org

7. Microsoft Corporation: C++ AMP: Language and programming model (2013). http://download.microsoft.com/download/2/2/9/22972859-15C2-4D96-97AE-93344241D56C/CppAMPOpenSpecificationV12.pdf

8. Microsoft Corporation "Reference (C++ AMP)" (2012). http://msdn.microsoft.com/en-us/library/hh28939028v=vs.11029.aspx

9. PathSCale Inc.: PathScale EKOPath Compiler & ENZO GPGPU Solutions (2016). http://www.pathscale.com

10. Sharlet, D., Kunze, A., Junkins, S., Joshi, D.: Shevlin Park: ImplementingC++ AMP with Clang/LLVM and OpenCL 2012 LLVM Developers' Meeting (2012). http://llvm.org/devmtg/201211#talk10

11. HSA Foundation: Bringing C++ AMP Beyond Windows via CLANG and LLVM (2013). http://www.hsafoundation.com/bringing-camp-beyond-windows-via-clang-llvm/

12. INCITE program. http://www.doeleadershipcomputing.org/incite-program/

13. CORAL fact sheet. http://www.anl.gov/sites/anl.gov/files/CORAL%20Fact%20Sheet.pdf

14. Bland, A.S., Wells, J.C., Messer, O.E., Hernandez, O.R., Rogers, J.H.: Titan: early experience with the cray XK6 at Oak Ridge National Laboratory. In: Proceedings of Cray User Group Conference (CUG) (2012)

15. SUMMIT: Scale new heights. Discover new solutions. https://www.olcf.ornl.gov/summit/

16. Walkthrough: Matrix multiplication. https://msdn.microsoft.com/en-us/library/hh873134.aspx

17. Kim, J., Esler, K.P., McMinis, J., Morales, M.A., Clark, B.K., Shulenburger, L., Ceperley, D.M.: Hybrid algorithms in quantum Monte Carlo. J. Phys.: Conf. Ser. **402**(1), 012008 (2012). http://stacks.iop.org/1742-6596/402/i=1/a=012008
18. Esler, K.P., Kim, J., Schulenburger, L., Ceperley, D.: Fully accelerating quantum monte carlo simulations of real materials on GPU clusters. Comput. Sci. Eng. **13**(5), 1–9 (2011)
19. Wong, M., Kaiser, H., Heller, T.: Towards Massive Parallelism (aka Heterogeneous Devices/Accelerator/GPGPU) support in C++ with HPX (2015). http://www.open-std.org/jtc1/sc22/wg21/docs/papers/2016/p0234r0.pdf
20. Wong, M., Richards, A., Rovatsou, M., Reyes, R.: Kronos's OpenCL SYCL to support Heterogeneous Devices for C++ (2016). http://www.open-std.org/jtc1/sc22/wg21/docs/papers/2016/p0236r0.pdf
21. Kaiser, H., Heller, T., Adelstein-Lelbach, B., Serio, A., Fey, D.: HPX: a task based programming model in a global address space. In: Proceedings of the 8th International Conference on Partitioned Global Address Space Programming Models, ser PGAS 2014, pp. 6:1–6:11. ACM, New York (2014). http://doi.acm.org/10.1145/2676870.2676883
22. Stone, J.E., Gohara, D., Shi, G.: OpenCL: a parallel programming standard for heterogeneous computing systems. IEEE Des. Test **12**(3), 66–73 (2010). http://dx.doi.org/10.1109/MCSE.2010.69

WOPSSS

Analysis of Memory Performance: Mixed Rank Performance Across Microarchitectures

Mourad Bouache[1(✉)], John L. Glover III[1], and Jalil Boukhobza[2]

[1] Yahoo! Performance Engineering Group, 701 First Avenue,
Sunnyvale, CA 94089, USA
{bouache, glover}@yahoo-inc.com
[2] Univ. Bretagne Occ. UMR 6285, Lab-STICC, F-29200 Brest, France
boukhobza@univ-brest.fr

Abstract. The two primary measurements for performance in storage and memory systems are latency and throughput. It is interesting to see how the memory DIMMs are populated on the server board impact performance. The system bus speed is important when communicating over the Quick Path Interconnect (QPI) to the other CPU local memory resources. This is a crucial part of the performance of systems with a Non-Uniform Memory Access (NUMA). This paper investigates the best practice approaches to optimize performance which have applied to the last few CPU and chipset generations.

1 Introduction

The modern evolution of CPU and memory showcase that Moore's law is still applicable to this day. The transistor count has been increasing every year, however, due to thermal and/or power constraints, the frequency or speed has not enjoyed the same growth and has barely doubled in the last decade. From 2000 to 2009, the CPU speed went from 1.3 GHz to 2.8 GHz. Transistor-count on the other hand increased from 37.5 million in 2000 to 904 million in 2009. This means that transistor count does not automatically translate in raw CPU speed increase. CPU frequency slowly but regularly increased until around 2004 when the heat build-up in the chips caused Intel to abandon the consistent speed improvement and move towards a design with multiple processors (cores) on the same CPU chip. The industry followed soon after. For memory subsystems, Moore's Law originally applied only to random access memory (RAM). It has been generalized to apply to the CPU and to disk storage capacity as well. Indeed, disk capacity has been improving by leaps and bounds; it has improved 100 fold over the last decade. Disks spin three times faster now, and are also 5 times smaller than they were 15 years ago; while the data rate has improved only 30 fold in the same timeframe.

Processor speed and core counts are important factors when designing a new server platform. However with virtualization platforms the memory subsystem can have an equal or sometimes even greater impact on application performance than the processor speed. The application performance is also linked to the Quick Path Interconnect (QPI) speed [1] as well as a Non-Uniform Memory Access (NUMA) [2].

© Springer International Publishing AG 2016
M. Taufer et al. (Eds.): ISC High Performance Workshops 2016, LNCS 9945, pp. 579–590, 2016.
DOI: 10.1007/978-3-319-46079-6_39

Memory configuration, or memory population, has a direct impact on server and application performance. The CPU type and generation impact the type of memory configuration and performance so when deciding on new server configurations there are a wide variety of options. Memory Channels, Memory bus frequency, and rank of DIMMs are just a selection of options you encounter. The number of DIMMs used and how the DIMMs are populated on the server board impact performance and the maximum supported memory capacities. All of which are taken into consideration when evaluating system or application performance.

Diagnosing and troubleshooting memory issues [3] in enterprise server configurations is an important process that can help prevent unnecessary replacement of hardware components. Having a troubleshooting methodology helps to accurately diagnose good from bad components as well as determine component mismatches that may boot but not run optimally. For example, frequency mismatches down clock to the lower frequency thus stranding performance on the faster DIMM. Standard diagnostic tools usually help in troubleshooting memory problems by successfully isolating the specific DIMMs causing the problem, which prevents replacement of unaffected DIMMs, or in some cases, entire banks of memory. In addition, systematic troubleshooting can help determine if a firmware or other software download can resolve a problem without replacing hardware.

Many server manufacturers do provide a diagram on how to populate DIMMs in the proper order to ensure the system will run Power On Self Test (POST) and have optimal performance across the memory controller but it does not make note of the performance degradations that occur when mixing DIMMs of different Ranks or Frequency. Since this mismatched state leads to performance differences across the same model server within a given application cluster we wanted to evaluate what those differences are so we can more accurately detect them in the larger Data Center Environment. While optimal memory placement is recommended dealing with the upgrades and reconfigurations that results in mismatches are common in a real world environment.

In this paper, through our testing and observation of several models of servers with several CPU generations running in Yahoo datacenters, we evaluate the performance of different DIMM use cases of single, dual, and a mix of both Ranks. The objective is to validate the best server configurations and performance for our applications and to identify performance deltas of systems that are using mismatched or unbalanced memory configurations.

For memory upgrades we validated a few best practices to optimize performance which have applied to the last few CPU and chipset generations: Upgrade to a balanced memory configuration that fits capacity needs, also lower Rank provides slightly lower latency due to rank access cycles, and finally frequency will down-clock to the slowest DIMM. We are going to explain all the previous approaches farther in this paper.

In Sect. 2 we give background and related work about memory architecture. Experimentation is covered in Sect. 3. In Sect. 4 we conclude and give some future work perspectives.

2   Background and Related Work

Today's CPU micro-architectures contain integrated memory controllers. The memory controller connects through multiple channels to the DIMMs. DIMM stands for Dual Inline Memory Module and contains the memory modules (DRAM chips) that provide 4 or 8 bits of data. Dual Inline refers to pins on both side of the module. Chips on the DIMM are arranged in groups called ranks that can be accessed simultaneously by the memory controller. Within a single memory cycle 64 bits of data will be accessed. These 64 bits may come from the 8 or 16 DRAM chips depending on how the DIMM is organized.

In this paper, we are evaluating the bandwidth of memory configurations that mix 1Rx4 and 2Rx8 DIMMs and also compare Single and Dual Ranked DIMMs. In the next section we go over the performance results of the Independent Memory mode while increase the number of DIMMs per channel (DPC). To measure memory latency and bandwidth, we used Intel Memory Latency Checker[1].

In this section, we are giving a background about the memory architecture, ranking, different types, frequency, generations and DIMM populations:

2.1   Ranked DIMMs

SR or Single ranked DIMMs [8] are typically least expensive DIMMs that are available. Intel generally recommends against using them in one DIMM per channel (1 DPC) configurations. When scheduling reads and writes to memory, one must observe large turnaround times between reads and writes on a given rank. If a channel only has a single rank, these turnarounds result in a significant decrease in peak throughput. When used on a 2 DPC setup, it is possible to hide these turnarounds (by using the other DIMM) and therefore achieve strong bandwidth (Fig. 1).

DR or Dual ranked DIMMs are highly recommended. They typically can achieve high frequencies and also avoid the turnaround problems that are possible with single rank DIMMs. Dual rank DIMMs work well in just about any topology. Using 2 DR DIMMs instead of 2 SR DIMMs will have additional rank turnaround time delays which reduces the bus efficiency at high utilizations. On the other hand, DR DIMMs provide more bank resources (and therefore high page hit rates). In general, 2 DR DIMMs should slightly outperform 2 SR DIMMs across a range of workloads. DR DIMMs are usually the best bet for most systems (with the exception of high capacity systems). They have great performance, high frequency, and tend to not cost too much. They can be used in 1DPC, 2DPC and 3 DPC setups.

QRDIMMs (Quad Ranked DIMMs) are generally not recommended for best performance. They have traditionally been used for high memory capacity workloads. Because of electrical issues, these DIMMS tend to run at relatively low frequencies.

---

[1] https://software.intel.com/en-us/articles/intelr-memory-latency-checker.

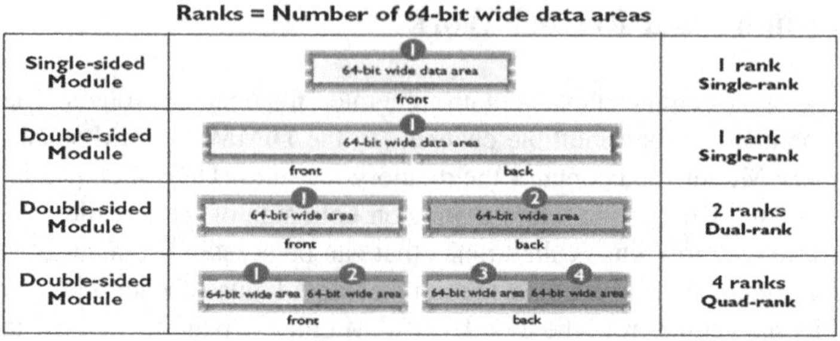

Ranks = Number of 64-bit wide data areas

Fig. 1. Single or dual rank memory (Dell server (http://en.community.dell.com/support-forums/)).

2.2 Types of DIMMs

Manufacturers of DDR-3 SDRAM DIMMs [9] produce two types of DIMMs: Unbuffered DIMMs (UDIMM) [10] and Registered DIMMs (RDIMM). Unbuffered DIMMs represent the most basic type of memory module and offer lower latency and (relatively) low power consumption but are limited in capacity. Unbuffered DIMMs are applicable for systems with low DIMM counts and where low power is required and large memory capacities are not required. RDIMMs offer larger capacities than UDIMMs and include address parity protection.

2.3 DIMM Population

"It is important to ensure that DIMMs with appropriate number of ranks are populated in each channel for optimal performance. Whenever possible, it is recommended to use dual-rank DIMMs in the system. Dual-rank DIMMs offer better interleaving hence better performance than single-rank DIMMs.

For instance, a system populated with six 8 GB dual-rank DIMMs outperforms a system populated with six 8 GB single-rank DIMMs by 7 % for SPECjbb2005. Dual-rank DIMMs are also better than quad-rank DIMMs because quad-rank DIMMs will cause the memory speed to be down-clocked.

Another important guideline is to populate equivalent ranks per channel. For instance, mixing one single-rank DIMM and one dual-rank DIMM in a channel should be avoided."[2]

2.4 Independent Mode DIMM Population

The Romley-EP platform implements a 4 channel memory controller that allows up to 4 DIMMs per channel on each CPU socket. Dual CPU socket systems can access each other's memory controller through the Intel QPI (Quick Path Interface) [1] at speeds up

---

[2] http://en.community.dell.com/support-forums/desktop/f/3514/t/19513761.

to 8.0 GT/s. While there are no compatibility restrictions on how DDR3 memory is populated there are guidelines[3] on how to populate for optimal performance in Independent mode. These guidelines were validated from the test methodology we used as explained in Sect. 3.1:

- For one DIMM per channel (1DPC) configurations, the Romley-EP platform requires DIMMs within a channel to be populated starting with the DIMMs farthest from the processor in a "fill-farthest" approach.
- For two DIMM per channel (2DPC) configurations, the Romley-EP platform requires DIMMs within a channel to be populated starting with the DIMMs farthest from the processor in a "fill-farthest" approach. Also pay attention when populating a Quad-rank DIMM with a Single- or Dual-rank DIMM in the same channel, the higher-rank DIMM must be populated farthest from the processor.
- When single, dual and quad rank DIMMs are populated for 2DPC, always populate the higher number rank DIMM first (starting from the farthest slot), for example, first quad rank, then dual rank, and last single rank DIMM.

2.5   Related Work

Much of the state-of-the-art work in this field has focused on simulation-based performance evaluations of DRAM and how to these concepts in the enterprise environment [4]. One study tried comparing differences between Bandwidth and Latency Row Hit Buffer Rates (RHBR) with memory level parallelism in multi and many cores architecture [5]; basically expanding performance by increasing memory channels in a virtual layer. Another interesting study was done creating a model (ANATOMY) [6], which has a queuing module helping to capture technological impact in memory system. These studies take a deep dive on modeling memory performance based on differences in the memory architecture but have been mostly theoretical. We expand on some of these research topics by testing on the actual memory controllers and micro-architectures currently in use in the Enterprise Data Center environment.

3   Experimentations

Since the introduction of the Intel Nehalem CPU architecture [11], memory has been managed by multiple controller channels, each channel containing the same number of banks. We were first introduced to this memory system in the Romley-EP chipset. During testing of different memory configurations on this chipset we noticed performance mismatches at the SpecInt level and diving further into the individual Spec benchmarks we could see that the memory intensive benchmarks were the main culprits of the low Spec rate. This led us to evaluate the effects of memory population as well as memory Rank and Frequency on bandwidth and latency performance. We will be

---

[3] http://www.intel.com/content/www/us/en/intelligent-systems/romley/embedded-intel-xeon-e5-2600-processor-series-with-intel-c604-c602-j-chipset.html.

experimenting with the Romley-EP and Haswell-EP microarchitectures since we know CPU has an impact on memory performance.

3.1   Experimental Methodology

Intel has been releasing new CPU architectures and updates to those architectures about every 18 months. During the Harpertown (E5420) generation, Intel had skipped an update cycle so the industry had been standardizing performance on DDR2 and the Penryn microarchitecture with its single memory channel controller. The single controller DIMMs slots could be filled in almost any order with no need to "balance" across CPU sockets. This resulted in a lower SpecInt performance index delta between different memory configurations and capacities.

We started this performance analysis on the Romley-EP microarchitecture since it brought such a big change to the memory platform. As our business units started deploying more Nehalem/Westmere CPU servers in production they started to notice some performance mismatches. Under further analysis we found that many of the performance differences were due to slight variations in the memory DIMM population. We started by booting the system with a single DIMM and testing the memory transactions performances. We then increased the memory by a DIMM at a time to evaluate how the performance scales and what population conditions give performance degradation as we scale DIMMs. Once we could find a trend in the performance scaling we started looking at how DIMM rank and frequency combinations affect performance (see Sect. 2.4 for Guidelines).

We expanded this benchmarking process to the Haswell-EP microarchitecture to see how moving to a 4 memory channel controller platform affects performance. Much like the previous generation the performance of the memory platform is very sensitive to the DIMM population and many of the same rules for matching rank and frequency carried over. Seeing as Memory will be changing to keep up with CPU advances will expect new advances to the memory platform in the near future that we will continue to evaluate for performance.

We used the stream_omp [13] benchmark since it performs predictable multi-core memory transactions that we could run standalone to exercise the memory platform. Stream_omp measures the bandwidth (in MB per second) for 4 of the main memory transactions:

> *Copy - $a(i) = b(i)$*
> *Scale - $a(i) = q*b(i)$*
> *Add - $a(i) = b(i) + c(i)$*
> *Triad - $a(i) = b(i) + q*c(i)$*
> *where a, b and c are vectors and q is a constant*

The multi-core memory access was not optimized so as to give a representation of a general application adding and moving data across the capacity of our memory space. From there, we just run the same benchmark script parameters while changing the memory configurations and capacities. This is how we derived the best practices for memory usage in a multi-controller platform using the Stream-scaling[4] performance tool.

3.2   Romley-EP Microarchitecture

The Romley-EP platform supports four different memory RAS (Row Access Select) modes [12]: Independent Channel Mode, Rank Sparing Mode, Mirrored Channel Mode, and Lockstep Channel Mode.

The rules on channel population and channel matching vary by the RAS mode used.

DIMM timings (RAS and CAS latencies) do not have to match but timings will be set to support all DIMMs populated (i.e., DIMMs with slower timings will force faster DIMMs to the slower common timing modes).

Independent Mode Memory Configuration. While there are performance and redundancy benefits of using Rank Sparing, Mirrored Channel, and Lockstep Channel Modes for specific applications, a majority of the enterprise applications are using the Independent Mode to get the largest memory capacity and most predictable performance due to having uniform CPU to memory locality. Since we use the memory controller in Independent Mode there should be no compatibility restriction on how memory is populated but there are guidelines on how to populate for best performance. This analysis will take a look at mixed rank DIMM population in the same channel and across sockets to validate the optimal configurations and communicate those guidelines to our procurement teams for HW orders and our site-ops teams that will ultimately be performing the memory upgrades.

Mixed Rank Performance. We have noticed from the Romley-EP server POST (Power On Self Test) that the memory controller accepts these mixed and non-mixed configurations. The fact that the server POSTs does not mean the DIMMs is populated for optimal performance so the DIMM population guidelines must still be followed.

The memory configurations performances are generated using an Open Source multi-threaded memory transaction benchmark: **stream_omp** [13].

Performance Analysis. With the memory populated for optimal performance the stream_omp benchmark generated the data in Table 1. The results for each metric of the stream_omp benchmark were plotted (see Fig. 2) to give a visual comparison. From the data we can see that the overall performance is not majorly affected by mixing different rank memory of the same frequency. If they are different frequencies then the memory controller will down-clock all DIMMs to match the lowest frequency DIMM.

The performance delta between non-mixed rank configurations (1Rx4 vs. 2Rx8) is ~9 % in favor of the dual rank 2Rx8. Although the single rank 1Rx4 should have a

---

[4] *Automate memory bandwidth testing with STREAM using varying core counts* https://github.com/gregs1104/stream-scaling.

Table 1. 1Rx4, 2Rx8 - 1600 MHz DDR3 mixed rank memory bandwidth

Memory configuration	Copy (MB/s)	Scale (MB/s)	Add (MB/s)	Triad (MB/s)
8x 1Rx4	32932.0169	32719.2726	28525.4034	34951.9265
6x 1Rx4, 2x 2Rx8	32398.6115	32673.0758	32526.5917	36919.6589
4x 1Rx4,4x 2Rx8	32238.3033	32686.6027	36584.8795	36297.9522
2x 1Rx4,6x 2Rx8	33246.0747	32394.7017	37166.3852	36439.4605
8x 2Rx8	36182.1615	35802.851	39649.1703	39479.6729

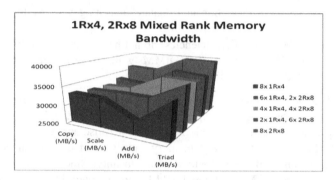

Fig. 2. Memory transaction bandwidth (mixed and non-mixed rank 1600 MHz DDR3 DIMM configurations)

lower latency (meaning that it can access all the modules during the same access transaction as opposed to needing 2 transactions to read all modules on dual rank or 4 transactions to access quad rank modules).

We start to see more comparable performance when we start evaluating the mixed rank configurations. Moving from 25 % to 75 % mixed rank configurations shows roughly ~4 % performance delta and a ~10 % lower bandwidth compared to the max non-mixed performance. 10 % may seem noticeable but that is on the highest end of the performance spectrum and many application may not be able to attain that memory bandwidth due to other resource contention (i.e. CPU needs to be shared for compute as well as memory transactions). For applications that are memory latency or bandwidth sensitive you may notice the performance loss in application SLA or QPS so a proper application analysis should be performed to determine if that performance loss can be balanced against the overall performance gain your application should receive from increasing memory capacity whether that increase results in a mixed rank configuration or not.

3.3   Haswell-EP Micro-Architecture

Performance Tool and Hardware Configuration. In this evaluation we used Stream-scaling[5] performance tool as it automates running the STREAM memory bandwidth test on Linux systems. It detects the number of CPUs and the size of each of their caches. The program then downloads STREAM, compiles it, and runs it with an array size large enough to not fit into cache. The number of threads is varied from 1 to the total number of cores in the server, so that you can see how memory speed scales as cores involved increase.

For the single and dual ranked tests we used a dual socket Intel Haswell CPU - Xeon E5-2680 v3 2.50 GHz (HT enabled, 24 cores, 48 threads) with 64 GB 2133 MHz of 8 × 8 GB and RHEL Server 6.5 Operating System in 1U form factor server. Figure 3 shows the memory population diagram on the test servers. We have been working with 8 GB memory DIMM in our experimentation study.

Performance Results

One DIMM-Per-Channel Configuration. In a one DIMM-per-channel configuration, dual-rank performs better than single-rank as we can see in Fig. 4. The dual rank

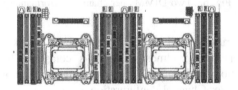

Fig. 3. One DIMM-per-channel configuration

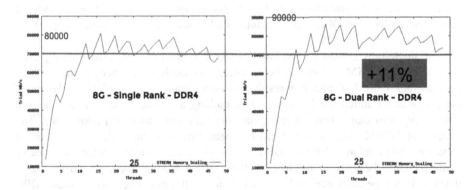

Fig. 4. One DIMM per channel performance

---

[5] *Automate memory bandwidth testing with STREAM using varying core counts* https://github.com/gregs1104/stream-scaling.

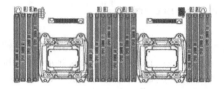

Fig. 5. One DIMM per channel configuration

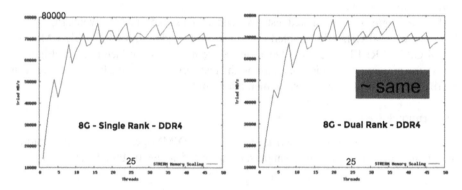

Fig. 6. Two DIMMs per channel performance

configuration is performing 11 % better. Where the dual-rank configuration in one DIMM-per-Channel is hitting almost 90K MB/s compared to only 80K for the single-rank configuration. In Fig. 3 we are presenting the memory population on the server for one DIMM-Per-Channel configuration.

Two DIMMs-Per-Channel Configuration. In a two DIMM-per-channel configuration, the performance of single and dual-rank will be almost identical (within the accuracy of the measurement) as you can see in Fig. 6. For the mixed ranked test, we found that bandwidth scales with DPC and were interested in tracking how it scales (Fig. 5).

The single-rank DIMM will be lower power than the dual-rank DIMM. Long-term, the single-rank DIMM will end up being lower cost and having better availability than the dual-rank DIMM. Typically it results in a better improvement of latency. However the performance difference between single ranking and dual ranking is minute and comes only into play when squeezing out the very last ounce of performance. The number of DIMM slots does not always mean that you can scale up to a certain capacity configuration. DDR3 LRDIMMs provide a great way to maximize capacity while retaining bandwidth. Beginning 2014, DDR4 was released, providing higher density, better performance and decreased drop off rates when using multi DPC configurations.

4   Conclusions and Future Works

This paper is meant to provide guidelines for evaluation of memory performance as affected by different factors such as microarchitecture, DIMM type, and DIMM population. Through this study we have provided the following recommendations to achieve optimal memory performance in the Romley-EP and Haswell-EP microarchitectures: (1) **Upgrade to a balanced memory configuration that fits capacity needs:** This requires being aware of your memory system and number of controller channels. Since the Intel Nehalem CPU architecture [11], memory has been managed by multiple controller channels and each channel will have the same number of banks. To "balance" memory we must populated the same number of channels and banks within the channels across each CPU socket. (2) **Lower Rank provides slightly lower latency:** Memory DIMMs have the same socket interface and their capacity is determined by the amount of DRAM chips connected through Ranks. A Rank is the series of DRAM chips connected to the same chip select and therefore accessible simultaneously. Dual Rank means that there must be 2 chip selects to access the entire capacity of the memory. Quad Rank requires 4 chip selects and each select incurs extra latency therefore single Ranks would have the lower latency of DIMMs of the same capacity and frequency. (3) **Frequency will downclock to the lowest DIMM:** Memory Frequency is another factor that affects latency and overall application performance. The frequency determines how fast the data can be accessed on the chip and since the OS allocates Virtual memory pages that stride across multiple physical DIMMs the access times need to be the same. That is why the BIOS of the server will down-clock all DIMMs to the Speed of the slowest DIMM. So even if you are upgrading from 2 to 8 DIMMs and bought the latest fastest memory for your server they will only run as fast as the 2 original DIMMs in the system. If latency is a concern then upgrade all the DIMM's to the same RANK and frequency.

Combining DRAM and NAND [14] at the system-level architecture provides the best of both worlds, which is why modern servers use DRAM as a memory/cache and NAND for storage. There is still a latency and capacity gap between DRAM and NAND, so the question arises: how do we combine the best of DRAM and NAND at the silicon level? The industry is developing a new type of memory that provides low latency and high endurance while offering a small and scalable cell size. Theoretically, NVDIMMs with 3D XPoint memory could provide similar bandwidth. Updates revealed at the Intel Developer Forum trade-show last year claim 3D XPoint NVDIMMs will only offer around 6 GB/s of bandwidth, hardly considered a breakthrough, the new Intel DIMMs based on 3D XPoint [17] will significantly improve performance of server-class storage sub-systems.

References

1. Ziakas, D., Dimitrios, Z., Allen, B., Maddox, R.A., Safranek, R.J.: Intel® quickpath interconnect architectural features supporting scalable system architectures. In: 2010 18th IEEE Symposium on High Performance Interconnects (2010)

2. Yang, R., Antony, J., Rendell, A.P.: A simple performance model for multithreaded applications executing on non-uniform memory access computers. In: 2009 11th IEEE International Conference on High Performance Computing and Communications (2009)
3. Bigelow, S.J.: Bigelow's Drive and Memory Troubleshooting Pocket Reference. McGraw-Hill, New York City (2000). Computing
4. Cuppu, V., Jacob, B., Davis, B., Mudge, T.: High-performance DRAMs in workstation environments. IEEE Trans. Comput. **50**(11), 1133–1153 (2001)
5. Chen, L., Licheng, C., Yongbing, H., Yungang, B., Guangming, T., Zehan, C., Mingyu, C.: A study of leveraging memory level parallelism for DRAM system on multi-core/many-core architecture. In: 2013 12th IEEE International Conference on Trust, Security and Privacy in Computing and Communications (2013)
6. Gulur, N., Nagendra, G., Mahesh, M., Raman, M., Ramaswamy, G.: ANATOMY. In: The 2014 ACM International Conference on Measurement and Modeling of Computer Systems - SIGMETRICS 2014 (2014)
7. Gulur, N., Nagendra, G., Mahesh, M., Raman, M., Ramaswamy, G.: ANATOMY. ACM SIGMETRICS Perform. Eval. Rev. **42**(1), 505–517 (2014)
8. Kaviani, K., Bucher, M., Su, B., Daly, B., Stonecypher, B., Dettloff, W., Stone, T., Prabhu, K., Venkatesan, P.K., Heaton, F., Kollipara, R., Yi, L., Madden, C.J., Eble, J., Lei, L., Nhat, N.: A 6.4 Gb/s near-ground single-ended transceiver for dual-rank DIMM memory interface systems. In: 2013 IEEE International Solid-State Circuits Conference Digest of Technical Papers (2013)
9. S. Prayaga and S. California State University: Design of DDR3 SDRAM Test Module (2007)
10. Joodaki, M., Mojtaba, J., Amir, A.: A radiated EMI measurement setup for un-buffered DRAM PCBs. In: 2014 International Symposium on Electromagnetic Compatibility (2014)
11. Berger, A.S.: The Intel x86 Architecture. In: Hardware and Computer Organization, pp. 265–294 (2005)
12. Jacob, B., Ng, S., Wang, D.: Memory Systems: Cache, DRAM, Disk. Morgan Kaufmann, Burlington (2010)
13. Li, H.F.: Bandwidth of fast memory in multiprocessing. Proc. IEEE **68**(5), 630–632 (1980)
14. DRAM. In: Low-Power CMOS Design (2009)
15. Jun, B., Byunghei, J., Dongkun, S.: Workload-aware budget compensation scheduling for NVMe solid state drives. In: 2015 IEEE Non-Volatile Memory System and Applications Symposium (NVMSA) (2015)
16. Xu, Q., Qiumin, X., Huzefa, S., Mrinmoy, G., Manu, A., Tameesh, S., Zvika, G., Anahita, S., Vijay, B.: Performance characterization of hyperscale applicationson on NVMe SSDs. In: Proceedings of the 2015 ACM SIGMETRICS International Conference on Measurement and Modeling of Computer Systems - SIGMETRICS 2015 (2015)
17. Dreslinski, R.G., Thomas, M., Korey, S., Reetuparna, D., Nathaniel, P., Sudhir, S., David, B., Dennis, S., Trevor, M.: XPoint cache. In: Proceedings of the 21st International Conference on Parallel Architectures and Compilation Techniques - PACT 2012 (2012)

Considering I/O Processing in CloudSim for Performance and Energy Evaluation

Hamza Ouarnoughi[1,2]([✉]), Jalil Boukhobza[1,2], Frank Singhoff[1,2], Stéphane Rubini[2], and Erwann Kassis[1]

[1] B-Com Research Institute of Technology, Plouzané, France
{hamza.ouarnoughi,jalil.boukhobza,frank.singhoff,erwann.kassis}@b-com.com
[2] Université de Bretagne Occidentale, UMR 6285, Lab-STICC, 29200 Brest, France
{boukhobza,singhoff,rubini}@univ-brest.fr

Abstract. This article presents an extension of the IaaS Cloud simulator *CloudSim*. Our *CloudSim* extension takes into account the processing of I/O workload generated by virtual machines within a Data Center and evaluates the overall performance and energy consumption. Indeed, storage systems energy consumption may represent up to 40 % of the total energy consumed in a Data Center. Then, we propose three contributions. First, we modified the time computation model of *CloudSim* to consider I/O operations. Second, we designed several models of storage system devices including Hard Disk Drives and Solid-State Drives, and finally, we considered the CPU and RAM used for I/O request processing. Our extensions have been evaluated using video encoding traces. First simulation results showed that a significant amount of energy, around 17 %, is consumed due to I/O workload execution, which shows the soundness of our *CloudSim* extensions.

Keywords: Cloud computing · CloudSim · Storage · Energy consumption

1 Introduction

IaaS Cloud Computing is an emerging technology supporting a new way of using hardware infrastructures. Cloud providers offer these infrastructures as virtualized hardware (i.e. CPU, storage, and network), managed by suitable software (i.e. virtualization technologies). They propose their services under the form of Virtual Machines (VMs), ready to be used on demand by Cloud customers.

Mastering the utilization costs of Cloud infrastructure represents a real challenge for Cloud providers. Power consumption cost is one of the main costs for a data center [9]. Several approaches have been proposed in order to minimize data center energy consumption. One of the most commonly used is VM placement optimization which aims to find the optimal allocation of physical machines of a data center (i.e. host servers) to customers' virtual machines. Most state-of-art VM placement optimization methods are based on CPU utilization [15].

© Springer International Publishing AG 2016
M. Taufer et al. (Eds.): ISC High Performance Workshops 2016, LNCS 9945, pp. 591–603, 2016.
DOI: 10.1007/978-3-319-46079-6_40

They consider that power consumption of a given host depends exclusively on its CPU load. However, several studies [4] have shown that other system components may greatly contribute to the overall host power consumption while others [12] emphasize that the power consumed by a storage system may represent up to 40 % of the overall data center power consumption. Therefore, we believe that it is necessary to consider storage systems and associated workload in VM placement optimization.

The work presented in this article is part of an energy-aware VM placement optimization project that considers storage systems and I/O workload execution. For performance evaluation sake, we used one of the most popular approach [3] as a comparison baseline. In this work [3], authors used the Cloud simulator *CloudSim* [5]. Unfortunately, *CloudSim* does not consider I/O processing related time and energy consumption.

Even if *CloudSim* considers transfer time of Cloud customer binary files to the Cloud storage system, it does not take into account I/Os related to VM image creation and I/O workload execution. Many state-of-the-art studies aimed to provide storage systems support in *CloudSim* [7,13,14,21]. To the best of our knowledge, none considered I/O workload processing.

This article presents an extension of the *CloudSim* storage system model. The proposed extension aims to take into account I/O workload processing in the overall simulation results. We then extended *CloudSim* as follows: (1) first, we modeled the VM I/O workload execution in the time computation model of *CloudSim*, (2) We extended the storage device entities of *CloudSim* to express both Hard Disk Drive (HDD) and Solid State Drive (SSD) devices performance and energy models, (3) We took into account CPU and memory I/O processing related time and energy consumption.

The remainder of this article is organized as follows. Section 2 presents the related works. Section 3 describes the contribution of this paper. Section 4 presents the extension evaluation and Sect. 5 concludes the article.

2   Related Work

In this section, we summarize state-of-the-art work for I/O and storage integration inside *CloudSim*. There are other work that aim to consider storage capabilities in other simulators used in Cloud context such as *SimGrid* in [11] but as they do not target VM-based concepts nor storage system energy consumption, they fall out of the scope of this paper.

CloudSim is a discrete event simulator that enables modeling and simulation of Cloud computing systems and application provisioning environments [5]. To the best of our knowledge, there are four state-of-the-art work that dealt with storage in *CloudSim*. In [14], the authors implemented *CloudSimDisk*, a *CloudSim* extension based on an analytical energy consumption model for three hard drives. This extension considers only transaction time and energy consumption related to adding and retrieving binary files executed by VMs. In [21], Sturm *et al.* target the simulation of a STaaS Cloud (STorage as a Service). This approach focuses on a pricing model of object storage in *CloudSim* [16], and gets around the usual use VM execution concept in *CloudSim*. The closest work to ours introduced several extensions for *CloudSim* in order to overcome resource over-utilization, and then to minimize costs [7]. For such a purpose, Grozev *et al.* focused on load balancing algorithms by considering all resources, including the storage parts. Finally, Long and Zhao [13] proposed an extension for *CloudSim* storage system in order to maximize system performance. This approach targets the integration of file replication over storage devices and data centers.

Approaches in [7,13,14,21] exhibit three main drawbacks:

- VM I/O workload processing is not considered in the time and energy models of *CloudSim*.
- the existing models do not consider time and energy generated by storage system devices' activities,
- when used in *CloudSim*, the storage system is limited to a shared SAN which relies only on one model of HDD.

In this work, we answer each of the three above mentioned issues. We propose an extension to simulate more accurate and realistic scenarios by considering I/O workloads and storage system performances. The next section details our extension for *CloudSim*. First, we present the concept of VM I/O workload execution and its related time and energy consumption. Second, we give an overview of our modeling of different classes of storage device in *CloudSim* storage system.

3 CloudSim I/O Processing and Storage System Support

3.1 Storage in CloudSim

CloudSim is a discrete event IaaS Cloud simulator developed in Java. It is composed of a set of entities: `Datacenter`, `DatacenterBroker`, `CloudInformationS-ervice` and `CloudsimShutdown`. Those entities model the main architecture element of a Data center. They communicate using predefined events (e.g. `VM_CREA-TE`, `VM_MIGRATE`, `VM_DESTROY`, etc.). Events can be external (i.e. between different entities) or internal (i.e. sent and received by the same entity). When received by an entity, each event is handled by the receiving entity before sending a acknowledgment (e.g. `VM_CREATE_ACK`, `VM_MIGRATE_ACK`, `VM_DESTROY_ACK`, etc.). A *CloudSim* simulation is based on the execution of a set of *Cloudlets*. A *Cloudlet* models a process with a CPU workload ran by a VM.

CloudSim allows users to simulate IaaS Cloud scenarios with different infrastructure architectures. It is usually used to experiment VM placement optimization strategies with a focus on energy efficiency or load balancing. From the storage system perspective, the latest *CloudSim* version uses a shared SAN (Storage Area Network), which is a set of similar hard drives [6], connected by a LAN (Local Area Network). From the I/O workload perspective, *CloudSim* mainly considers the time to store an input *Cloudlet* file during its submission. This time is obtained using hard drives performance metrics (latency and throughput), and the LAN throughput, but the related energy consumption is not accounted. In addition, the VM image and its I/O workload management are not considered.

The main objective of our contribution is to consider I/O workload execution of VM in an IaaS Cloud context. I/O workload impact on performance and energy consumption can be decomposed in two main elements, (1) the execution of the I/O workload on the storage devices containing the requested data, and (2) the execution of the I/O software stack for workload processing on host's CPU and RAM. Thus, executing I/O workload induces time and energy latencies on storage system devices, and also CPU and RAM. Our contribution can be summarized as follows:

Time and energy computations for I/O processing: In order to consider I/O workload execution, we have updated both VM time and energy computation models to take into account I/O processing. We have chosen to define I/O workload at the VM level. Indeed, on one hand defining workloads at the VM granularity corresponds to the targeted objective (placement of VM), and on the other hand, it is more convenient as in real platforms, tracing is achieved at the hypervisor level [10].

Storage device support: Our extension updates the model of storage system devices already used in *Cloudsim*, especially the `Storage` interface and the class `HardDriveStorage`. The additional material targets mainly performance and power characteristics.

I/O workload and CPU correlation: As discussed earlier, when executing an I/O workload, a given VM does not only solicit the storage system, but also uses the CPU and RAM for I/O requests processing. In *CloudSim*, RAM utilization is driven by CPU usage. Based on performance measurement, we developed empirical correlation models in order to evaluate CPU usage according to I/Os. The developed models mainly depend on I/O size, I/O access pattern, and storage device type.

3.2 Time and Energy Computations for I/O Processing

Time Computation. Simulated execution time in *CloudSim* depends on the time between sending an event by an entity and receiving the acknowledgment. Among the events that impact simulation time, we distinguish *Cloudlets* and VMs processing events (create, move, pause, resume, etc.). Figure 1 shows a simple scenario for the execution of a *Cloudlet* on a VM. The first phase is the creation of a *Cloudlet* on the storage device (CLOUDLET_SUBMIT event). This event is produced once for each *Cloudlet* in the beginning of the simulation. Its duration depends on *Cloudlet* file size and storage system performance. The second phase is to execute *Cloudlet* instruction. Its duration depends on the *Cloudlet* length (i.e. number of instructions), and CPU performances of both VM and host. There is another event that implies I/O which is the *Cloudlet* relocation (CLOUDLET_MOVE event). Figure 2 shows event sequence that affects simulation time after our extension integration.

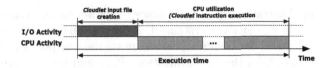

Fig. 1. Time model before the extension

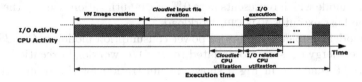

Fig. 2. Time model after the extension

Our contribution related to I/O time can be outlined as follows:

- VM*image creation:*VM creation is a data center internal event. We extended
  VM creation time by storing VM image on the storage device. This time varies
  depending on VM image size and storage device characteristics.
- I/O *execution:*we have introduced this concept in order to simulate I/O workload execution on the storage device and related energy consumption. VM I/O
  execution is a data center internal event. I/O execution time depends on characteristics of the VM I/O workload and the storage device on which the VM
  image is stored. An I/O workload is characterized by: (1) read rate, (2) sequential rate, (3) I/O request size, (4) I/O request arrival rate, and (5) the total
  amount of processed data. This characterization is widely used in state-of-art
  work, and specially in virtualized environment [8].

Energy Consumption. I/O workload execution does not affect only execution time, but also the system energy consumption. On the previous version of
CloudSim, energy consumption depended solely on hosts CPU load. Equation 1
shows how *CloudSim* gets the host power consumption $P(u)$, depending on its
CPU utilization u:

$$P(u) = k \cdot P_{max} + (1 - k) \cdot P_{max} \cdot u \qquad (1)$$

P_{max} denotes the maximum power of the host machine (i.e. when CPU utilization is equal to 100 %). k denotes the ratio between the maximum power and
the idle power (i.e. when CPU utilization is equal to 0 %). In [3], the authors consider that a host machine consumes 70 % of the maximum power in idle mode,
which means that $k = 0.7$.

The CPU utilization of a given host depends on VM CPU workload and the host
CPU performance. The CPU workload of a given VM is the sum of all *Cloudlets*
CPU workloads given in MI (Million Instructions). *CloudSim* uses the MIPS
(Million Instructions Per Second) as the only CPU performance metric.

Figure 3 is an illustrative figure that shows the power consumption with and without considering the storage system. The left timeline is obtained by the initial power model used in *CloudSim* that computes the host power consumption (CPU and RAM) only from the CPU utilization. P_{max} and k values are obtained from experimentations presented in [3]. This diagram illustrates three power phases for a given host. The first and the last phase show the power consumption during idle mode which represents here 0 % of CPU utilization. During the second phase, the host executes VMs CPU workload.

Our model completes the initial power consumption model in *CloudSim*, by adding the energy consumption related to VMs I/O workload execution.

The right time-line in Fig. 3 shows an illustration for the result after this update. Notice that a storage device in idle mode can consume power (e.g. up to 60 % of the power during operational mode [20]), and as consequence, the power in idle mode is also increased. During the second phase, the host alternates between I/O and CPU workloads execution. Storage system and I/O workload affect the consumed energy in terms of time and power.

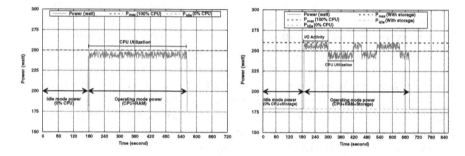

Fig. 3. Power model before and after the extension for HDD and SSD (with idle and operational power values variation but a similar behavior).

3.3   Storage Device Support

We extended the storage system of *CloudSim* by implementing two storage devices types: HDD and SSD (see Appendix Fig. 7). We classified the added attributes and methods in two main classes: (1) performance-related, and (2) power-related ones. For each storage device, performances depends on I/O work-load characteristics (e.g. read/write, sequential/random, I/O size, etc.), and device performances properties: latency, average seek time, data transfer rate (for sequential access), and IOPS (for random access). The energy consumed by a storage device depends on: its performances, I/O workload characteristics, and power properties (i.e. power for random/sequential and read/write operations, idle power, standby power). We also implemented a storage system energy consumption model that we have already presented in previous work [18].

3.4 I/O Workload and CPU Correlation

Simulating I/O workload execution does not only imply storage system activities, but also CPU utilization due to I/O software stack execution. In order to quantify and implement the CPU involvement in I/O processing, we have established a correlation model that gives CPU time depending on I/O workload characteristics. Our experiments have shown that CPU time related to synchronous I/O execution depends on four parameters: (1) storage device type (HDD and SSD), (2) I/O operation type (read or write), (3) I/O access pattern (random or sequential), and (4) I/O request size.

In order to design the CPU correlation model, we developed an I/O micro-benchmark that measures CPU time according to the total workload execution time. Fig. 4 shows results obtained for our hardware platform. Left and right charts represent obtained results for read and write operations respectively. For each experiment, we varied: (1) the storage device type (HDD, SSD), (2) the access pattern (sequential, random), and (3) the I/O size (x axis). We can observe that the CPU is more impacted in read operations as compared to writes. As SSD performance is higher than HDD, more I/O requests are processed by time unit making the CPU utilization higher. A linear regression was used to obtain the CPU correlation model. For example, the following equation gives the CPU time related to random writes on HDD:

$$Time_{CPU} = Time_{IO} \cdot [(7 \cdot 10^{-8} \cdot IO_{size}) + 9.7 \cdot 10^{-3}] \qquad (2)$$

As noted earlier, our VM I/O workload characterization includes a parameter representing the sequential rate [18]. Based on this parameter, an I/O workload may include interleaved random and sequential access. Therefore, random CPU correlation models are applied to the random parts, and sequential models are applied to the sequential parts.

4 Evaluation

This section presents the evaluation of our extension in two parts. The first one aims to validate the claim that I/O workload processing contributes highly in the energy budget while the second part validates the CPU correlation model.

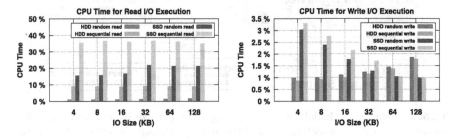

Fig. 4. CPU time for I/O execution

4.1   CPU, Memory and I/O Traces Simulation

This first evaluation assesses the storage system energy consumption of a real use case. To do so we proceeded in two main steps, Fig. 5 summarizes the methodology:

1. *Real workload execution*: we ran experiments in a real environment and we collected a set of measures on the CPU, memory load, and I/O requests.
2. *Workload simulation*: from the collected measures and traces, we replayed the same scenario in *CloudSim* by turning ON and OFF the storage system.

In this evaluation step, as the CPU utilization is obtained from traces, the CPU correlation models were not be used.

Real Workload Execution Phase: As mentioned above, the first evaluation phase includes two steps: (a) workload execution, and (b) measures collection.

(a) Workload execution: this step consists of running a workload in VMs (step 1 in Fig. 5). We chose an encoding video benchmark as a real use case of VMs in the Cloud as this is an ongoing project our institute. Virtual machines encode video from mov format [2] to several videos in TS (Transport Stream) format [19]. This process is used for video streaming using HLS (HTTP Live Streaming) protocol [1]. We used H264 for video encoding and HE-AAC for audio encoding. Eight VMs were used in this experiment, four of which were stored in HDD and four in SSD. We performed 4 experiments in which we varied the number of VMs running on (HDD, SSD) as follows: (1, 1), (2, 2), (3, 3), and (4, 4). Each VM has a 20GB image and all VMs have the same configuration.

(b) Trace collection: during workload execution, CPU and memory utilization were monitored, in the addition to I/O traces. CPU and memory traces were aggregated to an average value related to one unit of time (defined to 5 mn in

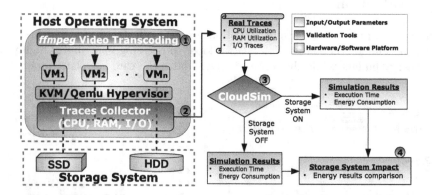

Fig. 5. Evaluation methodology. The four steps are: (1) run benchmarks, (2) collect measures, (3) collect simulation results with and w/o storage system effects, (4) compare the results.

CloudSim). Concerning I/O traces, each VM had its own I/O trace file gathered from I/O block level [17]. Each I/O trace file line includes five fields formatted as follows:

< data_amount >, < read_rate >, < random_rate >, < io_size >, < io_arrival_rate >.

First filed (i.e. < data_amount >) represents the total read and written amount of data. Second and third fields (i.e. < read_rate > and < random_rate >) denote rates of read requests and access pattern randomness respectively. Fourth field represents I/O request size in bytes. The last field denotes request arrival rate during sample interval.

Workload Simulation Phase. Simulation phase includes two main steps: (a) scenario simulation using CPU, memory, and I/O traces, and (b) comparing simulation results by activating and deactivating storage system.

(a) Simulation using real traces: in this step we used traces obtained from real workload execution phase. CPU and memory utilization are attached to hosts, while I/O traces are attached to VMs. Simulations were executed by varying the following parameter: (1) number of VMs per host, (2) storage system ON/OFF, and (3) storage device HDD/SDD (when storage system is ON). Configurations about the number of VMs were the same as for the real workload execution phase and we varied the number of hosts. The total number of VMs was set to 290 VMs as in [3]. The number of active hosts depends on the number of VMs per host (i.e. unused hosts are shutdown).

(b) Simulation results comparison: Storage energy consumption is used in order to show and quantify the impact of the storage system. Section 4.3 shows the obtained results from the evaluation.

4.2   CPU Correlation Model Validation

In order to validate the CPU correlation model, we used the same I/O traces used in the previous part. The objective of this step is to assess I/O workload processing energy consumption only with I/O traces, using the CPU correlation model (without using the CPU and RAM traces). Results obtained from this step were compared with the previous step (using CPU and RAM traces) in order to evaluate the correlation model accuracy. We used the same simulation configuration as the previous section. Results are presented in Sect. 4.3.

4.3   Evaluation Results

This section shows the obtained results from the two parts of the evaluation. Two metrics are shown, first, the energy consumption related to I/O workload processing which validates the impact of I/Os on the overall energy consumption. This metric is used for the simulation part that uses real CPU, memory and I/O traces. Second, the difference between simulations using real traces and the ones using the correlation model which validates the accuracy of the correlation model. Figure 6 shows the percentage of the energy consumed during

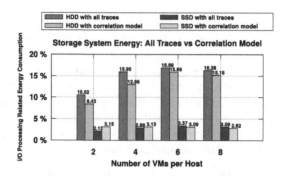

Fig. 6. Storage system energy consumption: traces vs correlation model

I/O processing, using all traces (i.e. CPU, memory, and I/O), and using our correlation model (i.e. using only I/O traces). In both cases, we keep the same Cloudlet length, in order to maintain the same simulation and real workload execution time. We can see that the energy consumption when processing I/Os grows according to the number of VMs per host, except for the last value (i.e. 8 VMs per host). This trend is due to the growth of I/O workload execution time (e.g. ~10 min for 2 VMs and ~13 min for 4 VMs) and host CPU utilization (e.g. ~23 % for 2 VMs and ~49 % for 4 VMs). The last value is due to the hardware experimental platform, where the host has an 8 CPU cores, each core is allocated to a VM (i.e. one vCPU per core). During the workload execution, all CPU cores are fully utilized, which implies less CPU time for the I/O processing (e.g. on HDD, ~335 IO/second for 6 VMs/host and ~260 IO/second for 8 VMs/host), and then less energy consumption due to I/O processing. The other observation is the difference between energy consumed in the HDD case and the SSD case. This is due to the difference between their respective performance (e.g. in 6 VMs/host case, 335 IO/second for HDD and 1607 IO/second for SSD) and their power consumption in operation mode (5 Watts fort HDD and 3.5 Watts for SSD). Figure 6 shows that our very basic correlation model gives good results. For example, in the case of HDD we have ~20 % of maximum error rate, ~6 % of minimum error rate, and the average error is ~12 %. The higher the number of VMs, the better the accuracy of our model (e.g. ~9 % error rate in the case of 8 VMs per host using SSD).

5   Conclusion

This paper presents an extension of *CloudSim* to take into account I/O workload processing. Our extension considers I/O workload execution time and energy consumption by: (1) updating the time and energy computation model of *CloudSim*, (2) taking into account different classes of storage systems (i.e. HDD and SSD), and (3) including a CPU correlation model that depends on I/O workload characteristics and storage device type in order to represent CPU and RAM I/O processing time and energy. Simulations with video encoding applications validated the impact of I/O processing on energy consumption to up to 17 % of total energy consumption. As a perspective, this implementation will be used in a VM placement optimization approach that takes into account I/O processing cost. We also plan to study and integrate the problem of interference between VMs sharing the same storage device.

Acknowledgment. This work has been achieved within the Institute of Research & Technology B-Com, dedicated to digital technologies. It has been funded by the French government through the National Research Agency (ANR) Investment referenced ANR-A0-AIRT-07.

Appendix

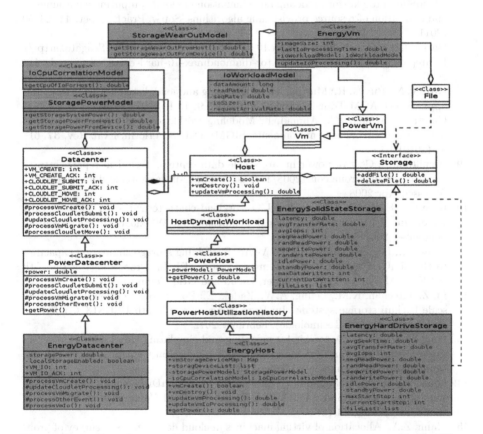

Fig. 7. UML Class diagram of the main added and modified elements in *CloudSim*. The diagram present only added or modified classes that impact storage system and I/O execution. All classes and interfaces with the green color have been added in our extension. Methods and attributes presented in this diagram (from the initial implementation) have been overridden by our extension. (Color figure online)

References

1. HTTP live streaming overview. https://developer.apple.com/library/mac/documentation/NetworkingInternet/Conceptual/StreamingMediaGuide/UsingHTTPLiveStreaming/UsingHTTPLiveStreaming.html. Accessed Apr 2016

2. Apple Computer, Inc.: Quicktime file format. Technical report (2001). www.apple.com, https://developer.apple.com/standards/qtff-2001.pdf

3. Beloglazov, A., Abawajy, J., Buyya, R.: Energy-aware resource allocation heuristics for efficient management of data centers for cloud computing. Future Gener. Comput. Syst. **28**, 755–768 (2012)

4. Bianchini, R., Rajamony, R.: Power and energy management for server systems. Computer **37**, 68–76 (2004)

5. Calheiros, R.N., Ranjan, R., Beloglazov, A., De Rose, C.A.F., Buyya, R.: CloudSim: a toolkit for modeling and simulation of cloud computing environments and evaluation of resource provisioning algorithms. Softw. Pract. Exper. **41**, 23–50 (2011)

6. Gasior, G.: Maxtor's diamondmax 10 hard drive. Technical report, Seagate. http://techreport.com/review/7903/maxtor-diamondmax-10-hard-drive. Accessed Jan 2016

7. Grozev, N., Buyya, R.: Multi-cloud provisioning and load distribution for three-tier applications. ACM Trans. Auton. Adap. Syst. **9**, 13:1–13:21 (2014)

8. Gulati, A., Kumar, C., Ahmad, I.: Modeling workloads and devices for io load balancing in virtualized environments. SIGMETRICS Perform. Eval. Rev. **37**, 61–66 (2010)

9. Hamilton, J.: Cost of power in large-scale data centers. Technical report. http://perspectives.mvdirona.com/2008/11/cost-of-power-in-large-scale-data-centers/. Accessed Apr 2008

10. Irfan, A.: Easy and efficient disk I/O workload characterization in VMware ESX server. In: IEEE 10th International Symposium on Workload Characterization, September 2007

11. Lebre, A., Legrand, A., Suter, F., Veyre, P.: Adding storage simulation capacities to the SimGrid toolkit: concepts, models, and API. In: Proceedings of the 15th IEEE/ACM Symposium on Cluster, Cloud and Grid Computing (2015)

12. Li, Z., Greenan, K.M., Leung, A.W., Zadok, E.: Power consumption in enterprise-scale backup storage systems. In: Proceedings of the Tenth USENIX Conference on File and Storage Technologies, February 2012

13. Long, S., Zhao, Y.: A toolkit for modeling and simulating cloud data storage: an extension to CloudSim. In: International Conference on Control Engineering and Communication Technology, Liaoning, China (2012)

14. Louis, B., Mitra, K., Saguna, S., Ahlund, C.: CloudSimDisk: energy-aware storage simulation in CloudSim. In: IEEE/ACM International Conference on Utility and Cloud Computing (2015)

15. Mann, Z.A.: Allocation of virtual machines in cloud data centers–a survey of problem models and optimization algorithms. ACM Comput. Surv. **48**, 11:1–11:34 (2015)

16. Mesnier, M., Ganger, G.R., Riedel, E.: Object-based storage. IEEE Commun. Mag. **41**, 84–90 (2003)

17. Ouarnoughi, H., Boukhobza, J., Singhoff, F., Rubini, S.: A multi-level I/O tracer for timing and performance storage systems in IaaS cloud. In: 3rd IEEE International

Workshop on Real-Time and distributed Computing in Emerging Applications (2014)

18. Ouarnoughi, H., Boukhobza, J., Singhoff, F., Rubini, S.: A cost model for virtual machine storage in cloud IaaS context. In: 24th Euromicro International Conference on Parallel, Distributed, and Network-Based Processing (2016)

19. Ruiu, D.: An overview of MPEG-2. Technical report, Hewlett Packard (1997). http://literature.agilent.com/litweb/pdf/5966-1031E.pdf

20. Seagate: Barracuda st1000dm003. Technical report, http://www.seagate.com, http://www.seagate.com/staticfiles/docs/pdf/datasheet/disc/barracuda-ds1737-1-1111us.pdf. Accessed Mar 2016

21. Sturm, T., Jrad, F., Streit, A.: Storage CloudSim - A simulation environment for cloud object storage infrastructures. In: Proceedings of the 4th International Conference on Cloud Computing and Services Science (2014)

Early Evaluation of the "Infinite Memory Engine" Burst Buffer Solution

Wolfram Schenck[1][✉], Salem El Sayed[2], Maciej Foszczynski[2],
Wilhelm Homberg[2], and Dirk Pleiter[2]

[1] Faculty of Engineering and Mathematics,
Bielefeld University of Applied Sciences, Bielefeld, Germany
wolfram.schenck@fh-bielefeld.de

[2] Jülich Supercomputing Centre, Forschungszentrum Jülich, Jülich, Germany
{s.el.sayed.mohamed,w.homberg,d.pleiter}@fz-juelich.de

Abstract. Hierarchical storage architectures are required to meet both, capacity and bandwidth requirements for future high-end storage architectures. In this paper we present the results of an evaluation of an emerging technology, DataDirect Networks' (DDN) Infinite Memory Engine (IME). IME allows to realize a fast buffer in front of a large capacity storage system. We collected benchmarking data with IOR and with the HPC application NEST. The IOR bandwidth results show how well network bandwidth towards such fast buffer can be exploited compared to the external storage system. The NEST benchmarks clearly demonstrate that IME can reduce I/O-induced load imbalance between MPI ranks to a minimum while speeding up I/O as a whole by a considerable factor.

Keywords: Burst buffer · Storage · Infinite Memory Engine (IME) · GPFS · NEST · IOR · Performance analysis

1 Introduction

Design of any future supercomputing systems face the challenge of maintaining a reasonable balance of compute performance versus performance of the I/O sub-system. In practice, this gap is growing and systems are moving away from Amdahl's rule of thumb for a balanced performance ratio, namely a bit of I/O per second for each instruction per second (see [1] for an updated version). Systems providing $O(10^{16})$ Flop/s compute performance typically feature an I/O bandwidth well below 10^{12} Byte/s.

The growing gap between compute and I/O performance is even more critical as the need for the latter is growing. This is partially due to new, more data-intensive application areas with need for scalable compute resources. A possibly even larger demand for I/O capabilities results from the emerging need for continuous check-pointing since the complexity of supercomputing systems is growing and they are becoming more likely to fail.

Today, disk drives are the predominant technology in modern high-performance storage systems. This technology has been showing impressive

© Springer International Publishing AG 2016
M. Taufer et al. (Eds.): ISC High Performance Workshops 2016, LNCS 9945, pp. 604–615, 2016.
DOI: 10.1007/978-3-319-46079-6_41

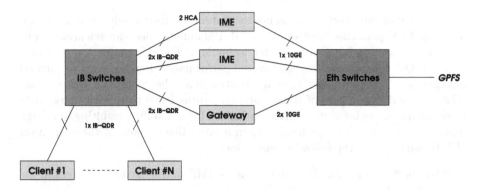

Fig. 1. Schematic overview of the integration of the IME servers at Jülich Supercomputing Centre (JSC).

capacity growth rates, but only moderate speed improvements. For this reason there is the need to move forward using other technologies, i.e. non-volatile memory (NVM) technologies. This technology allows for significantly higher bandwidth, however at significantly higher costs per unit capacity. Therefore, there is a growing interest in hierarchical approaches, where NVM-based storage devices and large capacity disk drives are combined to provide both, high bandwidth as well as large capacity.

Burst buffers [2] are such an architectural concept. It is based on the observation that HPC applications often do not exhibit a continuous but rather a bursty I/O pattern, i.e. short periods which are followed by longer periods without I/O. Adding a fast buffer which is able to store a full burst, one in principle could relax the bandwidth towards the large capacity storage system. An implementation of such a burst buffer has been developed by DDN under the name Infinite Memory Engine (IME). It is designed as an intermediate storage layer between a compute system and an external storage system and uses NVM-based storage devices as shown in Fig. 1. Burst buffers like IME are in principle especially beneficial for scientific applications which cause large amounts of I/O traffic during operation. In this regard, three main patterns can be identified:

- **Dominant read**: A large class of parallel scientific applications are concerned with processing data retrieved by experiments or collected by observatories, e.g. large-scale radio-astronomy facilities. Burst buffers can be used for pre-staging this data.
- **Dominant write**: A much broader class of scientific applications faces the opposite challenge: It generates a large amount of data which need to be written to storage for long-term archiving or later post-processing.
- **Transient write/read**: Furthermore, workflows exist where one application produces a significant amount of data which is consumed by the same or another application running on the same system. Often this data is transient in nature, i.e. does not have to be archived. Burst buffers would allow to keep this data within the system.

The goal of our study is to assess by systematic testing with real hardware how well IME performs in practice, and if it is able to speed up scientific applications by its underlying burst buffer technology. For this evaluation we ran a series of IOR benchmarks to assess overall performance. Furthermore, we carried out extensive tests with NEST, an application from the "dominant write" class. NEST is used in the field of computational neuroscience to simulate large networks of spiking point neurons. It is optimized for scalability, resulting in a huge number of processes writing local data in a burst-like fashion. In the evaluation of IME we consider the following questions:

- What performance can be achieved using IME and what is the potential for overall application performance improvement?
- What efforts are required to adapt applications?
- What features are missing at the current development stage of IME?

In the next section we highlight some of the related work. In Sect. 3 we describe the test setup we have been using. Our results are then presented in Sects. 4 (IOR) and 5 (NEST). Finally, we summarize our findings and draw our conclusions in Sect. 6.

2   Related Work

The term "burst buffers" has first been used in [2]. The authors do not claim having invented the concept of an intermediate storage layer, but rather claim having presented a concept for incorporating such buffers into the existing HPC storage software stacks. They proposed to use a combination of the check-pointing framework SCR [3] and the checkpoint file system PLFS [4].

An evaluation on how the parallel file system GPFS could be used for staging files in an intermediate, NVM-based storage layer or for flushing these to an external storage system was presented in [5]. GPFS comprises a policy engine which can be used to manage the available storage and handle data movement between different storage pools.

In [6] an attempt was made to explore the potential for burst buffers for a large-scale Blue Gene/P system under the assumption that it could be equipped with burst buffers. The resulting hypothetical architecture was modeled by an event simulator. The main benefit that had been identified for burst buffers was the opportunity to use a much less capable external storage system with no major impact on the I/O rates. This simulation-based approach was enabled by extensive analysis of I/O data collected during production runs [7], which was used as input for these simulations.

With the emergence of suitable NVM-based storage devices, a large number of papers have been published on how to integrate these technologies into HPC architectures in general and I/O architectures in particular. In [8] the use of NVM instead of DRAM for data staging is advocated. A prototype for the later realized Gordon architecture, which had been optimized for data-intensive applications by integrating SSDs, is presented in [9]. Several concepts have been

Table 1. Parameters used for IOR.

I/O API	POSIX
Number of MPI ranks per compute node	`NPROC` = 2, 4, 8
Transfer size	`TSIZE` = 4 MiByte
Overall amount of data	`BSIZE` = 24, 12, 6 GiByte (depending on `NPROC`)
Number of repetitions	5

developed for managing data staging within an HPC system, e.g. in an NVM layer. Examples are DataStager [10] and DART [11].

3 Test Setup

The IME test-setup (Fig. 1) at the Jülich Supercomputing Centre (JSC) comprised 2 IME scalable servers with 24 SSDs each. Each IME SU SSD has a capacity of 200 GiByte. Each IME server was connected via 2 IB-QDR links to the IB fabric of the JUDGE cluster. Additionally, each server was connected via a single 10-GE link to JSC's 10-GE fabric, which provided the connectivity to the central storage facility JUST. As parallel file system GPFS is used.

The meanwhile decommissioned JUDGE cluster comprised 206 IBM iData-Plex nodes. Each node consisted of 2 Intel Xeon X5650 (Westmere) processors and 48 GiByte of main memory. Each processor had 6 cores and supported via hyperthreading 12 hardware threads (providing overall 24 hardware threads per compute node).

Regular access to the external storage system JUST was realized through 1 gateway node. the time when the runs reported here have been executed. This was connected via 2 IB-QDR links to the IB fabric of the cluster and via 2 10-GE links to JSC's 10-GE fabric. The nominal network bandwidth to the IME servers was 128 Gbit/s. The direct path towards the external GPFS via the gateway nodes was limited by the 10-GE links to a nominal bandwidth ob 20 Gbit/s.

We used up to 60 iDataPlex nodes, which served as compute nodes, all running Scientific Linux 6.7. A pre-release version of IME was used, i.e. all results should be considered preliminary.

4 IOR Benchmarks

To measure I/O bandwidth and to explore the scalability of IME, we used the IOR benchmark (version 2.10.3; parameter settings in Table 1).

The total amount of data written and read per process (parameter `BSIZE`) was selected such that the aggregated amount of data per node was 48 GiByte, i.e. equal to the main memory capacity per node. We also performed runs, where

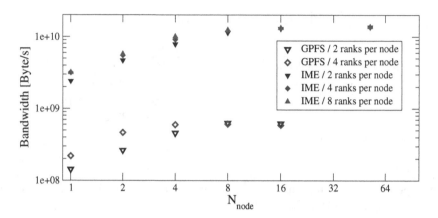

Fig. 2. Read bandwidth as a function of the number of nodes N_{node}.

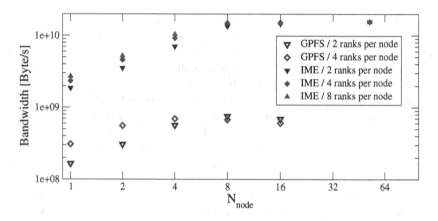

Fig. 3. Write bandwidth as a function of the number of nodes N_{node}.

less data was written and read, to confirm our expectation that the amount of data is large enough to minimize possible caching effects.

In Figs. 2 and 3 we plot the maximum measured bandwidth using the POSIX interface as a function of the number of nodes.[1] We performed the measurements for different numbers of MPI ranks per compute node. We make the following observations:

- To maximize read or write performance at least 4 MPI ranks per node should be involved in reading or writing.
- To fully saturate bandwidth at least 8 and 4 nodes are required when accessing IME or directly GPFS, respectively.

---

[1] For the setup that was put in place in December 2015, MPI I/O was not sufficiently stable to obtain coherent results for IOR using MPIIO or HDF5 as I/O API.

- For reading and writing to and from IME a bandwidth of up to 13.8 GByte/s and 15.63 GByte/s was measured, respectively, which corresponds to 86 % and 98 % of the nominal network bandwidth.
- The bandwidth to GPFS via the gateway nodes could not be fully exploited. We observed a bandwidth of 0.6–0.7 GByte/s, which amounts to about 25 % of the nominal network bandwidth. Due to the pending decommissioning of the cluster it was not possible to investigate this further.

5 NEST Benchmarks

5.1 Background on Application

NEST (the "NEural Simulation Tool") [12] is used in the field of computational neuroscience to simulate biological neural networks at the level of spiking point neurons. The focus is on the simulation of the dynamics of interactions between nerve cells. NEST was developed under the premise that it is both suited for small experiments on local machines and for large-scale simulations on the world's leading supercomputers [13]. This flexibility is achieved through a hybrid parallelization scheme using MPI and OpenMP threads.

A typical NEST simulation consists of two stages: First the network is wired up and connections (synapses) between neurons are established ("build stage"), and second the dynamics of the whole network is simulated ("simulation stage"). During the simulation stage, the generated data can be recorded and stored in the file system. For this purpose, two classes of virtual recording devices are provided, *spike detectors* and *multimeters*. Spike detectors register discrete signals emitted by neurons in irregular intervals (so-called "spikes"). In contrast, multimeters record in a continuous and deterministic fashion specific state variables, e.g. the membrane potential of single neurons. The user can freely choose the number of spike detectors and multimeters in the simulation, the sets of neurons connected to them for recording, and the sampling interval and set of state variables for each multimeter. Every recording device exists on every thread in the simulation, and for each thread-specific instance a separate file and C++ stream is used.[2]

The main program structure of the NEST simulation stage can be reduced to the following three steps which are repeated in an iteration loop:

(1) Thread-internal routing of spike events to their target neurons;
(2) updating of neuronal states and generation of spike events;
(3) exchange of spike events between MPI ranks.

During step (2), the recorded data is written to the file system. In step (3), MPI synchronization takes place between all ranks. In large simulations, step (1) takes a considerable amount of time [15], so that it is valid to state that NEST writes data in bursts during step (2).

---

[2] Because this I/O approach does not scale well on supercomputers, right now a new I/O subsystem for NEST based on libraries for parallel I/O is developed [14].

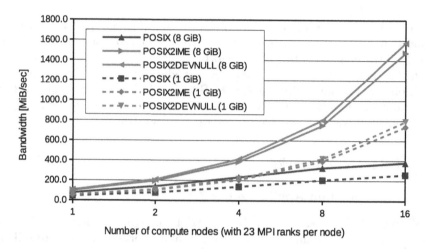

Fig. 4. Effective bandwidth consumed by NEST for the three settings described in the text as a function of the number of compute nodes. Solid lines: 8 GiByte of data per node written to the file system (corresponds to 22 multim. state vars.). Dashed lines: 1 GiByte of data per node (corresponds to 1 multim. state var.).

5.2   Workload Description

NEST was built with gcc 4.4.7 on the code base from revision 11903 in the main NEST SVN repository. To create benchmarking data, a random balanced network [16] was simulated over 100 ms of biological time. Such a network consists of an excitatory and an inhibitory population of neurons. Both populations were connected to a specific spike detector and a specific multimeter, thus overall there were four virtual recording devices. The amount of written data was varied through the number of state variables recorded by the multimeters from each neuron, ranging from 1 to 22. Spike data contributed less than one percent to the overall amount of written data.

5.3   Weak Scaling Analysis

To analyze the impact of using IME on the overall performance of the simulation stage of NEST, we determined the effective bandwidth, i.e. the ratio of the total amount of written data versus time-to-solution (also called "simulation time"), for the following settings:

POSIX: Write to files in GPFS using POSIX API

POSIX2IME: Write to files in IME using POSIX API.

POSIX2DEVNULL: Write to device /dev/null instead of writing to files.

The first setup corresponds to a standard run without IME, the second setup relies fully on IME for writing data, while the third setup mimics the ideal case

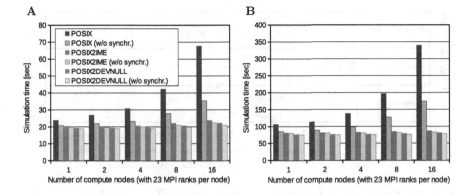

Fig. 5. Time-to-solution of the NEST simulation stage as a function of the number of compute nodes. **A:** Each node writes about 1 GiByte of data. **B:** 8 GiByte per node.

of an infinitely fast storage system. In addition to varying the amount of written data per neuron (see preceding subsection), we varied the number of compute nodes between 1 and 16 with the number of simulated neurons and synapses per node being constant (strict weak scaling). On each compute node, 23 MPI ranks were started. This is one less than the number of available hardware threads per node. The 24th hardware thread was left to the FUSE client which always ran at 100 % load (single-threaded).

5.4   Effective Bandwidth

Results are plotted in Fig. 4. Each data point is based on the minimum value of time-to-solution out of five independent runs. Our observations are:

- The effective bandwidth in the case POSIX2DEVNULL is only 5–10 % higher compared to the case POSIX2IME. This means that the performance of IME is close to the "ideal" performance.
- Good scaling is observed: The effective bandwidth in the case of POSIX2IME nearly doubles with every doubling of the number of compute nodes.
- On GPFS such scaling behavior could only be consistently observed up to 4 compute nodes. As a consequence the effective bandwidth on GPFS was nearly 4 times smaller compared to IME for the largest problem size and 8 GiByte of written data per compute node.
- As NEST is performing a large number of small, formatted I/O operations, the bandwidth is significantly smaller compared to IOR measurements.

5.5   Time-to-Solution

In Fig. 5 we compare time-to-solution as a function of the number of compute nodes. For each setting (POSIX, POSIX2IME, POSIX2DEVNULL), we show the full simulation time and the simulation time after subtracting the time required for

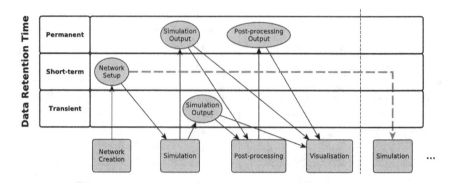

Fig. 6. Data retention time analysis for the NEST work-flow.

step 3 in the main simulation loop of NEST (bars in light color; "w/o synchr."). Step 3 covers mainly MPI synchronization between ranks and therefore reflects load imbalance between ranks. Generally, step 3 is very short, and in NEST simulations without I/O, load imbalance is not an issue. The simulation time after subtracting the time required for step 3 is called "effective simulation time" in the following. Three things can be observed:

- The larger the number of nodes, the larger is the advantage of writing to IME or to "/dev/null" instead of writing to GPFS. As observed before, the cases POSIX2IME and POSIX2DEVNULL show nearly ideal scaling behavior.
- The larger the number of compute nodes, the more suffers GPFS from I/O-induced load imbalance between ranks (visible in the increasing difference between full and effective simulation times). In contrast, writing to IME shows nearly the same pattern as writing to "/dev/null", thus there is no I/O-caused load imbalance. Further runtime reduction by reducing load imbalance between ranks is therefore barely possible via I/O improvements.
- These observations hold qualitatively both for 1 GiByte of written data per compute node (Fig. 5a) and 8 GiByte of written data per compute node (Fig. 5b).

6   Discussion, Conclusions, and Future Work

We carried out an empirical evaluation of the IME burst buffer technology. We collected both benchmarking data with IOR and with the HPC application NEST on a compute cluster with up to 64 nodes. The IOR results show that both for reading and writing data about 90 % of the nominal network bandwidth could be saturated when using IME. This number was already nearly reached with only eight compute nodes. Compared to GPFS attached via a small number of 10-GE links, an I/O speedup factor of more than 20 could be observed. This indicates that IME is a promising technology for various classes of applications (i.e., "dominant read", "transient write/read", "dominant write").

The NEST benchmarks corroborate this general finding but go one step further. NEST operates with a large number of small writes which occur in a burst-like fashion roughly simultaneously on all MPI ranks. When writing to GPFS, this behavior causes a considerable amount of load imbalance which increases with the number of compute nodes. With only 16 compute nodes, this load imbalance already nearly doubles the simulation time. When using IME instead of GPFS, two beneficial effects could be observed: The load imbalance nearly disappears, and in addition to this, the effective simulation time (not including time lost to load imbalance) is roughly halved on 16 compute nodes. NEST performance with IME comes very close to using NEST with an infinitely fast storage device, resulting in nearly perfect weak scaling behavior. This finding fully applies to the setting with only one multimeter state variable (corresponding to 1 GiByte of written data per node). Such a setting would be realistic for NEST production runs. Therefore we conclude that the incorporation of IME in compute clusters would be highly beneficial for users of NEST or other applications with similar I/O characteristics ("dominant write" in bursts). It also has to be emphasized that the switch from GPFS to IME did not require any changes in the source code of NEST, making the transition effortless and easy.

For sustained performance of the burst buffer over long simulation times, the bandwidth between burst buffer and external storage system needs to be large enough to avoid buffer overflow. Extrapolating the scaling behavior of NEST with IME from Fig. 4 for the realistic setting (one multimeter state variable corresponding to 1 GiByte of written data per node), an external bandwidth of about 3 GiByte/s would be required for a cluster with 64 compute nodes. Such a bandwidth is achievable with today's technology at reasonable cost, confirming the practical applicability of the burst buffer concept.

In this paper we mainly focused on today's implementation of work-flows, where data is written to an external storage system. Due to bandwidth limitations as well as growing data volumes we expect this not to be affordable anymore in future. To analyse such future work-flows we consider a data retention time analysis as proposed in [17] to be helpful. This analysis results in a classification of data used or generated by a user application depending on how long it will be retained. It includes the following data retention time classes: permanent, transient or short-term. Short-term data has a life-time that does not exceed job duration. Transient data has a limited life-time that exceeds job duration, e.g. output data that is used by a next job. Finally, permanent data is assumed to have unlimited life-time. For NEST a retention time analysis for the data created and re-used at different stages of the work-flow has been performed and is shown in Fig. 6.

For the further development of IME, we recommend to consider the following use cases and demands:

– *Data pre-fetching*: Applications that perform significant amount of reading from the external storage system would likely benefit from data being pre-fetched to IME before job start. Extensions of the batch queuing system, as implemented for the Cori system at NERSC, are a good starting point.[3]

– *Managing short-term and transient data*: IME data management tools should allow keeping short-term or transient data within IME. As this data is not meant to be stored permanently, it ideally never hits the external storage. This case could also be relevant for parallel performance tools that generate significant amount of transient data that is processed soon after job end.

– *End-to-end data integrity*: As the capacity of storage systems continue to grow also the risk of undetected data corruption grows [18]. To reduce this risk, storage solution providers did integrate end-to-end data integrity checks (see, e.g., IBM's parallel file system GPFS). Using IME in its current implementation as an intermediate storage layer in front of GPFS, end-to-end data integrity between producers and consumers is not provided. However, this would be highly desirable.

Regardless of these desired future improvements, we finally conclude that the IME burst buffer technology has reached a level of maturity that allows it to be used for running complex parallel applications. It allows to grow the I/O bandwidth at a faster speed than in the past and thus mitigate the risk of a further deepening gap between I/O and compute performance.

Acknowledgements. We would like to thank DDN for making an IME test system available at Jülich Supercomputing Centre. In particular, we gracefully acknowledge the continuous support by Tommaso Cecchi and Toine Beckers.

References

1. Gray, J., Shenoy, P.: Rules of thumb in data engineering, pp. 3–10 (2000)
2. Bent, J., Grider, G., Kettering, B., Manzanares, A., McClelland, M., Torres, A., Torrez, A.: Storage challenges at Los Alamos national lab. In: 2012 IEEE 28th Symposium on Mass Storage Systems and Technologies (MSST), pp. 1–5, April 2012
3. Moody, A., Bronevetsky, G., Mohror, K., de Supinski, B.: Design, modeling, and evaluation of a scalable multi-level checkpointing system. In: 2010 International Conference for High Performance Computing, Networking, Storage and Analysis (SC), pp. 1–11, November 2010
4. Bent, J., Gibson, G., Grider, G., McClelland, B., Nowoczynski, P., Nunez, J., Polte, M., Wingate, M.: PLFs: a checkpoint filesystem for parallel applications. In: Proceedings of the Conference on High Performance Computing Networking, Storage and Analysis, pp. 1–12, November 2009
5. El Sayed, S., Graf, S., Hennecke, M., Pleiter, D., Schwarz, G., Schick, H., Stephan, M.: Using GPFS to manage NVRAM-based storage cache. In: Kunkel, J.M., Ludwig, T., Meuer, H.W. (eds.) ISC 2013. LNCS, vol. 7905, pp. 435–446. Springer, Heidelberg (2013)

---

[3] http://www.nersc.gov/users/computational-systems/cori/burst-buffer/
example-batch-scripts/.

6. Liu, N., Cope, J., Carns, P., Carothers, C., Ross, R., Grider, G., Crume, A., Maltzahn, C.: On the role of burst buffers in leadership-class storage systems. In: 2012 IEEE 28th Symposium on Mass Storage Systems and Technologies (MSST), pp. 1–11, April 2012

7. Carns, P., Harms, K., Allcock, W., Bacon, C., Lang, S., Latham, R., Ross, R.: Understanding and improving computational science storage access through continuous characterization. In: 2011 IEEE 27th Symposium on Mass Storage Systems and Technologies (MSST), pp. 1–14, May 2011

8. Kannan, S., Gavrilovska, A., Schwan, K., Milojicic, D., Talwar, V.: Using active NVRAM for I/O staging. In: PDAC 2011, pp. 15–22. ACM, New York (2011)

9. He, J., Jagatheesan, A., Gupta, S., Bennett, J., Snavely, A.: Dash: a recipe for a flash-based data intensive supercomputer. In: 2010 International Conference for High Performance Computing, Networking, Storage and Analysis (SC), pp. 1–11, November 2010

10. Abbasi, H., Wolf, M., Eisenhauer, G., Klasky, S., Schwan, K., Zheng, F.: DataStager: scalable data staging services for petascale applications. In: HPDC 2009, pp. 39–48. ACM, New York (2009)

11. Docan, C., Parashar, M., Klasky, S.: Enabling high-speed asynchronous data extraction and transfer using dart. Concur. Comput. Pract. Exper. **22**(9), 1181–1204 (2010)

12. Gewaltig, M.O., Diesmann, M.: NEST (Neural Simulation Tool). Scholarpedia **2**(4), 1430 (2007)

13. Kunkel, S., Schmidt, M., Eppler, J.M., Plesser, H.E., Masumoto, G., Igarashi, J., Ishii, S., Fukai, T., Morrison, A., Diesmann, M., Helias, M.: Spiking network simulation code for petascale computers. Front. Neuroinform. 8, Article number 78 (2014)

14. Schumann, T., Frings, W., Peyser, A., Schenck, W., Thust, K., Eppler, J.M.: Modeling the I/O behavior of the NEST simulator using a proxy. In: Elgeti, S., Simon, J.W. (eds.) Conference Proceedings of the YIC GACM 2015, Aachen (Germany), pp. 213–216. Publication Server of RWTH Aachen University (2015)

15. Schenck, W., Adinetz, A.V., Zaytsev, Y.V., Pleiter, D., Morrison, A.: Performance model for large-scale neural simulations with NEST. In: SC14 Conference for Supercomputing (Extended Poster Abstracts), New Orleans (LA), November 2014

16. Morrison, A., Aertsen, A., Diesmann, M.: Spike-timing dependent plasticity in balanced random networks. Neural Comput. **19**(6), 1437–1467 (2007)

17. Lujan, J., et al.: APEX workflows. Technical report, LANL, NERSC, SNL (2015)

18. Rozier, E.W.D., Belluomini, W., Deenadhayalan, V., Hafner, J., Rao, K., Zhou, P.: Evaluating the impact of undetected disk errors in raid systems. In: IEEE/IFIP International Conference on Dependable Systems Networks, DSN 2009, pp. 83–92, June 2009

Motivation and Implementation of a Dynamic Remote Storage System for I/O Demanding HPC Applications

Matthias Neuer[1(✉)], Jürgen Salk[1], Holger Berger[2], Erich Focht[2],
Christian Mosch[1], Karsten Siegmund[1], Volodymyr Kushnarenko[1],
Stefan Kombrink[1], and Stefan Wesner[1]

[1] Ulm University, Ulm, Germany
{matthias.neuer,kiz.hpc-admin}@uni-ulm.de
[2] NEC, Munich, Germany
{holger.berger,erich.focht}@emea.nec.com

Abstract. I/O subsystem performance is becoming increasingly important for a wide range of applications. The demand can be met with a large memory capacity or fast local SSDs, but such solutions cause very high investment costs and are rather inflexible. Here, we investigate a multi-tiered approach, combining memory, local SSDs and InfiniBand-attached block storage connected via SRP (SCSI RDMA protocol). Different variants of this hybrid storage system are evaluated, and we present a method to analyze the I/O patterns of applications for choosing the best approach. We also demonstrate the integration of the dynamic remote storage facility into the scheduling system Moab. Our method allows for an on-demand provisioning of multi-tiered file systems of varying sizes, managing storage resources automatically with a broker software.

Keywords: Multi-tiered storage · I/O access patterns · Block-device cache · Logical volume concatenation · Job scheduling

1 Introduction

In a range of application domains, such as structural mechanics, computational biomechanics as well as computational chemistry, the performance of the I/O subsystem visibly influences the overall time to result. A possible approach to provide the necessary fast I/O is to use systems equipped with sufficient main memory or fast local storage solutions SSD devices. However, such solutions are only available at high costs as the systems must be built for the peak demand.

One way to compromise between performance demand and cost is a tiered storage solution with a high performance tier (e.g. based on SSDs) and a capacity tier (realized with HDDs) [1]. There are several different options to build the tiered system out of these building blocks as outlined later in Sect. 3.

The paper starts with an analysis of different I/O monitoring solutions and their applicability to understand the I/O pattern of applications. The choice of

© Springer International Publishing AG 2016
M. Taufer et al. (Eds.): ISC High Performance Workshops 2016, LNCS 9945, pp. 616–626, 2016.
DOI: 10.1007/978-3-319-46079-6_42

analyzed software is based on their application in the field of quantum chemistry (often abbreviated as QC). Sample jobs running Molpro [2] were chosen to prepare the graphs, but the same method could be applied to any other application.

Secondly, different options to build tiered storage systems are analyzed using the storage access patterns recorded in the first section. The following section introduces the Dynamic Remote Scratch implementation (DRS). This solution does not just use the fast local storage as a generic cache, but aims to combine local and networked attached storage in a more flexible way.

2 Typical I/O Demands of High End Quantum Chemistry Jobs

Thorough understanding of I/O patterns and identifying bottlenecks is the starting point for improving performance of I/O demanding HPC applications [3]. To do this, we analyze the I/O characteristics of a representative QC job on both, the storage device and the application level, respectively.

2.1 Monitoring Storage Device Utilization

The I/O dependency was verified by monitoring the utilization of the exposed storage devices while running a representative QC test job. The *iostat* command has been used to capture status information on the device activity at intervals of one second during runtime of the program. *Iostat* is a popular performance reporting tool that is part of the sysstat package [4].

Although *iostat* provides various metrics on device activity, we confine ourselves to the %util metrics in the study presented here. This metrics is the percentage of CPU time during which I/O requests were issued to the device, i.e. this value represents a measure for the utilization of the corresponding device. A value close to 100 % indicates device saturation. For this analysis, *iostat* has been invoked with the following options:

```
iostat -dkx 1 | tee ~/iostat.out
```

The -d option causes *iostat* to include storage device utilization metrics, whereas the -kx option causes extended statistics to be printed in kB/s.

The system requirements for the test application are known to amount to 13 GB in main memory (RAM) and 35 GB of disk space for temporary data during runtime. The device utilization has been recorded for two different test runs of the application: (1) on a compute node with 16 GB of RAM and (2) on a compute node with 48 GB RAM, both of which equipped with conventional spinning disk hard drives. The measured storage device activities for both test runs are shown in Fig. 1.

Figure 1 (a) shows that in run (1) the storage device was saturated for a large amount of the runtime, meaning that the application had to wait for the

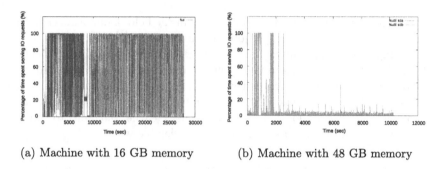

(a) Machine with 16 GB memory   (b) Machine with 48 GB memory

Fig. 1. Two runs of the same application on different nodes

data to become available. Figure 1 (b) shows the device utilization for test run (2), in which the observed storage device utilization was drastically reduced in comparison to test run (1). The ratio of the time being spent in serving I/O requests is in the order of 5 % (apart from some peak utilization in the starting phase of the program). This difference in device utilization can be attributed to page caching of the operating system: Unlike test run (1), the total amount of memory available in test run (2), was sufficiently large for the application itself (13 GB) and also for keeping its temporary data file (35 GB) fully within the page cache. Thus, most of the read requests issued by the application have not been served by the storage device itself but from data cached in memory. This resulted in a tremendous speedup of the application by a factor of 2.5.

This test case clearly indicates that I/O operations represent a major bottleneck for the application and optimization of the storage system is very likely to increase the performance for this kind of applications.

2.2 Tracing I/O Patterns at the Application Level

The results obtained by *iostat* from the previous section reflect the utilization of the underlying storage device but does not provide any deeper insight on the application's I/O behavior itself. Information is lacking on the type of I/O operations sent to the OS, specifically the ratio of write versus read operations, the number of I/O operations issued per second, the number of bytes (read or write) per operation and the exact access pattern: sequential streaming I/O versus random access. In order to gain a better understanding of the application's I/O pattern, we have used the *strace* command [5]. *Strace* is a diagnostic tool that intercepts and records the system calls which are called by a running process and the signals which are received by a process. The following command line has been used to capture the I/O related system calls of the test application:

```
strace -T -ttt -f -e trace=file,desc -o ~/trace.out prog < infile
```

The -T option causes *strace* to report the elapsed time for any system call. The option -ttt causes microsecond timing, the -f option causes all children

processes to be included and the -e trace=file,desc option has been used
to limit the trace to I/O related system calls in order to reduce the amount of
data written to the output file specified by the -o option. This measurement has
been performed on a compute node equipped with 48 GB RAM, i.e. within the
environment referred to as run (2) in the previous section. The recorded output
file contained 30 million lines that were finally post-processed and visualized by
means of a number of custom shell and Perl scripts.

Figure 2 depicts the performed
IOPS (I/O operations per second)
of the program for all read operations throughout the whole runtime.
The observed pattern reveals repet-
itive read access signatures, each of
which exposing a sub-pattern of bursty
read accesses with up to tens of
thousands read operations per second.
Obviously, these peak values exceed
the capabilities of current magnetic
hard disks. As the read requests in
the example are fully served from the
page cache instead of the physical storage device, the peak values observed
in Fig. 2 represent an upper limit for
what is generally achievable.

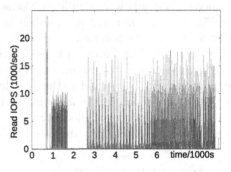

Fig. 2. IOPS during runtime

Figure 3 shows file descriptor offsets for every two consecutive read
operations. A zero offset indicates
sequential reads with the next block of
data located directly after the previous
one, whereas each non–zero offset indicates repositioning of the file pointer
before the subsequent read operation,

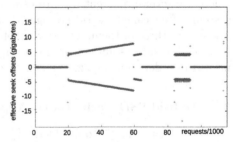

Fig. 3. Measured offsets between successive read operations.

i.e. that the next data chunk is located somewhere else in the file. The latter
translates to random access I/O which increases access times due to additional
seek latencies introduced by head repositioning for spinning hard drives. Further
investigation showed that the application reads data in a small number of discrete chunks sizes ranging from 19 kB up 352 kB. We have repeated this analysis
for other sub-samples for this test application, which all revealed the very same
behavior as the one described above.

The same analysis methods have been applied to various test cases that are
not presented in detail here. From our investigations we can draw a number of
conclusions: From the observation that there are more read than write operations we can deduce that cache based storage solutions represent a promising
approach to face I/O performance shortages as already demonstrated in the page
cache example of Sect. 2.1. Because the IOPS values of up to several thousand

exceed the capabilities of conventional hard disks, we have to take SSDs into consideration. However, as some jobs require up to 10 TB of storage, it would be too expensive to cover these peak-capacity demands at all nodes and all times purely by local SSDs. Thus, a tiered or hybrid storage facility consisting of local SSDs as core storage devices and supplementary hard disk devices for serving peak-capacity demands appear as a sensible approach.

Given that the observed I/O patterns reveal bursty but also highly discontinuous workloads with significant domains of only few read accesses (as seen in Fig. 2), the supplementary hard disks may even reside on a shared storage device that can be accessed remotely by multiple nodes at the same time. The SRP (SCSI RDMA Protocol) is used here as this fully preserves the local page caching mechanisms of the operating system without introducing overhead for cache coherence as it would be the case through e.g. the TCP/IP communication protocol. Therefore, in the following sections we focus on a hybrid solution of local SSDs and a central block storage system connected via SRP and the way these two storage facilities are joined.

3 Hybrid Storage System

There are several different ways to connect two storage devices to form a single system, often called hybrid storage or tiered storage, and in this chapter we investigate three of them. The trivial solution is mounting the two devices side by side. The other solutions are more sophisticated and careful configuration is needed in order to maximize the benefit of the SSDs.

3.1 Hybrid SSD Cache Based Approach

We chose flashcache [6] to use block devices as a cache for it is released under the GPL and seems to be the most stable solution currently available. The following benchmarks were run on a single node using just a single process as this is the typical way to do I/O for most of the applications in quantum chemistry. The node has 128 GB RAM, a RAID0 array of 4 SSDs with a total of 850 GB as cache, and as a backend device a NetApp E-5560, consisting

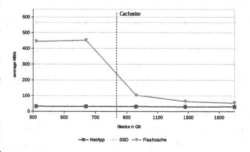

Fig. 4. Quantchem FIO benchmark

of conventional hard disks, connected via SRP over InfiniBand. Besides the standard sequential and random I/O benchmarks we used a custom-made benchmark called quantchem which models the behavior of typical QC jobs with random as well as sequential reads and different block sizes using FIO (Flexible I/O Tester) [7]. The block sizes and the mixture of sequential and random accesses was generated using *strace* analysis of quantum chemical applications like the ones presented in this paper. The benchmark reads from files with configurable size and Fig. 4 shows the results when this file size is successively increased from 320 GB to 1600 GB.

Evidently, as soon as the file size exceeds the size of the cache, the performance of flashcache drops rapidly, being only barely faster than the backend device at 1600 GB file size. This disappointing result is caused by the random disk access pattern of the quantchem benchmark which leads to a almost uniform access distribution. So there are many cache misses due to the unpredictability of the data accesses and so most of the data comes from the backend device. A similar result was seen in [8], where the same benchmark was used but on a smaller system with much smaller files. There, the performance decline was not quite as large when exceeding the cache size because the speed difference of the cache- and the backend device was smaller. In Fig. 5 we will see a block access pattern of a real QC job which makes it quite clear why it is so hard for a caching system to figure out what data to hold in the cache. When the whole file fits in the cache, there is still a performance gap between flashcache and a pure SSD, which was already seen in [9]. In all these caching solutions, the cache overlays the disk space and thus the space on the caching device does not provide any additional space for files. The solution presented in the next chapter does not have this drawback while showing a better performance than the cache based solutions with standard caching algorithms.

3.2   Hybrid Concatenated Storage Systems

In the approach using a hybrid concatenated storage system, both devices, a fast SSD and a slow HDD, are used to store data permanently. These devices can be connected via RAID0, which splits the disk and the SSD in small stripes and distributes the data evenly across both storage systems. Another way to connect these devices is via LVM, logical volume management, where a single logical volume is created by linearly concatenating the physical volume corresponding to the SSD and the physical volume corresponding to the conventional disk. Here we have to take care that data gets written to the SSD first. If the data written completely fits onto the SSD, we don't want parts of the data to be stored on the slower disk. To achieve this, two things have to be taken into account. First, the file system has to place files at the beginning of the device and second the first blocks of the LVM device have to correspond to the physical volume created from the SSD. To fulfill the second requirement, LVM can be told to create a logical volume with a smaller size using only the physical volume from the SSD and then extend the logical volume to the full capacity. This ensures that blocks with small numbers are placed on the fast storage system and blocks with high numbers are placed on the slow storage system.

Modern file systems have sophisticated methods to speed up file operations. Often, these methods are still tailored for spinning hard disks. For example, files are distributed across the whole device which hinders the efficient use of the concatenated file system. In RHEL 7.1 with kernel 3.10.0-229 we noticed that

XFS [10] evenly spreads out subdirectories on the file system by default but when using just a single directory XFS behaves much better for our intended use. A similar problem arises when old files are deleted and afterwards new files are created. In this case XFS reuses the disk space of the old file as we expected but ext4 [11] places the new file after the deleted file. This could lead to unused disk space on the high performance storage system which is the reason why we decided to focus on the XFS file system.

Figure 5 shows accessed block numbers in read operations over time of a real QC job. The job was monitored on block layer level in an LVM concatenated file system. The hybrid file system was created by joining a RAID0 of 3 SSDs and a remote block storage device connected via SRP – both storage systems are equally sized at 300 GB. The job started a Molpro LCCSD [12] calculation whose read operations proved to be mainly random and traverse a big portion of the file in a short amount of time. The concatenated storage system benefits from the distribution of the I/O operations because about 70 % of the data is read from the SSD. The fact that the program mostly reads from the beginning of the file can of course not be guaranteed for every QC job but we saw this behavior on multiple occasions.

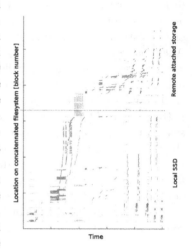

Fig. 5. Block accesses pattern of Molpro LCCSD run

4   DRS, a Dynamic Remote Scratch Implementation

4.1   Motivation

The usage of the remote storage configurations presented above in an environment with high throughput of production jobs requires a high degree of automation and flexibility for the assignment of the limited number of remote storage resources to the compute nodes. Ideally the remote storage resources would "float" freely in the cluster and be assignable to any of the nodes that needs them. This minimizes job waiting times and helps to increase resource usage compared to a fixed static setup, where only a small number of nodes has the additional storage capacity available. A dynamic approach allows to allocate vast resources to single job, or many comparably large resources to a larger number of nodes, depending only on user needs which can be expressed via batch system resource requests and without any administrator interaction.

4.2   Experimental Setup

The experiments and validation of the developments were done on a partition of the "JUSTUS" cluster at the University of Ulm, a system built with 444 nodes and a QDR infiniband interconnect. The resource management system is built with Torque and Moab. As backend storage we used a NetApp E-5560 with an additional disk enclosure with a total of 120 nearline SAS disks of 4 TB in 8U rackspace. The embedded dual redundant controllers offer a total of 4 QDR InfiniBand host connections, which can be used through SRP (SCSI RDMA protocol). The storage can sustain around 6 GB/s of bandwidth.

Volumes are created in a Dynamic Disk Pool (DDP) setup, which is NetApp's implementation of declustered parity RAID [13], offering fast rebuilds and high random access performance. Tests have shown that random access performance for small numbers of nodes is superior to traditional RAID6 volume group setups, sacrificing a little bit of bandwidth in the saturation for larger number of nodes.

4.3   Architecture

The flexible dynamic remote resource allocation is achieved by combining existing features of the Moab batch scheduler, a custom made, specialized broker software and a matching client, the SRP initiator in the Linux OS and the SRP target in a storage appliance.

The components involved in the setup, as depicted in Fig. 6:

Moab scheduler. The Moab batch scheduler's task is to schedule a job to execution hosts, considering the user's resource requests for remote storage which are expressed as requests for a global consumable resource. The broker acts as the central instance to decide which resources are available, and is queried by Moab similar to a license server for floating licenses.

torque prologue. A customized torque prologue which runs under with root privileges on the job execution nodes, decides which remote storage resources are requested for the job. *drs client* queries the *drs broker*, which makes those resources available and keeps track of the allocation. Finally, the SRP initiator is configured and the scratch filesystem is created and mounted.

torque epilogue. When the job ends, the torque epilogue is executed. It is used to unmount the scratch filesystem, clean up and signal to the broker that resources are no longer used.

drs client. The *drs client* is used for sending queries and commands to the central broker, for allocating, freeing and inquiring resources.

drs broker. The *drs broker* is the central instance that keeps track of remote storage resource allocations and configures the storage targets.

SRP initiator/target. The SRP initiator is presenting remote storage as a block device on the local machine. The target is the counterpart of the initiator. In the concretely investigated setup SRP targets were running within the controllers of a NetApp E-5560 device with IB host interfaces.

With the builtin Moab mechanisms we could not keep track of remote storage volume to node assignments. Floating licenses can not be distinguished or labeled according to our needs for managing remote volumes. Volumes carry additional properties like size, identifier and other attributes. The central *drs broker* fills the gap and adds the required flexibility while avoiding race conditions during allocation.

The listed components work together to allow a large number of nodes of a cluster to allocate flexibly remote storage from a limited pool of volumes without risking that resources are overcommited. Moab will only start a job if the specified resources are available. The interaction of the DRS components is depicted in Fig. 6.

4.4   Implementation

The broker and its client are implemented in the programming language *Go* [14] which makes them very easy to deploy, as they are static executables without dependencies on shared libraries and therefore OS version agnostic. *Go* offers a pretty high abstraction while maintaining type safety with a static type system, and showed a good development productivity. The communication between broker and client is implemented using *Go*'s very simple and elegant RPC mechanism. As a side effect, the broker is asynchronous as

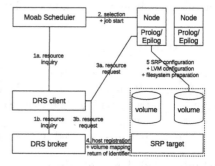

Fig. 6. Process flow for job submission

each request is running in it's own go-routine, *Go*'s implementation of lightweight green-threads. The broker maintains a record of available storage, which is configured with a configuration file listing the available storage targets and the volumes available on each of them. A volume can be flagged with attributes usable for selecting between different kinds of volumes like e.g. HDD and SSD based volumes, and with an additional property which represents an access channel to the volume. The later is used to achieve load balancing over the dual redundant controllers of the NetApp E-series devices, where each volume has a preferred owner among the controllers. The broker dumps the internal state to files at every change and reads them on restart, to make the system reboot and crash persistent. The client does all the interaction with the broker, it is also part of the administrative interface to the broker and can be used to inquire the state. It serves as the interface to the broker for the Moab scheduler and is called in the prologue and epilogue for resource allocation and deallocation. The broker tries to always end up in a clean state, if there is e.g. a problem in setting up a volume as part of a request for several volumes, it will roll back and free all resources and signal to the client that resource allocation could not succeed. A resource request can be associated with a walltime of the corresponding batch job, and resources will be freed by the broker after this time has elapsed. This way crashed nodes which didn't execute the epilogue will never leave stalled resources behind for unlimited time, administrator interaction for recovery is not required. In case a client freed some resources and the broker can not free them on the storage target for whatever reason, the volumes are marked as needing manual intervention and will not be candidates for allocation unless the state is cleared. The broker's architecture allows implementation of different target architectures. At the moment a testing dummy target and a target for the Netapp E-series IB SRP target are implemented, future additions could be e.g. iSER support for different vendors targets. Different and multiple targets can be supported by one single instance of the broker. The current implementation assumes existing volumes on the storage, it does not create the volumes but only manages them. The volumes are mapped on demand to hosts which are registered and deregistered in the SRP target. An enhanced implementation of the broker which also configures the volumes is in development. We expect slight performance regressions with this approach as the volumes initialization might not be finished when their usage starts, a tradeoff not available in the current setup.

4.5   Moab Interaction

As Moab can not be easily extended, we had to find a way to couple the scheduler with the external resources broker using existing features. We chose to treat the volumes as a Moab *shared cluster resource*, which is usually used e.g. for floating software licenses. Moab can call an external tool to check the availability of such a shared resource, and take that into consideration for scheduling decisions.

The implemented resource broker client offers an option to be called by Moab and return a resource status in the format required by Moab. As Moab queries the resource status very often (every 10 s in our configuration), this inquiry has to be fast and cheap, which is one of the reasons to store the resource state in a broker instead of querying the used NetApp storage directly. The direct query is heavy and expensive and takes about 5 s.

5   Conclusion

I/O demanding HPC applications, such as quantum chemistry codes, suffer from bottlenecks introduced by poor performance of pure spinning disk storage. Although SSDs provide good performance characteristics, pure SSD based solutions are currently too expensive. This I/O bottleneck challenge can be addressed in a cost-effective and flexible manner by means of a multi-tiered storage solution consisting of large memory, local SSDs as well as a shared on-demand HDD layer. SSD caching solutions built upon this system result in poor performance for the use cases investigated in this study. However, a concatenated hybrid filesystem using LVM reveals good performance if special care is taken in the order of the underlying physical volumes. A broker has been implemented and successfully integrated within the scheduling system of the cluster such that the remote storage resources can be dynamically assigned to the nodes according to the specific job demands. This facility supports various flavors of hybrid scratch file systems that are assembled and disassembled on-the-fly, transparently for the user.

References

1. Zhang, G., Chiu, L., Liu, L.: Adaptive data migration in Multi-tiered storage based cloud environment. In: Proceedings of the IEEE 3rd International Conference on Cloud Computing. IEEE Computer Society (2010)
2. Werner, H.-J., Knowles, P.J., Knizia, G., Manby, F.R., Schütz, M.: Molpro: a general-purpose quantum chemistry program package. Wiley Interdisc. Rev. Comput. Mol. Sci. 2(2), 242–253 (2012)
3. Byna, S., Chen, Y., Sun, X.-H., Thakur, R., Gropp, W.: Parallel I/O prefetching using MPI file caching and I/O signatures. In: Proceedings of the ACM/IEEE Conference on Supercomputing. IEEE Press, Article 44 (2008)
4. SYSSTAT package. http://sebastien.godard.pagesperso-orange.fr
5. strace, system call tracer. http://sourceforge.net/projects/strace
6. flashcache. https://github.com/facebook/flashcache
7. FIO: Flexible I/O Tester. https://github.com/axboe/fio
8. Neuer, M., Mosch, C., Salk, J., Siegmund, K., Kushnarenko, V., Kombrink, S., Nau, T., Wesner, S.: Storage systems for I/O-intensive applications in computational chemistry. In: Resch, M.M., Bez, W., Focht, E., Kobayashi, H., Qi, J., Roller, S. (eds.) Sustained Simulation Performance, pp. 51–60. Springer, Heidelberg (2015)
9. Hollowell, C., Hogue, R., Smith, J., Strecker-Kellogg, W., Wong, A., Zaytsev, A.: The effect of flashcache and bcache on I/O performance. J. Phys. Conf. Ser. 513, 2023 (2014)
10. Sweeney, A., Doucette, D., Hu, W., Anderson, C., Nishimoto, M., Peck, G.: Scalability in the XFS file system. In: Proceedings of the USENIX 1996 Technical Conference, San Diego, CA, USA, pp. 1–14 (1996)
11. Mathur, A., Cao, M., Bhattacharya, S., Dilger, A., Tomas, A., Vivier, L.: The new ext4 filesystem: current status and future plans. In: Proceedings of the Linux Symposium (2007)
12. Schütz, M., Werner, H.-J.: Low-order scaling local electron correlation methods. IV. linear scaling local coupled-cluster (LCCSD). J. Chem. Phys. 114(2), 661–681 (2001)
13. Holland, M., Gibson, G.A.: Parity declustering for continuous operation in redundant disk arrays. In: Proceeding of the 5th Conference on Architectural Support for Programming Languages and Operating Systems (1992)
14. The Go Programming Language. http://golang.org

Parallel I/O Architecture Modelling
Based on File System Counters

Salem El Sayed[1(✉)], Matthias Bolten[2], and Dirk Pleiter[1]

[1] Jülich Supercomputing Centre, Forschungszentrum Jülich, 52425 Jülich, Germany
s.el.sayed.mohamed@fz-juelich.de
[2] Institut für Mathematik, Universität Kassel, 34132 Kassel, Germany

Abstract. Keeping compute and I/O performance balanced is a major challenge for future cost-efficient HPC systems. Several architectural concepts and new technologies allow to address this challenge, however at the price of higher complexity. In this paper we propose a particular approach to exploring the design space using event simulation models that take I/O server-side performance counters as input. In this way real-life data can be used to explore architectural modifications. We apply our approach using data collected by a GPFS file system serving a petascale Blue Gene/P installation.

1 Introduction

Keeping future high-performance computing (HPC) systems balanced is one of the key challenges on the path towards exascale architectures. This, in particular, concerns the balance of compute and I/O sub-system performance [4], which becomes even more urgent as new, emerging HPC application areas are in need for significantly higher I/O performance. This includes, e.g., radio-astronomy [6] or light-source experiments [2]. These trends are not expected to change in the foreseeable future. Therefore, the design of the I/O sub-system using new emerging I/O architectures will be a key issue that needs to be addressed for future exascale architectures. As the design of new I/O architectures is very costly, performance models are an interesting approach for exploring performance behaviour when architectural parameters are changed or even more significant changes to the architecture are endeavoured.

For our approach we assume that the I/O sub-system comprises a parallel file system or other components, which allow for server-side logging of performance numbers like number of bytes read or written in regular intervals. Based on the hardware and software architecture a model is designed, which is suitable for event simulation and captures the most important features of the I/O sub-system but is kept as simple as possible. The parameters of the model are tuned such that it reproduces the performance counters.

This article makes the following contributions: (i) We develop a methodology for modelling I/O architectures using server-side performance monitoring data as input for a discrete event simulation model, (ii) We demonstrate how to apply this approach to the Blue Gene/P installation JUGENE, for which we

© Springer International Publishing AG 2016
M. Taufer et al. (Eds.): ISC High Performance Workshops 2016, LNCS 9945, pp. 627–637, 2016.
DOI: 10.1007/978-3-319-46079-6_43

collected file system statistics over a period of about 2 years, and (iii) Results are presented on how to apply the methodology for exploring architectural modifications. More specifically, we present model results for an hypothetical change of the Blue Gene/P I/O nodes with integrated non-volatile memory devices.

After introducing our methodology in Sect. 2 we use this to develop in Sect. 3 a model for a specific Blue Gene/P installation. We analyse the model parameters in Sect. 4, which is followed by an application of the model to an architectural design space exploration in Sect. 5. We draw our conclusions in Sect. 6.

2 Methodology

Modern I/O sub-systems are fairly complex, incorporating many components and implementing various interaction protocols. Modelling I/O sub-systems, therefore requires adequately representing the inherent functionality of the simulated system, while keeping the model reasonably simplified. This requires a close study of the modelled I/O sub-system internal components and the sum of their behaviour. Many I/O sub-systems allow for monitoring internal progress using performance counters. These collect information such as number of bytes read or written at one or more components in the I/O sub-system. When logged progressively over time the performance counters can reasonably represent the I/O behaviour, which the model can use to implement and validate it's functionality.

In this study we observe the I/O sub-system behaviour using file system monitoring tools. Specifically we employ a file system monitor which resides in the General Parallel File System (GPFS). The GPFS performance counters include, among other values, bytes read and written and number of read and write requests [1, Chap. 8]. The counters can be logged progressively at constant intervals in time. The resulting logged I/O behaviour is reformatted to facilitate analysis. Compared to other I/O monitoring methods, monitoring the I/O behaviour in the file system can reduce the complexity of the observed system and the resulting I/O model.

2.1 Model Creation and Validation

To build a model for a given architecture we perform the following steps: (i) Construct the model in terms of different components and associated model parameters, (ii) Determine model parameters based on known architectural parameters as well as empirically obtained performance data input, and (iii) Validate the model by comparing model predictions with performance data that was not used for constructing the model. Details on each of these steps are given in the remaining part of this section.

Simulation Model Design. The internal functionality of the I/O sub-system can be represented using a limited set of components, which themselves can be comprised of internal components. The term component can stand for any part of the I/O sub-system that exists to perform operations that will lead to the fulfilment of an I/O request. On construction of the I/O model the main issue is selecting the relevant components and the level of details to incorporate into the model to create the necessary internal functionality. The decision on complexity and details depends on various factors. These include availability of information on the inner processes and protocols of the I/O sub-system, the level of performance information collected and details of I/O monitoring information.

Each of the components has one or more associated parameters, which describe the capabilities and capacities of these components, e.g. data throughput. These can be determined from the I/O sub-system documentation, or using statistical methods for fitting the model parameters to empirically obtained performance data. The need for determining these parameters also impacts the number of components in the model and the level of detail. A too large number of parameters cannot be determined with a sufficient level of accuracy and confidence when validating the I/O model. This can lead it to suffer from parameter sensitivity and the risk of overfitting.

Creating the event list used to drive the simulation of the I/O model, requires incorporating an I/O Request Generator. This has the task of translating the available I/O monitoring data into I/O requests to drive the simulation. The internal operation of the I/O request generator depends on the I/O monitoring data and could require interpolation to determine missing values. For server-side I/O monitoring the details of size and temporal distribution of individual I/O requests is unknown. This leads the event generator to create all requests with the average size and at the beginning of the I/O monitoring interval.

Model Parameter Determination. The parameters associated with each component have to be determined to simulate the I/O model. The values of these parameters can be determined using known architectural information. Overall parameters can be determined by aggregation of individual or internal component performance. However, it is not always possible to determine the parameters in this way. A component is only an abstract representation of several system components and simple performance number aggregation may not be possible. In this case the parameters need to be fixed by training the model. Training here means that server-side performance counters are used as input to the model to check whether it can reproduce, to some degree of accuracy the behaviour of the modelled system. An overview over the procedure for determining the model parameters is shown in Fig. 1.

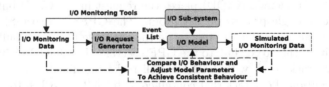

Fig. 1. Procedure for determining the I/O model parameters.

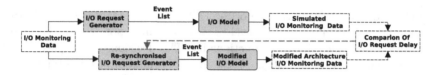

Fig. 2. Architecture exploration using the I/O model.

Model Validation. Model validation has several aspects. The most important one being a comparison of model predictions with a test data set, i.e. a data set that was not used for determining model parameters. The procedure is similar to the one depicted in Fig. 1, except that the comparison between measured performance data, which is also used as input to the model, matches the performance data "predicted" by the model. Another aspect concerns the comparison of model parameters with expectations. While this leads only to a weak validation of the model, it is nevertheless necessary to reduce risks related to overfitting.

2.2   Architecture Exploration

Driven by real I/O behaviour the model can help predict the impact of architectural changes of the I/O sub-system on performance. The architectural changes can be implemented through changing parameters such as bandwidth and delays or by adding or removing I/O model components. By comparing the simulated I/O monitoring data and the modified architecture I/O monitoring data, predictions on performance of new I/O architectures can be made. The process of architecture exploration is depicted in Fig. 2.

Changing the model may require modifying the set of I/O requests in order to respect timing constraints or causal relations. We thus introduce a "re-synchronized I/O request generator" (see Fig. 2).

3   Model for Blue Gene/P

JUGENE was a Blue Gene/P system that had been operated at Jülich Supercomputing Center (JSC) from 2008 until 2012. An overview on it's I/O sub-system is given in Fig. 3. More details have been published in [3].

The Compute Nodes (CN) forward I/O requests to the I/O node (ION). The Control and I/O daemon (CIOD) places the request in the CIOD buffers, each dedicated to a single process on CN group. The GPFS Network Shared Disk (NSD) client can place the I/O request in the available page-pool buffer, before forwarding it on the 10 GE link to the GPFS servers. The JUGENE installation comprised 72 racks each with 1024 CN. All racks contained a total of 8 ION, with the exception of one rack that contained 32 ION. The GPFS storage cluster featured an aggregate bandwidth of 66 GByte/s.

For server-side I/O monitoring we employed the GPFS I/O counters [1, Chap. 8]. These counters are accumulated for an extended period of time and

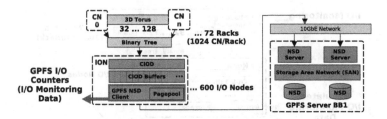

Fig. 3. Blue Gene/P I/O sub-system using GPFS (JUGENE), adapted from [3]

logged periodically every 120 s by each ION. On JUGENE 6 different I/O counters have been collected: bytes read and written, number of read and write requests as well as open and close commands. By combining the I/O monitoring data with the job information it is possible to relate I/O behaviour to jobs that ran on the system.

3.1 Blue Gene/P I/O Sub-system Model

In Fig. 4 we show the simulation model that we constructed following the procedure described in the previous section on the basis of the Blue Gene/P I/O sub-system architecture as shown in Fig. 3.

Our model comprises several types of data links along which data is moved between Compute Nodes (CN) and disks:

Internal component link Zero delay link connecting internal components.
Binary tree link Connects the CN forming a binary tree that ends at the ION.
10 GE Ethernet link Connects the ION to the GPFS server.
Storage link Connects the GPFS server with the disk to model the aggregate storage bandwidth of the GPFS storage cluster.

For our model we have defined the following components (as shown in Fig. 4 from top to bottom):

I/O Request Generator Creates the event list based on the I/O monitoring data. The request is assigned to one CN within the group of CN attached to a given ION in round-robin fashion.
CN Sequentially receives the I/O request from the I/O generator over an internal component link and forwards it over the binary tree.
CIOD Forwards the I/O request to the corresponding CIOD buffer.
CIOD buffer Buffers the I/O request and could either forward it to the bypass if the 10 GE link is free or, for write requests, forward it to the pagepool if it has sufficient space.
Pagepool Operates as a write buffer if the 10 GE link is busy. Once the 10 GE becomes free it will forward the I/O requests to the bypass.
Bypass Receives the I/O requests from the CIOD buffers or the page-pool only if the 10 GE is free to be used.

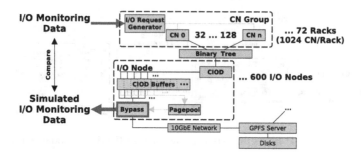

Fig. 4. Model for the Blue Gene/P I/O sub-system.

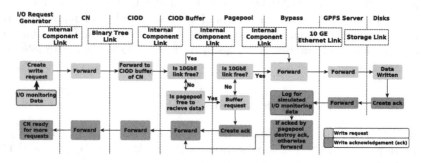

Fig. 5. Flow chart for Blue Gene/P I/O sub-system model describing overall model protocol for write requests and acknowledgements.

GPFS server Receives the I/O requests on the 10 GE and forwards it to the disks.

Disk Fulfils received requests with no read or write delay, both of which are represented in the disk bandwidth.

An I/O request message traversing the model can be one of four types: (i) write request, (ii) write ack, (iii) read request, (iv) read data. Only messages containing data have a lower priority and exhibit delay when forwarded over links with limited bandwidth. Both, the write and read requests are generated by the I/O Request Generator. However, only the write request contains data. A write ack contains no data and represents an acknowledgement, which is generated by the disk or the page-pool on receiving a write request. Finally, the read data is generated by the disk on receiving a read request and contains the data to be read. As the messages traverse the links, the described components have to react with the appropriate behaviour. Figure 5 depicts a flow chart describing the resulting overall protocol for write requests and acknowledgements.

The behaviour of read requests and read data messages are similar to the write operation. The only exception is the lack of buffering in the page-pool for read data. This is because any read after write or re-read of the same data cannot be detected using this I/O monitoring method. The model also assumes no handshakes exist and the number of meta-data operations being small. Although meta-data operations are time consuming for some applications, in this I/O model we focus on overall data movement. Meta-data operations could be regarded for future improvements of the I/O model. Here we consider the chosen parameters sufficient to tune to represent the overall I/O sub-system behaviour.

To perform the discrete event simulation the model is implemented using the ONNeT++ framework [7]. The design of the OMNeT++ is intended for the simulation of networks and is written in C++. The here described model is a set of communicating components reacting to discrete events forwarded on channels with determined delays or bandwidth. This makes OMNeT++ as a modular network discrete event simulator a suitable framework to describe the presented I/O sub-system model.

4   Model Parameters

Many of the parameters are determined by studying the system specifications and former studies of the Blue Gene/P and GPFS architecture such as [3]. The parameters are mostly set to the architectural design values dictated by the Blue Gene/P I/O sub-system. However, due to the use of file system monitoring data in the form of GPFS I/O logs, some model parameters are adjusted. The empirical results available in [3] have not been integrated into the model, as the recorded behaviour should be represented by the sum of the chosen parameter values.

The parameters used in the Blue Gene/P model are given in Table 1. Only the number of CIOD buffers has been reduced to CN group size instead of the number of process that can run on the CN group [3]. This is due the GPFS I/O counters not logging the CN process that initiated the I/O request.

4.1   Model Validation

The validation cycle described in Sect. 2.1 is used to validate the Blue Gene/P I/O sub-system model, with the parameters given in Table 1. The GPFS I/O logs are employed as the I/O monitoring data to compare model predictions with I/O sub-system behaviour. The validation ran for 24 h simulated time, simulating the full Blue Gene/P system of 73,728 CN and 600 ION. The I/O monitoring data used comprises the I/O requests from 4,418 arbitrary jobs that ran during these 24 h.

Table 1. Blue Gene/P model parameters and values

Binary tree link bandwidth	10 GE link bandwidth	Storage link bandwidth	CIOD buffer size	Number of CIOD buffers	Page-pool buffer size
850 MByte/s	1.25 GByte/s	66 GByte/s	4 MiByte	32/128 (CN group size)	1024 MiByte

Four of the GPFS I/O counters are used and measured to determine validity of model parameters, write bytes, write requests, read bytes and read requests. It was observed that the model achieves a high correlation to the measured GPFS I/O logs. The highest mismatch was measured for the write requests with the average difference between simulated and measured GPFS I/O performance counters being 2 % for the 24 h of simulated time. The remaining counters have a mismatch average of less than 1 %.

Given the accuracy obtained, the parameter values selected are considered adequate to represent the I/O behaviour of the Blue Gene/P I/O sub-system and no further parameter training is considered needed. These parameter values are used for the subsequent design space exploration.

5   Design Space Exploration

A promising improvement on the I/O bandwidth can be achieved using burst buffers [5]. These are high bandwidth non-volatile memory closely placed to the compute cluster that temporarily stores data before evicting it to the storage system. Generally burst buffers have the task to hide delays exhibited by slow link for relatively short bursts of I/O. To accelerate the read path the burst buffers have to operate similar to a cache or a data pre-fetching mechanism has to be employed.

5.1   Burst Buffer I/O Sub-system Model

The Blue Gene/P I/O sub-system model shown in Fig. 4 is modified for the use of burst buffers. These are connected internally to the bypass component of the ION by an internal link and to the GPFS server by an external link. Introducing the burst buffer component to the model adds three parameters, bandwidth of internal link, bandwidth of external link and burst buffer size. The internal link is considered to be similar to the binary tree link, therefore choosing it's bandwidth to be 850 MByte/s. This leaves two parameters, the external bandwidth and the burst buffer size, to be used for architectural exploration.

The introduction of new components to the I/O model in the form of burst buffers changes the overall I/O sub-system behaviour given in Fig. 5. Both the CIOD buffer and the pagepool cannot forward the write requests unless the internal link is free and the burst buffer has sufficient space for the written data. The bypass has no longer a direct link to the GPFS server, as all I/O requests and data flow through the burst buffer. On receiving a write request the burst buffer stores the data and creates the corresponding write ack which it passes back to the bypass. Finally the data to be written is forwarded to the GPFS server when the external link becomes available.

With the exception of a few differences the read path behaves similar to the write path. However, on receiving a read request, the burst buffer does not create a corresponding read data as read buffering or caching is not modelled.

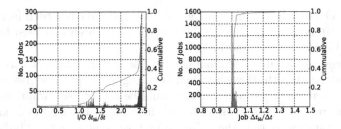

Fig. 6. Histogram (blue columns) and cumulative distribution function (red line) for the relative change in I/O time (left) and overall job execution time (right) for case (A). δt and Δt are the original I/O and job time, respectively, while δt_{bb} and Δt_{bb} are burst buffer I/O and job time, respectively. (Color figure online)

5.2 Simulation Results

As a design space exploration, we investigate the reduction of cost by decreasing the external link bandwidth, thus replacing the 10 GE cards, which represent a significant cost factor. Burst buffers are used to improve on possible performance degradation. For this purpose two configurations of burst buffer size and external link bandwidth are used. Case (A) sets the external link to 500 MByte/s and the burst buffer size to 16 GiByte, representing the use of a burst buffer with 4 GE as an external link, which can be achieved using 4×1 GE links. Meanwhile, case (B) sets the external link to 125 MByte/s and the burst buffer size to 64 GiByte, which represents the use of a burst buffer with a single 1 GE as an external link.

To asses the two cases, the cycle for architecture exploration given in Fig. 2 is used. For that purpose the same 24 h of GPFS I/O logs used for the validation is fed to the modified model.

The results of comparing case (A) with the unmodified model is given in Fig. 6. As seen in Fig. 6 (left panel) the I/O time of jobs has been significantly increased, with the I/O time becoming upto 2.5 times longer. This is consistent with our expectations as the bandwidth of the external link has been throttled by a factor 2.5 and the burst buffers cannot be exploited in all cases. However as seen in Fig. 6 (right panel), this has only a marginal effect on the overall job time, with 90 % of the jobs having suffered less than 5 % slow down. In comparison, Fig. 7 shows the results of comparing case (B) to the unmodified model. As seen

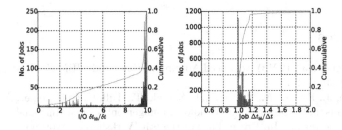

Fig. 7. Similar to Fig. 6, but for case (B).

both the I/O and job time have increased. The I/O time has been increased by a factor of 10, however the overall job time has only been increased by around 10 % for 90 % of the simulated jobs.

The given results might discourage the use of burst buffers with reduced external link bandwidth. However when factoring in the possible cost reduction, the overall decrease in job performance could be acceptable. Additionally, considering future I/O sub-systems where an increase in external link bandwidth could be no longer an option, these simulation results indicate burst buffers being a good architectural choice.

6 Summary and Conclusions

In this paper we presented a methodology for constructing discrete event simulation models for simulating I/O sub-systems using server-side performance data on input. We used this method to develop a model for a large-scale Blue Gene/P system comprising 73,728 Compute Nodes and 600 I/O Nodes. We could show that the model parameters can be tuned such that the model becomes self consistent, i.e. for event lists created from performance data collected on all I/O Nodes the model could reproduce these performance data with satisfactory accuracy.

Simulating a modification of the architecture, which has been explored, concerned the integration of buffers based on non-volatile memory technologies. The goal of this study was to assess the overall performance impact caused by a significant reduction of the external storage bandwidth at presence of such burst buffers. The results indicated that replacing one 10 GE link per I/O node by multiple 1 GE links would have impacted the overall performance by a few percent. The model itself only depends on the modelled system architecture. The performance characteristics of applications using that system architecture enter the modelling procedure through performance data obtained on the modelled system.

Acknowledgments. This work has been performed in the context of the Exascale Innovation Center at Jülich Supercomputing Center. It was partially funded by the state of North Rhine-Westfalia ("Anschubfinanzierung zum Aufbau des Exascale Innovation Center (EIC)"). We acknowledge furthermore the help of Wolfgang Frings, Michael Hennecke and Willi Homberg for collecting and managing JUGENE's I/O performance data.

References

1. GPFS Version 3.5 (2013) Advanced Administration Guide. IBM Publication, (SC23-5182-08), June 2013
2. Deslippe, J., Essiari, A., Patton, S.J., Samak, T., Tull, C.E., Hexemer, A., Kumar, D., Parkinson, D., Stewart, P.: Workflow management for real-time analysis of light-source experiments. In: Proceedings of the 9th Workshop on Workflows in Support of Large-Scale Science, WORKS 2014, pp. 31–40. IEEE Press, Piscataway (2014)

3. Frings, W., Hennecke, M.: A system level view of petascale I/O on IBM Blue Gene/P. Comput. Sci. - Res. Dev. **26**(3–4), 275–283 (2011)
4. Kunkel, J., Kuhn, M., Ludwig, T.: Exascale storage systems - an analytical study of expenses. Supercomput. Front. Innov. **1**(1), 116–134 (2014)
5. Liu, N., Cope, J., Carns, P., Carothers, C., Ross, R., Grider, G., Crume, A., Maltzahn, C.: On the role of burst buffers in leadership-class storage systems. In: 2012 IEEE 28th Symposium on Mass Storage Systems and Technologies (MSST), pp. 1–11, April 2012
6. Quinn, P.J., Axelrod, T., Bird, I., Dodson, R., Szalay, A., Wicenec, A.: Delivering SKA Science. In: PoS, AASKA14:147 (2015)
7. Varga, A., et al.: The OMNeT++ discrete event simulation system. In: Proceedings of the European Simulation Multiconference (ESM 2001), vol. 9, p. 65. sn (2001)

User-Space I/O for μs-level Storage Devices

Anastasios Papagiannis[1,2]([✉]), Giorgos Saloustros[1], Manolis Marazakis[1], and Angelos Bilas[1,2]

[1] Institute of Computer Science, FORTH (ICS), Heraklion, Greece
{apapag,gesalous,maraz,bilas}@ics.forth.gr
[2] Department of Computer Science, University of Crete, Heraklion, Greece

Abstract. System software overheads in the I/O path, including VFS and file system code, become more pronounced with emerging low-latency storage devices. Currently, these overheads constitute the main bottleneck in the I/O path and they limit efficiency of modern storage systems. In this paper we present *Iris*, a new I/O path for applications, that minimizes overheads from system software in the common I/O path. The main idea is the separation of the control and data planes. The control plane consists of an unmodified Linux kernel and is responsible for handling data plane initialization and the normal processing path through the kernel for non-file related operations. The data plane is a lightweight mechanism to provide direct access to storage devices with minimum overheads and without sacrificing strong protection semantics. *Iris* requires neither hardware support from the storage devices nor changes in user applications. We evaluate our early prototype and we find that it achieves on a single core up to 1.7× and 2.2× better read and write random IOPS, respectively, compared to the *xfs* and *ext4* file systems. It also scales with the number of cores; using 4 cores *Iris* achieves 1.84× and 1.96× better read and write random IOPS, respectively.

Keywords: NVM · I/O · Storage systems · Low latency · Protection

1 Introduction

Emerging flash-based storage devices provide access latency in the order of a few μs. Existing devices [14] provide read and write latencies in the order of 68 and 15 μs respectively, and these numbers are projected to become significantly lower in next-generation devices. Phase Change Memories (PCM) [21], STT-RAM [11], and memristors [15] may provide even lower access latency, at the scale of hundreds or tens of nanoseconds [8].

Given these trends, the software overhead of the host I/O path in modern servers is becoming the main bottleneck for achieving μs-level response times application I/O operations. Instead of storage device technology setting the limit in increasing the number of I/O operations per second (IOPS), as was the case until recently, we now have to deal with limitations on the rate of serving I/O operations, per core, due to software overhead in the I/O path. Therefore, in this

© Springer International Publishing AG 2016
M. Taufer et al. (Eds.): ISC High Performance Workshops 2016, LNCS 9945, pp. 638–648, 2016.
DOI: 10.1007/978-3-319-46079-6_44

new landscape, it becomes imperative to re-design the I/O path in a manner that it will be able to keep up with shrinking device and network latencies and to allow applications to benefit from increasingly fast storage devices.

In this paper, we explore the design of a storage I/O stack that is placed in user-space and in the largest part within the address space of the application itself. An important design aspect is the separation of the control and data planes [5,20]. This idea comes from the area of networking and several frameworks designed in order to take advantage of fast network devices [12]. The control plane is responsible for taking decisions regarding resource allocation and routing, while the data plane, also termed as the forwarding plane, forwards network packets to the correct destination according to control plane logic. In our storage I/O context, the control plane should decide if an I/O operation should be accelerated by our framework or it should go through the standard I/O path in the Linux kernel. More specifically, our control plane consists of an unmodified Linux kernel which is responsible for normal processing for non-file related operations and the configuration of several independent data planes. Our data plane provides a lightweight mechanism to enable direct access the storage devices without sacrificing strong protection semantics. We use traps in the data plane for protection rather than using a separate trusted process [24] or server for enforcing protection. Our approach has the advantage that it does not require any context switches or network messages in the common I/O path. The premise behind our design is to allow the application to operate as close as possible to locally-attached storage devices.

The key features of our design are as follows:

1. We intercept file-related calls from applications at the runtime level and convert them to key-value store requests.
2. We serve block operations from a key-value store. The key-value store in our current prototype is build directly over memory-mapped devices and makes extensive use of copy-on-write for failure atomicity, concurrency, and relaxed-update semantics.
3. We rely on virtualization support in modern processors (Intel's VT-x [23] and AMD's SVM [1]) to provide strong protection between different processes that access the same storage devices. These technologies have already been used to improve the performance of virtual machines. In this paper we use them for providing protected, shared access to our key-value store from multiple applications in each server.
4. Finally, we use a kernel-space module for initialization and coarse-grain file operations that do not affect the common I/O path.

We present a proof-of-concept prototype, *Iris*, for Linux servers and provide preliminary performance results. For our experiments we use PMBD [8,16], a custom block device that emulates PCM latencies. We show that, per-core, our approach achieves a 1.7× improvement in read IOPS, and 2.2× in write IOPS.

We also show that our design scales well, providing up to 1.84× and 1.96× improvement for random read and write IOPS respectively using 4 cores. We compare *Iris* with the state-of-art Linux kernel file systems, *xfs* and *ext4*.

The rest of this paper is organized as follows. In Sect. 2 we present the design of *Iris*, and in Sect. 3 a preliminary evaluation. Section 4 reviews related work. Section 5 concludes the paper and discusses the future work.

2   *Iris* Design

We implement a custom I/O path over fast persistent devices that removes most of the overheads from the Linux kernel I/O path. Figure 1 shows the top-level architecture of our system. *Iris* consists of three main parts:

- the key-value store, responsible for storing file blocks, providing atomic semantics, and handling failure scenarios (e.g. system crashes),
- the *Iris* kernel, which handles accesses to the key-value store and performs permission checks, and
- the I/O interposer which handles I/O processing at the user-space and generate key-value requests.

2.1   Key-Value Store

Our key-value store is designed primarily for fast storage devices, and is mainly based on Tucana [18]. Its API provides methods for inserting a <key, value>

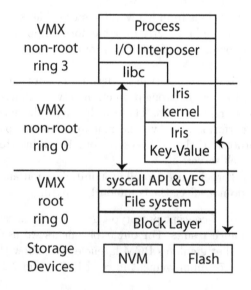

Fig. 1. Top-level architecture of *Iris*.

pair and for retrieving a <value> based on a <key>. It also supports range queries which return keys in sorted order. We use range queries in order to enable better performance for sequential file accesses. At its core, it implements a variant of B^ϵ–tree [6], a write-optimized indexing data structure. It supports multiple databases over a single or multiple devices. Since it operates at the device level, it implements its own allocation mechanism for space management over storage volumes. It maps the underlying devices in memory, and access them as memory regions.

Its persistence mechanism is based solely on the Copy-On-Write (COW) mechanism [22]. Common key-value stores use journaling for consistency purposes. In this case, for each update the mutation is first appended in a log and then updated in-place in the primary storage space. Our store operates differently: It creates a copy of the new value and subsequently modifies it. More specifically, each modification to the tree data structure requires the update of a set of nodes. Instead of updating them in-place, we create a copy of the old nodes and updates only the copy. This procedure begins from a leaf node, where a new <key, value> inserted, and goes recursively up to the root of the tree. At any point in time, there are two root nodes: The first one is read-only, while the second one is where all data updates occur.

Our system is capable of batching a series of updates which subsequently are written to the device in an atomic manner, thus reducing actual I/O operations. After a period of time has elapsed or the application explicitly instructs to make its changes persistent, the key-value store with an atomic operation will update the read-only root to be the new persistent view of the database. Finally, keeping versions of the database is supported by keeping pointers to previous versions of the tree-structured index.

We keep both file blocks and file metadata in the key-value store. To distinguish different files, we use the persistent and unique inode number provided by VFS for each file. The key for accessing a file block in the key-value store is formed by the concatenation of the file's inode number and the requested block number. In our implementation, we use a block size of 4KB, but this is a parameter configurable by the system administrator. The value returned by the key-value store is a block of the actual data of the file. We also keep persistent metadata for each file that is present in the key-value store. These include the inode number, the file path and the name of the file, a *struct stat* that also contains the size of the file, and the file ownership and permissions information.

We rely on the key-value store to provide data and metadata consistency upon failures. By guaranteeing a series of update operations to be atomic, we ensure that file data and metadata will not be in an inconsistent state after a failure. Current state-of-art file systems use a journaling mechanism to provide data integrity after a failure. Each write has to be done first on the journal device and then on the primary device. When a failure occurs, the file system has to replay the log. We use a different approach for failure handling. By using the copy-on-write technique, we remove the overhead to perform a write on both the journal device and then to the primary device. After a failure, only the last consistent view of our key-value store is visible to applications.

Our key-value store is designed to be mapped to multiple applications, allowing shared storage. Therefore, it has to support concurrent *get* and *put* requests. To maintain POSIX semantics, for each file the results of the last write must be returned to any subsequent read operation. Although these can be easily implemented using coarse-grain locking, we have implemented a more sophisticated locking protocol to support concurrent reads and writes for different files.

2.2 *Iris* Kernel

The *Iris* kernel is the heart of the system. It maps a fast storage device to the application process address space. Therefore, in the common path *Iris* avoids the overheads of system call processing, VFS, and in-kernel file system processing. The main drawback of moving all I/O processing into user space is the lack of protection that Linux kernel provides. To address this concern, we rely on processor virtualization virtualization features. Intel VT-x [23] virtualization technology provides two different privilege domains: VMX-root and VMX non-root. Each of them supports the standard privilege rings (0 to 3). The purpose of this separation is to better support Virtual Machine Managers (VMMs). Normally, the VMM runs on VMX-root, ring 0, while the guest OS of each virtual machines runs on VMX non-root, ring 0, and guest processes on VMX non-root, ring 3. In our work, we use this privilege separation for a different purpose, following the idea behind the Dune [4] prototype. The Linux kernel runs on VMX-root, ring 0, the protected I/O path code runs on VMX non-root ring 0, and user processes (issuing I/O requests) run on VMX non-root ring 3. By using this privilege separation we provide strong protection semantics to access shared storage devices, similar to the unmodified Linux kernel.

The *Iris* kernel runs on VMX non-root ring 0, thus it is protected from user processes that run on VMX non-root ring 3. When I/O interposer issues a *get* or *put* request, it checks if the specified process has sufficient privileges to access the file with the specific inode number. If not, an error is returned to the interposer and then to the user.

2.3 I/O Interposer

The purpose of this part is to intercept I/O system calls to libc. We provide our own dynamically linked library that replaces these libc calls and ensure that our library gets priority over libc (via *LD_PRELOAD*). Therefore, applications run unmodified, while our I/O interposer handles all open file descriptors and translates I/O requests to key-value requests: *get* and *put*. For each open file, we maintain state related to the file, which allows us to handle *ftruncate, fallocate, stat, lseek* and their variants.

Except from the persistent file metadata that are stored inside the key-value store, the interposer also uses in-memory metadata. These metadata include open file descriptors and the current read/write offset in each file. These meta-data are also not persistent in the case of the unmodified Linux kernel. After a failure, applications do not expect to have the files descriptors that are available before a failure. We also keep an in-memory copy of persistent metadata, to accelerate metadata operations but without sacrificing correctness.

3 Evaluation

In this section we provide a preliminary evaluation of *Iris*. Our testbed consists of two Intel Xeon E5620 processors running at 2.40 GHz and 24 GBytes of DDR3/1333 DRAM organized in 2 NUMA nodes, each of them with 12 GBytes of DDR3 DRAM. In our experiments we pin the benchmark threads on a single NUMA node in order to remove NUMA-related effects. We run experiments with *FIO* [2] to measure random-access read and write IOPS, with a block size of 512 bytes, a device queue depth equal to 1, and direct I/O to bypass the page cache. We vary the number of I/O issuing threads from 1 to 4. Each thread performs I/O on a separate file of size equals to 128MB. We use the PMBD [8,16] block device driver to emulate the access latencies of a PCM memory device over DRAM. We dedicate 8GBytes of the testbed's DRAM for use as PMBD's storage space. We compare *Iris* with the current state-of-art file systems provided by the Linux kernel, *EXT4* and *XFS*. For both of these filesystems, we also use PMBD as the underlying block device.

Table 1 shows the number of random IOPS for both reads and writes using a single thread. The results obtained from *Iris* have very small variance between the runs. Regarding random read IOPS, *Iris* provides 1.65× and 1.7× higher

Table 1. Single thread random IOPS (thousands).

	EXT4	*XFS*	*Iris*
read	269	261	445
write	203	199	439

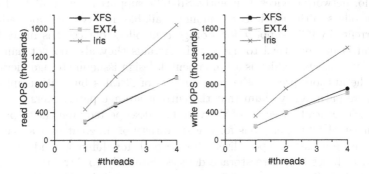

Fig. 2. Random read/write IOPS scaling.

number of IOPS compared with *EXT4* and *XFS*, respectively. For random write IOPS the improvement is 2.16× and 2.2×, respectively.

Figure 2 shows how random IOPS scale while increasing the number of threads from 1 to 4, compared to *EXT4* and *XFS*. Using 4 threads, *Iris* provides 1.84× and 1.82× for reads and 1.96× and 1.8× for writes higher number of IOPS respectively. These results show that while we increase the number of threads the performance improvements remains almost the same. With *Iris*, we serve around 400 KIOPS per thread (i.e. processor core in this evaluation experiment), almost 2× more than what is achievable with *EXT4* and *XFS*, without sacrificing protection guarantees and failure resilience.

In this work, we have focused the evaluation on small random read/write accesses, to better highlight overheads and the improvements achievable with *Iris*. Optimizations focusing on throughput, especially for sequential accesses, are outside the scope of this paper, but we expect significant improvements for such access patterns as well. These improvements are a consequence of the design decision to build out key-value store on top of a B^ϵ–tree, rather than more commonly used hash-based data structures. To serve sequential accesses, *Iris* issues range queries to its underlying key-value store, which then returns the requested blocks in sorted order. This helps *Iris* to accelerate sequential accesses. We leave this optimization and its evaluation as a future work.

4   Related Work

Recent papers have addressed the issue of how to optimize accesses to fast I/O devices. The Arrakis [19,20] and IX [5] operating systems are based on the concept of separating the control and data planes. The control plane is responsible of managing the hardware resources in a protected and isolated manner, while the data plane is a low-overhead mechanism that allows direct but safe access to the hardware resources, specifically I/O devices.

Arrakis, which is based on Barrefish [3], achieve this by relying on SR-IOV [17] hardware features. SR-IOV allows a single physical PCI-Express device to export several virtual devices that are isolated from one another. Although they present the idea of it on both network and storage devices, their evaluation is mainly for network devices. Currently, SR-IOV support is not available for storage controllers, although it is commonly available in server network adapters. The current SR-IOV support for storage controllers/devices has many limitations and is not practical to use yet. In Arrakis they also do not handle the case of data sharing, which is a fundamental design issue in storage hierarchies. In [19] the authors present the key concepts of Arrakis but with emphasis on the storage path. They claim that the current storage path suffers from many sources of overheads because of the very broad-scope requirement to provide a common set of I/O operations for a wide variety of different user applications. They propose a custom specialized storage path for different kinds of applications, with direct access to storage devices. Similarly to Arrakis, they require hardware virtualization support from storage devices (SR-IOV), which however is not practical today.

Compared to Arrakis, we only require hardware virtualization support from the processor (e.g. Intel's VT-x in our prototype), but not from the I/O devices. We also use an unmodified Linux kernel, thus we still support user applications that do not require I/O acceleration. The operations that our custom data plane cannot handle (e.g. network accesses) still go through the normal path inside the kernel.

IX uses the unmodified Linux kernel as the control plane and implement a lightweight OS abstraction for the data plane. It uses Dune [4] to provide privilege separation between the control plane, the data plane and the normal processes, to provide safe access to the hardware devices. They do not require SR-IOV virtualization support, but they propose a solution and evaluation only for network devices. Authors provide an event-driven API (libIX) that provides run to completion with adaptive batching, zero-copy API and synchronization free processing. These optimizations targeting throughput and the new event-driven API require changes to the applications. We also use Dune for protected accesses to hardware devices but our main contribution is to minimize latency, and we don't require changes to the user applications. Thus IX (i.e. network-specific) optimizations are not suitable for *Iris*, a latency-optimized storage path.

Moneta-D [7] uses specialized hardware for fast access to I/O storage devices with strong protection semantics. All the metadata operations still go through the normal I/O path in the Linux kernel. They optimize read/write operations in a way that does not require crossing the kernel for permission checks. Moneta-D provides a private, virtualized interface for each process and moves file system protection checks into hardware. As a result applications can access file data without operating system intervention, eliminating OS and file system costs entirely for most accesses. In our work, we only require virtualization support in the processor, rather than in the interface to storage devices.

Another approach to access fast storage devices appeared in Aerie [24]. This work assumes byte-addressable NVM placed on the memory bus. The key idea in this work is that the NVM is directly mapped in the user's address space. Using this approach, user application can read/write data and read metadata directly; however, the metadata updates have to be performed by a separate trusted process, the *Trusted FS Process*. This approach has the disadvantage that metadata updates, which are done by a centralized process, can limit scalability. We don't have this limitation in our approach, as multiple applications can update their metadata concurrently.

In Mnemosyne [25] and NV-Heaps [9] the authors propose ideas on how to use NVM for a persistent replacement to volatile memory that user applications can use, i.e. applications can rely on in-memory data-structures that can survive system crashes. Mnemosyne and NV-Heaps provide an API for NVM allocation and deallocation, with failure handling provisions. They also implement persistent data structures and atomic semantics (transactions) to leverage NVM from user applications. These works are orthogonal to our approach. In principle, we can apply these techniques to optimize access to NVM from our key-value store.

Other works like BPFS [10], PMFS [13], NOVA [27] and SCMFS [26] try to optimize in-kernel file systems. They use the standard VFS layer, and try to optimize the file system data structures to access NVM. We don't compare with these approaches as we propose an alternative way to access NVM, different from the common system call and VFS layer approach.

5   Conclusions and Future Work

In this paper we propose *Iris*, a custom storage system for providing direct access to fast storage devices and minimize system software overheads without sacrificing strong protection semantics. We implement a key-value store for storing file data and metadata, and guarantee both atomicity and recoverability. The key-value store is designed to scale-out by utilizing fast storage devices at several nodes. We use processor virtualization features to provide protected accesses to our key-value store. In the preliminary evaluation, we show improvements up to 1.7× for random read IOPS and 2.2× for random write IOPS as compared with state-of-art Linux kernel file systems using a single core. Performance scales with the number of cores, with up to 1.84× and 1.96× improvement for random read and write IOPS, respectively, using 4 cores

Our future work includes the full implementation of *Iris* and its extensive evaluation using real applications, including On-Line Transaction Processing (OLAP) and On-Line Analytical Processing (OLTP) workloads.

Acknowledgments. We thankfully acknowledge the support of the European Commission under the Horizon 2020 Framework Programme for Research and Innovation through the ExaNeSt project (grant agreement 671553).

References

1. AMD: Secure Virtual Machine Architecture Reference Manual
2. Axboe, J.: Flexible I/O Tester (2005). https://github.com/axboe
3. Baumann, A., Barham, P., Dagand, P.E., Harris, T., Isaacs, R., Peter, S., Roscoe, T., Schüpbach, A., Singhania, A.: The multikernel: a new OS architecture for scalable multicore systems. In: Proceedings of the ACM SIGOPS 22nd Symposium on Operating Systems Principles SOSP 2009, pp. 29–44. ACM, New York (2009). http://doi.acm.org/10.1145/1629575.1629579
4. Belay, A., Bittau, A., Mashtizadeh, A., Terei, D., Mazières, D., Kozyrakis, C.: Dune: Safe user-level access to privileged cpu features. In: 10th USENIX Symposium on Operating Systems Design and Implementation (OSDI 2012), pp. 335–348. USENIX, Hollywood (2012). https://www.usenix.org/conference/osdi12/technical-sessions/presentation/belay
5. Belay, A., Prekas, G., Klimovic, A., Grossman, S., Kozyrakis, C., Bugnion, E.: IX: a protected dataplane operating system for high throughput and low latency. In: 11th USENIX Symposium on Operating Systems Design and Implementation (OSDI 2014), pp. 49–65. USENIX Association, Broomfield, October 2014. https://www.usenix.org/conference/osdi14/technical-sessions/presentation/belay

6. Brodal, G.S., Fagerberg, R.: Lower bounds for external memory dictionaries. In: Proceedings of the Fourteenth Annual ACM-SIAM Symposium on Discrete Algorithms, SODA 2003, pp. 546–554. Society for Industrial and Applied Mathematics, Philadelphia (2003). http://dl.acm.org/citation.cfm?id=644108.644201
7. Caulfield, A.M., Mollov, T.I., Eisner, L.A., De, A., Coburn, J., Swanson, S.: Providing safe, user space access to fast, solid state disks. In: Proceedings of the Seventeenth International Conference on Architectural Support for Programming Languages and Operating Systems, ASPLOS XVII, pp. 387–400. ACM, New York (2012). http://doi.acm.org/10.1145/2150976.2151017
8. Chen, F., Mesnier, M., Hahn, S.: A protected block device for persistent memory. In: 2014 30th Symposium on Mass Storage Systems and Technologies (MSST), pp. 1–12, June 2014
9. Coburn, J., Caulfield, A.M., Akel, A., Grupp, L.M., Gupta, R.K., Jhala, R., Swanson, S.: NV-Heaps: making persistent objects fast and safe with next-generation, non-volatile memories. In: Proceedings of the Sixteenth International Conference on Architectural Support for Programming Languages and Operating Systems, ASPLOS XVI, pp. 105–118. ACM, New York (2011). http://doi.acm.org/10.1145/1950365.1950380
10. Condit, J., Nightingale, E.B., Frost, C., Ipek, E., Lee, B., Burger, D., Coetzee, D.: Better i/o through byte-addressable, persistent memory. In: Proceedings of the ACM SIGOPS 22nd Symposium on Operating Systems Principles, SOSP 2009, pp. 133–146. ACM, New York (2009). http://doi.acm.org/10.1145/1629575.1629589
11. Dieny, B., Sousa, R., Prenat, G., Ebels, U.: Spin-dependent phenomena and their implementation in spintronic devices. In: International Symposium on VLSI Technology, Systems and Applications VLSI-TSA 2008, pp. 70–71, April 2008
12. DPDK: Data plane development kit (2016). http://dpdk.org/
13. Dulloor, S.R., Kumar, S., Keshavamurthy, A., Lantz, P., Reddy, D., Sankaran, R., Jackson, J.: System software for persistent memory. In: Proceedings of the Ninth European Conference on Computer Systems, EuroSys 2014, pp. 15:1–15:15. ACM, New York (2014). http://doi.acm.org/10.1145/2592798.2592814
14. FusioIO: ioDrive2/ioDrive2 Duo Datasheet (2014). http://www.fusionio.com/load/-media-/2rezss/docsLibrary/FIO_DS_ioDrive2.pdf
15. Ho, Y., Huang, G., Li, P.: Nonvolatile memristor memory: device characteristics and design implications. In: IEEE/ACM International Conference on Computer-Aided Design - Digest of Technical Papers, ICCAD 2009, pp. 485–490, November 2009
16. Intel: Persistent memory block driver (PMBD) v0.9. (2013). https://github.com/linux-pmbd/pmbd
17. Kutch, P.: PCI-SIG SR-IOV primer: An introduction to SR-IOV technology, Intel application note, 321211–002 (2011)
18. Papagiannis, A., Saloustros, G., González-Férez, P., Bilas, A.: Tucana: Design and implementation of a fast and efficient scale-up key-value store. In: 2016 USENIX Annual Technical Conference (USENIX ATC 2016), USENIX Association, Denver, June 2016. https://www.usenix.org/conference/atc16/technical-sessions/presentation/papagiannis
19. Peter, S., Li, J., Zhang, I., Ports, D.R.K., Anderson, T., Krishnamurthy, A., Zbikowski, M., Woos, D.: Towards high-performance application-level storage management. In: 6th USENIX Workshop on Hot Topics in Storage and File Systems (HotStorage 2014). USENIX Association, Philadelphia, June 2014. https://www.usenix.org/conference/hotstorage14/workshop-program/presentation/peter

20. Peter, S., Li, J., Zhang, I., Ports, D.R.K., Woos, D., Krishnamurthy, A., Anderson, T., Roscoe, T.: Arrakis: the operating system is the control plane. In: 11th USENIX Symposium on Operating Systems Design and Implementation (OSDI 2014), pp. 1–16. USENIX Association, Broomfield, October 2014. https://www.usenix.org/conference/osdi14/technical-sessions/presentation/peter

21. Raoux, S., Burr, G., Breitwisch, M., Rettner, C., Chen, Y., Shelby, R., Salinga, M., Krebs, D., Chen, S.H., Lung, H., Lam, C.: Phase-change random access memory: a scalable technology. IBM J. Res. Dev. **52**(4.5), 465–479 (2008)

22. Rodeh, O.: B-trees, shadowing, and clones. Trans. Storage **3**(4), 2: 1–2: 27 (2008). http://doi.acm.org/10.1145/1326542.1326544

23. Uhlig, R., Neiger, G., Rodgers, D., Santoni, A., Martins, F., Anderson, A., Bennett, S., Kagi, A., Leung, F., Smith, L.: Intel virtualization technology. Computer **38**(5), 48–56 (2005)

24. Volos, H., Nalli, S., Panneerselvam, S., Varadarajan, V., Saxena, P., Swift, M.M.: Aerie: Flexible file-system interfaces to storage-class memory. In: Proceedings of the Ninth European Conference on Computer Systems, EuroSys 2014, pp. 14:1–14:14. ACM, New York (2014). http://doi.acm.org/10.1145/2592798.2592810

25. Volos, H., Tack, A.J., Swift, M.M.: Mnemosyne: lightweight persistent memory. In: Proceedings of the Sixteenth International Conference on Architectural Support for Programming Languages and Operating Systems, ASPLOS XVI, pp. 91–104, ACM, New York (2011). http://doi.acm.org/10.1145/1950365.1950379

26. Wu, X., Reddy, A.L.N.: SCMFS: a file system for storage class memory. In: Proceedings of 2011 International Conference for High Performance Computing, Networking, Storage and Analysis, SC 2011, pp. 39:1–39:11. ACM, New York (2011). http://doi.acm.org/10.1145/2063384.2063436

27. Xu, J., Swanson, S.: Nova: a log-structured file system for hybrid volatile/nonvolatile main memories. In: 14th USENIX Conference on File and Storage Technologies (FAST 2016), pp. 323–338. USENIX Association, Santa Clara, February 2016. https://www.usenix.org/conference/fast16/technical-sessions/presentation/xu

Scaling Spark on Lustre

Nicholas Chaimov[1]([⊠]), Allen Malony[1], Costin Iancu[2], and Khaled Ibrahim[2]

[1] University of Oregon, Eugene, OR, USA
{nchaimov,malony}@cs.uoregon.edu
[2] Lawrence Berkeley National Laboratory, Berkeley, CA, USA
{cciancu,kzibrahim}@lbl.gov

Abstract. We report our experiences in porting and tuning the Apache Spark data analytics framework on the Cray XC30 (Edison) and XC40 (Cori) systems, installed at NERSC. We find that design decisions made in the development of Spark are based on the assumption that Spark is constrained primarily by network latency, and that disk I/O is comparatively cheap. These assumptions are not valid on Edison or Cori, which feature advanced low-latency networks but have diskless compute nodes. Lustre metadata access latency is a major bottleneck, severely constraining scalability. We characterize this problem with benchmarks run on a system with both Lustre and local disks, and show how to mitigate high metadata access latency by using per-node loopback filesystems for temporary storage. With this technique, we reduce the shuffle time and improve application scalability from $O(100)$ to $O(10,000)$ cores on Cori. For shuffle-intensive machine learning workloads, we show better performance than clusters with local disks.

Keywords: Spark · Berkeley data analytics stack · Cray XC · Lustre · Shifter

1 Introduction

Apache Spark [14] is a data analytics framework which provides high-level constructs for expressing computations over datasets larger than the system physical memory. The runtime provides elastic parallelism, i.e. resources could grow or shrink without requiring any change to application code, and provides resilient execution, which allows automatic recovering from resource failures.

Spark is part of the Berkeley Data Analytics Stack [6], which includes storage, resource management and scheduling infrastructure, such as the Hadoop Distributed File System (HDFS) [11] and the Hadoop YARN resouce scheduler [12]. High-level application-domain libraries are built on top of spark, such as GraphX for graph analytics [7], Spark SQL for database queries [3], MLLib for machine learning [10], and Spark Streaming for online data processing [15].

Spark targets directly cloud or commodity clusters compute environments, which have latency-optimized local disk storage and bandwidth-optimized network, relatively few cores per node, and possibly little memory per node.

© Springer International Publishing AG 2016
M. Taufer et al. (Eds.): ISC High Performance Workshops 2016, LNCS 9945, pp. 649–659, 2016.
DOI: 10.1007/978-3-319-46079-6_45

HPC systems such as the Cray XC series, in contrast, feature diskless compute nodes with access to a high bandwidth global filesystem, large core counts, large memory sizes per compute node, and latency-optimized networks designed for use with HPC tightly coupled applications. The question remains if design decisions made for cloud environments translate well when running Spark on HPC systems and whether the latter can bring any value to analytics workloads due to their superior and tightly integrated hardware. In this paper, we present a comparative performance analysis of Spark running on Cray XC HPC systems and on a system (Comet) designed for data intensive workloads with large local SSDs.

We discuss the design of the Spark runtime, showing where file I/O occurs and what file access patterns are commonly used. On Cori, a Cray XC40 system installed at NERSC [1], we show that the use of the Lustre filesystem to store intermediate data can lead to substantial performance degradation as a result of expensive metadata operations. Initial Spark scalability is limited to $O(100)$ cores. To reduce I/O impact we extend Shifter, a lightweight container infrastructure for Cray systems, to mount a per-node loopback filesystem backed by Lustre files. This reduces the impact of the metadata operations by many orders of magnitude. With loopback, single node Spark performance on Cray XC improves by $6\times$ and it becomes comparable to that of single Comet node with SSDs. Even more exciting, loopback allows us to scale out to $O(10,000)$ cores and we observe orders of magnitude improvements at scale. We use the `spark-perf` benchmark suite, consisting of a set of core RDD benchmarks and a set of machine learning algorithm benchmarks using `MLLib`. After calibrating and obtaining equivalent node performance on the Cray and Comet, we can compare the performance across the two system architectures.

Overall, these results are very encouraging. Simple configuration choices make HPC systems outperform architecures specifically designed for data analytics workloads with local SSDs: a global file system that provides a global name space can provide good performance. This indicates current system HPC designs are good to execute both scientific and data intensive workloads. The performance differences between the Cray XC and Comet may provide incentive for the aquisition of HPC systems in the "commercial" domain.

2   Spark Architecture

Spark implements the Map/Reduce model of computation. From the application developer's perspective, Spark programs manipulate *resilient distributed datasets* [13] (RDD), which are distributed lists of key-value pairs. The developer constructs RDDs from input data by reading files or parallelizing existing Scala or Python lists, and subsequently produces derived RDDs by applying *transformations* and *actions*. Transformations, such as `map` and `filter`, declare the kind of computation that could occur, but does not actually trigger computation; rather, a *lineage* is constructed, showing how the data represented by an RDD can be computed, when the data is actually required. *Actions* actually retrieve values from an RDD, and trigger the deferred computation to occur.

During *map* tasks, all data dependencies are intra-partition. During *reduce* tasks, inter-partition dependencies can occur, and it is only during reduce tasks that inter-node communication occurs. This occurs through a *shuffle*. During a shuffle, the ShuffleManager sorts data within each partition by key, and the key-value pairs within each partition are written to per-partition shuffle data files on disk. Each executor then submits requests for blocks, which are either local or remote. Each node then requests blocks, both locally and from other executors. When a block is requested which is owned by a remote executor, the local BlockManager makes a remote request to the owning BlockManager, which maintains a queue of requests which are serviced once the shuffle data is written to the corresponding shuffle file.

3 Disk I/O Patterns in Spark

Disk I/O can occur in almost every stage of a Spark application. During the construction of input stages, disk I/O occurs to read the input data. In a traditional Spark installation, the input data would be stored in an HDFS overlay built on top of local disks, while on the Cray XC input data is stored directly on the Lustre filesystem available to all compute nodes. Output data is similarly stored either in HDFS or in Lustre, depending on the installation. When data is stored outside of HDFS, there is one file per partition, so as a minimum, there must be at least as many file opens and file reads as there are partitions. Additionally, each file is accompanied by a checksum file used for verifying integrity, and an index file indicating file names and offsets for specific blocks. Simple file readers such as the text file reader perform two file opens per partition: one for the checksum file and one for the partition data file. More complex file format readers perform more file operations; for example, the Parquet compressed columnar storage format performs four file opens per partition: first the checksum is opened, the partition data file is opened and the checksum computed, and both closed. Each partition data file is then opened, the footer is read, and then the file is closed. Finally, the file is opened again, the remainder of the file is read before closing the file again.

During every phase, BlockManager I/O can occur. If a block is requested while being stored on disk, the corresponding temporary file is opened and the data read and stored in memory, potentially triggering an eviction. When an eviction occurs, the corresponding temporary file is created, if necessary, and is written to. If sufficient memory is available that problem data fits in RAM, BlockManager disk I/O does not occur.

During shuffles, files are created storing sorted shuffle data. As originally designed, each shuffle map task would write an intermediate file for each shuffle reduce task, resulting in $O(tasks^2)$ files being written. The very large number of files produced tended to degrade performance by overwhelming the `inode` cache [5], so this was replaced with a single file per shuffle reduce task. However, as tasks are not supposed to affect the global state of the runtime except through the BlockManager, every map task writing to a per-reduce-task file opens the file, writes to it, and closes it. Similarly, every shuffle reduce task opens the file, reads from it, and closes it. Thus, although the total number of files has been reduced to $O(tasks)$, the number of *metadata operations* remains $O(tasks^2)$. Shuffle intermediate files are *always* written regardless of the amount of memory available.

4 Spark Performance on Lustre

Previous work on porting Spark to the Cray platform [9] running under Cluster Compatibility Mode revealed that performance of TeraSort and PageRank was up to four times worse on a 43 nodes of a Cray XC system compared to an experimental 43-node Cray Aries-based system with local SSDs, even though the experimental system had fewer cores than the Cray XC (1,032 vs 1,376). To mitigate this problem, the authors redirected shuffle intermediate files to an in-memory filesystem, but noted that this limited the size of problem that could be solved, and that the entire Spark job fails if the in-memory filesystem becomes full. Multiple shuffle storage directories can be specified, one using the in-memory filesystem and one using the Lustre scratch filesystem, but the Spark runtime then uses them in a round-robin manner, so performance is still degraded.

On Cori we compare directly Lustre with in-memory execution performance. On Comet we compare Lustre with SSD storage. To illustrate the main differences we use the GroupBy benchmark which is a worst-case shuffle. GroupBy generates key-value pairs with a limited number of keys across many partitions, and then groups all values associated with a particular key into one partition. This requires all-to-all communication, and thus maximizes the number of shuffle file operations required, as described in Sect. 3, above.

Figure 1 shows the results on Cori. On a single node (32 cores), when shuffle intermediate files are stored on Lustre, time to job completion is 6 times longer

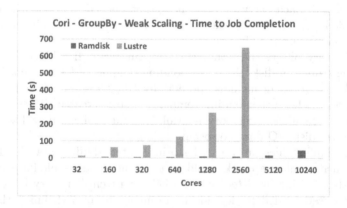

Fig. 1. GroupBy benchmark performance (worst-case shuffle) on NERSC Cori, with shuffle intermediate files stored on Lustre or RAMdisk. Number of partitions in each case is $4 \times cores$.

than when shuffle intermediate files are stored on an in-memory filesystem. The performance degradation increases as nodes are added: at 80 nodes, performance is 61 times worse on Lustre than the in-memory filesystem. Runs larger than 80 nodes using Lustre fail.

Results on Comet are shown in Fig. 2. On one node, shuffle performance is 11 times slower on Lustre than on the SSD; however, the performance penalty does not become worse as we add nodes. Because Comet compute nodes feature local SSDs, there is less contention for the Lustre metadata server, as other jobs running on the system tend to make use of the SSD for intermediate file storage.

Figure 3 shows the performance of the spark-perf benchmarks [2] on SDSC Comet. The *scheduling-throughput* benchmark runs a series of empty tasks without any disk I/O; its performance is unaffected by the choice of shuffle data directory. The *scala-agg-by-key*, *scala-agg-by-key-int* and *scala-agg-by-key-naive* benchmarks perform aggregation by key: they generate key-value pairs and then apply functions to all values associated with the same key throughout the RDD; this requires a shuffle to move data between partitions. The version using floating point values (*scala-agg-by-key*) and the integer version (*scala-agg-by-key-int*) are designed to shuffle the same number of bytes of data, so that the number of values in the integer version is larger than for the floating point version, increasing the number of shuffle intermediate file writes. The *scala-agg-by-key-naive* benchmark first performs a groupByKey, grouping all values for each key into one partition, before performing partition-local reductions, so that shuffles move a larger volume of data than for the non-naive versions, giving larger shuffle writes. The three *scala-agg-by-key* benchmarks have degraded performance

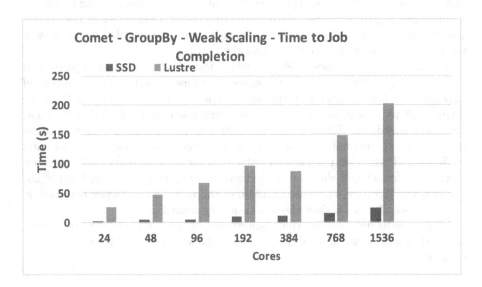

Fig. 2. GroupBy benchmark performance (worst-case shuffle) on SDSC Comet, with shuffle intermediate files stored on Lustre or local SSD. Number of partitions in each case is 4 × *cores*.

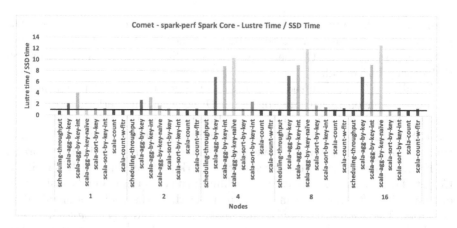

Fig. 3. Slowdown of spark-perf Spark Core benchmarks on Comet with shuffle intermediate data stored on the Lustre filesystem instead of local SSDs.

when intermediate data is stored on Lustre, which continue to degrade as more nodes are added; at 16 nodes, performance for *scala-agg-by-key-naive* is 12 times worse than on SSD. The remaining benchmarks involve little or no shuffling and so are unaffected by shuffle directory placement.

As described in Sect. 3, shuffle intermediate files are opened once for each read or write. When shuffle intermediate files are stored on Lustre, this causes heavy metadata server load which slows the overall process of reading or writing. Figure 4 shows the slowdown that results from opening a file, reading it, closing it, and repeating this process, as compared to opening a file once and performing multiple reads. For read sizes under one megabyte, Lustre filesystems show a penalty increasing with decreasing read size.

Spark-perf also provides a set of machine learning benchmarks implemented using MLLib [10]. Figure 5 shows the slowdown of using Lustre storage instead of SSD for these benchmarks. Iterative algorithms – those which perform the same stages multiple times, and therefore have multiple rounds of shuffling – show the worst slowdown. The *lda* (Latent Dirichlet allocation), *pic* (power iteration clustering), summary statistics, *spearman* (Spearman rank correlation) and *prefix-span* (Prefix Span sequential pattern mining) benchmarks all show subsantial slowdown when shuffle files are stored on Lustre rather than local SSDs. These are all iterative with the exception of the summary statistics benchmark, which has smaller block sizes than the other benchmarks.

These results demonstrate that shuffle performance is a major cause of performance degradation when local disk is not available or not used for shuffle-heavy applications.

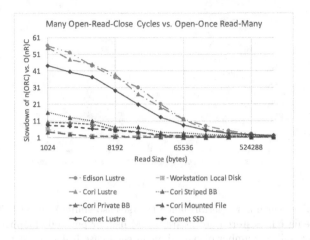

Fig. 4. Slowdown from performing open-per-read rather than single-open many-reads for reads of different sizes on various filesystems on Edison, Cori, Comet, and a workstation with local disk. The penalty is highest for the Lustre filesystems.

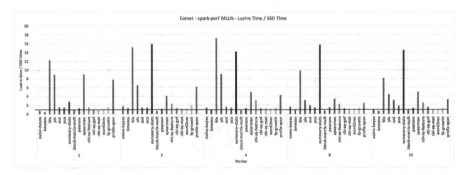

Fig. 5. Slowdown of spark-perf MLLib benchmarks on Comet with shuffle intermediate data stored on the Lustre filesystem instead of local SSDs.

5   Localizing Metadata Operations with Shifter

To improve the file IO performance, ideally we need to avoid propagating metadata operations to the Lustre filesystem because these files are used solely by individual compute nodes. On Cray XC systems, we do not have access to local disk, and using in-memory filesystems limits the problem sizes. We have previously described a file-pooling technique [4] which maintains a pool of open file handles during shuffling to avoid repeated opens of the same file. However, this requires modifications to the Spark runtime, and affects only operations coming from the Spark runtime. Other sources of redundant opens, such as high-level libraries and third-party file format readers, are not addressed. Furthermore, each file must be opened at least once, still placing load on the Lustre metadata server, even though the files are only needed on one node.

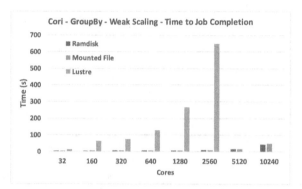

Fig. 6. GroupBy benchmark performance (worst-case shuffle) on NERSC Cori, with shuffle intermediate files stored on Lustre, RAMdisk, or per-node loopback filesystems backed by Lustre files. Number of partitions in each case is $4 \times cores$.

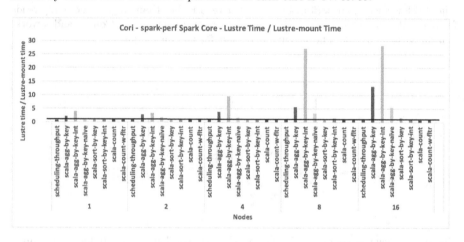

Fig. 7. Slowdown of spark-perf Spark Core benchmarks on Cori with shuffle intermediate data stored on the Lustre filesystem instead of Lustre-backed loopback filesystems.

To keep metadata operations local, we have previously experimented with mounting a per-node loopback filesystem, each backed by a file stored on Lustre. This enables storage larger than available through an in-memory filesystem while still keeping file opens of intermediate files local; only a single open operation per node must be sent to the Lustre metadata server, to open the backing file. This approach was not feasible, however, for ordinary use, as mounting a loopback filesystem requires root privileges.

Shifter [8] is a lightweight container infrastructure for the Cray environment that provides Docker-like functionality. With Shifter, the user can, when scheduling an interactive or batch job, specify a Docker image, which will be made available on each of the compute nodes. In order to do this, Shifter provides a mechanism for mounting the image, stored on Lustre, as a read-only loopback

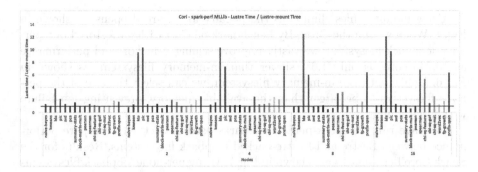

Fig. 8. Slowdown of spark-perf MLLib benchmarks on Cori with shuffle intermediate data stored on the Lustre filesystem instead of Lustre-backed loopback filesystems.

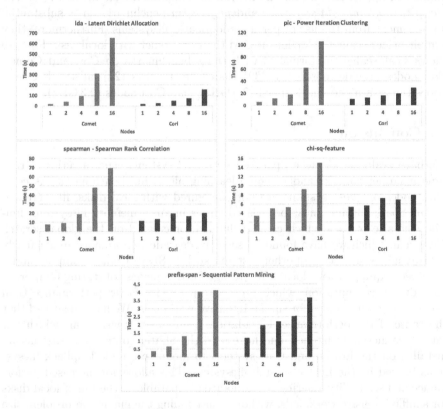

Fig. 9. Weak scaling for the MLLib benchmarks most sensitive to shuffle performance on Cori with per-node loopback filesystems and on Comet with local SSDs.

filesystem on each compute node within the job. Motivated by our work, Shifter was recently extended to optionally allow a per-compute-node image to be mounted as a read-write loopback filesystem.

Using mounted files eliminates the penalty for per-read opens, as shown in Fig. 4. When we run the GroupBy benchmark on Cori with data stored in a per-node loopback filesystem, we vastly improve scaling behavior, and performance at 10,240 cores is only 1.6× slower than in-memory filesystem, as shown in Fig. 6. Unlike with the in-memory filesystem, we can select the size of the per-node filesystem to be larger than the available memory, preventing job failure with large shuffles.

We have run the spark-perf benchmarks used in Sect. 4 to compare performance between Lustre and Lustre-backed loopback file systems. Results for the Spark Core benchmarks are shown in Fig. 7. Using per-node loopback filesystems improves performance at larger core counts for the *scala-agg-by-key* and *scala-agg-by-key-int* benchmarks, particularly for the latter which performs a larger number of opens. Results for the MLLib benchmarks are shown in Fig. 8. The *lda, pic, spearman, chi-sq-feature* and *prefix-span* benchmarks show substantial improvement from the use of per-node loopback filesystems. Furthermore, they exhibit better scaling behavior on Cori than on Comet with local disk. Figure 9 shows weak-scaling performance with those benchmarks on Cori and Comet. Cori nodes provide more cores (32) than Comet nodes (24), although Comet nodes run at a higher clock speed (2.5 GHz) than Cori nodes (2.3 GHz).

6   Conclusion

We have evaluated Apache Spark on Cray XC systems using a series of runtime microbenchmarks and machine learning algorithm benchmarks. As compute nodes on these systems are not configured with local disks, files created by the Spark runtime must be created either in an in-memory filesystem, limiting the size of data which can be shuffled, or created on the global scratch filesystem, which we have found to severely degrade performance, particularly as more nodes are used. On other systems, such as SDSC Comet, compute nodes have been equipped with local SSD storage for the purpose of storing temporary data during computation, which provides up to 11× faster performance than using a Lustre filesystem for shuffle-intensive workloads. We have identified that the cause of the performance degradation is not read or write bandwidth but rather file metadata latency, and have used the Shifter container infrastructure installed on the Edison and Cori systems to mount per-node loopback filesystems backed by the Lustre scratch filesystem. This allows for increased performance and scalability, offering performance comparable to the use of local disks for shuffle-intensive workloads, without constraining the maximum problem size as with the in-memory filesystem. This technique is a promising approach for deploying Apache Spark on Cray XC systems.

References

1. National Energy Research Scientific Computing Center. https://www.nersc.gov
2. spark-perf benchmark. https://github.com/databricks/spark-perf

3. Armbrust, M., Xin, R.S., Lian, C., Huai, Y., Liu, D., Bradley, J.K., Meng, X., Kaftan, T., Franklin, M.J., Ghodsi, A., Zaharia, M.: Spark SQL: relational data processing in spark. In: Proceedings of the 2015 ACM SIGMOD International Conference on Management of Data, SIGMOD 2015, pp. 1383–1394. ACM (2015). http://doi.acm.org/10.1145/2723372.2742797

4. Chaimov, N., Malony, A., Canon, S., Iancu, C., Ibrahim, K.Z., Srinivasan, J.: Scaling spark on hpc systems. In: Proceedings of the International Conference on High-Performance Parallel and Distributed Computing (2015)

5. Davidson, A., Or, A.: Optimizing shuffle performance in spark. http://www.cs.berkeley.edu/kubitron/courses/cs262a-F13/projects/reports/project16_report.pdf

6. Franklin, M.: Making sense of big data with the berkeley data analytics stack. In: Proceedings of the Eighth ACM International Conference on Web Search and Data Mining, WSDM 2015, pp. 1–2. ACM, New York (2015). http://doi.acm.org/10.1145/2684822.2685326

7. Gonzalez, J.E., Xin, R.S., Dave, A., Crankshaw, D., Franklin, M.J., Stoica, I.: Graphx: graph processing in a distributed dataflow framework. In: Proceedings of OSDI, pp. 599–613. https://www.usenix.org/system/files/conference/osdi14/osdi14-paper-gonzalez.pdf

8. Jacobsen, D.M., Canon, R.S.: Contain this, unleashing docker for hpc. In: Cray Users Group (2015)

9. Maschhoff, K.J., Ringenburg, M.F.: Experiences running and optimizing the berkeley data analytics stack on cray platforms. In: Cray Users Group (2015)

10. Meng, X., Bradley, J., Yavuz, B., Sparks, E., Venkataraman, S., Liu, D., Freeman, J., Tsai, D.B., Amde, M., Owen, S., Xin, D., Xin, R., Franklin, M.J., Zadeh, R., Zaharia, M., Talwalkar, A.: MLlib: machine learning in apache spark. http://arxiv.org/abs/1505.06807

11. Shvachko, K., Kuang, H., Radia, S., Chansler, R.: The hadoop distributed file system. In: 2010 IEEE 26th Symposium on Mass Storage Systems and Technologies (MSST), pp. 1–10 (2010)

12. Vavilapalli, V.K., Murthy, A.C., Douglas, C., Agarwal, S., Konar, M., Evans, R., Graves, T., Lowe, J., Shah, H., Seth, S., Saha, B., Curino, C., O'Malley, O., Radia, S., Reed, B., Baldeschwieler, E.: Apache hadoop YARN: yet another resource negotiator. In: Proceedings of the 4th Annual Symposium on Cloud Computing, SOCC 2013, pp. 5:1–5:16. ACM (2013). http://doi.acm.org/10.1145/2523616.2523633

13. Zaharia, M., Chowdhury, M., Das, T., Dave, A., Ma, J., McCauley, M., Franklin, M.J., Shenker, S., Stoica, I.: Resilient distributed datasets: a fault-tolerant abstraction for in-memory cluster computing. In: Proceedings of the 9th USENIX Conference on Networked Systems Design and Implementation, NSDI 2012, p. 2. USENIX Association (2012). http://dl.acm.org/citation.cfm?id=2228298.2228301

14. Zaharia, M., Chowdhury, M., Franklin, M.J., Shenker, S., Stoica, I.: Spark: cluster computing with working sets. In: Proceedings of the 2nd USENIX Conference on Hot topics in Cloud Computing, vol. 10, p. 10. http://static.usenix.org/legacy/events/hotcloud10/tech/full_papers/Zaharia.pdf

15. Zaharia, M., Das, T., Li, H., Shenker, S., Stoica, I.: Discretized streams: an efficient and fault-tolerant model for stream processing on large clusters. In: Proceedings of the 4th USENIX Conference on Hot Topics in Cloud Ccomputing, HotCloud 2012, pp. 10–10. USENIX Association, Berkeley (2012). http://dl.acm.org/citation.cfm?id=2342763.2342773

VHPC

Accelerating Application Migration in HPC

Ramy Gad[1]([✉]), Simon Pickartz[2]([✉]), Tim Süß[1], Lars Nagel[1], Stefan Lankes[2],
and André Brinkmann[1]

[1] Zentrum für Datenverarbeitung, Johannes Gutenberg-Universität Mainz,
Mainz, Germany
{gad,suesst,nagell,brinkman}@uni-mainz.de
[2] Institute for Automation of Complex Power Systems,
E.ON Energy Research Center, RWTH Aachen, Aachen, Germany
{spickartz,slankes}@eonerc.rwth-aachen.de

Abstract. It is predicted that the number of cores per node will rapidly
increase with the upcoming era of exascale supercomputers. As a result,
multiple applications will have to share one node and compete for the
(often scarce) resources available on this node. Furthermore, the growing number of hardware components causes a decrease in the *mean time
between failures*. Application migration between nodes has been proposed
as a tool to mitigate these two problems: Bottlenecks due to resource
sharing can be addressed by load balancing schemes which migrate applications; and hardware errors can often be tolerated by the system if faulty
nodes are detected and processes are migrated ahead of time.

Virtual Machine (VM) migration currently seems to be the most
promising technique for such approaches as it provides a strong level of
isolation. However, the migration time of virtual machines is higher than
the respective migration time on the process level. This can be explained
by the additional virtualization layer in the memory hierarchy.

In this paper, we propose a technique for the acceleration of VM
migration. We take advantage of the fact that freed memory regions
within the guest system are not recognized by the hypervisor. Therefore,
we fill them with zeros such that zero-page detection and compression
can work more efficiently. We demonstrate that the approach reduces
migration time by up to 19 % with a negligible overhead for some applications.

1 Introduction

With the continually growing demands of HPC applications for more computational power, supercomputers are moving towards the exascale era. Compared to
today's systems, this performance gain will not only be achieved by an increase
of the node count but also by a rising amount of cores per node. The efficient
exploitation of such exascale systems requires the usage of all the available cores
of a node. Single applications typically stress one specific resource on a compute
node, like the CPU, the memory, or the IO. The sharing of nodes by multiple
applications can overcome the resulting scaling limitations within a node, and it

© Springer International Publishing AG 2016
M. Taufer et al. (Eds.): ISC High Performance Workshops 2016, LNCS 9945, pp. 663–673, 2016.
DOI: 10.1007/978-3-319-46079-6_46

has been shown that co-scheduling multiple applications with different resource requirements on the same node can increase the overall system utilization and energy efficiency [4,26]. However, as applications have varying resource demands over time, a dynamic load balancer is required to avoid that resources get congested.

The migration of jobs across the cluster is necessary to support dynamic load balancing. A migration mechanism can also help to improve the systems' resiliency, as in the case of imminent failures an evacuation of affected nodes can be performed by a migration of the respective processes [18,28]. In previous studies we investigated different migration techniques and found full virtualization based on Kernel-based Virtual Machine (KVM) [14] to provide a high flexibility while providing performance results comparable to a native execution [20]. A drawback is the high migration time caused by the transfer of partly unnecessary memory regions. This is the result of the additional level in the address translation that comes with full virtualization. The hypervisor is not capable of detecting memory that has been freed by applications running within the VM.

In this paper, we propose an approach to accelerate VM migration in the HPC context by a reduction of the transmitted data volume. While we concentrate on the case of virtual machines in this paper, our approach can also be applied to other migration techniques. The migration time of VMs is mainly determined by the network bandwidth [13] and the size of the virtual machine image comprising the guest operating system and the application's processes. For a reduction of the VM image size and an acceleration of the migration, hypervisors apply compression [27] and zero-block detection [9]. We leverage this by transmitting only what is required to resume the VM on the target node.

When executed within a VM the release of memory does not affect the amount of data that is transferred during a migration since these regions are only freed within the guest system but not returned back to the host. Therefore, we overwrite these freed regions with zeros. This way, the zero-page detection and the compression algorithm are able to further reduce the VM image size. In our approach, we substitute the memory operations *realloc* and *free* to place zeros in every freed memory region. We evaluate the approach by running a set of HPC applications from various domains within VMs based on KVM. We demonstrate that our approach can boost the migration time by up 19 % with a negligible overhead for some applications.

The remainder of this paper is structured as follows: After discussing related work, we explain our approach in Sect. 3 and evaluate it in Sect. 4. Finally, in Sect. 5 we draw our conclusion and outline future work.

2   Related Work

Application migration is used for fault tolerance and load balancing. Nagarajan et al. propose a fault tolerance scheme for MPI applications based on proactive migration [18]. They monitor the health of computing nodes in order to detect deteriorating behavior and to anticipate node failures. In such a case the monitoring system triggers the migration of the node's processes to healthy nodes.

Application migration for load balancing is seldom exploited in HPC, but quite common in cloud computing. Load balancing strategies can include the current load distribution in the data center, historical data on the load and/or information about renewable energy [12,17]. Randles et al. present a comparison of distributed load balancing strategies [23].

There exist different migration techniques in HPC, for example, *process-level migration*, *virtual machine migration* and *container-based migration*. Process-level migration is based on the checkpoint/restart (c/r) mechanism, which allows an application to save a snapshot of its current state so that it can be restarted from that point on the same or another node. The simplest approach is *system-level c/r* which performs a memory core dump. It can be implemented in kernel space (see BLCR [8]) or in user space (see DMTCP [1]). The advantage of system-level checkpoint/restart is that it is transparent to the application and that the checkpoint can be taken at arbitrary points. However, these tools produce relatively large checkpoints because they include data that is not required for restarting the computation.

Application-level c/r was introduced to get checkpoints of smaller size, but it is also more complex and involves the application programmer. The programmer must know the data structures to be included into the checkpoint and has to add this information to the code. In order to ease the process, the programmer is assisted by special libraries and compilers. The `Libckpt` library, e.g., provides transparent c/r, but requires user directives that mark the checkpoints' locations and data [21]. Bronevetsky et al. provide a source-to-source compiler tool that automatically instruments the code to save and restore its own state. The tool coordinates c/r for parallel OpenMP [5] and MPI programs [25].

The virtualization overhead is often seen as the main reason why virtual machine migration is rarely used in HPC. Youseff et al. show that this overhead can be neglected and that the performance of virtual machines is relatively close to native execution [29]. Pickartz et al. demonstrated that virtual machine migration can also be beneficial in HPC because of its flexibly and even improved performance [20].

A lot of effort has been spent on accelerating these virtual machine migrations, either focusing on increasing the bandwidth between source and destination nodes or on finding better algorithms for copying data between the nodes. None of the studies investigated what is contained in the virtual machine image and whether it is needed: Huang et al. propose a high performance virtual machine migration design that uses RDMA (Remote Direct Memory Access) over InfiniBand [13]. In this way, they are able to increase the available bandwidth for migration and reduce the migration overhead by 80 % with respect to TCP/IP. Satyanarayanan et al. propose a suspend/resume approach for virtual machines, in which a suspended virtual machine saves its volatile state to a file [15,24]. This file is copied to a remote node where the virtual machine can be resumed.

Live migration is a technique for moving virtual machine between computing nodes with almost zero downtime. There are different techniques for live migration, for example *precopy* and *postcopy*. Hirofuchi et al. propose live migration with postcopy in which the content of a virtual machine is copied after its process state has been sent to the target node [11]. Once the process state starts execution on the target node, virtual machine memory pages are fetched on demand from the source node. The precopy approach proposed by Clark et al. first copies the whole memory state of the virtual machine from the source to the destination node [6]. As this memory might get updated after being copied from the host node, updated memory pages are iteratively copied to the source node before finally the process state can be copied to the target node. Precopy works better with read-intensive applications; write-intensive applications accessing large amounts of memory can make migration impossible [11]. Precopy is also more resistant to faults because the source node still holds an updated copy of the virtual machine. On the other hand, postcopy typically experiences the shortest downtime.

3   Methodology

This section describes our proposed solution for an accelerated migration of VMs in detail. First, we give an overview of the migration mechanism inside QEMU / KVM. Afterwards we introduce our preload library implementing the zeroing of freed memory. Finally, we provide a brief description of selected HPC application benchmarks that we use for an evaluation of the presented approach.

3.1   Virtual Machine Migration

The migration of VMs based on KVM is implemented by the user-space emulator QEMU [2] which does not have any knowledge of the actual page mapping within the VM. QEMU supports both *cold* and *live* migration. However, as the underlying migration mechanism is very similar in both modes, we focus on the former in the scope of this work.

QEMU has to traverse the whole virtual memory region representing the guest physical address space. Memory blocks that are not mapped into the virtual address space of a process running within the VM resemble from QEMU's point of view memory regions only containing zeros. A mechanism to detect these regions and to avoid unnecessary data transfers of whole zero-pages is part of QEMU since Version 1.6.0. This zero-detection is realized by an unrolled loop that can easily benefit from vector operations.

Furthermore, QEMU supports the migration of compressed VMs. This is a rather new feature that has been integrated in Version 2.4. If enabled, the RAM pages of a VM are compressed prior to the migration and they are decompressed on the destination node. A fine-tuning of the performance of the compressed migration is possible modifying the parameters *compress-level* and *(de-)compress-threads*.

3.2   Virtual Machine Memory Zeroing

Placing zeros in the free memory regions inside the VM is done using a newly developed *zeroing preload library*. This library is loaded before the application is executed inside the VM. The library intercepts memory deallocation operations like *realloc* and *free*. For each memory deallocation, an approximated size of the freed memory is fetched from the *glibc* library. Zeros are placed in these memory regions before committing the deallocation operation.

For each memory allocation, the *glibc* library generates an *allocated chunk*. This *allocated chunk* encapsulates the user data and a size field which contains the size of this allocated chunk. For memory alignment reason, the *glibc allocated chunk* size is usually larger than the user requested memory. Our approach was tested with glibc version 2.17.

Setting deallocated memory to zero, is the main source of the runtime overhead introduced to the application by our zeroing library. The runtime overhead depends on the size of the deallocated memory and the number of deallocation operations.

3.3   HPC Application Benchmarks

The following is a brief description of the HPC applications which we have tested with our approach:

- NAMD [19] is a parallel molecular dynamics simulator for large biomolecular systems. NAMD can simulate a hundred million atoms utilizing up to 500 k cores.
- mpiblast [7] is the MPI parallel version of the Basic Local Alignment Search Tool (BLAST). It compares nucleotide/protein sequences to sequences in a database and computes statistics about the matching results. mpiblast boosts the performance of BLAST and can scale up to hundreds of processors.
- gromacs [22] is a computational chemistry application that performs molecular dynamics simulation. It can solve Newton's equations of motion for systems with hundreds to millions of interacting particles.
- LAMMPS [10] is also a molecular dynamics simulator. In addition to molecules, LAMMPS models / simulates atomic, polymeric, biological, metallic, granular, and coarse-grained systems using a variety of force fields and boundary conditions. It parallelizes the computation by spatially decomposing the simulation domain.
- PhyloBayes [16] is a parallel implementation of Bayesian Markov chain Monte Carlo (MCMC) sampler for phylogenetic inference. The program uses nucleotide, protein, or codon sequence alignments to perform phylogenetic reconstruction.

4   Evaluation

In this section we evaluate the proposed approach in terms of runtime overhead and checkpoint size. We show that the reduction of the checkpoint size descreases the migration time.

We have used two NUMA nodes for the evaluation. Both nodes have 32 virtual cores on two sockets with 8 physical cores each. The nodes are equipped with Intel SandyBridge CPUs (E5-2650) clocked at 2 GHz and connected by a Gigabit Ethernet fabric. Both systems have the same software stack and run an unmodified CentOS 7.2 installation with a 3.10.0 Linux kernel. The virtualization framework is based on KVM and QEMU version 2.5.1.

4.1   Zeroing Preload Library Overhead

The zeroing preload library introduces runtime overhead to our sample HPC applications which is mainly the time required to place zeros in the freed memory regions. It thus depends on the application, *i.e.*, the number of times memory is freed as well as the size of the affected memory regions.

We ran each of our test application benchmarks inside of a VM and measured the execution time with and without the preload library. Each run was repeated ten times. PhyloBayes was excluded from the test because its runtime is longer than four days. Figure 1 shows the normalized execution time of our test applications. The runtime was normalized with respect to the maximum runtime.

While mpiblast has a rather large preload library overhead of 6.6%. For gromacs, NAMD and LAMMPS, the overhead is negligible with less than 0.3%. The negative value of -0.11% for NAMD can only be explained by noise.

Finding: The runtime overhead of the preload library depends on the application and ranges roughly from 0% to 6.6% for the sample applications.

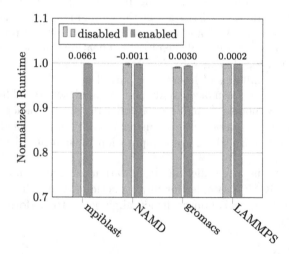

Fig. 1. Impact of the preload library on the runtimes of selected HPC applications. The bars represent the normalized execution time, the median as well as the upper and lower quartiles. The numbers above the bars are the difference between the medians for zeroing being enabled and disabled.

4.2   VM Image Size

The migration time of a running application inside a VM is affected by the size of the VM image which mainly depends on the size of the application's memory image. We studied the effect of our zeroing preload library on the size of the VM image and examined whether compression and zero-page detection algorithms benefit from it.

Since KVM performs checkpointing as a memory core dump, a checkpoint is a good measure for the VM's image size. Again we ran each of our application benchmarks inside a VM with and without the zeroing preload library. We performed three checkpoints at 5 min intervals and compressed them logging the checkpoint size before and after compression.

The zero-page detection algorithm is applied by the hypervisor with every checkpoint. So we log the number of these detected zero pages.

Observing the results in Fig. 2, we see that, with compression disabled, all applications have a smaller checkpoint size when zeroing is enabled. Also all applications experience a larger number of zero pages when zeroing is enabled. With compression enabled, the checkpoints of all application except gromacs are smaller when zeroing is enabled.

From the results we can derive that, for all applications, the zero-page detection algorithm found additional zero blocks generated by the preload library. The compression algorithm is applied after the zero-page detection algorithm. For all applications except gromacs, compression benefitted from the additional partial zero pages generated by the preload library.

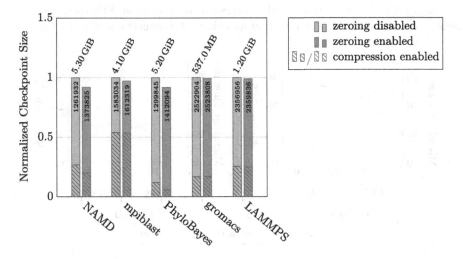

Fig. 2. Impact of the preload library on the checktpoint size. The values are normalized to the checkpoint size with disabled preload library and without compression. The values above the bars are the absolute size with disabled preload library and without compression. The values inside the bars are the number of detected zero pages in the checkpoint image.

Finding: The benefit of zeroing depends on the number of full/-partial zero memory blocks detected within the application.

4.3 VM Migration Time

The primary goal of our work is to investigate if zeroing of unused memory regions results in an improved migration time. We therefore compare the migration times of HPC application benchmarks with and without the preload library enabled. For the experiment we selected NAMD and PhyloBayes because, looking at the results of the previous section, they seem to be promising candidates that might benefit from our approach.

We ran each of the two applications for more than half an hour and migrated it back and forth between the two cluster nodes every 5 min. Therefore, we used a VM with 10 GiB of guest physical memory and performed a mapping of the virtual CPUs matching the host's topology [3]. We used the Gigabit Ethernet link for data transfer and QEMU for the migration of the VMs with compression enabled or disabled and with default parameters, *i.e.*, 8 compression threads, 2 decompression threads, and a compression level of 1. To get stable results we repeated this test 10 times and averaged the results. For both applications, zeroing accelerated the migration time by up to around 19 % (cf. Fig. 3).

The results perfectly match our findings of the previous section. Zeroing accelerates migration whether compression is enabled or not. However when compression is enabled, we have much more savings with respect to migration time. This can be explained by the fact that compression also benefits from partial zero pages.

Although we only regarded the migration over Gigabit Ethernet, the presented approach might be interesting for other interconnects as well. In any case

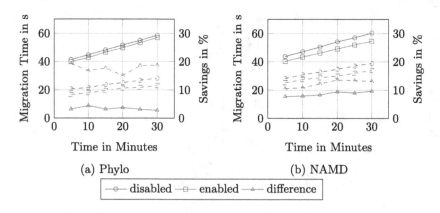

(a) Phylo   (b) NAMD

—◦— disabled —▫— enabled —▵— difference

Fig. 3. Migration time with *enabled* and *disabled* memory zeroing. The absolute results are displayed by means of the red and blue curves on the left y-axis respectively. The green curves correspond to the values on the right y-axis and represent the savings obtained when enabling memory zeroing with respect to normal execution. The dashed curves represent measurements with enabled compression.

the overhead generated by the preload library has to be balanced against the savings that can be achieved with the given link speed.

Finding: The migration algorithm of KVM benefits from the zeroing approach in all cases whether compression is enabled or not. Using compression is advisable because then zeroing accelerates the migration time even if none of the pages is completely zeroized.

5   Conclusion and Future Work

In this paper we have considered the migration of virtual machines and presented a new approach for reducing the size of the data transmitted. This approach zeros unused data so that zero-page detection and compression schemes work more efficiently. Our evaluation shows that this technique can indeed accelerate migration and reduce network traffic. In particular we have demonstrated that it is suitable for HPC environments by testing it with parallel applications encapsulated in VMs.

In future work, we want to eliminate the runtime overhead (time of placing zeros) of the current implementation of the preload library. When zeroized freed memory regions are allocated again before migration, the zeroing has been done in vain adding overhead without contributing to the acceleration of the migration. Instead of zeroing pages, we consider discarding unwanted pages, *i.e.*, completely deallocated memory pages. We are planning to implement this technique as a kernel module in the guest OS or in the hypervisor.

Acknowledgment and Availability. This work was supported by the German Ministry for Education and Research (BMBF) under project grant 01|H13004 (FAST).

The zeroing preload library is publicly available under https://version.zdv. Uni-Mainz.DE/anonscm/git/memory-zeroing/memory-zeroing.git.

References

1. Ansel, J., Arya, K., Cooperman, G.: DMTCP: transparent checkpointing for cluster computations and the desktop. In: 23rd IEEE International Symposium on Parallel and Distributed Processing (IPDPS), pp. 1–12 (2009)
2. Bellard, F.: Qemu, a fast and portable dynamic translator. In: FREENIX Track: 2005 USENIX Annual Technical Conference, pp. 41–46 (2005)
3. Breitbart, J., Pickartz, S., Weidendorfer, J., Monti, A.: Viability of Virtual Machines in HPC. In: Euro-Par 2016: Parallel Processing Workshops. LNCS. Springer (Accepted for publication) (2016)
4. Breitbart, J., Weidendorfer, J., Trinitis, C.: Case study on co-scheduling for HPC applications. In: 44th International Conference on Parallel Processing Workshops (ICPPW), pp. 277–285 (2015)
5. Bronevetsky, G., Marques, D., Pingali, K., Szwed, P.K., Schulz, M.: Application-level checkpointing for shared memory programs. In: 11th International Conference on Architectural Support for Programming Languages and Operating Systems (ASPLOS), pp. 235–247 (2004)

6. Clark, C., Fraser, K., Hand, S., et al.: Live migration of virtual machines. In: 2nd Symposium on Networked Systems Design and Implementation (NSDI), pp. 273–286 (2005)

7. Darling, A., Carey, L., Feng, W.C.: The design, implementation, and evaluation of mpiBLAST. ClusterWorld Conference & Expo and the 4th International Conference on Linux Cluster: the HPC Revolution 2003, pp. 13–15, June 2003

8. Duell, J.: The design and implementation of berkeley lab's linux checkpoint/restart. Technical report, Lawrence Berkeley National Laboratory (2003)

9. Dusser, J., Seznec, A.: Decoupled zero-compressed memory. In: 6th International Conference on High Performance Embedded Architectures and Compilers (HiPEAC), pp. 77–86 (2011)

10. FrantzDale, B., Plimpton, S.J., Shephard, M.S.: Software components for parallel multiscale simulation: an example with LAMMPS. Eng. Comput. (Lond.) 26(2), 205–211 (2010)

11. Hirofuchi, T., Nakada, H., Itoh, S., Sekiguchi, S.: Reactive consolidation of virtual machines enabled by postcopy live migration. In: 5th International Workshop on Virtualization Technologies in Distributed Computing, VTDC@HPDC 2011, pp. 11–18 (2011)

12. Hu, J., Gu, J., Sun, G., Zhao, T.: A scheduling strategy on load balancing of virtual machine resources in cloud computing environment. In: 3rd International Symposium on Parallel Architectures, Algorithms and Programming (PAAP), pp. 89–96 (2010)

13. Huang, W., Gao, Q., Liu, J., Panda, D.K.: High performance virtual machine migration with RDMA over modern interconnects. In: IEEE International Conference on Cluster Computing, pp. 11–20 (2007)

14. Kivity, A., Kamay, Y., Laor, D., Lublin, U., Liguori, A.: kvm: the Linux virtual machine monitor. In: Linux Symposium, pp. 225–230, June 2007

15. Kozuch, M., Satyanarayanan, M.: Internet suspend/resume. In: 4th IEEE Workshop on Mobile Computing Systems and Applications (WMCSA) (2002)

16. Lartillot, N., Lepage, T., Blanquart, S.: Phylobayes 3: a bayesian software package for phylogenetic reconstruction and molecular dating. Bioinformatics 25(17), 2286–2288 (2009)

17. Mäsker, M., Nagel, L., Brinkmann, A., Lotfifar, F., Johnson, M.: Smart grid-aware scheduling in data centres. In: 2015 Sustainable Internet and ICT for Sustainability (SustainIT), pp. 1–9 (2015)

18. Nagarajan, A.B., Mueller, F., Engelmann, C., Scott, S.L.: Proactive fault tolerance for HPC with xen virtualization. In: 21st Annual International Conference on Supercomputing (ICS), pp. 23–32 (2007)

19. Phillips, J.C., Braun, R., Wang, W., et al.: Scalable molecular dynamics with NAMD. J. Comput. Chem. 26(16), 1781–1802 (2005)

20. Pickartz, S., Gad, R., Lankes, S., Nagel, L., Süß, T., Brinkmann, A., Krempel, S.: Migration techniques in HPC environments. In: Lopes, L., Žilinskas, J., Costan, A., Cascella, R.G., Kecskemeti, G., Jeannot, E., Cannataro, M., Ricci, L., Benkner, S., Petit, S., Scarano, V., Gracia, J., Hunold, S., Scott, S.L., Lankes, S., Lengauer, C., Carretero, J., Breitbart, J., Alexander, M. (eds.) Euro-Par 2014. LNCS, vol. 8806, pp. 486–497. Springer, Heidelberg (2014). doi:10.1007/978-3-319-14313-2_41

21. Plank, J.S., Beck, M., Kingsley, G., Li, K.: Libckpt: transparent checkpointing under UNIX. In: USENIX 1995 Technical Conference on UNIX and Advanced Computing Systems, pp. 213–224 (1995)

22. Pronk, S., Páll, S., Schulz, R., et al.: GROMACS 4.5: a high-throughput and highly parallel open source molecular simulation toolkit. Bioinformatics **29**(7), 845–854 (2013)
23. Randles, M., Lamb, D.J., Taleb-Bendiab, A.: A comparative study into distributed load balancing algorithms for cloud computing. In: 24th IEEE International Conference on Advanced Information Networking and Applications Workshops (WAINA), pp. 551–556 (2010)
24. Satyanarayanan, M., Gilbert, B., et al.: Pervasive personal computing in an internet suspend/resume system. IEEE Internet Comput. **11**(2), 16–25 (2007)
25. Schulz, M., Bronevetsky, G., Fernandes, R., Marques, D., Pingali, K., Stodghill, P.: Implementation and evaluation of a scalable application-level checkpoint-recovery scheme for MPI programs. In: ACM/IEEE SC Conference on High Performance Networking and Computing, p. 38 (2004)
26. Süß, T., Döring, N., Gad, R., Nagel, L., Brinkmann, A., Feld, D., Schröder, E., Soddemann, T.: Impact of the scheduling strategy in heterogeneous systems that provide co-scheduling. In: 1st COSH Workshop on Co-Scheduling of HPC Applications, COSH@HiPEAC 2016, pp. 37–42 (2016)
27. Svärd, P., Tordsson, J., Hudzia, B., Elmroth, E.: High performance live migration through dynamic page transfer reordering and compression. In: IEEE 3rd International Conference on Cloud Computing Technology and Science (CloudCom), pp. 542–548 (2011)
28. Wang, C., Mueller, F., Engelmann, C., Scott, S.L.: Proactive process-level live migration and back migration in HPC environments. J. Parall. Distrib. Comput. **72**(2), 254–267 (2012)
29. Youseff, L., Wolski, R., Gorda, B.C., Krintz, C.: Evaluating the performance impact of xen on MPI and process execution for HPC systems. In: Proceedings of the 1st International Workshop on Virtualization Technology in Distributed Computing (VTDC@SC) (2006)

Migrating LinuX Containers Using CRIU

Simon Pickartz[✉], Niklas Eiling, Stefan Lankes, Lukas Razik,
and Antonello Monti

E.ON Energy Research Center, Institute for Automation of Complex Power Systems,
RWTH Aachen University, Aachen, Germany
{spickartz,neiling,slankes,lrazik,amonti}@eonerc.rwth-aachen.de

Abstract. Process migration is one of the most important techniques in
modern computing centers. It enables the implementation of load balancing strategies and eases the system administration. As supercomputers
continue to grow in size, according mechanisms become interesting to
High-Performance Computing (HPC) as well.

Usually, migration is accomplished by means of hypervisor-based virtualization. However, container-based approaches are an attractive alternative for HPC to minimize the performance penalties. In contrast to
virtual machine migration, the migration of operating system containers
is mostly unexplored in the context of HPC until today.

In this paper we present a prototype implementation of a libvirt driver
enabling the migration of LinuX Containers. We evaluate the driver in
terms of overhead added by the additional software layer and compare
its migration performance with that of virtual machines based on KVM.

Keywords: LinuX Containers · CRIU · Migration · HPC

1 Introduction

Virtualization techniques are already widely employed in today's data centers.
In conjunction with migration mechanisms they allow for the facilitation of
load balancing strategies, an improvement of fault resiliences, and a simplified system administration [3,10]. These aspects become likewise important for
High-Performance Computing (HPC) as supercomputers continue to increase in
size. However, migration techniques did not find much adoption in this field of
research, yet. This is mainly due to two reasons: (1) the mechanisms are usually implemented in conjunction with hypervisor-based virtualization. Despite
providing great flexibility and satisfactorily performance [14,15], there is still a
little performance hit compared to native execution which does not comply with
the goals of HPC; and (2) migration on the process-level, e. g., by using Berkley
Lab Checkpoint / Restart (BLCR) [6], has to cope with the problem of residual
dependencies [10].

Containers are an attractive alternative combining the best of two worlds:
on the one hand they provide a similar level of isolation compared to Virtual Machines (VMs). On the other hand containers are able to offer superior

© Springer International Publishing AG 2016
M. Taufer et al. (Eds.): ISC High Performance Workshops 2016, LNCS 9945, pp. 674–684, 2016.
DOI: 10.1007/978-3-319-46079-6_47

I / O- and CPU performance [16–18]. However, in contrast to the well established field of hypervisor-based migration, the relative young field dealing with the migration of containers in HPC is mostly unexplored.

Libvirt[1] allows for the management of different virtualization solutions (e. g., KVM or Xen) via an unified and stable interface. This forsters the adoption of the individual virtualization facilities since users only have to deal with one toolchain. However, the support for container-based virtualization including their migration is only partly available. Therefore, we propose a prototype implementation of a libvirt driver for the management and migration of LinuX Containers (LXC)[2]. For the latter we build upon Checkpoint / Restore In Userspace (CRIU)[3], a tool for checkpointing processes or groups thereof. This allows for the implementation of cold- and live-migration features. The main contributions of this work can be summarized as follows:

– an analysis of CRIU and an examination how its page server can be leveraged for an implementation of container migration and
– the implementation of container-based virtualization via the long-term stable API of libvirt with the goal of fostering the adoption of containers in HPC.

The paper is structured as follows: The next section covers background information on container-based virtualization. After an introduction to our driver implementation in Sect. 3, we present the evaluation results in Sect. 4. Before concluding the paper, we discuss related work in Sect. 5.

2 Background

This section discusses the requirements for the implementation of our work. We start with an introduction to container-based virtualization and the *libvirt* toolkit. Finally, we present CRIU which enables the migration of containers.

2.1 Container-Based Virtualization

This virtualization approach creates the impression of multiple operating systems by using isolation and control mechanisms for the separation of user-space instances, i. e., containers [18]. In contrast to hypervisor-based virtualization, the abstraction is provided at the system call level, i. e., a single kernel is shared among all containers, reducing the overhead of multiple kernel instances running at the same time [17]. Therefore, containers are an attractive alternative to VMs for HPC workloads.

Namespaces and Cgroups are means for isolation and control features provided by the Linux kernel and form the basis for containers [1]. Namespaces allow

---

[1] http://libvirt.org/.
[2] https://linuxcontainers.org/.
[3] https://criu.org/.

for the isolation and partitioning of specific resources to containers, e.g., with the *pid* namespace the separation of different process groups is possible [4]. This facilitates the migration of containers across nodes since the IDs of the processes running therein do not have to be adapted on the target systems. In contrast to namespaces, the cgroup subsystems are applied to process groups for the tracking and the limitation of specific resources [9], e.g., the *cpuset* subsystem allows for the assignment of individual CPUs to all processes of a cgroup [12]. This becomes especially important when scheduling multiple containers concurrently on the same node.

LinuX Containers is one of the first solutions for container-based virtualization that exclusively uses the cgroups and namespaces. It is implemented in user-space and requires at least the Linux kernel version 2.6.32 although certain features depend on more recent versions. An LXC instance consists of a set of processes to which the same namespaces apply. A limitation of its resources is realized by means of cgroups. The management of containers is either possible via a C API, or a set of command-line tools.

2.2   Domain Management Using Libvirt

Libvirt is an open source domain-management library written in C. Originally a wrapper around Xen, now it supports a variety of virtualization solutions such as QEMU, VMware ESX, and OpenVZ by now [2]. Furthermore, it provides a long-term stable API and a unified domain configuration via XML files. This enables an isolation from changes to the virtualization layer. Internally, libvirt is divided into a domain-dependent and a domain-independent layer (cf. Fig. 1). The former is implemented by means of *drivers* for each virtualization solution[4]. The domain-independent layer separates these drivers from the user interfaces. On the one hand, this eases the driver development as common functionality is

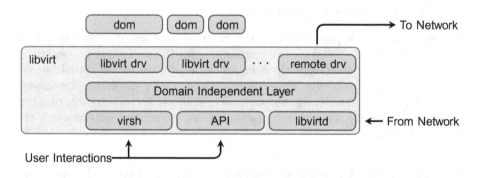

Fig. 1. Overview of libvirt

---

[4] The libvirt upstream sources comprise a driver called *lxc*. However, this is not based on the LXC API discussed in the previous section and lacks migration support.

available on the domain-independent layer. On the other hand, users are provided a consistent interface to the different virtualization solutions.

In addition to the domain drivers, libvirt provides the special *remote* driver. This enables the remote management of domains even if the underlying virtualization tool lacks according support. Therefore, the driver redirects calls addressing domains on different machines to the appropriate *libvirtd* daemon on the remote node.

2.3   Checkpoint/Restore in Userspace

Checkpoint/Restore In Userspace enables the checkpointing of Linux processes or a group thereof. In this work we leverage its capabilities for the implementation of container-based migration. CRIU is mainly implemented in user space and depends on features of the Linux kernel that have been gradually made available since version 3.11.

The Checkpoint/Restart Procedure saves the state of a process to a set of files forming the checkpoint, i. e., the process (the *dumpee*) is said to be *dumped*. Therefore, CRIU retrieves the necessary information from the /proc file system, e. g., file descriptors, memory maps, child processes, and threads. Finally, *ptrace* is used for the injection of code into the dumpee for the gathering of memory and credentials, e. g., the process ID, the user ID, etc. Due to the code injection, CRIU requires root privileges.

After checkpointing, the injected code is removed and the dumpee may either continue or stop its execution. Thereby a live-migration mechanism can be realized. In conjunction with the kernel support for the tracking of memory changes, CRIU is able to implement the post-copy live-migration approach [7]. For the restoration, CRIU reads the image files and rebuilds the process tree with all necessary resources, e. g., timers, credentials, threads. Finally, the memory is rebuilt from within the execution context of the processes and it may resume its execution.

The Page-Server is a mechanism of CRIU that allows for a reduction of the overhead generated by using the file system. Usually, the migration via CRIU requires all dump files to be stored in the local file system of the source node and then transferred to the destination node. This may be avoided by leveraging the page-server: it is started on the destination node and directly receives the memory content of the migrated process from the source node. Thereby, the largest part of the migration data, i. e., the memory content, only has to be stored within the file system of the destination node. However, the page-server does not allow for the transfer of the metadata created by CRIU (cf. Fig. 2) in its current implementation. This has to make the detour via the local file system of the source node. Unfortunately, the bypassing of the file system of both nodes for all dump data is not possible with the current version of CRIU.

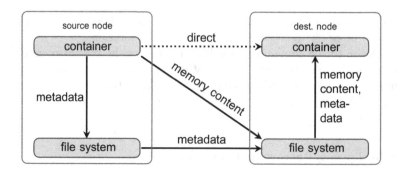

Fig. 2. Migration using the CRIU page-server

3   Libvirt LXC Driver

This section presents our prototype implementation of a novel libvirt driver for the management of LXC instances and their migration. This driver not only improves the usability and provides better access to LXC containers for future research but also enables remote management capabilities of LXC instances via the libvirt toolchain. To avoid naming conflicts with the upstream libvirt lxc driver, we call our driver *lxctools*.

3.1   Container Management

For the integration of the new driver into libvirt, we only had to modify seven existing source files and link libvirt against liblxc, i. e., the LXC C API. The implementation of the driver API is realized by filling a predefined struct with function pointers that reference the driver implementation. Furthermore, our lxctools driver implements a driver object that is used for data exchange between different consecutive driver calls. The members include a list of all available containers (cf. Listing 1.1) which allows for the effortless translation of multiple libvirt API calls to list operations, e. g., searching for a container or accessing the domain configuration.

```
struct lxctools_driver {
    const char* path;                        //LXC configuration path
    virDomainObjListPtr domains;             //list of containers
    int numOfDomains;                        //num. available domains
    virCapsPtr caps;                         //driver capabilities
    struct lxctools_migrate_data* md;        //data req. for migration
};
```

Listing 1.1. Driver struct

A domain is always referenced by its name as parameter to the function calls. Therefore, our driver first has to search the respective container within the above mentioned list, e. g., when starting or stopping it. Subsequently, it ensures that the container is in a state appropriate for the requested operation, i. e., a container that shall be shut down has to be in *running* state. On success, the driver invokes the LXC API call and updates the domain struct with the new state.

Besides the management of domains, a libvirt driver is in charge of providing domain-specific information. For example, on the execution of the *virsh dominfo* command, details on the respective domain are presented. The acquisition thereof is realized by leveraging the LXC API directly interacting with the cgroup subsystems.

3.2   Migration Using CRIU

Checkpoint/Restart (C/R) mechanisms can be regarded as generalization of process migration, i. e., the restart from a checkpoint on a different node than the one the checkpoint was taken on, is effectively a migration of that process. We leverage this fact for the implementation of the migration support for our lxctools driver.

As the LXC API does not support a full migration procedure for containers, our lxctools driver has to mediate between LXC and the libvirt migration API. The domain-independent layer of libvirt provides a skeleton for the migration feature. This successively executes several functions alternating on the source and the destination node and establishes a communication path between the two nodes. The individual steps have to be implemented by the drivers realizing the actual migration.

The Cold Migration is implemented by following the path provided by the migration skeleton. Initially, the driver and container state are validated on the source node and then on the destination node. Subsequently, the migration environment is prepared, i. e., for the avoidance of unnecessary overhead a *tmpfs* mount is created for the dump files. The preparation step on the destination node additionally includes the execution of the CRIU page-server and a file server that is used for the transfer of remaining dump files that are not copied by the page-server (cf. Sect. 2.3). The dump itself is created using the LXC API which in turn executes CRIU. In doing so, the memory content is directly transmitted to the destination node and stored in the local tmpfs, as we exploit the page-server facility of CRIU with our lxctools driver.

Once the metadata is transferred to the destination node as well, the container can be restored from the dump via the LXC API. Finally, the driver performs various cleanup tasks, such as unmounting the tmpfs on both nodes. The driver does not handle the transfer of the filesystem of a container. Thus, we expect the root file systems of containers to be present in a shared file system.

The Live Migration is similar to the cold migration. However, instead of creating a single dump only, several dumps are created during the live migration procedure. The number of dump iterations may either be set statically or be determined dynamically, i.e., when the pre-dump execution time reaches a

certain bound. For the evaluation of the performance of the driver, we used a
dynamic number of iterations with stops when the last iteration required less
than 1 s. This value proved to result in a good detection of unchanged memory.
In CRIU terminology, all but the last dump are so called pre-dumps which only
contain the container's memory pages for a reduction of the overhead.

For each dump an individual folder is created on the tmpfs by the lxctools
driver. This way we can reuse the mechanism for transfering metadata that
already served for the cold migration. However, due to limitations of CRIU's
implementation, the page-server itself has to be restarted by the driver after
each dump. This is realized by using a thread that immediately restarts the
page-server once it finished accepting a dump.

4   Evaluation

For evaluating our work we used two NUMA nodes each possessing two sockets
with eight physical cores. As each core exhibits two hardware thread contexts,
each node exposes 32 virtual cores in total. These are equipped with Intel Ivy-
Bridge CPUs (E5-2650 v2) clocked at 2.6 GHz. The nodes are connected by a
Gigabit Ethernet network which is used for transferring migration data.

The systems run the same setup employing a 4.4.4-301 Linux kernel of a
standard Fedora 23 installation. We use a modified libvirt 1.2.16 version that
embodies our lxctools driver[5]. This is used for all measurements, i. e., VM migration based on KVM as well as migration of LXC instances.

4.1   Driver Overhead

We started with an analysis of the overhead generated by the integration of LXC
into libvirt. Therefore, we compared the execution time of the four commands
start, *shutdown*, *save*, and *restore* when using libvirt including our lxctools driver

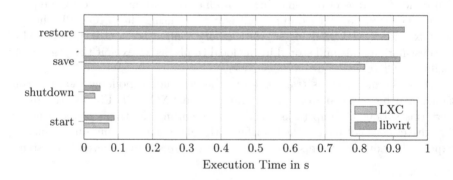

Fig. 3. Command execution times of libvirt and lxc

---

[5] This has been made available on GitHub: https://github.com/RWTH-OS/libvirt.

to the direct invocation of the LXC Command Line Interface (CLI) (cf. Fig. 3). As the migration is not supported by LXC natively, no execution time could be measured for this command. The presented results are averaged over 200 runs. The *save* and *restore* commands have been executed on a container with a memory load of 1 GiB. The results indicate a small overhead generated by the additional software layer. This is caused by the invocation of libvirt which needs to load our driver and set up the environment, e. g., read the XML configuration. However, the generated overhead is in the range of a few tens of milliseconds and is therefore outweighed by the advantages we get from the full libvirt support.

4.2   Migration

Our lxctools driver enables the migration of LXC containers via the interfaces provided by libvirt. Therefore, we can directly use the *virsh* command for a comparison of the cold migration time of LXC containers to that of VMs based on KVM (cf. Fig. 4). By performing a migration of empty VMs or containers, i. e., freshly started instances with n Bytes of guest physical memory (cf. Fig. 4a), we can obtain best-case results. Again averaged over 200 runs, we can see that the migration of a VM with 256 MiB of guest physical memory is already 35 % slower than that of a container. This is due to the memory consumption of additional kernel running within the VM. Furthermore, raising the guest physical memory to 4 GiB results in an increased migration time of up to 44 %. This is due to KVM's migration mechanism. Instead of transferring only those pages that are actually mapped into the virtual address space of the KVM process, its virtual memory representing the guest physical memory is traversed and checked for non-zero pages, i. e., the migration time grows linearly with the amount of guest physical memory.

Figure 4b presents a similar study including memory load within the migrated domain. Here, the transfer of the additional memory pages mainly determines the migration time. For smaller workloads of up to 2 GiB the overhead of the kernel

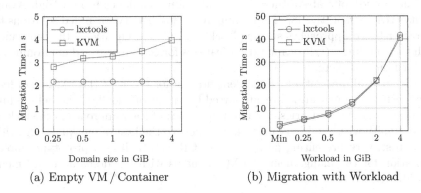

(a) Empty VM / Container   (b) Migration with Workload

Fig. 4. Comparision of migration time for VMs run under QEMU and LXC containers. The results are averaged over 200 iterations per meter point.

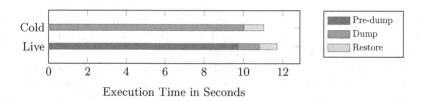

Fig. 5. Runtime analysis of the live and cold migration implementations

within VMs prevails. With a rising workload KVM's highly optimized migration mechanism starts to outperform our implementation that still relies on passing all data through at least one tmpfs. However, we observe an acceptable overhead of around 3 % for a workload of 4 GiB.

Finally, we analysed our live-migration implementation. Therefore, we migrated a container with 1 GiB of memory load 20 times between the cluster nodes back and forth (cf. Fig. 5). As the load was allocated only once and remained unchanged during the migration, the second pre-dump (cf. the small red box at around 9.5 s) required less than 1 s. This results in a total of two pre-dump iterations. In the final dump only the metadata is gathered and transferred to the destination node which takes 1.96 s on average depicting the actual downtime.

Since the live-migration of a comparable VM requires around 0.06 s, this demonstrates that our prototype implementation has still room for performance improvements.

5   Related Work

The migration of operating system containers among computers used for HPC is a rather young field of research. However, there have been several studies comparing the performance of containers to that of VMs [5,13,17,19]. Li et al. present a study of state-of-the-art virtualization techniques from a High Availability (HA) perspective [8]. They compare several hypervisor-based solutions to container-based approaches such as Docker, LXC, and OpenVZ[6]. In accordance with their findings, C/R or migration features for container-based environments are far from complete.

Mirkin et al. present a C/R implementation for OpenVZ [11]. Although features such as live-migration are supported by means of a loadable kernel module and some user-space utilities, the main drawback of their approach is the lack of compatibility with the Linux upstream kernel. To the best of our knowledge this is the first work presenting an analysis of CRIU as well as a prototype implementation for the mangament of LXC domains with the domain-management tool libvirt.

---

[6] https://openvz.org/.

6 Conclusion

In this paper we present the first libvirt driver that enables the migration of LXC instances via this management tool. In doing so, we investigate CRIU in detail and show how its page server can be leveraged for an accelerated migration.

In accordance with our results, the invocation of the container management facilities through libvirt and hence our driver only adds small overhead compared to the CLI. Thereby libvirt offers further capabilities to the user such as the remote management of containers. The evaluation of container-based migration could show that our driver is competitive to VM migration over Gigabit Ethernet based on KVM. The migration of a container with a workload of 4 GiB is only around 3 % slower than that of a comparable VM. For smaller workloads container-based migration is even up to 44 % faster than that of VMs.

For future work we plan to work on downtime reduction for live-migration. Therefore, we will avoid the detour of the transferred data over the local file system. Furthermore, we will investigate how faster interconnects can be leveraged for an acceleration of the migration.

Acknowledgment. This research and development was supported by the Federal Ministry of Education and Research (BMBF) under Grant 01|H13004B (Project FaST).

References

1. namespaces(7) Linux Programmer's Manual, Sept 2014. http://man7.org/linux/man-pages/man7/namespaces.7.html
2. Bolte, M., Sievers, M., Birkenheuer, G., Niehörster, O., Brinkmann, A.: Non-intrusive virtualization management using libvirt. In: Proceedings of the Conference on Design, Automation and Test in Europe, pp. 574–579 (2010)
3. Clark, C., Fraser, K., Hand, S., Hansen, J.G., Jul, E., Limpach, C., Pratt, I., Warfield, A.: Live migration of virtual machines. In: Proceedings of the 2nd Conference on Symposium on Networked Systems Design & Implementation - vol. 2, pp. 273–286 (2005)
4. Dua, R., Raja, A.R., Kakadia, D.: Virtualization vs containerization to support PaaS. In: 2014 IEEE International Conference on Cloud Engineering (IC2E), pp. 610–614 (2014)
5. Felter, W., Ferreira, A., Rajamony, R., Rubio, J.: An updated performance comparison of virtual machines and linux containers. In: 2015 IEEE International Symposium on Performance Analysis of Systems and Software (ISPASS), pp. 171–172 (2015)
6. Hargrove, P.H., Duell, J.C.: Berkeley lab checkpoint/restart (BLCR) for linux clusters. J. Phys. Conf. Ser. **46**, 494 (2006)
7. Hines, M.R., Gopalan, K.: Post-copy based live virtual machine migration using adaptive pre-paging and dynamic self-ballooning. In: Proceedings of the 2009 ACM SIGPLAN/SIGOPS International Conference on Virtual Execution Environments, pp. 51–60 (2009)

8. Li, W., Kanso, A.: Comparing containers versus virtual machines for achieving high availability. In: 2015 IEEE International Conference on Cloud Engineering (IC2E), pp. 353–358 (2015)

9. Menage, P.: Kernel Documentation, cgroups. kernel.org. https://www.kernel.org/doc/Documentation/cgroups/cgroups.txt

10. Milojičić, D.S., Douglis, F., Paindaveine, Y., Wheeler, R., Zhou, S.: Process migration. ACM Comput. Surv. (CSUR) **32**, 241–299 (2000)

11. Mirkin, A., Kuznetsov, A., Kolyshkin, K.: Containers checkpointing and live migration. In: Proceedings of the Linux Symposium, pp. 85–90 (2008)

12. Ondrejka, P., Silas, D., Prpi, M., Landmann, R.: Red Hat enterprise Linux 7 resource management guide. Technical report, Red Hat, Inc. (2015)

13. Padala, P., Zhu, X., Wang, Z., Singhal, S., Shin, K.G.: Performance evaluation of virtualization technologies for server consolidation. HP Labs Technical report (2007)

14. Pickartz, S., Breitbart, J., Lankes, S.: Implications of process-migration in virtualized environments. In: Proceedings of the 1st COSH Workshop on Co-Scheduling of HPC Applications, pp. 31–36, January 2016

15. Pickartz, S., Gad, R., Lankes, S., Nagel, L., Süß, T., Brinkmann, A., Krempel, S.: Migration techniques in HPC environments. In: Lopes, L., et al. (eds.) Euro-Par 2014. LNCS, vol. 8806, pp. 486–497. Springer, Heidelberg (2014). doi:10.1007/978-3-319-14313-2_41

16. Regola, N., Ducom, J.C.: Recommendations for virtualization technologies in high performance computing. In: 2010 IEEE Second International Conference on Cloud Computing Technology and Science (CloudCom), pp. 409–416 (2010)

17. Walters, J.P., Chaudhary, V., Cha, M., Jr., S.G., Gallo, S.M.: A comparison of virtualization technologies for HPC. In: 22nd International Conference on Advanced Information Networking and Applications (AINA 2008), pp. 861–868 (2008)

18. Xavier, M.G., Neves, M.V., Rossi, F.D., Ferreto, T.C., Lange, T., Rose, C.: Performance evaluation of container-based virtualization for high performance computing environments. In: 2013 21st Euromicro International Conference on Parallel, Distributed, and Network-Based Processing, pp. 233–240 (2013)

19. Xavier, M.G., Veiga Neves, M., de Rose, F., Augusto, C.: A performance comparison of container-based virtualization systems for MapReduce clusters. In: 2014 22nd Euromicro International Conference on Parallel, Distributed, and Network-Based Processing, pp. 299–306 (2014)

Providing Security in Container-Based HPC Runtime Environments

Holger Gantikow[1]([⊠]), Christoph Reich[2], Martin Knahl[2], and Nathan Clarke[3]

[1] science + computing ag, Tübingen, Germany
gantikow@gmail.com
[2] Hochschule Furtwangen, Furtwangen, Germany
Christoph.Reich@hs-furtwangen.de, Martin.Knahl@hs-furtwangen.de
[3] Plymouth University, Plymouth, UK
N.Clarke@plymouth.ac.uk

Abstract. Virtualization at the operating system level utilizing container technologies provides reduced performance overhead over Type-1 hypervisors for HPC and also adds many possibilities to significantly improve the often demanded flexibility of such an installation. This paper discusses technologies and concepts on several layers that can be applied to securely integrate container-based virtualization in a multitenant HPC environment, requiring both security and high performance.

Keywords: Virtualization · Container · Docker · HPC · Security

1 Introduction

Current installations of all sizes used for High Performance Computing (HPC) require flexible and resilient architectures, which need to be easy to install and administer, all while providing high performance.

The use of virtualization can solve several of these requirements and improve the flexibility of an architecture, but there are often shortcomings performance-wise compared to a bare-metal installation, as several studies, including [3] and [8] have shown over the years. Even with improved hardware support, narrowing this performance gap for Type-1 hypervisors (ESXi, KVM, Xen), the most common way to deploy HPC installations is still bare-metal, leaving virtualized HPC mainly in the focus of public cloud providers. Although hypervisor-based virtualization is widely adopted it is not the only way to virtualize.

1.1 Container-Based Virtualization for HPC

Over the course of the last three years container-based virtualization has gained a lot of interest, especially by the popularity of Docker[1]. Even though Linux Containers (LXC)[2] are available since 2008 and there are several alternatives,

---

[1] Docker - https://www.docker.com/.

[2] Linux Containers - https://linuxcontainers.org/.

© Springer International Publishing AG 2016
M. Taufer et al. (Eds.): ISC High Performance Workshops 2016, LNCS 9945, pp. 685–695, 2016.
DOI: 10.1007/978-3-319-46079-6_48

including Rocket (rkt)[3] and to a certain extent systemd-nspawn, Docker seems the most reasonable representative. By providing tools and an ecosystem around its core components it made workflows around containers straightforward to use.

Contrasting virtual machines (VMs) containers do not start a full operating system (OS). All containers on one host share the same Linux kernel, which results in near bare-metal performance, as [11] has shown.

Containers provide an appropriate technology for solving the issue of application dependencies and conflicting requirements when providing a wide variety of different applications or several versions of one application on the same system, as often encountered in HPC environments. Furthermore they can be used to run legacy code on current systems. Their suitability for *containerizing* complex workflows [15] in one portable entity that is convenient to share with third parties and can be managed independently of content, gained the interest of many scientific communities, requiring reproducible research [5], or dealing with complex pipelines, as in genome sequencing [10].

Given their advantages in lifecycle management and the circumstance that HPC technologies like GPU-computing[4] and Infiniband are available in a containerized environment, containers are to be considered a lightweight virtualization building block for HPC environments, where a 1–2% overhead is acceptable for increased flexibility [12].

1.2 Containers and Security

As, unlike VMs, containers all share the same host kernel and have thus to be considered less secure, they should not be seen as a drop-in replacement for VMs, especially when requiring strong isolation. They share the same three major threats with any other virtualization technique:

Privilege Escalation An attacker gaining access to a container could be able to break out of the container and access the host system and other containers.
Denial-of-Service One container using up all resources of the host could starve out other containers on the same host and the host itself.
Information Leak Confidential details about other containers, as running applications, or the host itself could be leaked and used for further attacks.

While most of these threats are mitigated to a certain extent by the basic underlying kernel features *cgroups* and *namespaces* (see Sect. 3.2), Docker has put strong development focus on improving security in recent versions, as security concerns are still the most limiting barrier to adoption in production [9].

In a pure batch-processing oriented HPC-environment risks can be reduced by utilizing containers as *Application Containers*, prohibiting user access into the container and also restricting access to the Docker commandline interface (CLI) by the use of wrapper scripts. As [13] has shown, this substantially reduces the

---

[3] Rkt - https://coreos.com/rkt/.
[4] GPU-Enabled Docker Container - http://www.nvidia.com/object/docker-container. html.

attack surface over so-called *System Containers*, which provide more unrestricted access. System Containers are rather comparable to VMs and often requested by users for interactive access to applications.

The current mechanisms and technologies to secure the usage of container-based virtualization in an HPC environment, considering both application and system containers, are introduced in Sect. 3.

They can be applied in pieces for improving the security of specific aspects, such as image vulnerability scanning, or could be combined to a framework, where configurations and preconditions are generated according to selected security and isolation requirements at job submit time.

2   Related Work

As technology securing containers is currently under steady development, the work published is usually blog posts focussing on single aspects or features and presentations. For example [13] presented an overview of the vulnerabilities of Xen (paravirtualized), KVM/QEMU and containers that occured in 2014.

Besides [6], that covers an overview of an unnamed older Docker version's isolation mechanisms, there are two current extensive publications, covering many details in depth out of scope for this paper. To be specific the recently updated best-practises security document [7], which was implemented in most parts in *Docker Bench* tool (see also 3.2) and a whitepaper [14], that covers many security aspects of Docker, LXC and Rkt in great depths and lengths and contrasts their default configurations. Another useful resource is [4], focussing on vulnerability exploitation in Docker Container environments.

3   Applicable Security for Container-Based Virtualization

Adopting container-based virtualization in an HPC environment does not require a complete redesign of existing security policies, but rather their extension. There are usually processes and mechanisms already in place to improve security and privacy, which are basically independent of container usage, among them firewalls and measures to provide secured and isolated access to data.

Going beyond that, multiple technologies and tools to improve the security of container utilization can be applied to both the *Provision Mode* (Sect. 3.1), responsible for providing images, and the *Operation Mode* (Sect. 3.2), related to runtime and operational aspects. The modes are further devided into layers with the applicable technologies collated accordingly.

3.1   Provision Mode

Containers are the running, stateful instances of an image. The possibility to quickly build new images based on existing ones using Dockerfiles and upload them on the public registry *Docker Hub*[5], is one of the main reasons for the popularity of this platform, but also implies that security is a pivotal aspect of provisioning images. Figure 1 shows the tools and technologies applicable to the Provision Mode, explained in the following.

Fig. 1. Applicable security tools and mechanisms in *Provision Mode*

(a) Image Provenance and Distribution Layer. While pulling one of 100.000+ ready to run images straight from Docker Hub is convenient, there are several constraints to consider when using Docker in production. As software running inside a container can have elevated rights compared to running straight on the host system, there need to be guarantees and trust about the images' origin, who created them and that they remained untampered during transit and storage. This implies that the images need to be signed after build and that transport layer security is used during transit. There are several possibilities to support these requirements:

Official Repositories Docker's concept of verified repositories with signed and validated images is called *Official Repositories* and consists of curated base images of distributions and popular applications, such as databases or webservers. These are considerable as trustworthy base for own images, when building own base images is not an option, but requires trusting Docker's developers and the contributors to these images.

Trusted Registries For environments demanding on-premise registries due to security and compliance requirements, there is the possibility to run a so-called *Trusted Registry* (TR), that provides LDAP/AD user authentication and Role Based Access Control (RBAC).

Private Registry As TR is a *subscription-based product* it is often preferred to install a private registry, which is also favourable for integrating in audits and vulnerability scans. In cases neither Docker Hub, alternative repositories such as Quay.io[6], or a private onsite registry are an option, the possibility to load images straight from an internal storage remains.

---

[5] Docker Hub - https://hub.docker.com/.

[6] Quay - https://quay.io/.

Content Trust Docker's approach to image signing and verification is called *Content Trust* and uses *Notary*[7], an open source tool that is based on *The Update Framework (TUF)*[8]. Images should be signed locally before uploading them to a remote registry, as is done with the Official Repositories. The use of signed and verified images should be enforced by enabling content trust in the configuration, as this ensures the image comes from a trusted party and remained unmodified during transfer.

Usage of signed images, curated and stored by an Operations Team in a dedicated private software library, as the only source of trusted software for improved security and reproducibility, is highly recommended and transferable to all sorts of software repositories. Images failing these requirements could be treated with increased isolation.

(b) Image Content Layer. Ensuring images are free from known vulnerabilities is important, as it decreases attack vectors that can lead to security breaches. Especially when dealing with legacy code that might depend on a vulnerable library that cannot be updated it is essential to be aware of potential risks. To mitigate these, availability of vulnerable images should be limited to certain users and containers based on these images could be placed on hosts in a different security zone providing stronger isolation. Possibilities include limited network connectivity, placing containers of one tenant on one host, adding an additional layer of virtualization or even applying means to detect application anomalies. There exist several options to detect vulnerable images:

Clair Clair[9] is an analysis engine, that scans each image layer for vulnerabilities based on the Common Vulnerabilities and Exposures (CVEs) database[10]. It currently only supports Debian, Red Hat and Ubuntu images, as it relies on their native package manager for gathering information about installed software. Clair can be used locally or remotely via an REST-API and is integrated in the Quay registry.

Docker Security Scanning (formerly Project Nautilus) Docker provides a quite similar tool called *Docker Security Scanning*. It also analyses software packages installed as DEB and RPM, but it furthermore scans each binary for known vulnerabilities[11]. As opposed to Clair it is not available standalone and only as an add-on service for Docker Cloud private repositories and used for Official Repositories on Docker Hub.

Even though neither of these tools inspect running containers, the possibility to analyse images in a repository is vital. As layers can be shared and reused

---

[7] Notary - https://github.com/docker/notary.

[8] The Update Framework - https://theupdateframework.github.io/.

[9] Clair - https://github.com/coreos/clair.

[10] Common Vulnerabilities and Exposures - http://cve.mitre.org/.

[11] Docker Security Scanning safeguards the container content lifecycle - https://blog.docker.com/2016/05/docker-security-scanning/.

already one vulnerable base image can lead to multiple vulnerable containers. CoreOS[12] has shown that 80 % of the images hosted on Quay were vulnerable to Heartbleed. As Clair is Open Source Software, we expect support for software installed bypassing DEB/RPM packages or using the Perl/Python package manager in future releases, as well as checks for leaked information (passwords and keys), and an overall support for a higher diversity of distributions.

This would especially help with the shift from traditional distributions to optimized distributions. While Debian, Red Hat and derivates are widely used, their base image size of 200 MB is rather large compared to lightweight distributions such as Alpine Linux with 5 MB. The use of stripped down images also improves security by benefiting from a reduced attack surface.

Further improvements would result from the integration of means to trigger an automated patch management process once a CVE for any component within an image is reported. While this might limit reproducibility, it would reduce security risks and improve auditability of such changes.

3.2   Operation Mode

Once image security is established securing operation has to be ensured. Figure 2 shows the applicable tools and technologies on the corresponding layer, futher explained in the following section.

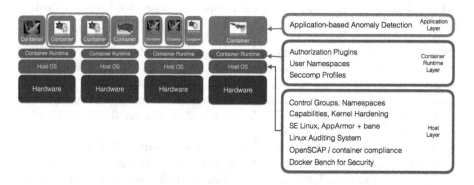

Fig. 2. Applicable security tools in *Operation Mode.*

(a) **Host Layer.** The host layer provides several possibilities to improve the security that go beyond general hardening recommendations such as applying patches and updates whenever possible, especially kernel updates, or removing unrequired services from the host system to reduce the attack surface.

---

[12] CoreOS Introduces Clair: Open Source Vulnerability Analysis for your Containers - https://coreos.com/blog/vulnerability-analysis-for-containers/.

Kernel Features. Control Groups, Namespaces are no *additional* tool that can be applied to containers, but should be introduced here very briefly, as they are the core components providing isolation.

Control Groups (cgroups) Cgroups are a Linux kernel feature to provide performance isolation (CPU, Memory and I/O resources) on a collection of processes and are shortly described as powerful alternative to ulimits/rlimits to ensure that containers cannot starve the host or each other by denial of service attacks. They are also required for prioritzing shares of resource utilization, accounting of usage and for checkpoint + restart of process groups. They are also applicable in HPC environments without containers[13].

Namespaces Namespaces provide processes and spawned child processes their own limited view of the system. Namespaced resources are mapped to separate values on the host, so it appears to processes within the namespace that they have their own isolated instance of the global resource. PID 1 for instance in a container is not PID 1 on the host or another container, and processes in a container cannot see processes of another container or the host. Currently not all kernel features are namespaced, which can present a risk for information exposure and attacks. The latest namespace added was the *user namespace* in 2013, with support by Docker starting 2016.

Capabilities Linux kernels capabilities can be used to assign certain coarsely grained privileges to processes. By default containers run with a reduced set but require additional ones for example for inserting kernel modules. In terms of security it is advisable to reduce available capabilities as much as possible and only add required ones. Identifying safely droppable privileges by trial and error and a test suite is cumbersome, but currently the only way to do so. For a HPC environment this approach can be feasible as compute jobs for one application should have constant capabilities requirements.

Kernel Hardening Deployment of hardened kernels, using patches as *grsecurity*[14], which protects against programs modifying memory with the aim to trigger buffer overflows, and PaX[15], which adds patches to RBAC and auditing, might be useful in some scenarios. In HPC environments their use is questionable, as the security checks and measures can induce performance overhead and PaX conflicts with applications generating code at runtime.

Linux Security Modules (LSM) / Mandatory Access Control. The LMS framework supports a variety of security modules, including Smack, TOMOYO Linux and Yama - and the widely used ones AppArmor and SELinux.

Security Enhanced Linux (SELinux) SELinux is installed on many distributions by default and usually preconfigured to protect the host and containers from each other, by limiting access to resources. By applying specific labels

---

[13] Resource Management with Linux Control Groups in HPC Clusters - http://slurm.schedmd.com/pdfs/LCS_cgroups_BULL.pdf.

[14] Grsecurity - https://grsecurity.net/.

[15] Pax - https://pax.grsecurity.net.

to a container it is also possible to create policies limiting communication to specific ports or creating secret and top-secret containers for processing sensitive data[16].

AppArmor + Bane While less granular than SELinux, AppArmor is more straightforward to configure and still provides a high level of protection from containers attempting to access critical system resources, by providing pathname-based access control. The default profile can be overwritten with a custom container-specific profile at container startup. These profiles can be generated using the custom AppArmor profile generator *Bane*[17].

The use of SELinux and AppArmor is not always straightforward, but can provide strong additional security assurance preventing privilege escalation by restricting access to resources. This is especially required in cases where user namespaces are not applicable yet.

Auditing. Running regular audits on images, containers and hosts is essential to ensure that no security breaches have occurred.

Linux Auditing System The Linux Auditing System is used to record events, which can be used to detect misuse and unauthorized activities. Auditing Docker daemon related activities, such as starting containers and changes to configurations files, certificates and keys, should extend audits in place and analysis of logs files needs to be integrated in security monitoring facilities.

OpenSCAP - container compliance The OpenSCAP[18] project provides a collection of tools required for implementing and enforcing the NIST *Security Content Automation Protocol* (SCAP). By the use of OpenSCAP container compliance[19] these policy-based security audits can be performed on images and containers. As these audits also includes CVE scans, there might be redundancy with tools such as Clair (see 3.1). As Clair is easier to integrate in image registries and compliance audits based on SCAP are often already established, the primary use of this tool might be in custom security policy audits and on-demand scans of potential malicious containers.

Docker Bench for Security The Docker Bench for Security tool[20,21] based on the CIS Docker Benchmark best-practises [7] automates the validation of configuration details, such as file permissions or the use of trusted registries. This tool might be a good start for auditing the host configuration, as it can be extended with custom checks and policies and could be included as precondition for running containers with additional security requirements.

---

[16] Tuning Docker with the newest security enhancements - https://opensource.com/business/15/3/docker-security-tuning.

[17] Bane - https://github.com/jfrazelle/bane.

[18] OpenSCAP - https://www.open-scap.org.

[19] Container-Compliance - https://github.com/OpenSCAP/container-compliance.

[20] Docker-Bench-Security - https://github.com/docker/docker-bench-security.

[21] Alternative: Actuary - https://github.com/diogomonica/actuary.

(b) Container Runtime Layer. Recent versions of Docker include several features that improve the possibilities to lock down containers, access to them and the granularity to control what containerized applications are allowed to do.

Authorization Plugins The integration of authorization plugins enables fine granular role-based access policies to interact with the Docker daemon. As opposed to the out-of-the-box *all or nothing* authorization model where any member of the *docker* group can run any command, resulting in severe possibilities to escalate rights, this approach provides a finer level of granularity, given development of suitable authorization plugins. For example members of an audit team could only access readonly commands, while an operations team could issue container lifecycle commands. The contribution of the AuthZ authorization framework[22] is an essential option in a multitenant environment where possibilities to directly interact with the Docker daemon need to be provided while separation of access to resources is required.

User Namespaces Docker finally added support for *Phase 1* of user namespaces in version 1.10, which currently only remaps the root user. *Phase 2* will allow full per-container UID remapping and allow a stronger tenant separation and improve per-user accounting capabilities in future. While some limitations apply, such as a privileged user, or member of the docker group, is still required to interact with the Docker engine and the feature is disabled by default, the root user remapping makes it harder to perform privilege escalation with the help of the filesystem and it is now possible to apply the nproc cgroup[23] to a container, as these limits did not apply to root.

Secure computing mode (seccomp) Profiles Starting v1.10 Docker supports the kernel feature *seccomp*, which restricts available syscalls within the container. If supported by host kernel the default seccomp profile can be used, which disables around 40 out of 300+ system calls. While still providing wide application compatibility, this feature could be used to tightly lock down processes inside a container. By using a container-specific whitelist of syscalls generated during a regular non-malicious run of a container, malicious code would then fail by requiring a wider set of syscalls.

(c) Application Layer. Options to increase security at the application layer are rather limited using an universal, non application-specific approach. As the use of tools discussed in Sect. 3.1 is suitable to mitigate certain potential risks by the detection of software vulnerabilities during provision, focus should be placed on detecting application *runtime anomalies* at this layer.

The internal nature of containers simplifies gathering information about processes running inside a container, as containerized processes can be monitored in detail from the host by tracing their system calls using `strace`. This can be used for detecting anomalous behaviour without any modification to either the

---

[22] Docker AuthZ Plugins - https://www.twistlock.com/2016/02/18/docker-authz-plugins-twistlocks-contribution-to-the-docker-community/.

[23] Fork bomb prevention - https://github.com/docker/docker/issues/6479.

container or the host kernel or prior knowledge of the application running inside the container. This method is proposed by Abed [1,2] as a host-based intrusion detection system (HIDS). His work uses a frequency-based approach, dropping the sequence of occurrence and only keeping track of the frequency of occurrence of each distinct system call. Even though this requires far less storage space than a sequence-based approach, it is to assume that this might still impose too much performance degradation in a multi-core, multi-host computation with several thousand syscalls per process - per second.

The overall approach of system call tracing might be applicable with image-specific seccomp profiles. This would provide the possibility to narrow down whitelist of allowed syscalls, based on the results of a learning phase.

4 Future Work

While Docker's security features have strongly improved, there still are several areas that need further work. Among them improvements to the granularity of access to the Docker daemon for multitenant environments, the expected implementation of Phase 2 of user namespaces and the possibility to provide security profiles as part of the image specification. There is also a need for improved namespace-awareness of the Linux kernel. Many features, including devices, kernel ring buffer (dmesg), time, along the proc and sys pseudo-filesystems are not namespace-aware yet and can present at least a risk of information exposure.

Furthermore an evaluation of the runtime performance overhead induced by mechanisms such as seccomp profiles, as well as an evaluation of orchestration frameworks from a security point of view would provide further insight.

5 Conclusion

Containers are a possible building block and core component for flexible HPC environments. Given their low performance-overhead they are suitable for onsite HPC installations with a wide set of different applications and possibly even for *HPC-cloud* bare-metal providers, enabling them to provide customized applications in a timely manner. For IaaS-Cloud-based HPC resources they can be used as way to deploy the required application stack and configuration.

Most of the described security measures can be established without inducing further runtime performance overhead and only need to extend existing regular baseline security and vulnerability scans.

Even though container-based virtualization is technically still to be considered less secure than hypervisor-based virtualization: for an HPC environment most possible risks are preventable by providing audited container images from a trusted source, that are run on systems patched on a regular base, following the principle of least privilege. Meaning in this case utilizing only *Application Containers* without interactive user access to the container, and the application itself running under a non-privileged user, with further improvement by applying a container-specific seccomp profile and limiting access to the Docker daemon using authorization plugins. If required required workloads from multiple tenants could also be isolated on host-level for additional isolation.

Utilizing containers no longer neccessarly means running untrusted code downloaded off the internet as *root*: csontainerized environments can be more secure than the equivalent environment without containers, if configured right.

References

1. Abed, A.S., Clancy, T.C., Levy, D.S.: Applying bag of system calls for anomalous behavior detection of applications in linux containers (2015)
2. Abed, A.S., Clancy, C., Levy, D.S.: Intrusion detection system for applications using linux containers. In: Foresti, S. (ed.) STM 2015. LNCS, vol. 9331, pp. 123–135. Springer, Heidelberg (2015). doi:10.1007/978-3-319-24858-5_8
3. Bakhshayeshi, R., Akbari, M., Javan, M.: Performance analysis of virtualized environments using HPC challenge benchmark suite and analytic hierarchy process. In: 2014 Iranian Conference on Intelligent Systems (ICIS), pp. 1–6, February 2014
4. Bettini, A.: Vulnerability exploitation in docker container environments, pp. 1–13 (2015). https://www.blackhat.com/docs/eu-15/materials/eu-15-Bettini-Vulnerability-Exploitation-In-Docker-Container-Environments-wp.pdf
5. Boettiger, C.: An introduction to docker for reproducible research. SIGOPS Oper. Syst. Rev. **49**(1), 71–79 (2015)
6. Bui, T.: Analysis of Docker security. CoRR abs/1501.02967 (2015). http://arxiv.org/abs/1501.02967
7. Center of Internet Security: CIS Docker 1.11.0 Benchmark. Technical report, Center of Internet Security (2016). https://benchmarks.cisecurity.org/tools2/docker/CIS_Docker_1.11.0_Benchmark_v1.0.0.pdf
8. Chakthranont, N., Khunphet, P., Takano, R., Ikegami, T.: Exploring the performance impact of virtualization on an HPC cloud. In: 2014 IEEE 6th International Conference on Cloud Computing Technology and Science (CloudCom) (2014)
9. ClusterHQ, DevOps.com: The Current State of Container Usage-Identifying and Eliminating Barriers to Adoption. Technical report (2015). https://clusterhq.com/assets/pdfs/state-of-container-usage-june-2015.pdf
10. Di Tommaso, P., Palumbo, E., Chatzou, M., Prieto, P., Heuer, M.L., Notredame, C.: The impact of Docker containers on the performance of genomic pipelines. PeerJ **3**, e1273 (2015)
11. Felter, W., Ferreira, A., Rajamony, R., Rubio, J.: An updated performance comparison of virtual machines and linux containers (2014)
12. Gantikow, H., Klingberg, S., Reich, C.: Container-based virtualization for HPC. In: Proceedings of CLOSER 2015, March 2015
13. Jackson, I.: Surviving the Zombie apocalypse-security in the cloud containers, KVM and Xen (2015). http://xenbits.xen.org/people/iwj/2015/fosdem-security/slides.pdf
14. NCC Group: Whitepaper Understanding and Hardening Linux Containers. Technical report, NCC Group (2016). https://www.nccgroup.trust/globalassets/our-research/us/whitepapers/2016/april/ncc_group_understanding_hardening_linux_containers-10pdf
15. Zheng, C., Thain, D.: Integrating containers into workflows: a case study using makeflow, work queue, and Docker, vol. 2, pp. 31–38 (2015)

Author Index

Printed in the United States
by Bookmasters

Printed in the United States
By Bookmasters